The COMPLEAT ANGLER'S CATALOG

by Scott Roederer

Johnson Books: Boulder

Spring Creek Press: Estes Park

©Copyright 1985 by Scott Roederer

Cover design: Steven R. Lester

Cover art by Wm. Van Dyke Jones

First Edition
1 2 3 4 5 6 7 8 9

ISBN 0-933472-93-5
LCCCN 85-804-07

Printed in the United States of America by
Johnson Publishing Company
1880 South 57th Court
Boulder, Colorado 80301

Contents

Preface

A LOT OF THE CREDIT FOR this book goes to my Uncle Bill. He took me fly fishing when I was a youngster and showed me how to dap for browns in the Cache La Poudre with a Renegade. More importantly, he let me buy equipment from his shop at 40% off, and that allowed me to support my fly fishing habit on a paper boy's budget.

That was 20 years ago. My fascination with fly fishing, with its equipment, and with good bargains continues unabated today. When you combine a hardcore fly fisherman with a hardcore shopper, you get someone who wants a book like this one. It took over a year to compile, even with the aid of a computer, but now, for the first time, I can sit down and have all the choices in front of me when I want a new rod, reel, or (almost) anything else.

I hope a number of fly fishermen will share my compulsion to own equipment that's just right. I want equipment that fits my needs and my fishing style, not just the equipment that happens to be available. This book will help me find that equipment and will help you do the same. It will also save you some money, if that's important.

Besides, my taste in equipment has improved over those 20 years. If enough of you buy this book, I may just be able to afford the Bogdan reel I now covet. (Warning: This book may be hazardous to your pocketbook, instead of helpful, if not used carefully.)

I know that most readers don't bother with prefaces, and I hope you're anxious to get on with the book, but let me tell you about the people who helped. Dave Cleveland gave me the idea for the book and was clever enough not to get involved with its production. Writer-friend David Morgan introduced me to the fine people at Johnson Books and also retired discreetly from the scene.

The fly fishing lady in my life, fortunately, did not retire from the scene. My Dame Juliana tolerated a year without many fishing trips and without much of my company and did not once complain about missing either one. I'm pretty sure that's good. She substituted proofreading for reading the water, and that's a great sacrifice. She deserves the Ross Reel she covets, and I'll be able to buy her one if you buy this book.

Greg Kielian gave me the short course in computers that got me started, returned all my desperation calls, and finally got my machine to talk to their machine, the outcome of which was typeset words.

Within the industry, Nick Lyons has been very helpful and supportive. There is no finer, nor more generous, gentleman in the sport. (He's also an excellent fly fisherman.)

And finally, there are the people in the business who sent me their catalogs and product information sheets in good faith. We have a great group of people working for us out there. Without their help, of course, this book could not have been done. Special thanks go to those who allowed use of illustrations from their catalogs, especially Bob Jacklin's Fly Shop, Thomas & Thomas, and The Fly Shop. Others are recognized within the book.

I hope you'll find lots of things you can't live without in this book, and if you deal with any of the companies directly, let them know you read about their product in the book.

It's April and springtime in the Rockies. The yellow-rumped warblers have returned to the backyard balsam poplars, and the red-winged blackbirds sing from their perches above Fish Creek behind my house. It doesn't snow very often now, and there wouldn't be ice in the guides if I were to head down to the Big Thompson. The midges have been hatching every morning at ten, and the rainbows are particularly handsome at this time of year. I think it's time for a little equipment field testing.

Scott Roederer, April 1985

Index to catalog sources

1. The Compleat Angler's Outfit

FLY FISHING IS A SPORT with many levels. There are thousands of duffers who own a fly rod and use it sparingly, sometimes as a last resort and sometimes on a whim. On the other hand, there are thousands of experts who can tell an *Emphemerella dorothea* from a *Pothamanthus distinctus* at dusk from 30 paces. In between are the rest of us, hundreds of thousands of fly fishermen, each enjoying the sport at his or her own level.

Most of us started fly fishing because it "looked like fun". We were already fishermen of some sort, usually spin fishermen who took up that sport because it looked like more fun than bait fishing. It was, and fly fishing was even more fun than spin fishing.

Something drew us initially to fly fishing. Perhaps it was the gracefulness of the fly fisherman's line in the air. Perhaps it was the obvious intent with which fly fishermen pursued their sport. It may have even been because we were outfished by a fly fisherman. As for me, I remember seeing a fly fisherman release a fish, a keeper. That seemed strange to me. Why would anyone try to catch a fish only to let it go? The sole conclusion I could draw was that the activity itself was reward enough. I didn't feel that way about spin fishing, so I decided there must be something special about fly fishing. And, of course, there is.

I can't explain what makes fly fishing so special. Perhaps nothing will ever be written that fully accounts for the fascination most fly fishermen feel for their sport. If you're a fly fisherman, you understand that fascination. You share, with me and others in the sport, that special anticipation of a day astream. You know that there is nothing quite like fly fishing, and there doesn't have to be.

Nowhere in the sport is that fascination so clearly evident than in the fly fisherman's love of his equipment. Consider for a moment the fly reel, a simple mechanical device that lets line out, brings line in, and stores it in the meantime. Except in extraordinary fishing situations, the Cortland Crown does the job simply and efficiently

at a retail cost of under $30. Were fly fishing a simple sport, the Crown and other comparable reels might be the only ones on the market.

Instead, there are many reels of differing quality and style. Many of those are for special purposes, but most of the multitude of reels, about 150 of them, are layers on top of the basic design represented by the Crown. They extend upward in quality to the Bogdan reels, which are handmade to order and cost over $300.

The same can be seen in rods. A Lamiglas G1000 rod or a Cabela's Fish Eagle rod will cast a fly line comfortably and efficiently in most fishing situations and will do it for less than $75. A few minutes of browsing through the pages of this book will uncover rods of much greater sophistication and cost. The Thomas & Thomas Presentation bamboo rod and the Montagne rectangular bamboo rod, for instance, both cost nearly $1,500 or 20 times the basic rod.

So, whether fly fishing is a simple hobby for you, something akin to gardening, or a way of life, separating you from more respectable people, the equipment you use reflects your interest, your level in the sport. When your interest, and therefore your level of involvement, in the sport of fly fishing increases, the first symptom is the desire for new and better equipment.

Equipment is so much a part of the serious fly fisherman's life that it sometimes seems more valuable to him or her than the activity itself. There is nothing so cherished in a fly fisherman's life, for instance, as a fly rod that becomes part of him, that operates automatically in ways that defy his explanation, that will cast and place a fly as if he were dropping it on the water himself from directly above.

Nor is there anything quite like the feel and sound of a trusted reel taking in and giving out line. Nor anything like the deep patina of a landing net's wood, magnified by water droplets and glistening in the sun. Nor the feel of the old familiar vest as it's hauled on the shoulders.

1

This book exists to help fly fishermen find equipment that will be special in those ways. But before we get further into equipment, it may be wise to try to understand more completely (or compleatly, if you prefer) the sport and the men and women who pursue it.

Understanding fly fishermen. Ardent fly fishermen make up a subculture. The fact that no sociologist has studied fly fishermen is evidence only that sociologists don't visit trout streams as often as they should. If they did, they'd find men and women dressed up in costumes talking in a strange tongue.

If the waders, vests, and funny hats didn't convince the sociologists they were in the midst of a subculture, the odd use of the English language would. "Cast" is not a theatrical term. "Double haul" is not a big moving day. "Strike" has nothing to do with baseball or labor unions. "Leaders" are not to be followed by anything but fly lines.

Most certainly, the sociologists would witness the fly fishermen's rituals and thus confirm their deepest suspicions about the group. The most obvious rituals include The Tying of the Blood Knot, The Prayer-Position Cast, and The Mayfly Collection Dance.

Most holy of all the rites, however, is The Baptism, which privilege is bestowed on fly fishermen by powers beneath the surface of the water. The sociologists would witness much attention given the angler who experiences this rite and would hear him or her speak of the mystery of it.

The reverence given equipment would also impress the sociologists. They might suggest that a good fly rod, for instance, is worshipped by fly fishermen. (The place of worship, of course, is most prudently the local fly shop, for thou shalt not covet thy neighbor's fly rod.)

But before I carry this analogy so far as to suggest that because I'm writing about equipment, I'm writing Holy Scripture, let me simply say that this book is "devoted" to fly fishing equipment—rods, reels, lines, waders, vests, flies, and every other piece of equipment the fly fisherman uses in pursuit of his or her reality.

How to use this book. In this book, you'll find listings of every piece of fly fishing equipment I could find—the good and the bad, the beautiful and the ugly. I've given sources for each of these products, so you can use the listings to locate hard-to-find equipment and supplies, everything from French silk fly lines to Horse Leech salmon flies to Silver Monkey hair.

These sources are, for the most part, the catalog companies listed in Chapter 14. They are listed by a three-letter code, which is usually the first three letters of the company's common name. "Kau", for instance, is the code for Kaufmann's Streamborn from Oregon. A few are listed a bit more cryptically ("T&T" stands for Thomas & Thomas, for example), but all will be easily found in the alphabetical listings.

If you find a source not listed in Chapter 14, as you will in the chapter on flies, for instance, the source will be listed in the introduction to the chapter you're in or described under the product listing itself or a similar one above it. In some instances, products were so popular that I didn't list every source. If there were more than 15 sources, you'll find the sources listed as "many catalogs". If there were more than 20 sources, it will say "most catalogs".

I've also listed the range of prices for each product. The range represents the lowest price and the highest price found in current catalogs. Thus, you can also use the listings to compare prices, both between competitive products and between retail sources for each product.

Some products will have only one price or a very limited range. These products come from manufacturers who practice price controls. Basically, those manufacturers refuse to supply retailers unless they agree to sell the products at a standard price or with very limited discounting. This is an unfortunate practice from the consumer's standpoint, and one that has been successfully challenged in court in other areas of the economy.

Some of our most prominent companies, including Sage, Cortland, Orvis, Scott, and Ross, among others, do it. It helps control the type of retail outlet that carries the product and thus protects the stature of the product line. And although it reduces competition in the marketplace, it has one positive effect. Price controls help small fly shops compete, and that's good for fly fishermen.

The price ranges, when given, can help you save a lot of money, often much more than the cost of this book. A Fenwick Boron-X 7½' rod, for instance, has a price range of $186-$328. That means that at least one catalog offered it for $186, or $142 less than at least one of the other catalogs. If you're a careful shopper, you can have your Boron-X rod and a new Ross reel to go with it for about the same money that someone else might spend on the rod alone.

I haven't listed the prices offered by individual catalogs. The decision not to do that rested in part on the complications that would have been caused in gathering information for the book. It also rested in some sense of fair play. If I told you who charges $328 for the Fenwick rod mentioned above, you'd never send for the catalog, and that would probably be unfair. Other prices in the catalog are competitive, and there are many unusual products in that catalog that you'd miss out on.

I also consider shopping to be somewhat like fishing— those people who work at it are rewarded. I may tell you that The Big Brown is waiting for you in the Fryingpan River, but I'm not sure I should have to point to the rock where it lives. As it is, in Chapter 14 I've described all the rocks, and you can probably figure it out for yourself.

I am in favor of consumerism, and I don't expect you to go out of your way to pay more for a product than you must, especially if you deal with catalog companies. That's one reason for this book. I do believe in the local fly shop, however, and in the fact that having a shop is worth a lot. The few extra bucks you may spend in that local shop will be returned to you in service, advice, instructions,

directions, and fish stories, and I suggest you deal with them whenever possible.

As a point of consumer information concerning this book, the prices in this edition were gathered during 1984 and 1985. They will be out of date to some degree when you read the book. For that matter, some of the products may have disappeared into the back rooms of The American Museum of Fly Fishing and new ones taken their place. In the delayed world of book publishing, this cannot be avoided.

Prices vary from year to year. Mostly, of course, they go up, but in the two year period I worked on the book, some prices came down. The prices of foreign-made products, for instance, fluctuate with the value of currencies. A new federal excise tax added to wholesale prices also caused a change in prices between 1984 and 1985. The full impact of the tax is not clear, except that prices have gone up because of it.

The studies I've done on price changes show such wide variations as to make predictions useless, but if I thought the actual prices were the most important part of the book, I'd have dropped the project long ago. The range of prices is important, and it will remain fairly consistent even though the base prices change. Furthermore, price comparisons between products will be possible even if the prices for the products change.

Besides the list of sources and the price range for each product, I've also given a brief description. Often that is based on my own experience, but more frequently, it's based on catalog descriptions. There is also introductory information in many of the chapters that is designed to help you select appropriate equipment.

In addition to equipment, you'll also find listings of books, magazines, and fishing art along with information about organizations for fly fishermen, descriptions of catalog companies, and lists of fly shops, fly fishing schools, and state game and fish departments. If you can think of anything I left out, I'd be glad to hear from you.

For that matter, let me make it easy to do that. If you have a comment about the book, experiences you'd like to relate about equipment, or if I left your product or organization out of the book, please write me in care of Spring Creek Press, Box 1848, Estes Park, Colorado 80517.

With that business out of the way, let's take a brief look at the compleat angler's equipment.

The compleat angler's outfit. First, let's reduce to a minimum the number of items we fly fishermen need. We need a fly rod, reel, line, leader, and a fly. That's the absolute minimum, and of course, it's not a workable outfit. However, we need add only a few items to make it workable.

First, add hip boots or waders, depending on the requirements of the water. The mobility afforded by boots makes proper presentation possible, and that's central to our success. We must also carry more than one leader and more than one fly (because we occasionally lose one or the other), so let's add some terminal tippet material and an extra complete leader, along with a small fly box containing a few carefully chosen patterns. Some floatant to help keep our dry flies dry is important, too.

To make leader and fly changes easier, let's attach a pin-on retractor reel with a set of clippers to our shirt. To help us release our fish, let's also put a pair of forceps on our retractor. An Insta-Net will also aid in handling fish.

And that's all we need, really need. Of course, the rest of the gear we all typically carry is stuff we can't live without!

So, what do we end up with streamside? The answer has thousands of variations, but let's take a look at two sample fishermen. We'll call one of them the Very Compleat Angler and the other one the Almost Compleat Angler. Let's outfit them from top to bottom with the "basics" in two styles.

And which fisherman will catch the most fish? This list can't answer that question.

Very Compleat Angler

Irish Knit Hat—$33
Action Optics Sunglasses—$79
Hal Janssen Fishing Shirt—$44.95
Trout Bandana—$5.95
Fothergill Vest—$92
Chatillion Spring Balance—$39
Walton's Thumb Clippers—$34.95
Hy-Point Power Sharpener—$11.50
Bio-Quip Pocket Net—$8
Hardy Thermometer—$19.95
Seidel's 700 Floatant—$3.50
Gehrke's Xink—$3.60
Starrett Micrometer—$74.95
North Fork Dispenser—$29.95
Wheatley #1609 Fly Box—$110
Handmade Wood Fly Box—$39.95
Brodin Scrimshaw Net—$101
Orvis Deluxe Stretch Waders—$315

French Silk Line—$65
Bogdan Trout Reel—$300
Kustin Ultimate Rod—$3,000

Total Cost—**$4,411.25**

Almost Compleat Angler

Columbia Up-Downer Cap—$9.95
Fisherman's Sunglasses—$8.95
Mirafiori T-Shirt—$7.95

Columbia McKenzie Vest—$29.95
Zebco De-Liar—$2.10
Drugstore Clippers—$.49
Bear Stone Hook Hone—$1.15
Minnow Dip Net—$.45
Taylor Thermometer—$7.95
Paraffin/Gasoline Mix—$.50
Toothpaste—$.98
Multus Gage-It—$4.75
Dennison Dispenser—$6.95
Fly-Rite Fly Box—$6.49
Perrine #100 Fly Box—$9.75
Insta-Net—$10.95
Red Bal Sportsters—$17.95
River Systems Shoes—$34.50
Air Cel Supreme Line—$15.95
Cortland Crown II Reel—$26
Lamiglas G1000 Rod—$44.40

Total cost—**$248.11**

A word about buying equipment. Like most other fly fishermen, I appreciate quality in the equipment I use. My time spent fly fishing is quality time, and I don't like to spend it with inferior gear. The failure of a piece of equipment is also frustrating, and I get enough frustration at work.

At the same time, I'm a good consumer. I buy only what I need, and I buy equipment to match my abilities, my experience, and the demands of the sport. I'm not trendy, and I have little notion of fashion streamside (except in hats). Too many people buy expensive equipment when they don't need it. A novice fly fisherman with a T&T Presentation Rod is just a show-off. He hasn't earned the rod, and he can't appreciate the rod.

So, buy the highest quality equipment you need and can afford. Don't be taken in by advertisements or the claims of catalog companies or shop clerks. Judge equipment on the basis of your own needs, tastes, and budget. If you're a beginner, you have little to go on and much to learn. May your lessons be cheap. If you're an expert, fall not into the trap of impressing others. But when you've earned and can appreciate quality gear and when you can afford it, buy it. May that time come soon for you.

Whatever level you're at in the sport, whatever your needs and desires, fly fishing equipment manufacturers have probably made it for you. We're fortunate to have a wealth of innovative people out there working to bring their ideas of the ultimate rod or reel or what-have-you to us. Most work on their own or in close consort with a few other good people and not for some big company. That has kept our marketplace healthy and us happy. It has given us more choices, and like having many trout rising at once before us, that makes it all the more fun.

Enjoy the sport. Enjoy the book. And good shopping to you.

2. Fly Rods

PERHAPS IT WON'T SURPRISE YOU that there are over 1,000 rods listed in this book. If it doesn't, you're either in the business of making rods and know the competition or you're an experienced fly fisherman and have reason to own at least half that number of rods.

The nature of the sport does require a lot of different rods. Just as a hunter wouldn't use a .357 magnum to hunt rabbits, a fly fisherman wouldn't use a 10', 12-weight rod for bluegill. The reverse is even more ludicrous. How about a .22 for grizzly or a 7', 2-weight for tarpon? So, the requirements of matching your tackle to your sport make it necessary to have about 25 rods (on the market, not in your closet) in different lengths and line weights. But what about the other 975?

They're on the market because a rod must not only suit its intended use, it must also suit an angler's personality and fishing style. (And there are more than 975 different personalities and fishing styles wading around our streams and lakes.) The rod is the most important piece of equipment for the fly fisherman and the most personal. The choice of a rod depends on its usage, certainly, but just as importantly it depends on the tastes and casting style of the angler. Too little attention is paid to this fact by fly shop owners, catalog ad writers, and rod companies. All of these people tend to hype their favorite rod as the "best" rod, when indeed it may not be even suitable for the customer and his fishing style.

Later in this introduction, I'll be describing some of the criteria for selecting a rod. Some of it is rudimentary, like selecting the proper line weight and length for the type of fishing you'll be doing. Some of it is fairly esoteric, like choosing rod action and material. All of it, however, won't add up to the perfect rod.

What I want to tell you now may sound like "Zen and the Art of Fly Fishing". Your rod is an extension of your arm. It was added to the sport so that you can fish farther away from yourself than the 10 feet you could throw a fly line unassisted. The rod adds power to your casts, and it adds control. In fly fishing, you must cast the weight of the line, rather than the weight of a lead sinker or a spinner. A simple flick of the wrist will not send out 40 feet of fly line. It must be worked out gradually and controlled in the air in the meantime. It is the control of that line, as it is cast and placed, that determines in large part your success as a fly fisherman.

Control comes from a fly rod that acts just as you want it to. Some fly rods require you to make constant adjustments to get the fly where you want it. Others simply have a mind of their own (and they are invariably half-wits). I have a couple of both varieties in my closet—I can't even bear to give them away to someone. Unlike these rods, the rod you are searching for will respond to your wishes, just as your own arm does.

Reach over and pick up your coffee cup. Did you have to think about it? Did you tell your arm to go four inches farther, your fingers to open and close on the handle? Of course not. It was automatic. And that's how you want your fly rod to behave on the stream.

As for the Zen of it all, I can stand in the stream, look at the undercut bank where The Big Brown waits, and put my fly there without thinking about how I'm going to do that. This is not because I'm the world's best caster. I'm not. It's because my rod somehow knows (excuse the anthropomorphism) exactly what I want from what is telegraphed through my hand, wrist, and arm muscles. That rod, like those muscles, has a direct link to my mind.

Dave Hughes relates the same idea in *An Angler's Astoria*. In describing a particularly difficult presentation, he writes: "My eye and mind calculated the backcast and forecast. Then hand, wrist, arm, and the split bamboo moved quickly and precisely in ways that are mysterious even to me."

Before you dismiss the idea of your fly rod being an extension of your psyche, give the concept some consideration. If you're a beginner, you'll need a few years and a few rods before you understand. If you're a veteran and don't know what I'm talking about, you're missing a great deal of satisfaction in the sport and you'd better start rod shopping.

It was 10 years before I found a rod that came close to what I'm trying to describe. It was another five years before I found the perfect rod for me. (For me, it was a Scott PowR-Ply 8½' for a 5-weight line, but that doesn't make it the rod for you.) It won't take you as many years or as many rods as it did me, because you now know what's possible and you'll look for it. I didn't.

For beginners who have been down to the local discount store to shop for a rod, this may be doubly difficult to understand. You've seen the $13.95 weeping willows and the $17.95 2x4s. There's not much Zen in them. But take a browse through the catalog listings. You'll find among them a $3,000 bamboo rod from Barry Kustin and many other expensive, hand-crafted rods. This lends some credence to what I'm telling you.

Think about your friend who does serious shotgunning. He wants a gun that comes up correctly on the shoulder every time, without his thinking about it. He wants to be able to pull the gun up, look at the target, and shoot. There's no aiming, no thinking about where the gun's pointed. There is only the activity and the result. So it should be with the fly fisherman's cast. Just as the shotgunner is willing to spend the money to get a gun that works like that for him, the fly fisherman is willing to make the same investment in a fly rod.

Not that you need to spend a tremendous amount on your first fly rod. You'll find some very adequate (although probably not ideal) rods for around $50-$75. I spent $160 for my favorite rod some years ago. That was a small fortune for me, but I'd tried out 30 rods and I knew it was the right one for me. I fish well over 200 hours a year with that rod, have for five or more years, will for many more years. Movies cost a hell of a lot more per hour and are generally far less entertaining.

Whether you're spending $50 or $3,000, I invite you to go on a quest for a rod that will cast well and become part of you, a rod you can respect, a rod you can appreciate as you would anything of quality in your life.

Selecting a rod. This is the most difficult equipment choice for the fly fisherman, beginner or veteran. It's a lot easier to catch fish than it is to pick the correct fly rod.

Most people entering the sport make a big mistake on rod selection. They base their selection entirely on cost. They want to try out the sport as inexpensively as possible (and I don't blame them). They go down to the local discount store, pick up fly rods one after the other, and check their price tags. They wiggle them self-consciously, since they don't have any idea what makes a good rod. The resulting threat to fellow shoppers is enough to cause them to make a hasty, and poor, choice.

This kind of rod selection has caused many fly fishermen in the making to give up the sport. For those of us who survived the process, myself included, it has filled our tackle closets with rods we now realize are more suited to holding up tomato plants in the garden than to casting a fly line.

So let's get one thing settled. You should spend at least $50 on your first fly rod, more if you can afford it. That will buy a rod that will cast well enough that you won't get discouraged. If you're not ready to spend $50 on a rod, you don't want to learn fly fishing badly enough. If you invest in a rod and decide later that it's not the sport for you, you'll at least have a rod that is decent enough to hand down to a niece or nephew who wants to learn.

I've found about 25 rods significantly under $50, but I'm not including them. They aren't worth the frustration. If you already own one, I'm sorry to have insulted your rod, but I'm also quite sure you'll retire it the moment you try any of the rods I'm suggesting for a first rod.

Just to help you narrow things down, here is a list of rods I feel comfortable in recommending for the beginner. I can't recommend rods for the experienced fly fisherman, since personal taste plays such an important role in selecting one.

Rods for the beginner that cost about $50: Cortland 2000 ($42), Fenwick Fiberglass ($49), Fisher Fiberglass (about $58), and Lamiglas G1000 (about $50). The last rod is graphite, and because of the material, I'd recommend it above the others. The G1000 is usually about $90, but Hook & Hackle offers it within our price constraints. The G1000, however, does not come with a bag or tube, something you'll want to add.

If you can spend a bit more or can build a rod, take a look at Cabela's Fish Eagle rods. Like the Lamiglas, these are graphite rods, and like the Lamiglas, the Cabela's rods that I've cast have been impressive for the price (about $80). The Fenwick Eagle graphite rod is also worthy of your attention, as are some of the less expensive Cortland graphite rods.

Even with these recommendations and what you'll read about rods in the rest of this chapter, you should never buy a rod without trying it out. Would you buy a car without first driving it?

Try out your friends' rods, visit the fly shops in your area, get as many rods in your hand as you can, even if you're sure from the ads that you're going to love Brand X. Your local fly shop is a good place to get started. The shop personnel will give you the personal attention necessary to get you into a rod that fits, and they'll let you try it out before you buy. If you don't know how to cast, they'll probably help you with that, too. But, please, don't take advantage of them by trying out rods there and ordering them from a catalog. The advice and help you'll get from a good shop will be worth the extra bucks (if any) over the years.

If you don't have any friends (who fly fish, that is) and you don't have any fly shops within a day's drive, you may have to deal directly with a catalog company or rod maker without having cast their rods. If that's the case, call them first and discuss your needs. Tell them the rods you've used before and your reaction. Elicit their advice and support in your rod selection. Then see if they have a return policy that will allow you to exchange the rod (undamaged and unfished) for another if necessary. All reputable companies have a return policy.

A number of smaller rod companies offer that exchange up front. Dave Sylvester of Deerfield, for instance, will let you try out his rods for 10 days with full return or exchange privileges. Other companies offer some kind of exchange program, but they may not advertise it. You have to ask, and ask you should.

Choosing a rod, whether it's your first or your fifteenth, is always an adventure. My last big buying trip took me to every fly shop in Boulder and Denver. I tried out at least 30 rods. The one I bought was the first one I tried that day. It was handed to me without a sales pitch, and it didn't need one. But I wasn't sure until I'd tried out the other 29.

I guess I could get on the soapbox about advertising. Every rod is the finest, the longest casting, the best. Hogwash. Yes, there are many fine fly rods on the market, but the one that's right for you can't be located by reading the ads.

You can narrow your choices down by following the guidelines below. These general rules for rod selection will help get you started, but the heart of your selection still depends on trying out the rods and finding the one that speaks to you.

Line weight. Rods are designed to throw a specific weight line, and the combination of line weight and rod length determines, in part, the action of the rod. The kind of fishing you'll be doing determines what line weight you'll need, and that, in turn, begins the rod selection process. If you're buying a rod and don't know what you want, the first thing a fly shop clerk will ask you is what kind of fishing you'll be doing. The following set of guidelines gives you the line weights in general categories and the kind of fishing for which they are preferred.

Line weights 2,3,4. These are very lightweight lines. (Indeed, casting a 2-weight line feels like you're casting monofilament.) That means they land on the water without as much disturbance as heavier lines. Since trout, especially, are very sensitive to vibrations, line weight becomes a concern on some waters.

Beaver ponds, spring creeks, and the flats of some of our more prestigious streams like the Battenkill, the Firehole, and the South Platte are some of the areas where a lighter weight line is preferred for its delicacy of presentation.

Some anglers prefer the lightweight lines when fishing for smaller fish, such as bluegill and brook trout, because rods designed for the light lines are more sensitive and make playing the fish more exciting. Others choose a light line and a miniature rod to go with it just for the fun of going lightweight.

The lighter line weights are not as easy to cast as heavier ones, so the beginner probably should put off the purchase of such a rod until he's got confidence in his casting.

Line weights 4,5,6. The "medium" weights are appropriate for most trout fishing situations. They are easy to cast and can be managed in breezy conditions. At the same time, they are still light enough to provide a reasonable presentation that will not spook trout.

Some of the more wind-resistant flies used in trout fishing are easier to cast with these medium weight lines, and yet the lines and rods do not weigh so much as to tire out the beginning caster in a day's fishing time.

My all around rod is a 5-weight graphite. If I'm careful, it's delicate enough for fishing the #24 white midges in the Firehole. If I need to, I can throw a streamer or weighted nymph in the Bighorn. A lighter line would work better on the Firehole, perhaps, and a heavier one would certainly help in casting the heavier flies, but the 5-weight can do either job in a pinch.

A beginner who will only own one rod for the time being should probably buy one designed for one of these line weights, and I have leanings toward the 6-weight as the true all-around line weight.

Line weights 6,7,8. These heavier lines will cast big, bushy flies better than the lighter lines will. They are preferred by bass fishermen and weighted-nymph fishermen for this reason. They'll also cast better in the wind. Western fishermen who face big waters and high wind need heavier line weights. Big waters also require lots of long distance casting, and heavier line weights are better in those situations.

Most freshwater fly fishermen will never need to use anything heavier than an 8-weight. It will control poppers the size of mice and nymphs the weight of Quarter Pounders.

Line weights 8,9,10. Now we're getting into the heavyweight division. Most of the rods designed for these line weights are for steelhead and salmon fishermen. They are also used for light saltwater fishing. Rods built for these purposes are generally long, stiff, and heavy, and they wouldn't be much fun for six inch brook trout in the beaver ponds.

Line weights 10,11,12, and even 13. These line weights and the rods that throw them are designed primarily for the salmon and saltwater fisherman. Long-distance casting without a lot of false casting is required in this part of the sport, and these heavies will do that in the hands of an experienced caster. However, bigger is not better for the novice.

Any rod you pick up these days is marked with its length and line weight. Many rods bear two recommended line weights. In many cases, this means the rod is capable of handling either line weight with the preference up to the caster. The heavier line will slow the rod down in comparison to the lighter line. You should try both line weights before selecting one of these rods.

Other rods bearing two line weights are really designed for one weight. You may use either a double taper line in the lighter weight or a weight forward line in the heavier. (For a discussion of line tapers, see the chapter on fly lines.) In any case, most rods will handle a line weight above and below the one they specify. If you have a rod that isn't quite right, you may get a pleasant suprise if you try a different line weight on it.

After selecting the appropriate range of line weights, your next job is to pick the rod length.

Rod length and weight. The rods listed here range in length from Ed Shenk's 5½' Flea rod to the 16' Rodon Boron rod designed for saltwater and salmon use. Those two rods represent the extremes in rod weights, too, at 1¼ oz. for the flea and 12½ oz. for the Rodon rod.

Choosing your rod's length is not nearly as difficult as these extremes of the offerings would seem to make it, because most of the rods in use today range from 7' to 9', with 8' and 8½' being the most common.

Rod length is matched to the kind of fishing you'll be doing, just as is line weight. Personal taste and casting ability also play important roles in selecting the proper length rod. Let's take a very general look at rod lengths to help you out.

5'-7'. Shorter rods have no practical advantage over longer rods. They are, however, a lot of fun to cast. A fly fisherman who owns a short rod may tell his buddies that he bought it for the small stream down the road a piece, but it's probably just a fun rod to own.

In the 1960s, short rods were in fashion. The up-to-date fly fisherman had to have at least one short rod, say 6½'. Their light weight was supposed to make a 6" brook trout feel like a miniature tarpon. They were also supposed to be better rods for small, brushy streams. When graphite arrived with its light weight and extreme sensitivity, the first argument for a short rod became less compelling.

The second reason for buying a shorty was faulty, I think. It was a theoretical notion, rather than one based on experience. I fish small, brushy streams with a friend who uses a 7' rod. I use an 8½' rod. I can steeple cast better than he can (because of the rod's length), so I stay out of the trees better. My rod allows better roll casts with more accuracy. In addition, I can reach pockets with a flick cast that he can't, and I can mend line easier to improve my drift in the swift streams we fish. I can reach around trees better and dap farther away than he can. The only advantage he has is during the walk to the stream and in some very tight casting situations that I'd rather skip anyway. So much for short rods on small streams.

The shorties are fun, however, and you'll be amazed at the line you can throw with one. As a third or fourth rod, they're worth some thought.

7'-9'. The rods in these lengths will cover the requirements of every kind of fishing except some steelhead, salmon, and saltwater fishing. Within this range, you can find line weights from 2 to 10.

Most people use rods of 8' or 8½'. Longer rods can feel cumbersome, especially to a beginner, and shorter ones require more finesse and better timing.

At one time, as I've noted, short rods were in fashion. Now, the fashion pendulum has swung the other way and longer rods are in fashion. If you were the first on your block with a 9' rod, you were the envy of fellow fly fishermen. Part of this swing in favored rod lengths had to do with the development of graphite as a rod material. Its full advantages are not realized in short lengths.

Even during passing fancies like the short-rod craze, fly fishermen still favored the 8' to 8½' lengths, and they may always. The rods are easy to handle, yet offer adequate line control and power for most fishing situations. The ideal rod for a beginning trout fisherman is probably an 8½' for a 6-weight line.

9' and over. These are generally the workhorse rods. Not that they aren't fine casting machines with the capability of delicate presentations for their line weight— they are that, too.

Many rods over 9' are designed for line weights of 8 and above. That combination of length and line weight is required by fishermen who cast to steelhead, salmon, and saltwater gamefish. In very long lengths, rods are sometimes two-handed models.

Many of the rods in these lengths have fighting butts. Fighting butts extend the rod's butt so that it can be carried in the angler's belly and the fish fought with extra leverage. There are two varieties. One is an internal part that is pulled down when a fish is on. The other is an external extension that is inserted by the fisherman when the time is right. The former is more convenient, but it adds to the rod weight. The latter gives the rod a lighter weight, but requires carrying in a pocket. The resultant fumbling for the extension can cost you a good fish or an overboard fighting butt.

I won't spend any more time on rod lengths. I'm also not inclined to spend a lot of time on rod weight. This was a much more important consideration when fiberglass was the primary rod material. Today's graphite rods are very lightweight. People in my fishing classes who have been using older fiberglass rods or production bamboo rods from the 1940s are astounded at the light weight of graphite.

Let me give you some quick comparisons for 8½' rods designed for a 6-weight (or 6/7-weight) line. The Cortland 2000 (fiberglass) weighs 4 oz. The same size Fenwick fiberglass weighs 3¾ oz. The Winston fiberglass weighs 3⅜ oz.

Graphite rods are generally lighter. How much lighter depends on the tapers used and kind of graphite. The inexpensive Lamiglas G1000 graphite rod, for instance, weighs 3 oz. The Sage GFL 686 weighs 3⅛ oz., and their Graphite II rod weighs 3³⁄₁₆ oz. Cabela's Fish Eagle in this length and line weight comes in at 3.3 oz., while Fenwick's HMG Graphite weighs more at 3½ oz. Cortland's Black Diamond is lighter at 2¾ oz. The Orvis Limestone weighs just 2⅝ oz., as does the Winston graphite, but the Scott PowR-Ply G85-6 squeaks in under both to win lightweight honors at 2½ oz.

You won't be able to feel the weight difference between the Scott and the other ultralight rods, but you will be able to tell them apart in hand from the heavier graphite rods and certainly from the fiberglass models.

Boron rods, incidentally, generally weigh a little more than the graphites in the same lengths and line weights. The Fenwick HMG Boron-X weighs 3⅞ oz. The Orvis Boron/Graphite weighs 3⅜ oz. The Rodon Boron rod, a three-piece, weighs 3⅛ oz. The Lamiglas Boron, on the other hand, weighs just 3 oz., the same as their graphite rod.

You won't find much information about rod weights from makers of bamboo rods. The rod makers don't wish to compete on that basis, and a potential purchaser of a bamboo rod is buying it for reasons other than its weight. Stated bamboo weights range from 2⅝ oz. to 4¼ oz. for the 8½', 6-weight models.

All this may be more confusing than it should be. You'll choose a rod based on its "feel", as well as other considerations. Weight will play a part in this, but so will the rod's action.

Rod action and material. Slow, medium, and fast. Those wonderfully simple descriptions of rod action are not very useful today, I'm afraid. They developed as ways to talk about a rod's action when bamboo was about the only rod material in use.

A slow rod was designed for wet flies and nymphs. It was limber and felt "soft" in casting. The timing required a longer wait between backcast and forward cast. Line speed was less. A fast rod was supposedly for dry-fly fishing. It was stiffer. The timing was quicker, and line speed was greater. A medium action rod was between the extremes and did both kinds of fishing with compromises.

When there was only one rod material, all slow-action rods behaved in relatively the same manner. That descriptive system began to change when fiberglass entered the market in the 1950s, and its credibility has eroded and continues to erode as newer materials, such as graphite and boron, are used for fly rods.

The newer rods, which are hollow tubes, did not easily fit into that convenient classification sytem based on the solid construction of a bamboo rod. And each of the new materials is different in action simply because of the characteristics of the material. Fiberglass rods are the "slowest", high modulus graphite rods the "fastest".

This confusion concerning rod action is further aggravated by the fact that all graphite rods, to my knowledge, use fiberglass in combination with the graphite. There are also many varieties of graphite. All boron rods have graphite in them, and the differing percentages used by manufacturers change rod action.

Furthermore, taper designs have become more and more varied partly because of the workability of the newer materials. Thus, a manufacturer could have two rods of the same length and line weight, made of the same material, and each could have a different action. (Fortunately, none of them do this.)

So, can we say anything about rod action? Yes, we can. However, everything that's said must be relative. We can call a fiberglass rod "fast" only with the understanding that it's not as fast as say a "medium" graphite rod. One thing you should immediately understand from this is that any such descriptive phrase used in an advertisement is to be taken with a block of salt.

Let's take a brief look at rod materials and their actions. That may help you choose the material for your new rod.

Bamboo. Arundinaria amabilis. That's Latin for fine fly rods. Bamboo has a long tradition as a fly rod material. Before bamboo, rods were made of other woods. With the advent of bamboo as a rod material, rods became more responsive and much lighter.

The bamboo used in quality fly rods comes from China. Various attempts at starting bamboo "plantations" in other parts of the world have failed to produce the dense, straight-fibered cane that China is known for. Even so, rod makers often reject much of the cane during quality inspections. Orvis, for instance, keeps only a small percentage of the cane it imports, even after an initial inspection overseas.

The select bamboo used in quality rods is typically tempered by a heating process. Then the poles are cut to suitable lengths and split into segments roughly triangular in shape. These segments are milled to close tolerances, and six of them are fitted and glued together to form a hexagonal rod. A notable exception to this process are the rods of M. Montagne, which are rectangular when finished.

Many bamboo rods are then finished with a waterproof varnish. Bamboo rod owners must maintain this finish to assure that the rods do not take in water and become warped or lose the bond between segments. Other bamboo rods are impregnated with a finish and do not require that routine inspection and maintenance.

Bamboo rods are beautiful, as are all things made of wood. Pride of ownership is high, and every rod is distinctive. They remain the favorite casting tools of many fly fishermen. Newer materials are capable of throwing longer lines, perhaps, but they cannot match the grace and beauty of bamboo.

Since the material is expensive and the hand crafting extensive, a good bamboo will cost some money. H.L. Leonard's least expensive model, the Deluxe, is $600. The Orvis Madison series begins at $550.

Those are the economy models. Their price is based on the appearance of the bamboo and the rod components used. Standard models cost more. Orvis Battenkills start at $775, while Leonard's Standard rods are $800. The Thomas & Thomas Classics retail for $635, with Weir & Sons rods starting at $650. Winston bamboo and Ron Kusse rods are $695 and $690 respectively. Of course, you can spend much more for the bamboo rod that suits you. M. Montagne rods are $1,300, Foster's Anglia is $1,250, and Barry Kustin's hollow-built Ultimate is $3,000.

A bamboo rod is a worthwhile purchase for those anglers who appreciate its heritage and beauty. The values of the rods increase with time, making them worthy of the investor's or collector's interest. (The retail price of new Orvis rods, for instance, rose about $200 in one year recently.)

At the same time, the worst investment you can probably make in a rod is a cheap bamboo. I've seen some in sporting goods stores that come with a "set" (a bend in the rod) already established so you don't have to worry about getting one. These rods commonly sell for $125. Your money is much better spent on a rod of a different material until you can afford a quality rod.

I'm often asked to evaluate older bamboo rods. Out in the West, I don't find many of outstanding value. Most are the production rods of the 1940s. These are generally three piece, 9' rods with aluminum reel seats. Some have reinforcement wraps the length of the rod.

Rods such as these were produced in mass just as fiberglass rods were in the 50s and inexpensive graphite rods are now. They are not very good casting tools, generally, and are of limited interest to collectors. My suggestion to the people who bring a rod like this in is that it be retired to a place of honor on the wall of the den. It served grandfather well and thus has sentimental value much beyond its monetary worth.

If you have an older bamboo rod, however, you should have it evaluated at several fly shops. It could be a Payne or Garrison worth thousands of dollars to an earnest collector.

The action of bamboo rods varies considerably according to the rod maker's designs, but the rods are generally neither as fast nor as light as graphite. (For an interesting exception, see the Kustin rods.) They offer excellent line control, however, and with casts of short to medium length, they are perhaps the most accurate and delicate of the materials.

Fiberglass. The first of the "modern" materials, fiberglass offered one immediate benefit over bamboo—it was less expensive. It was also lighter and could be made into any length rod.

There was an initial lack of acceptance of fiberglass by those anglers already in the sport. Indeed, the first glass rods were inferior to the bamboo rods they were accustomed to. However, some fine rod makers began working with the material. Their improvements in design and construction filtered down, and soon even production rods were sound casting instruments.

Courtesy of Ron Kusse Rods

Russ Peak, Harry Wilson at Scott PowR-Ply, the R.L. Winston Co., and others created excellent glass rods, and still do. As a quality rod material, though, fiberglass lives in the shadow of graphite. Winston's first-class fiberglass rods, for instance, retail for $160, and a good graphite rod can be purchased for that amount. Most fishermen prefer the graphite.

Fiberglass is lighter than bamboo, but heavier than graphite. It is not as strong as either. It's only advantage today is that it's inexpensive. Graphite as a material costs up to 10 times as much.

Many fiberglass rods, I'm afraid, are real clunkers. A number of these come from manufacturers who deal mostly in spin fishing and bait casting equipment. Their fly rods were not developed independently of that heritage. They are very tippy with little flex in the lower section.

Fiberglass rods are manufactured by rolling fiberglass cloth onto mandrels. These metal rods represent the hollow area inside the rods. After the process is complete, the mandrel is removed, leaving a hollow fiberglass blank.

One thing to check in a fiberglass rod is the ferrule (the joint between sections). Metal ferrules were originally used on fiberglass rods, and many inexpensive models still use them. They affect the action of the rod. Since the metal doesn't flex, there will be a dead spot right in the middle of the rod. More sophisticated ferrules use fiberglass but are still bulkier than the rod itself. The best ferrules (at least in terms of action) are built internally, so that the outside diameter of the rod shaft does not change.

Fiberglass will probably be around a long time as an inexpensive beginner's rod. Fiberglass rods are also preferred by some anglers for nymph fishing, due in part to their slower action and resistance to breakage. Fiberglass has reached its peak of development, however, and the expensive glass rods are being built only for those anglers who simply prefer the material. Except on the basis of personal taste, it's difficult to build a case for even the expensive glass rods when good graphite rods are available for the same money.

Graphite. Developed for the space program, graphite is now the most popular fly rod material. It is stiff, strong, and very lightweight. When built with a carefully designed taper, it also creates a very delicate rod. Graphite is much more sensitive and responsive than other materials, making it possible to feel hits better. Finally, with the development of graphite came the possibility of creating long rods for light line weights, something that had not been practical with previous materials.

You'll hear a lot about graphite's high modulus of elasticity. That means it resists bending. Pick up any true graphite rod in the store and it will feel very stiff compared with rods of the previous materials we've discussed.

Notice that I specified a true graphite rod. Some manufacturers call their rods graphite rods even if they have a relatively small percentage of graphite in them. I'm also suspicious of the rods that say 100% graphite, because even Orvis claims only 94-96% pure graphite in their rods.

Even if you know the rod is truly a graphite rod, you still can't be sure of exactly what you're getting. There are high modulus and low modulus graphites, and everything in between. Fly rod construction has always been a complicated art/science, and the advent of graphite only made it more complicated.

I don't think it would help if manufacturers marked all their rods with something like "94.6% pure K-3 graphite". You'd still not know exactly what the thickness of the wrap was or the design of the taper. The only reliable test is to try out the rod and see if it works for you.

Graphite is another material that had some early difficulty in angler acceptance. It was first thought to be appropriate only for long-distance casting (sounds a bit like boron's reputation today). For years, anglers talked of graphite rods as tippet busters because of their power when setting the hook. I've had fly shop owners tell me not to buy graphite if I wanted to fish anything finer than 4x tippets.

This period of awkward adolescence for graphite had something to do with the rod makers and their use of the material and something to do with anglers and their inability to adjust to it. I still break off a couple of 6x tippets with my graphite rods if I've been using a bamboo or fiberglass rod. (Of course, I also miss a lot of fish on the bamboo rod after fishing the graphite because the bamboo is so much slower.)

Now, rod makers have developed graphite into a marvelous rod material that will delicately present and protect 7x tippets. Part of that development was the design of new tapers that took advantage of graphite and still retained delicacy. For a while, graphite rods were built on the same mandrels as fiberglass rods, and that didn't work. (Some manufacturers, I believe, still do this, and it still doesn't work.)

The most important thing I can probably tell you about graphite rods is that the material doesn't make the rod. Too many manufacturers are riding the fashion formula and selling rods just because they're made of graphite. Big deal. Graphite rods still must be designed properly, with specially created mandrels and appropriate ferrule systems.

Boron/graphite. Boron is the newest rod material. It is an incredibly stiff material, so stiff that many rod makers will not even work with it. Indeed, the boron must be "cut" with graphite to make it a viable rod material. Percentages of graphite in current rods run from 20-40% depending on length and line weight of the rod.

Because of its stiffness (and resulting power), boron/graphite rods are generally longer length rods for heavier lines. Current rod design in boron is also producing rods suitable for light lines and delicate tippets. However, as a special use rod for long distance casting or heavy wind situations, boron/graphite is the most powerful material you can find on the market.

You might assume, as I did, that boron rods are extremely fast because of the stiffness of the material. This is not necessarily true. Rodon's boron/graphite rods, for instance, are relatively slow, developing their power over the full length of the rod. They are pleasant to use and, indeed, may feel more like a fiberglass or bamboo rod in action. The punch that they deliver, however, is quite different.

Maybe you've read this section on materials hoping to get the final word on rod action. Now you may understand that although materials put some inherent characteristics into a rod's action, they do not determine it completely. Only vague generalizations can be made about action based on the material, and rod design can negate most of them.

The real way to determine a rod's action, the only way in fact, is to try it out. No magazine ad can tell you in a thousand words what your hand can tell you in 30 seconds.

Test Driving a Fly Rod. You can get your money's worth from this book just by following one piece of advice I've already given you. Don't buy a fly rod based on a magazine ad or a shop clerk's recommendation alone. Try out the rod first. Compare rods. Look for the one that fits you (and your pocketbook).

If you fly fish already and have for a number of years, you probably know exactly what you want in a rod, but if you're a novice, it's very difficult to know where to start, what questions to ask, what to look for in the rods you're considering. From this introduction you'll have some idea of the line weight and rod length you want. You may also have decided on a rod material. That will still leave you many rods from which to choose.

The restraints of pocketbook may limit your choice somewhat, at least at any one shop, but there are often many shops around. You should visit all of them before deciding. Remember that this is your most important decision in equipment selection, and it's a fun one to make if you do it right.

In your introductory discussions with a shop owner or clerk, tell him (sorry, I still haven't run across a her selling rods) what kind of fishing you'll be using the rod for and what line weight and length you think is most appropriate. He may suggest a few other combinations based on your experience and what you look like during the casting. Give them a try.

He'll also want to know how much you want to spend. If you say less than $100, you won't have much of a selection probably, and most of the rods will be fiberglass If you say less than $250, you'll probably be able to look at most of the stock, including quality graphite rods. Even if you are willing to spend that much, it's a good idea to look at the less expensive rods, also. Right now, you can't tell what will please you the most, and some of the less expensive rods are not as demanding on the caster. You may be more comfortable driving a Chevy as your first car instead of a Ferrari.

You can do a preliminary quality check based on the rod's appearance. First, check the number of guides. An 8½' rod in a high quality line will have as many as 10 guides plus the tip top. A rod that has fewer guides than the number of feet in its length is suspect.

Next check the windings on the guides. They should be uniform, well-wound, and smoothly finished. Trims should be done with thread, not paint. Then put the rod together and check the alignment of the guides. It may not be perfect but it should be damn close.

A brief word about putting rod sections together. Rods with metal ferrules (bamboo for the most part these days) should be aligned before they're snugged. The two sections should then be brought together in a straight line. Rods with fiberglass or graphite ferrules should be aligned about a quarter turn off. The sections are then brought together, and the final snug made with a turning motion that aligns the guides. Some of the more thoughtful manufacturers will have marked the alignment point with dots on both sections at the ferrule.

You should also look the blank itself over for imperfections. Any that you find will probably be cosmetic blemishes, but they may affect your feelings for the rod. It's not much fun to find them after you've bought the rod.

Now take a look at the cork handle and the reel seat. On a high quality rod, the cork will be smooth, although there are always some pits. Lower quality rods have lots of pits and other imperfections that will cause blisters on your hand. You may have to look closely because handles are filled in much the same way that wood is sometimes filled. Large fillings may come out after the handle is wet a few times.

At this time, you should begin considering the style of handle you prefer. The fact that there are so many styles suggests that this is another area where personal taste is involved. The handle should be comfortable, whatever style it is. You hand should fit all the way around it, but your fingers should not touch the palm of your hand. If they do, the handle is too small, and blisters will develop. Blisters are the result of friction and its heat. A smooth hold on the rod handle, without wrinkles in your skin, will eliminate blisters.

The reel seat can give you some indication of the rod's quality, also. Make sure the reel sits in perfect alignment to the guides. Sloppy work on the handle and reel seat often shows up in alignment first. Take a look at the hardware used. A few comparisons between rods of known quality and ones you're not familiar with will allow you to judge the materials and workmanship in the reel seat.

Reel seats are either "down-locking" or "up-locking". Down-locking seats place the reel at the very bottom of the rod. The tightening nut or slip ring is close to the cork. Up-locking seats place the foot of the reel under the cork handle. The hardware is at the bottom of the rod and moves up to tighten the reel.

You may not at first have a preference on reel seat style. It will probably be one of the least important considerations for a beginner. More expensive rods built with the experienced fly fisherman in mind usually give the buyer a choice in both handle styles and reel seats.

I've had a preference on reel seats from the beginning. I've always thought the down-locking looked better. After all, a fly reel belongs at the bottom on the rod. More practical considerations have reinforced that preference. Up-locking seats leave the rod butt exposed below the reel. It attracts fly line, and that can cost you a fish. I've also discovered over the years that occasionally the difference between reaching that rising fish on Fan Lake and falling short is the two or three inches that I can scoot my hand down if I have a down-locking reel seat. Just that much extra leverage can increase the distance of my cast. So much for my preferences. You can start developing your own.

All these superficial quality checks will give you some indication of the rod's quality and will allow you to compare rods in the same price range. The real test comes in the casting.

Unfortunately, there seems to be only one thing on the mind of a person trying out rods—how far can I cast with this rod? That should only be a curiosity for you unless you spend all your time casting that much line. So, the first thing to do is to shake off that almost automatic desire to put out 60' of line. A rod must perform up close if it's to be of any value to you.

Courtesy of R.L. Winston Rods

By way of example, I cast a friend's rod recently and just for fun tried to put out all the fly line (30 yds.). To my surprise, I could. Now, this is not an earth-shaking event for high class casters with good equipment, but it was kind of the highlight of my day. I was even more surprised because the rod was a $39.95 special. It was a 8½' rod for a 7-weight line and was supposed to be 100% graphite. You'd recognize the brand name as that of a well-known reel manufacturer, but for a rod, it was an off-brand.

Having gotten the macho casting demonstration out of the way, I went to work really trying the rod out. I couldn't hit a 5' circle 10' away with it. It was a dog, a real clunkerstick. It didn't load properly (more on loading later). It was top heavy and boorish. It would do only one thing well—put out a lot of line. It makes a good boat rod—especially because it wouldn't hurt too much to have it go overboard—but that's all it's useful for.

So, in trying out rods, save the distance casting for last. It's occasionally very important to throw a lot of line, and the rod should do that well, but it's more important that it exhibit good line control at short to medium distances. I'd recommend that the first part of your casting concentrate on accuracy at distances of 15'-30'. Look at a place and try to cast to it. You won't be too successful at first; nobody is with a new rod. But the rod should respond quickly to your wishes, and you should be hitting the mark soon.

One thing you're looking for during the accuracy casts and false casting you'll be doing is how the rod "loads". You'll hear this term frequently in discussions of rods.

The weight of the fly line as it's backcast, for instance, bends the rod. That's the load. The resulting spring back to center by the rod material provides a lot of the power of the cast. The clunkerstick I mentioned earlier loaded well at great line lengths, but it didn't load at all at short line lengths. Might as well have been casting with a broom handle.

So, in part, you're looking for a rod that loads well at all casting distances. This characteristic is determined by proper design of the rod's taper and careful manufacturing. On short casts, you should feel the power of the rod and not have to force the line out. On longer casts, the rod should flex far into the butt section and give the power necessary to throw the long line. You may wish to have the shop clerk cast while you watch the rod, because you can see the load on the rod, at least partly. The real test, again, is casting.

As you feel the rod working, it should respond to the load and the lack of a load. That is, it should recover from the load properly. At one end of the spectrum, you may find a rod that does not finish a cast properly. Evidence of this is a consistently piled leader. The final punch is not there. At the other end, you may find rods that "overpower". These rods go past center as they recover from a load. The telltale sign of this is a feeling of the rod being top heavy, of moving forward after you've finished the cast. There's one big name rod maker whose every rod feels like that to me. Control is lacking on the recovery.

It takes a practiced hand to judge loading properly, but if you pay attention to the rods you're trying out, you'll begin to understand. The next characteristic you should be judging is not as subtle, and it's more a matter of taste than the quality of the rod.

The action of a rod amounts to its personality, and it must match yours. I discussed action briefly as part of rod materials. It was only covered briefly there because so many other factors go into the creation of a rod's action.

First, let's make sure we know what we're talking about when we say "action". The action of a rod is a description of how long it takes to load and recover during casting. A "slow" rod takes a longer time to load for the pick up of line, longer to throw it into the backcast, longer to load there, and longer to recover into the forward cast. A "fast" rod takes less time to do all this.

What this all amounts to for the caster is a difference in timing during the cast. It does not necessarily reflect on a rod's power or accuracy, although a fast action rod is often built for power and a slow action rod is easier to aim for some anglers. The timing you prefer as a caster seems to be something inherent in you. That's why I often refer to it as a matter of personality.

I can relate this to myself, in any case. I get my relaxation from the sport of fly fishing and its intensity for me. When I'm on the stream, it's difficult for anything else but the casting and the fishing to enter my consciousness. I like a fast rod. It fits my desire to fish hard and forget it all.

Other anglers, I know, get to the stream and practically fall over asleep from the relaxation they feel just from being there. Their entire attitude is relaxed, and so is their casting style. Those people like a slower rod.

This is cheap psychology and only that. All I'm saying is that the timing required by a rod to work properly varies from rod to rod, and some rods suit some anglers more than other rods because of that.

You'll have to determine over a period of time what kind of action you like in a rod, but you should begin while you're trying out rods. You might, for instance, start by asking the shop clerk to separate out the fastest and the slowest rods. That way you can try both extremes and learn the difference. It's very possible you won't like either of the them, but you'll like one more than the other and that will give you a start.

Now you know how to begin. You may have noticed that I didn't give you any way to judge a rod by wiggling it in the store. There isn't any way. Take the rod outside and cast it. Cast every rod you can, especially as a beginner. Do not be swayed by advertising or the clerk's personal preferences. Keep the macho, long distance casting to a minimum. And, most importantly, enjoy the adventure.

What's in a rod name? Rod companies can be divided into two groups: those that name their rod models and those that don't.

Now, I have a lot of respect for Scott, Sage, and other companies that send their rods out with unglamorous titles like G85-5 and GFL 8100-3. When they sell a rod, they don't have to lie awake at night wondering if it was the rod the customer bought or its name.

Still, they've missed a lot of fun naming their rods, and their rod owners are a bit deprived, not in rod quality, certainly, but in mystique. Consider, for instance, the aura created by owning the Rivermaster from Orvis. I'd stand tall in my waders with that rod.

I get the same kind of image from Deerfield's Tarponeer. I can see myself now, standing in the bow, swashbuckler boots and chinos. My hat is a Capt. Hook special (but in light tan to reflect the heat). I have a black patch over one eye, but the other eye is intent in its search for the big fish. And back on shore, I could carry the four-piece Tarponeer in a sheath on my side, ready for action.

Hardy's pack rod gives me shudders of anticipation whenever I hear its name: Smuggler. This rod would require secret agent attire: overcoat and dark sunglasses. I'd feel sneaky everytime I took the rod out. I could carry it everywhere in my overcoat pocket. But it would cause trouble, because sooner or later I'd have to try to smuggle it into Crocker Ranch, our local invitation to trespassing.

Other rods have names that describe their nature. Orvis has the Far and Fine, a name that bespeaks delicacy. Both Orvis and Ed Shenk of Letort Ltd. have a Flea rod. At 5½', Ed's is a bit more flea than the Orvis rod at 6½'. Foster's of England has an even more inviting

name for their small rod: Wisp. And then there are rods that speak of status and power. Thomas & Thomas has the Classic rod. R.L. Winston offers an Executive travel rod, but the executive might also be lured by the Advantage or Advantage-Plus from Orvis. And for the real power hungry, there's Champion from Fosters of England, Powerhouse from Orvis, and Kustin's Ultimate. The classiest name has to belong to the Sans Pareil from Thomas & Thomas.

Finally, there's a large group of names that are simply pleasant and inviting. From Orvis, Shooting Star, Tight Loop, and Osprey. From Lamiglas, Esprit and Centuria. The Stalker from Winston, Skip Morris's Finesse. Enthusiast, Specialist, and Traditionalist from Thomas & Thomas. Super Delicate from Doug Brewer at Big Sky. And one of my favorites, Golden Shadow from H.L. Leonard.

Of all the rod names, one has stuck as my absolute favorite. It describes exactly how someone should feel about his or her favorite fly rod. The rod is made by Skip Morris. He calls it the Companion.

FLY RODS

Although there are well over 1,000 rods listed here, the list is by no means complete. Let's say these are the 1,000 most available rods, those listed in catalog companies or advertised by rod makers in fly fishing magazines.

The rods are listed alphabetically with no price categories. If no sources are listed in a table, the only source is the rod manufacturer. Rod weights are given when available.

Apple Rod Company
11560 North Riverland Road
Mequon, Wisconsin 53092
(414) 242-2384

Jon Apple makes quality graphite rods finished with oxidized nickel silver fittings, impregnated wood reel seats, extra select cork handles, and black guides. He offers a 10-day return policy on rods that are unfished and undamaged.

Model	Length	Line	Weight	Price
603	6	3,4	1½	$185
703	7	3,4	1¾	$185
704	7	4,5	1⅞	$185
803	8	3,4	2¼	$195
804	8	4,5	2⅜	$195
805	8	5,6	2¾	$195
902	9	2,3	2⅜	$195
903	9	3,4	2½	$195
904	9	4,5	2⅝	$195
905	9	5,6	3	$195
Four-piece rods				
904	9	4,5	2¾	$230
905	9	5,6	3⅛	$230

Beartooth Fly Rods
Box 734
West Yellowstone, Montana 59758
(406) 646-9023

Beartooth Fly Rods are relatively new on the fly fishing scene, but like a number of other new companies, they are producing high quality rods from the start. Daniel Delekta, in the introduction to his catalog, talks of rods from the large rod makers: "The high quality we once knew had vanished." And so, he started Beartooth.

Using blanks from REC in Vermont, Beartooth produces rods of exceptional visual beauty. The "Diamondback" model name comes from the braided overwrap on the graphite. That, in combination with the rich colors the rods come in, gives them a distinctive, quite handsome look.

The rods cast well. They develop their power stroke smoothly and recover without over-casting. They are exceptionally strong rods, and I think they're controllable. I've tried the rods, and I think they're different enough in design and feel to warrant the consideration of the serious angler shopping for a top-line graphite rod.

Two lines of graphite and one of boron/graphite are listed. You may be able to try out the rods at a fly shop (probably in the West) or at your nearest Expo or Conclave. If you meet Dan, you'll get to hear one man talk about his product with confidence and pride, and that's always a good experience.

Beartooth Diamondback and Carbonite fly rods carry a lifetime guarantee. Beartooth will replace tip or butt sections, no matter how they are damaged.

Model	Length	Line	Price
Boron	8½	6,7	$238
Boron	8½	7,8	$238
Boron	9	4,5	$252
Boron	9	5,6	$252
Boron	9	6,7	$252
Boron	9	7,8	$252
Boron	9	8,9	$252
Graphite			
Carbonite	7½	5,6	$170
Carbonite	8	5,6	$175
Carbonite	8½	5,6	$180
Carbonite	8½	6,7	$180
Carbonite	9	5,6	$185
Carbonite	9	6,7	$185
Carbonite	9	7,8	$185
Carbonite	9	8,9	$185
Diamondback	7	4,5	$197
Diamondback	7½	4,5	$204.50
Diamondback	8	4,5	$211
Diamondback	8	5,6	$211-$217
Diamondback	8½	4,5	$218
Diamondback	8½	5,6	$218-$224
Diamondback	8½	6,7	$224
Diamondback	8½	7,8	$224
Diamondback	9	3,4	$225
Diamondback	9	4,5	$225
Diamondback	9	5,6	$225-$238
Diamondback	9	6,7	$238
Diamondback	9	7,8	$238

Model	Length	Line	Price
Diamondback	9	8,9	$248
Diamondback	9	9,10	$248
Diamondback	9	10,11	$248
Diamondback	9½	5,6	$232-$252
Diamondback	9½	6,7	$252
Diamondback	9½	7,8	$252
Diamondback	9½	8,9	$262
Diamondback	9½	9,10	$262
Diamondback	9½	10,11	$262
Pack	8½	6,7	$224
Pack	9	5,6	$238
Pack	9	6,7	$238
Pack	9½	5,6	$252

Browning Rods

Browning was at one time a popular fiberglass rod manufacturer. They produced the Browning Silaflex rods. Their participation in the market, at least as far as our fly fishing catalogs show, has been reduced to only a few rod models, including boron rods and Midas graphite rods.

Model	Length	Line	Weight	Price	Source
Boron	7½	4,5,6	2	$98.30	Dun
Boron	8	3,4,5	2.2	$84-$106.50	Dun, AnW
Boron	8½	5,6,7	2.7	$87.25-$114.73	Dun, Fol, Cus
Midas	8	5	3.3	$45-$56	AnW, Dun
Midas	8½	6,7	3.8	$59.80	Dun

Cabela's
812 13th Ave.
Sidney, Nebraska 69160
(800) 237-4444 (orders)
(800) 237-8888 (customer service)

Cabela's offers a very affordable line of graphite fly rods under their Fish Eagle name. The rods were originally endorsed by Lefty Kreh (who now endorses another brand), and his comments in their catalog may help you pick out the most appropriate rod. The rods are American made by an independent rod maker.

The 8½' rod for a 5,6-weight line is an outstanding value for the beginner at $74.95, and Cabela's will let you try out a rod for 30 days with full return privileges. They are, incidentally, good at taking care of their customers, so you can trust the guarantee.

They have rods ranging from a 7' for a 4,5-weight to a 10½' for an 8,9-weight. The most recent additions to the line are the Fish Eagle II rods. These are high modulus graphite rods in the vein of Sage Graphite II.

Model	Length	Line	Weight	Price
Fish Eagle	7	3,4	2.4	$64.95
Fish Eagle	7	4,5	2.5	$64.95
Fish Eagle	7½	3,4	2.5	$67.95
Fish Eagle	7½	4,5	2.6	$67.95
Fish Eagle	7½	5,6	2.8	$67.95
Fish Eagle	8	4,5	2.8	$72.95
Fish Eagle	8	5,6	3	$72.95

Model	Length	Line	Weight	Price
Fish Eagle	8	6,7	3	$72.95
Fish Eagle	8½	5,6	3.1	$74.95
Fish Eagle	8½	6,7	3.3	$74.95
Fish Eagle	8½	7,8	3.6	$74.95
Fish Eagle	9	4,5	3.5	$79.95
Fish Eagle	9	5,6	3.6	$79.95
Fish Eagle	9	6,7	3.6	$79.95
Fish Eagle	9	7,8	3.9	$79.95
Fish Eagle	9	8,9	4.4	$82.95
Fish Eagle	9	10-12	5.5	$82.95
Fish Eagle	9½	8,9	4.9	$86.95
Fish Eagle	10	8,9	5	$89.95
Fish Eagle	10½	8,9	5.1	$92.95
F. Eagle II	7½	4,5		$119.95
F. Eagle II	8	5,6		$124.95
F. Eagle II	8	6,7		$124.95
F. Eagle II	8½	5,6		$129.95
F. Eagle II	8'8"	6,7		$129.95
F. Eagle II	9	6,7		$134.95
F. Eagle II	9	7,8		$134.95
F. Eagle II	9	8,9		$134.95

Cairnton Rods

Box 908
Woodland, Washington 98674
(206) 225-9231

Cairnton offers rods designed by Russ Peak and endorsed by Lefty Kreh. A complete catalog is available for $1.

North Fork carries River Dee rods by Cairnton. These graphite rods have two different tips, each of which can handle three line weights. Thus, the 8' rod will throw a 4-, 5-, or 6-weight line with one tip and a 5-, 6-, or 7-weight line with the other. The catalog claims a six line capacity, but it's likely you'll commonly use just two lines, one for each tip. Compare with Deerfield's Over-and-Under, a four-piece rod with three tips for six line weights.

Model	Length	Line	Price	Source
River Dee	8	4-6, 5-7	$325	Nor
River Dee	8½	5-7, 6-8	$325	Nor
River Dee	9	5-7, 6-8	$325	Nor

Cortland Rods

Cortland, maker of fine fly lines, has also developed a line of fly rods. These begin with the 2000 series, a fiberglass rod that is suitable for beginners. The GRF-1000 rods begin the graphite rod offerings, which continue with the higher quality Signature, LTD Graphite, and Black Diamond rods.

Model	Length	Line	Weight	Price	Source
Fiberglass					
2000	7	5,6	3¼	$42	Kau, Mer
2000	7½	5,6	3½	$42	Kau, Mer
2000	8	6,7	3½	$42	Kau, Mer
2000	8½	6,7	4	$42	Kau, Mer
2000	8½	7,8	4½	$42	Kau, Mer, Hig
2000	9	8,9	6	$42	Kau, Mer
2000 Pack	7	6		$52	Edd, Hig

Model	Length	Line	Weight	Price	Source
Graphite					
GRF-1000	7½	5,6		$39.95	Nor
GRF-1000	8	5,6		$39.95	Nor
GRF-1000	8½	6,7		$39.95	Nor
GRF-1000	8½	7,8		$39.95	Nor
Signature	7½	5	2½	$79.95	Edd, Mer, T&T
Signature	8	5,6		$85	Edd
Signature	8	6	2⅝	$79.95	Edd, Mer, T&T
Signature	8½	6	2¾	$79.95	Edd, Mer, T&T
Signature	8½	6,7		$85	Edd
Signature	8½	7	2⅞	$79.95	T&T
Signature	9	6	3	$79.95	Edd, Mer, T&T
Signature	9	8	3½	$79.95	T&T
Signature	9	8,9		$85	Edd
LTD Graphite	7½	5	2¾	$119.95	Hun, Pen, T&T
LTD Graphite	8	6	3	$119.95	Hun, Pen, T&T
LTD Graphite	8½	6	3	$119.95	Hun, Pen, T&T
LTD Graphite	8½	7	3⅛	$119.95	Hun, Pen, T&T
LTD Graphite	9	6	3⅜	$119.95	Hun, Pen, T&T
LTD Graphite	9	8	3½	$119.95	Pen, T&T
Black Diamond	7½	5	2⅛	$170	Edd
Black Diamond	8	5	2½	$175	Edd
Black Diamond	8½	6	2¾	$175	Edd
Black Diamond	8½	7	3½	$175	Edd
Black Diamond	9	6	3⅛	$175	Edd
Black Diamond	9	7	3¼	$175	Edd
Black Diamond	9	8	3½	$175	Edd
Black Diamond	9	9	3⅞	$185	Edd
Black Diamond	9	10	4½	$185	Edd

Deerfield Rod Co.

70-A Arcadia Rd.
Hackensack, New Jersey 07601

Perhaps your experience with pack/travel rods has been no better than mine. I have a fiberglass monster around here someplace, one of the production models, a $39.95 special. It was bad enough to make me want to backpack to places that didn't have any fishable waters. I finally convinced myself that a full length aluminum case made a good walking stick (which it doesn't), so I could carry my regular rod.

Those negative experiences are a thing of the past, and pack/travel rods have come of age. The rods from Deerfield are a case in point.

Dave Sylvester, owner of Deerfield, has come up with an exceptional graphite rod in four pieces (and sometimes in six or eight pieces, but more on that later). A blindfold test would make it difficult, if not impossible, to tell the rod from a conventional two-piece rod. The rods utilize an internal tip ferrule that adds just enough extra weight to help the ferrule areas flex with the rod.

Deerfielder models are designed for trout fishing with lengths of 7½'-9' for line weights 4-7. Each rod designates two line weights. I found the lighter weight line to give the rod a fast pulse that I like, but the rods seem to load a bit better with the heavier line. I found myself using the lighter line for streams where short to medium length casts were required. On the lakes and bigger rivers, the heavier line made use of the rod's power for the longer casts required in that type of fishing.

In addition, there's the Salmoneer I and II and the Tarponeer, longer rods for heavier weights. I've cast the

9' for 7,8-weight lines, and it's got the backbone to handle more line than I can. It will pick up an amazing amount of line. These models range from 8 ½'-10' with line weights of 7-13.

The most interesting Deerfield rods are the Side-by-Sides and Over-and-Unders. The Side-by-Sides are four-piece rods with two tips. The second set of tips (the top two sections) is designed to throw a line one weight heavier. And so, the Side-by-Side I 8' rod is made for a 3,4 and 5,6 line. On some models, this has required plugging of sections. In others, the taper and design has pulled it off. In either case, the rods work well with both sets of tips, with only a little compromise occasionally showing in one set of tips or the other.

The benefits of such an outfit are obvious. Now you don't have to decide which line weight you'll need before your trip. Backpackers will be particularly fond of this feature, since it means having a 7-weight line for the lakes and a 5-weight for the nearby streams. Two rods for the extra half ounce of tips and extra bag material. (If you think fly fishermen are sensitive about weight, backpackers are worse, and a backpacking fly fisherman can end up fishing the funny farm pond.)

On the Side-by-Side models, the two tip sections are told apart by a discrete trim wrap of a different color, and an explanation is inscribed on the rod above the handle.

In production now is the Over-and-Under, a rod with three tip combinations. I was skeptical about the Side-be-Side, but it works well, so I suspect I'll be pleasantly surprised by the Over-and-Under, too.

The rods, not incidentally, are finished very well and come in top quality aluminum cases (which are too heavy for backpacking but ideal for traveling). Although Deerfield rods are available at a few stores here and there, you'll probably have to deal through the mails for the rods, either with Dave directly or with Tidewater Specialties. Dave will give you 10 days to try the rod out with full refund or exchange privileges.

Model	Length	Line	Weight	Price	Source
Deerfielder	7½	4,5	2¼	$225	Dee
Deerfielder	8	5,6	2½	$225	Dee, Tid
Deerfielder	8½	5,6	3½	$225	Dee
Deerfielder	9	6,7	3¾	$225	Dee
Salmoneer I	8½	7,8	4	$225	Dee, Tid
Salmoneer I	9	7,8	4⅛	$225	Dee
Salmoneer I	9½	7,8	4¼	$245	Dee
Salmoneer I	10	7,8	4¼	$245	Dee
Salmoneer II	9½	8,9	4¾	$245	Dee, Tid
Salmoneer II	9½	9,10	5	$255	Dee
Salmoneer II	10	8,9	4⅞	$245	Dee
Salmoneer II	10	9,10	5½	$255	Dee
Tarponeer	9	10,11	5½	$270	Dee
Tarponeer	9	12,13	6½	$280	Dee
Side-by-Side I	8	3-6	2½	$270	Dee, Tid
Side-by-Side I	8½	4-7	3½	$270	Dee
Side-by-Side I	9	4-7	3¾	$270	Dee, Tid
Side-by-Side II	8½	5-8	4	$285	Dee
Side-by-Side II	9	5-8	4⅛	$285	Dee, Tid
Side-by-Side III	9	7-10	4¼	$325	Dee

Model	Length	Line	Weight	Price	Source
Side-by-Side II	9½	5-8	4¼	$310	Dee
Side-by-Side III	9½	7-10	5	$325	Dee, Tid
Side-by-Side III	10	7-10	5½	$325	Dee
Over-and-Under	8½	2-7		$375	Dee
Over-and-Under	8½	5-10		$375	Dee
Over-and-Under	9	5-10		$395	Dee
Over-and-Under	9½	5-10		$395	Dee

E.F. Roberts, Custom Rodmaker
21C Seymour Rd.
East Granby, Connecticut 06026
(203) 651-8402

E.F. Roberts is one of the few one-man bands in the rod making industry. From his shop in Connecticut, he turns out a limited number of rods each year, working in cane, graphite, and boron/graphite.

In his catalog, you'll find a list of standard bamboo models, but he spends a majority of his time on one-of-a-kind, custom rods. An example he gives is the 7'9" cane rod he built in three sections. The rod had an extra mid-section and tip designed to throw a heavier line. The buyer ended up with a five-piece bamboo rod for line weights 4 and 6. That's a custom rod.

In addition to his bamboo work, Ed also builds graphite, graphite saltwater, and boron/graphite rods. Again, there's a standard model list here, but variations in fittings and grips are possible.

If you're interested in a custom bamboo rod, call the phone number above in the evening. Ed's a mechanical engineer in real life, so he can provide a lot of technical data on your new rod, if you're so inclined.

Model	Length	Line	Price
Standard	7¼	4	$600
Standard	7½	5	$600
Standard	7½	6	$600
Standard	8	5	$600
Standard	8	6	$600
Graphite	7	3,4	$200
Graphite	7½	4,5	$200
Graphite	8	4,5	$210
Graphite	8	5,6	$210

Model	Length	Line	Price
Graphite	8½	6,7	$212
Graphite	9	4,5	$224
Graphite	9	5,6	$224
Graphite	9	6,7	$224
Graphite	9	7,8	$224
Graphite	9	8,9	$224
Graphite	9½	8,9	$235
Graphite SW	9	7,8	$240
Graphite SW	9	8,9	$240
Graphite SW	9½	8,9	$260
Graphite SW	9½	9,10	$260
Boron	7½	5,6	$280
Boron	8	4,5	$280
Boron	8	5,6	$280
Boron	8½	6,7	$291

Fenwick/Woodstream
Box 729
Westminister, California 92683

These are probably the most popular fly rods in the country. They are definitely offered by more catalog companies than any other rod make.

Fenwick is one of the long-time American companies that everyone associates, one way or another, with fishing. The company manufactures all types of rods, and part of the popularity of their fly rods is based on satisfaction with the performance of their rods in other kinds of fishing. Most of us were spin or bait fishermen before we became fly fishermen, and when we made the switch, it was a confidence builder to stay with a rod brand we recognized.

Fenwick fiberglass rods are still around, but the company also has a long history of graphite rod construction and now produces boron rods.

The fiberglass models retail for around $50. They are fairly slow rods, but they have good power for fiberglass. Some people who have switched to graphite for their dry fly fishing still keep their semi-retired Fenwick fiberglass rods for nymphing and bass fishing where the slow power stroke helps in pick-up.

Fenwick's graphite series is led by the HMG Graphite rods, which retail for about $150. The Eagle graphite rods are similar in construction but do not have the appointments of the HMGs. At about $65, they should be considered by the beginner looking for a good starter rod in graphite. Fenwick graphite rods are heavier than most comparable graphite rods, and their action is slower than most. The power of graphite and the sensitivity are there, however. This combination obviously appeals to many fishermen.

Fenwick's boron/graphite line is also popular. The Boron-X series has 14 models. The rods are constructed of an internal rod of boron fibers covered by graphite. The rods retail for about $200.

And price is something you must be concerned with. The range of prices for all Fenwick rods is great simply because they are offered by so many companies. You can save as much as $140 (almost the price of a second rod) on a Boron-X by shopping around.

Model	Length	Line	Weight	Price	Source
Fiberglass					
FF705	7	5		$49	AnW
FF755	7½	5	3⅛	$49.35-$69.95	Cab, Cus, Fol, H&H, Kau, Ram, Sim
FF756	7½	6	3⅛	$49-$69.95	Kau, Cus, Pen, Cab, Sim, Ram, AnW, H&H, Fol
FF805	8	5	3⅛	$49-$69.95	AnW, Cus, Pen, H&H, Sim, Cab, Fol, Kau, Ram
FF806	8	6	3⅜	$49-$69.95	Sim, Ram, Pen, H&H, Cab, Cus, AnW, Fol, Kau
FF856	8½	6	3¾	$49-$69.95	Cab, Cus, Pen, H&H, Sim, Ram, AnW, Kau
FF857	8½	7	4⅜	$49.35-$69.95	Kau, Cus, Pen, H&H, Sim, Ram, Fol, Cab
FF858	8½	8	4⅜	$49-$69.95	Kau, Cab, Pen, H&H, Sim, Ram, AnW, Cus, Fol
FF909	9	9	4½	$49.35-$69.95	Kau, Cus, Pen, Ram, Sim, H&H, Fol, Cab
Eagle Graphite					
E70-5F	7	5		$64	AnW
E75-6F	7½	6	2⅝	$64-$67.98	AnW, Pen, Sim
E80-6F	8	6	3	$63.70-$100	Cus, Bud, AnW, Fol, H&H, Pen, Sim, Wul
E85-6F	8½	6	3⅛	$64-$100	Pen, Bud, Cus, H&H, AnW, Sim
E85-7F	8½	7	3¼	$63.70-$100	Bud, Cus, Fol, H&H, Pen, Sim
E90-8F	9	8	3⅜	$63.70-$67.98	Cus, Fol, H&H, Pen, Sim
HMG Graphite					
GFF755	7½	5	2⅞	$116.75-$198	H&H, Cus, Pen, Dan, Sim, Kau, Fol, Cab
GFF756	7½	6	2⅞	$115-$198	Sim, Pen, Dan, Bud, AnW, Fol, Kau, Cab
GFF805	8	5	3	$120.60-$204	H&H, Cus, Pen, Dan, Bud, Cab, Sim, Kau, Fol
GFF806	8	6	3⅛	$118-$204	Dan, Cus, Pen, Kau, Bud, Sim, Cab, H&H, AnW
GFF856	8½	6	3½	$120-$210	Cus, Kau, Pen, Dan, Bud, Sim, H&H, Fol, AnW
GFF857	8½	7	3½	$124.50-$210	Kau, Cus, Pen, Dan, Bud, Sim, H&H, Cab
GFF858	8½	8	3½	$120-$210	Fol, Cus, Pen, Dan, Bud, Kau, Cab, H&H, Sim, AnW
GFF905	9	5	3⅝	$125-$218	H&H, Cus, Pen, Dan, Bud, Sim, AnW, Fol, Cab, Kau
GFF906	9	6	3¾	$128.50-$218	Cus, Pen, Cab, Dan, Bud, Sim, Kau, H&H

Model	Length	Line	Weight	Price	Source
GFF907	9	7	3⅝	$128.50-$218	Kau, Cus, Pen, Dan, Bud, Sim, H&H, Cab
GFF908	9	8	4	$128.50-$218	Cab, Sim, Pen, Dan, Bud, H&H, Cus, Kau, Fol
GFF9010	9	10	5	$128.50-$218	Kau, Cus, Pen, Dan, Sim, H&H, Fol, Cab
GFF959	9½	9	4¾	$128.50-$218	Pen, Cus, Kau, Dan, H&H, Sim, Cab
Boron-X					
XF755	7½	5	3⅛	$186-$328	Kau, Cus, Pen, Dan, H&H, Sim, AnW, Cab
XF756	7½	6	3¼	$193.25-$328	Cus, Pen, Dan, H&H, Sim, Cab
XF806	8	6	3¼	$186-$328	Bud, Cus, Pen, Dan, Cab, Sim, H&H, AnW, Kau
XF855	8½	5	3⅞	$194.75-$328	Cus, Pen, Dan, H&H, Cab
XF856	8½	6	3⅞	$193.75-$328	Wul, Bud, Cus, Pen, Dan, H&H, Kau, Cab, Sim
XF857	8½	7	3⅞	$193.25-$328	Cab, Pen, Cus, Dan, Bud, Sim, H&H, Kau
XF858	8½	8	3⅞	$193.25-$328	Kau, Cus, Pen, Dan, Sim, H&H, Cab
XF904	9	4	3⅞	$194.75-$328	Cus, Pen, Dan, H&H, Cab
XF905	9	5	4	$186-$328	AnW, Cus, Pen, Dan, Bud, H&H, Kau, Sim, Cab
XF906	9	6	4	$194.75-$328	Cab, Cus, Pen, Dan, H&H, Kau
XF908	9	8	4⅜	$193.25-$328	Sim, Cus, Pen, Dan, Bud, H&H, Cab, Kau
XF9010	9	10	5¼	$194.75-$328	Cus, Pen, Dan, H&H, Cab
XF9012	9	12	5⅞	$194.75-$265	Kau, Cus, Pen, H&H, Cab
XF959	9½	9	5½	$194.75-$328	Dan, Pen, Cus, H&H, Cab

Fisher Rods

Box 3147
Carson City, Nevada 89702
(800) 334-FISH (orders)
(702) 246-5220

J. Kennedy Fisher is a prominent name in fly rods. Not only do they create rods under their own name, they also manufacture rods to specification for respected rod companies such as Scott PowR-Ply and Deerfield.

Fisher rods are moderately priced and well-made, and Fisher blanks are a favorite of rod builders. They offer a line of fiberglass rods, designated by FG in the list, graphite rods, and boron rods. The rods listed here have aluminum reel seats and do not include a rod tube. Models with wood insert reel seats and tubes are available from Fisher. A Fisher rod is an excellent investment for a beginner and the favorite rod for many experienced anglers.

Model	Length	Line	Price	Source
Fiberglass				
FG	7	3,4	$65	Mur
FG	7	4	$58.18-$75.95	JKF, Mer
FG	7	5	$75.95	JKF
FG	7½	3	$65	Mur
FG	7½	4	$58.18-$75.95	JKF, Mur, Mer
FG	7½	5	$58.18-$75.95	Mur, JKF, Mer
FG	8	5	$55-$75.95	Mur, Edd, JKF
FG	8	6	$58.18-$75.95	JKF, Mur, Mer
FG	8	7	$58.18-$75.95	Mer, JKF
FG	8½	6	$58.18-$75.95	Mer, JKF, Fly
FG	8½	7,8	$55-$75.95	Mur, JKF, Edd, Fly
FG	8½	8	$63.25-$80.95	JKF, Edd, Mer
FG	9	6	$75.95	JKF
FG	9	8	$69.95-$80.95	JKF, Fly
FG	9	9	$59-$80.95	Edd, Mer, JKF
FG	9	10	$63.25-$80.95	JKF, Mer
FG	9	13	$89.95	JKF
FG Pack	7	6	$95.95	JKF
FG Pack	7½	6	$95.95	JKF
FG Pack	8	6	$65.95-$95.95	JKF, Edd
Graphite				
Graphite	7	2,3	$128	JKF
Graphite	7½	2,3	$128-$129	Nor, JKF
Graphite	7½	3,4	$107.07-$128	JKF, Mur, Mer
Graphite	7½	4,5	$107.07-$128	Mer, JKF
Graphite	8	4,5	$107.07-$129	Nor, JKF, Mur, Edd, Mer
Graphite	8	5,6	$107.07-$129	Mur, Nor, JKF, Edd, Mer, Fre
Graphite	8	6,7	$107.07-$129	Nor, Mer, JKF
Graphite	8½	4,5	$107.07-$128	JKF, Mur, Mer
Graphite	8½	5,6	$107.07-$129.95	Edd, Mer, Nor, JKF, Fre
Graphite	8½	6,7	$107.07-$128	Edd, JKF, Mer, Fly
Graphite	8½	7,8	$107.07-$128	Fly, Mer, Edd, JKF
Graphite	9	4,5	$120-$128	JKF, Fly
Graphite	9	5,6	$119.95-$129.95	Mur, Nor, JKF, Edd, Fly, Fre
Graphite	9	6,7	$119.95-$128	Mur, JKF, Edd, Fly

Model	Length	Line	Price	Source
Graphite	9	7,8	$119.95-$129	Mur, Nor, JKF, Edd, Fly
Graphite	9	8,9	$107.07-$129.95	Edd, Mer, JKF, Fly, Fre
Graphite	9	9,10	$107.07-$129	Edd, Nor, JKF, Mer, Fly
Graphite	9	11,12	$132.07-$158	JKF, Mer
Graphite	9	12,13	$158	JKF
Graphite	9½	5,6	$148	JKF
Graphite	9½	6,7	$129.95-$148	JKF, Nor, Fre
Graphite	9½	7,8	$148	JKF
Graphite	9½	8,9	$148	JKF
Graphite	9½	9,10	$154	JKF
Graphite	10	4,5	$148	JKF
Graphite	10	5,6	$148	JKF
Graphite	10	6,7	$148	JKF
Graphite	10	7,8	$129.95-$148	Fre, JKF
Graphite	10	8,9	$148-$149	Nor, JKF
Graphite	10	9,10	$148	JKF
Boron				
Boron	9	6,7	$159-$169.95	JKF, Mur, Fre
Boron	9	7,8	$159-$169.95	Mur, JKF, Fre
Boron	9	8,9	$159-$169.95	Mur, Fre, JKF
Boron	10	8,9	$179.95	Fre, JKF
Four-piece rods				
Graphite	9	5,6	$179	JKF, Nor
Graphite	9	6,7	$179-$180	JKF, Fly, Nor
Graphite	9	7,8	$179-$180	Fly, JKF, Nor
Graphite	9	8,9	$179	JKF
Graphite	9½	7,8	$207	JKF
Graphite	9½	8,9	$207-$210	JKF, Nor
Graphite	9½	9,10	$215	JKF
Graphite	10	7,8	$207	JKF
Graphite	10	8,9	$207	JKF
Graphite	10	9,10	$215	JKF

Fosters of England
Anglia Company
1901 Philtower
Tulsa, Oklahoma 74103

A newcomer on the American side, Fosters of England has been making quality bamboo rods since 1763. Ten models are now imported for the Yank market by the Anglia Company.

I've not had the opportunity to try out the rods, or even to see one, but from the pictures in the catalog, I think you'll find the rods distinctive compared to rods offered by American manufacturers, at least in style of finish and furnishings.

The first thing you're bound to notice is the intermediate wraps (thread wrappings on the rod between guides) on all models except the Wisp and Dove. These give the rods an antique look. And although you may not notice this, the wraps are done in silk.

The cork handles also give the rods a distinctive look. The Airsprite has a fairly typical cigar-shaped handle, but the other models feature a "scroll-shaped" handle (standard and elongated) which is unlike any other handle I've seen. Again, the feeling of an antique rod is there.

The rods, if they cast as well as they are appointed, will find a place in the hearts of American fly fishermen who favor the traditional and yearn for the days of the tweed jacket.

All models, except the Dove and the Anglia, are single tip, with extra tips available at costs of from $100-$225 depending on length. The Anglia is a special edition model limited to 25 rods. The Dove and the Anglia come with a leather-covered aluminum case, the others with aluminum tubes.

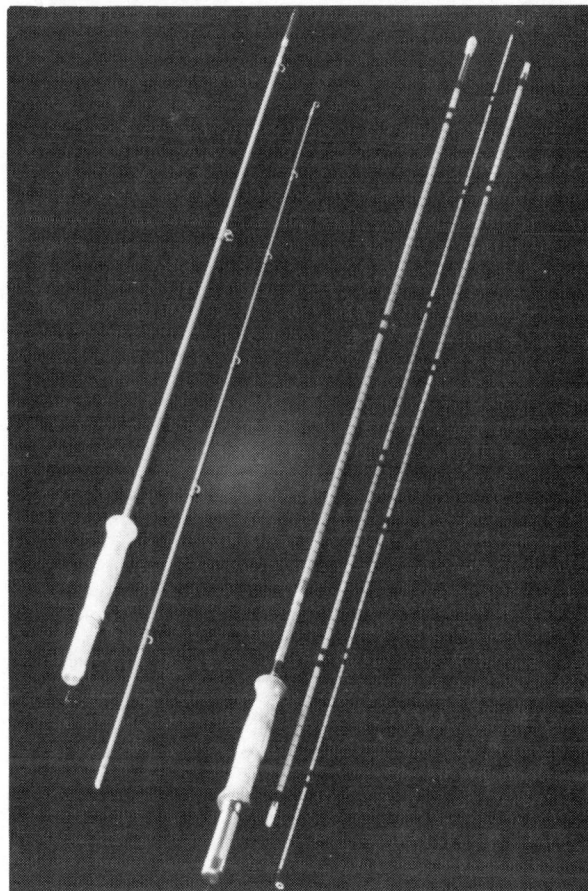

Model	Length	Line	Weight	Price
Wisp	6	3,4	2¼	$350
Wisp	6½	3,4	2½	$350
Airsprite	7	4,5	3¼	$475
Airsprite	7½	4,5	3½	$475
The Anglia	7¾	5,6	5½	$1,250
Dove	7¾	5,6	5½	$1,250
Champion	8	5,6	4⅞	$550
A.E.M.	8	5,6	5¼	$675
A.E.M.	8½	5,6	5½	$675
England's Favorite	8½	5,6	6	$750

Gillie Custom Rods
111 John St.
Kelso, Washington 98626
(206) 577-6071

Gillie Custom Rods is the only source of Gary Loomis graphite rods that I have for you. The Gillie line is custom wrapped from the G. Loomis blanks.

I've listed the standard grade rods here. They include chrome stripper guides and standard Glenn Struble reel seats. A deluxe grade with silicone carbide strippers and deluxe Struble reel seats is available for about $20 more.

Both models come with aluminum tube. The rods have a lifetime warranty against defects. Purchasers have a five-day examination period during which they may return the rod (unfished and undamaged, of course) for a full refund.

Gillie often shows up at fishing shows and expositions, and that may give you an opportunity to try out one of the rods.

Model	Length	Line	Price
Custom	7	3,4	$140
Custom	7	4,5	$140
Custom	7½	3,4	$140
Custom	7½	4,5	$140
Custom	7½	5,6	$140
Custom	8	4,5	$145
Custom	8	5,6	$145
Custom	8	6,7	$145
Custom	8¼	5,6	$145
Custom	8½	5,6	$145
Custom	8½	6,7	$145
Custom	8½	7,8	$145
Custom	9	3,4	$150
Custom	9	4,5	$150
Custom	9	5,6	$150
Custom	9	6,7	$150
Custom	9	7,8	$150
Custom	9	8,9	$150
Custom	9	11,12	$160
Custom	9½	6,7	$155
Custom	9½	7,8	$155
Custom	9½	8,9	$155
Custom	10	6,7	$160
Custom	10	8,9	$160

Hardy Rods
Hardy (USA)
123 Sylvan Ave.
Newark, New Jersey 07104

Hardy of England, maker of fine reels, also produces quality fly rods, including one of my favorites, the Smuggler. All the rods listed here are manufactured from graphite, but you can expect to see other materials and many other models available on the American side in up-coming years. Hardy has a new distributor, and soon every product in the Hardy catalog will be on hand for American customers. For now, you'll have to be content with the listings of the basic graphite rod and the Smuggler.

The Smuggler is a nifty pack/travel rod that breaks down to six pieces for the 7' model, seven pieces for the 8'2 ½" model, and eight peices for the 9'5" rod. It seems incredible, with the experience of fiberglass in our heritage, that a rod with so many small sections can be functional, but it is. It's not only functional, by all reports, it casts very well. Since the Smuggler fits in a briefcase, it is especially convenient for air travel as carry-on baggage. I'd suggest you give one of the rods a try if you do a lot of traveling to places where there's fishing to be done after business.

Model	Length	Line	Weight	Price	Source
Graphite	7½	4,5	1¾	$184	Dun
Graphite	8	5,6	2¼	$189.50	Dun
Graphite	8½	6,7	2¾	$199	Dun
Graphite	9	4,5	3¼	$215	Dun
Graphite	9	5,6	3½	$215	Dun
Graphite	9	6,7	3½	$215	Dun
Graphite	9	7,8	3½	$215	Dun
Graphite	9¼	7,8	4	$220	Dun
Graphite	9½	6,7	4½	$230	Dun
Graphite	9½	8,9	4¾	$235	Dun
Graphite	10	6,7	4½	$235	Dun
Graphite	10	9,10	4¾	$240	Dun
Graphite	10½	7,8	4¾	$240	Dun
Smuggler	7	5	1¾	$250-$290.50	Cab, T&T, Dun
Smuggler	8'2.5"	6	2½	$255-$308.50	T&T, Cab, Dun
Smuggler	9'5"	7	3½	$275-$326.50	T&T, Dun, Cab

H. L. Leonard Rod, Inc.
Central Valley, New York 10917
(914) 928-2303

Since 1881 the H. L. Leonard Rod, Inc. has been making high quality fly fishing rods. The company was started by Hiram Lewis Leonard. He brought together some of the best rod makers in the world, Payne, Edwards, and the Hawes brothers, to create rods that are truly classics. Older Leonards are collector's items of great value. Today's Leonards are fine casting instruments and collector's items of the future.

According to the Leonard catalog, which you can ask for, the bamboo rods for which the company is best known require 50 man-hours of labor. Leonard also makes two lines of graphite rods under the names Sterling and Golden Shadow.

Leonard Deluxe rods (formerly Red Wrap rods) are the least expensive rods in the line. They have a maintenance-free acrylic finish. They feature nickel silver cap and ring seats and are wrapped in light green. Since Red Wraps are still offered through some catalogs, I've left them in.

Standard models feature a varnish finish and medium action. They are available in two-piece (#36-40) and three-piece (#46-51). The Catskill Series rods are dry-fly action rods, "the ultimate in simplicity and understatement". The Hunt Series rods feature open-flamed cane that gives a darker color to the rod. These are among the top lines offered by Leonard. They are available in two-piece and three-piece with the same numbering system as the Standard rods. Tournament Series rods are built to order. They are strong rods with medium fast action.

Where more than one line weight is listed, rods should be ordered by specific line weight desired, except for the Sterling series.

Model	Length	Line	Price	Source
Graphite				
Sterling	7½	3,4	$235	HLL
Sterling	7½	4,5	$235	HLL
Sterling	8	4,5	$235	HLL
Sterling	8	5,6	$235	HLL
Sterling	8½	4,5	$235	HLL
Sterling	8½	5,6	$235	HLL
Sterling	8½	6,7	$235	HLL
Sterling	9	4,5	$235	HLL
Sterling	9	5,6	$235	HLL
Sterling	9	6,7	$235	HLL
Sterling	9	7,8	$255	HLL
Sterling	9	8,9	$255	HLL
Sterling	9	9,10	$255	HLL
Sterling	9½	8,9	$255	HLL
Sterling	9½	9,10	$255	HLL
Golden Shadow	7	4	$270-$300	Don, HLL
Golden Shadow	7	5	$270-$300	Kau, Don, HLL
Golden Shadow	7	6	$270-$300	Don, HLL
Golden Shadow	7½	5	$270-$300	Kau, Don, HLL
Golden Shadow	7½	6	$270-$300	Don, HLL
Golden Shadow	8	5	$270-$300	Kau, Don, HLL
Golden Shadow	8	6	$270-$300	Kau, Don, HLL
Golden Shadow	8½	5	$270-$300	Don, HLL
Golden Shadow	8½	6	$270-$310	Don, HLL, Wul
Golden Shadow	9	6	$270-$300	Kau, Don, HLL
Golden Shadow	9	8	$270-$300	Kau, Don, HLL
Bamboo				
Red Wrap	6½	4	$450-$500	Kau, Don, Hun
Red Wrap	7	4	$450-$500	Kau, Don, Hun
Red Wrap	7½	5	$450-$500	Kau, Don, Hun
Red Wrap	8	6	$450-$500	Kau, Don, Hun
Deluxe	6½	4	$600	HLL
Deluxe	7	4	$600	Nor, HLL
Deluxe	7½	4,5	$600	HLL, Nor
Deluxe	8	5	$600	HLL
Standard Series				
36	6	3	$800-$950	Kau, Don, HLL, Hun
37	6½	3,4	$800-$950	Kau, Don, HLL, Hun
38	7	3-5	$800-$950	Kau, Don, HLL, Hun
39	7½	4-6	$800-$950	Kau, Don, HLL, Hun

Model	Length	Line	Price	Source
40	8	4-6	$800-$950	Kau, Don, Hun
41	8½	5,6	$800-$950	HLL, Hun
46	6	2-4	$800	Kau, Don, HLL
47	6½	3,4	$800	Kau, Don, HLL
48	7	4,5	$800-$950	Kau, Don, HLL, Hun
49	7½	4-6	$800-$950	Kau, Don, HLL, Hun
50	8	4-6	$800-$950	Kau, Don, HLL, Hun
51	8½	6,7	$800-$950	Kau, Don, HLL, Hun
Catskill Series				
36	6	2,3	$875-$985	Kau, Don, HLL, Hun
37	6½	3,4	$875-$985	HLL, Kau, Don, Hun
38	7	3,4	$875-$985	Kau, Don, HLL, Hun
39	7½	4,5	$875-$985	HLL, Kau, Don, Hun
40	8	4,5	$875	HLL, Kau, Don
46	6	3	$875	Kau, Don, HLL
47	6½	3,4	$875	Kau, Don, HLL
48	7	3,4	$875	HLL, Kau, Don
49	7½	4,5	$875	HLL, Kau, Don
50	8	4,5	$875	HLL, Kau, Don
Hunt Series				
36	6	3	$950-$1,075	Kau, Don, HLL, Hun
37	6½	3,4	$950-$1,075	Kau, Don, HLL, Hun
38	7	3-5	$950-$1,075	Kau, Don, HLL, Hun
39	7½	4-6	$950-$1,075	Kau, Don, HLL, Hun
40	8	4-6	$950-$1,075	Kau, Don, HLL, Hun
41	8½	5,6	$950-$1,075	HLL, Hun
46	6	3	$950	Kau, Don, HLL
47	6½	3,4	$950	Kau, Don, HLL
48	7	4,5	$950-$1,075	Kau, Don, HLL, Hun
49	7½	4-6	$950-$1,075	Kau, Don, HLL, Hun
50	8	4-6	$950-$1,075	Kau, Don, HLL, Hun
51	8½	6,7	$950-$1,075	HLL, Hun
Tournament Series				
48	7	3-5	$1,050	HLL
49	7½	4-6	$1,050	HLL
50	8	4-6	$1,050	HLL
51	8½	5-7	$1,050	HLL

Kusse Rods
Rena Marie Circle
Washingtonville, New York 10992
(914) 496-7187

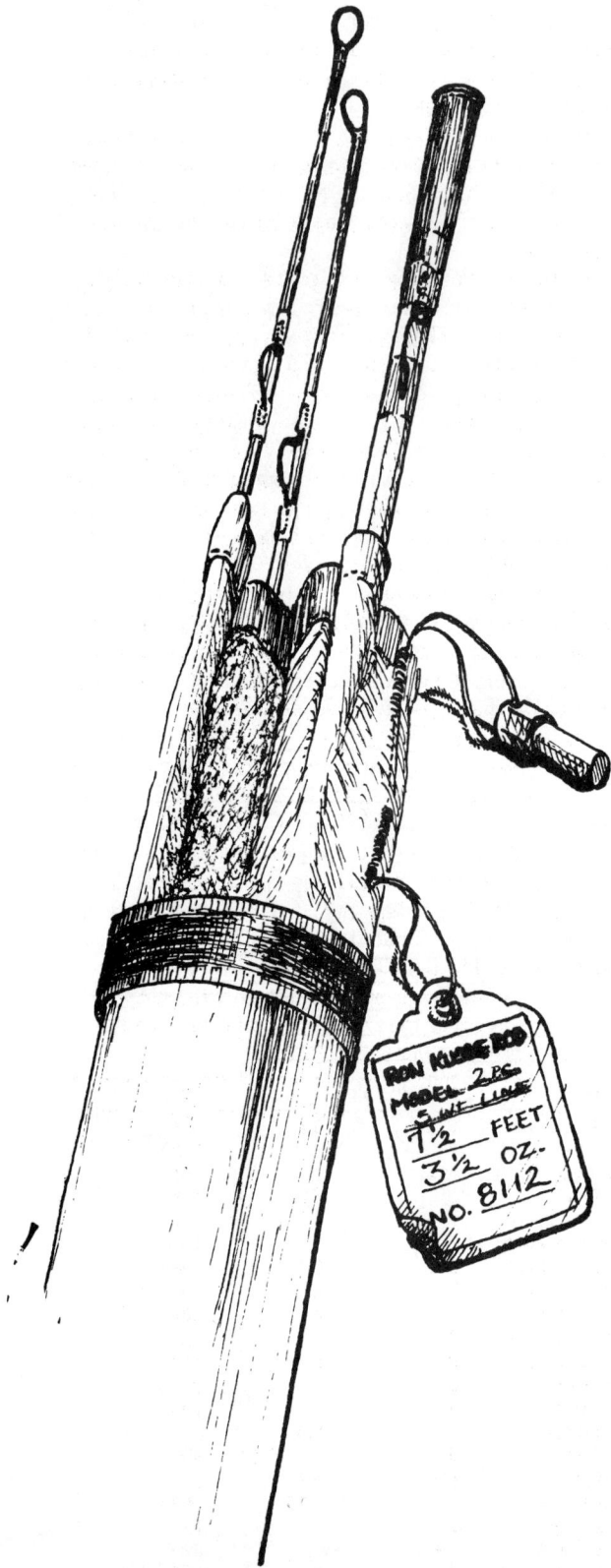

By way of introduction to Ron Kusse and his rods, let me give you a quote from his catalog that sums up what he and the handful of other independent rod makers are trying to do:

"The difference between a rod used simply as a tool to catch fish, and one of the rare rods that seems to become part of you, can easily be summed up as craftsmanship, the understanding of rod action and cosmetic appeal.

"There are a few individual craftsmen making a limited number of split cane rods each year. These rod makers, working by themselves, will split the cane, bevel the cane, cut their own hardwood reel seats, machine their own nickel silver fittings, do their own windings, varnish the rods, and even put their own finishing touches on the rod cases. These craftsmen work alone. They enjoy each aspect of their work, and most times would find fault with a subordinate craftsman's efforts when his own name is going to appear on their rods. Rod actions and each maker's idea of cosmetics will vary, but these individual craftsmen have one thing in common: they are dedicated to handcrafting the finest fly rods they are capable of making."

A few years ago, Ron Kusse (pronounced "coo-see") left his executive position with the H.L. Leonard Rod Co. to make rods independently and individually. His desire to have every aspect of rod building directly under his control is evidenced by the fact that he does everything on a rod himself, right down to turning the reel seats and varnishing the rod. When you buy a Kusse rod, you get a rod made by Kusse.

The cane rods come with two tips, select cherry reel seats, jewelry-grade nickel silver fittings, and Super Z ferrules. The base price is about $690. Although he often makes customized rods featuring hardwood presentation cases and other finery and costing well over $1,000, no rod he makes casts any better than the standard model. His only rod is his best rod.

Ron describes the action of his rods as "a crisp modified dry fly action that has a progressive or medium taper". He will build custom rods with faster or slower tapers. He has specific recommendations for rod length. He considers the 7 ½' rod to be the "epitome of rods for general fishing", and his standard rod list includes only 6'-8' rods. Other lengths, of course, can be ordered.

Expect to wait if you want a Kusse rod. Last time I checked, he was seven months behind in his orders.

Ron also finishes graphite and boron/graphite rods. He believes that the finish work and choice of components on rods of modern materials makes the difference between the rod being a very ordinary casting tool and being a rod that "seems to become a part of you". The graphite rods are created from Loomis Composites blanks. The boron/graphite rods are done from Rodon blanks. He lavishes the same care and attention on the finish of these rods as he does on the cane rods he makes from scratch. They have blued nickel silver fittings, black walnut reel seats, and black chrome guides. Ron gets high marks from other rod makers for all his finish work.

All Kusse rods come with some unusual guarantees. First, you have full return privileges if the rod does not please you. Second, for as long as Kusse is making rods, he will repair or replace any rod that breaks or fails to perform adequately due to workmanship or defects in materials. Third, he will replace one section of a rod broken by any means, car doors or falls in the stream, free during the first five years of ownership.

Ron also does limited repair and restoration of quality cane rods. Call first. He accepts some trade-ins toward the purchase of a rod. As a result, he does offer a list of good quality reels, rods, and "interesting fishing artifacts" for sale through his shop. Ask for it when you request his catalog.

Model	Length	Line	Price
Graphite	7	4	$245
Graphite	7	5	$245
Graphite	7½	3	$245
Graphite	7½	4	$245
Graphite	7½	5	$245
Graphite	8	4	$245
Graphite	8	5	$245
Graphite	8	6	$245
Graphite	8½	5	$245
Graphite	8½	8	$245
Graphite	9	6	$245
Graphite	9	8	$245
Graphite	9	9	$245
Graphite	9½	9	$245
Boron	7	4	$275
Boron	7	5	$275
Boron	7½	3	$275
Boron	7½	4	$275
Boron	7½	5	$275
Boron	8	4	$275
Boron	8	5	$275
Boron	8	6	$275
Boron	8½	5	$275
Boron	8½	8	$275
Boron	9	6	$275
Boron	9	8	$275
Boron	9	9	$275
Boron	9½	9	$275
Bamboo	6	3	$690
Bamboo	6½	4	$690
Bamboo	7	4	$690
Bamboo	7	5	$690
Bamboo	7½	4	$690
Bamboo	7½	5	$690
Bamboo	7½	6	$690
Bamboo	8	6	$690

Kustin Rods
22105-4 Burbank Blvd.
Woodland Hills, California 91367
(818) 992-5747

Perhaps the most innovative among bamboo rod builders is Barry Kustin (pronounced "cuss-tin"). He has broken with traditional design by producing hollow

bamboo rods. The traditional rod, of course, is solid. Sample sections of the hollow bamboo appear pretty fragile. The sidewalls are thin, thinner than those of most synthetic rods. But Barry will explain to you that the strength of the bamboo comes from the outer fibers. The pith adds nothing but weight.

It remains only to explain how Barry manages to keep those thin strips together. It requires, as he says, a "short glue line" and that requires a special epoxy glue. Barry has spent a lot of research time selecting that critical component.

With the thin sidewalls, these rods are amazingly light, fast, and sensitive. I've never cast a bamboo rod with a finer touch. The rod has the aesthetic appeal and the feel of bamboo with some of the action and weight-to-power ratio of graphite. It's unique among the rods listed here.

If the hollow-built rods sound interesting, there are other Kustin rods you'll find fascinating. They are the Comp I and II rods, featuring hollow-built bamboo with an inner layer of graphite fibers. This unnatural marriage is another unique idea, although Kustin gives credit to Maine's Cecil Pierce for the concept.

I haven't tried the Comp rods, but it's that kind of innovation that keeps rod building alive and healthy. Such a combination of synthetic and organic materials may create the ultimate casting tool. And speaking of ulitmate, Barry makes the most expensive rod listed in this book. He calls it what it better be, The Ultimate. It is all-bamboo, hollow-built, and cosmetically perfect due to a special invisible scarfing method that removes all nodes. Retail price for each of the 10 rods in this limited edition: $3,000.

Of the rods listed here, the Superlight and The Argo are hollow-built. The Letort rods are three-piece models. The Double Built is hollow-built but uses two layers of bamboo. The Comp I and II are composite bamboo and graphite rods. The Comp I has graphite under all six sides. The Comp II has graphite under three sides, making it slower than the Comp I (but still very fast for bamboo). Prices are for two tip rods.

Model	Length	Line	Price
The Argo	6½	3,4	$595
The Argo	7	4,5	$595
The Argo	7½	5,6	$595
The Argo	8	6,7	$595
The Argo	8½	7,8	$595
Superlight 20/20	6	3	$595
Superlight 20/20	6½	3,4	$595
Superlight 20/20	7	4	$595
The Double Built	8	6,7	$895
The Double Built	8½	7,8	$895
The Double Built	9	8,9	$895
The Letort	9	3	$995
The Letort	9	5	$995
The Comp I	7½	5,6	$995
The Comp I	8	7,8	$995
The Comp I	8½	8,9	$995
The Comp I	9	9,10	$995
The Comp II	8	7	$795
The Comp II	8½	8	$795
The Comp II	9	9	$795
The Ultimate	n/a	n/a	$3,000

Lamiglas, Inc.
Box U
Woodland, Washington 98674
(206) 225-9436

Lamiglas was best known for its use of S-glass in fiberglass rods. Before the advent of graphite, S-glass was the hot new material for rods. Lamiglas has continued its development as a rod manufacturer with a complete line of graphite rods and now a line of boron

S-glass is a stiffer material than the fiberglass that was typically found in rods. Speaking technically, it had a modulus of about 13 million pounds per square inch, compared to 10.5 million psi for other fiberglass material. Graphite, by comparison, ranges in the 30s. With the movement to lighter, faster rods, graphite became the material of choice.

This is evident in the fact that I could find no mail order source for Lamiglas fiberglass rods, although the blanks are still available through a number of catalogs. It's certainly not a reflection on Lamiglas fiberglass rods, but it gives some indication of where the industry is going. Boron, with further development, may replace graphite, or another space-age material may come along and bump both out of the lead.

One reason that Lamiglas fiberglass rods are difficult to find is that the company makes a fine, moderately priced graphite rod, the G1000. With graphite as the material and a price tag as low as $50, the G1000 itself would be competition for the S-glass rods. The G1000 has an aluminum reel seat and simple fittings, and the price does not include a rod bag or case. Although I could not find them listed in any catalog, the Lamiglas catalog also shows an even more economical rod series, the G500, that you may see in a local fly shop or in a catalog in the future. Expect fewer guides and inexpensive fittings, of course.

I've tried the G1000 and found it a nice rod for the $95 price tag it had on it. It's an even better fly rod for the $50 price tag found in Hook & Hackle. Hope it wasn't a misprint, because this rod compared to the fiberglass rods in that price category is a "best buy" as a beginner's rod or a back-up or special-use rod. The action is clean and fairly crisp. You'll find it to be slow enough to be forgiving of a beginner's mistakes but quick enough to keep line speed and line control. Try it out for yourself, but keep in mind that you'll probably want to spend about $20 more on bag and tube (which might be included with other rods in the $75-$100 range).

Two other graphite models are in the Lamiglas line, the Esprit and the Centuria. The Esprit is a dressier version of the G1000. It has a walnut reel seat and better quality guides. It includes a bag and aluminum rod case. The Centuria is new, but the price tag suggests a different line competing with Fenwick and other makers. Also included in the Lamiglas line is the Esprit Boron (listed here simply as Boron). It also has a moderate price tag that might make it worth considering for the fly fisher with a limited budget who wants a boron rod for a few special fishing situations.

Model	Length	Line	Weight	Price	Source
G1000	7½	5	2¾	$42-$78	H&H, Ram, Ste
G1000	8	6	3	$44.40-$83	H&H, Ram, Ste
G1000	8½	6	3	$45.35-$85	H&H, Ram, Ste
G1000	8½	7	3⅛	$45.35-$85	H&H, Ram, Ste
G1000	9	6	3⅜	$48.25-$91	H&H, Ram, Ste
G1000	9	8	3½	$48.25-$91	H&H, Ram, Ste
G1000	9½	9	4⅝	$59.10	H&H
Esprit	7½	5	2¹/₁₆	$88.35-$175	H&H, Ste
Esprit	7½	6	2⅛	$175	Ste
Esprit	8	5	2⁹/₁₆	$180	Ste
Esprit	8	6	2¹³/₁₆	$90.75-$180	H&H, Ste
Esprit	8	7	2¹⁵/₁₆	$180	Ste
Esprit	8½	5	2⅞	$190	Ste
Esprit	8½	6	2¹⁵/₁₆	$95.50-$190	H&H, Ste
Esprit	8½	7	3¹/₁₆	$95.50-$190	H&H, Ste
Esprit	8½	8	3⅜	$198	Ste
Esprit	9	4	2⅞	$100.30-$200	H&H, Ste
Esprit	9	5	3¹/₁₆	$100.30-$200	H&H, Ste
Esprit	9	6	3³/₁₆	$100.30-$200	H&H, Ste
Esprit	9	7	3⁵/₁₆	$100.30-$200	H&H, Ste
Esprit	9	8	3¹⁵/₁₆	$104.10-$208	H&H, Ste
Esprit	9	9	4¹/₁₆	$208	Ste
Esprit	9½	7	3⅝	$210	Ste
Esprit	9½	8	4	$218	Ste
Esprit	10½	9	4⅛	$238	Ste
Centuria	7½	5		$175	Ste
Centuria	8	5		$180	Ste
Centuria	8	6		$180	Ste
Centuria	8½	6		$190	Ste
Centuria	8½	7		$190	Ste
Centuria	9	5		$200	Ste
Centuria	9	6		$200	Ste
Centuria	9	8		$200	Ste
Centuria	9½	7		$210	Ste
Centuria	9½	8		$210	Ste
Boron	8	6	2⅞	$119.10	H&H
Boron	8½	6	3	$123.85	H&H
Boron	8½	7	3⅛	$123.85	H&H
Boron	9	6	3¾	$133.40	H&H
Boron	9	8	4	$133.40	H&H
Boron	9	9	4¹¹/₁₆	$133.40	H&H
Boron	9½	7	3⅞	$142.95	H&H
Boron	9½	9	4⅝	$142.95	H&H

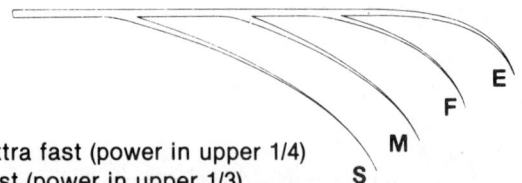

E - extra fast (power in upper 1/4)
F - fast (power in upper 1/3)
M - medium (power in upper 1/2)
S - slow (power spread progressively entire length)

L.L. Bean, Inc.
Freeport, Maine 04033
(207) 865-4761

The entry of L. L. Bean into the fly fishing marketplace is a recent one, but the company's longstanding reputation in the outdoor field assures that the product line is of the highest quality. Bean's fly fishing product line is being developed under the guidance of well-known writer Dave Whitlock, and that provides another recommendation for those products.

The major rod line is graphite with a braided overwrap in the style of the rods of its supplier, REC, Inc. The rods feature aluminum oxide stripping guides and hard chrome-plated snake guides. The much-appreciated ferrule line-up dots are included. These are not just convenient—they also save wear on the ferrule from the realignment often needed when they are lacking. Rubber butt caps are grooved to allow you to keep your leader secure while transporting the rod. All rods have uplocking reel seats. The "Trout" models have a wood insert and nickel silver hardware. The special bass and light saltwater rod (8¾' for 7,8 line) and the heavier rods have corrosion-resistant aluminum reel seats and fighting butts.

A line of fiberglass rods is also available (designated here with the code FG), as are pack/travel rods in both fiberglass and graphite. And there's one boron/graphite rod. If you call or write for a catalog, you should ask for the fly fishing issue.

Model	Length	Line	Weight	Price
Double L FG	7½	5		$75
Double L FG	8	6		$75
Double L FG	8½	7		$80
Double L	7	3,4	1¾	$175.50
Double L	8	5,6	3½	$189
Double L	8½	3,4	3½	$189.50
Double L	8½	5,6	3½	$189.50
Double L	8½	6,7	4	$189.50
Double L	9	5,6	4	$198.50
Double L	9	8,9	5½	$206
Double L	9½	9,10	6½	$214.50
Dbl.L (Boron)	8¾	7,8	4	$227.75
FG 4-pc.	7	5		$82.50
FG 4-pc.	8	6	3.6	$85.50
FG 4-pc.	8½	7		$86.50
Double L 3-pc.	7	3,4		$198.50
Double L 4-pc.	8	5,6	4	$206.50
Double L 6-pc.	8	5,6		$247.50
Double L 4-pc.	8½	6,7	4.2	$209.50
Double L 4-pc.	9	5,6		$224.50
Double L 4-pc.	9½	9,10		$237.50
Dbl.L (B) 4-pc.	8¾	7,8		$247.50

M. Montagne, Rodmaker
Box 64
Olema, California 94950
(415) 663-1573

If you write Montagne (pronounced "mon-tane") for his catalog, you'll receive a most intriguing scientific dissertation on fly rod dynamics and the physics of casting. By the time you've studied the work, you'll have picked his brain about rods, and you'll understand why he makes rods the way he does far more clearly than I could hope to tell you here.

And the rods require explanation, for they are unique. Montagne makes rectangular bamboo rods. Even the cork handle is different from any other you'll find, and the reel seat is his own innovative design. You'll notice in the catalog's photographs the brevity of the seat and the fact that finished cane shows between handle and seat. The entire rod is the product of Montagne's drive to create the ultimate casting and fishing tool.

He claims: "The Montagne Section is the most powerful, fastest recovering section in the history of rodmaking." His theme throughout the catalog is that design, not material, accounts for the action of the rod. He has many negative things to say about high modulus materials (i.e. graphite and boron), and many of his comments about the design of those rods are worthy of consideration.

"Design is essential to effective utilization of a material and consequent performance." Montagne's design work is intriguing. Until recently, the bamboo fibers in his rods were built around a base of Sitka Spruce, which gave the rods stiffness and greater weight savings. Now, he has begun "radical hollow-building" to reach the same end: greater line speed and control. (See Kustin rods for a comparison.)

Such talk is alien to our thinking about bamboo rods. We are in the space age, and space-age materials give us more line speed than bamboo ever could. Bamboo is for gentle folk casting gentle lines on gentle water. Montagne debunks that notion pretty thoroughly in print. It's for you to decide if his rods make the debunk complete.

Model	Length	Line	Price
Standard	7½	4	$1,300
Standard	8	5	$1,300
Standard	8¼	6	$1,300
Standard	8½	7	$1,300

The Orvis Company, Inc.
10 River Road
Manchester, Vermont 05254
(802) 362-1300

If you don't already know Orvis and its rods, consider yourself a beginner in fly fishing. From fiberglass to fine bamboo, Orvis offers the most complete line of rods in the business.

The reputation of the people in Manchester was built by Charles Orvis in the 1800s and has been enhanced by rod builders like Wes Jordan along the way. No other company stands as a symbol of American fly fishing as does Orvis.

Although today's operation is considerably larger than it was in the years of Wes Jordan (currently about 15,000 rods and plenty of other fishing equipment sold each year), the quality of the line has been maintained.

Graphite rods, which account for about 11,000 of the rods sold by Orvis, are featured first in their catalog. They have everything from the new Ultra Fine 2-weight to the 15' Two-Handed Spey for an 11-weight line. After their introduction several years ago, Orvis graphite rods were considered "eastern" rods by westerners who had to battle wind and big water. A year or two ago, Orvis supplemented its line with a Western Series. These were designed with a stiffer butt section for more power in the wind but with suitable tip action for short casts.

You'll find the Orvis graphite rods to be among the smoothest in action and the most delicate in presentation. The 2-weight Ultra Fine, in case you're wondering, casts and fishes well. You'll find it difficult to work in the wind, certainly, and it takes more effort to cast than does a heavier line-weight rod, but for those who seek the ultimate lightweight experience, the rod will come as a pleasant surprise. It's great fun and makes those Rocky Mountain National Park brookies feel like Florida Keys tarpon.

Orvis offers pack/travel rods in the following models: Traveler, Tight Loop, Spring Creek, All Rounder, and 9x9. All are four-piece rods.

Orvis has also entered the boron/graphite market with models from 8½' to 9½'. The 9½' rods utilize a 80/20 mix of boron and graphite. The shorter rods are 60% boron and 40% graphite (by weight). The ferrules are external graphite. Because the ferrules are "softer" than the boron/graphite mix yet are thicker than the rod, the dead spot associated with ferrules should be negligible. In return, the external ferrules are stronger in hoop strength, an important consideration when casting a long line to big fish. Boron rods start at $285. There is considerable change in the offerings right now, so send for the current catalog for accurate listings.

The other man-made material, fiberglass, is also represented in the Orvis line with the Fullflex rods. Back when fiberglass and bamboo were the only readily accessible materials, I bought one of these rods when I wanted a "good" rod but couldn't afford bamboo. It was fast and light compared to other fiberglass rods I knew

then, and I was pleased with the rod and used it almost exclusively for several years. If you're just beginning your fly fishing career and don't have much money, consider a Fullflex glass rod at $79.

You'd expect a company who's been making rods since 1856 to carry a full line of bamboo, and Orvis won't disappoint you. Their catalog says they retain only 5% of their imported cane for use in the rods. Beyond this initial care in selection, they also grade their finished rods according to appearance.

The C.F. Orvis "125" rods are their top line, selected for this distinction because of the perfection of their color uniformity. Cane that is unblemished but not of "125" grade goes on to become Battenkill rods. Cosmetic imperfections cause a rod to be graded a Madison or MCL rod. Special use rods, such as the Flea, are of Battenkill grade unless preceded by the MCL code. The Madison/MCL rods come with single tip, all others with two tips. Rod performance does not differ between Battenkill and Madison rods, which makes the Madison a bargain for the rod buyer with a limited budget. But buy quickly. The price of Orvis bamboo rods rose $200 between 1984 and 1985. This may indicate a supply problem.

Wherever your desire in a fly rod may lead you, Orvis has a model you should consider. (Note: Some of the rods listed here do not appear in the current Orvis catalog. Most of them have been discontinued, but you may still find them in fly shops or other catalogs.)

Model	Length	Line	Weight	Price	Source
Fiberglass					
Fullflex	7	5	2½	$79	Orv, Kau
Fullflex	7½	6	2¾	$79	Kau, Orv
Fullflex	8	7	3¼	$79	Orv, Kau
Fullflex	8½	6	.3⅞	$79	Kau, Orv
Fullflex	8½	8	3½	$79	Orv, Kau
Graphite					
Otter	7	5	1⅝	$210	Hun, Kau, Fly, Orv
Otter-Option	7	5	2	$210	Kau, Orv
Traveler	7	6	3	$230	Kau
Tippet	7½	3	1½	$215	Fly, Bud, Kau, Orv
Brook Trout	7½	4	1⅝	$215	Fly, Hun, Kau, Orv
Trout	7½	6	2⅛	$210	Kau, AnR, Hun, Fly, Orv
Ultra Fine	7¾	2	1½	$230	Kau, Orv
Far and Fine	7¾	5	2⅛	$210	Bud, AnR, Kau, Hun, Fly, Orv
7/11	7'11"	4	2⅞	$215	Kau, Orv
Tight Loop 4-pc.	8	4	2½	$270	Kau, Orv
Trout	8	6	1⅞	$210	Fly, AnR, Kau, Hig, Orv
Trout-Option	8	6	2¼	$210	Kau, Dan, Bud, AnR, Hun, Fly, Orv
Trout-3pc	8	6	2½	$215	Hun, Fly, Kau, Hig

Model	Length	Lines	Weight	Price	Source
All Rounder-4-pc.	8	7	3	$270	Hun, Kau, Fly, Orv
All Rounder	8¼	7	2½	$230	Bud, Dan, Fly, Hig, Orv, Kau, AnR, Hun
All Rounder-Option	8¼	7	2⅞	$237	Hun, Kau, Fly, Orv
Henry's Fork	8½	5	2½	$237	Dan, Kau, Bud, Hun, Fly, Orv
Limestone Special	8½	6	2⅝	$237	AnR, Hig, Dan, Kau, Orv, Bud, Fly, Hun
Powerhouse	8½	8	2⅞	$237	Kau, Bud, AnR, Hun, Orv
Zephyr	9	4	2⅞	$235	Fly, Orv
Spring Creek-4-pc.	9	5	3⅝	$270	Kau, Orv
Performer	9	6	3	$237	Bud, Dan, Kau, Hun, Fly, Orv
Shooting Star	9	9	4¼	$265	Kau, AnR, Hun, Orv
9x9	9	9	3⅛	$242	Kau, Orv
9x9-4-pc.	9	9	4¼	$297	Kau, Hun, Orv
Bonefish Special	9	9	4⅝	$265	Kau, Orv
Spring Creek	9¼	5	2¾	$237	Let, AnR, Bud, Orv, Kau, Fly, Hun
Advantage	9¼	7	3⅛	$242	Hun, Bud, Kau, Fly, Orv
Advantage-Plus	9¼	7	4¼	$265	Hun, Kau, Fly, Orv
Osprey	9½	6	3½	$235	Fly, Kau, Hun
Lt. Salmon/Salt.	9½	8	4⅛	$265	Hun, AnR, Kau, Orv
Rivermaster	9½	8	3⅝	$230	Kau, Bud, AnR, Hun, Orv
Salmon 2-Hand	10	9	4⅝	$285	Hun, Kau, Orv
Salmon 2-Hand	13½	10	9¼	$315	Kau, Orv
2-Hand Spey	15	11	12	$340	Kau, Orv
Western	8	4	2½	$215	Kau, Let, Dan, Bud, Hun, Orv
Western	8¾	5	2⅞	$237	Kau, Hig, Orv
Western	8¾	7	3¼	$237	Dan, Hun, Kau, Bud, Hig, Orv
Western Bass	8¾	8	3½	$237	Kau, Orv
Western	9	4	2¾	$237	Orv, Kau
Western	9	6	3⅛	$237	Hun, Kau, Bud, Hig, Orv
Western	9¼	8	3⅞	$237	Kau, Orv
Western	10	7	3½	$270	Hig, Hun, Kau, Orv
Boron/graphite					
Boron	8¼	7	3¼	$285	Kau
Boron	8½	6	3⅜	$340	Orv, Kau, Hig, Hun
Boron	8½	8	3⅝	$310	Kau
Boron	8½	8	4	$345	Kau, Hun
Boron	8¾	7	3¾	$345	Orv, Kau, Hun, Hig
Boron	8¾	7	4⅜	$380	Orv, Hun, Kau
Boron	9	8	4	$340	Orv, Kau
Boron	9	9	4	$375	Orv, Kau
Boron	9	9	4⅝	$415	Orv, Kau, Hun
Boron	9	10	5½	$415	Orv, Kau

Model	Length	Lines	Weight	Price	Source
Boron	9	12	5⅞	$415	Orv
Boron	9¼	8	4⅛	$345	Hun, Hig, Kau
Bamboo					
Madison	7½	5	3¼	$550	Orv
Madison	7½	6	3½	$550	Kau, Hun, Orv
Madison	8	6	3¾	$575	Kau, Hun, Orv
Madison	8	7	4	$575	Orv, Kau
MCL Flea	6½	4	2⅜	$525	Kau, Orv
MCL 7/3	7	3	2¾	$550	Orv, Kau
MCL Midge	7½	5	3¼	$550	Kau, Orv
Flea	6½	4	2	$750	Kau, Orv, Hun
Bamboo	7	3	2⅜	$775	Orv, Kau
Bamboo	7	4	2¾	$950	Kau, Orv
Battenkill Midge	7½	5	3⅝	$775	Kau, Hun, Orv
Battenkill	7½	6	3⅞	$775	Orv, Kau, Hun
Battenkill-3-pc.	8	6	4⅛	$800	Hun, Kau, Orv
Battenkill	8	6	4½	$950	Kau, Hun, Orv
Battenkill	8	7	4⅜	$800	Orv, Kau
Far and Fine	7½	5	3⅞	$900	Orv
"125"	6½	4		$900	Kau, Orv
"125"	7	3		$925	Orv, Kau
"125"-3-pc.	7	4		$1,100	Kau, Orv
"125"	7½	5		$925	Orv, Kau
"125"	7½	6		$925	Kau, Orv
"125"	8	6		$950	Orv, Kau
"125"-3-pc.	8	6		$1,100	Kau, Orv
"125"	8	7		$950	Orv, Kau

Powell Rod Co.

Box 3966
Chico, California 95927-3966
(916) 345-3393

Spanning over 80 years and three generations, the Powell Rod Company is a part of America's fly fishing heritage. Begun by E.C. Powell, the company was passed down to Walton, his son. Now, Walton's son, Press, is in charge.

Powell is best known for its bamboo rods, including the Golden Signature Companion rods with two butts and three tips. The standard Signature rods include a full range of rod sizes and line weights. Many options are available. Check their catalog for details.

Graphite is also part of the Powell line. They offer single or two-tips, and the range of prices given here represents the cost for single or two-tip rods. The graphite line now includes the West Branch series, economical rods for the cost-conscious angler. They are available in single tip only. Custom orders are also possible.

Model	Length	Line	Weight	Price
Graphite				
DF 70-1	7	4,5	2⅝	$185-$250
DF 76-1	7½	4,5	2¾	$185-$250
DF 76-2	7½	5,6	2⅝	$185-$250
DF 80-1	8	4,5	2⅞	$185-$250
DF 80-2	8	5,6	2¾	$185-$250
DF 83-2	8¼	5,6	2⅞	$185-$250
DF 86-1	8½	4,5	2⅞	$185-$250
DF 86-2	8½	5,6	3	$185-$250
WB 86	8½	5,6	2⅞	$125
LTSH 86	8½	7,8	3⅛	$190-$255

Model	Length	Line	Weight	Price
DF 90-1	9	4,5	3	$185-$250
DF 90-2L	9	5,6	3⅛	$185-$250
DF 90-2H	9	6,7	3⅛	$185-$250
WB 90T	9	6,7	3⅛	$125
LTSH 90	9	7,8	3⅜	$190-$255
COHO 90L	9	8,9	3⅞	$195-$260
WB 90SH	9	8,9	4⅛	$130
COHO 90	9	9,10	4	$195-$260
Tarpon	9	11,12	5	$225
DF 96-1	9½	4-6	3½	$185-$250
DF 96-2	9½	6-8	3¼	$185-$250
LTSH 96	9½	7,8	3⅝	$190-$255
COHO 96	9½	9,10	4⅛	$195-$260
LTSH 100	10	7,8	3⅞	$190-$255
COHO 100	10	9,10	4¼	$195-$260
DF 86-4	8½	5-7	3	$235
DF 90-4	9	5-7	3⅛	$235
DF 96-4	9½	6-8	3¼	$240
COHO 90-4	9	8,9	4	$245
Bamboo				
Walton 70	7	4,5	3¾	$600
Walton 76	7½	5,6	4	$600
Walton 80	8	5,6	4¼	$600
Walton 83	8¼	4,5	4⅜	$600
Walton 86	8½	6,7	4½	$600
Walton 810	8'10"	5,6	4⅜	$600
Walton 90	9	7,8	5¼	$600
Golden Signature Companion rods				
Walton 70-80	7,8	4,5	3¾,4¼	$1,000
Walton 76-86	7½,8½	5,6	4¼,4¾	$1,000
Walton 80-90	8,9	6,7	4¾,5¼	$1,000

Powell Rods
from Big Sky Custom Flies
Box 4981
Missoula, Montana 59801

Doug Brewer has developed a series of three graphite rods with the help of Press Powell of Powell Rod Company. They are all 9' rods with models for line weights 2,3 through 6,7.

Model	Length	Line	Price
Super Delicate	9	2,3	$180
Delicate	9	4,5	$180
All Western	9	6,7	$180

Rodon Manufacturing Co., Inc.
123 Sylvan Ave.
Newark, New Jersey 07104
(201) 481-0027

Rodon is unusual in that it makes rods of only one type, boron/graphite. Rodon is another company with a limited history in rod building, but they entered the market with a definite idea of what they wanted and with an experienced rod maker, Ted Simroe, in house.

Rodon wanted a rod that was "moderate", i.e., slower in action than graphite rods, but they wanted to retain the power of graphite rods. The solution was to build a slow taper rod (which would have lacked power had it

been built in graphite only) with a layer of boron in it. The boron gives the rod strength and power, the taper gives it the slower action.

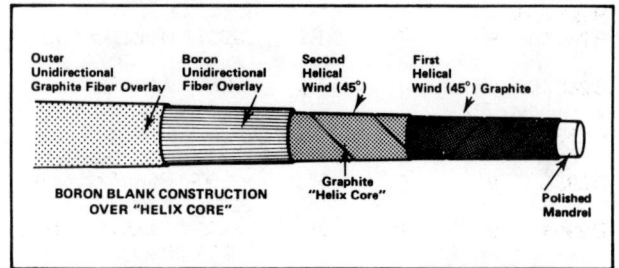

The rods are constructed with a base of graphite wound on the mandrel in the conventional way. Boron fibers are then laid over this, and a final coat of graphite is added to enable finishing of the rod. The technical data on the process, plus a complete explanation of the way the rod works in hand, is given in the excellent Rodon catalog.

In short, Rodon hopes their rods have the feel of bamboo with the power of graphite—a happy marriage. After trying out the rods, I think they've been very successful. The rods are powerful, smooth, and relatively slow. If you don't favor the fast lane of traditional graphite but want the power, try one. They offer a full range of sizes and line weights. Many models are offered in two-, three-, and four-piece rods. The number of sections is indicated by the first digit of the model number.

Model	Length	Line	Weight	Price	Source
Trout rods					
T 2704	7	4	1¾	$235-$252.35	Rod, Ram, Don, Mer
T 2753	7½	3	1⅞	$235-$252.35	Ram, Don, Rod, Mer
T 2755	7½	5	2⅝	$245-$262.65	Rod, Ram, Don, Mer
T 2804	8	4	2	$235-$252.35	Kau, Rod, Ram, Don, Mer
T 2806	8	6	2⅞	$245-$262.65	Kau, Rod, Ram, Don, Mer
T 2807	8	7	3⅛	$255-$272.95	Rod, Don, Mer
T 2855	8½	5	3	$245-$262.65	Kau, Rod, Ram, Don, Mer
T 2857	8½	7	3½	$255-$272.95	Kau, Rod, Don, Mer
T 2906	9	6	3¼	$245-$255	Rod, Ram, Don, Kau
T 2908	9	8	3⅝	$255-$272.95	Rod, Don, Mer, Kau
T 2957	9½	7	3¾	$255-$265	Kau, Rod, Don
T 3856	8½	6	3⅛	$285-$295	Rod, Don
T 3857	8½	7	3⅛	$315-$320	Kau, Rod
T 3906	9	6	3½	$285-$295	Kau, Don, Rod
T 3908	9	8	3¾	$315	Rod
T 3957	9½	7	3⅞	$315	Rod
T 4806	8	6	3	$315-$325	Rod, Don, Kau

Model	Length	Line	Weight	Price	Source
T 4857	8½	7	3¾	$335	Rod
T 4908	9	8	4⅛	$350	Kau, Rod
Bass rods					
B 2807	8	7	3¼	$260-$270	Rod, Don
B 2857	8½	7	3⅝	$260-$270	Rod, Don
B 2858	8½	8	3¾	$260-$270	Rod, Don
B 2907	9	7	3⅜	$260-$278.10	Kau, Rod, Don, Mer
B 2908	9	8	3⅞	$265-$283.25	Rod, Don, Mer
B 2959	9½	9	4⅛	$265-$275	Kau, Rod, Don
B 2008	10	8	4¼	$265-$275	Rod, Don
B 3857	8½	7	3¾	$320	Rod
B 3908	9	8	3⅞	$320	Kau, Rod
B 3959	9½	9	4¼	$330	Rod
B 4908	9	8	4⅛	$360	Rod
Steelhead rods					
H 2858	8½	8	3⅞	$280	Rod
H 2908	9	8	4	$280	Rod
H 2959	9½	9	4⅜	$285	Rod
H 2008	10	8	4⅝	$285	Rod
H 2010	10	10	5¼	$295	Kau, Rod
H 2059	10½	9	5	$295	Rod
H 3908	9	8	4⅛	$335	Rod
H 3959	9½	9	4½	$345	Kau, Rod
H 3008	10	8	4¾	$345	Rod
H 3010	10	10	5⅜	$355	Rod
Salmon rods					
S 2858	8½	8	3¾	$265-$275	Rod, Don
S 2907	9	7	3⅜	$265-$283.25	Rod, Don, Mer
S 2908	9	8	3⅞	$265-$283.25	Mer, Don, Rod, Kau
S 2957	9½	7	4	$265-$275	Kau, Don, Rod
S 2959	9½	9	4⅛	$270-$288.40	Rod, Don, Mer
S 2008	10	8	4¼	$270-$280	Don, Rod, Kau
S 2059	10½	9	4⅜	$270-$280	Rod, Don
S 3908	9	8	3⅞	$320-$330	Rod, Don
S 3957	9½	7	4⅛	$320-$330	Kau, Don, Rod
S 3959	9½	9	4¼	$330-$340	Don, Rod
S 3008	10	8	4½	$330-$340	Rod, Don
S 4857	8½	7	3⅞	$350-$360	Rod, Don
S 4908	9	8	4⅛	$350-$360	Rod, Don
Double-handed salmon rods					
D 3211	12	11	8½	$445	Kau, Rod
D 3412	14	12	10½	$545	Kau, Rod
D 3613	16	13	12½	$675	Kau, Rod
Saltwater rods					
W 2959	9½	9	4⅝	$290	Kau, Rod
W 2952	9½	12	5½	$335	Kau, Rod
W 2008	10	8	4⅞	$290	Rod
W 2010	10	10	5½	$300	Kau, Rod
W 2054	10½	14	6½	$395	Rod

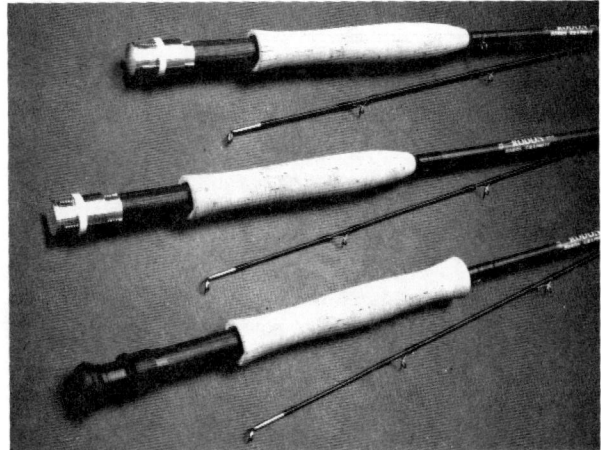

Model	Length	Line	Weight	Price	Source
W 3950	9½	10	4¾	$350	Rod
W 3008	10	8	4⅞	$350	Rod
W 3010	10	10	5⅝	$360	Rod
W 3051	10½	11	5¾	$380	Rod

Sage
9630 NE Lafayette St.
Bainbridge Island, Washington 98110
(206) 842-6608

Sage, a relative newcomer in the business, is currently a big name in rods. They established themselves quickly with major advertising campaigns and the endorsement of world class caster Steve Rajeff.

Their initial line was the GFL series of graphite rods. They are well-appointed, handsome rods of moderate action. A full line of GFL lines is available.

Added to the Sage line in 1984 was the Graphite II series. These rods are produced from higher modulus (stiffer) graphite. They are powerful rods designed to control long casts.

The high modulus material got a lot of press and sparked some controversy. Other rod makers took particular exception to Sage's claim that the Graphite II rods were "stronger, lighter, and more sensitive than any other rod on the market".

Indeed, the Graphite II rods are not lighter than other rods of the same length and line weight. Here's a comparison of finished rod weights for an 8½; 6-weight rod: Scott—2½ oz.; Orvis, Thomas & Thomas, Winston—2⅝ oz.; Lamiglass Boron—3 oz.; Sage GFL, Rodon Boron—3⅛ oz.; Sage Graphite II—3 3/16 oz.; Orvis Boron/Graphite 3⅜ oz.; Fenwick HMG Graphite—3½ oz. (Variations in components account for slight differences in rod weights.

Further reading in the Sage catalog, however, explains more clearly what Sage's claims for the new Graphite II rods are— "We can make lighter rods for the same power . . ." If a rod maker were to build a rod of the same stiffness as the Graphite II rod using a lower modulus graphite, it would probably weigh a lot more.

The question of power in a fly rod is interesting and one you'll have to settle on your own. Boron proponents might argue that their rods are more powerful than even Graphite II, for instance. No one would argue that the two materials develop their power much differently. If you're looking for a thunderstick for long casts or for fighting the gales, you should try both types of rods.

Graphite II rods may have found a niche in the market as an economical alternative to boron. Other rod companies, notably G. Loomis and Cabela's, are now producing rods from higher modulus graphite.

Sage offers a full line of GFL models and a developing line of Graphite II rods. New models were not yet listed in our catalogs, but they will be now. You can also write Sage for their catalog, if you wish.

Model	Length	Line	Weight	Price	Source
Graphite					
GFL 470	7	4	2¼	$202	Don, Pen, Kau, Mer, Fly
GFL 476	7½	4	2⅜	$208	Mer, Pen, Don, Ram, Kau, Fly
GFL 576	7½	5	2½	$208	Kau, Pen, Don, Ram, Fly, Mer, Bob
GFL 580	8	5	2⅝	$216	Bob, Pen, Don, Bud, Ram, Kau, Mer, Fly
GFL 680	8	6	2¾	$216	Kau, Pen, Don, Bud, Bob, Fly, Mer, Ram
GFL 586	8½	5	3	$225	Bob, Pen, Don, Ram, Fly, Mer, Kau
GFL 686	8½	6	3⅛	$225	Mer, Pen, Don, Dan, Kau, Fly, Bud, Bob, Ram
GFL 786	8½	7	3¼	$225	Pen, Fly, Don, Kau, Bud, Bob, Dan, Mer
GHFL 789	8¾	7	3½	$228	Kau, Pen, Don, Bud, Mer
GFL 490	9	4	3⅛	$234	Dan, Pen, Fly, Kau, Bud, Bob, Mer, Don
GFL 590	9	5	3¼	$234	Pen, Mer, Fly, Don, Bud, Ram, Kau, Bob, Dan
GFL 690	9	6	3⅜	$242	Bud, Pen, Don, Fly, Bob, Mer, Kau
GFL 790	9	7	3½	$246	Bud, Pen, Don, Kau, Fly, Mer, Bob
GFL 890	9	8	3⅝	$246	Kau, Fly, Don, Bud, Bob, Mer, Pen
GFL 896	9½	8	4	$255	Bud, Don, Kau, Fly, Bob, Mer
GFL 996	9½	9	4⅜	$255	Kau, Don, Bud, Mer, Fly
GFL 1096	9½	10	4½	$255	Don, Fly, Kau, Mer, Bud
Graphite II					
GFL 379RP	7¾	3	2⅛	$235	New model
GFL 480RP	8	4	2½	$240	Bob, Kau, Don, Fly, Mer, Pen
GFL 586RP	8½	5	3	$253	New model
GFL 686RP	8½	6	3³⁄₁₆	$253	Bob, Pen, Don, Bud, Kau, Mer, Fly

Model	Length	Line	Weight	Price	Source
GFL 789RP	8¾	7	3⅜	$257	New model
GFL 390RP	9	3	3⅛	$260	New model
GFL 490RP	9	4	3¼	$260	New model
GFL 590RP	9	5	3⅜	$262	Hig, Pen, Don, Bud, Dan, Bob, Mer, Fly, Kau
GFL 690RP	9	6	3½	$262	Dan, Pen, Don, Bud, Mer, Bob, Fly, Kau, Hig
GFL 790RP	9	7	3⅝	$266	Don, Pen, Kau, Bud, Dan, Bob, Mer, Fly, Hig
GFL 890RP	9	8	3¾	$266	Kau, Fly, Pen, Don, Dan, Bob, Mer, Bud
GFL 990RP	9	9	3⅞	$270	Dan, Pen, Don, Kau, Fly, Mer
GFL 1090RP	9	10	4¾	$276	New model
GFL 1190RP	9	11	5¾	$335	Don, Pen, Fly, Kau, Mer
GFL 1290RP	9	12	6	$342	Mer, Pen, Don, Kau, Fly
GFL 496RP	9½	4	3⅜	$263	New model
GFL 596RP	9½	5	3½	$267	Pen, Kau, Fly, Mer, Don
GFL 696RP	9½	6	3⅝	$267	Kau, Fly, Don, Mer, Pen
GFL 796RP	9½	7	3¾	$271	Pen, Kau, Fly, Mer, Don
GFL 896RP	9½	8	4	$271	Don, Pen, Mer, Fly, Kau, Hig
GFL 996RP	9½	9	4⅛	$274	Mer, Pen, Kau, Fly, Don
GFL 1096RP	9½	10	5¼	$274	New model
GFL 7100RP	10	7	4¼	$274	Mer, Don, Kau, Fly
GFL 9100RP	10	9	4¾	$276	New model
Three-piece rods					
GFL 589-3	8¾	5	3½	$258	Bud, Pen, Don, Fly, Mer, Kau
GFL 693-3	9¼	6	3¾	$264	Kau, Pen, Fly, Bud, Mer, Don
GFL 796-3	9½	7	4⅛	$272	Don, Pen, Kau, Fly, Mer, Bud
GFL 699-3	9¾	6	3⅞	$265	Kau, Mer, Don
GFL 8100-3	10	8	4¾	$285	Mer, Pen, Kau, Don, Fly
GFL 10106-3	10½	10	4⅝	$318	Pen, Mer, Don, Kau, Fly
Four-piece rods					
GFL 583-4	8¼	5	3	$252	Kau, Pen, Don, Dan, Bob, Mer
GFL 783-4	8¼	7	3½	$257	Kau, Pen, Don, Dan, Bob, Mer

Scott PowR-Ply
765 Clementina Street
San Francisco, California 94103
(415) 864-1611

Despite the numerous ads you see for Scott rods, the company is not a massive conglomerate. If you call the company to check on the progress of your rod, you may very well end up talking to Harry Wilson, the president. He'll yell over to the people in the next room to see if it's done. At some of the other big name rod companies, you'd

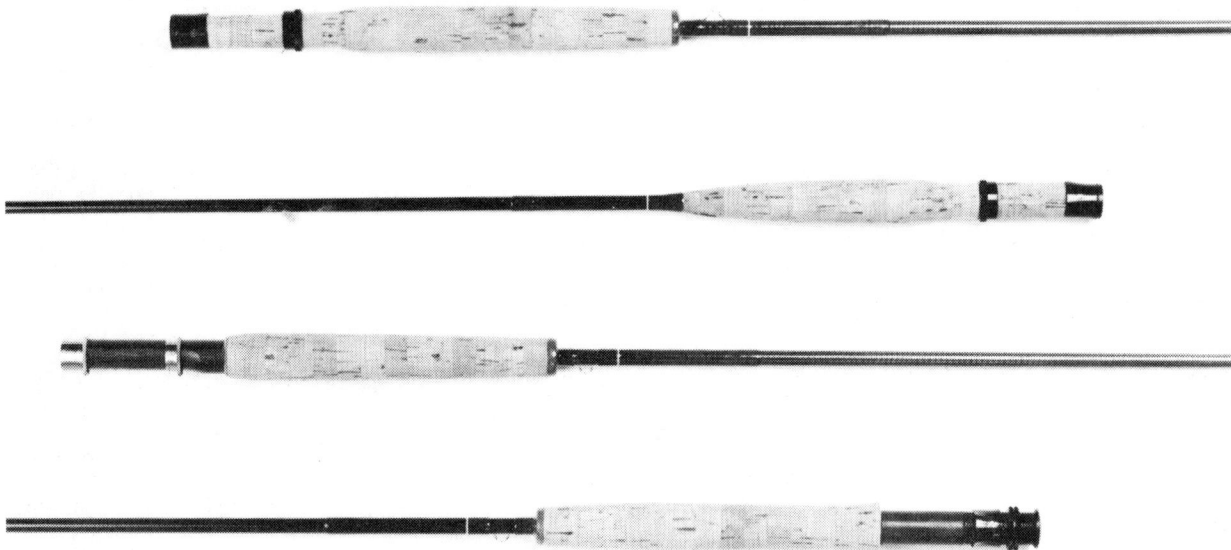

© Bill Acheson, 1982

be lucky to get a call through to someone who knew the president's name.

That fact speaks something about this company's style. Harry hasn't let things get out of control. He has people he trusts working for him, and there aren't so many of them that he can't look over their shoulders anytime he thinks it's necessary. It's almost a family operation.

The quality control and fine workmanship may also remind one of the small companies working with bamboo. Such care and attention to detail hasn't always been associated with graphite rods. Many companies got on the graphite bandwagon (as they are getting on the boron bandwagon now) without knowing the material. They used the same tapers that they had used for their fiberglass rods. They were interested in sales, not quality.

That didn't happen to Harry Wilson's company. Harry made fiberglass rods (and still does on special order), but he developed his graphite rods independently. One result of his careful research with the material is the "flex rating" system. By using that system, tip sections can be matched to butt sections to compensate for individual inconsistencies in manufacture. Each rod that comes from Scott has gone through the flex rating procedure.

As part of that flex rating, you may select from three actions for any model. Light action rods are a bit softer, strong action a bit stiffer. The standard action rod rests in between. Even the standard rod is considered fast action. It's built to have plenty of power, but it's also very accurate. It does require more finesse in casting than slower rods, but in return, it casts superbly.

The blanks for Scott rods come from the Fisher factory, but the graphite is different from that used in Fisher rods. The tapers and designs are unique to Scott.

Some makes of rods vary considerably in action from model to model, but these rods are very much alike in feel and action, within the bounds of line weight and rod length. They are the lightest rods made in each category, almost without exception.

Also important is Scott's ferrule system. It utilizes an internal sleeve, thus the rod diameter in the ferrule section is the same as the rest of the rod. Some rod makers would argue that it's not as strong as other ferrules, but few would disagree that it gives the best rod action.

Scott has a full line of graphite rods, including several pack/travel rods. These are indicated in the model numbers by a "/" followed by the number of sections. The rods range from 6'10" to 10' with line weights of 3-10. Models designated by a B are bass rods which feature a softer butt section and stiffer tip section to make casting air-resistant poppers easier.

Model	Length	Line	Weight	Price	Source
G75-3	7½	3	1.8	$250	Sco, Mur, Cus, AnR
G75-4	7½	4	1.9	$250	Sco, AnR, Cus, Fly, Mur, Hun
G75-5	7½	5	2	$250	Sco, Mur, Cus, AnR, Hun
G80-3	8	3	2.1	$250	Sco, AnR, Cus
G80-4	8	4	2.2	$250	Sco, Hun, Cus, AnR, Mur, Fly
G80-5	8	5	2.3	$250	Sco, Fly, Mur, AnR, Hun, Cus
G80-6	8	6	2.4	$250	Sco, Mur, Hun, AnR, Cus
G85-4	8½	4	2.3	$260	Sco, Cus, AnR
G85-5	8½	5	2.4	$260	Sco, Dan, AnR, Cus, Hun, Mur, Fly, Hig
G85-6	8½	6	2.5	$260	Sco, Mur, Hun, Dan, Hig, AnR, Fly, Cus
G85-7	8½	7	3.2	$280	Sco, Cus, Mur, AnR, Hun

Model	Length	Line	Weight	Price	Source
G90-3	9	3	2.3	$260	Sco, Fly, Cus, Mur, Hig, Dan, AnR
G90-4	9	4	2.4	$260	Sco, AnR, Cus, Hig, Fly, Mur, Hun, Dan
G90-5	9	5	2.5	$260	Sco, Mur, AnR, Cus, Fly, Hun, Hig
G90-6	9	6	2.6	$260	Sco, Cus, Fly, Dan, AnR, Hun, Mur, Hig
G90-7	9	7	3.3	$280	Sco, AnR, Cus, Dan, Fly, Mur, Hun, Hig
G90-8	9	8	3.4	$280	Sco, Wul, Cus, AnR, Hun, Mur, Hig
G95-8	9½	8	3.6	$290	Sco, Mur, Dan, AnR, Fly, Cus, Hig
G95-9	9½	9	3.9	$290	Sco, Hun, Dan, Fly, Mur, Cus, AnR, Hig
G95-10	9½	10	4.7	$295	Sco, Mur, Fly, Cus, AnR
G100-4	10	4	2.8	$270	Sco, Cus, Mur, AnR, Fly
G100-5	10	5	2.9	$270	Sco, Fly, Mur, AnR, Cus, Hig
G100-6	10	6	3.4	$290	Sco, Cus, Fly, AnR, Hun, Mur, Hig
G100-7	10	7	3.5	$290	Sco, Mur, Cus, Fly, AnR, Hun, Hig
G100-8	10	8	3.6	$290	Sco, Hun, Mur, Cus, Fly, AnR
Bass rods					
G85-7B	8½	7,8	3.1	$290	Sco, Mur, Cus, AnR, Hig
G90-7B	9	7,8	3.3	$290	Sco, Fly, Mur, AnR, Cus, Hig
G95-8B	9½	8,9	3.4	$295.50	Sco, Cus, AnR, Mur
Three-piece rods					
G70-4/3	6'10"	4	1.7	$275	Sco, Mur, Cus, AnR
G70-5/3	6'10"	5	1.8	$275	Sco, Cus, AnR, Mur
G70-6/3	6'10"	6	1.9	$275	Sco, Wul, Cus, AnR, Mur
G75-4/3	7'7"	4	2	$280	Sco, Cus, AnR, Mur
G75-5/3	7'7"	5	2.1	$280	Sco, Cus, AnR, Mur
G95-5/3	9½	5	2.7	$325	Sco, AnR, Cus, Hun, Fly
G95-6/3	9½	6	3.3	$345	Sco, Cus, AnR, Hun, Fly
G95-7/3	9½	7	3.4	$345	Sco, Hun, Cus, Fly, AnR
Four-piece rods					
G90-5/4	9	5	2.7	$325	Sco, Hun, Cus, AnR, Fly, Mur, Hig
G90-6/4	9	6	2.8	$325	Sco, Hun, Fly, AnR, Cus, Hig, Mur

Model	Length	Line	Weight	Price	Source
G90-7/4	9	7	3.5	$345	Sco, Fly, Cus, Mur, AnR, Hig
G100-7/4	10	7	3.9	$360	Sco, AnR, Cus, Hun, Mur, Fly
G100-8/4	10	8	4	$360	Sco, Cus, Fly, Mur, AnR
A five-piece rod					
G84-5/5	8⅓	5	2.4	$325	Sco, Cus, AnR

Skip Morris

Box 30312
Portland, Oregon 97223
(503) 620-7460

Skip Morris is unusual among independent, custom rod builders in that he works entirely with graphite and fiberglass. Instead of a second line behind bamboo, the man-made materials are his first choice.

You'll find his standard models listed here. They include the Metolius series, relatively fast-action rods for the "quick-paced" caster, the Trout series, slow-action rods for those with "an easy, unhurried casting style", and the Deschutes series, moderate-action rods for those folks in between. The Companion rods are multi-piece fiberglass and graphite rods, and the Basser rods are slow-action rods with stout tips for setting hooks in the tough mouths of bass.

If you request Skip's brochure, I think you'll like his style. This is not glossy hype, so I like it. He tells the story of his involvement with rod building as if you were sitting in his living room with him.

Skip designs his own rod tapers and shaft dimensions, and his rods will be different from production models on the market from larger companies. In his brochure, he gives three reasons for going out on his own.

"The first was so that I could create rods tailor-made for the many individual tastes and needs of different flyfishers. The second reason . . . was my fascination with fly rod action. My third reason, and a very compelling one, was my dissatisfaction with many of the rods on the market. Some were too heavy; others lacked power where it was needed; still others were just poorly designed and lacked the smooth, effortless performance a fine fly rod must offer."

You begin to get a picture of just what Skip Morris wants in a fly rod after reading his brochure. You may want the same thing, and if you do, try one of his standard models. If they don't appeal to you, but you still agree with Skip about production rods, then he'll make a rod for you to your specifications. There's even a questionnaire included to help you describe your needs.

Some of the possibilities include: "rods for certain angling situations, two-tipped rods for two different actions or line weights, a favorite bamboo rod reproduced in fiberglass or graphite, a favorite rod reproduced in a multi-piece or 'pack' design, a rod with a feel or action not available over the counter, or perhaps a rod designed just to suit you."

Guess that covers the territory of custom rod building.

I've listed Skip's standard models in the basic Whitetrim style. A fancier model is available (Silvertrim) for about $20 more in each model. Skip will also send you a list of rods on his "rod rack", experimental rods that were developed on the way to a custom rod or just for fun.

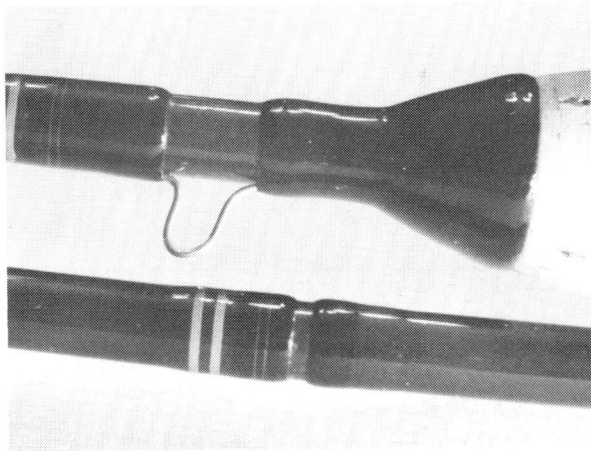

Model	Length	Line	Price
Finesse	7½	4	$109
Metolius	7½	5	$109
Deschutes	8	5	$109
Deschutes	8	6	$117
Trout	8	6	$117
Basser	8	7	$117
Graphite			
Miniature	6	4	$219
Basser	8¾	8	$227
Brown Trout	8	4	$219
Metolius Light	8¼	5	$219
Trout	8½	5	$219
Metolius	8½	6	$227

Model	Length	Line	Price
Trout	8¾	6	$227
Metolius	8¾	7	$227
Deschutes	9	5	$219
Deschutes	9	6	$227
Deschutes	9	7	$227
Trout	9	7	$227
Multi-piece rods			
Companion	7	4	$137
Companion	7½	5	$139
Companion	8	6	$147
Companion	8½	6	$253
Deschutes Pack	9	6	$249

Thomas & Thomas
Box 32
Turner's Falls, Massachusetts 01376
(413) 863-9727

Thomas & Thomas is a well-respected rod manufacturer best known for their high quality bamboo rods. They also offer a full line of graphite rods.

The T&T bamboo rod offering begins with the Classic series at $635. These are two-piece rods with an extra tip. They feature walnut reel seat spacers and nickel silver fittings. The Individualist series retails for about $850. Unlike the Classic rods, which are impregnated, these rods carry a varnish finish. All have an extra tip. A three-piece series is available in this line.

At the high end of the market are the Sans Pareil rods. At a base price of about $1,000 for a two-piece rod, these are T&T's best. They are custom built to a customer's special needs. The series includes one-piece (to 9'6"!), two-, three-, and four-piece rods. A special Presentation Sans Pareil retails for about $1,400.

The company also offers graphite rods. These include two-rod sets called the Brace series. The finish work on the graphite rods is just as fastidious as the work done on the bamboo rods.

I've cast T&T rods, and they are impressive. A friend owns several T&T rods, and he's like a convert trying to get everyone to join the T&T religion.

Model	Length	Line	Weight	Price
Graphite				
Supra-Lite	7½	4	2	$280
Special Dry Fly	8	4,5	2⅜	$280
Trouter	8	5	2½	$280
Enthusiast	8½	5	2½	$280
General				
Practitioner	8½	6	2⅝	$280
Iliaska Special	9	7	3⅝	$290
Basser	9	7	3⅞	$290
Salmo	9½	7	3⅝	$295
Gaspe	9½	8,9	4	$295
Bamboo				
Classic	7	4	2⅜	$635
Classic	7½	5	3¼	$635
Classic	8	5	3¾	$635
Classic	8	6	4	$635
Classic	8½	7	4½	$635

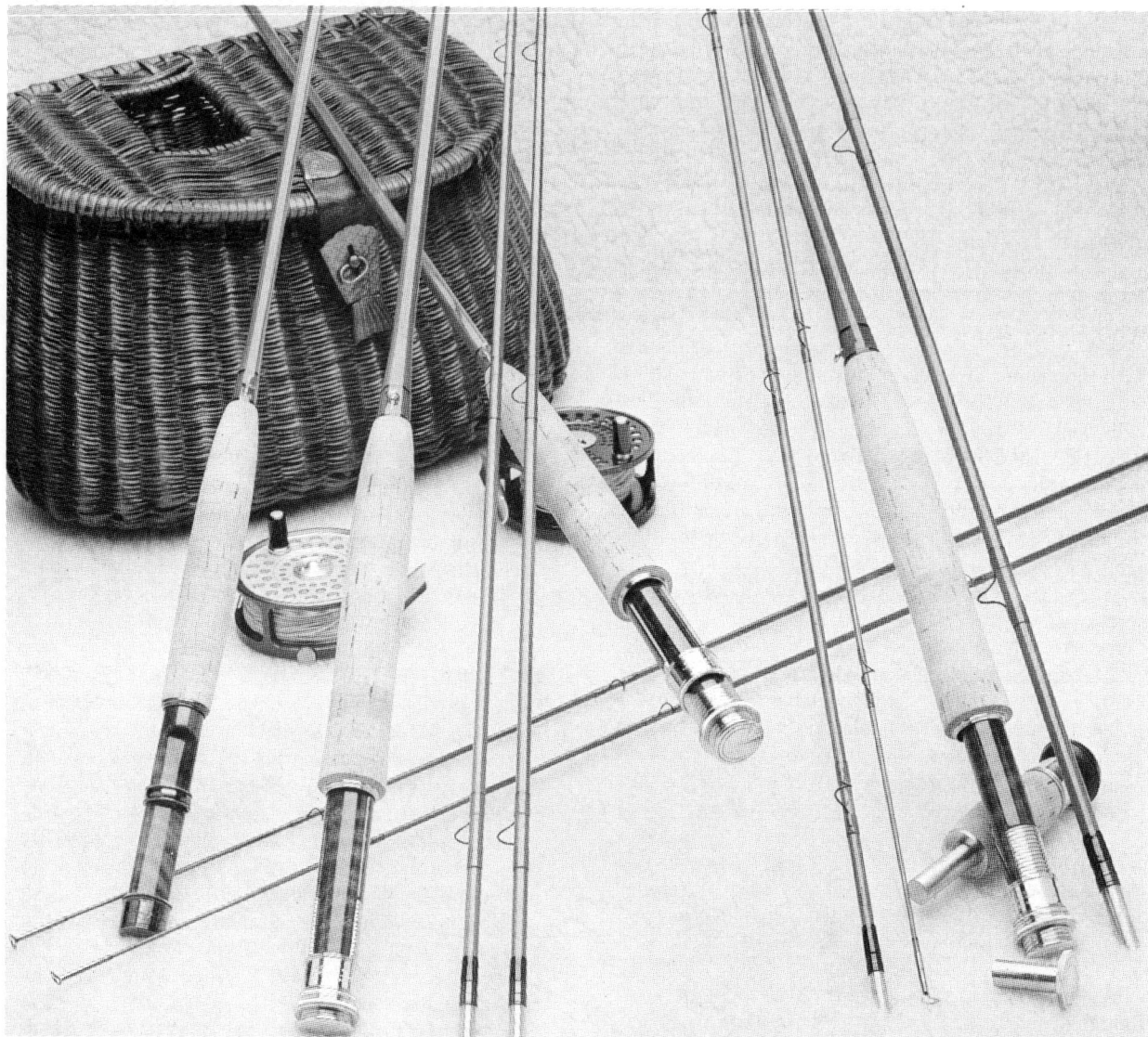

Model	Length	Line	Weight	Price
Individualist Series, bamboo				
Midge	7	4	2⅜	$850
Caenis	7½	3	2⅞	$850
Specialist	7½	4	3⅛	$850
Specialist	7½	4	3¼	$900
Hendrickson	7½	5	3⅜	$850
Hendrickson	7½	5	3½	$900
Limestoner	8	4	3⅝	$850
Beaverkill	8	5	3⅞	$850
Beaverkill	8	5	4	$900
Paradigm	8	5	3¾	$850
Traditionalist	8	6	4⅛	$850
Traditionalist	8	6	4½	$900
Henry's Fork	8½	5	4¼	$850
Montana	8½	6	4½	$850
Montana	8½	6	4⅝	$900
Salmon	8½	7	4¾	$960
Salmon	8½	8	4⅞	$960
Salmon	8½	8	5⅛	$960
Salmon	9	9	5¾	$960
One-piece bamboo				
Sans Pareil	6	3-6		$850

Model	Length	Line	Weight	Price
Sans Pareil	6½	3-7		$960
Sans Pareil	7	3-7		$1,070
Sans Pareil	7½	3-7		$1,180
Sans Pareil	8	3-7		$1,290
Sans Pareil	8½	4-8		$1,400
Sans Pareil	9	4-9		$1,500
Sans Pareil	9½	6-9		$1,600
Two-, three-, four-piece bamboo				
Sans Pareil	7-9½	3-9	2-pc.	$1,070
Sans Pareil	7-9½	3-9	3-pc.	$1,180
Sans Pareil	7-9½	3-9	4-pc.	$1,290
Presentation	6-9½	3-9	2-pc.	$1,400
Kosmic	8½	5	2-pc.	$1,950
Two-rod sets, graphite				
Eastern Brace	8	4,6		$775
Western Brace	9	4,6		$795
Travelers Set—Trout	9	5,6		$895
Travelers Set—Salmon	9½	7,9		$925

Vince Cummings

A line of fiberglass rods designed and built by Vince Cummings is offered by Fred Reese (see address Chapter 14).

Model	Length	Line	Price	Source
FL460	6	3,4	$95	Fre
FL465	6½	3,4	$95	Fre
FL470	7	4,5	$95	Fre
FL475	7½	4,5	$95	Fre
FL480	8	5,6	$95	Fre

Walt Carpenter

Harry Murray at Murray's Fly Shop offers a selection of bamboo rods from one of the country's leading rod builders, Walt Carpenter. The lower price is for one-tip rods, the higher for two-tip rods.

Model	Length	Line	Price	Source
Highlander 63	6¼	3,4	$450, $575	Mur
Highlander 66	6½	4	$450, $575	Mur
Highlander 70	7	4,5	$450, $575	Mur
Highlander 73	7¼	4,5	$450, $575	Mur
Highlander 756	7½	5	$450, $575	Mur
Highlander 766	7½	6	$450, $575	Mur
Highlander 806	8	6	$450, $575	Mur

Weir & Son
2455 The Alameda
Santa Clara, California 95050
(408) 247-3122

Although they produce a line of graphite rods, Weir & Son is known for bamboo rods. This is a small company centering around the Weir family. The rods are completely designed and built in-house. Even the hardware is constructed in the Weir & Son workshop.

The bamboo rods come in four actions: lightweight for light lines and tippets; medium for overall use; dry fly for fast action and accuracy; and special for bass, steelhead, and salmon fishing. The rods are varnished and come with a choice of high quality reel seats.

In addition, the company offers true custom rod building services to those who want a rod not listed in the catalog. Possibilities include custom grips, custom tapers, and use of pre-embargo cane. Contact the company for details.

Weir & Son also sells blanks as well as reel seats and hardware. They offer full repair and restoration services on all makes of bamboo rods. One unusual service is the ability to replicate an existing reel seat that may have been damaged.

Model	Length	Line	Price
Graphite			
Black Hawk	7½	3,4	$250
Black Hawk	7½	4,5	$250

Model	Length	Line	Price
Black Hawk	7½	5,6	$250
Black Hawk	8	4,5	$250
Black Hawk	8	6,7	$250
Black Hawk	8½	6,7	$250
Black Hawk	8½	7,8	$250
Black Hawk	9	4,5	$250
Black Hawk	9	6,7	$250
Black Hawk	9	7,8	$250
Black Hawk	9	8,9	$250
Black Hawk	9½	8,9	$250
Black Hawk	10	8,9	$250
Black Hawk	10	9,10	$250
Bamboo			
Dry Fly	6½	3	$650-$700
Dry Fly	7	4	$650-$700
Dry Fly	7½	5	$650-$700
Dry Fly	8	6	$650-$700
Dry Fly	8½	6	$650-$700
Lightweight	7	3	$650-$700
Lightweight	7½	4	$650-$700
Lightweight	8	5	$650-$700
Lightweight	9	6	$650-$700
Medium Action	7½	5	$650-$700
Medium Action	8	6	$650-$700
Medium Action	8½	7	$650-$700
Special	9	8	$900
Special	9	11	$900
Special	9½	10	$900

Winston
Box 248
Twin Bridges, Montana 59754
(406) 684-5533

"A bamboo rod is more than a fine fishing and casting tool. It represents our angling heritage, the dedication to craftsmanship, the beauty of design, and the development of natural materials."

The philosophy of the R. L. Winston Rod Co. is clearly stated in their catalog. Throughout that catalog, which makes excellent reading on its own, I'm impressed with the thought and care that goes into Winston rods. The description of the process used to make a bamboo rod is enough in itself to make you want one. Did you know there are over 150 feet of edges in a two-tip, 8' rod? And every one must be perfect.

The catalog describes each model, giving a description of the action and a range of casting distances appropriate to the rod. This is the best, most informative rod catalog published and should be a model for all rod makers. The preliminary information about choosing line weight, material, rod action, and length is a rod buyer's primer.

But before this turns into a book review, let's get back to the rods. Winston makes a line of quality bamboo rods divided by line weights into three groups: Light Trout (3,4); Trout (5-7); and Steelhead and Atlantic Salmon (8-10). The Trout and Steelhead rods utilize a fluted, hollow construction. All rods have a varnish finish. According to the catalog, they range in action from fast to slow depending on line weight and length.

If it were not enough for a company of four people to create these fine cane rods, they also make fiberglass and graphite rods with excellent reputations for design and quality of manufacture.

Winston is one of the few companies that still takes fiberglass seriously. They are aware of its limitations, but they are also aware of certain benefits. How about the suggestion that you might be better off with two fiberglass rods to meet your specific angling needs, instead of one compromise graphite rod? The rod blanks used are made to Winston's specifications by J. Kennedy Fisher. They have the same model names as the bamboo rods with two additions. There's a pair of big game rods for saltwater use and a series of three- and four-piece travel rods. A two-rod travel set with two 8 ½' rods for line weights 6 and 8 finishes the fiberglass series.

Winston's graphite line offers rods from 7 ½' to 10' for line weights 3-12. Like the fiberglass line, there are models for saltwater and a travel rod series. The travel rods are three-piece 8 ½' and 9' in length. The Executive Travel Set contains two 9' rods with a choice of line weights from 5-8. The two rods are packaged together in a leather case. These rods are distinctive in color (deep green) and action. They are certainly a rod you should try out if considering graphite.

All rods are subject to a five-day inspection by you. Return the rod unfished and undamaged for an exchange or refund.

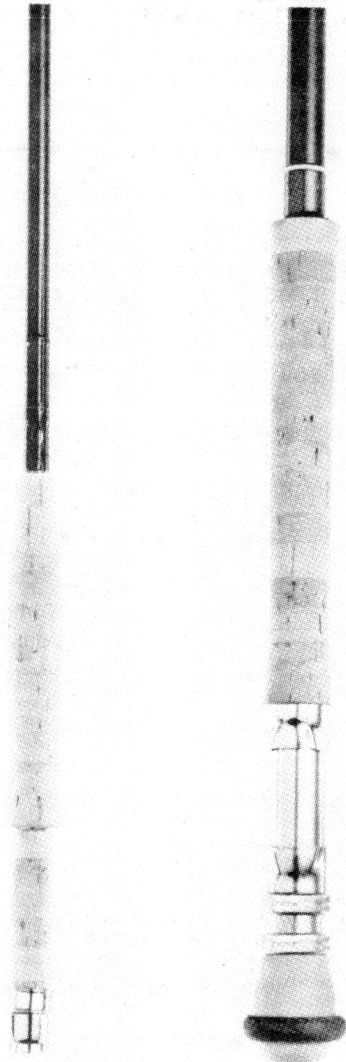

Model	Length	Line	Weight	Price	Source
Fiberglass					
Stalker	6½	2,3	1⅔	$160	RLW
Stalker	6½	4	1⅞	$160	RLW
Stalker	7	2,3	1¾	$160	RLW
Stalker	7	4	2⅛	$160	RLW
Stalker	7½	2,3	1⅞	$160	RLW
Stalker	7½	4	2⅜	$160	RLW, Bud
Stalker	8	2,3	2⅜	$160	RLW
Stalker	8	4	2⅝	$160	RLW
Stalker	8½	4	2⅞	$160	RLW
Trout	7	5	2⅛	$160	RLW
Trout	7½	5	2⅜	$160	RLW, Bud
Trout	7½	6	2⅞	$160	RLW
Trout	8	5	3⅛	$160	RLW, Bud
Trout	8	6	3⅛	$160	RLW
Trout	8	7	3¾	$160	RLW
Trout	8½	5	3⅜	$160	RLW
Trout	8½	6	3⅜	$160	RLW
Trout	8½	7	4	$160	RLW
Trout	9	6	3¾	$160	RLW
Trout	9	7	4¼	$160	RLW
Trout	9¼	5	3⅞	$160	RLW

Model	Length	Line	Weight	Price	Sources
Steelhead	8¾	7	4½	$165	RLW
Steelhead	9	7	4⅝	$165	RLW
Steelhead	9	8	4¾	$165	RLW
Steelhead	9	9	4⅞	$165	RLW
Steelhead	9	10	5⅝	$165	RLW
Saltwater	9	10	6	$175	RLW
Saltwater	9	11,12	7½	$175	RLW
Graphite					
Light Trout	7½	3	1¾	$280	RLW, Dan, Bud
Light Trout	7½	4	1⅞	$280	RLW, Dan, Bud
Light Trout	7½	5	1⅞	$280	RLW, Dan
Light Trout	8	3	1⅞	$280	Fly, RLW, Bud
Light Trout	8	4	2	$280	RLW, Dan
Light Trout	8	5	2⅛	$280	RLW, Fly, Hig, Dan, Bud
Light Trout	8½	3	2	$280	RLW, Bud, Fly
Light Trout	8½	4	2⅛	$280	Fly, RLW
Light Trout	8½	5	2½	$280	Dan, RLW
Light Trout	9	3	2⅛	$280	RLW, Bud, Fly
Light Trout	9	4	2¼	$280	Fly, RLW, Bud
Light Trout	9	5	2¾	$280	RLW, Fly, Bud, Hig
Trout	8	6	2½	$280	RLW, Bud, Fly, Dan
Trout	8½	6	2⅝	$280	RLW, Bud, Dan, Fly, Hig
Trout	8½	7	3	$280	Fly, RLW, Bud
Trout	9	6	2⅞	$280	RLW, Fly, Bud Hig
Trout	9	7	3¼	$280	RLW, Dan, Fly
Trout	9½	6	3⅜	$280	RLW, Bud
Steelhead	9	7	3½	$290	Fly, RLW, Dan
Steelhead	9	8	3⅝	$290	RLW, Fly
Steelhead	9	9	3⅞	$290	Fly, RLW
Steelhead	9½	7	3½	$290	RLW, Fly, Bud
Steelhead	9½	8	3¾	$290	Fly, RLW, Bud
Steelhead	10	9	4⅜	$295	RLW
Saltwater	9	10	4¼	$295	RLW
Saltwater	9	11,12	6¼	$300	RLW
Executive	9	5,8	2 rods	$610	RLW, Bud
Bamboo					
Light Trout	5½	3	1¾	$695	RLW
Light Trout	5½	4	2	$695	RLW
Light Trout	6	3	2	$695	RLW
Light Trout	6	4	2¼	$695	RLW
Light Trout	6½	3	2⅛	$695	RLW
Light Trout	6½	4	2½	$695	RLW
Light Trout	7	3	2½	$695	RLW
Light Trout	7	4	2⅝	$695	RLW, Bud
Light Trout	7½	3	2¾	$695	RLW
Light Trout	7½	4	2⅞	$695	RLW
Light Trout	8	4	3⅛	$695	RLW
Trout	6½	5	2¾	$695	RLW
Trout	7	5	2⅞	$695	RLW
Trout	7½	5	3	$695	RLW, Bud
Trout	7½	6	3½	$695	RLW
Trout	8	5	3¾	$695	RLW, Bud
Trout	8	6	4	$695	RLW, Bud
Trout	8½	5	4⅛	$695	RLW
Trout	8½	6	4¼	$695	RLW, Bud
Trout	8½	7	4½	$695	RLW
Trout	9	6	4⅞	$695	RLW
Trout	9	7	5	$695	RLW
Steelhead	8¾	7	4⅞	$695	RLW
Steelhead	9	7	5⅛	$695	RLW
Steelhead	9	8	5¼	$695	RLW
Steelhead	9	9	5½	$695	RLW
Steelhead	9¼	8	5½	$695	RLW
Steelhead	9¼	9	5¾	$695	RLW

Model	Length	Line	Weight	Price	Sources
Steelhead	9½	9	6	$695	RLW
Multi-piece rods, fiberglass					
Travel	7½	5		$162.50	RLW
Travel	8	5		$162.50	RLW
Travel	8	6		$162.50	RLW
Travel	8½	6		$162.50	RLW
Travel	8½	6,8	2 rods	$250	RLW
Multi-piece rods, graphite					
Travel	8½	5	2½	$285	RLW, Bud, Hig
Travel	8½	6	2⅝	$285	RLW, Fly, Bud
Travel	9	5	2¾	$285	Fly, RLW, Bud
Travel	9	6	2⅞	$285	RLW, Hig, Bud
Travel	9	7	3⅜	$285	RLW, Bud
Travel	9	8	3⅝	$285	RLW, Bud

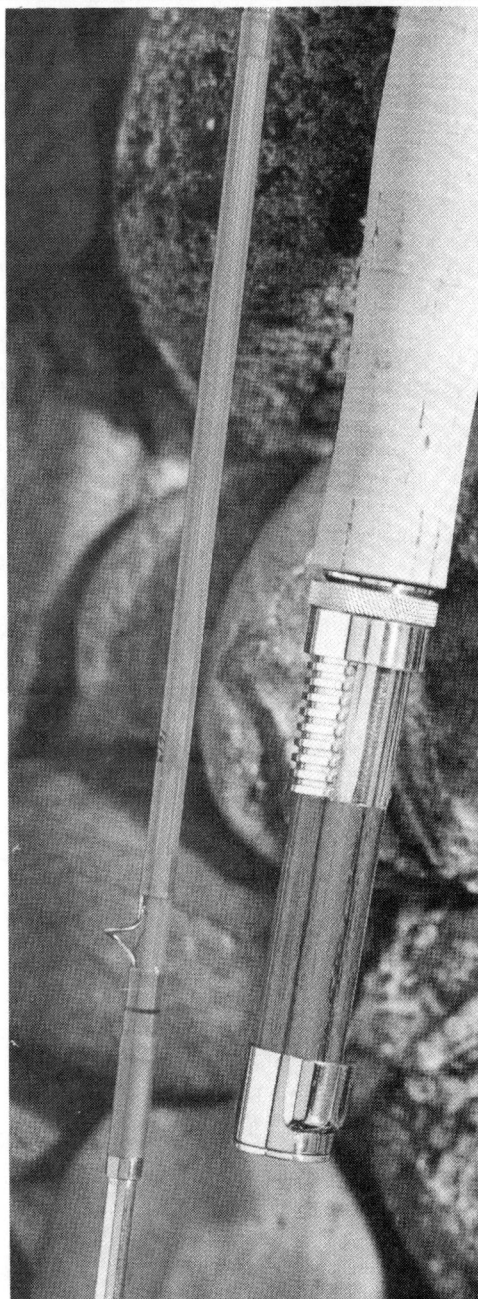

ROD ACCESSORIES

There are a number of accessories designed primarily for the fly rod, and most of them deal with carrying and protecting rods.

Aluminum Rod Tubes

Aluminum tubes are your best protection against rod breakage during transit or storage. (If you have a closet like mine, storage is just as dangerous as transit.) The tubes are listed alphabetically.

Cal Air Custom Grade. *Aluminum with gold anodized collars; 7'-9' rod lengths.*
$23.75-$26.25 Dan
Champion. *Aluminum; 22"-61".*
$24-$36 Orv
Clemens pack rod tube. *Aluminum with plastic cap; 23½"; 2" diameter.*
$10.95 Dal
Cumings. *Telescoping aluminum case; 4" diameter; adjusts 39"-72"; up to eight rods.*
$66.65 Dan
Fenwick Texhyde tubes. *Aluminum tube covered in brown vinyl; quick-opening plastic cap; 1⅝" and 2⅝".*
$18.90-$35 Dal, Sho, H&H, Sim

Rodon. *The most popular traditional brushed aluminum tubes and a nice-looking brown anodized tube (direct from Rodon only); regular screw-top aluminum caps or brass collars and caps; 1⅝" or 2" diameter; lengths and prices for the 1⅝" tubes given; add about $8 for brass fittings or for 2" diameter, about $4.50 for the brown anodized finish; special sizes available from Rodon (see address in rod listings).*

Tube Length	Rod Length	Price
37"	6'	$11.85-$13.80
40"	6½'	$12.11-$14.20
43"	7'	$12.46-$18.95
46"	7½'	$12.87-$18.95
49"	8'	$13.14-$18.95
52"	8½'	$13.49-$18.95
55"	9'	$13.83-$19.00
58"	9½'	$14.18-$18.95
61"	10'	$14.53-$18.95

Edd, Dan, Kau, Ram, Bud, Sim, Hun, Mer, H&H, Pen, Don, Pfe, Fly, AnJ

Leather-Covered Aluminum Tubes

Cabela's. *Cowhide-covered aluminum tube; 44"-59".*
$64.95-$79.95 Cab
Orvis. *Saddle stitched russet leather case over aluminum tube; sizes for rods from 6½' 3-piece to 9½' 2-piece.*
$90-$138 Orv

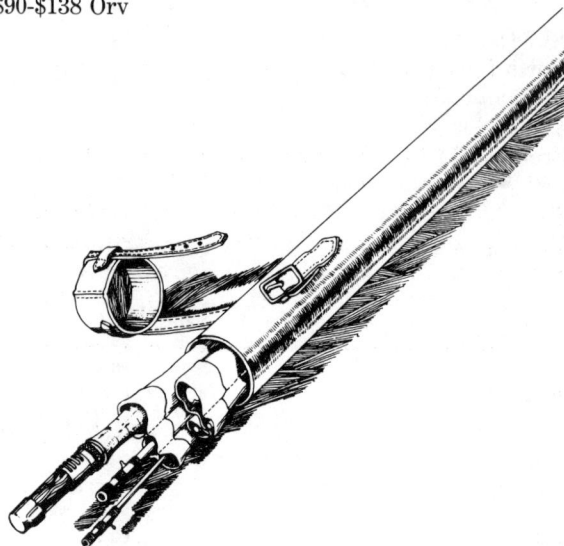

Walker. *Top grain leather over 1⅝" or 2½" aluminum tube; available in any length; can be personalized at $.75 a letter.*
1⅝"—$105; 2½"—$125 RLW

Tubes of Other Materials

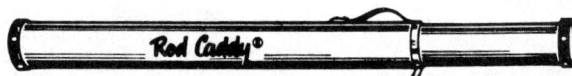

Rod Caddy. *Best known brand of plastic tubes; Model 204—2" diameter, adjusts from 34"-65", holds two or three rods; Model 203—3", adjusts 38"-65", holds three or four rods; Model 202-A—4¼", adjusts from 46"-72", holds six to eight rods; Model 202-96—similar to the 202-A but adjusts from 59"-96".*
204—$9.75; 203—$14; 202-A—$28; 202-96—$31 AnW, Sim, Orv
Rod Caddy. *Model 707; rectangular; 1½"x2½" in lengths of 46"-72".*
$5.75-$6.75 Cor
Zoom-Lok. *Telescoping plastic case; 3", 4½" models with a variety of extension capabilities.*
$20-$40 Cor
Plano. *Adjustable polypropylene tube; 4¼"; adjusts from 48"-72".*
$26.95 Ram
Dunn's Rod Safe Fly Tote. *ABS plastic; described (incredibly?) as "baggage-handler-proof"; 3¾", 56" long.*
$44.95 Dun
Plastic pack rod case. *2"diameter, 24" long.*
$5.49 Dal

Telescoping plastic pack rod case. *2"; adjusts from 16"-27".*
$8.75 Bul

North Fork pack rod case. *Hard foam with green Cordura cover; 32".*
$13.95 Nor

Scott. *Rigid PVC rod carrier; 3"; will carry four rods with bags or six without.*
$55 Scott PowR-Ply (See address under Scott rods.)

Presentation Cover. *Tan vinyl cover for homemade PVC cases or for protection of aluminum case; snap closure and place for identification card; sizes from 44"-60".*
$4.61-$5.99 Dal

Rod and Reel Cases

To some of us, a case that will hold a rod hooked up with the reel in place is as important in our insurance package as an aluminum rod tube. Some people view us as lazy, since we won't case our rods between stops on the river, but I think we're just too excited by the fishing to stop and unhook. In any case, this piece of equipment beats throwing your rod in the trunk or leaning it out the sunroof. Simply take down the rod with reel still attached (and hook snugged to tip top or hookkeeper) and place in case.

Humdinger. *Black vinyl with artificial fleece lining; ¼" steel insert for protection; 53" length (up to 8½' rods).*
$15.95 Cab

The Great Escape Works. *Constructed of 10.1 oz. duck canvas with heavy pile liner; ¼" steel shaft; more resistant to tears than vinyl and no cold cracking; sizes for rods to (but not including) 8½' and 8½' to 10'.*
$40-$43.75 (plus $3.75 shipping) The Great Escape Works, 1995 McKinzie Drive, Idaho Falls, Idaho 83401 (208) 522-6475

Wray's Soft Rod Cases. *Ballistic nylon with ⅜" foam padding; red; sizes for rods to 8½', to 9½'.*
8½'—$21.50; 9 ½'—$22.50 Bud

Rod Bags, Sacks, or Socks

By any name, these bags are made to cover your rod while in the case. Most are simply made of poplin, but we're now seeing some options in fashion and materials.

Rodon. *50% polyester, 50% cotton oxford (won't require ironing); tan; available in all lengths (including custom lengths direct from Rodon); 3-piece bags also available.*
$4.50-$6.00 Rodon, T&T, Ram, Bud, Sim, Hun, H&H, Pen

Lamiglas. *Quality bags available in local fly shops; tan and plaids; (I bought a brown Rodon tube and brown plaid Lamiglas bag to match, and I'm the fashion talk of the stream); couldn't find these in any catalog by brand name (check Dale Clemens for his plaid bags), but you should pick out your own anyway.*
About $5 Local shops

Pack rod bags. *20" for 6'-7½' 4- or 5-piece rods.*
$4.79 Dal

Pack rod bags. *20" 4-piece bag, 22" 5-piece bag.*
$6 Cor

Fenwick's Texhyde bags. *Same material used to cover the Texhyde tubes; single cavity.*
$9 Sim

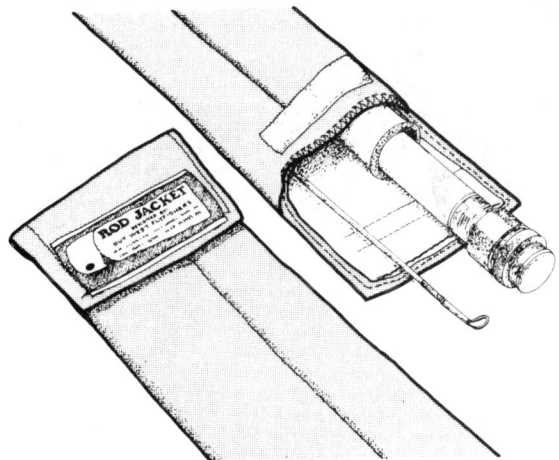

Rod Jacket. *Nylon outer layer, urethane foam middle layer, tricot inner layer; especially useful for transporting rods in the bigger travel cases where several rods may be knocking around together without tubes; available in all common sizes.*
$8.95 T&T, AnJ, Hun

Bullard Bag. *Designed to cushion rods; Cordura nylon with fleece lining.*
$14.95-$20.40 Bul

Rod Blanket. *Holds four rods in eight sections rolled up together; fleece-lined Cordura; 50" long.*
$36.50 Bul

Orvis stretch nylon gun socks. *To protect your aluminum tube during transit (you've heard of tube socks, right?); if you display your tubes in a rack, these keep them looking new forever; in three colors, red, gold, or blue stripes against black.*
$4.25 Orv, Bud

Carry Bags and Shipping Cases

Most of these items are bags designed to carry cased rods. They are convenient for car travel and can be used for airline travel. Some people prefer hard-sided shipping cases for airlines for reasons almost any air traveler can explain in lurid detail.

Rod Safe. *Heavy urethane-coated Cordura with five sleeves for tubes up to 2" in diameter and 9½' in length; tubes are inserted, then rolled up; adjustable straps secure them; carrying handle; a nifty rod carrier.*
$31.95-$42.50 Ram, Dan, Kau, Pen, Don, T&T

Scott. *Rust-colored Cordura carrier; complete with locks, name tag containers, sling strap, center handle, and foam end plugs; in 59" or 62" lengths.*
$24 Scott PowR-Ply (see address under Scott rods)

Padded carrying case. *For fly rods up to 9½'; outer layer 8 oz. coated parapec; reinforcements of plastic and foam;*

case lined in coated nylon; two colors, rust and forest green.
Three rod case—$40; four rod—$45; five rod—$50 Bud, RLW

Simms. *Cordura nylon reinforced with rigid plastic and foam; holds cased rods to 9½'; same three sizes as above; rust.*
$50, $55, and $60 Pen

Thomas & Thomas. *Heavy gauge, brown Cordura nylon with tanned leather reinforced corners; leather handle or shoulder strap; for six rods up to 9½'.*
$59.95 T&T

Traveler's Rod Bag. *Urethane-coated Cordura; heavy duty lockable zipper; two outside pockets for reels, fly boxes; blaze orange or brown; two to eight rods; 56" for rods to 9'; 60" for rods to 10'.*
56"—$57.50; 60"—$59.50 Orv, Bud, Hun

Carry-On Bag. *For pack/travel rods; styled to match Orvis Battenkill luggage; two outside 9" pockets carry extras; for two 2" tubes holding 4-piece rods up to 9'.*
$59.50 Orv

Cabela's shipping cases. *ABS plastic with "egg carton" foam; 4" steel hinges; three steel latches with key lock; dust proof; meets FAA requirements for commercial air travel; holds up to 12 2-piece rods by layering them in foam; 6½" wide by 5" deep; two lengths, 55", 67".*
55"—$44.99; 67"—$49.99 Cab

Cabela's rod and tackle case. *Holds six rods on one side and equipment in compartments on other side; high-impact plastic; 6½" wide by 7½" deep by 55" long.*
$64.99 Cab

Cabela's aluminum transport case. *Anodized, extruded aluminum body, brass hardware, egg-carton foam padding; collapsible handle; key lock; holds four rods without tubes; 3¼"x3½"; two lengths, 55", 68". (Note: This case is not listed in current catalog; call for availability.)*
55"—$49.95; 68"—$56.95 Cab

Royal Cadee. *Extruded aluminum transport case similar in features to Cabela's; holds up to six rods; 60" length for rods up to 9½'.*
$69.50 T&T

Thomas & Thomas aluminum transport case. *The ultimate in protection for the traveler's fly rods; up to six rods in tubes; quality locks; continuous piano hinge for durability; weathertight gasket; 4"x9"x60"; for rods up to 10' in length.*
$195 T&T

Car-Top Racks

Hardy Car-Top Rod Clamp. *Sponge rubber lined, stainless steel; gutter clamps.*
$18.95 Pen
Orvis car-top rack. *For three or four rods with reels mounted; stainless steel; attached with vinyl clamps to car's rain gutters.*
$28.50 Orv
Wheatley Rod Carriers. *Two models, both secured by gutter clamps; vertical carrier holds a single rod; horizontal model holds two or three rods and has suction cup for stability.*
Vert.—$19.95; horiz.—$24.95 T&T

Utilitarian Rod Racks

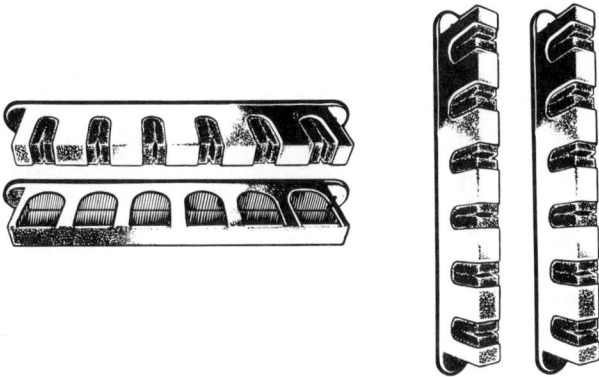

Berkley rod rack. *White plastic; foam inserts; horizontal and vertical models; both hold six rods; not designed for moving vehicles.*
$4.99-$6.99 Fol, AnW, Dal, Cab
Universal Rod Holder. *Heavy duty horizontal rack with secure holders; adjustable for rod size after mounting.*
2-rod—$9.95; 4-rod—$15.95 Cab
Cabela's Rod Holder. *Aluminum with secure neoprene holders; two horizontal models (for two rods or three rods) for use in boats, as well as campers and trailers; overhead model holds four rods securely on ceiling of camper or boat.*
2-rod—$6.95; 3-rod—$7.85; overhead—$21.95 Cab

Rod Display Racks

Here's an area in which there seems to be a deficiency of offerings, an unusual phenomenon in fly fishing. A good quality wall rack for multiple rods is not available through any of the major catalogs, although there is one (the FSM) from an independent mail order firm. Perhaps there are a lot of woodworkers among fly fishermen . . .

FSM Rod Rack. *Oak wall rack for nine rods; rod butts rest in cork-lined recesses, tips lean against latex-covered hooks; I have one of these and like it because it shows off the rods instead of the rack; unfinished or finished.*
Unfin.—$33.50; fin.—$47.50 Fishing Specialities Mfg., 1010 4th & Pike Bldg., Seattle, Washington 98101 (206) 624-6960
Antique Rod Rack. *An exceptional display case for that special rod; hardwood frame with choice of laminated backboards in mahogany or oak to complement light or dark rods; holders are felt-lined; fitted with brass decorative strips; designed to show an extra tip but may be ordered without that feature; specify rod length and number of sections when ordering, as well as backboard wood.*
6½'-7' or 7½'-8' (2-pc.)—$34.95; 8½' (2 pc.) or 8'-8½' (3-pc.)—$36.95; 9'-9½' (3-pc.)—$38.95; 10' (3-pc.)—$39.95 T&T
Revolving rack. *For you anglers with so many rods the local fly shop is afraid you'll open your own business; a revolving display rack; circular with 24 rod capacity; 24" tall for freshwater rods.*
$19.95 Cab
Fenwick revolving rack. *Similar to Cabela's rack but in wood; with Fenwick logo, too; holds 24 rods.*
$99.95 Fenwick (see address under rods)

Tube Racks

The last type of rack stores your rods in their tubes. Holes cut in an upper shelf hold the tubes upright.

Thomas & Thomas. *For eight tubed rods; oil-finished mahogany; 2⅛" holes.*
$44 T&T

Miscellaneous Rod Accessories

Among the most clever rod accessories is another rack. I've listed it here because it's not the kind of rod rack you'd be looking for in the rod rack section.

Rod Saver. *Hooks on an open car window to hold four rods during the lunch break; saves car paint as well as rods; a great idea from Thomas & Thomas.*
$9.95 T&T

Some Help For Sticky Ferrules . . .

Rod Grips. *Textured rubber pads; 3½"x6½"; used to take apart sticky rod sections without putting force on guides.*
$2 T&T
Ferrule Treatment. *Lubricates sticky ferrules.*
$3.95 T&T
Pro-Tec. *Lubricates and protects ferrules.*
$2.89 Dal

And Cork Handles . . .

Cork sealant. *Penetrates to prolong the life of cork, prevents chipping, and eases cleaning.*
$2.89-$4.07 Dal, Ste, Mer

For That Personal Touch . . .

Heat embossing pen. *Used to personalize any rod that does not have an exterior finish.*
$18.99 Dal
Rod ink. *Opaque ink for regular drawing pen; white and gold.*
$1.40 Dal

Or to Make Your Fish Stories Credible...

Fishscale. *White-lettered rule decal; apply to rod above handle to provide measurement of fish to be released; can also be applied to net; handy for checking tippet lengths.*
$3.95-$5 Pen

Finally, Something to Aid Your Casting . . .

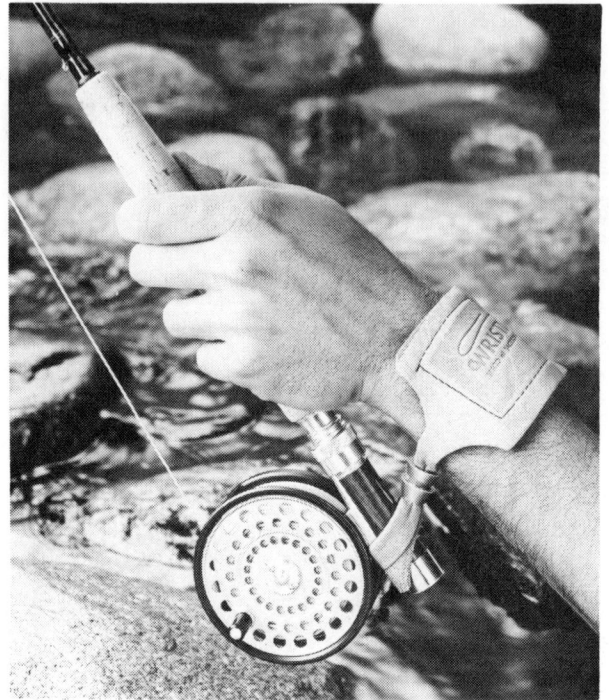

Wristlock. *Leather device; attaches to your wrist and to the butt of your rod; prevents wrist from "breaking" during casting; bad habits should be corrected by technique, not a crutch, but in the initial stages of learning or of breaking a habit, this may be beneficial; also used by fly fishermen who must cast long lines all day; helps prevent fatigue.*
$10 Pen, Bud, Kau, T&T
Fly-O. *3' rod with 15' of yarn line; imitates action of a fly rod but can be used indoors. (Note: I know that some of you have living rooms the size of gymnasiums and cathedral ceilings higher than Steve Rajeff can steeple cast, but do you want to move all the coat racks everytime you practice casting?)*
$18.50-$20 Wul, Pen
Casting Mate. *Developed by Joe Humphreys to improve muscle tone and strength of grip; looks like a big priest or fancy billy club.*
$6.95 Pen

3. Fly Reels

IF A REEL WERE only a device for holding line conveniently out of the way while you cast, selecting one would be very easy. For one thing, there'd probably be only one or two models on the market. However, the moment you strip off line for that first cast, your reel becomes much more than a device for holding line, and selecting the right reel is an important (and not very easy) task. Complicating that selection is the fact that there are over 150 models of reels currently on the market.

How important the reel is becomes apparent the first time you lay into a fish large enough to take line off the reel. Let me give you an example. Let's say you hook a 20" Bighorn rainbow on 5x tippet. You can't turn that large a fish on that light a tippet, so off it goes on the first long run. Let's assume it can make five miles an hour. Since you can comfortably walk three miles an hour and a big trout can outdistance a fisherman scrambling along the bank, five miles an hour is probably slower than that rainbow is moving.

At five miles an hour, the trout is taking 440' of line a minute or 87.9" of line every second. If your reel spool with line on it has a 3" outside diameter, it will rotate at 746 RPM at the beginning of the run. If the run continues until the diameter is reduced to 1", the spool will be rotating at about 6,723 RPM. To withstand that kind of use, the reel had better be well made.

Many of you are now thinking that you'll never get into a fish like that. You're the ones who'll hook Old Mossyback in the local put-and-take stream.

Big fish aside, there's the matter of reliability that everyone must consider. I've spent time fishing with people who had reel trouble, and let me tell you, they had *real* trouble. One fellow spent the day turning the spool with his finger when his reel handle fell off. Another had a reel that would let line out but wouldn't wind it in, and he carried line in his hands all day. I learned a lot of new words both days.

My last (and I do mean last) cheap reel broke down on a stream miles from home and miles from a fly shop. The check pawl gave way when a rivet broke, allowing the line to be pulled from the spool by the force of the current. I spent a miserable day. I hate to have miserable days when I'm fishing—I get enough of those at work. I can't say how much I would have paid for that day's fishing, but I know that that amount plus what I paid for the cheap reel would have bought me a decent one.

A good reel not only assures the pleasure of a day's fishing, it adds to it. A quality reel is a joy to own. My best reel feels good, sounds good, and has never let me down. I trust it. And I'll probably be able to pass it on when I get too old to tell a bed pan from a trout stream.

Selecting a reel. Your fly reel, like your rod, should be chosen with care. Ordering one sight-unseen from a catalog company is a poor second to trying one out at a fly shop or borrowing a friend's to try out. All the glossy ads and pretty write-ups in fishing magazines may tell you a lot about the reel, but they can't tell you that you'll like it. Among all the reels on the market, many may suit your needs. One one or two may also suit your taste.

So, like the rod you select, your reel must meet your needs and still be a pleasant tool. The following guide to selecting a fly reel should help you find a reel that will meet your needs and that will be of the highest quality you can afford. If you don't know your taste in reels yet, you will after you've handled a dozen or so.

Reel capacity. The primary consideration in reel selection is line capacity. Your reel must hold a line of the weight your rod requires, *plus* backing. Before you scoff at the idea of backing because it's only needed for big fish, please read on. Backing does protect you from losing a fish that takes out your entire fly line (something that has yet to happen to me in trout fishing, unfortunately). It also protects you, your line, and your reel from unnecessary wear and tear.

45

By putting backing on a reel, you increase the winding diameter of the spool. That keeps your line from being wound into such tight coils that it requires stretching. It also means fewer turns of the reel to retrieve line, which cuts down on reel wear and makes it easier on you. The faster retrieve made possible by the increased diameter can also be very important when playing a fish (the big one you think you'll never catch) off the reel.

Line capacities are confusing. In my descriptions of the reels, I've given you the capacities specified by the manufacturers or given in catalogs. Unfortunately, the two sources are not always consistent, nor is either necessarily accurate. To further complicate things, some sources specify 18 pound backing, some 20 pound. In the listings I've assumed the source was using 18 pound backing, and you can assume the same, unless the first line capacity listed specifies another backing size.

The simplest solution is to deal with a fly shop. The salesman will know from experience the proper amount of backing for the reel you've selected and will usually attach backing and line for you at no charge. If you do this yourself with only the manufacturer's capacities as your guide, use those capacities to buy the proper amount of backing. To be sure of getting the correct amount of backing on, you'll need to put the fly line on the reel first, attach the backing, wind on backing to fill the reel, remove the works and reverse it. With a weight forward line, this process is even more wearisome because the line must be removed from its spool before winding onto the reel spool, since it comes from the factory with the end to be attached to backing exposed.

Reel weight. Another consideration, and one that gets more inconclusive discussion than any other, is weight. A reel should balance the rod it's attached to. With the new, lighter rod materials such as graphite and boron, reel weight has become a critical consideration to many anglers. Indeed, the old reliable reel that weighs 7 oz. and balanced the now-retired fiberglass rod may feel like angle iron on the new 2 oz. graphite rod.

Using the lightest reel possible makes some sense, since you're constantly moving the weight of the reel while casting. An ounce of weight carried through the casting motion all day makes pounds of difference. However, you can go too light. A heavy rod or a very long rod will be better balanced, and therefore easier to cast, with a heavier reel. Even line weight plays a part in all this, since it's part of both the reel weight and the rod weight.

There's no formula I can give you on this. There are simply too many variables. I picked up a fishing book written in 1898 and found a section on matching rod and reel. They did give a formula: the reel should weigh one and a half times the rod. Such a formula, however, ignores important things like rod length and that means ignoring the idea of a fulcrum and that means throwing physics out the window. I wouldn't want to do that.

Another unscientific method is to mount the reel on the rod and check the balance point. People who subscribe to this method suggest that if the balance point is about half way up the cork handle, the outfit is balanced.

The best way may be to try out several reels. Your local fly shop may have several different kinds of reels outfitted for its customers to try on rods or you may be able to go from fishing friend to fishing friend trying out their reels. A reel that's too light will make the rod feel tip heavy. One that's too heavy will make the rod feel too light and fast, too fast for good line control. Fortunately for all of us, there seems to be a fairly wide range of reel weights that will work well on a given rod.

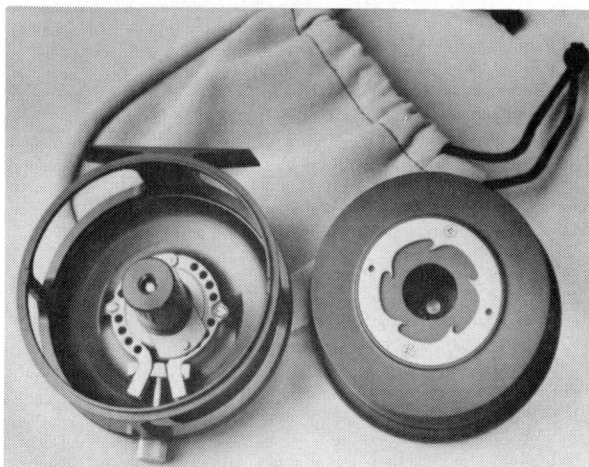

Disc Drag, Courtesy of Ross Reels

Drag systems. Drag is tension applied to the reel spool as it lets out line. Every reel has some type of device to prevent overrun of the line as it's pulled from the reel. If pressure can be applied to that device, it's a drag system. Almost all the reels have a drag designed to be used in playing a fish off the reel.

The basic drag system uses a triangular-shaped pawl held against a geared wheel on the reel spool by a spring. Tension on the spring can be adjusted to increase or decrease the drag. The Hardy L.R.H. Lightweight is a typical example of this type of drag. Take the spool out and you'll see two pawls, one to be engaged for left-hand retrieve, one for right-hand retrieve. They are held against the geared wheel of the spool by a leaf spring. An adjustment knob located on the outside of the reel frame moves that leaf spring up and down to adjust the tension.

Less expensive reels sometimes use only one pawl. This can cause difficulty in reversing the retrieve unless they are carefully manufactured. With inexpensive reels, the drag system is likely to be weak and offer little adjustment.

Other reels, such as Scientific Anglers Systems One, have a check-pawl drag with a palming rim for additional drag pressure. With a palming rim, the outside edge of the reel spool is exposed so that the angler can use his hand as a brake. With experience, a palming rim can afford almost perfect drag control. In the meantime, you'll lose some fish.

More sophisticated drag systems use discs, somewhat similar to disc brakes on a car. The materials and specifics differ, but the theory is the same. A pad applies pressure to a smooth wheel as line is given out. Technology has made these drags virtually indestructable. For an example of the testing that some of the reels have undergone, read the description of the Ross Reels. Next time you're in the fly shop, pick up a Marryat reel as an example of a very strong disc drag. Crank the drag full down and compare it to the drag afforded by a check pawl system. You'll understand why a disc drag is favored by big game fishermen.

A reel's drag system is important to you. It's when that big fish is on and line is streaming off the reel that the drag counts, and that's the most important moment in your fishing life. The care given over to the drag system will also show you the quality of the reel itself.

Reel features. Most reels are kept pretty simple, and the number of additional features is minimal. I discussed one of them, the palming rim, in the previous section.

Another feature you may wish to shop for is the counterbalanced spool. The weight of the handle can cause a reel to wobble when a fish takes line out at a fast clip. The resulting vibration could loosen a reel seat and send your reel into the water in the middle of things. Nothing would be more disconcerting. To compensate for the handle, a weight is added opposite the handle. But many of the best reels skip this feature, so it's safe to assume it's not a biggy.

The position and type of drag adjustment may make a difference to you. Some knobs are rim-mounted, others side-mounted. It's important that the knob be easily adjusted, and that it's placement make sense to you.

Reels come in many finishes. Baked enamel is commonly used. It's a handsome finish, but it will show scratches. Anodizing is used on more expensive reels. It serves as a protection against corrosion.

Reel construction. Fly reels are commonly constructed in one of the following ways:
1. assembled from stamped parts;
2. molded from plastics or graphite;
3. cast in aluminum, magnesium, steel, or an alloy;
4. machined from solid bar stock;
5. or a combination of these.

There's not a lot you can tell about the quality of a reel from the type of construction alone. If it's machined from bar stock, the most expensive process, you can be sure the reel is top-line. The other processes are used on reels throughout the range of quality and price.

Stamped parts, for instance, are used on the least expensive reels, those costing $10 or so. The same process is used to build Pflueger reels (at $35-$50) and Valentine reels (around $100), but it's carried out with much greater precision and care. The same goes for cast reels. The quality of the casting and the tightness of the fit of the parts will vary considerably between a low-end $25 reel and a $135 reel.

Those reels that are machined from bar stock begin as a block of solid metal, usually aircraft-grade aluminum. In a time-consuming and therefore expensive process, they are cut down to the reels you hold in your hand. The tolerances on these reels are incredible, and the strength of the material unsurpassed. Reels machined from bar stock include Bogdan, Catino, Fenwick World Class, Fin-Nor, H.L. Leonard, Marryat, North Fork, Orvis Saltwater CFO and SSS, Pate, and Ross. The least expensive of these starts at about $135. You can spend $400 or more in this class, but these are the Rolls Royces and their quality is impeccable.

Reel costs. A final, and very important, consideration in reel selection is cost. If you don't need to worry about cost, you've already gone into the fly shop and asked for the best. I'm sure they were happy to accommodate you. For the rest of us, I've divided the reels into three broad price categories: under $50, $50-$100, and over $100.

As it turns out, these mathematically convenient categories also lump reels by quality and performance pretty well. There's a definite jump in quality and features as you move up in categories. It is possible, however, to find a workable reel for less than $50.

An inexpensive reel will have limitations. If you're fishing in saltwater, for instance, you'll have to have a reel designed for that use and it will be more expensive. The demands of steelhead and salmon fishing require a heavy duty, large capacity reel the likes of which you won't find in the under-$50 range. In trout fishing, it's not as easy to determine the requirements for a reel, but there's a big difference between the reel I need for fishing for the 6" brook trout in Fish Creek in the backyard and the one I need for the 20" browns on the Bighorn River in Montana.

It's my feeling that if you spend all your time close to home and the streams you fish hold mostly small trout, say 15" or smaller, then you can comfortably purchase a reel in the under-$50 category. On the other hand, if you invest in travel to get to your fishing or if you fish water that holds larger trout, you'd be better off in the $50-$100 category for the sake of reliability, ruggedness of construction, and versatility. Unless you have special needs, such as saltwater fishing, you don't need to go above $100. However, the reels in that category are wonderful. Pride of ownership plus the fact that the reel will probably outlast you may make the extra investment worth it. With inflation, those reels can commonly be resold for more than the original price in just a few years.

Test driving a reel. Whichever reels you're considering, there are a few things you can check in the fly shop before you make a purchase. Not all of these tests are appropriate to every reel. Don't, for instance, abandon the Ross Reel because it doesn't pass the click test—it's not supposed to click.

First, make sure all the parts fit tightly. Close tolerances are the mark of a quality reel. Check first for play between the spool shaft and the reel's spindle. Grasp the edge of the spool and try to wobble it on the spindle. There should be no play. Try this test on a $100 reel so you know what you're looking for.

Release the spool (a procedure which should be simple) and slowly remove the spool from the spindle. As you do this, continue to check for play. A reel with exact tolerances will show very little play even with the spool halfway off the spindle. Next, try out an extra spool. It should fit as well as the original. Perform the same tests with the extra spool to get some idea of how consistent the manufacturer is in his quality checks.

Check out the spool release carefully. Look inside the spool shaft hole while you work the release to make sure it works smoothly. It should be a metal part, not plastic. If the release breaks or wears, there's often nothing to do but get a new spool. When you return the spool to the shaft, you should feel or hear when the release catches. Avoid a reel without a good spool release.

If the reel has a full-frame, you can easily inspect tolerances between spool and frame as another quality check. Look directly at the handle side of the reel as you rotate the spool slowly. As you look in one spot, the gap between the spool and frame should stay the same. That tests the spool tolerance. Looking around the rim as you rotate the spool will check the frame tolerance. Exposed rim models are more difficult to examine, but try looking at an angle to where the back of the spool fits into the frame.

Next, check the entire reel for imperfections in casting, stamping, or machining. Your fingers are more sensitive than your eyes for this test. Run your fingers over the spool and frame searching for imperfections. Pay special attention to the line guard which must be smooth to protect your fly line.

Finally, check out the drag system. Rotate the spool very slowly forward. In the best reels, there is very little play between clicks, and you won't feel the pawl go "over center" on the teeth of the geared wheel. By applying a steady pressure, you should be able to rotate the spool one click at a time. While you're carrying out this test, make sure the handle rotates on its spindle smoothly and without excessive wobble.

Then put the drag through its paces. Test it at its lightest setting and then its heaviest setting to see the range it will give you. Rotate the spool slowly backwards to make sure it works smoothly that way. Remove the spool and observe the internal operation of the adjustment knob. Watch for play and make sure the adjustment at its lightest setting will not allow the spring to loosen so much that a pawl or other part can come free (which happened to me with one reel).

Disc drags are more difficult to check, but on better quality reels, you can trust them if they work smoothly and have a wide adjustment range. The real test is whether they'll take the long run of a big fish in stride,

and for that test, you'll need to buy the reel.

If you intend to reverse a reel, make the necessary adjustments specified by the manufacturer and carry out the tests with the reel reversed. I've found one reel that doesn't work well reversed, the Ryobi 355MG. Incidentally, most reels come from the factory ready for right-hand retrieve. Some people prefer not to change rod hands in order to reel in line and they "reverse" the reel so that it can be worked with the left hand. I've tried both ways and still like to reel with my right hand; it's faster for me. The reversal process usually entails changing the pawl set-up and moving the line guard. Some reels come only in right-hand retrieve, some can be ordered in either mode but can't be reversed.

The tests I've given you will help you walk out of the shop with a reel of the best quality you can afford. They won't, however, tell you how well a reel will hold up. Other fishermen are a good source of information here, but you may also wish to call a reel repair service and talk to them about specific models. Repair people know more than anyone about what goes wrong with reels, and they're usually not reluctant to tell you since they're not in the business of selling them. While you're talking to them, ask them about parts availability.

The range of reels. The more than 150 reels listed here cover a wide range of sizes, line capacities, and prices.

The smallest reel, by weight, is the Orvis CFO II which weighs in at just 2 oz. The Cortland CG 1 follows closely at 2¼ oz. Ryobi's 255MG and Hardy's Flyweight are also-rans at 2.3 and 2⅜ oz. respectively. Of these, the Hardy is the smallest by diameter at just 2½". The Orvis reel is only ¹⁄₁₆" larger.

The heaviest reel is the Bogdan 300-M at 15 oz. Bogdan's #2 weighs 14 oz. and his #1, 13 oz. Other contenders in the heavyweight division are Tycoon/Fin-Nor's #3 and #4 at 12 oz. and 14 oz. The Billy Pate and Catino Tarpon models each weigh 12 oz. The Catino has the largest diameter of any reel listed at 4⅜".

Line capacities range from the Orvis CFO II's DT2F (plus 50 yards of backing) to the big boys' capacities which reach to a 12-weight line plus over 300 yards of 30 pound backing.

The range of prices is equally impressive. The winner in the least expensive category is the Martin 62 which retails for $6.25. Runners-up are also Martins. The model numbers 63 and 65 list for about $10. At the other end of the spectrum, you can pick up an Orvis SSS 11/12 Anti-Reverse for five big bills. You can also spend that much for a Catino Tarpon (but it can be found for $100 less). A Billy Pate Tarpon will cost you $495, and Bogdan reels are as much as $433.

With this range of offerings, you really ought to be able to find one that suits your needs and your pocketbook.

Reels described here. For the most part, the reels I've included are the ones found in fly shops and catalog companies catering to fly fishermen. You may find a fly reel at your local discount store that isn't included here. That doesn't mean it isn't a good reel (although there's a good chance of that). Most fly shops and catalog companies stay away from equipment sold to discount stores because they can't compete on price. In general, that equipment is low-end merchandise of inferior quality, and reputable dealers don't want to mess with the complaints and unhappy customers.

Most of the reels are single action, which means that one turn of the handle rotates the spool one turn. If you fish for big game fish, you may need a multiplier. A turn of its crank will rotate the spool more than one turn, usually two turns. This is helpful in retrieving the large amount of line taken out by a fish on the run. Because of the extra hardware involved and because these reels are built for the heavy-duty needs of steelhead and salmon fishermen, as well as saltwater anglers, they are heavy. Leave the purchase of a multiplier until you need one and then spend some money on it.

I haven't included automatic reels in the book. Perhaps I'm showing some prejudice, and old-timers might like to argue with me about it. I just can't see an automatic reel for the serious fly fisherman today. They have only one advantage—they'll pick up slack quickly. You can't play a fish off them, they're very heavy, and they're complicated mechanically. That invites every kind of breakdown, including coming unsprung in midstream. I used one when I was a kid, but I outgrew it.

The reels are listed alphabetically under the price categories mentioned before. I've given the reel weight, the diameter of the reel, the manufacturers' line capacities (see page 71 for codes), and the origin of manufacture when those specifications were available. Prices noted in parenthesis are for spare spools, when available. In the descriptions, I've tried to stick to the facts, interjecting my opinion only when I thought it was based closely on those facts and not a matter of personal taste. After all, I can't pick out the reel that's right for you.

REELS UNDER $50

Until a few years ago, there were very few decent reels in this price range. Many of us, in fact, remember when we could only find one make of reel in our local sporting goods stores, Pflueger. Fortunately, it was a good reel, and the old standby Pflueger is still offered (although it's now made in Japan).

Many other companies are now trying to find a niche in the under-$50 range. In fact, there are probably too many, and some may disappear in the next few years. For now, new reels continue to enter the market. Besides Pflueger, you'll find reels from such well-known American companies as Martin, Cortland (reels made in England), and Berkley. Daiwa and Ryobi, two Japanese firms better known for their spinning reels, are also included.

A new entry in 1984 was the Scientific Anglers Systems One reel (made in Japan). With rugged construction and

a reasonable price tag (about $35), it promises to be one of the most popular reels in this category.

Although there are several good reels represented here, it's more difficult to shop for a reel under $50 than it is for a more expensive one. Quality varies considerably from manufacturer to manufacturer, from model to model, and even from individual reel to individual reel. Carefully follow the tests outlined in the introduction to this chapter when choosing one of these reels.

So much for warnings. The good news is that there are some decent reels for the money here. Design and manufacturing improvements developed for more expensive reels have worked their way down. Most of us started with a reel from the low end of the market. If we picked a good one, we still have it, even though it may have been retired for a fancier model. If we picked a poor one (like the imitations of name-brand reels often found in discount stores), it fell apart, and we spent more money on our next one. In any case, nobody needs to apologize for thrift.

ABU Garcia

Sweden seems an unlikely place to come up with a fly reel, but here's one manufactured there. The reel uses a disc drag which operates smoothly but has a lot of parts to it. The payment for this feature is weight. At about 5 oz. for a reel with DT6F capacity, it's heftier than comparable reels.

The tolerances on the reels I checked were not exceptional, just about what I'd expect from a disc drag reel in this price range. Compare the reel with the Scientific Anglers Systems One and the Pflueger Medalist 1494 before buying.

I couldn't find this reel in any catalog, but I did find it in a discount drug store. Don't expect the pharmacist to be able to get you extra spools or spare parts. For that matter, your local fly shop will probably be unable to help either.

Diplomat 158. *5 oz.; 3"; DT6F + 25.*
About $35 Sporting goods dealers and discount stores
Diplomat 178. *6 oz.; 3⅝"; WF8F + 75.*
About $40 Sporting goods dealers and discount stores

Berkley Specialist

Berkley was one of the first companies to bring out a newly designed reel for the low-end market. At the time of introduction, Specialist reels were probably the lightest in their price range. Because of that, they were popular with anglers wishing to match up a light reel to their new graphite rods without further damage to their pocketbooks.

These reels use a cast aluminum half-frame and a "graphite-filled" spool (replacing the older molded plastic spool). A three-position check pawl prevents overrun but is not strong enough to be considered a real drag system.

Drag can be accomplished by palming the exposed rim. The reels are reversible.

Removal of the spool is very easy. Just pull it off. The spool is held on the spindle by a friction fit on a rubber part which can be adjusted for wear with a screwdriver. When wear occurs and is not compensated for by that adjustment, the spool can work its way off the spindle during use.

Other lightweight reels have come on the market in this price range since introduction of the Specialists, and Berkley may have lost a share of the market. Acceptance of the plastic spool, which was serviceable and very sturdy, was never high among fly fishermen used to the look and feel of full metal reels. The move to the graphite spool may stem further erosion of Berkley's share of the market.

Many people are pleased with their Specialists. The reel is nifty and fairly tough, and it is inexpensive. The only broken Specialist I've seen is one that was chewed up by a fly shop mascot. I know of many fly shops that use the reels for their customers to try out rods with.

You may already own a Specialist, since the company gave one away free with the purchase of any Specialist fly line (priced as low as $11.50). Such a promotion made me suspicious that the reels were not long for this world, but Berkley officials have assured me that the reel will remain in their product line. The new graphite spool backs that up.

There are three models with capacities of WF5F to WF9F plus backing. The reels are American-made. Spool prices are given in parentheses.

554. *2.9 oz.; 2⅜"; WF5F + 30.*
$18.15-$32.75 ($5.95-$10.55) Dan, Cab, Dal, Mer, Mur, Pen, Tac, H&H, Cus
556. *3.5 oz.; 3"; WF6F + 100, WF8F + 50.*
$19.10-$33.95 ($6.20-$11) Cus, H&H, Tac, Pen, Mur, Mer, Dal, Cab, Dan
558. *5.9 oz.; 3¼"; WF9F + 150.*
$19.95-$35.45 ($7-$12.45) Dal, Mer, Cab, Dan, Pen, H&H, Cus

Cortland Crown II and Rimfly

The Crown II and Rimfly are simple, lightweight reels constructed of cast silicone aluminum alloy. Both feature an exposed rim for palming.

The Crown II is Cortland's basic adjustable-drag reel. It's not fancy, but it does the job. There are few parts, so reliability should be high. Screws are used internally to secure the pawls, and they should be checked periodically for tightness.

For even greater economy, consider the Rimfly. It's similar to the Crown II but does not have an adjustable drag.

The tolerances on these reels are remarkable. Their English origin is obvious. I'd certainly recommend that you consider these reels if you're looking to get into the sport with a minimum of cost and a maximum of value for your money.

There are three sizes in the Crown II line and two in the Rimfly. The reels are available through Cortland Pro Shops and authorized catalog dealers. Prices are controlled by Cortland, but they are bargain enough as it is.

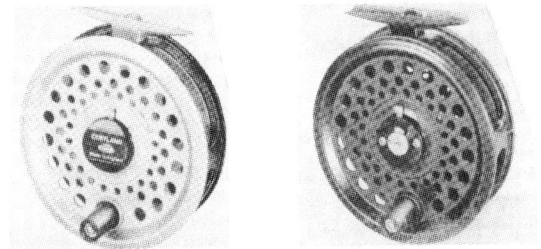

Crown II Small. *2½ oz.; 3¼"; WF6F + 90 (20#).*
Crown II Medium. *3½ oz.; 3½"; WF7F + 120 (20#).*
Crown II Large. *5 oz.; 3⅝"; WF8F + 170 (20#).*
$26 ($11) AnR, Bud, C&C, T&T, Kau, Dan, Pen, Fly, Bob, Cus
Rimfly Small. *Same as Crown II Small.*
Rimfly Medium. *Same as Crown II Medium.*
$17.50-$19.95 ($9) Bud, C&C

Cortland CG Graphite

Cortland's intermediate reels are made of graphite. The material may not take the hard knocks a metal reel will, but it is very lightweight. These English-made reels are reversible and feature a palming rim.

Although they are still available in some shops and catalogs, Cortland's current catalog does not include the CG. As with any orphaned product, parts and extra spools may become a problem in the future.

CG I. *2¼ oz.; 2⅞"; DT5F + 0.*
$36 ($11) Mer, Pen
CG II. *2½ oz.; 3¼"; DT6F + 20 (20#)*
$38 ($11) Pen, Mer
CG III. *3½ oz.; 3½"; DT7F + 30 (20#).*
$40 ($11) Mer, Pen

Regal Strike Series™ SF 706 reel

Daiwa Regal Strike Series Reels

These reels may be one of the better bargains in this price range. The SF706 and SF708 are essentially identical to the Scientific Anglers Systems One 4,5,6 and 7,8,9 reels (which are made by Daiwa), but they retail for considerably less.

The Daiwa reels lack the counterbalanced spool (a minor issue for everyday fishing). The only other difference, apparently, is paint and logo, although listed weights differ. Extra spools are not listed in the Daiwa catalog, but an S/A spool should fit if my information is correct. Please try out the idea before purchasing an extra spool.

The reels have a cast aluminum half-frame and spool. The adjustable drag utilizes two pawls for ease in changing retrieve. The spool has an exposed rim for palming.

Daiwa does not direct its marketing toward fly fishermen. The mainstay of their company is spin and bait fishing equipment, and the reel is marketed through high volume retailers. I couldn't find the reels locally, but I did find two catalog sources for the reels. For the price, you can't go wrong.

SF706. *4.9 oz.; 3¼"; DT7 + 70 (20#).*
$17-$19.95 AnW, Sim
SF708. *5.1 oz.; DT8 + 50.*
$22.60 Sim

Martin Reels

Martin reels have only been around for about 15 years, but that's long enough to make them old timers in the under-$50 category.

There are many models in the Martin line, almost too many to keep track of. I've included 12 models commonly available through mail order houses. You may find others at local sporting goods dealers or in catalogs. Many of the less expensive models will not be found in fly shops, since they're inexpensively made and don't appeal to the serious fly fisherman. They may make a good reel for a youngster, however.

The other Martin reels are serviceable, plain-Jane models. For people who associate Martins with the Model 62 and other inexpensive reels they've picked up in discount stores, the better reels will come as a pleasant surprise. They have a good feel, although they're rather clunky and unsophisticated. This may add to their appeal. They aren't sexy, but they'll do the job. The tolerances are appropriate to the price range.

If you're not into ultralight reels and if you don't care about the latest in technology and engineering, you'll find Martins a good buy. Compare them with Pflueger and decide for yourself.

I've given a brief description of each reel. All are reversible. None have palming rims (probably considered a fad). Most have spare spools available, although they may be difficult to find. Most of the reels use a check pawl drag of varying degrees of sophistication. The multipliers use a Teflon and metal disc drag.

Model 62. *Deep drawn alloy; cup frame; epoxy finish; on/off click; the least expensive reel in the book; 3½ oz.; 3"; DT6.*
$6.25-$12.60 Sim, AnW, Tac, EJH
Model 63. *One piece cup frame of aluminum alloy; non-adjustable drag; 3¾ oz.; 3"; WF6F.*
$7.35-$12.80 ($5.20-$5.98) EJH, Cus, Tac, Sim, Pen
Model 65. *Assembled from stamped parts; check pawl drag that can be turned off but not adjusted; described by Dan Bailey's as "an excellent kids' reel"; 5 oz.; 3 5/16"; WF9F + 130.*
$10-$14.70 ($5.10-$5.95) Cab, Dan, Sim, H&H, Cab

Model 66. *Similar to the 65 but with twin, plated line guards; 5½ oz.; 3⅛"; WF9F + 130.*
$11.50-$19.95 Tac, Fly, EJH, AnW

Model 67-A. *Adjustable drag; lots of screws that need to be checked periodically to assure field reliability; 5½ oz.; 3 5/16"; WF9F + backing.*
$15.90-$23.95 ($7.15-$10.70) Pen, Dan, Mur, Sim, EJH, H&H, Bob, Cus

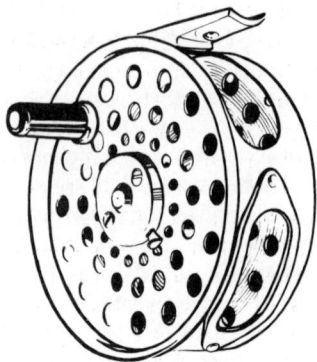

MG-3. *Smallest of the more expensive Martins, but still holds a DT8F; deep drawn, one-piece cup frame; two-pawl adjustable drag controlled by coil springs; 2¾ oz.; 3"; DT8F.*
$21.50-$36.80 ($11.98-$15.99) AnW, Dal, Pen, EJH, Sim, Tac, H&H

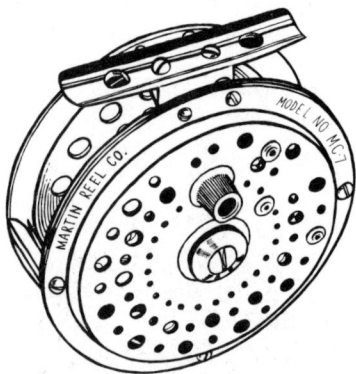

MG-7. *Offered by more catalog companies than any other Martin; assembled from stamped parts; adjustable drag; 4 oz.; 3 5/16"; DT8F + backing.*
$24-$44.95 ($11-$17) H&H, Bob, Cus, EJH, Fly, Tac, Dan, Cab, AnW, Dal, Pen, Sim

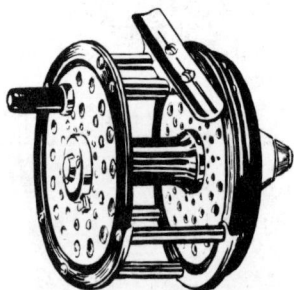

MG-7/5. *360 degree, one-way disc drag with on/off click; 6 oz.; WF9F + 150.*
$28.60-$29.95 ($13.30-$16.95) Cab, AnW, H&H, Cus

MG-8. *Similar to MG-7/5 above; 6¾ oz.; WF9F + 200.*
$29.95-$32.95 ($13.30-$16.95) H&H, Cab
MG-9. *Saltwater/salmon reel; adjustable disc drag with on/off click; spool counterbalanced; limited five year warranty; 9.8 oz.; 4"; WF10F + 300.*
$35.50-$41 ($13.05-$17.60) H&H, AnW

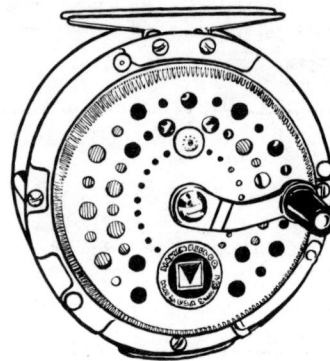

MG-10. *Multiplier with 3:1 ratio for very fast retrieve; for bass or large trout; fully adjustable coil spring-powered pawl drag; lightweight for a mulitplier; compare to MG-72 and Shakespeare's Speedex; 5¾ oz.; 3 5/16"; WF9F + backing.*
$33.50-$59 ($11-$13.95) Cus, EJH, H&H, Sim, Pen, Cab, Dan, AnW

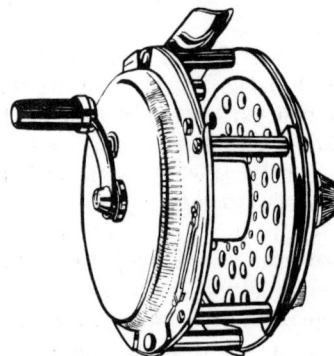

MG-72. *Multiplier with fast 3:1 ratio; Teflon and metal disc drag with on/off click; 9 oz.; WF9F + 150.*
$29.95-$42.98 ($12.75-$16.95) Sim, Cab, Pen, Tac, H&H, Cus

Orvis Madison

The least expensive Orvis reel series, the Madison, just sneaks in under the $50 mark. The current Madisons are fairly new, replacing a stodgy full-frame model that looked like (and could have been) a Martin. The new models use a half-frame with an exposed rim for palming.

The Madisons are handsome reels. They're cast from aluminum and have a black finish. They use a single pawl drag. They are not particularly lightweight reels. The IV, for instance, weighs 4¾ oz. The Orvis Battenkill Mark IV, their intermediate reel with the same line capacity, weighs only 3¼ oz. Other reels in the under-$50 category weigh as little as 2 ½ oz. You can also go the other way and look at the Pflueger Medalist 1494½ at 6 oz.

Screws are used to attach internal parts, the cover on the spool release, and other parts, and these need to be checked periodically for tightness. The reels come in a poplin bag and are made in England. Prices on Orvis products are controlled by the company, and distribution is through authorized dealers only.

Madison III. *4⅜ oz.; 3¼"; WF6F + 50 (20#).*
$38.50 ($12.50) Orv, Hig
Madison IV. *4 ¾ oz.; 3 ½"; WF7F + 100 (20#).*
$41 ($13) Orv, Hig
Madison V. *5¼ oz.; 3¾"; WF9F + 100 (20#).*
$43.50 ($13.50) Orv, Hig
Madison VI. *7½ oz.; 4"; WF9F + 200 (20#).*
$50 ($16) Orv, Hig

Pflueger Medalist Reels

Pflueger Medalists have a long tradition among American fly fishermen. Many of us grew up with a Medalist, and many fly fishermen shun the more technologically advanced reels in favor of this very conservative design. A 1495 picked off the shelf will still look, act, and feel just like the one your father picked off the shelf many years ago.

Indeed, there were no startling changes in this line for many years. But Pflueger no longer makes the reels. Medalists are now manufactured in Japan under the guidance of Shakespeare. They still look and feel the same, however. Still, the new origin of manufacture will startle long time Pflueger fans.

The reels are built to last forever, with little consideration given to faddish things like lightweight alloys or palming rims. There is one new model, the 1499, a saltwater reel capable of handling up to a 12-weight line and backing. It departs from the standard check pawl drag with a full-circle drag washer. It's sealed against corrosion and employs nylon bearings.

The rest of the line, from the 1492 to the 1498, is cut from the same cloth. The reels have an aluminum alloy full-frame, stainless steel line guards and spindle, and an adjustable check pawl drag. All are reversible, except the 1492 and 1492½. Extra spools are available, and parts are accessible. However, it remains to be seen if the changeover to the Japanese manufacturing system will cause some problems.

There are lots of screws used to hold the frame together. These are potential problem areas on any reel and should be checked regularly. Replacement screws and pawls are available from Bud Lilly's Trout Shop. The reels are heavy for the line weights they carry. (That doesn't bother Pflueger—they even boast that BB shot can be inserted into the reel to increase weight.)

The line capacities given by the company must go back to the time when nearly everyone used a level line. Unless a catalog company gave me better figures, I've had to stick with the company's unsatisfactory descriptions. You'll have to be wary of extremes if you want backing.

The reels are solidly built. They have virtually no sex appeal, but they'll keep putting out line and taking in line for a long time with only minor maintenance. Perhaps the hardest thing for the modern fly fisherman to accept about the reels is their weight. They will balance with an old Montague three-piece bamboo, certainly, but the delicate graphites will feel better with a lighter reel.

To me, it's too bad that these old timers in the American reel business didn't put their expertise at building reliable reels together with advances in technology and design to better meet the needs of modern American fly fishermen. Pflueger could have given the English and the Japanese manufacturers something to think about. Martin still has that opportunity.

If you're conservative in your approach (and in your spending), Pflueger will provide you with a workhorse reel, and you won't have to apologize about owning one to anyone who knows his fly fishing.

The reels are numbered from 1492 to 1499 with the progression showing increase in size and capacity. The half numbered models have a 1" spool width (compared to ¹³⁄₁₆" on the whole number models), giving them slightly greater line capacity. Again, all models except the 1492 and 1492½ are reversible.

1492. *4 oz.; 2⅞"; 4-5.*
$19.99-$34 ($8.90-$13.95) Cor, Cus, H&H, Fly, Bud, Cab, Dal, Mer, Pen, Sim, AnW
1492 ½. *4.5 oz.; 2⅞"; 4-6.*
$19.99-$34 ($8.90-$13.45) Cab, AnW, Cor, Bud, Mer, H&H, Mur, Cus, Pen, Sim
1494. *5 oz.; 3¼"; DT4F + 70, DT5F + 50, WF5F + 100, DT6F + 20, WF6F + 80, WF7F + 60.*
$21.95-$37.25 ($8.90-$15.95) Many catalogs

1494½. *6 oz.; 3¼"; DT5F + 100, DT6F + 70, WF6F + 140, DT7F + 40, WF7F + 120, DT8F, WF8F + 110.*
$21.95-$37.25 ($8.90-$15.95) Many catalogs
1495. *6 oz.; 3⅝"; 5-10 (approx. same as 1494½).*
$24.50-$41.95 ($9.95-$15.95) Many catalogs
1495½. *6.4 oz.; 3⅝"; 6-11.*
$24.50-$41.95 ($9.95-$15.95) Many catalogs
1498. *6.8 oz.; 4"; DT7F + 180, WF7F + 260, DT8F + 150, WF8F + 240, DT9F + 120, WF9F + 220, DT10F + 10.*
$29.99-$48.25 ($11.45-$17.95) AnW, Dan, Cab, Dal, Cor, Kau, Bud, Mer, Bob, Pen, Sim, Ste, Fly, H&H, Cus

Ryobi MG Series Reels

The MG stands for the magnesium these reels are cast from. The good news about magnesium is its light weight. The bad news is that it doesn't do to drop this reel, because magnesium is more breakable than aluminum. The reel foot is integral to the frame, and that will probably be the part that hits the ground if you drop the reel.

Okay, you've been warned. Now, I'll tell you that I own a Ryobi 355MG, and that I find it a very pleasant reel. I like its light weight, palming rim, and the feel of its check pawl. As on many of the inexpensive reels, the drag is marginal. The adjustment on this one works on a cam that tightens the spring. It's difficult to set it to anything but full-on or full-weak, but it needs to be full-on anyway.

The only real problem with these reels is the reversal to left-hand retrieve. They employ a single check pawl which is supposed to be reversed for left hand retrieve. That works fine on the 255MG, but for some reason does not work on the 355MG. I've tried it on several reels, and the drag and forward click both become messed up. A reel repair service told me that this is a problem that can be corrected by adjusting the spring. Better check it out before you buy a 355MG if you intend to reverse it.

This is a handsome reel with potential in the marketplace, but like the Daiwa reel described herein, it has not been marketed to fly fishermen. I bought mine from

a general sporting goods dealer. You'll find them now at a few fly shops, but I couldn't locate a mail order source for you.

If you want a very lightweight reel without the Hardy price tag, try to find one of these reels. When you're shopping around, you may want to take a look at the Cortland Crown II for comparison.

255MG. *2.3 oz.; 3"; DT5F.*
355MG. *3 oz.; 3½"; DT8F + 20, WF9F + 50.*
357MG. *3.7 oz.; 3¾"; DT8F + 130, WF9F + 170.*
455MG. *4 oz.; 4"; DT10F + 150 (30#), WF10F + 175 (30#).*
About $30-$40 (about $10-$15) Fly shops or sporting goods dealers

Ryobi FLY Series Reels

Along with the MG series, Ryobi makes a more traditional, all aluminum reel. It features a cast full-frame with an exposed palming rim. Screws are used to attach various parts. They must be periodically checked for tightness.

The reel has a single check pawl drag. Because of an error in design, the drag adjustment mechanism, at least on early models, can be adjusted so loose that internal parts may come apart. This isn't much of a problem since the drag is weak and will probably be set at its strongest setting.

I bought one of these reels for bass fishing. I didn't want to spend a lot of money, and Pfluegers are just too heavy for me. In the model with the same capacity, they weigh an ounce more. The Ryobi has a tighter feel to it, but I don't think it will compare to Pflueger for reliability. The reels are commonly found in sporting goods stores and discount stores.

FLY355. *5.7 oz.; 3½"; DT8F + 20, WF9F + 50.*
FLY455. *7 oz.; 4"; DT10F + 150 (30#), WF10F + 175 (30#).*
About $25 (about $8) Sporting goods dealers

Scientific Anglers Systems One Reels

S/A's re-entry into the reel market came in 1984 with the Systems One reel. They previously imported the Hardy Marquis reels under their name as the well-known Systems reels. The current Systems One hits a different part of the market.

The reels are made in Japan for S/A (see the text on Daiwa reels for an interesting note). The parts are cast in aluminum, and the reel has an attractive enamel finish. Extra spools are available at a reasonable price. In a touch designed to get the attention of anglers who usually spend more on their reels, the spool is counterbalanced to eliminate wobble that may cause a reel to come unseated.

The drag is a traditional two-pawl system with a fairly wide range of adjustment. The rim is exposed for additional drag through palming. All parts are metal.

There is no free lunch, and the apparent ruggedness of the reels is paid for in weight. The 4,5,6 weighs 4.6 oz. Other reels of similar capacity in this price range weigh as little as 2.5 oz. By comparison, the Pflueger 1494 weighs 5 oz.

This reel has a cleaner feel than the Pflueger (in part because it has more clicks to the turn) and with the exposed rim is more versatile and "modern". At $35-$40, it looks like a reasonable bargain. You should compare it to the Pflueger, the Orvis Madison (slightly heavier and a few dollars more), the Cortland Crown (considerably lighter and less expensive), and the Daiwa SF reels. In your comparison, follow the testing procedures outlined in the introduction to this chapter.

4,5,6. *4.6 oz.; 3⅛";* DT4F + 60 (20#), WF4F + 100, DT5F + 50, WF5F + 90, DT6F + 40, WF6F + 70, DT7F + 20, WF7F + 60.
$31.49-$44.60 ($11.73-$16.10) Many catalogs
7,8,9. *4.9 oz.; 3⁷/₁₆";* DT6F + 110 (20#), WF6F + 150, DT7F + 70, WF7F + 120, DT8F + 50, WF8F + 110, DT9F + 25, WF9F + 90.
$32.80-$46.50 ($12-$17.10) Many catalogs

Shakespeare Speedex Multiplier

This inexpensive multiplier barely makes it into the under-$50 category. Its frame is cast aluminum, and it has a steel spindle ("positively anchored", according to Shakespeare's brochure). The line guard is chrome-plated, and gears are made of high-impact nylon.

Multipliers retrieve line quickly, an advantage with big fish that make extended runs. The Speedex retrieves at a 2:1 ratio. Spools are interchangeable, and the reel reverses for left-hand retrieve.

The drag is a basic two-pawl system. For extra drag, both pawls can be engaged. In addition, there's a palming rim. All this makes for interesting combinations, and a suitable drag setting should be found.

Multipliers are generally used by salmon and steelhead fishermen (as well as saltwater anglers), but a reel in this price range is suspect for the kind of use demanded by that type of fishing. One of the catalog companies advertises the reel as a bass reel and specifically recommends that it not be used for salmon and steelhead. I'd have to agree. With the money and time you'll invest in that kind of fishing, spend some more on your reel.

There are two models, differing only in spool width and line capacity. Speaking of which, you'll have to take the figures here with a shaker of salt. Shakespeare's catalog uses the wonderfully descriptive phrase "up to #7" for line weights, as if there were only level lines in the world. The catalog companies give two different figures, and I've decided to list both instead of buying a Speedex and experimenting.

2801. *7 oz.; 3½";* WF7F + 30 (30#) or WF8F + 35.
2803. *7.2 oz.; 3½";* WF7F + 100 or WF10F + 120.
$39.95-$68.50 ($13.95-$19.95) Hun, Cab, Hig

REELS $50-$100

Welcome to comfortable shopping territory. You really can't go wrong with any of the reels listed in the $50-$100 category.

Reels in the lower price range are chancy. There are good bargains, but there are also clunkers. Reels in the over-$100 price range are good, there's little doubt, but the investment is so high that it takes some intense browsing and contemplation to end up with a reel that's going to please you for the 30 years it's going to last. The reels in the $50-$100 price category may also last 30 years, but the cost is not so prohibitive that you're going to feel bad if you retire one in 10 years in favor of a fancier model.

There are not a tremendous number of reels here. As usual, the middle of the market is ignored by manufacturers in favor of the high volume of the low end and the high profit of the upper end. But what they lack in numbers, these reels make up for in quality. I've owned one of them, a Hardy L.R.H. Lightweight, for about 10 years now. We have quite a history together. Many miles of streams and many hours on the lakes. Never has it flinched, never failed. It doesn't look new now—too many bangs on the bottom of the canoe, too many drops to the sandy riverbank—but it still works like new. It's one of the best investments I've made in my fishing life.

The other reels listed here are, I'm sure, of just as high a quality as the Hardy. The Orvis Battenkill series has been around forever, and there's good reason for its longevity. The Hardy Marquis series also has a long history with American anglers, formerly as the Scientific Anglers Systems reels. Valentine reels have a solid reputation, especially among eastern fishermen.

In short, if you're looking for high quality equipment without extremely high prices, this is the place. Happy shopping.

As with the under-$50 reels, spool prices are given in parentheses. Backing listed under capacities is assumed to be 18 pound unless indicated otherwise in the first listing.

Cortland LTD Graphite

The Cortland LTD Graphite reel is constructed of high tech materials and uses sophisticated engineering and design. The result is a reel that departs from the traditional without sacrificing function and form.

According to the Cortland literature, the reel is made of "high technology materials reinforced with graphite fibers". The materials along with the half-frame design make these reels lightweight. The smallest LTD will hold a WF6F and 80 yards of backing, and it weighs only 3 oz. The comparable Hardy, the L.R.H. Lightweight, weighs 3¾ oz.

The LTD features a disc drag which asserts pressure only while putting line out. The reel's click mechanism can be switched off for silent running. Metal parts are corrosion-resistant which allows the reel to be used in saltwater.

In addition to the high tech body materials, the reel uses Delrin gears treated with silicone and Teflon. The line guard is made of something called borosilicate (which sounds like it ought to be the latest material in rods). A chemist must have helped put the reel together.

For a high tech, "modern" reel, the price is right, too. Take a look at this reel at your nearest Cortland Pro Shop. There are three models with capacities of WF6F to WF9F plus backing.

The Cortland SS Magnum, a salmon, big game reel, is also listed here. It has large capacity and a palming rim.

LTD Small. *3½ oz.; 3¼"; DT5F + 50, WF5 + 100, WF6 + 50.*
$45 ($20) Kau, Fly, Nor, T&T, Cab, Mer
LTD Medium. *4 oz.; 4½"; DT7 + 50, WF8 + 110, WF9 + 50.*
$50 ($20) See LTD Small
LTD Large. *4½ oz.; 4½"; DT9 + 50, WF9 + 125, WF10 + 75.*
$55 ($20) See LTD Small
SS Magnum. *WF9F + 325 (20#).*
$70 ($20) T&T, Pen

Hardy Hydra

Introduced in 1984 and removed quickly from the market, this was Hardy's attempt to reach the economy end of the market. Since the reel is a Hardy and since it's no longer available, there is the chance that it will become a collector's item in the future. If you bought one, you might consider setting it aside.

I've found the reel in one catalog, but it's unlikely they'll still have it by the time you read this. Might be worth a try, however.

Hardy Hydra. *WF7F + 110.*
$49.95 Pen

Hardy Lightweight Series

I think I can call these reels classics. I try to use the word carefully . . . most things so described are classy, not classic.

The Lightweight series reels are traditional in design. They have a cast aluminum full-frame with a simple check pawl drag utilizing the two-pawl system which allows easy reversal from right to left retrieve. I'll let the simplicity of design stand as one mark that makes the Lightweight series reel a classic.

That simplicity also makes for a very reliable reel. There is virtually nothing that can go wrong unless some damage is done to the reel.

Of course, that simplicity must be coupled with quality of construction and materials, and the Hardy Lightweight reels get high marks in both categories. The tolerances on these reels are remarkable for their price. They will pass all the tests I outlined in the introduction. In fact, I'd recommend using these reels as a standard against which other reels, both less and more expensive, should be judged.

As for the quality of the materials, I can only say that after 10 years of hard use (with less care and maintenance than it deserves), my L.R.H. Lightweight still has excellent spool tolerance. There is no apparent wear on the check pawl, which is one of the first places where poor materials will show up, and the line guard is still smooth.

The Lightweights are not trendy. They've been the same forever. If you're into high fashion and the latest gadgets, these will not please you. With the check pawl system, they don't have strong drags, and since there is no palming rim, you'll have to add drag through use of your line control hand. On the other hand, this is one reel that will always be there when you need it. Harry Murray of Murray's Fly Shop has only one comment in his catalog about the Lightweights: "Unless you want to spring for a Bogdan, I feel these are the finest reels you can buy." Would that make them classics, Harry?

There are five models with line capacities ranging from DT2F to DT10F. The reels are made in England. (Incidentally, I just learned the answer to one of the pressing questions of my angling life—L.R.H. stands for left- or right-hand retrieve.)

(Note: Hardy recently began to exercise some price control pressure in order to reduce discounting. They have "asked" retailers to limit discounts to 10%. Hook & Hackle, a major discounter, dropped the reels in 1985, perhaps in response. In any case, the range of prices here may now be a source of consumer nostalgia. Hope you already bought your Hardy reels.)

Flyweight. 2⅜ oz.; 2½"; DT4F + 0, WF4F + 50 (20#), WF5F + 30, WF6F + 10.
$63.30-$95 ($35-$53) Most catalogs
Featherweight. 3 oz.; 2⅞"; DT4F + 40 (20#), DT5F + 0, WF5F + 60, WF6F + 40.
$67.80-$100 ($36.15-$53) Most catalogs
L.R.H. Lightweight. 3⅜ oz.; 3³/₁₆"; DT4F + 70 (20#), DT5F + 50, WF5F + 90, WF6F + 20, WF6F + 80, WF7F + 60.
$72-$106.50 ($37.98-$60) Most catalogs
Princess. 4¾ oz.; 3½"; DT5F + 100 (20#), DT6F + 70, WF6F + 140, DT7F + 50, WF7F + 120, DT8F + 0, WF8F + 110.
$75-$113 ($37.98-$60) Most catalogs
St. Aidan. 6 oz.; 3¾"; DT7F + 180 (20#), WF7F + 250, DT8F + 150, WF8F + 240, DT9F + 120, WF9F + 220, DT10F + 10.
$80.98-$120 ($39.98-$65) Many catalogs

Hardy Marquis Series

These reels were formerly marketed by Scientific Anglers as the respected "Systems" reel series. They are handsome reels known for their reliability and quality construction.

The major difference between the Marquis series and the Lightweight series is the exposed rim on the Marquis reels. The Marquis spools have a polished rim designed for palming. Like the Lightweights, they are made of aluminum and have exceptional tolerances. Materials and quality control follow the Hardy tradition of excellence.

The spools from the S/A Systems reels are interchange-able with the new Marquis series spools. The S/A numbers correspond directly with the Marquis numbers through model 7. Conversion for the remainder of the line is as follows: Marquis Model 8/9 = S/A 8; 10 = S/A 9; Salmon 1 = S/A 10; Salmon 2 = S/A 11.

Models range from the Marquis 4 to the Salmon 2 which will handle a DT9F plus plenty of backing. Hardy also offers multipliers in the Marquis series. The Marquis Multipliers 6,7, and 8 will handle those line weights in a weight forward taper with adequate backing. The retrieve is 1⅔ to 1.

The Marquis series reels are made in England. (Note: See remarks about price range under Hardy Lightweight series above.)

Marquis 4. 3¼ oz.; 2¾"; DT4F + 0, WF4F + 40, WF5F + 10.
$67-$105 ($36.15-$54) Many catalogs
Marquis 5. 3¾ oz.; 3"; DT4F + 20, WF4F + 75, DT5F + 0, WF5F + 55, WF6F + 35, WF7F + 15.
$69-$105 ($37.30-$56) Many catalogs
Marquis 6. 4¼ oz.; 3¼"; DT5F + 20, WF5F + 75, DT6F + 0, WF6F + 60, DT7F + 0, WF7F + 45, WF8F + 30, WF9F + 15.
$71-$108 ($38.40-$58) Many catalogs
Marquis 7. 4½ oz.; 3⁷/₁₆"; DT6F + 40, WF6F + 105, DT7F + 0, WF7F + 95, DT8F + 0, WF8F + 75, WF9F + 55, WF10F + 35.
$74-$113 ($39.55-$58) Many catalogs
Marquis 8/9. 5¾ oz.; 3⅝"; DT7F + 50, WF7F + 120, DT8F + 25, WF8F + 105, DT9F + 0, WF9F + 95, WF10F + 70.
$79.10-$120 ($40.70-$61) Many catalogs
Marquis 10. 6½ oz.; 3¾"; DT8F + 35, WF8F + 135, DT9F + 0, WF9F + 120, WF10F + 90, WF11F + 25.
$81.40-$120 ($41.80-$60) Many catalogs
Marquis Salmon 1. 7¾ oz.; 3⅞"; DT9F + 110, WF9F + 215, DT10F + 50, WF10F + 185, DT11F + 0, WF11F + 175.
$85.90-$130 ($48.50-$80) Many catalogs
Marquis Salmon 2. 8¾ oz.; 4⅛"; DT9F + 215, DT10F + 60, WF10F + 240, DT11F + 0, WF11F + 200.
$90.45-$135 ($48.50-$80) Pen, LLB, Kau, Mer, Cab, Sim, Cus, Hun, Dan, AnR, Don, H&H
Marquis Multiplier 6. 4⅝ oz.; WF6F + 110.
$83.98-$92.46 ($31.98-$34.84) Pen, Mer

Marquis Multiplier 7. *5¾ oz.; 3⁷/₁₆"; WF7F + 125.*
$85.90-$130 ($30.50-$46) Cus, Cab, H&H, Mer, Pen, Dan
Marquis Multipler 8/9. *7 oz.; 3⅝"; WF8F + 175.*
$89.30-$135 ($31.65-$46) Pen, Mer, H&H, Dan, Cab, Cus

Hardy Sunbeam Series

Sunbeam reels are rather flashy models. The dark metal of their spools is contrasted by a bright palming rim.

The reels are slightly heavier than other Hardy reels of comparable line capacities in this price range. Like the other Hardy reels, however, they are machined to close tolerances. The drag system has a wide range of adjustment. The Sunbeam reels have a steel spindle, like the other models, but the spool rides on bronze bearings. The line guard on these reels is ceramic.

These reels are apparently out of production and may not be in current catalogs. There are five models in the series. Line capacities range from WF5F to WF9F plus adequate backing. The reels are made in England.

Sunbeam 5/6. *4¼ oz.; 3"; WF5F + 100.*
$85.98-$94.41 ($39.98-$46.75) Dal, Mer
Sunbeam 6/7. *4⅝ oz.; 3¼"; WF6F + 120.*
$89.98-$96.96 ($40.98-$48.51) Mer, Dal
Sunbeam 7/8. *5⅜ oz.; 3⁷/₁₆"; WF7F + 140.*
$91.98-$99.51 ($41.98-$52.92) Dal, Mer
Sunbeam 8/9. *6⅛ oz.; 3⅝"; WF8F + 170.*
$94.98-$103.77 ($48.98-$57.33) Mer, Dal
Sunbeam 9/10. *7½ oz.; 3⅞"; WF9F + 230.*
$99.98-$108.87 ($49.98-$60.86) Tac, Dal, Mer

Other Hardy Reels

The St. John is a large capacity reel. It is a unique model among the Hardy reels, although some catalog companies run its listing with the Lightweight series.

The St. John is made for heavy duty fishing, like that encountered in steelheading. The aluminum is heavier gauge, and the drag springs and pawls are carbon steel. Line capacity ranges to a DT8F plus 140 yards of 20 pound backing. Reel weight is necessarily high at 8½ oz. Like all Hardy reels, it is machined to close tolerances and is manufactured in England.

I've found some miscellaneous Hardy models in the catalogs. At this time, I'm not sure where they fit in the scheme of things. The St. George is a large capacity reel offered by R.L. Winston. The Zenith is listed in the Dale Clemens catalog as the largest of the Lightweight series. The Husky is a Zenith with disc drag. So "unavailable" are all of these reels, except the St. John, that you may not find them in any catalog.

St. John. *8½ oz.; 3⅞"; DT7F + 160, DT8F + 140, WF8F + 220, DT9F + 120, WF9F + 200, DT10F + 10.*
$74.60-$110 ($37.30-$56.50) AnR, Fol, Let, Hun, Pen, Kau, Mer, Sim, H&H

St. George. *7¾ oz.; WF9F + 180.*
$103 ($51) RLW
Zenith. *7¼ oz.; 3⅜".*
$90.72-$120 (46.20-$54.95) Dal, Tac, Fly, Let
Husky. *Similar to Zenith but with disc drag.*
$145 Let

Orvis Battenkill Mark Series

The Orvis line of basic and intermediate reels has undergone some changes in recent years. The Madison, their basic reel, is much improved over the former Madison model. The Battenkill, their intermediate reel, has also been improved.

The Battenkill is cast from a magnesium alloy for less weight. It features a half-frame design, allowing the angler to palm the exposed rim of the spool for additional drag. The internal drag is a single pawl with the adjustment on the back of the frame.

The light weight of this reel, plus the exposed palming rim, make it a very modern, practical tool for the fly fisherman. With its black finish and white lettering, it's also an attractive reel. Best of all for many of us, its price tag is competitive. The Hardy reels and Valentine reels in this price category are closer to $100.

The reels come with a vinyl case and spare spool bag. They are made in England. As with all magnesium reels, they must never be used in saltwater. Saltwater melts magnesium. The reels come in three models, Mark III, Mark IV, and Mark V, with line capacities ranging from WF6F to WF9F plus backing.

Mark III. *3 oz.; 3¼"; WF6F + 50 (20#).*
$65 ($31) Orv, Fre, Let, H&H, Hig, Ste, Kau, Bud, AnR
Mark IV. *3¼ oz.; 3½"; WF7F + 100 (20#).*
$65 ($31) See III
Mark V. *4 oz.; 3¾"; WF8F + 200 (20#). (Note: This model is not included in the current Orvis catalog.)*
$69.50-$77.50 ($33.50-$36.50) Fre, Let, H&H, Hig, Ste, Kau, Bud, AnR

Orvis Magnalite

If you're looking for an inexpensive multiplier, this is certainly a model you should consider.

As I've said before, it's poor judgment to spend thousands of dollars on a salmon fishing trip and take an inexpensive reel with you. But for bass fishing or big water/big fish angling that doesn't require a large monetary investment to get to, this reel is a good bet.

There are two sizes with line capacities from WF7F to WF9F and backing. The reels are geared to retrieve 2:1 and are reversible for left-hand retrieve.

Magnalite Medium. *5 oz.; 3½"; WF7F + 100 (20#).*
$47.50 ($15) Orv, Ste
Magnalite Large. *6¼ oz.; 3¾"; WF9F + 100 (20#).*
$50 ($16) Orv, Ste

Pflueger Medalist 1499

Pflueger's newest model, the 1499, shares only the name with the other Medalists. It doesn't look like a Medalist and it doesn't cost like a Medalist.

The 1499 is Pflueger's entry in reels for saltwater. It's sealed against corrosion, and the spool is anodized. Coupled with these necessary features is a disc drag. Pflueger claims it's the "largest, full-circle drag washer ever incorporated into a fly reel". In another departure from standard Medalist fare, the 1499's spool is machined.

There is one similarity between the 1499 and other Medalist models—it weighs a lot. At 12.5 oz., it weighs as much as the Bogdans and Catinos. Of course, as a saltwater reel, it's supposed to weigh a bunch.

The reel will carry a "#12" line with 200 yards of 15 pounds backing.

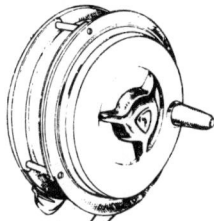

1499. *12½ oz.; 4"; 12 + 200.*
$89.95 Ram

Valentine Reels

If you sat down to design a traditional reel with built-in reliability and a drag that really works, you'd probably end up with a Valentine.

The premise behind these reels is obvious. They are built to be workhorses. Valentine reels are not dainty, nor are they fancy, faddish, or even fashionable. But they are tough, and they'll go on putting out line and taking it in for many, many years.

There are no cast parts in Valentine reels. Cast parts have a tendency to crack when impacted. Stamped parts of strong aluminum are tougher, and if they are impacted (that means dropped on the stoney banks of your local river), they'll probably dent or bend, and you'll probably be able to fish with the reel after some quick streamside repairs. Later, you can replace the parts easily with the aid of a screwdriver.

You'll need a screwdriver handy to tighten the several screws on a Valentine reel. The trade-off for this periodic maintenance is reliability and toughness. Before you begin to liken this reel to the reels using assembled, stamped parts that were listed in the under-$50 category, stop. The quality of the stamping is higher, and the assembly is better.

The real difference between the inexpensive reels and the Valentine is the drag. This reel has a drag that will nearly stop you from pulling line off the reel. The drag

is comparable to those of reels in the higher-priced category, reels like the Marryat. Like those reels, the Valentine uses a disc system. This one uses a Teflon washer against a stainless steel disc. It's smooth and sensitive.

The reels also have a counterbalanced spool to eliminate wobble during runs. This is a feature of limited interest to most of us, but it shows once more that the Val-Craft Co. intended to design a reel that works and works right. In the process, they've given up a lot in the weight category. The Model 76, for instance, weighs in at 4¾ oz. Compare that to the Hardy Featherweight of similar line capacity. It weighs 3 oz.

The only complaint I'd have as a Valentine owner is the reel's looks. If I spent nearly $100 on a reel, I wouldn't want it to look like a $39.95 Pflueger. That's what a quick look at a Valentine reel will remind you of. It's the white handle and center emblem. Pfluegers are too imbedded in the consciousness of all American fly fishermen to escape the connection. In fact, until I researched the reels, I'd always written them off as an over-priced Pflueger, and that is not at all an accurate perception of the Valentine product.

There are five models with capacities from WF5F to WF11F plus backing. The reels are American-made.

Model 76. *4¾ oz.; 3"; WF5F + 75 (20#).*
$82 ($27) Mer
Model 83. *5½ oz.; 3¼"; WF6F + 100.*
$83 ($27) Mer
Model 89. *6¼ oz.; 3½"; WF7F + 150.*
$84 ($29) Mer
Model 95. *6½ oz.; 3¾"; WF9F + 200.*
$86 ($29) Mer
Model 101. *7¼ oz.; 4"; WF11F + 300.*
$88 ($30) Mer

REELS OVER $100

And now the top quality reels available on the market today. These are the Mercedes, the Rolls Royces, the Porsches of fly reels. Try not to drool on the glass countertop at your local fly shop while you take a look at the Orvis CFO, the Ross RR, the Hardy Perfect, and the Marryat. If you're after a big-game reel, try not to fondle the Catino or the Fin-Nor too long.

These reels need little introduction. Your dreams are or will be introduction enough. If you are ready for a lifetime reel that will fill even fishless days with pleasure, if you can afford a dream, this is the place. You'll find classy reels here. Some are even classics, and others are classics in the making.

All the reels here are extremely functional and well-designed. Many of them are beautiful. Shopping for a reel in this price range can be as exciting as owning one. Enjoy.

The reels are listed in alphabetical order. Spare spool prices are listed in parentheses. Backing specifications are for 18 pound material unless noted otherwise.

Bogdan Reels

Bogdan reels have been a hallmark for discriminating anglers since the 1950s. They are individually handcrafted from scratch upon receipt of an order. The Bogdan line was until recently restricted to big-game and saltwater fishing needs. There are now Bogdan reels for trout and steelhead fishing.

When you deserve a Bogdan and can afford one, you should also be prepared to wait for one. According to Hunter's Angling Supply, the only retail source for Bogdan's that I could find, you may have to wait up to 24 months. As a fine craftsman who gives individual attention to every detail of a reel's construction and who limits his output to allow that, Stan Bogdan is not about to hurry an order for anyone. Hunter's quotes him as saying, "The reel will be ready when it is ready."

So, forget mass production and the profit motive. But also, forget shoddy workmanship. Bogdan's approach is very refreshing in light of what has happened to many fine craftsmen who have given in to mass production and satisfying the every demand of the consumer. In fact, it makes me want one of these reels very badly. Perhaps in a few years . . . (Maybe I should place my order now, just in case.)

The ordering instructions for Bogdan reels are too extensive to include here. If you're interested, I suggest you start by sending for the Hunter's catalog. Incidentally, if you buy a Bogdan, I'm envious.

Single Action Reels

Trout. *5 oz.; 3¼"; WF5F + 20 (30#).*
$300 Hun
Large Trout. *5½ oz.; 3¼"; WF7F + 50.*
$310 Hun

Steelhead. *6 oz.; 3¼"; WF9F + 75.*
$318.50 Hun
Large Steelhead. *7½ oz.; 3½"; WF9F + 150.*
$332.75 Hun
50. *9 oz.; 3½"; WF9F + 110.*
$382.50 Hun "

Multipliers, 2:1

00. *10 oz.; 3¼"; WF9F + 75.*
$387 Hun
0. *11 oz.; 3¼"; WF9F + 150.*
$398 Hun
100-M. *11 oz.; 3½"; WF9F + 110.*
$398 Hun
150. *12 oz.; 3½"; WF10F + 150.*
$406.50 Hun
1. *13 oz.; 3¾"; WF10F + 150.*
$414 Hun
2. *14 oz.; 3¾"; WF11F + 225.*
$425 Hun
300-M. *15 oz.; 3¾"; WF12F + 225.*
$433 Hun

Catino Reels

Catino's two models, the Bonefish and the Tarpon, are designed with the saltwater fly fisherman in mind. They feature corrosion-resistant materials, large capacities, and an oversize disc drag.

The reels are machined from aluminum bar stock and the finish is hard-anodized. Needle-and-thrust bearings and a Teflon bushing give the spool a smooth, reliable ride. These are direct-drive reels with an exposed rim for palming during those long runs.

Although the reels are designed for saltwater fishing, the steelhead and salmon angler will find them very appropriate for their sport. The reels must be ordered in either right- or left-hand retrieve. The left-hand retrieve models entail an extra charge with some companies. Apparently, the other companies just charge the higher price for both models.

Catino reels are American-made.

Bonefish. *6¼ oz.; 3½"; WF8F + 200 (20#), WF9F + 150 (30#).*
$350-$400 ($150-$200) Hun, Orv
Tarpon. *12 oz.; 4⅜"; WF12F + 325 (30#).*
$450-$500 ($165-$225) Orv, Hun

Dennison Fly-Spin Combination Reel

The Combination Reel is unique in that it allows the angler to switch between fly and spin fishing while using the same reel. An offshoot of the Fly-Spin reel, which is designed for the spin fisherman using a fly rod to cast his monofilament, the Combination has a spool for fly line as well as a spool for mono.

Although an oddity, the reel may appeal to fly fishermen who also do some spin fishing (or vice versa). The reel is available from Dennison Research, 2220 S.W. Troy, Portland, Oregon 97219 (503) 246-6576.

Fly-Spin Combination. *2 to 1 retrieve; 10½ oz.; 5¼"; line weight 7 plus backing.*
$142 Dennison

Fenwick World Class Reels

Fenwick's entry into the reel marketplace may come as a surprise to those anglers used to thinking of the company as middle-class and moderately priced. These reels are designed for the top line market. They come in against Marryats and Ross reels.

Like their competitors in this price range, the World Class reels are machined from aluminum bar stock. They are good-looking reels, finished in black and brass, and are fully anodized for corrosion protection.

The most distinctive feature of the reels is the drag set-up. The smallest model uses a double check pawl, the others a multiple disc drag, but on all the reels, the adjustment for the drag is separate from the adjustment for the click.

The double-pawl drag on the World Class 2 with its separate adjustments will allow reversal in record time, since no switching of pawls is necessary. This, however, is a minor advantage since most anglers already know their retrieve side or experiment at a more leisurely pace. The other models are also easy to reverse.

The multiple disc drag on the larger models uses metal plates, hardened steel against impregnated bronze. Fenwick claims maximum heat dissipation from the metal discs. In addition, the oil impregnated in the bronze "weeps out" when the disc becomes hot, thus providing self-lubrication.

The reels come in four models. The World Class 2 is a basic trout model with ventilated spool. The WC 4 has a larger capacity and carries a solid spool. The WC 6 is the companion to the WC 4 but features an anti-reverse handle. The WC 8 is a large capacity, anti-reverse reel suitable for saltwater gamefish. On the anti-reverse

models, Fenwick suggests purchasing extra spools with clutch, bearings, brake control, and handle as one unit to make changing spools easier and quicker.

The reels are American-made and carry a lifetime guarantee.

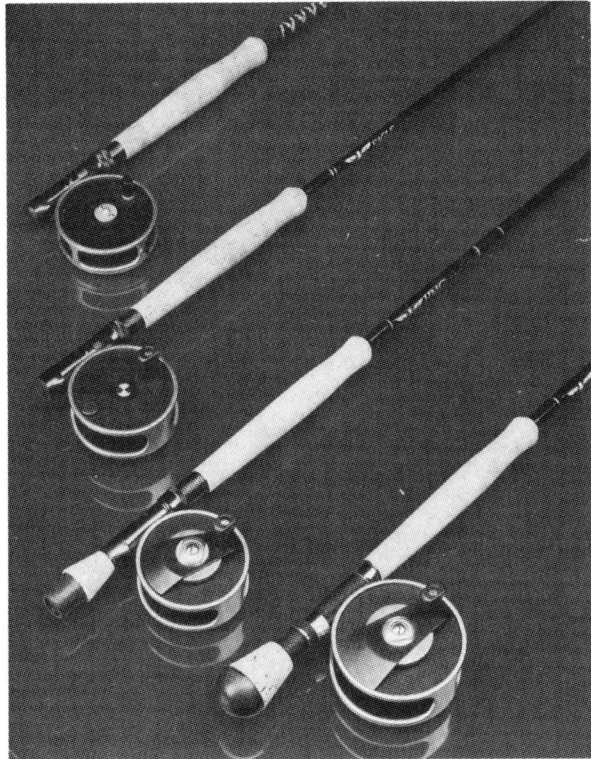

World Class 2. *4.6 oz.; 3⅛"; WF7F + 150 (20#).*
$115.85-$160 ($39.95-$69.95) Fol, Cus, Fly, Sim, Cab, Pen, Dan, Don
World Class 4. *6.6 oz.; 3⅛"; WF9F + 200.*
$194.35-$265 ($64.95-$98) See World Class 2
World Class 6. *9.2 oz.; 3⅛"; WF9F + 200.*
$194.35-$265 ($64.95-$98) See World Class 2
World Class 8. *12 oz.; 3⅝"; WF13F + 370.*
$284.95-$370 ($64.95-$98) See World Class 2

Hardy Perfect Reels

A manufacturer has to have some confidence to call one of its products "perfect". For one thing, the name invites critics.

You won't find a critic here. I'm going to let the Perfect rest on its long history—since 1891—and on the reputation of its maker. The reels are of heavier construction than the Lightweight and Prince models. Stainless steel ball bearings have been used to give the reel a smooth ride.

The Perfects feature an agate line guide housed in nickel silver. It is not reversible, and the reel is available in right-hand retrieve only. The reel has an adjustable drag, and additional drag can be applied by palming the back side of the spool.

These reels are machined to exceptional tolerances. They are handsome reels and definitely worthy of your consideration. A few turns of the handle may sell you. Nothing sounds quite like the Perfect.

The only thing you'll give up if you buy a Perfect is weight. The 3⅜" model weighs 6½ oz. Compare that to the Hardy Princess at 4¾ oz.

There are three models, designated by spool diameter, with capacities of WF5F to DT8F plus backing. The reels are made in England.

Perfect 3⅛. *5½ oz.; 3⅛"; DT4F + 35 (20#), DT5F + 0, WF5F + 60.*
$96.10-$145 ($24.85-$38) Hun, Pen, Kau, Mer, Sim, Fly, Let, H&H, Fol, Cus, Dan, Bud, AnR, Don
Perfect 3⅜. *6½ oz.; 3⅜"; DT5F + 95, DT6F + 70, WF6F + 135, WF7F + 120.*
$97.20-$145 ($26-$38) See Perfect 3⅛
Perfect 3⅝. *6½ oz.; 3⅝"; DT7F + 160, WF7F + 250, WF8F + 230.*
$99.90-$150 ($27.10-$38) See Perfect 3⅛

Hardy Prince Reels

Hardy introduced a new design in reels when it brought out the Prince in 1984. In an engineering coup, Hardy placed the check pawl drag system entirely within the arbour (the center of the spool).

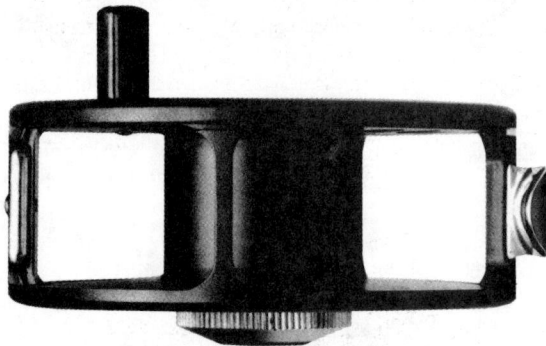

When you pull the spool off the Prince's spindle, you'll find the check pawl sticking straight out from the frame. Its tension mechanism is placed within the enlarged spool center, and the pawl sits perpendicular to the spool gear. This leaves the full reel width available for line capacity, giving greater capacity for reel weight.

You can see the difference in weight with a few quick comparisons with reels of similar capacity. The Hardy Princess (from the Lightweight series) weighs 4¾ oz., and the Marryat 8 weighs 4¼ oz. In comparison, the Prince 5/6 weighs 3¾ oz. On the other hand, the Orvis CFO IV comes in under the Prince at 3½ oz. The other

advantage of the Prince's enlarged spool center is a quicker line retrieve.

The Prince comes in two freshwater models. The saltwater model, the Ocean Prince, is listed separately. Like the other Hardy reels, these are made in England.

Prince 5/6. *3¾ oz.; 3"; DT5F + 135, WF5F + 155, DT6F + 95, WF6F + 140, DT7F + 65, WF7F + 110, WF8F + 95.*
$89-$140 ($42-$68) Bob, Don, Fre, Hig, T&T, Sim, AnR, Bud, Dan, Hun, Pen, Kau, Mer, Dun, Ram
Prince 7/8. *4¼ oz.; 3¼"; DT6F + 195, WF6F + 270, DT7F + 160, WF7F + 245, DT8F + 125, WF8F + 230.*
$92-$145 See Prince 5/6

Hardy Ocean Prince Reels

Hardy's recent entry into the big-game reel market is the Ocean Prince, and it looks like a very competitive model.

The Ocean Prince, like other quality big-game reels, is machined from aluminum. It features a disc drag with a full adjustment range and a palming rim for maximum control. The materials are corrosion-resistant and coated with a corrosion-proof finish, making the reel suitable for saltwater use.

The spool is free wheeling when line is taken out, a feature you can appreciate only if you've tried to grab hold of a reel handle while a big fish is running. The reel is easily reversible, and spools can be changed quickly without the use of tools.

The Ocean Prince comes in one model. Capacities range from WF9F to WF12F plus backing. It's manufactured in England (see note on prices, page 57).

Ocean Prince. *3¾"; WF9F-WF12F + backing.*
$207-$292.50 ($89.95-$134.50) Pen, T&T, Sim, Mer

H.L. Leonard Reels

Leonard recently introduced this modernized replica of its original reel. Although it's constructed of anodized aluminum and stainless steel, the reel looks somewhat like an antique reel. The frame pillars are raised from the spool in the fashion of reels of years past.

The reel features a full-circle disc drag and quick-release spool, so it's entirely modern in function. The distinctive feature remains its appearance. The angler who collects or is interested in antique equipment cannot help but enjoy the thought of fishing with a modern tool that looks very much like an antique reel someone found in his attic, new and in the box. I'm certain it would be a perfect reel for an elderly (or brand new) cane rod, a Leonard perhaps.

The reel is hefty at 8 oz., but beauty never has come cheap. The Leonard reel is American-made.

Leonard. *8 oz.; 3⅛".* *(Note: Capacities were not available.)*
$250 ($85) Don

Marryat Reels

I can tell you two things about the Marryat reel from picking one up in the local fly shop. They are among the classiest-looking reels on the market, and they have one of the best drags.

The reels are machined from aircraft-grade aluminum which has been cold-forged and anodized. They are reported to have tolerances of .0025". The reels are fully anodized and suitable for saltwater use. The Marryat has a roller clutch drag which is smooth and very strong. With the drag full-on, the spool can barely be turned using the handle.

The trouble, if any, with the reels is that they are almost too pretty to be taken out in the field. With the excellent anodized finish, of course, there's nothing to worry about if the reel is given reasonable care. You can order your Marryat in either bronze or gold. Good luck deciding.

The reels are reversible, and extra spools are available. Although they were originally made in America, the reels are now manufactured in Japan. Five models are made with capacities ranging from DT4F to WF9F with backing. The three larger models have a counterbalanced spool.

Marryat 7. *3½ oz.; 2¹¹⁄₁₆"; DT4F + 35 (20#).*
$92.50-$127.50 ($48-$56.95) LLB, T&T, Nat, Dan, Bea, Fly
Marryat 7.5. *4 oz.; 2⅞"; DT5F + 40.*
$95-$132.50 ($50.25-$58.70) T&T, Fly, Dan, Bea
Marryat 8. *4¼ oz.; 3"; WF7F + 140.*
$96-$137.50 ($52.50-$61.80) See Marryat 7
Marryat 8.5. *5 oz.; 3⅛"; WF8F + 235.*
$97-$142.50 ($56.25-$64.80) See Marryat 7
Marryat 9. *5¼ oz.; 3¼"; WF9F + 320.*
$99-$147.50 ($59.50-$68.25) See Marryat 7

Monarch Reels

Monarch Reels are relatively new on the market. They have a one-piece full frame machined from aluminum and they are designed to withstand the rigors of big-game fishing. A large cork disc provides the drag. All parts are corrosion-resistant, making the reels suitable for saltwater use.

There are three models with capacities of WF5F-WF12F plus backing. The reels are available from Saracione Manufacturing, 7210 Jordan Ave. Box B-84, Canoga Park, California 91303.

M30. *7 oz.; WF5F + 175 (20#).*
$350 Saracione
M35. *Weight and capacity unavailable.*
$375 Saracione
M40. *13 oz.; WF12F + 250 (30#).*
$400 Sarcione

North Fork Reels

You can order your North Fork reel in a velvet-lined walnut box (with brass inlay), and the reels look worthy of this kind of treatment. The reels are very attractive, following the same styling lines as Bogdans and Fenwick World Class reels but with their own flair and distinctive lines. As might be expected for a reel in this price range, they are machined from solid aluminum. The spool is anodized aluminum, and the fittings and screws are brass.

The drag system for the three larger models is an adjustable check pawl. The two smaller models have a non-adjustable check pawl system to prevent overrun.

Even with all the trimmings, the reels come in at a reasonable weight, heavier than Marryats and Ross RR reels, lighter than Hardy Perfects. With five models, you can get a North Fork for every line from a DT3F to a DT8F plus backing. The walnut box, incidentally, will cost you an additional $70.

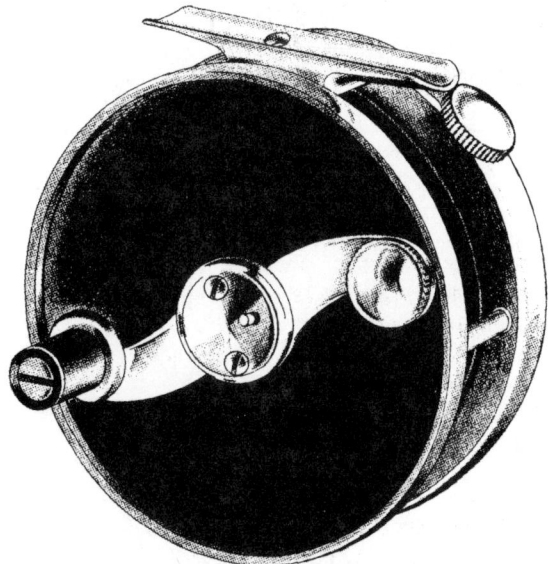

North Fork 3/4. *3.7 oz.; 2.26"; DT3F + 20.*
$125 ($35) Nor
North Fork 4/5. *4.1 oz.; 2.4"; DT4F + 40.*
$125 ($35) Nor
North Fork 6/7. *4.8 oz.; 2.77"; DT6F + 60.*
$135 ($40) Nor
North Fork 7/8. *5.7 oz.; 3.1"; DT7F + 80.*
$145 ($45) Nor
North Fork 8/9. *6.4 oz.; 3.25"; DT8F + 100.*
$145 ($45) Nor

Orvis CFO Reels

Orvis is justifiably proud of its CFO fly reels. They are handsome reels built to exacting standards.

The reels are cast from aluminum alloy. They use a half-frame which leaves the spool rim exposed for palming. That feature complements the check pawl which is adjustable on all models except the tiny CFO II. The nickel silver line guard is symmetrical to make reversal even more simple. The reels come in a fleece-lined suede case.

There are five models with capacities ranging from DT2F to DT11F plus backing. The reels are made in England. The CFO, incidentally, stands for Charles F. Orvis, the founder of the company. It's a distinction the reel deserves.

CFO II. *2 oz.; 2⁹/₁₆"; DT3F, WF4F.*
$97.50 ($39) Orv, AnR, Kau, Bud, Fly, Hig, H&H, Let, Fre
CFO III. *3¼ oz.; 3"; WF4F + 100 (20#), WF5F + 75.*
$100 ($41) See CFO II
CFO IV. *3½ oz.; 3⁶/₁₆"; WF7F + 100 (20#), WF8F + 50.*
$105 ($43.50) See CFO II
CFO V. *4¼ oz.; 3⁷/₁₆"; WF9F + 200 (20#), WF10F + 150.*
$110 ($46) See CFO II
CFO VI. *9¾ oz.; 4"; DT11F + 200 (30#).*
$115 ($47.50) Orv, AnR, Let

Orvis Saltwater CFO Reels

The big brother to the CFO freshwater reels is a single action reel designed for the angler wishing to get into a big capacity, saltwater reel for a moderate price.

The reel shares the same basic design as the little CFOs. It has a half-frame with exposed spool rim. The frame and spool, unlike the freshwater models, are machined from aluminum bar stock. It has an anodized gold finish. The reels utilize a double pawl drag which is fully adjustable.

There are three sizes with line capacities from WF7F to WF10F with backing.

Light. *5 oz.; 3¼"; WF7F + 150 (20#).*
$177.50 ($97.50) Orv
Medium. *6 oz.; 3¾"; WF9F + 200.*
$190 ($105) Orv
Large. *6⅞ oz.; 4"; WF10F + 200.*
$205 ($115) Orv

Orvis Presentation Reels

The recently-introduced Presentation series reels are machined from aluminum bar stock and anodized for corrosion resistance. They have supplanted the CFO as the top line reel in the Orvis line.

The reels utilize a two-pawl drag. One pawl is powered by a light spring for normal use and for use with fine tippets. The second pawl has a heavier spring for additional drag. The switch from one drag system to the other can be made "with a flick of your finger". The spools are counterbalanced for vibration-free runs. Presentation reels are available in either full-frame or exposed rim construction. Exposed rim models are indicated by EXR.

The reels are made in Argentina (probably on the banks of one of the great rivers there). Although Orvis is listed as the only source, you will undoubtedly find these reels in many of the catalogs listed under CFO reels.

Exposed Rim Models

Presentation EXR I. *3 oz.; 2⅞"; WF3F + 50 (20#).*
$125 ($53) Orv
Presentation EXR II. *3⅜ oz.; 3"; WF5F + 75.*
$130 ($63) Orv
Presentation EXR III. *3⅞ oz.; 3¼"; WF6F + 100.*
$135 ($72) Orv
Presentation EXR IV. *4⅜ oz.; 3½"; WF8F + 150.*
$140 ($78) Orv
Presentation EXR V. *5 oz.; 3¾"; WF10F + 150.*
$150 ($85) Orv

Full-Frame Models

Presentation II. *3¼ oz.; 2⅞"; WF5F + 75.*
$125 ($60) Orv
Presentation III. *3¾ oz.; 3⅛"; WF6F + 100.*
$130 ($69) Orv
Presentation IV. *4 oz.; 3⅜"; WF8F + 150.*
$135 ($75) Orv

Orvis SSS Series Reels

Salmon. Steelhead. Saltwater. The SSS series is designed for the special needs of the big-game angler and the saltwater angler.

The reels are machined from aluminum bar stock for close tolerances. All components are anodized aluminum, stainless steel, or naval bronze for corrosion resistance. The drag is a multi-stage disc utilizing cork and Teflon for smoothness and strength.

The SSS reels are available in direct-drive and anti-reverse. A series of anti-reverse multipliers with 2.3:1 retrieve is also available. (The handles turn on direct-drive reels when a fish is running. On anti-reverse models, the handle remains stationary.) All models feature an audible click when line is running either direction.

The unique feature of these reels is the exposed rim on anti-reverse models. Traditional design of anti-reverse reels prevents leaving the spool rim exposed. The reels are lighter than many comparable saltwater reels, but at least one reel comes to mind as being lighter than the SSS reels, the Ross S.

Weight is generally not a big concern for the salmon, steelhead, saltwater fishermen. They have big rods that need the heavier weight for balance, and they are much more concerned with reliability. Orvis understands this fact, and they presently offer a guarantee that the buyer will find the SSS reels to be superior to heavier and more expensive reels. Money back. No questions.

There are four models with line capacities from WF6F to WF12F with backing. The reels are not reversible but may be ordered in either right- or left-hand retrieve.

Anti-Reverse Models

SSS 6/7 A-R. *5⅞ oz.; 3⁵/₁₆"; WF6F + 150 (20#).*
$375 ($160) Orv
SSS 7/8 A-R. *6¾ oz.; 3½"; WF8F + 200 (20#).*
$400 ($175) Orv
SSS 9/10 A-R. *8½ oz.; 3¾"; WF10F + 200 (30#).*
$425 ($185) Orv
SSS 11/12 A-R. *10 oz.; 4"; WF12F + 300 (30#).*
$550 ($230) Orv

Direct-Drive Models

SSS 7/8 D-D. *6¾ oz.; 3½"; WF8F + 200 (20#).*
$325 ($140) Orv
SSS 9/10 D-D. *8½ oz.; 3¾"; WF10F + 200 (30#).*
$375 ($155) Orv
SSS 11/12 D-D. *10 oz.; 4"; WF12F + 300 (30#).*
$500 ($215) Orv

Anti-Reverse Multipliers

SSS 6/7 M. *6½ oz.; 3⁵/₁₆"; WF6F + 150 (20#).*
$450 ($150) Orv
SSS 7/8 M. *7½ oz.; 3½"; WF8F + 200 (20#).*
$475 ($165) Orv
SSS 9/10 M. *9¼ oz.; 3¾"; WF10F + 200 (30#).*
$500 ($175) Orv
SSS 11/12 M. *10¾ oz.; 4"; WF12F + 300 (30#).*
$625 ($220) Orv

Pate Saltwater Reels

Billy Pate reels are machined from corrosion-resistant aluminum. They have a disc drag and double click mechanism with distinctive tones for incoming and outgoing line (handy for anti-reverse models).

The reels have a lifetime guarantee. As with other smaller volume manufacturers, delays may be experienced in orders and repairs. You must specify left- or right-hand retrieve and direct-drive or anti-reverse when ordering.

There are two models. The reels are made in America.

Salmon. *9 oz.; WF9F + 200 (20#).*
$365 Kau, Fly
Tarpon. *12 oz.; WF12F + 300 (30#).*
$395 Fly, Kau

Ross RR Reels

A conversation with Ross Hauck is all you'd need to be convinced that these reels have been designed and manufactured with the pride and attention to detail that will make them American classics.

Ross builds his reels to last a lifetime and guarantees his work, in writing, to the original owner. He works from a three pound block of aluminum bar stock that has been rolled under tremendous pressure so it has grain almost like wood. From this block, he machines a reel of great beauty and exacting tolerances. With the exception of the reel foot screws and the stainless steel bearings, everything is made in the family shop under Ross's watchful eye.

Ross drove over one of his reels with his Jeep to test its ruggedness. Only the handle broke. You may not believe that from the look of the reels. They are delicate in appearance, having an antique look to them. Don't be fooled by that—these are tough reels.

The disc drag uses a spring-loaded Delrin button. It's been subjected to a most remarkable test. At full drag, Ross ran the reel at 4,250 R.P.M. for over 24 hours (about 6,000,000 revolutions). There was no appreciable heat rise, and wear on the drag amounted to .003". On the freshwater models, the drag is not particularly strong, compared to a Marryat, for instance, but it is as reliable and durable as reels designed for saltwater and costing much more.

The only objection some anglers might have is the lack of a click. The reels run silent both ways. Ross would probably tell you that the click is an unnecessary piece of machinery that can break down. My guess is that you won't miss it after a few minutes on the stream.

The other feature that may raise an eyebrow is the spool release. You must loosen a screw (a dime works fine) to remove the spool. You can be sure there's a good reason for this. For one thing, the spool is attached to the shaft (which is an integral part of the reel body rather than the spool) by the screw, so there's no worry about extra spools fitting properly. And, I'd guess that also helps keep down the price of extra spools. With the careful design typical of Ross reels, the screw does not come free from the spool when loosened.

The reels come in four models with capacities to WF9F plus backing. The largest model, the 3.5, has a solid spool with counterbalanced handle.

RR 1. *3.14 oz.; 2 13/16"; DT4F + 30, WF4F + 60, DT5F + 0, WF5F + 40.*
$150 ($46) Tid, Cus, Nat, RLW, Fly, Kau, Bud
RR 2. *3.38 oz.; 3 1/16"; DT5F + 25, WF5F + 100, DT6F + 0, WF6F + 75.*
$155 ($48) See RR 1
RR 3. *3.68 oz.; 3 ⅜"; DT7F + 60, WF7F + 100, DT8F + 20, WF8F + 80.*
$160 ($50) See RR 1
RR 3.5. *4.2 oz.; 3 ⅜"; DT8F + 165, WF8F + 250, DT9F + 130, WF9F + 215.*
$170 ($52) Tid, Kau

Ross S Reels

Like the freshwater Ross reels, the saltwater model has been carefully engineered for reliability. The reels are direct-drive, single action.

The Ross S reels use a disc drag which relies on a collar of self-lubricating polymer material. The collar is replaceable. The drag has been subjected to the same kind of testing that the freshwater Ross reels underwent with the same positive results. With 41 times the surface area of the freshwater models, this drag will be heavy enough for big fish. The saltwater reels also allow palming

control. The reels are, incidentally, fairly easy to reverse with the aid of a screwdriver.

The selling point for these reels, other than the Ross reputation, is their weight. If you've been waiting for a lightweight, reliable saltwater reel, get out the checkbook. The biggest model, the S Three, weighs only 7.8 oz. A quick comparison of the other saltwater reels capable of handling a 12-weight line will show the weight advantage of the Ross. The traditional favorite Fin-Nor #4 weighs 13 oz., and the Catino Tarpon 12 oz. Closest to the Ross is the comparable Orvis SSS which weighs 10 oz.

If weight is not an important factor to you, maybe cost is, and the Ross S models compare very favorably. The only reel you can get for less is the Fin-Nor.

Of course, the Ross does not look like a Fin-Nor or a Catino. It looks like a Ross. That means the traditionalists may steer away from the Ross... at least until it becomes a tradition among saltwater fly fishermen. That could be very soon.

The reels come in three sizes with capacities of WF8F to WF12F plus adequate backing. They are, of course, American-made.

S 1. *7.2 oz.; 3.2"; WF8F + 150 (20#).*
$310 ($100) Kau, Bud, Nat, RLW, Fly
S 2. *7.45 oz.; 3.45"; WF10F + 175.*
$335 ($105) Kau, RLW, Nat, Tid
S 3. *7.8 oz.; 3.7"; WF12F + 300.*
$365 ($115) Kau, RLW, Fly, Nat

Sage Reels

The essential difference between the Sage reels and other traditional English reels, the Hardy Marquis for example, is that the Sage is machined from aluminum bar stock. This gives the reel additional strength compared to the reels that are cast aluminum.

The Sage reel is anodized a rich brown and is dressed with nickel silver components. It comes in a suede leather case, and each reel is factory registered and carries a serial number.

So much for the reasons why this reel costs $146. It is a beautiful reel with excellent tolerances and quality materials. It has a very crisp feel, and it sounds good. You'll have to decide whether these features, many of them emotional, warrant the cost.

I'd suggest you compare these reels with the Ross RR and the Marryat, both of which feature disc drags. For pure function, compare the Sage with the Marquis which has the double-pawl drag and exposed palming rim and costs about $100. You can anticipate, of course, differences in machining in the less expensive model.

However, if you decide on the Sage after these comparisons, the decision will be based on the uncompromising quality of the reels and their aesthetics. Nobody can argue your choice, and the pride of ownership will be worth the additional cost.

Sage reels come in three sizes with capacities ranging from WF7F to WF9F plus backing.

505. *4¾ oz.; 3³⁄₁₆"; DT4F + 70 (20#), DT5F + 55, WF5F + 90, DT6F + 20.*
$146 ($68) Cor, Fly, Bob, Mer, Kau, Pen, Bud
506. *5⅛ oz.; 3½"; DT5F + 110, DT6F + 70, DT7F + 50, WF7 + 120.*
$152 ($70) See 505
509. *7⅝ oz.; 3¾"; DT8F + 150, WF8F + 250, DT9F + 120, WF9F + 240.*
$162 ($75) See 505

Stutz Estuary Reels

The Stutz is a light saltwater reel with clutch drag and a palming brake. It features a silent retrieve with a click when line is taken out. It is finished in an anodized bronze color.

Estuary. *5½ oz.; 3⁵⁄₁₆"; WF9F + 150 (20#).*
$239.50 ($89) Kau, Fly

Tycoon Fin-Nor Reels

The Fin-Nor reels are perhaps the best known saltwater reels. They have an excellent reputation among anglers, and they come in at a relatively moderate price. (If you think $250 is a lot for a reel, take a look at some of the other saltwater reels.)

The reels are machined from aluminum bar stock and fully anodized for corrosion resistance. They feature a disc drag system that is considered one of the most sensitive made.

Tycoon Fin-Nor makes four models. Models are available in either direct-drive (D-D) or anti-reverse (A-R). They must be ordered for either left- or right-hand retrieve. The reels are American-made.

Direct-Drive Models

1 D-D. *8 oz.; 3"; WF7F + 125 (20#), WF8F + 85.*
$216-$265 ($81-$105) RLW, Sim, Cus, Cab, Bul, Kau, Pen, Hun, Dan, Don
2 D-D. *9½ oz.; 3½"; WF8F + 125 (30#).*
$231-$330 ($86.40-$110) Fly, Fol, Dan, Don, Cus, Cab, Bul, Hun, Pen, Kau, RLW, Sim
3 D-D. *11½ oz.; 4"; WF9F + 250 (20#), WF10F + 150 (30#).*
$252-$355 ($91.50-$115) See 2 D-D
4 D-D. *12½ oz.; 4"; WF12F + 250 (30#).*
$285.95-$360 ($97.20-$125) Don, Hun, Pen, Kau, Bul, Cab, RLW, Sim

Anti-Reverse Models

1 A-R. *8½ oz.; 3⅛"; WF7F + 150.*
$232.20-$272 ($81-$84.95) Pen, Bul, Sim
2 A-R. *10 oz.; WF9F + 150 (20#).*
$246.75-$340 ($86.40-$105) Kau, Bul, Cab, RLW, Sim,
Pen, Hun, Dan, Don, Fly, Cus, Fol
3 A-R. *12 oz.; 3½"; WF10F + 150 (30#).*
$262.50-$370 ($91.80-$115) See 2 A-R
4 A-R. *13 oz.; WF12F + 300 (30#).*
$297-$352 ($97.20-$119.95) Sim, Bul, Pen

Valentine Planetary Drive Reels

These reels are unique in the industry. They use a planetary drive to turn the spool, and the advantages are obvious.

For one thing, the planetary drive acts as a multiplier. One turn of the crank will give the angler 1½ turns at the spool. The retrieve is much like any other reel for the fisherman, except that a constant pressure must be applied to the handle itself. The gearing behind the handle is doing the actual work of retrieving line. Thus, when line is taken out by a fish, only the handle turns. The spool sideplate remains stationary. This feature helps keep whirring spool handles from catching loose line and saves busted knuckles.

Another advantage comes when you want an extra spool for your reel. Because of the construction employed, extra spools are very simple and very inexpensive. You can pick up this reel with an extra spool for much less than that combination in reels costing less initially.

The reels are constructed of precision stamped parts. That allows quick disassembly with a screwdriver, but that same screwdriver must be used periodically to tighten the screws. The reels are made of gold anodized

aluminum with bronze bearings and stainless steel line guards. They are suitable for saltwater use.

The reels are relatively lightweight for their line capacity, coming in someplace between the lighter Ross S and the slightly heavier Orvis SSS. They are considerably less expensive than either.

The reels may be ordered in either left- or right-hand retrieve. They come in a leather case. There are three models with capacities of WF7F to WF11F plus backing. They are American-made.

350. *7½ oz.; 3½"; WF7F + 150 (20#).*
$110 ($24) Mer
375. *9 oz.; 3¾"; WF9F + 200.*
$118 ($26) Mer
400. *9½ oz.; 4"; WF11F + 300.*
$125 ($28) Mer

Walt Carpenter Reel

Styled to resemble the Vom Hoffe and Walker reels of yesteryear, the Carpenter reel will appeal to those anglers who cherish the heritage of the sport. It is offered in either left- or right-hand retrieve.

Carpenter. *2⅝"; DT3F-DT5F + backing.*
$175 Mur

REEL ACCESSORIES

Reel Cases and Carrying Bags

Reel cases include everything from neoprene pouches to sheepskin-lined suede cases. Any padded case should do, but for those in search of a touch of class, there are lots of fancy models to choose from. I've listed the cases by type and by material used.

Drum-Shaped Cases

Cotton duck. *Zipper closure, piped leather seams, "fleecy" lining; sizes for salmon reels.*
$11.90-$12.90 Don

Suede leather. *Zippered, lined with fleece or artificial fleece; sizes: 3¼"-5".*
$4.69-$12.35 Many catalogs
Suede leather. *Double deckers in same style and diameters as above; for two reels or reel and extra spool.*
$5.95-$15 T&T, Fly, Sim, Dal, Hun, Bud, Cab, Pen, Orv, Kau
Vinyl. *Zippered; 3 ½"x3¼"x3½" and 4x5x7".*
$1.70-$2.26 AnW, Fol
Hardy. *Vinyl reel cases with Hardy logo; padded, zippered; 3½", 4¼", 4¾".*
$8.35-$9.95 Mer, Fol

Reel Pouches

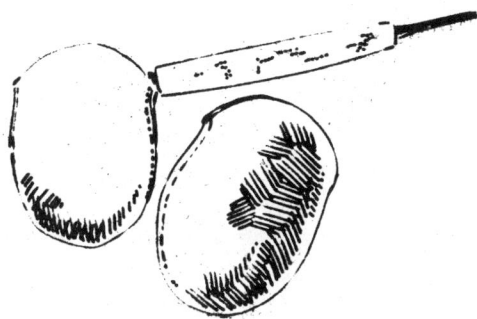

Reel Deal. *Neoprene pouch from Simms; slips over reel on or off rod; floats, supposedly with reel; several colors allow organization by reel size or line weights; sizes: S,M,L.*
S—$5-$7; M—$7-$10; L—$9.94-$12.50 Fly, Big, Bob, Bud, Kau, Pen, Ram, Hig
Cotton/polyester pouch. *Double layer material; spare spool bag.*
$3.21-$3.50 T&T, Dal, Orv
Canvas pouch. *Sheepskin-padded, suede bottom; regular and large.*
$11.50 T&T
Leather pouch. *Suede or buckskin; drawstring close; 4"x6"-9"x11".*
$2.40-$6.49 AnW, Bud, Kau, Cus, Fol, Dal, Tid, Dan

Rod and Reel Pouch

Vinyl. *Pouch to be placed over rod handle and reel; 8x14" and other sizes.*
$2.45-$3.35 Fol, AnW

Reel Carrying Bags

These products are for that acquaintance of mine who has a duffle bag full of reels and can never find the right one in the tangle of lines and leaders.

Reel Bag. *Looks like a large shaving kit; Cordura nylon; six pockets for reels and spools; (my acquaintance needs about four of these bags); center divider protects reels, provides two envelope pockets for leaders and reel lube; 6½"x13".*
$19.95 Pen
Deluxe Reel Bag. *Larger size and capacity; 8 pockets for reels; 14"x10"x6".*
$34.95 Pen

Miscellaneous Reel Accessories

Antique Reel Display Case

Thomas & Thomas. *Display case for your reel collection, antique or brand new; wood; 10 compartments; reels are visible through brass-hinged, picture frame door with brass corner accents; a handsome case; 14"x17"x5".*
$58.75 T&T

Line/Leader Minders

There are two devices on the market to tend the loose leader ends while a reel is not in service. One type attaches to the side of your reel. It's rather clunky looking, but it will save you those most frustrating moments—trying to find the end of your leader while fish are rising. The other type is designed for spare spools. It's a fancy replacement for a big rubber band, but it works better, doesn't get lost as easily, and won't crack or break. You'll order one the first time your line comes unspooled.

Tip-Tac. *Velcro "button" that sticks to the side of your reel; pull apart and run the leader through it; five buttons.*
$1.50 Bob, Bud, Dan, T&T, Dal, Nor, Wul
Line Minder. *Simple rubber or neoprene band that slips over extra spool while it's out of the reel.*
$1.50-$5.00 Bob, Bud, Kau, Pen, Ram, T&T

Reel Lubes

Not much is made of reel lubes, but they are vital to the continued health of a piece of equipment subjected to extremes of heat and cold and the ravages of sand, silt, and water. Silicones seem the favorite lubricant now. They are less likely to pick up dirt and grit or to become sluggish in cold weather, but they need to be applied more frequently. Reel lubes are too numerous to mention by name.

$.85 to $2.34 Bud, Cus, Sim, T&T, Fol, Mer

Reel Rags

If these are good enough to add the final polish to Ross Reels, they're good enough for any reel you'll ever own. Cleans even anodized aluminum.

$2.00 Kau

Reel Parts and Repairs

Bud Lilly's Trout Shop and Thomas & Thomas are the only catalogs that offer spare parts for reels. It can't be very profitable, but it makes their service much more like your local fly shop's. The Trout Shop offers Pflueger frame screws and check pawls and Hardy line guard screws, check pawls, and line guards. T&T offers refurbishing/repair kits for Hardy reels.

For repairs beyond the replacement of minor parts, try Coren's Rod and Reel Service, 6424 N. Western, Chicago, Illinois 60645. You should call ahead to see if they can do the work your reel requires. Call (312) 743-2980.

The following reel repair shops may also be able to help, but call ahead to be sure they work on your make of reel and have parts on hand for it.

Glenn's Reel and Rod Repair
2210 E. Ninth St.
Des Moines, Iowa 50316
(515) 262-2990

Tackle Unlimited
555 Miller Ave.
Clairton, Pennsylvania 15025
(412) 233-9072

Bucko's Parts and Service
191 Stafford Road
Fall River, Massachusetts 02724
(617) 674-7900

Bob's Reel Service
406 South Lincoln Ave.
Loveland, Colorado 80537
(303) 667-1107

John's Sporting Goods
1913 Broadway
Everett, Washington 98201
(206) 259-3056

Ollie Damon, Inc.
4530 S.E. Hawthorne
Portland, Oregon 97215
(503) 232-3193

Okiebug Rod and Reel Repair
3501 S. Sheridan
Tulsa, Oklahoma 74145
(918) 664-1026

De Ketts Tackle and Parts
2710 State Street
Saginaw, Michigan 48603
(517) 790-0330

Your local fly shop is perhaps the best place to begin if you need reel repairs, especially if they carry the make you own. They may do the repairs themselves or have someone who does them locally. In any case, they'll know where you should send it. If all else fails, contact the manufacturer. They will refer you to a repair service in your area or do the repairs themselves.

4. Fly Lines and Leaders

FLY LINES HAVE BENEFITED more from technological advancements than any other part of the fly fisherman's tackle, except perhaps rods. With the advent of plastic-coated lines in the 50s, nearly everything became possible. Lines could float without grease. They could sink. Part of them could float, part sink. They could sink slow, or they could sink fast. And they could have every conceivable configuration.

After 30 years of development, things are still happening to the fly line. The plastic coating, first introduced by Scientific Anglers in 1954, is used on floating lines to trap "microspheres" of air. The density of a floating fly line is actually less than water, making it unsinkable unless it gets dirty or cracks develop allowing water to permeate the braided core. Now coatings on Scientific Anglers Ultra lines are actually water-repellent, making the lines ride even higher on the water. (All this on the way to the ultimate line, which, of course, would hover just above the water's surface.)

Meanwhile, Cortland is working on refinements in the fly line's stiffness/suppleness qualities to improve casting distance and accuracy. Through a special coating, they have developed a line, the 444SL, with increased stiffness for greater casting lengths.

Other lines have been developed for special uses. They often rely on taper to do the job for which they are designed. There are bass bug tapers, saltwater tapers, and shooting tapers. Sinking and sink tip lines meet the needs of the nymph and streamer fisherman.

Rodon has even developed a line specially designed for boron/graphite rods. They make a pretty good case for conventional lines being inadequate for the new rod material.

And, in the midst of all this modern technology, you'll find a silk line like that used by our fishing forefathers. In short, there's something for everyone in fly lines today, and more to come tomorrow.

For the beginner, this can all be very confusing.

After all, all you want, as a novice, is to get a fly line and go out and catch fish. I'll try to help keep it simple for you with a special beginner's section later. First, let's go through the basics of choosing a fly line.

Codes on fly line boxes. As confusing as today's coding system may seem to a novice, we should all be grateful for it. It's much easier to deal with than the old system. (More on that in the section on line weights.)

All fly lines are marked with a three-part code, such as DT5F. The letter or letters at the beginning of the code designate the line's configuration or taper: L = level, no taper; DT = double taper; WF = weight forward; ST = shooting taper. A more complete explanation follows in the section on line tapers.

The middle part of the code is a number designating the weight of the line. These range from 2-weight (the lightest) to 15-weight.

The final part of the code describes the line's floating/sinking characteristics. The code goes like this: F = floating; I = intermediate sinking; S = sinking; F/S = floating with sinking tip.

As far as it goes, the code is very good. However, there are so many variations within the coding boundaries that you can't rely on the code alone. For instance, a "WF" may be a conventional weight forward taper, a bass bug taper, or Rodon's special boron/graphite rod taper. Sinking lines may sink 1"/second or 5"/second. A sink tip may have 5' or 30' of sinking line. The message is simple. You must know the line company's products before you can choose a line, especially a special use line, to meet your needs. The listings here should help.

Now let's take a look at each of the line characteristics as if you were selecting a line.

Fly line tapers. The first letters of the fly line code describe the line's taper or lack of it. The various tapers have much to do with a line's performance in the field.

The easiest to understand is the level line. It's designated by an "L". The level line has no taper. It's always the cheapest line because it requires no "machining". It's also virtually useless as a casting tool. I haven't even included level lines, because they are such a poor investment.

Line Tapers Courtesy of Cortland

Let me give you a bit of casting physics by way of explanation. When you cast a line, you exert a specific amount of energy to the line through the rod's action. Once the casting motion is complete, you cannot add any energy. As the line moves forward, it uses up that "X" amount of energy. With a tapered line, this is no problem, because as the line uses the casting energy, it becomes smaller and lighter and thus requires less energy to be moved.

A level line, on the other hand, has the same diameter throughout. As energy is used up, there comes a point where there is too little to move the line, and it falls in a pile. The caster may overpower the cast to compensate, but there's no way to control the delivery when that's done. As you know by now, line control is at the essence of the sport, and you won't have any control with a level line. You can get a level line for about $5. Spend an extra $6 for a beginner's tapered line. If you already have a level line, throw it out. It's ruining your chances of liking the sport. Throwing out a level line is one of the cheap lessons in fly fishing.

The next line taper is the double taper ("DT"). This line is tapered at both ends symmetrically. Where delicacy of presentation and line control is paramount, the double taper is the preferred line. Because it has a long level section in the center, line control is generally better than that of other tapers, most of which put a heavy section forward. This superior line control, with the tapered front, allows more accurate and delicate presentations. It's also the best taper for roll casts, especially at longer distances.

So why doesn't everyone use a double taper? The primary reason is distance casting. The double taper will not shoot as well as weight forward tapers. In addition, a double taper at 60' weighs considerably more than a weight forward at 60'. This adds to the difficulty of maintaining line in the air.

I use a double taper for all my stream fishing and for any situation, like beaver ponds, where delicacy is essential. Another recommendation for a double taper is that it's only half as expensive as the other tapers. Since you usually have only the first 30'-40' of a fly line in the water, that's what wears out. When it finally cracks and quits floating, you only need pull your double taper off the reel and reverse the line. Since it's the same front and back, you have the equivalent of a new line.

Lake fishermen and others who do long distance casting

favor the next taper, the weight forward ("WF"). Most of these lines have a heavy front taper that decreases to a long, relatively small diameter level section. With the weight up front and a small, light line behind, it's possible to cast farther more easily than with a double taper. However, some delicacy is lost, and so, too, is some accuracy, in my opinion. You cannot make subtle changes with the weight forward, as you can with the consistently-sized double taper.

It is in lake fishing that the weight forward shines. You can pick up a weight forward and shoot it to a rising fish much more quickly than you can a double taper, which requires more false casting to reach the same distance. In lake fishing, delicacy is not as critical (if you give the cruising fish enough room). Saltwater anglers find the weight forward especially helpful. They need to be able to shoot a great deal of line quickly to the fast moving bonefish and tarpon, and a weight forward is just the ticket. Special saltwater tapers are made in heavy line weights.

In addition, bass fishermen have special weight forward tapers made for them. These feature "blunter" tapers. This configuration allows better pick up of the big, bushy poppers and streamers bass men (and women) are fond of throwing at the largemouths (and smallmouths). These lines, in conjunction with one of the specially designed bass rods, make fly casting for bass as easy and enjoyable as dry fly casting for trout.

The final taper is the shooting taper (''ST''). This is somewhat the equivalent of a weight forward cut off before it tapers back to the small diameter level line. A shooting taper is attached to a running line to provide the ultimate in distance casting. With the entire weight at the front, the shooting taper can pull off amazing amounts of running line. There is, however, a considerable loss of control when you're shooting line like that. Accuracy and delicacy have little to do with a shooting taper.

Still, this line serves its purpose. Salmon, steelhead, and saltwater fly fishermen prefer a weight forward or a shooting taper (often called a shooting head), because of the ease of casting long distances all day long. Some lake fishermen will also use shooting tapers when they finally get tired of having fish rise 10' farther out than they can cast. (Shooting tapers are cheaper than belly boats.)

Shooting tapers are attached to running lines which are designed for light weight and smooth shooting. One type you'll see in the fly line listings is a small diameter (usually about .030") floating fly line, packaged in 100' coils . Some fly shooters prefer an even lighter running line, and they go to one of the monofilament running lines (listed in line accessories).

Fly line weights. Prior to the advent of modern fly lines, lines were graded by diameter. This was a workable system, since silk lines were consistent in weight for a given diameter. You may still find an older rod with the diameter grades on it. It will say something like "HDH" (the equivalent of a double taper 6-weight).

When plastic-coated lines came in, diameters no longer correlated well with line weight, and a new system was established. The first 30' of a fly line (arbitrarily set as the length of the average cast) is now weighed to establish the line's weight designation. In case you're interested in the specifics, here's the chart of line weights as specified by the American Association of Fishing Tackle Manufacturers.

Line weight	Weight (in grains)
1	60
2	80
3	100
4	120
5	140
6	160
7	185
8	210
9	240
10	280
11	330
12	380
	(437.5 grains = 1 oz.)

The choice of line weight is the beginning place for all equipment choices, except waders and vests, which have more to do with your weight than the line's. The chapter on rods has an explanation of the application of line weights to fishing situations, and you may wish to take another look at that.

As further amplification, line weight must be matched to fly size. The Orvis Company has a nice chart explaining this visually in their booklet "Choosing an Orvis Fly Line" which you can request from them. The generally accepted combinations of unweighted fly sizes and line weight are given below:

Line weight	Range of fly sizes
3	16-28
4	14-26
5	12-22
6	8-20
7	6-16
8	4-14
9	1/0-10
10	3/0-8
11	4/0-4
12	6/0-1/0

A lot depends on the action of your rod and other factors. A light line weight cannot power big flies. A heavy line weight will snap the light leaders required for small flies.

You can see the correlation between the information here and that in the chapter on rods. Trout fishing with dry flies usually requires flies in sizes 12-28, and the corresponding line weights are those recommended in the rod chapter.

So, by deciding the kind of fishing you'll be doing and the size flies required for it, you'll decide on a line weight. From that, you'll choose a rod and reel to match. Of course, you're not really done with fly line selection. You must determine the correct taper and decide the floating/sinking issue.

Fly line specific gravity. The last part of the fly line code tells you whether the line floats or sinks or does some of both.

Floating lines ("F") are used for dry fly and wet fly fishing and for limited nymph fishing when working fairly shallow water. It's essential that your fly line float when fishing dries. Otherwise, the line will pull the dry fly under. In some wet fly fishing and nymph fishing, a floating line allows detection of strikes that cannot be directly seen. You watch the end of the line for any hesitation that might indicate a strike. Cortland makes a nymph tip line that has a brightly colored tip to aid in seeing that often subtle hesitation.

To aid in getting a nymph or wet fly down to the fish's level, the floating/sink tip line ("F/S") was created. These lines feature a sinking front section on a floating line. Since extreme depth is not required in situations for which this line was designed, the floating line is a real asset, allowing easy pick-up and mending.

The length of the sink tip is important and is not given in the code. Sometimes it's not given in catalogs or even on the box label. You'll want a short sink tip for small streams and pocket water. The Teeny Mini-Tip has the shortest sink tip at 5'. The standard length is 10'. Scientific Anglers and Cortland both make a series of sink tips with lengths of 10', 20', and 30'. The longer tips, which are often called sinking heads, are useful in big rivers and in lakes.

The sink tip lines have a light-colored floating section and a dark-colored sinking section.

The next code is for intermediate sinking ("I") lines. These lines sink over their entire length, but the sink rate is so slow that they will normally be only an inch or two under the water during a drift. Neither fish nor fowl, these lines are not used a great deal. One situation in which they are favored is when the water surface is wind-chopped. On days like that, it helps keep contact with the fly to have the line underwater where it can lie straighter than it could on the surface.

The final type of line is the sinking line ("S"). Again, the code will not tell you much, except that the full line sinks. Here, you'll have to rely on the manufacturer to tell you the sink rate. The leading line makers give those rates in inches/second. A slow sinking line drops about 1

½"/sec. A very fast sinking line goes down at the rate of 4½"-5"/sec. S/A and Cortland are good about stating their sink rates, although the catalogs are not good about reporting them. The lists here should help you in ordering.

Sink rates are always given in a range for any one line. This range represents the difference between the lightest and heaviest weights offered in that line.

Full sink lines are used most commonly on lakes. Fish may be found feeding at varying depths, and by experimenting with time between cast and retrieve, you can determine the correct depth for the most action. Count the seconds before you begin the retrieve, and when you start to get fish, use that depth for succeeding casts.

The line that sinks the fastest and farthest is the lead core, which is useful only under extraordinary situations where extreme depth is necessary.

The beginner's fly line. First, let's start with a fact. The most useful line is a floating line. To begin with any other type would be foolish and would handicap your casting to boot.

Second, line weight is up to you and your fishing needs. I hope that as a beginner you can stick with line weights 5-7. Choose the 5-weight line and rod if you will be doing mostly trout fishing. Choose the 7-weight if you'll be after bass. Choose the 6-weight if you'll be doing some of both or if you can't tell a trout from a bass.

Third, let's end with a prejudice. I think you ought to buy a double taper. That makes me an oddball casting to the beat of a different drummer, because most line manufacturers suggest the weight forward for beginners. It's true that weight forward lines make long casts easier, and therefore reward the beginner in his first goal, casting a long way. Many schools use weight forward lines for this reason.

My suggestion to the beginner is that long casts are not as important as accurate casts with delicate presentations. It's my feeling that the double taper allows greater success in those areas than does the weight forward. The weight forward line feels awkward to me even after many years of casting both lines. As the line extends past the taper, it feels as if there's a dead weight at the end of the line, rather than a continuous weight throughout.

I don't want the beginners in my fly fishing classes to start by casting great distances. I don't want them to sacrifice line control for distance. I don't want them to fish very far away from themselves in the stream. A long cast may impress friends and fishermen, but it won't catch more fish, at least not in the beginning.

In addition, the double taper is the most economical tapered line, since it can be reversed. This is important to most beginners since they have a large initial investment to make and since they are more likely to make mistakes that can damage a line.

It seems popular today for line companies to offer "beginner's lines". Although many of these are designed with beginner's casting problems in mind, some are simply the lower quality lines from a manufacturer. To me, the fly line is nearly as important as the fly rod. I'd recommend looking for a good bargain on a quality line rather than settling for a cheap line that will be frustrating to cast and that will probably be worn out in the first season or two.

Inexpensive and "beginner's" lines retail for $9-$13. You can order a Scientific Anglers AirCel Supreme double taper (or weight forward, if you're still not convinced) from Simon Peter, Hook & Hackle, Cabela's, or Bullard's for under $16. You can even find Ultra lines for around $23 by careful shopping. It's worth the extra money to have a good line. Spring for a Cortland, if you'd rather, but get a good line.

Fly line care. Unless you're getting one of the French silk lines from Blue Ribbon Flies, there's not a lot of line care that needs to be done. The most common need is for cleaning, and you'll find a number of accessories to help with that. All lines should be cleaned, but floating lines need regular cleaning. Clean them whenever they look dirty or show signs of sinking. A quick line cleaning should restore their normal buoyancy. It's simply a matter of removing the extra weight of the dirt.

Lines should never be cast without a leader, no matter how anxious you are to try out a new line. That can cause cracking. They should not be cast on gravel or concrete. If cast on grass, they should be cleaned afterwards.

Avoid any chemicals except line cleaner. This includes fly sprays, insect repellents, and any other new-fangled thing you may be carrying streamside.

If you feel a line has failed without due cause, contact the manufacturer. They will analyze the problem and tell you what they've found. If it's your fault, you'll know better next time. If it's theirs, they'll often replace the line.

A short history of fly lines. Fly lines used to be made of twisted horse hair. Eventually, someone began mixing silk with the horse hair, and that material gradually took over as the standard for years. After World War II, man-made materials took the forefront. Nylon became popular, and most recently, plastic-coated lines have dominated.

And a quote from antiquity. "I prefer quite a heavy braided silk line, which has been dressed in boiled linseed oil under an air-pump for some ten days, and then stretched moderately tight between supports in a dry place where the air is fresh and about sixty degrees. The superfluous oil should be wiped off with chamois leather as many as three or four times during the first week or so, and then allowed to dry naturally, till it is quite free from evaporation. This will require several weeks to harden, but must in no case be hurried."
—from *Guns, Ammunition, and Tackle*. Money, et al. MacMillan, London. 1912.

Choosing a fly line color. Fly lines are available in many decorator colors: lemon yellow, fluorescent lime, sky blue, snow white, ripe peach, chocolate brown, forest green, and nearly every other color that "art directors" at line companies can dream up.

This wild variety of hues may present a dilemma to the uninitiated fly fisherman. The fly line is such an obvious part of the act, arcing through the air above streams and riding the water currents, that its color must be important. With so many colors, the beginner might even imagine he needs several colors in each line to meet specific angling situations, maybe sun-kissed orange for sunny days or deep purple for nymphing.

So what is the best color for a fly line? As usual, there are two schools of thought about the issue. One suggests that it's wise to buy a line the angler can see. The other school argues that it's best to have a line that the fish can't see.

For floating lines used in dry fly fishing and in many nymph fishing situations in streams, I want a line I can see. In low light, it's often necessary to use the end of the line to judge where the fly is, and in any light a bright color lets me keep track of what nasty tricks the current is playing, without having to take my eye off the fly itself. Nymphing often requires watching the tip of the line for movement. A bright color, whatever it might be, is better.

At the same time, a line floating on the water probably looks the same to fish no matter what color it is. It appears as a dark line in the surface film. Since there's no direct light source from beneath the water, it's unlikely that the fish can tell a mauve from an emerald line. And either one, or battleship gray, for that matter, will often scare fish. That's one reason we use leaders.

For sinking lines, I'll stick to the second school of thought. Under the water's surface, color is more visible to the fish, and grays, blacks, browns, and dark greens can be more easily ignored in that element. Fluorescent lime cannot. When I use a sinking line in lakes for nymphing and in streams for streamer fishing, I rely on feeling the hit rather than seeing it. A bright color has no advantage over a dull color. The first underwater camo line should be out any time now.

The choice of specific colors, however, is up to you, and indeed, it may "say" something about you. As for me, my current floating lines are peach-colored. That's about as trendy as I want to be. (If you ask me, fluorescent colors are a passing fad having something to do with new wave haircuts and break dancing.) My sinking line is dark green, and I try to imagine it looks like a string of water weed trailing through the current.

The best thing is to pick a line on some other basis than color. If the line you want comes in more than one shade, pick the one that will look best with your favorite fishing shirt.

FLY LINES

Berkley Specialist Lines

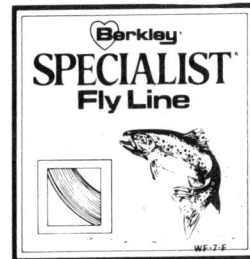

Berkley produces a series of fly lines that retail for about $15. They must be described by price first, because these lines are not the same quality that you'll find in Cortland 444s and Scientific Anglers AirCel Supremes. Those lines, however, are $8-$10 higher.

You must understand that Berkley's main thrust is not fly fishing, and they aim for the beginner's market. As a beginner's line, these are okay. You may also wish to purchase a special use line in an economical brand such as Berkley.

My main objection to the lines is their stiffness and their retention of coiling. This trait is especially evident in cold weather and cold water (both of which we have a lot of in Colorado). They shoot well, probably because of the stiffness, but you must continually stretch them to keep coils from catching on guides.

All of this is given as warning. You won't get a 444 for $15 by buying a Berkley, but nobody is really saying you will, including Berkley. You may have a Berkley line right now. There have been two years of promotional sales on the lines. The first year there was a $10 rebate, and I got a line for $2.88. Last year, Berkley gave away a reel with every line. I don't quite understand these giveaways, but there are now a lot of people, many of them beginners, who have a Berkley reel and line.

In addition to the catalogs listed here, you'll find Berkley lines in discount stores. (Note: In addition to the lines listed here, Berkley also offers a weight forward sinking and a shooting taper sinking. Neither line is offered by catalog companies.)

Specialist. *Double taper floating; DT3F-DT10F; 90';
colors: ivory, fl. yellow, fl. orange.*
$11.75-$16.95 AnW, Fol, Cus, Tac
Specialist. *Weight forward floating; WF4F-WF10F; 90';
colors: ivory, fl. yellow, fl. orange.*
$13.30-$16.95 Fol, Tac, Cus
Specialist Blunt Tip. *Bass bug/saltwater weight forward
floating; WF7F-WF11F; 90'; color: ivory.*
$15.50 Cus
Specialist Sinking Tip. *Weight forward floating/sink tip;
WF5F/S-WF10F/S; sink rate: "extra fast"; 90'(10' sink
tip); color: yellow floating, brown sinking.*
$16.95 Tac

Specialist Sinking. *Double taper sinking; DT5S-DT10S; sink rate: "extra fast"; 90'; color: deep brown.*
$11.75-$16.95 AnW, Tac

Cortland Lines

An unimposing factory in New York turns out what many consider to be the finest fly lines made. Quality control on the lines is faultless, and the company continues to make advancements in line design.

The newest line in Cortland's offerings is the 444SL. It features a coating that gives the line extra stiffness for distance casting. There is a fine line (so to speak) to be drawn in making a fly line that is supple enough to move and shoot properly yet stiff enough that it does not sag in the guides. Most of us have had lines that were too stiff. These are usually cheaper lines. They coil up on themselves like snakes in love. They don't shoot well because they catch on the guides and coils catch fingers and reels.

With that background, it's to be forgiven if the only thing the typical fly fisherman looks for in a fly line is suppleness. But a line can be too supple and lose its integrity as it moves through the guides and into the casting motions. Cortland's 444SL is an attempt, and a successful one, to add stiffness without producing a line that will coil and catch.

The Cortland line begins with the economy 333HT series. The top quality lines are the 444 and 444SL. Cortland protects the prices on its top lines, so don't expect any bargains except the quality your investment will mean. I consider Cortland lines to be the most durable on the market.

I've listed the lines by type. In sinking and sink tip lines, Cortland uses a numbering system to designate sink rates. The 444 lines are available through selected catalog companies and Cortland Pro Shops. The 333 lines are available in discount stores.

Cortland Floating Lines

333HT. *Double taper floating; DT4F-DT10F; 90'; colors: medium green, hot yellow, white.*
$11.49-$15 T&T, Cab

333HT Rocket Taper. *Weight forward floating; WF5F-WF9F; 105'; colors: medium green, hot yellow, white.*
$11.49-$15 T&T, Cab

333HT Bug/Saltwater. *Special weight forward floating; WF7F-WF11F; 105'; colors: medium green, hot yellow, white.*
$11.49 Cab

444. *Double taper floating; DT3F-DT10F; 90'; colors: peach, fl. red.*
$26 Many catalogs

444 Rocket Taper. *Weight forward floating; WF4F-WF11F; 105'; colors: peach, fl. red.*
$26 Many catalogs

444 Nymph Tip. *Weight forward floating; WF4F-WF9F; 105'; color: peach with 6" red/orange strike indicator.*
$27 Kau, Edd, Cus, Bob, Dan, Tac, Bud, Hig, Pen, Mer, Fly, Nor

444 Bug Taper. *Special weight forward floating; WF7F-WF10F; 105'; color: peach.*
$26 Mer, Nor, Hun, AnR, Fly, Cab, Hig, Tac, Edd

444. *Shooting taper floating; ST6F-ST11F; 30' (with factory spliced loop); color: peach.*
$13 Kau, Mer, Cab, Edd

444 Running Line. *Running line floating; diameter: .031"; 100'; color: peach.*
$8.50-$9 Mer, T&T, Kau

444SL. *Double taper floating; DT4F-DT9F; 90'; color: fl. mint green.*
$30 Pen, Mer, Hun, AnR, Hig, Bud, Dan, RLW, T&T, Bob, Edd, Nor, Cus, Kau

444SL Rocket Taper. *Weight forward floating; WF4F-WF12F; 105'; color: fl. mint green.*
$30 Many catalogs

444SL Saltwater Taper. *Special weight forward floating; WF7F-WF12F; 105'; color: fl. mint green.*
$30 Nor, Edd, T&T, Fly, AnR, Hun, Mer, Kau

Cortland Sink Tip Lines

333HT. *Double taper floating/sink tip; DT4F/S-DT9F/S; sink rate: 3.5"-4.5"/sec.; 90'; color: green floating, dark green sinking.*
$21 (often discounted) Retail stores

333HT Rocket Taper. *Weight forward floating/sink tip; WF5F/S-WF11F/S; sink rate: 3.5"-4.5"/sec.; 105'; color: green floating, dark green sinking.*
$21 (often discounted) Retail stores

444 #3. *Double taper floating/sink tip; DT5F/S-DT10F/S; sink rate: 3.5"-4.5"/sec.; 90'(10' sink tip); color: peach floating, brown sinking.*
$27 Kau, Pen, Edd, Bob, Mer, Hun, Dan, T&T, Tac

444 Rocket Taper #1. *Weight forward floating/sink tip; WF5F/S-WF9F/S; sink rate: 1.25"-1.75"/sec.; 105'(10' sink tip); color: peach floating, green sinking.*
$27 Mer, Hig, Cus

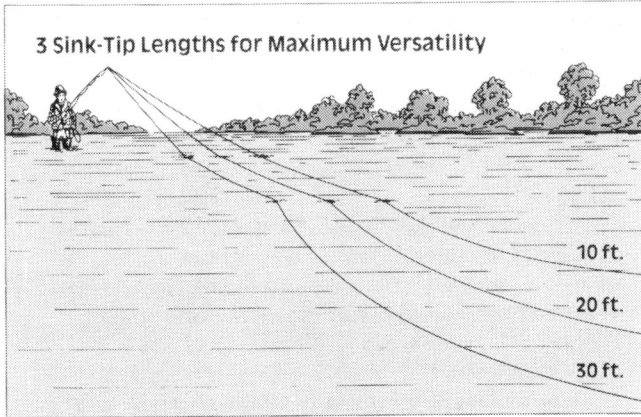

3 Sink-Tip Lengths for Maximum Versatility

444 Rocket Taper #3-10'. *Weight forward floating/sink tip; WF4F/S-WF11F/S; sink rate: 3.5"-4.5"/sec.; 105'(10' sink tip); color: peach floating, brown sinking.*
$27 Kau, Bob, Edd, Hig, Bud, Dan, T&T, Cab, Tac, Fly, AnR, Hun, Mer, Pen
444 Rocket Taper #3-20'. *Weight forward floating/sink tip; WF5F/S-WF11F/S; sink rate: 3.5"-4.5"/sec.; 105'(20' sink tip); color: peach floating, brown sinking.*
$27 Cab, T&T, Nor, Mer, Kau
444 Rocket Taper #3-30'. *Weight forward floating/sink tip; WF6F/S-WF11F/S; sink rate: 3.5"-4.5"/sec.; 105'(30' sink head); color: peach floating, brown sinking.*
$27 T&T, Mer, Kau, Nor
444SL Rocket Taper. *Weight forward floating/sink tip; WF5F/S-WF9F/S; sink rate: 3.5"-4.5"/sec.; 105'(10' sink tip); color: fl. mint green floating, brown sinking (it'll remind you of mint chocolate chip ice cream).*
$30 Mer, Cus, Edd, Dan, Bud, Hig, Fly, AnR, Kau

Cortland Intermediate Sinking Lines

444 Rocket Taper. *Weight forward intermediate sinking; WF5I-WF12I; sink rate: 1.15"-1.5"/sec.; 105'; color: ice blue.*
$26 Mer, AnR, Hun, Kau, T&T
444 Saltwater Taper. *Special weight forward intermediate sinking; WF7I-WF13I; sink rate: 1.15"-1.5"/sec.; 105'; color: ice blue.*
$26 Kau, Mer, Nor, Fly, Hun
444 Shooting Taper. *Shooting taper intermediate sinking; ST7I-ST12I; sink rate: 1.15"-1.5"/sec.; 30'(with factory spliced loop); color: ice blue.*
$13 Mer, Nor

Cortland Sinking Lines

333HT. *Double taper sinking; DT5S-DT9S; sink rate: 2.5"-3"/sec.; 90'; color: dark green.*
$11.49 Cab
333HT Rocket Taper Fast Sink. *Weight forward sinking; WF5S-WF9S; sink rate: 2.5"-3"/sec.; 105'; color: dark green.*
$19 (often discounted) retail stores

333HT Rocket Taper Extra Fast Sink. *Weight forward sinking; WF6S-WF11S; sink rate: 3.5"-4"/sec.; 105'; color: dark green.*
$19 (often discounted) retail stores
333HT Shooting Taper. *Shooting taper sinking; ST6S-ST11S; sink rate: 2.5"-3"/sec.; 30'; color: dark green.*
$10.50 (often discounted) retail stores
444 #2. *Double taper sinking; DT5S-DT9S; sink rate: 2.5"-3"/sec.; 90'; color: medium brown.*
$26 Tac, Mer
444 #3. *Double taper sinking; DT6S-DT11S; sink rate: 3.5"-4"/sec.; 90'; color: dark brown.*
$26 T&T, Hun, Mer, Kau
444 Rocket Taper #1. *Weight forward sinking; WF5S-WF12S; sink rate: 1.25"-1.75"/sec.; 105'; color: light brown.*
$26 Bud, Mer, Edd
444 Rocket Taper #2. *Weight forward sinking; WF5S-WF11S; sink rate: 2.5"-3"/sec.; 105'; color: medium brown.*
$26 Mer, Hig, Nor, Bud, Cab, Tac, Edd
444 Rocket Taper #3. *Weight forward sinking; WF5S-WF11S; sink rate: 3.5"-4"/sec.; 105'; color: dark brown.*
$26 Kau, Edd, Cus, Bob, Cab, T&T, Bud, Dan, Hig, Mer, Hun
444 Rocket Taper #4. *Weight forward sinking; WF6S-WF12S; sink rate: 4.25"-5"/sec.; 105'; color: very dark brown.*
$26 Fly, Nor, Hig, T&T, Cab, Edd, Kau, Mer, Hun
444 #1. *Shooting taper sinking; ST8S-ST11S; sink rate: 1.25"-1.75"/sec.; 30'; color: light brown.*
$13 Mer, Fly
444 #2. *Shooting taper sinking; ST6S-ST11S; sink rate: 2.5"-3"/sec.; 30'; color: medium brown.*
$13 Mer, Nor, Fly, Cab
444 #3. *Shooting taper sinking; ST6S-ST12S; sink rate: 3.5"-4"/sec.; 30'; color: dark brown.*
$13 Mer, Fly, Hig, Dan, Cab, Bob, Edd, Cus, Kau
444 #4. *Shooting taper sinking; ST7S-ST12S; sink rate: 4.25"-5"/sec.; 30'; color: very dark brown.*
$13 Kau, Mer, Nor, Fly, Bud, T&T, Edd
Kerboom. *Lead core shooting taper; 450 and 550 grains; sink rate: would beat Lusitania down; colors: 450—green; 550—red.*
$12 Mer, Bud, Nor, T&T, Kau
Lead Core. *Open stock level lead core; 13 grains/foot; sink rate: see Kerboom; length: pick your own; color: gray.*
$.06/foot Mer

French Silk Lines

If you find something lacking in all the plastic-coated miracles of modern chemistry in this chapter, here's a bit of relief for you. Blue Ribbon Flies of West Yellowstone offers an authentic silk line in double taper, sizes 4-7.

How a silk line from France found its way to Montana is a mystery. You might expect such a line to be offered by Thomas & Thomas, but not by Blue Ribbon Flies. Anyway, a break from talk of microspheres and special coatings is welcome. This is an opportunity to escape back to the time of tweeds and gentle folk with cane rods.

Meanwhile, this sounds like a very nice line. In their catalog, the Mathews call the French line "the best casting line" they've used. (Could they be suggesting that the wonders of modern living aren't all they're cracked up to be? If so, I often agree. How about a greenheart rod in the next catalog?)

According to the catalog, the lines do not require drying after each use. For given weights, the lines are smaller in diameter than plastic lines, making them less air resistant, a plus in the wind. The tips are extra long allowing for trimming to exact weights.

The lines require dressing three times a day while breaking them in and about twice a day thereafter, but the process only takes a moment or two. The line can be left untreated for use with nymphs. The silk lines are stiff until broken in, so be prepared to spend some time working with the line to develop suppleness. (Things worked for are more appreciated than things bought pre-packaged.)

If you've been looking for a silk line for that antique rod and reel, you're in luck. So are the rest of us who might forget where we came from. Thanks, Blue Ribbon.

French Silk. *Double taper floating (if dressed), intermediate (if not), sinking (after a day's fishing without line dressing); DT4F-DT7F; length: n/a; color: n/a.*
$65 Blue Ribbon Flies, Box 1037, West Yellowstone, Montana 59758

Gudebrod Fly Lines

Gudebrod, better known for their rod building finishes and supplies, also makes a fly line. It's offered through Reed's.

G-5. *Double taper floating; DT4F-DT10F; 90'.*
$19.50-$20 Ree
G-5. *Weight forward floating; WF4F-WF10F; 90'.*
$19.50-$20 Ree

Orvis Lines

The pale green color that is the signature of Orvis fly lines has been on our streams and lakes for many, many years. I'd guess that it was with some reluctance that Orvis added another color, fluorescent yellow, but it's now popular enough that it's easily recognized as an Orvis line, too.

Orvis carries only top quality lines, manufactured to their taper and color specifications by Scientific Anglers. On all the lines that will take one an epoxy connection and 12" of butt material have been added. This saves you the agonies of a nail knot and provides the smoothest line/leader connection available. Since Orvis charges $4

for the same type of splice to be added between line and backing, you can assume the service adds about that much to the cost of the line.

Besides the traditional lines, Orvis offers two lines that are worthy of extra description here. The "SSS" lines are floating lines designed for saltwater, salmon, and steelhead fishing where long casts are required all day long. The finish on these lines is harder to reduce friction and slack in the line as it goes through the guides. In addition to a shorter front taper, the line has a longer belly to enable the caster to keep more line in the air. The line is longer overall (107') than other lines, too.

The Orvis Shooting Head is a high-density sinking head, 30' in length, attached to a floating running line, 100' in length. The lines are attached with an epoxy connection.

As an additional note, the Hy-Flote lines are similar to Scientific Anglers Ultra lines. They feature the line coating that repels water. The lines stay up nicely on the water and are very supple.

Orvis. *Double taper floating; DT3F-DT11F; 82'; color: pale green.*
$26 Orv
Orvis. *Weight forward floating; WF3F-WF12F; 82'; colors: pale green, fl. yellow.*
$26 Orv
Hy-Flote. *Double taper floating; DT2F-DT11F; 90'; color: pale fl. yellow.*
$35 Orv
Hy-Flote. *Weight forward floating; WF3F-WF12F; 90'; color: pale fl. yellow.*
$35 Orv
"SSS". *Special taper weight forward floating; WF5F-WF12F; 107'; color: pale blue.*
$27.50 Orv
Orvis. *Weight forward floating/sink tip; WF4F/S-WF12F/S; sink rate: 1 ½"-2 ½"/sec.; 82'(10' sink tip); color: tan floating, dark brown sinking.*
$26 Orv
Hy-Flote. *Weight forward floating/sink tip; WF5F/S-WF12F/S; sink rate: 3 ½"-5 ½"/sec.; 90'(15' sink tip); color: pale fl. yellow floating, dark brown sinking.*
$42 Orv
Orvis. *Weight forward intermediate sinking; WF3I-WF13I; sink rate: 1"-1 ½"/sec.; 3-7—82', 8-13—107'; color: amber.*
$27.50 Orv
Orvis Fast Sinking. *Weight forward sinking; WF5S-WF12S; sink rate: 2"-3"/sec.; 82'; color: dark green.*
$22.50 Orv
Orvis Super Fast Sinking. *Weight forward sinking; WF6S-WF12S; sink rate: 3 ½"-5 ½"/sec.; 82'; color: dark brown.*
$30 Orv
Orvis Shooting Head. *Shooting taper sinking; ST8S-ST12S; sink rate: 2 ½"-4"/sec.; 130' (30' shooting taper,*

100' floating running line); color: dark brown with white running line.
$30 Orv

Rodon Borkast Lines

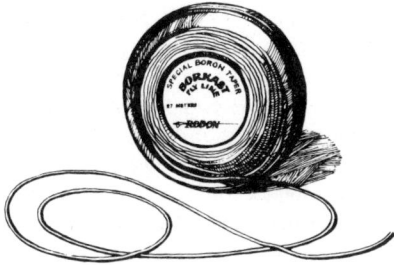

Rodon's Borkast lines were specially developed for use with boron/graphite rods (specifically their own rods, of course). They decided that the new rod material did not cast as well as it might with traditional line tapers, so they designed their own.

A double taper line, for instance, will not shoot line as well as a weight forward line, and one of the strengths of boron/graphite rods is distance casting. But, according to Rodon, traditional weight forward lines also did not perform well with the faster rods. The long level section at the front of a weight forward could not hold the tight loop required for good presentations at a short distance and it collapsed at longer distances. In addition (and here's one that I consider true for any rod), the 30' front taper overpowers the level section and makes delicate presentations difficult at longer distances.

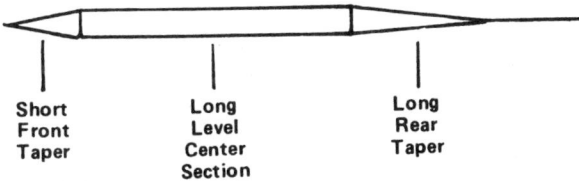

| Short Front Taper | Long Level Center Section | Long Rear Taper |

So, Rodon redesigned the weight forward line. They eliminated the level section in the front taper and created a continuous taper to the line point. They shortened the front taper for quicker turn-over. Then they increased the length of the center level section from about 15' to over 30' and added a longer rear taper. This gives the Borkast line a forward section of about 52' before running line is encountered.

If you've experienced the casting difficulties described here, you might give this new taper a try, especially if you are a distance caster. The lines are made for Rodon by Scientific Anglers, so you can be assured of quality. The lines are available from catalogs or directly from Rodon. Their address is listed in the chapter on rods.

Borkast. *Special weight forward floating; WF3F-*
WF14F; 88½'; color: light gray.
3-9—$24.95-$27.50; 10-14—$24.95-$30.50 Kau, Don, RLW
Borkast Long Haul. *Special shooting taper floating; ST6F-ST12F; 36'-44'; color: light gray.*
6-10—$14; 11-12—$15.50 Kau
Borkast Shooting Line. *Running line floating; diameters: .030" (for line weights 6-9), .035" (10-14); 98'; color: light gray.*
.030"—$9.75; .035"—$12 Kau
Borkast Sink Tip. *Special weight forward floating/sink tip; WF5F/S-WF12F/S; sink rate: 3½"-4½"/sec.; 88½'(10' sink tip); color: light gray floating, neutral gray sinking.*
$24.95-$30.50 Kau, Don
Borkast Sinking. *Special weight forward sinking; WF5S-WF14S; sink rate: 3½"-4½"/sec.; 88½'; color: medium neutral gray.*
5-10—$27.50; 11-14—$30.50 Kau
Borkast Long Haul. *Shooting taper sinking; ST6S-ST14S; sink rate: n/a; 36'-46'; color: medium gray.*
6-10—$14; 11-14—$15.50 Kau
Borkast Shooting Line. *Running line sinking; diameter: .035" (for line weights 10-14); 98'; color: medium neutral gray.*
$12 Kau

Scientific Anglers Lines

Scientific Anglers has been making quality fly lines since before my time . . . 1945 to be exact. Their catalog now offers 250 different lines.

In 1954, S/A introduced the first "modern" fly line, utilizing plastic coating filled with microspheres of air. Those lines were named AirCel. Seven years later, they improved that line by perfecting a coating with even more air trapped in it. That was dubbed AirCel Supreme.

Most recently, the AirCel Ultra hit the market. The company has heralded it as a "new technology" in fly lines. They claim that the chemical formulation of the coating actually repels water. This feature should make the line float higher, thus aiding in picking up and mending line.

Although the Ultra lines cost as much as $9 more than the comparable style and size in AirCel Supreme, the lines are selling well. They seem to float and shoot with the best of the lines I've used, but whether they are worth 40% more in initial cost will depend on their durability.

One thing you can have confidence in is the company's reputation for taking care of people who experience problems with their lines. When I was a youngster at the sport, I had an AirCel crack within a few months. I sent it back to S/A, and they replaced it. The kicker is that it was my fault. I had used a loop in the line to attach my leader. That loop had put excessive strain on the material near the end of the line. That was all explained to me in a very kind letter accompanying the new line. I got good service from the new line after I learned the nail knot.

S/A also makes a line they call Concept. It is an economical line designed for the beginner. It features a shorter front taper than conventional lines. That is supposed to help the beginner with his line control during casting. The lines are also short, 57', which will not work well for the experienced fly fisherman but should be plenty long for those first years of fishing.

Cortland is the only other line that comes close to S/A in popularity, and because distribution of Cortland lines is limited to authorized dealers, S/A lines are offered in more catalogs than any other. Their prices are not controlled, as Cortland's are, so you can get a bargain by shopping around. You may even find S/A lines, especially the Concept, in discount stores. The price range given here represents the prices found in the catalogs listed. Keep in mind that line prices do not vary by weight, except in specialized lines such as the Deepwater Express.

Scientific Anglers Floating Lines

Concept. *Double taper floating; DT5F-DT8F; 57'; color: yellow.*
$8.30-$11.95 H&H, Fly, Mer, Cor, Cus, Tac, Let
Concept. *Weight forward floating; WF5F-WF8F; 57'; color: yellow.*
$7.75-$9.10 Mer, Fol, H&H, Cor, Cus, Tac, Let
AirCel. *Double taper floating; DT4F-DT9F; 82'; colors: white, pale green.*
$13-$22.50 Dan, Cor, Sim, Ran, EJH, Cus, Edd, Tac, Mer, Fol, Hun, H&H
AirCel. *Weight forward floating; WF5F-WF9F; 82'; colors: white, pale green.*
$13-$22.50 Mer, Edd, Cus, EJH, Ran, Sim, Cor, Dan, Fol, H&H, Hun
AirCel Bass Bug. *Special weight forward floating; WF6F-WF9F; 82'; colors: pale green, fl. orange.*
$13.25-$27 H&H, Hun, Hig, Kau, Mer, Bul, LLB, Tac, Edd, Cus, Mur, Sim, Cor
AirCel. *Shooting taper floating; ST7F-ST10F; 30'; color: white.*

$8.85-$14 Hun, H&H, Cor, Sim, Don, Cus, Edd, Tac, Mer, Kau, Dal
AirCel Shooting Line. *Running line floating; diameter: .029"; 100'; colors: pale green, fl. orange.*
$5.55-$9.50 Dal, Pen, Dan, Edd, Tac, Cab, Don, Cor, Hun, H&H, Bud, Fly, Fol, Kau, Mer
AirCel Supreme. *Double taper floating; DT3F-DT11F; 82'; colors: ivory, mahogany, fl. orange, fl. yellow (availablility of colors depends on line weight).*
$15-$26 Most catalogs
AirCel Supreme. *Weight forward floating; WF4F-WF10F; 82'; colors: ivory, mahogany, fl. orange, fl. yellow.*
$15-$26 Most catalogs
AirCel Supreme Saltwater. *Special weight forward floating; WF8F-WF13F; 82'; colors: ivory, non-glare gray.*
$15-$27 Kau, RLW, Dan, Fol, Hun, H&H, Mer, Dal, Tac, Cab, Let, Bul, Cus, Don, Cor
AirCel Ultra. *Double taper floating; DT3F-DT11F; 82'; colors: buckskin tan, sunrise orange.*
$21.45-$31.50 Most catalogs
AirCel Ultra. *Weight forward floating; WF3F-WF11F; 82'; colors: buckskin tan, sunrise orange.*
$19.95-$31.50 Most catalogs
AirCel Ultra Bass Bug. *Special weight forward floating; WF6F-WF13F; 82'; color: buckskin tan.*
$21.98-$30 Fly, Hun, Don, Mur, Cus, Edd, Tac, Cab, T&T, Mer, Kau, H&H, Pen
AirCel Ultra Saltwater. *Special weight forward floating; WF8F-WF13F; 82'; color: gray.*
$21.98-$30 Pen, Hun, H&H, Don, Cus, Edd, Dal, Fly, Kau, Mer

Scientific Anglers Sink Tip Lines

AirCel Wet Tip. *Double taper floating/sink tip; DT4F/S-DT8F/S; sink rate: 1½"-2"/sec.; 82'(10' sink tip); color: two-tone green.*
$15.70-$25.50 Dan, Kau, Mer, H&H, Dal, Hun, Cor, Ran, Don, EJH, Cus, Edd, Tac
AirCel Wet Tip. *Weight forward floating/sink tip; WF5F/S-WF10F/S; sink rate: 1½"-2"/sec.; 82'(10' sink tip); color: two-tone green.*
$14.75-$25.50 Kau, Sim, Ran, Don, Cab, Tac, Edd, Cus, EJH, Mer, H&H, Dan, Dal, Fly, Hun
AirCel Wet Tip Hi-D. *Weight forward floating/sink tip; WF5F/S-WF10F/S; sink rate: 2½"-4¼"/sec.; 82'(10' sink tip); color: yellow floating, dark green or orange sinking.*
$15-$25.50 Most catalogs
AirCel Wet Tip Hi-D Bass Bug/Saltwater. *Special weight forward floating/sink tip; WF7F/S-WF13F/S; sink rate: 2½"-4¼"/sec.; 82'(10' sink tip); color: yellow floating, dark green sinking.*
$15-$25 Fol, H&H, Dal, Hig, Kau, Cor, Don, Cus, Tac, Cab, Bul, Hun

AirCel Wet Belly Hi-D. *Weight forward floating/sink tip; WF7F/S-WF10F/S; sink rate: 3"-4"/sec.; 82'(20' sink tip); color: yellow floating, dark green sinking.*
$15.70-$23 Kau, Dal, Hun, Dan, Hig, H&H, Cus, Tac, Cab, Mer, Fly

AirCel Wet Head Hi-D. *Weight forward floating/sink tip; WF7F/S-WF10F/S; sink rate: 3¼"-4¼"/sec.; 82'(30' sink tip); color: yellow floating, dark green sinking.*
$15.70-$24 Cus, Tac, Dan, Dal, Mer, Bud, Kau, Hun, H&H

AirCel Ultra Wet Tip Hi-D. *Weight forward floating/sink tip; WF5F/S-WF10F/S; sink rate: 2½"-4¼"/sec.; 82'(10' sink tip); color: sunrise orange floating, dark green sinking.*
$21.98-$33.35 Fly, Mer, Dan, Pen, H&H, Cus, Let, LLB, Bud

AirCel Ultra Wet Tip Hi-Speed Hi-D. *Weight forward floating/sink tip; WF5F/S-WF10F/S; sink rate: 3¾"-5¼"/sec.; 82'(10' sink tip); color: buckskin tan floating, gray sink tip.*
$19.95-$33.35 Most catalogs

Scientific Anglers Intermediate Sinking Lines

WetCel. *Double taper intermediate sinking; DT4I-DT10I; sink rate: 1¼"-1¾"/sec.; 82'; color: kelly green.*
$15.10-$18.80 H&H, Mer, Cus, Edd, Tac

WetCel. *Weight forward intermediate sinking; WF5I-WF13I (weights 11-13 are Saltwater Taper); sink rate: 1½"-1¾"/sec.; 82'; color: kelly green.*
$14.95-$21 Hig, Mer, Fly, H&H, Kau, Bul, Cus, Cab, Tac, Edd

Scientific Anglers Sinking Lines

Concept. *Special weight forward sinking; WF5S-WF8S; sink rate: n/a; 57'; color: green.*
$8.30-$11 H&H, Cor, Let

WetCel I. *Double taper sinking; DT5S-DT10S; sink rate: 1¾"-2½"/sec.; 82'; color: medium green.*
$15.10-$21 Pfe, H&H, Dan, Mer, Kau, Cus, Tac

WetCel I. *Weight forward sinking; WF5S-WF10S; sink rate: 1¾"-2½"/sec.; 82'; color: medium green.*
$14.95-$21 Fly, Dan, Pfe, Kau, H&H, Cus, Tac, Cab, Mer

WetCel I. *Shooting taper sinking; ST7S-ST11S; sink rate: 1¾"-2½"/sec.; 30'; color: medium green.*
$9.25-$12 Cus, Tac, Fly, H&H, Mer, Kau

WetCel II. *Double taper sinking; DT4S-DT11S; sink rate: 2"-3"/sec.; 82'; color: dark green.*
$14.10-$24.50 Many catalogs

WetCel II. *Weight forward sinking; WF4S-WF12S; sink rate: 2"-3"/sec.; 82'; color: dark green.*
$14.10-$24.50 Most catalogs

WetCel II. *Shooting taper sinking; ST6S-ST11S; sink rate: 2"-3"/sec.; 30'; color: dark green.*
$8.95-$13.50 Kau, Dan, Bud, Fly, Cus, Edd, Tac, Cab, H&H, Hun

WetCel Hi-D. *Double taper sinking; DT7S-DT10S; sink rate: 3¼"-4¼"/sec.; 82'; color: greenish black.*
$15.10-$24.50 Hun, H&H, Dal, Ran, Cus, Edd

WetCel Hi-D. *Weight forward sinking; WF6S-WF10S; sink rate: 3¼"-4¼"/sec.; 82'; color: greenish black.*
$14.95-$24.50 Dan, Hig, Fly, Kau, Dal, H&H, Cab, Tac, Edd, Sim, Ran, Cus, Pen, Mer, Hun

WetCel Hi-D. *Shooting taper sinking; ST7S-ST11S; sink rate: 3¼"-4¼"/sec.; 30'; color: greenish black.*
$8.85-$14 Hun, Dan, Mer, Hig, Sim, Edd, Cus, Cab, H&H, Fly, Kau

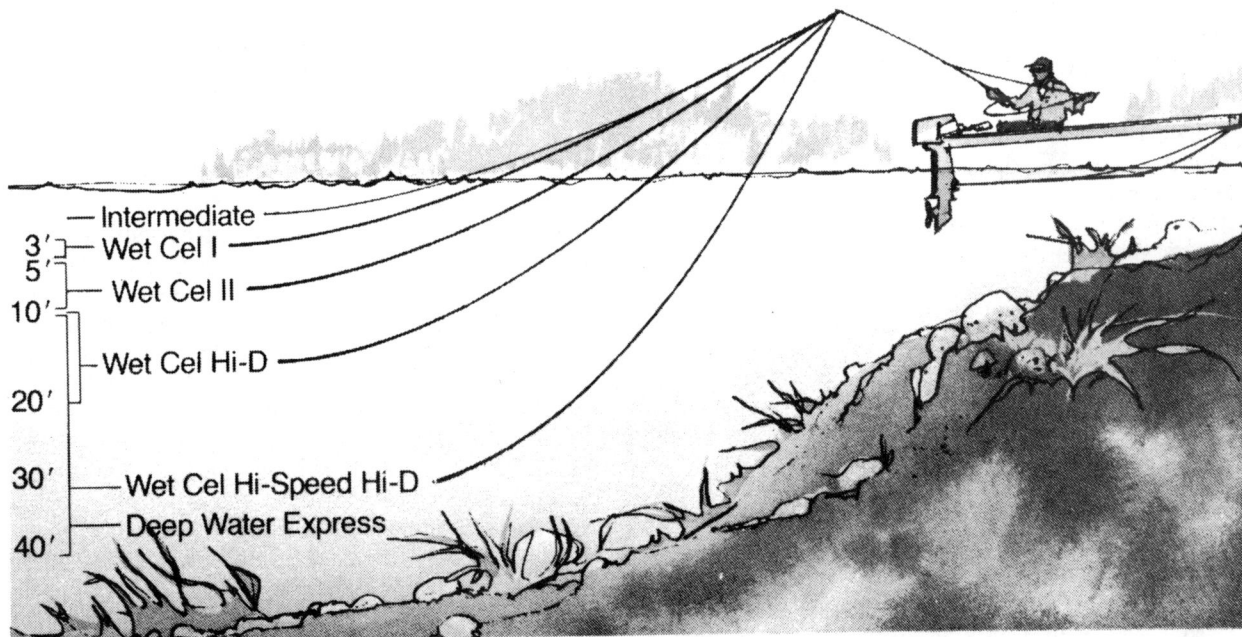

Intermediate
3' — Wet Cel I
5' — Wet Cel II
10' — Wet Cel Hi-D
20'
30' — Wet Cel Hi-Speed Hi-D
40' — Deep Water Express

WetCel Hi-Speed Hi-D. *Weight forward sinking; WF6S-WF13S; sink rate: 3¾"-6½"/sec.; 36'; color: gray.* $17-$29.50 Dan, Bud, Kau, H&H, Hun, Fly, Ran, Cus, Edd, Cab, Bul, Fol, Hig, Mer
WetCel Hi-Speed Hi-D. *Shooting taper sinking; ST6S-ST15S; sink rate: 3¾"-6½"/sec.; 30'; color: gray.* $9.85-$15 Many catalogs
Deep Water Express. *Tapered sinking; 550, 700, and 850 grains; sink rate: 7"-10"/sec (550—7"-8"; 700—8"-9"; 850—9"-10"); 30' (lines can be cut for different weights); color: 550—light gray; 700—brown; 850—black.* $12-$17.95 (Note: In some catalogs, price depends on weight.) Cus, Edd, Ste, Fly, Kau, Dan, Bud, H&H, Mer

Shakespeare Sigma Lines

Shakespeare makes an economy beginner's line that competes with Berkley Specialist, S/A Concept, and Cortland 333HT.

It's only offered by one catalog, Custom Fishing Tackle, but you may also run across it in discount stores and sporting goods shops. The lines come in a plastic box suitable for use as a fly box.

The one notable line here is the Mono-Core, a heavyweight line with a nylon polymer core. The core adds stiffness, which should give the line greater casting distance.

Sigma. *Double taper floating; DT4F-DT10F; 90'; colors: white, fl. green.* $13.95 Cus
Sigma. *Weight forward floating; WF5F-WF10F; 90'; colors: white, fl. green.* $13.95 Cus
Sigma Mono-Core. *Weight forward floating; WF10F-WF12F; 105'; color: white.* $20.65 Cus
Sigma. *Weight forward floating/sink tip; WF5F/S-WF10F/S; 105'; color: fl. green floating, black sinking.* $13.95 Cus
Sigma. *Double taper sinking; DT5S-DT10S; sink rate: n/a; 90'; color: black.* $13.15 Cus
Sigma. *Weight forward sinking; WF5S-WF9S; sink rate: n/a; 90'; color: black.* $13.15 Cus

Teeny Nymphline

Jim Teeny has made his way in the fly fishing world by catching a lot of big trout on nymphs, mainly those of his own creation, the Teeny Nymph. It follows that his Nymphlines are designed for fishing with nymphs, as well as wet flies and streamers.

The Teeny Mini-Tip is a weight forward with a short (5') sink tip merged to a level floating line. This unique design makes it ideal for fishing nymphs in small stream

pocket water where a longer sink tip doesn't allow for line mending and control.

The Teeny Nymphlines feature a sinking head 24' long merged to 58' of 4-weight level floating line. There are two weights, 300 grain and 400 grain. The Teeny 300 is suitable for "stronger" rods made for 7- to 10-weights. The Teeny 400 is for rods using 8- to 12-weights.

The lines are made for Teeny by Scientific Anglers. They are available directly from Jim Teeny (Box 970, Gresham, Oregon 97030) or from Stewart Custom Tackle. Expect to see them in other catalogs soon.

Teeny Mini-Tip. *Weight forward floating/sink tip; WF6F/S-WF8F/S; sink rate: "very fast"; 82'(5' sink tip); color: n/a.* $29.95 Ste
Teeny 300, 400. *Special weight forward floating/sink head; 300 and 400 grains (see note above); sink rate: "fast"; 82'; color: n/a.* $29.95 Ste
Teeny Level. *Running line floating; one size fits all; 82'; color: n/a.* $7.95 Ste

Wulff's Triangle Taper Lines

The intrepid Lee Wulff has designed a refined weight forward line that may represent the best of both worlds, double taper and weight forward.

The lines are called Triangle Tapers. Unlike conventional weight forward tapers, they taper continuously from the tip to the point at which they drop to a running line. A typical weight forward tapers abruptly (in comparison) to a heavy level section and then drops to the running line.

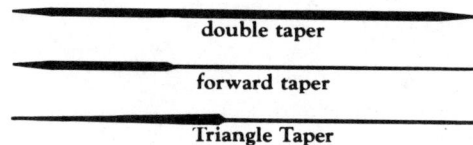

double taper

forward taper

Triangle Taper

The tapered head on the Triangle Tapers is 40', compared to about 30' on conventional weight forward lines. The continuous taper over a longer distance should give the lines a more delicate presentation. Line control should be enhanced at all distances, while the shooting qualities of a weight forward are retained. You should be able to roll cast this line up to 40' with as much ease or more than with a double taper line.

This sounds like an excellent fly line. With Lee Wulff's name behind it, you can be assured that it's been carefully thought out and fully tested. There's no gimmick here, just solid engineering and innovative design.

Presently the line is available in only three sizes: 4/5, 6/7, and 8/9. The double weights are unconventional, but they reflect, in part, the fact that many rods today are weighted using the same system. Also in the works is a Long Belly fly line, but no details were available.

Triangle Taper. *Special weight forward floating;
WF4/5F, WF6/7F, WF8/9F; 90'; color: white.*
$30 Wul
Long Belly. *Special weight forward floating; WF5F-
WF7F.*
$32 Pen, Wul

LEADERS

Now that fly lines do not require dressing and stretching, leaders use up more streamside fussing time than any other part of the fly fisherman's equipment. They are vital, the final link between angler and fly, and an angler's success depends heavily on his understanding and use of leaders.

If today's leaders require a lot of time and work, it's still nothing compared to the good old days. I quote from a book entitled *Guns, Ammunition, and Tackle* published in 1912:

"Most flies are tied on silkworm gut. It need hardly be said that this is the unspun gut of the *Bombyx mori* silkworm, and that the worm is taken when ready to make its cocoon and immersed in vinegar and the gut drawn out between pins, being allowed to dry and harden; after which it is boiled and the scale or outer skin drawn from it, usually through the teeth of the Murcian operator."

Today, it need hardly be said, we just go down to the fly shop and pick up a spool of leader material straight from a monofilament-making machine. Although some anglers yearn for the days of silk lines and greenhearts, few of them, if any, would return to the gut leader. It had to be kept wet to eliminate a natural stiffness, and it was not nearly as strong as monofilament.

In his wonderful *Standard Fishing Encyclopedia*, A.J. McClane gives comparative ratings of silkworm gut and nylon. A few examples of break points (in pounds): 2x, gut—1.8, nylon—7; 4x, gut—1.2, nylon—3.5; 6x, gut—.5, nylon—1.8. And nylon's break points have improved since this 1965 report.

Almost all leader material today is nylon, extruded to fine diameters by machines. The main source of leader material is European countries, notably France and West Germany. The exception on both counts is Aeon leader material, a Japanese product made of copolymers.

Leader types. Packaged leaders are of two varieties: knotted and continuous taper. Knotted leaders are constructed of lengths of level leader material. These begin with large diameters and decrease to small diameters. It's essential that a leader taper in this manner for the same reasons that it's essential that a fly line be tapered. Without the taper, a leader would not "turnover", i.e. would land in an uncontrollable pile.

Knotted leaders can be created with very exacting tapers. They have the advantage of an easily recognized tippet (leader end section). As you change flies, you know exactly what your tippet diameter is. You can restore the leader to its original length and tippet size at any time.

This is not so easy on continuous-taper leaders. Since the leader tapers uniformly, it takes a sharp eye or a leader micrometer to tell the exact size of your tippet. They do have a couple of advantages over knotted leaders, however.

One obvious advantage is the lack of knots that may fail. Not only may a knot be incorrectly tied, knots wear out leader material. There's a certain amount of hinging action at a knot. Over a period of time, this hinging will cause structural weakness in or near the knot. Although this is not a great problem with a properly tied leader, the smaller diameter knots should probably be re-tied occasionally.

Continuous-taper leaders have another advantage that makes them the choice of bass fishermen. There are no knots to catch moss and other water weeds.

Most fishermen use a tapered leader straight from the package, discarding it after fly changes have increased its tippet diameter. I was satisfied for many years with a system using a continuous-taper plus additional tippet material. I'd use the tippet of the leader down to the next size, then add a section of level tippet material that matched the original in size and length. This was largely an economy measure, and turnover is not perfect.

For trout fishing, I now prefer a knotted leader. Since they are sometimes difficult to find on the shelves, I've begun tying my own. You'll find leader kits listed in this section of the book, and if you should wish to tie your own, you should start with such a kit. It will give you leader recipes and a full selection of diameters.

With proper storage, a kit will last two or three years. I would suggest replacing the smaller diameters, 4x-7x, every year, since nylon deteriorates with time. That's one reason to avoid buying material from discount stores or from the sale bins at fly shops. It's probably old. Aeon material, interestingly, is not subject to the same deterioration, since it's not conventional nylon.

Leader length. Most fly fishing is done with leaders 7½'-9' in length. Remember that one of the jobs of the leader is to keep distance between the heavy line and the fly. In trout fishing, where you can count on the fish to be spooked by the fly line, a longer leader in this range is preferred. In bass fishing, where bass bugs are heavy and difficult to control, a shorter leader within the range of 7½'-9' is the choice.

Leaders less than 7½' are considered short. They have a few special uses, all of them for below-surface flies. Some people shorten the leader to as little as 3' or 4' when fishing streamers with a sink-tip or sinking line. This allows more direct contact with the fly and lets the line pull the streamer down to the desired depth. A method of nymph fishing also uses short leaders of 5' or 6'. Again, the same advantages are there.

Leaders over 9' are useful when casting over very spooky trout or fishing in low, slow water where even relaxed trout may be spooked by a line nearby. Some experienced casters regularly use leaders of 12' and sometimes extend them to 15'. Certain types of nymph fishing with a floating line also require leaders of this length.

In general, a beginner would be wise to use 7½' leaders for smaller streams and 9' leaders for lakes and larger rivers. Leaders shorter than 7½' and longer than 9' can come along in the repertoire as needed.

Tippet size. When you buy a packaged leader, you must select length and tippet size. The tippet size is the final diameter of the leader. The numbering system is somewhat confusing for beginners. Packaged leaders generally range from 2x to 6x, with the higher numbers being smaller diameters.

The "x-numbers" correspond to diameters according to the following scheme:

x-size	diameter
1x	.010″
2x	.009″
3x	.008″
4x	.007″
5x	.006″
6x	.005″
7x	.004″
8x	.003″

Since some manufacturers have not caught on to the x-numbers, you may have to remember which is which by diameter. That's easy enough if you can remember the Rule of 11. Subtract the number given in thousandths of an inch from 11 and you get the x-number. Example: .007″—subtract 7 from 11 = 4x.

The tippet size must match up to the kind of fishing you're doing and the size of fly you're using. Trout are notoriously "leader shy", especially with dry flies. Using too large a tippet diameter is the number one equipment problem for beginning trout fishermen. Most of them have graduated from bait or spin fishing or from warmwater fishing. Leader size is not as crucial in those sports.

The sign of too large a tippet diameter is the flash of a trout beneath the fly. Either the fly or the leader is too big. Start with a 5x leader for trout. If you're using a graphite rod and you've been fishing stouter leaders, you'll go through an adjustment period during which you break off flies when setting the hook, but at least you'll be getting strikes. After that adjustment period, you won't have any trouble with breakage under normal fishing. Bigger trout require some finesse, but I use 5x regularly on the Bighorn where the browns and 'bows weigh in over three pounds and the current is strong. I don't lose fish due to the fine leader (but I have a long list of other reasons).

With fidgety trout, 6x and even 7x can help. I'd leave the 8x trout for somebody who owns a fly factory.

The other factor here is fly size. Your tippet size must match your fly size. If you fish a small fly with a tippet too large, you won't get a proper presentation. Of course, there's also the problem of trying to get a 2x tippet through the eye of a #20 fly. If you fish a fly too large for the tippet, it will hinge on the knot and break off, sometimes without any provocation but always when The Big Brown rises to your fly.

So, here's another rule, the Rule of 4. Divide your fly size by 4 and you'll get the largest tippet you should use. Therefore, if you're fishing a #16 Adams, you should use a 4x (or finer) tippet. In their catalog, Orvis publishes this range of fly sizes for each tippet:

x-size	fly size
0x	1/0-2
1x	4-8
2x	6-10
3x	10-14
4x	12-16
5x	14-20
6x	18-24
7x	20-28

Working from tippet size to fly size, I can give you a rather flaky rule I'll call the Rule of 2+2. Take your tippet size and multiply by 2 and then add 2. That's the largest fly you should use on that tippet. With the same 4x tippet, then, you'll get 8 by multiplying and 10 by adding. That's the largest fly size for a 4x tippet that I'd recommend. This rule is not so crucial with heavier tippets (3x and heavier), and with light tippets (6x and lighter), it's better to add 4. (I told you the rule was flaky.)

Of course, these rules are only starting places for the fly fisherman. In reality, we are often called upon to break rules. Fishing the Green Drake hatch requires #8 dry flies, but it's done over trout that are wary (although less so during that hatch). Leaders of 4x and 5x are commonly used. When you use a finer leader than recommended for the fly size, you should re-tie knots frequently.

One caution is in order. If you fish extra-fine leaders, you'll have to play the fish more carefully and longer. That can cause exhaustion and possibly death later. Not only for your own landing success but also for the released fish's survival chances, use the stoutest leader you can.

Leader set-ups. Leaders are attached to the fly line in a variety of ways. The basic set-up involves tying a section of leader butt material (.020″ or so, depending on line size) about 12″ long directly on the fly line. This butt material is then attached to the leader. The butt material rather than the fly line is used up in leader changes. Fly line to leader butt knots are more difficult to tie in the field anyway.

The knot commonly used for leader to fly line is the nail knot. It's not an extremely difficult knot, but it's best tied in the comfort of your den (or in the garage if tender ears are around). Here's the knot:

Step 1: You'll need a small tube for this knot. Some people cut their children's ball-inflating tube down for this, but you can use a bobbin threader or you may find

plastic Q-tips in the house. These are hollow and can be cut easily to 1"-1 ½". Match the end of the tube to the end of the fly line and hold them parallel and together. Lay your leader on top of them with the end and plenty of extra material facing toward the body of the line.

Step 2: Take the leader end and wrap it back on itself and the line and tube. This is the step that requires some concentration. Make six wraps.

Step 3: Insert the end, now near the tip of the line, into the tube at the line end so that it is within the knot.

Step 4: Remove the tube carefully and keep pressure on the leader end. Begin tightening the knot by alternately pulling on the tip of the leader and on the long end of the leader so that it cinches on the line. Keeping control of the wraps during this process is important. They must tighten without overwrapping each other.

Step 5: Finish tightening by pulling both ends of the leader material. Then test the knot by pulling fly line against leader end. The leader material must bite into the fly line coating to hold well. When assured of tightness, trim the ends of both leader and line. You may wish to make the knot smoother by adding a coat of Pliobond.

Since it relies on the bite of monofilament on the fly line's plastic coating, this knot is useful in only this application. To add leader to butt material or to add leader materials of similar diameter, you'll need the blood knot. This is a nifty knot that is smooth and strong.

Step 1: Cross the two materials and hold the junction between thumb and forefinger. Take the end of the heavy leader. Wrap it around the other leader five times (more with smaller diameters).

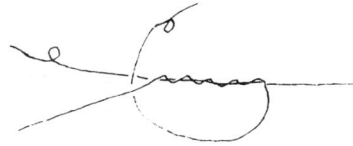

Step 2: Hold that end while sliding your thumb and forefinger away from the turns. Insert the end you've just wound through the gap at the junction between the two leaders. Hold it there with your other thumb and forefinger.

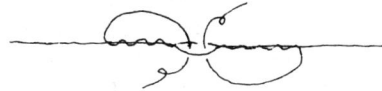

Step 3: Release your original grip and use those fingers to repeat the process with the second leader end. After wrapping, insert the end the opposite way through the junction. The leader ends should be pointing away from each other.

Step 4: Hold the ends (this is where teeth can help) while pulling both sections of leader away from each other. The tips should be trimmed as close as 1½ times the diameter of the material. Real close, in other words. An interesting variation of the blood knot will allow you to use droppers. This is more of an extension than a variation. Simply use a much longer end on the leader section you wish to use for a dropper, 4"-6" as a minimum. When you've completed the knot, do not trim this long end. It's your dropper. Droppers allow use of two or more flies. The practice was common when wet flies were in vogue, but with the current emphasis on dry fly fishing, the dropper has been dropped. It's too bad, because the system can allow you to try two flies or fish an emerger and a dry at the same time.

The blood knot and the nail knot described above and the improved clinch knot are the only knots the average fly fisherman needs to know. They are, however, very important to learn and be familiar with. You'll have to tie the blood and clinch knots while fish are rising, and that's the most demanding knot-tying situation.

Selecting leader material. There are a number of excellent leader materials on the market: Nylorfi, Maxima, Kroic, Aeon, Mason, and others. Choosing between them is difficult, since you can't tell much about a leader from its looks. On the other hand, you will find all of the leading brands fairly similar in quality.

It would be nice to be able to go by break-point ratings in picking leaders, but there is no industry standard for testing break points so you'd have to rely on the individual companies to do the testing. Even if they were standardized, there are other considerations in selecting a leader. In short, don't be too swayed by the break-point advertised on leader packages.

A leader's knot-holding qualities must also be considered. If you use a leader that breaks consistently at the knot or within the knot or pulls out of knots, then you've discovered a leader with knot-holding problems.

Finally, a leader must be judged on its stiffness. In the larger diameters, you will want a leader material to be fairly stout to aid in transmission of energy for efficient turnover, but in the smaller diameters, you'll want more suppleness. A single brand may be excellent in the heavier diameters but too stout in the lighter ones.

That may explain why many fly fishermen, myself included, prefer different brands for different leader diameters. And that fact may help you understand that picking a leader material is a long process based on experience with each brand.

Leaders are the final frontier. The quest for the perfect leader material for all diameters continues. And that's why more fussing time is spent on leaders than on any other part of the angler's gear.

The leaders are listed here in alphabetical order. Please note that several catalog companies require minimum purchases of three or more packaged leaders.

Aeon Leaders

Aeon leaders are not made of the traditional nylon material. They are a copolymer nylon. The material is shinier and slicker than regular nylon. The leaders have exceptional break points and are very limp in smaller diameters. The reported knot strength is 70%. An excellent material, Aeon is offered by more catalogs than any other material. The only caution necessary with these leaders deals with knot slippage. Because they are so slick, they will slip out of a knot. Like many of the catalog companies, I recommend an extra turn or two for additional strength on all knots tied with Aeon leader material.

Aeon Continuous Leaders

Butt	Tippet	Lb. Test
.021	0x	10
.021	1x	9
.021	2x	7
.021	3x	6
.021	4x	5
.021	5x	4
.017	6x	3
.015	7x	2
.013	8x	1.3

6', 7½', 9', 12' Aeon Leaders
$1.10-$1.25 Many catalogs

Extra Heavy Aeon Continuous Leaders

Butt	Tippet	Break
.023	.015	16
.023	.014	15
.023	.013	14
.023	.012	12
.023	.011(0x)	10

9', 12' Extra Heavy Aeon Leaders
$1.10-$1.25 Pen, T&T, Cus, Dal, Fly, AnR, Hun, H&H, Wul

Aeon Tippet Material

Aeon tippet material. *Available in 25 meter spools in sizes from 0x-8x; break points listed above.* $1.45-$1.85 Many catalogs

Berkley Specialist Leaders

Berkley offers four continuous-taper leaders. Not-A-Knot leaders are traditional tapered leaders. Qwik Sink leaders are treated with a chemical to make them sink. For wet fly and nymph fishermen, these are ideal, but the dry fly angler who likes his leader to sink may find that they pull the fly under, so well do they sink. It's probably better to apply a leader sink to the first 12" of a traditional tippet for use with dry flies.

Berkley's other two tapered leaders are the Flat Butt and the Knotless Heavy. The Flat Butt has just that, and it helps turn the leader over properly. The Knotless Heavy leader has the traditional round butt material, but the tippets are heavier for use in bass, salmon, steelhead, and saltwater fishing.

Berkley Not-A-Knot and Qwik Sink

Butt	Tippet	Lb. Test
.018	0x	6
.018	1x	5
.018	2x	4
.018	3x	3
.018	4x	2.5
.018	5x	2
.018	6x	1.75

7½', 9' Not-A-Knot
$.60-$.89 H&H, Pen, Tac, Cab, Cus, AnW, Mer, Egg, Fol, Sim, Ram, Edd, Bob
7½', 9' Qwik Sink
$.85-$1.35 H&H, Bud, Pen, Cab, Tac, Fol, Cus, Mer, Dal, Edd, Dal

Berkley Flat Butt Leaders

9' Flat Butt. *Available in 0x-6x; butt "diameter" .022"x.014"; break points listed above.* $.90-$1.45 Bud, Kau, Tac, Cus, Edd, H&H

Berkley Heavy Taper Leaders

Butt	Tippet	Lb. Test
.022	.015	10
.022	.013	8

7½', 9' Heavy Taper. *Available in 0x-4x; break points given above.*
$.70-$.83 H&H, Cab, Cus, Edd

Berkley Tippet Material

Berkley tippet material. *Available in 25 yard spools in sizes .015", .013", and 0x-7x; most break points identical to those listed above, but here are break points not included: 7x = 1#, .013" = 12#, .015" = 15#.*
$.75-$.90 H&H, Cus, Fol

Climax Leaders

Introduced in 1984 by Fred Arbona's Streamlife Innovations, Climax leaders and leader material come from France. The material is being described as having stiffness comparable to Maxima in larger diameters and suppleness comparable to Aeon in finer diameters. Published break points compare to Aeon's.

The price of Climax is less than any other material. For about the same money, spools of Climax hold four times the usual amount of material, 100 meters. Before you get too excited, remember that material, especially in small diameters, should be replaced every year. A hundred meters makes a lot of 12" tippets. As a side note, Streamlife Innovations is claiming a shelf life of two years without deterioration, so there's a second opinion (as usual) on the need to replace material every year.

Climax Flat Turnover Leaders are fairly conventional knotted dry fly leaders, utilizing Climax's stiffness in sizes to 3x and limpness in smaller diameters to create a leader with good turnover.

The Butt-As-Indicator Nymph Leaders have butt sections dyed red. This helps the angler see strikes while fishing nymphs. They are available in 0x-5x tippets.

Climax Knotted Leaders

7½', 9', 12', 16' Climax Flat Turnover Leaders. *Break points given in chart below.*
$1.25-$1.75 Str, Pen, Nor

7½' Climax Butt-As-Indicator Nymph Leaders. *Butt diameter .020"; available in 1x-5x.*
$1.25 Pen, Nor, Str

Climax Leader Material

Size	Lb. Test
.021	28
.019	25
.017	20
.015	17
.013	15
0x	13
1x	11
2x	9
3x	6.5
4x	5.5
5x	4.4
6x	3.2
7x	2.4

$1.85-$1.98 Nor, Pen, Str

Climax Leader Kit

Climax Leader Kit. *Contains 12 spools (.021"-5x) with break points of 3.2 to 28 pounds; instructions included.*
$19.95-$27.50 Str, Nor, Pen

Cortland Leaders

Cortland produces an unusual leader called the 444 Twin-Tapered. It features two tapered sections knotted together. The butt section is a hard nylon designed for strong turnover. It's 5½' in length. The tippet section is soft material for improved drift and delicate presentation. It's 4½' long. Each package comes with one butt section and two tippets. In addition, packages of three tippets are available.

A recent addition to the Cortland line are knotted leaders tied with Nylorfi (pronounced Ni-LOR-fee), an outstanding leader material imported by Cortland from France. Nylorfi is strong and very supple in small diameters. If there's a standard in the field, it's Nylorfi. It's also available in 27.4 yard (25 meters) spools in sizes of .015" to 8x. If all the different brands of leader material are confusing to you, just buy Nylorfi until you get far enough into the sport that you can see advantages in some of the other brands.

Cortland also offers a continuous-taper leader, the Cortland Crown.

Cortland Knotted Leaders

10' 444 Twin Tip Leaders. *Available in tippet sizes of .013" to 6x. (Note: No specifics are given in any of the catalogs, including Cortland's, concerning butt diameters or break points for these leaders. Sorry.)*
$1.35 (0x-.013"—$1.65) Bud, Nor, T&T, Edd, Hig, AnR, Hun, Mer

4½' 444 Twin Tip Leader Tippet Sections. *Three to a package in sizes .013" to 8x.*
$1.35 AnR, Mer, Nor, Hun, Hig, Bud, Edd, T&T
10' Nylorfi Knotted Leaders. *Break points same as listed below for Nylorfi leader material. (Note: No specifics concerning butt diameters are given in the catalogs.)*
$1.35-$1.50 Bud, T&T, Mer, Edd, Hig

Cortland Continuous Leaders

7½', 9', 12' Crown Knotless Leaders. *Sizes: 1x-6x. (Note: Break points unfortunately not available.)*
$.85 Edd, Bob, AnR, Dun, Mer, Hun
9' Crown Knotless Bass/Salmon. *Sizes: 0x-.013".*
$1.30-$1.35 Mer, Hun, AnR

Nylorfi Leader Material

Size	Lb. Test
.015	17.2
.013	12.3
0x	10.8
1x	9.4
2x	8
3x	5.9
4x	4.8
5x	3.9
6x	2.4
7x	1.7
8x	1.1

$1.35-$1.50 Bud, Nor, Pen, T&T, Nat, Mer, Bob, Hig, Fly, AnR, Hun

Dennison Leader Material

Dennison, maker of the popular leader dispensers, also offers tippet material pre-wound on spools to fit the dispensers. Available in 0x-7x, it's sold under the trade name Den-X. The spools contain 25 yards of material. No break points are given.
$1 Mer

Gladding Leaders

Gladding is a West German leader material. Continuous-taper leaders and tippet material by the spool are available under the trade name Gladyl.

Since Dan Bailey's Platlon Tapered Leaders use tippets of Gladyl, they are included here. The larger diameter strands in these knotted leaders are of stiff material to aid turnover. Thus, the design is somewhat similar to Cortland's continuous-taper 444 Twin Taper.

Gladyl Continuous Taper Leaders

Butt	Tippet	Lb. Test
.024	0x	9
.024	1x	7.2
.024	2x	6.3
.019	3x	5.2
.019	4x	4.3
.017	5x	3.3
.017	6x	2.1

7½', 9' Gladyl. *Break points above.*
$1-$1.10 Dan, Hig, Ran
9' Gladyl Salmon. *Sizes: .013"-.015".*
$1.40-$1.45 Dan, Ran

Gladyl Knotted Leaders

7½', 9', 12' Dan Bailey's Platlon Leaders. *Butt sections begin at .024"; break points identical to those above.*
$1.25 Dan, Bob
Platlon Leaders. *20" tippets. Price/doz.: $.50 Dan*

Gladyl Tippet Material

Gladyl Tippet Material. *Specifications identical to those listed above.*
$.65 Dan, Ran

Kroic Leader Material

Kroic comes from the longstanding Pezon & Michel company of France. Since the labels also bear the name "Luxor", you may know it by that name.

Dan Bailey's catalog describes it as having a stiffness something between domestic soft nylon and hard nylon material. They consider it to be stronger than many other brands that are rated higher in break point.

There are two types, Kroic and Kroic GT. The GT is rated stronger and is limper, making it the choice for small diameter tippets. The material comes on the traditional 27.4 yard/25 meter spool.

Since the Thomas & Thomas and Dan Bailey's knotted leaders are tied with Kroic, they are included here. They are the only pre-tied Kroic leaders available. Bailey's are marketed under the name "Dan Bailey's French Nylon Tapered Leaders", which, if nothing else (and these leaders are something else), is the sexiest name for a leader we've heard (except maybe Climax). The leaders use Kroic for larger diameters and Kroic GT for diameters of 0x and smaller. The T&T leaders are tied throughout with regular Kroic.

Kroic Knotted Leaders

9', 12' Dan Bailey's French Nylon. *Available in 0x-7x; break points given in the chart for Kroic GT below.*
$1.35 Dan, Hig
7½', 9', 12' T&T Leaders. *Butt diameter of .021"; 7 ½' leaders have terminal diameters of 0x-5x; 9' leaders available in 0x-7x; 12' leaders come in only 5x-7x; for break points, see Kroic Leader Material chart below.*
$2 T&T
9' T&T Salmon/Steelhead/Bass Leaders.

Butt	Tippet	Lb. Test
.023	.015	14
.023	.013	10
.023	.011	8

$2.25 T&T

6', 9' T&T Saltwater Leaders. *With a 1' shock tippet of Fibersteel.*

Butt	Tippet	Lb. Test
.023	.017	18
.023	.015	14
.023	.013	10
.023	.011	8

$2.50 T&T

Kroic Leader Material

Size	Lb. Test
.023	36
.021	25
.019	20
.017	16
.015	12
.013	9
.012	7.9
0x	6.8
1x	5.7
2x	4.8
3x	4
4x	3.3
5x	2.6
6x	1.5
7x	1.2
8x	0.8

$1.35-$1.60 Dan, T&T, Mur

Kroic GT Leader Material

Size	Lb. Test
0x	9.6
1x	8.3
2x	7.2
3x	6.1
4x	4.1
5x	3.25
6x	2.4
7x	1.8

$1.75-$1.95 Dan, Bud, Mur, Hig

Mason Leader Material

Mason is best known for hard (stiff) leader material. Many fly fishermen prefer harder material for all but the finer diameter sections of their leaders. With bigger, bushier flies, they may use this stiff material all the way down. It eases turnover, especially with the larger flies.

Mason material is available in hard and soft materials, and kits are available for tying your own leaders.

Mason Hard Material

Size	Lb. Test
.025	32
.023	25
.021	22
.019	18
.017	15
.015	12

Size	Lb. Test
.013	9
.012	8
0x	7
1x	6
2x	5
3x	4
4x	3
5x	2

Mason Hard Material. *See text above for details.*
$.65-$.90 H&H, Bud, Pen, Dan, Kau, EJH, Mer, Let, Cus, Dal, AnR, Hun
Mason Freshwater Kit. *12 spools with break points of 2-22 pounds.*
$6.75-$9.95 H&H, Mer, Kau, Pen, Let, EJH, Cus, AnR, Hun
Mason Saltwater Kit. *12 spools with break points of 5-32 pounds.*
$6.75-$9.95 H&H, Hun, Mer, AnR, Pen, Cus, EJH, Kau

Mason Soft Material

Size	Lb. Test
.025	40
.023	30
.021	25
.0185	20
.0165	17
.015	15
.013	12
.012	10
0x	8
2x	6
3x	4
5x	2

Mason Soft Material. *See text above for details.*
$.65-$.67 Mer, H&H
Mason Soft Kit. *12 spools with break points of 2-40 pounds.*
$6.75-$7.52 H&H, Mer

Maxima Leader Material

Maxima Chameleon leader material can be picked out of the crowd due to its color. Each size is chemically dyed one of a variety of shades of green and brown. Although it's probably done with camouflage in mind, it also helps the angler determine his terminal tippet size.

Maxima is a good material with excellent knot-holding characteristics. It is, however, fairly stiff in comparison to other materials. I've used it in the larger sizes, down to 4x. For the smaller diameters, I prefer a limper material. Because of the stiffness, turnover is very good with leaders built of Maxima.

Maxima, a West Germany company, is one of those brands that does not bear the x-numbers. You'll have to remember the Rule of 11 (see introduction to leaders) when buying, unless the fly shop or catalog company has done you the courtesy of converting the sizes.

Maxima comes in individual spools of 27.4 yards (25 meters). The Maxima Leader Kits contain 12 spools of material and instructions for tying your own. The freshwater kit contains sizes from .020" to 7x. The saltwater kit contains sizes from .028" to 5x.

Maxima knotted leaders are now available in 7½' and 9'lengths. Doctor's Choice Leaders are knotted leaders tied from Maxima and offered by Bob Jacklin.

Maxima Knotted Leaders

7½', 9' Maxima Knotted Leaders. *1x-7x tippets available; break points listed below.*
$1.25 Pen
9' Doctor's Choice Leaders. *2x-6x tippets; break points given below.*
$1.25 Bob

Maxima Chameleon Leader Material

Size	Lb. Test
.024	40
.022	30
.020	25
.017	20
.015	15
.013	12
.012	10
1x	8
2x	6
3x	5
4x	4
5x	3
6x	2
7x	1

Maxima Leader Material. *25 meter spools.*
$1.10-$1.70 Many catalogs
Maxima Leader Kits, Freshwater. *12 spools, instructions; .020"-7x.*
$13-$24 Many catalogs
Maxima Leader Kits, Saltwater. *12 spools, instructions; .028"-5x.*
$13-$17.95 Mer, H&H, T&T, Kau, Hun, AnR, Fly, Dal, Pen, Cus

Orvis Leaders

As you might expect, Orvis has a complete line of leaders, including such esoteric items as a compound taper wet fly leader with Kwik-Klips for easy, no-knot fly changes. Those leaders include a dropper clip. Orvis also handles braided leaders, but these are included in a separate section.

Published break points differ for knotted leaders and continuous-taper leaders. The chart below gives the break points for each. Orvis tippet material, offered in 50 yard spools in lighter diameters and 25 yard spools in heavier diameters, has slightly different break points, so a second chart is given for those.

A new material, the "666" series, is a blend of two types of nylon. Orvis claims an increase of 96% in tensile strength over regular Orvis tippet material. The "666" material retains 50% of its strength when knotted and wetted, compared to 15% for traditional material, according to Orvis.

Orvis also offers a leader kit that contains 18 spools. Considering the 50 yard size of the smaller diameters, this kit is a good buy. You can expect the instructions to be first rate.

Many of the leaders may be ordered in quantities of six or more at a discount averaging about 10%. See the Orvis catalog for details.

Orvis Knotted Leaders

Size	Knotted Lb. Test
.019	18.75
.017	14.5
.015	11
.013	8
.012	n/a
0x	6
1x	5
2x	4
3x	3.5
4x	3
5x	2
6x	1.25
7x	1

7½', 9', 12' Hand-tied leaders. *Butt section diameters are as follows: 7½'—.019"; 9' and 12'—.021"; available in the following tippet sizes: 7½'—0x-4x; 9'—0x-6x; 12'—4x-7x.*
$1.75 Orv, Kau, Ste
6' Special Leaders. *For sinking lines; tied with .021" butts in sizes 0x-2x and .019" butts in 3x-5x.*
$1.75 Orv
7½',9' Compound Wet Fly Leaders. *With Kwik-Klips, including a dropper clip; available in 0x-3x.*
$1.85 Orv
7½', 9', 12' Salmon and Saltwater Leaders. *Butt diameters of .021" and final diameters ranging from .011" to .019".*
$1.75 Orv

Orvis Continuous Taper Leaders

Size	Continuous Lb. Test
.015	16
.013	14
.012	12
0x	10
1x	9
2x	7
3x	6
4x	5
5x	4
6x	3

7½', 9', 12' Knotless Tapered Leaders. *.021" butt sections; available in the following sizes: 7½'—0x-4x; 9'—0x-6x; 12'—4x-6x; see chart above for break points.*
$1.65 Orv, Let
9' Knotless Salmon Leaders. *Butt .023" with terminal diameters of .011" to .015".*
$1.65 Orv

Orvis Leader Material

Size	Lb. Test
.023	34.4
.021	23.7
.019	19.2
.017	15.1
.015	11.6
.013	8.6
.012	7.5
0x	6.5
1x	5.5
2x	4.5
3x	3.8
4x	3.1
5x	2.4
6x	1.4
7x	1.1
8x	.75

Orvis Leader Material. *Sizes 0x-8x are 50 yard spools; other sizes 25 yard spools.*
$1.50 Orv, Kau, Ste
Orvis Leader Kits. *18 spools, including 3 of .021", 2 of .019" and .017", and one of other sizes.*
$20 Orv, Kau

Orvis "666" Material

Size	Lb. Test
0x	13
1x	11
2x	9
3x	7
4x	5
5x	4
6x	3
7x	2

Orvis "666" Material. *25 yards spools; break points above.* $2.85 Orv

Tortue Leader Material

Letort Ltd. touts this material as being very soft, limp, and strong, i.e. "the best leader material on the market". They use it on their knotted leaders listed in the section below on miscellaneous leaders.

It costs more, $4.55, but you get more, 110 yards (100 meters). They list the break points (but no corresponding x-numbers) as follows: ¾, 1, 1½, 2, 2½, 3, 4, 5½, 6, 7. You may order by the x-number, and they'll take care of getting you the correct size.
$4.55 Let

Some Miscellaneous Leaders of Interest

Several catalogs have house specials that you may find interesting. In many cases, the producers of the nylon used in the leaders has not been identified. That's too bad, I think, since buyers would have more confidence in the products knowing who made them. I've included only leaders of special interest here. You may find conventional leaders with a house brand on them, and I'd recommend against those unless the catalog gives the manufacturer's name.

Pennsylvania Outdoor Warehouse

Here's a wet fly leader for those traditional Rocky Mountain downstream fishers. It's made of stiff nylon and has loops for three flies. Unfortunately, no length is given.

Unsnelled Wet Fly Leader. *Available in 4#, 6#, and 8# test.*
$.89 Pen
Snelled Wet Fly Leader. *Tied in 6 # test only.*
$.89 Pen

The second leader of interest from Pen is a knotted leader for heavy flies, such as streamers, large wet flies, and weighted nymphs. It's described as a "weight-forward" or convex-taper leader. Maxima material is used in constructing this unusual leader.

7½', 9', 12' Convex-Taper Leaders. *Available in 1x-5x; see Maxima chart, above, for break points.*
$1.75 Pen

Letort Outfitters

Three leaders of interest are offered by the folks at Boiling Springs.

First is a Hi-Viz leader, designed for nymph fishing. The butt is knotless, flat nylon dyed a fluorescent yellow. A clear tippet is added. Second is a knotted leader tied to Joe Humphrey's specifications. It's tied with Mason hard nylon butt sections and tippets of Tortue soft material. The tippets are extra long for natural S-curves, which give a longer drag-free drift. Third, Letort Brand Tapered Leaders are conventional knotted leaders using the same materials as the Special Leaders.

10½' Hi-Viz Leaders. *Fl. yellow butt; available in 3x-6x.*
$2.25 Let
7½', 10½' Special Leaders. *Extra long tippets; 7½' has 4x tippet, 10½' has 4x or 5x tippet.*
$1.25, $1.30 Let
7½', 9', 12' Letort Brand Leaders. *Knotted leaders using Mason Hard for butts and Tortue for tippets; no break points given.*
$1, $1.10, $1.25 Let

Murray's Fly Shop

Specially designed for nymph fishing, Murray's Bright Butt Leaders have a dyed butt section.

9' Bright Butt Leaders. *Available in 0x-6x.*
$1.95 Mur

Thomas & Thomas

There are no buts about the special Extra Heavy Butt material offered by T&T. You'll get 15 yards of heavy material suitable for salmon and saltwater leaders.

T&T also has Flat Mono Butts in 20 or 25 pound test. The lighter is suitable for leader butts on fly lines of 3-weight to 6-weight. The heavier is suitable for 7-weight and heavier lines.

At the other end of the leader are two products of interest, Ultimate Tippets and Fibersteel. The Ultimate Tippet is a "collection" of 32" tippets carried in a special tube package that can hang from a clip (inside your vest to protect leaders from deterioration and you from funny looks). The tippets are color coded. There are two selections. The 90-tippet package contains 20 each of 4x, 5x and 10 of 1x-7x. The 100-tippet package has 40 of 4x and 20 each of 3x, 5x, and 6x.

Fibersteel, that remarkably flexible yet strong Kevlar material, is particularly well-suited for shock tippets on saltwater set ups, and T&T is the only source of Fibersteel I could find. (I didn't look through all the spin/bait catalogs where it may also appear.) It's available in the following lb. test/diameter combinations: 15#/.010", 20#/.012", 30#/.016", 42#/.020".

Extra Heavy Butt Material. *15 yard spool; sizes:
.023"-.025".*
$.95 T&T
Flat Mono Butts. *5 yard spools of flat material; 20 or 25 pound test.*
$.65 T&T
Ultimate Tippets. *Color coded 32" tippets; see text above for details.*
$6.95 T&T
Fibersteel. *5 yard coils of Kevlar material, for shock tippets; see text above for sizes.*
$2.50 T&T

Braided Leaders

Pow. Smash. Bang. Braided leaders made a big splash (so to speak) in 1984. Orvis introduced the new leaders but had supply problems. Beartooth Fly Rod Co. soon thereafter introduced its own line and had them in many fly shops, at least in the Rocky Mountain states. Blue Ribbon Flies has something they call French woven leaders, which may be the same. Now Cortland offers braided leaders and a braided leader kit.

The leaders work, supposedly, on the "Chinese finger torture" theory. A hollow braid is positioned over the shaved end of the fly line. This braid compresses as tension is applied. However, Super Glue must be applied to the connection (something which is neither necessary nor a good idea with Chinese finger torture devices).

A smaller diameter section of braid follows on the Beartooth braided leaders, and leader material is knotted to this. The Orvis leaders have a single section of braid with leader material "electronically welded" (i.e. melted) to it. Both brands are thereafter fairly conventional leaders.

The braided butts are supposed to have several advantages. They do stretch more than nylon monofilament, and that characteristic may help cushion the hook setting blow that often breaks fine tippets. Although it's more supple than traditional hard nylon butt material, it turns over very well (perhaps because of extra weight?). The suppleness aids in giving a drag-free drift.

I've fished with a braided leader, and I can vouch for the good turnover and for the fact that you can control a longer final tippet section with the leaders. I can also vouch for several disadvantages.

First, the Super Glue connection is stiff and causes a hinging effect which may, over time, weaken the material or cause cracks in the fly line. If you use Super Glue to reinforce the second braid connection on Beartooth leaders, you'll get another annoying stiff section there. Second, I'm suspicious of knots between braid and leader. That knot failed on my Beartooth leader, and so did a second knot that I tied. If a special knot is needed, they should make sure consumers know it. The Orvis "electronically welded" connection may be superior.

Third, the braid is supple and sinks, but it sinks so well that in fast moving streams, it can get caught in the currents and sink your fly. Hard nylon is stiffer and may affect your drift, but it allows for a more direct connection to your tippet. I think I may have broken off more tippets by losing that direct connection and having to pull farther and harder to regain it when setting the hook.

Fourth, I think the braid could get caught on rocks or snagged by an errant hook and start to unravel. This began to happen on my leader, but I abandoned it because of the knot failure before I could find out if the unraveling was a problem. Super Glue may become part of the tackle in your vest or bag if you experience unraveling.

Fifth, and most minor, it's a pain to attach the leaders to your fly line.

The initial cost of these leaders is high, but of course, that doesn't matter if they work well for you. You'll probably have to try one, so different are they, and perhaps your impressions will be more positive than mine. A lot of fly fishermen swear by the braided leaders. Certainly if you need a long, fine tippet, you may find them superior to conventional leaders and worth the extra effort of maintaining them.

As for me, I'll stick to a well-designed traditional leader.

7½', 9', 12' Beartooth Braided Leaders. *See text above*

for details.
$4.50 (plus $2 for Super Glue) Bea, Pen (and probably many more to come)
9' Beartooth Strike Indicator Braided Leaders. *Bright butt for use in nymphing.*
$4.50 Pen, Bea
7½' Beartooth Lead Core Braided Leaders. *Weighted for use with nymphs and streamers.*
$4.95 Bea, Pen
12' Orvis Braided Leaders. *See text above for details.*
$6.50 Orv
9' Orvis Sinking Braided Leaders. *Available in sinking, fast sinking, and extra fast sinking; designed for use with wet flies, nymphs, and streamers.*
$6.50 Orv
12½' Cortland Braided Butt Leaders. *Available in 3x-6x.*
$3.95 Nor (and many more to come)
Cortland Braided Butt Kits. *All you need to tie your own.*
$11.95 Nor (and many more to come)

LINE AND LEADER ACCESSORIES

You'll find a lot of accessories for lines and leaders in fly shops and catalogs. That's because lines and leaders are important and also because they cause more stream-side concern than things like rods and reels.

Included here are backing lines, running lines, leader dispensers, leader wallets, leader straighteners, chemicals to float and sink lines and leaders, knot-tying tools, clippers, split shot and other weights, and a number of miscellaneous items. I've tried to keep the list as simple as I could, partly by lumping things such as leader straighteners that are similar but may vary slightly from catalog to catalog and partly by eliminating items that were not well-described or for which no manufacturer was given.

Backing

Backing should be wound on your reel behind the fly line. The primary reason typically given for the need for backing is that a large fish on the run can take all your fly line out. That doesn't happen everyday (or ever, for some of us), but when it does, backing will save the day.

The other reasons for using backing are just as important. Because it fills up the inside diameter of your spool, it keeps the line from being wound into tight coils which must be straightened. With the increased spool diameter created by adding backing, line retrieve is quicker, which is advantageous. Since fewer turns of the spool are required, there's less wear and tear on you and on your reel.

Dacron is the material of choice for backing. It's durable and pliable, and it will move through the guides smoothly. Backing is offered in sizes ranging from 12 pound to 30 pound. The break point itself is fairly irrelevant since leaders are invariably more breakable. The lighter backing is promoted as being suitable for lighter fly line weights. The heavier backing is preferred by some anglers, especially those after large game fish, because it doesn't cinch down on itself during a retrieve under high tension. Overall, 18 or 20 pound is the standard backing size.

The best way to get the correct amount of backing is to go to your local fly shop and let them hook you up. They're experienced and have winding machines that measure length. If you have to do it on your own, you can start with the reel manufacturer's recommendations. Don't trust them too far, however. The most accurate method is to wind your fly line on your reel backwards. Attach your backing to the rear of the line and fill the reel, leaving a quarter inch or so of free space. Then simply pull the whole rig off the reel, attach the backing to the spool, and rewind. This may sound like a lot of work, but it's easier than doing the job over and over in an effort to get it right.

Backing is listed here alphabetically by brand name. There doesn't seem to be a lot of difference in the backing lines, except that some are more supple than others. Most people end up getting whatever backing their local fly shop has, and it will probably be a well-known brand name. Prices are for 100 yards of material, the most universal offering, unless noted otherwise. Generally, backing is wound on 50 yard spools that are connected in a package of two. Some of the backing lines, Berkley, Cortland, and Orvis, for instance, can be bought in large quantities at more economical prices.

Ashaway Lifeline. *18#, 20# dacron.*
$5.80 Ran
Berkley Backing. *18# dacron.*
$2.30-$5.50 Tac, Ram, Sim, Cus, Dal, AnJ, Cab, H&H
Cortland Micron Backing. *12#, 20#, 30#.*
12#—$3.95-$5.50 T&T, Ram, Kau
20#—$3.79-$5.60 Many catalogs
30#—$3.79-$6 T&T, Kau, Tac, Dan, Cus, Ran, Hun, Pen, Fly, Hig, Edd

Gudebrod Backing. *15#, 20#, 30# dacron.*
15#—$4.20-$4.30 H&H, Cus
20#—$2.60-$5.25 H&H, Cus, Sim, Mur
30#—$5.50-$5.65 H&H, Cus
Martin Backing. *18# dacron.*
$3.25 Cus
Orvis Backing. *12#, 20#, 30# dacron.*
12#—$2.15 (50 yds.) Orv, Ste
20#—$4 (100 yds.) Orv, Ste
30#—$4.35 Orv, Ste

Running Line

Running line is attached to the back of a shooting taper fly line to provide a lightweight, nearly friction-free line for long distance casting. Backing is then typically attached behind the running line to fill the reel.

Running lines are most often a special monofilament line. It's made to be supple—the best of them don't sit in coils so rigidly that they tangle and hang in the guides. And they have a slick coating for shooting line with a minimum of energy dissipation.

As an option, some people use a small diameter fly line attached to their shooting taper lines. These lines are described in the section on fly lines.

The monofilament lines are listed in alphabetical order. Since this set-up is so specialized, you'll probably have to try out a line or two before you find the one that works best in the fishing situations you face.

Berkley Flat Shooting Mono. *20#, fl. clear/blue, 110 yds.*
$2.95-$3.20 Cus, H&H
Cortland Cobra Flat Mono. *20#, 30#, red or mist blue, 50 yds.*
$1.90-$3 Mer, Fly, Mur, Hun, Bud, Edd
Cortland Plion Mono. *20#, 25#, 30#, fl. yellow/green, 50 yds.*
$2.50-$3.33 Hig, Fly
Gudebrod Super Shooter. *20#, sunburst orange, 200'.*
$2.65-$3.06 Dal, Cus
Sunset Amnesia. *15#, 20#, 25#, 30#, 40#, black, yellow, or fl. red, 200'.*
$1.30-$3.25 (depending, in part, on size) Kau, Dan, Cus, Mur, Bud, Fly, Bob

Leader Dispensers

Surprisingly, there are only a few dispensers available from catalog companies. Three of these are for specific brands of leaders, but the other three can be used with any kind of leader material.

Orvis and Cortland both offer molded nylon leader dispensers that fit their leader wheels (Nylorfi for Cortland's box). The dispensers hold four wheels, and the leader material feeds out through protective rubber. There are no cutters on the box. Be warned, molded nylon is heavy. Maybe it's my backpacking experience, but I tried one of Cortland's dispensers and gave it up. It weighed as much as two fly boxes, a paperback novel, and three Baby Ruths, and I'd rather carry those items.

Aeon Indispenser holds nine spools of Aeon material. It's color coded to aid in identifying sizes.

Two of the other dispensers come from Dennison Research. The basic model is molded plastic. It's a circular

container 4" in diameter and 1" deep. It opens on a sturdy plastic hinge; my hinge shows no wear after four or five years of use. Inside, you'll find six spools on spindles. You load the spools with your favorite leader material (or buy Den-X material already spooled), feed the end out the nearby hole, and latch the end under the stainless steel cutter.

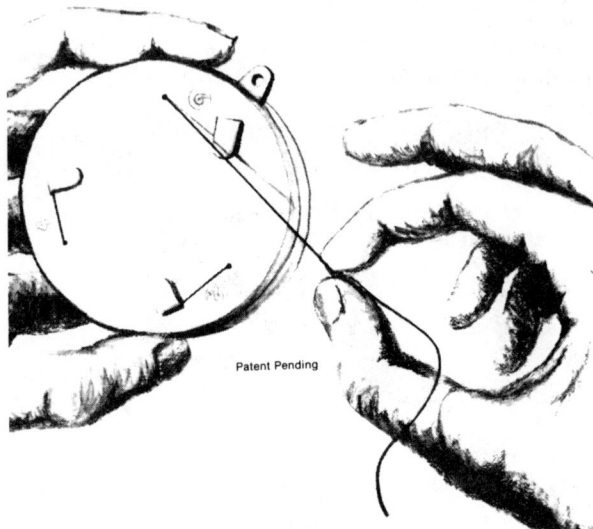

Patent Pending

When you need material, simply grasp the end extended between hole and cutter and pull out what you need. To cut, pull it under the cutter. The end will (usually) stay put, ending the problem of loose leader material. The dispensers come with a molded ring for attaching to your vest (which nobody does although a forgetful friend of mine attaches a cord to his and puts it in his pocket that way).

I've had very good luck with my Dennison dispenser. One spool got warped and didn't turn well, but I fixed that with my knife. The only other complaint I have is the numbering system molded on the dispenser's surface. Must be for people who remember pound test or something. Anyway, most anglers I know either write the correct x-number on the box with a marker or use some kind of self-adhesive tag. I found tiny circular tags at the office supply store. They cover up the funny numbers on the box. This is a small complaint, and the Dennison box remains one of the best bargains on the market for the convenience and durability it affords. It's available in three fashionable colors: blue, red, and black. (Blue's for the mellow fellow. Red suits the sporty guy or gal. Black is for the angler who's all business.)

The other Dennison dispenser is the Omni Box. It's made of aluminum and features four spools for tippets and room for fly storage. The Omni plus clippers would let you hit the stream fast and light. I like that. The box measures 3"x3"x1¼".

The final dispenser is a wooden one from North Fork. From the illustration in the catalog, it appears to use spools similar to those in the Dennison boxes. It holds four spools, and like all wood products, it's very attractive.

Orvis Tippet Dispenser. *Molded nylon; for Orvis material.*
$7.25 Orv, Ste
Nylorfi Tippet Dispenser. *Molded nylon; for Nylorfi material.*
$6.95-$7.95 T&T, Mer, Nor, Fly, Hig, Bob
Aeon Indispenser. *For nine spools of Aeon material; color coded.*
$8.95 Pen
Dennison Leader Dispenser. *Circular plastic box with cutters.*
$3.50-$6.95 Kau, Fly, Dan, Hig, H&H, T&T, Cus, Ram, Mur, Let, Mer, Dal, Bud, Hun

Omni Box. *Aluminum box with room for flies.*
$10-$15.95 Let, Mer, Bud, Hun, Bob

Wood leader box. *A handsome box.*
$29.95 Nor

Leader and Line Wallets

What fly fishermen lack in leader dispensers, they can make up for in "wallets" designed to carry ready-made tapered leaders.

There are so many of these that it's difficult to organize them for you. Basically, there are inexpensive vinyl wallets, more expensive nylon ones, and cowhide or leather wallets. Many of them feature zip-lock bags which can be replaced. I omitted wallets without brand names unless they were distinctive.

Cortland Leader Pack. *Soft vinyl with six double pockets; your basic leader wallet.*
$2.45 Mer, Edd

River Systems Leader Wallets. *Nylon pack material laminated with foam and tricot for flotation and protection; 5 zip-lock pockets plus license holder and other pockets; Velcro closure; tan with black binding, blue lining.*
$6.98-$9 Cus, Pen, Ram, H&H
Orvis Leather Wallet. *5 zip lock bags; traditional style.*
$8.75 Orv
Accordian Leather Wallet. *Under name of Cortland or Common Sense; brown cowhide; 6 bellows; 5"x4¼".*
$7.80-$13.75 Tac, Dan, Mer, Bud, Hun, Fly, AnR, Edd, Ree
Flat leader wallet. *Leather, opens flat, folds to 4"x4"; 3 pockets in each corner; nifty looking but maybe not as convenient (who cares?).*
$7.14-$14.95 Dal, Don
River Systems Line Wallet. *For 5 shooting heads; nylon/foam/tricot (see RS leader wallet); 5"x5". (Note: Since no brand name is given in some catalogs, can't be sure these are all made by RS.)*
$9.95 Fly, AnR, Kau

Line and Leader Chemistry

As I look over my worksheet, I'm amazed at all the line and leader dressings we have. And to think that I survived for years without any of this better fishing through chemistry.

Of course, we should all feel grateful for modern fly lines that require little care and for nylon leaders that don't have to be kept wet and be stretched before each use. The chemistry we have now is just icing on our collective cake.

You'll find two sections of chemistry here and one of associated hardware. The first section deals with fly line cleaners and floatants. The cleaners (which are often mixed with silicone as a floatant) come first, because they are really essential. Fly lines, particularly floating lines, must be cleaned regularly. Without cleaning, they will not shoot through the guides smoothly and floating lines will not float. Line cleaners are used on the first 30' or 40' of the line, the section that gets dirty quickly.

Cleaning is really the only thing you should have to do to a line, but there are a number of fly line "floatants". Since the specific gravity of a new floating fly line is less than that of water, these may seem superfluous, and they are in many cases. I can think of two situations where a silicone treatment may help. If you're trying to extend the life of a line that has a few cracks in it, the line dressing may help. It is also useful should you want to keep an intermediate sinking line on the surface. That would, admittedly, be an unusual situation. Many fly floatants are touted as line conditioners, too, but since their main function is floating a fly, they are considered in the chapter on flies.

The second section of chemistry deals with leader sinks. Most fly fishermen like their tippets to sink. It makes them less visible in smooth water. However, nylon leader material does not sink well on its own. Mostly it's a matter of surface tension. The chemistry in leader sinks helps pull down the tippet. These products are also used on flies to help them sink.

An organic alternative is a product called, affectionately, "Mud". It's an improvement on an old solution to the problem, rubbing the leader in streamside mud. Like toothpaste, another home remedy, this roughs up the surface of the slick leader material and somehow makes it sink. Carrying a tube of toothpaste is not fashionable and finding the correct consistency of streamside mud is difficult, hence we "need" leader sinks such as "Mud".

Leader sinks are used for the tippet material. Most fly fishermen prefer to have the leader butt floating to aid in line control.

The final section, dealing with hardware, features a collection of applicators for line cleaners. They're pretty clever devices, all of them, and if they make it convenient enough that you'll clean your line often, they're worth the investment.

Fly Line Cleaners and Floatants

These are arranged in random order. Most are liquid or paste that can be applied with one of the "appliances" listed at the end of this section. Some come in a tin with a felt applicator. The line is run through the saturated felt. It should then be run through a clean side of the felt to remove excess cleaner/conditioner. Use only an official line cleaner since some detergents can damage lines.

As an addendum to this section, there are some products designed to put a very slick coating on your line to make it shoot better. These may or may not work better than Armor-All, that wonderful product designed for use on car interiors. I was a little suspicious of it for use on fly lines, but I've tried it without detrimental effects (and my car interior looks nice, too).

Russ Peak Line Dressing. *A liquid from one of the foremost rod makers in the country—must be good stuff; 1 oz.*
$3.75-$5 Mer, Fly, Kau

Weber's Silicone Fly Line Conditioner. *Paste in a flip-top tub.*
$1.20-$1.75 Fol, AnW, Cus, Edd

Mucilin. *The old-time favorite; order with or without silicone, in paste or liquid form; still an excellent dressing.*
$1.75-$3 Dan, Kau, Cus, Mur, EJH, Ste, Ran, Pen, Bud, Fly, Bob

Clean-Kote Fly Line Cleaner. *A new product from Superior Fly Products; liquid form; 1 oz.*
$2.40-$3.30 Dan, T&T, Cus, Pen, Nor

Cortland Fly Line Cleaner. *Paste in tin with felt applicator.*
$1.25 Ram

Orvis Fly Line Dressing. *Liquid; adds slick coat for better shooting, 1 oz.*
$5 Orv

Seidel's 500, Fly Line Conditioner. *With silicone; liquid; one of the best product lines in fly fishing chemistry.*
$2.25-$3.25 Cus, Hun, Fly, Sim, H&H, Fol

Custom Fly Line Cleaner. *House brand from Dale Clemens.*
$1.79 Dal

Lamiglas Fast Coat. *Cleaner with coating for improving shooting distance; takes 30 min. to dry (which makes me think it must be a serious product for the serious angler); 1 oz..*
$3.49 Dal

Shoot-Eze Line Polish. *To improve slickness of line for longer casts.*
$1.95 Dal

Speed Cast. *Another lubricant/polish to improve line's movement through guides; with chamois applicator.*
$2.50-$2.95 T&T, Mer

Armor-All. *Will make your line very slick, but can't guarantee effect on coating.*
$.99-$1.49 Local discount stores

Leader Sinks

These products are designed to make your leader sink. Generally, a drop is put on your fingers and rubbed on the sections of tippet you wish to sink.

Sink-Kote Fly And Leader Sink. *A product of Superior Fly Products; liquid, 1 oz.; no drying time.*
$2.49-$3.30 Orv, Dan, Nor, Cus, AnJ, Pen, Bud
Seidel's 600 Leader Sink. *A popular leader sink in liquid form; 1 oz.*
$1.85-$3.50 Kau, H&H, Cus, EJH, Dal, Hun, Fly, Sim, Edd
Lamiglas Speed Sink. *Liquid; 1 oz.*
$3.49 Dal
Gallaher Fly Sink. *Liquid.*
$1.85-$2.10 Edd, Sim
Magic Sink. *Fly-Rite's leader sink.*
$2 Mer, FlR
Gehrke's Xink. *A long-time favorite of many fishermen; liquid; 1 oz.*
$2.50-$3.60 Dan, Edd, H&H, T&T, Cus, Cab, Let, EJH, Dal, Pen, Bud
"Mud". *A mysterious, dark paste; organic material; sinks leaders well but not suitable for flies (except the Cow Dung?); offered under Orvis, Simms, and other brand names but probably the same stuff (can't be that many commercial "Mud" producers).*
$1.75-$2.50 Orv, Kau, Let, Pen, Ste, Hig

Hardware

These devices are used to apply line dressing. Simple and ingenious, they will make cleaning your line much more convenient, and that means you'll do it more often.

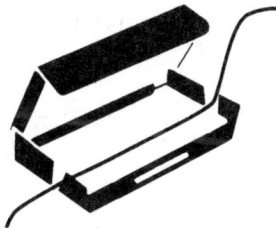

Stone Fly Line Dressing Box. *A nifty high-impact polypropylene box; add favorite dressing to four felt pads which may be rotated, reversed, and finally replaced; line is closed in box and pulled through; tension regulated by pressure on box; thoroughly workable; 3¼"x1⅞"x¾" so fits in vest easily; replacement pads from Stone Fly Products, Glide, Oregon 97443 for $1.95 (or local fly shops).*
$3.95 Orv, Big, Pen, or direct from Stone Fly

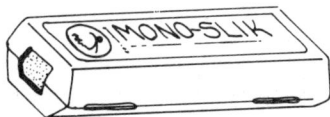

Mono-Slik. *Produced by Maxima using the same idea as Stone Fly box above; foam pads with dressing already added; can be refilled; 4⅜"x1⅛"x¾".*
$2.50-$4 Kau, H&H, T&T, Dal, Pfe, Fly

T&T Line Dresser. *A section of split suede; can be filled with dressing and line run through; washable; seems potentially messy to carry in vest.*
$3.50 T&T

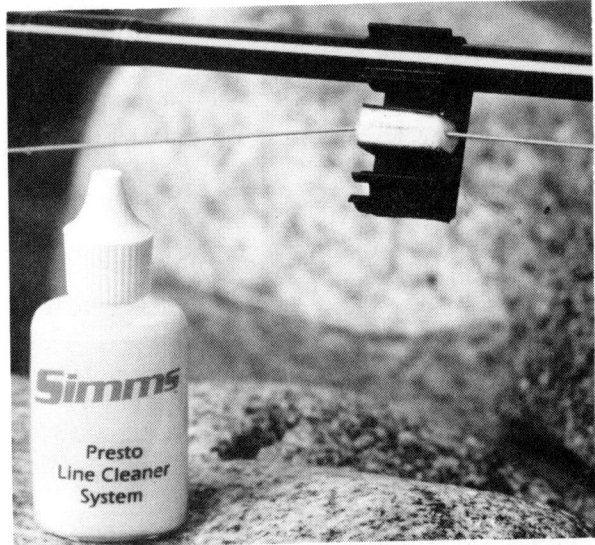

Simms Presto Line Tender. *Attaches to rod so line can be reeled in through felt pads of Tender; includes Simms line cleaner to be applied to pads; no word on replacement pads, though; looks like a nifty device.*
$5 Pen, Kau
World's Quik Line Cleaner. *A small circular device with felt pads; can be rotated for clean pads; you apply favorite cleaner.*
$2-$2.95 EJH, AnJ

Leader Straighteners

Another "necessary" item for the fly vest is a leader straightener. It's traditionally two pieces of rubber sandwiched between cowhide. A ring or grommet is provided for attaching a retractor. The leader is pulled through the rubber under tension to remove the kinks.

Remember as you straighten a leader this way that it works in part by heat created by the friction. If you create too much heat through too much tension or too fast a pull, you'll weaken the leader. Some people prefer leather leader straighteners since heat build-up is not as great.

Orvis Leader Conditioner. *Rubber with leather cover, retractor included.*
$5.75 Orv, Hig
Cortland Leader Straightener. *Rubber with leather cover, retractor included.*
$6.50 Mer
Generic leader straighteners. *These are the same style as the two above but don't include a retractor; some bear company names.*
$1.75-$3.50 Dan, H&H, T&T, AnJ, Pen, Fly, AnR, Bob, Mer, Mur, Cus

Leather Straightener. *Simply a piece of leather with a grommet for attaching to retractor.*
$1.50 T&T

Terminal Tactics Straightener. *An ingenious little piece of rubber with slits cut into it through which leader is pulled; adhesive back allows attachment to fly box; 1" x 1½".*
$2.10-$2.50 Dan, T&T, Cus

Fisherman's Clippers

You can skip this section if you do what I do . . . buy the drugstore's best clippers at 49 cents, use the hell out of them, and replace them once every year or two.

Lots of people do otherwise, however. They want their clippers, in the fashion of Swiss Army Knives, to include tools for lots of things, from unsticking glued fly eyes to opening bottles. For those people, this section offers everything from the basic Pal clippers at 99 cents to Walton's Thumb at $25. Such gadgets are neat and not that more expensive (except the Thumb). And who knows? Sometime one of them might save the day for you.

Pal Angler's Clip. *By far the most popular clipper; includes knife, hook disgorger, and awl; lanyard (also offered in most catalogs with retractor for $2.50-$3 more).*
$.99-$2 Most catalogs

Big Pal Angler's Clip. *Same features as above with bottle opener and screwdriver; larger size.*
$1.89-$3.40 Bob, Sim, Bud, AnJ, EJH, Cab, Fol, Tac, Dan, H&H, AnW, Cus

Cortland Fisherman's Helper. *See Pal for features; sold with retractor.*
$6.20-$7.29 Tac, Mer

Walker's Fisherman's Clipper. *Includes can opener, awl, hook disgorger; two sizes.*
Small—$1.40; large—$1.75 Cus

Orvis Fly Fisherman's Snip. *With needle; silver or black finish; will clip very fine material but check for perfect closure since they are expensive.*
$4.50 Orv, Hun, Ste, Hig, Fly

Orvis Nipper Knife. *Scissors (instead of clippers), knife, file; 2¼"x1"x½".*
$12 Orv, Kau, Bud, Hun, Ste

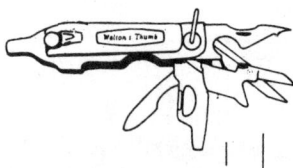

Walton's Thumb. *Clipper plus knife, tweezers, pincer nose, split ring opener, knot tag crimper, stiletto, scissors, screwdriver, and split shot opener; lacks small color tv.*
$22.50-$34.95 Ram, Cab, LLB, Fly

Leader Micrometers

"Miking" leaders has become great sport. It's always a thrill to find out that a famous leader material is really .002" off its stated size.

Outside of the sport involved, leader mikes come in most handy for checking terminal leader material for size. Seldom can you remember exactly what tippet size you were using last week. And continuous taper leaders grow steadily larger with or without your awareness. It's also handy to know where to start rebuilding if you break a leader at one of the intermediate blood knots.

It's a worthy endeavor to be a perfectionist about your leaders, and these are essential to perfect leaders.

Mike-Rite. *Rotate to desired sizes and check by inserting leader in gap; simple and compact, the standard mike; with leader formulas.*
$5.49-$8 Cab, Edd, Pen, Bob, Kau, Dal, Bud, Fly

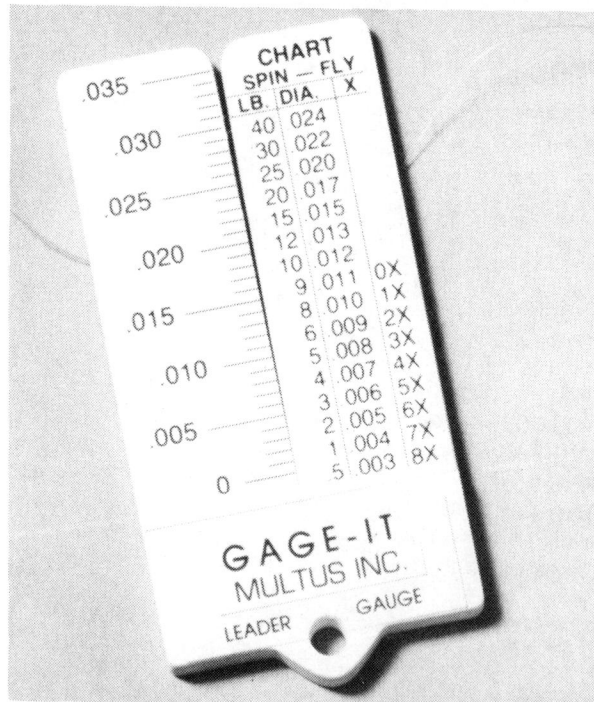

Multus Gage-It. *A simplified mike; insert leader in "V", where it stops is correct size; engraved markings won't scratch or wear off; like Mike-Rite, can be attached to vest with retractor or lanyard; 1½"x3½"x⁵/₃₂"; from Multus, Box 445, Medfield, Massachusetts 02052.*
$4.75-$6.50 Orv, Bob, Ram, Pen, Nor, Dan, H&H, T&T, Cus, Let, Bud, AnJ, Pen, or direct from Multus.

Cortland Leader Gauge. *No details available*
$7.95 Hig
Micrometer Leader Gauge. *No details, but priced like a "real" micrometer.*
$14.95 Mur
Starrett Micrometer. *Even more "real" that above; about the size of a pocket watch.*
$74.95 Pen

Knot-Tying Tools

Whenever there's a problem to be solved, whether it be how to get a man to the moon or how to thread a 7x tippet through the eye of a #26 midge pupa in a wind storm at dusk (guess which is more difficult), there are engineering wizards at work on it. Here are the results of their efforts for fly fishermen.

Unfortunately, I didn't have the opportunity to try these out. Some of them are fascinating just to look at. Just be sure that any knot-tying tool you may use does not pinch or otherwise damage your leader material. In any case, if you have trouble tying knots, you may wish to try one of these tools... or invent your own.

Moodus Angler's Tool. *Stainless steel tool for needle knots and blood knots; 4" long with pocket clip.*
$10.50-$10.85 Orv, Kau, Dan, Bud

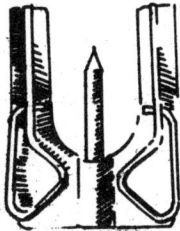

Courtesy of Bob Jacklin

Dennison Blood Knot Tyer. *A popular tool by a respected company.*
$6.95-$8.95 AnR, Bob, Hun, Kau, Dan, Cus, Mer, Bud, T&T
Blood Knot Machine. *Helps tie blood, clinch, dropper knots; instructions include leader formulas.*
$4.98 Pen
Orvis Fly Threader. *A nifty device for getting that tippet through the hook's eye, even in darkness.*
$5.25-$5.50 Kau, Hun, Orv

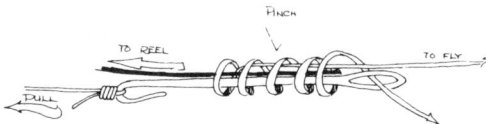

Nail Knot Tool. *A simple wire tool to ease the pain of tying the line/leader connection.*
$1.25 Bud
Ty-Rite Fly Holder. *A ballpoint pen type of device to hold fly while attaching leader; handy for tying clinch knots.*
$2.95 Bud, Dan

Cinch-Tie. *A brass tool for help in several tools.*
$7.95 AnJ
Needle 'N Tube. *Another fairly simple tool for help with nail knots and needle knots.*
$3.75-$5.95 Fly, Nor, Pen, LLB, T&T, Dal, Bud, Hun

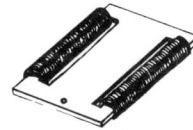

E-Z-"X" Blood Knot Tyer. *For help with the difficult blood knot.*
$3 T&T

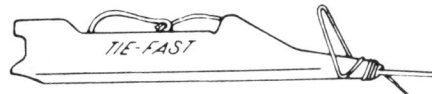

Tie-Fast Knot Tyer. *For nail and blood knots.*
$2.95-$3 Kau, Fly, Pen

Jiffy Blood Knot Tyer. *The "third finger" needed for blood knots; compact at 1"x¾"x5/16"; with instructions.*
$4.95 EJH

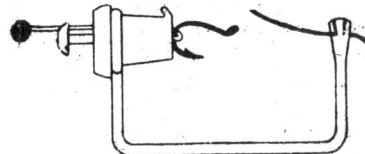

Leader Tyer. *A device to hold fly on one side and leader on the other (or two leaders); rotates to form knots; instructions included.*
$2 EJH

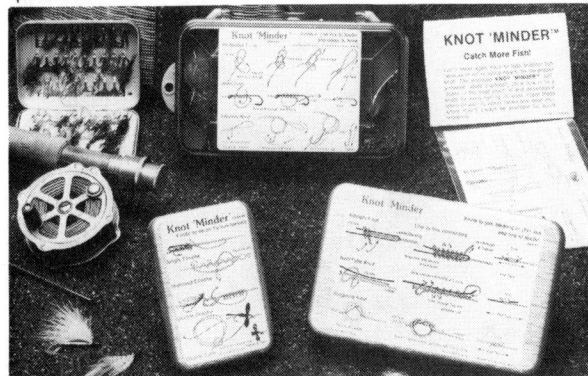

Knot Minder. *Although not actually a tool, these adhesive-backed vinyl cards will help your knot tying immensely; four cards printed with over a dozen common knots; designed to be stuck to fly boxes for easy reference;*

made by Sierra Outdoor Products, 92 Southern Heights, San Rafael, California 94901.
$3.95 Pen, Hig, Bud or direct from Sierra Outdoor Products

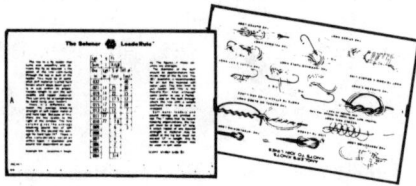

Solunar Leader-Rule. *Formulas for leader construction given in slide-rule form, along with common knots and hook sizes; flexible and waterproof.*
$2 Pen

Leader-Attached Weights

Traditional split shot remains the favorite weight for many fly fishermen, but there are now several other types of weights on the market.

One that is simply an improvement (and an excellent one, I believe) on the split shot is Water Gremlin's removable shot. Tiny levers are positioned counter to the opening. The shot is closed on the leader in regular fashion. When you want to remove it, you simply squeeze the levers together, thus opening the shot. Nifty. I don't find any disadvantage to the system although you might catch more weeds with the extra lead material. Unfortunately, the Water Gremlin shot is not made in very small sizes.

Another weighting system that is easily removed for weight adjustment, in whole or in part, are Twist-Ons. These strips of lead are packaged in a matchbook cover. You can tear out whole strips or tear strips in sections to suit your depth requirements. Twist-Ons are attached according to the instructions provided in their name. They are finer in diameter on the leader and thus less likely to catch on stones and weeds than is shot.

Fly-Rite Lead Sleeves are also designed to be "low profile" in the water. They are fairly flexible and are crimped on the leader. They come in a variety of sizes.

If you prefer more simplicity, there's lead wire for wrapping around leader.

Finally, there's Shape-A-Wate lead putty. It's moldable and obviously can be kept to a weed-free profile. It's also infinitely adjustable in terms of how much weight you can put on.

If you want midge-size shot, look for Pezon-Michel or Star shot (which may be identical). Both come in amazingly small sizes. They are packaged in "wheels" for easy dispensing.

The idea is to adjust the amount of weight you have on so that the nymph (or wet fly or streamer) rides at the proper depth. Often this means right at the bottom, and at that depth, it's important not to have excessive weight on or you'll end up stuck on rocks and everything

else besides fish. Your strike indicator will tell you when you're bumping bottom without getting continually hung up.

Since weight adjustments are made according to current speed and depth, many adjustments may be necessary during the course of a day astream. A weighting system that's convenient to change can be very handy. If you favor traditional split shot, you may wish to procure a tool for splitting them open.

Pezon-Michel Split Shot. *Very small diameter shot in wheel dispenser.*
$3.95-$4.10 Dal, EJH
Star Split Shot. *6 sizes in very small diameters, wheel dispenser.*
$2.95-$3.50 LLB, Let, Ram, Hun, T&T, Pen, Orv
Water Gremlin Split Shot. *Removable shot in sizes B to 7/5; packaged in zip-lock bags by individual size.*
$.40-$.65 T&T, Hig, AnW, Bud, EJH, Cus
Water Gremlin Split Shot. *Removable shot in wheel dispenser; variety of sizes.*
$.90-$2.50 AnW, AnJ, Fol
Twist-Ons. *Lead strips packaged in matchbook cover.*
$.25-$.50 Cus, EJH, Fly, Kau, Hig, Dan, Dal, Bob, Hun, Pen, Bud
Fly-Rite Lead Sleeves. *Wheel dispenser with varying sizes.*
$2.90-$4.25 H&H, Fly, Let, FlR, Mer, Bud, T&T, Kau
Lead Wire. *To be wrapped around leader much in the fashion of weighting a nymph.*
$.70-$2.95 (widely varying lengths; see catalogs) Bud, AnJ
Shape-A-Wate Lead Putty. *A moldable putty, re-usable; four 2½" leads.*
$.95-$1.50 Fly, Ram, Dal, T&T

Unusual Connectors

Although the following items are carried by a lot of catalog companies, I don't know anyone who uses them. I'm not sure why, since they appear to be sound devices. I've used the Leader-Link and find it very satisfactory. Maybe there's more security, at least in the angler's mind, with traditional knots.

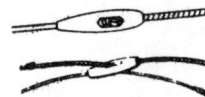

Leader-Links. *Designed to eliminate the nail knot; simply insert the line and the leader in opposite ends of the plastic Leader-Link, knot the ends so they can't pull back through, and go fish; available in either white or fl. orange.*
$.60-$1 (for 3) Tac, Kau, H&H, T&T, Cus, Dan, Mur, EJH, Pen, Bud

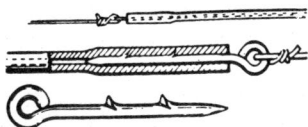

No-Knot Eyelets. *Another nail knot eliminator; barbed needle is inserted into the end of the fly line; eyelet allows an easy improved clinch knot for leader attachment.*
$.12-$.40 each (in packages of 2 or 3) Tac, Dan, Cus, EJH, Pen, Bud, Fly, Sim

Snap Hooks and Kwik-Klips. *Hook-like clips used by wet-fly fishermen to attach flies without using knots; quick and easy, but I think I'd rather have the less visible knots.*
$.79/12-$.35/3 Tac, Bud

Other Line and Leader Accessories

Stripping baskets. *Holds slack fly line or running line off the ground and away from distractions while you're casting; designed to be worn around the waist by use of a waist strap or by attaching to your wader belt; most are about 12" square and about 5" deep and have mesh bottoms to promote drainage. (Note: There is some diversity in design, so you should check specific catalogs for details.)*
$13-$23.75 Orv, Kau, Dan, H&H, T&T, Cus

Strike indicators. *Used with a nymph set-up to aid in detecting strike; adhesive-backed piece of foam that may be attached to line or leader by bending it back over itself with the line in the fold; easily attached and removed, but somewhat air-resistant and won't travel through the guides.*
$1-$1.50 (for about 20) T&T, Orv, Mer, Pen, Hig, Bud, Fly, Bob, Dal

Sleeve-type indicator. *Hollow sleeve that is slipped over the leader; flexible and can be treated to float.*
$1-$1.95 (for about 6) Bob, Fly, Bud

Leader-Loc and Tip-Tac. *These devices for holding your loose leader ends to your reel are listed under reel accessories.*

Plio-Bond. *Flexible, waterproof glue used to coat nail knots at the line/leader connection; helps the knot go smoothly through the guides and protects the knot.*
$1.25-$2.50 Kau, Hun, AnR, Dan, Fly, Cus, Mur, Bud

Supersplice Epoxy Kits. *Helps create the epoxy connection between leader and line; contains all necessary instructions, tools, and appropriate epoxy.*
$9.95-$11 Kau, T&T

5. Waders and Hip Boots

WHERE WOULD FLY fishermen be without waders? On the stream bank, of course, or in the hospital with pneumonia.

A spin or bait fisherman may get by without waders because he can cast farther and because he is not so concerned with a drag-free drift. But waders or hip boots are essential to the fly fisherman who uses the mobility afforded by them to reach distant fish-holding water and to improve his presentation to any water.

Until a few years ago, the subject of waders was a rather mundane one. With one or two exceptions, the angler's only choice was boot-foot waders or hippers. Then came Red Ball's Flyweight stocking-foot waders, and a whole new world seemed to open up. The current culmination of the market excitement is neoprene waders popularized by James-Scott and Simms. Now, with nearly 60 models of waders available, some explanation of the choices present is necessary.

Types of waders. Basically there are only two types of wading systems: the boot-foot wader and the stocking-foot wader.

The boot-foot wader is the traditional wader with boot and waterproof uppers manufactured as a single unit. Convenience is the greatest advantage of this type of wader. They can be slipped on instantly, and you can be fishing while others are still lacing. With some exceptions, they are generally made of tougher materials than stocking-foot waders. This makes them more resistant to punctures and snags.

The disadvantages of boot-foot waders include their weight and bulkiness. Since the materials used are heavier than stocking-foot wader materials, the boots weigh a lot. They don't fold up well, either, making them difficult to pack in the trunk, more difficult to take on the plane, and impossible to backpack.

It's also much more critical, and much more difficult, to get a correct fit with boot-foot waders. Comfort is one thing, but the life of the wader is dependent on correct fit, too. The most common problem is incorrect fit in the crotch and legs. This allows the legs of the wader to rub together while you're walking. The resultant chaffing wears through the materials and causes the waders to fail. At the same time, the waders must fit loosely enough to permit free movement. It's a slim line. If you decide on boot-foot waders, you should buy them from a dealer so that you can try them on with assistance from a clerk. If that's not possible, consider the size charts given by manufacturers carefully, especially if you're a bit odd in body size or shape (and who isn't?).

The last consideration is the longevity of the wader. Leaving aside the fact of streamside life that waders get punctured and torn, boot-foot waders using rubber will generally have a shorter life span than stocking-foot waders using man-made materials. Rubber is subject to deterioration from ozone and ultraviolet light. The result is known as weather-checking, and that spells the demise of a pair of waders. Advances in chemistry have given rubber boots a much longer life expectancy, but they will still bite the dust sooner than stocking-foot waders of man-made materials such as nylon and neoprene.

Stocking-foot waders require a wading shoe to be worn over the foot of the wader. They have several advantages that have made them the favorite of many fly fishermen.

First among those advantages is comfort. Stocking-foot waders are lighter and fit better than the stiffer, comparatively awkward boot-foot waders. They fit like a pair of coveralls instead of a tent. The neoprene waders stretch to give you even more mobility.

Stocking-foot waders weigh very little due to the lightweight nylon or neoprene generally used in them. They are compact when folded or rolled up, so they travel well and can be backpacked. The materials used in lightweight stocking-foot waders are more subject to punctures and tears than the fabric-covered rubber used in many boot-foot waders, but those tears are remarkably easy to repair. A self-adhesive nylon tape will fix nylon waders, and neoprene requires only a tube of cement.

In addition, the materials used are not as subject to deterioration. You won't find nylon weather-checking. If you do ruin or wear out a stocking-foot wader or a wading shoe, you need only replace the worn out part, not the entire system as you would with a boot-foot wader.

The disadvantage, of course, is the extra effort required to get into the water. Five minutes may not seem like a lot as you read this book, but streamside it can seem like hours. But that's a matter of mind control, folks, and shouldn't be the deciding factor.

Lightweight waders like Red Ball's Flyweights are also extremely cold when you're in the water, unless you wear long johns. As a trade-off, they're not as hot and clammy out of the water as boot-foot waders. Of course, neoprene is much warmer in the water and also has some insulating value against hot weather.

One advantage of stocking-foot waders is the choice of shoes for different wading situations. With one pair of waders and two pairs of shoes (one with felt soles, the other with rubber cleats), you can meet any wading situation. However, you'll have a difficult time locating cleat-sole wading shoes these days. I have a pair of Red Ball wading shoes with good cleat soles, but I didn't see them in any catalogs. High-top tennies or canvas hiking boots are an acceptable substitute, but they seldom have good, knobby soles.

The same advantage can be had with boot-foot waders by purchasing waders with cleat soles and adding a wading sandal when felt soles are needed.

Waders or hip boots? It's a relatively easy matter to decide between waders and hippers. Lake fishing and deep rivers require waders for the most complete access. At the same time, it's silly to burden yourself with waders if you're fishing small streams.

I use hippers for 75% of my fishing here in Colorado. Most of the streams are fairly small and not too deep, and the ones that are bigger and deeper are often too swift for safe wading over knee depth. I own waders for lakes, and I take them with me to the bigger streams. They are necessary on trips to the Bighorn, Madison, and other large rivers.

An interesting compromise are the waist-high waders from James-Scott. They should take care of 90% of your wading needs while being comfortable and giving access to pants pockets.

Felt soles or cleat soles? Felt soles give superior traction in streams, but poor footing in muddy-bottomed lakes and beaver ponds. Cleat soles are safer in mud but afford dangerously slick footing in most streams.

If you buy only one type of sole, choose it based on the kind of fishing you'll be doing the most. However, I'd recommend owning and using both types of sole. Your life can rest on your wading ability, and that is often determined by your boot soles.

In short, don't compromise in wading equipment.

Develop a wading system for every situation you'll face. If you fish mainly lakes, buy your boot-foot waders with cleats. Add a pair of felt-soled wading sandals or Korkers for streams. For stocking-foot waders, buy cleat-sole wading shoes (or substitute tennis shoes or canvas hiking boots) and felt-sole wading shoes.

A few rivers require even more care, so slippery are they. For them, add Stream Cleats, Kleet Feet, or boot chains. Don't mess around. Get the best footing you can. The most pleasant outcome of a mistake in equipment choice here will be an unpleasant dunking and a ruined day. The worst can be your death by drowning. It has happened to the best.

And while we're on the subject, carry a wading staff for additional safety.

The beginner's wading system. If you'll be fishing in small streams for the most part, you may wish to begin with a pair of hippers. You'll want felt soles for safety. Economics enter into your choice next. I'd recommend spending some money on your boots. It's really false economy to buy cheap boots that will need to be replaced in a year or that come with leaks so you don't have to bother creating your own.

With that in mind, I'd recommend the Ranger full-rubber hippers with felt soles. They are available from your local dealer or from Simon Peter for $48.60. You will find cheaper boots, but I can't recommend them. The last pair of full-rubber Ranger hip boots I bought lasted about five years, and I do a lot of fishing.

If hippers are your first choice but you think you'll soon need waders, you may wish to buy stocking-foot hippers and wading shoes. Red Ball Master S/T hippers are about $30, and the River Systems shoe with felt soles is about $35 (both from Hook & Hackle). Later you can add stocking-foot waders.

If you've decided to begin with chest waders, there's an economical way to get started. Red Ball (Hampshire) makes a nylon stocking-foot wader, the Sportster, that seems durable enough. We've had a pair in the family for a couple of years, now, and they've been entirely satisfactory. Considering the $17.95 price (from Hook & Hackle again), you can hardly go wrong. With a pair of old tennies, you're ready for the lakes. With the River Systems shoe, you've got a decent wading system for the streams at just over $50.

Care of waders and hippers. This is pretty simple. Keep the inside of your boots dry so that the green fuzzy stuff doesn't grow in them. A hanger that lets the boot air out is the answer, but people in damper climates and people who fall in a lot like boot dryers. (My "boot dryer" is a pile of newspapers. Wadded up and jammed into the boot, they'll absorb a lot of water pretty quickly.)

Store your waders out of the light and away from sources of ozone (electric motors). A black plastic garbage bag tied shut is pretty good protection.

It also pays to avoid barbed wire fences, the bunji sticks of beaver ponds, and your companion's backcast.

BOOT-FOOT WADERS AND HIPPERS

Boot-Foot Waders

The waders listed alphabetically here are one-piece, boot-foot, chest-high waders. All require suspenders to hold them up and some include them. A wading belt is recommended by many manufacturers, and belt loops are provided on many of these boots.

In selecting a wader, be sure that the company offers a size to fit you. It's best to try on the waders at a fly shop (and then buy them there), rather than buying through the mail. Correct fit is difficult and essential. If the waders are too small, you won't have any mobility. If they end up too big, parts will chaff together and wear out (and you'll look funny in the meantime).

Some waders offer a pouch just inside the wader top which is handy for items usually carried in pants pockets. Don't economize on boot-foot chest waders. It's not worth it. If you feel it necessary to do that, consider the suggestion for chest waders for beginners in the introduction.

An interesting variation on the traditional boot-foot wader is the Over-the-Shoe Wader available from Tidewater Specialties. It's a full length overshoe to be slipped right over regular shoes.

It's best to buy rubber products that are fresh from the factory since the primary cause of wader failure is weather-checking, which is a function of how long the wader has been out in the air and light. The best time to buy locally, then, is in late spring or early summer when your nearby shop has its new merchandise in. Try to get your old waders to wear out at the right time of year.

Keep in mind that not all sources listed for a product carry all available sizes. If you're beyond the standard deviation, you may have to do some shopping around.

Gra-Lite Waders. *Boot foot of heavy-duty vinyl; uppers shiny vinyl; cleat soles; 5 year warranty; repair kit, suspenders included; sizes: 8-13 in short, reg., and long.*
$160 Let

Hodgman Wadewell Waders. *3-ply fabric/rubber/fabric; cleat soles or felt soles; pouch; made in Orient; treated against ozone deterioration; sizes: reg.—5-13, long—9-13.*
$55.95-$89.95 (add about $5 for felts) Cus, Dan, AnW, Mur, Fol, Bob

Hodgman Rod and Reel Waders. *Rubber-surfaced; fabric-lined; pouch; treated for ozone deterioration; reinforced seams; insulated or non-insulated; sizes: see above.*
$41.60-$75 Cus, AnJ, Fol, Sim, Nat

Hodgman Brighton Waders. *Nylon surfaced with rubber layers; pouch; cleat sole; sizes: men's—7-13, women's—5-9.*
$51.95-$59.95 Cus, Fol, Ram, Bud (women's only and the only one to carry women's)

LaCrosse Waders. *Double-coated nylon uppers; rubber*

lowers; foam-insulated; cleat soles; sizes: 5-15.
$87 Dun

Marathon Waders. *Four layers of rubber on outside; inside layer on nylon; steel shank; felt soles; suspenders, repair kit included; sizes: 5-14.*
$96-$99.95 LLB, Dan

Marathon Insulated Waders. *Inside coating of neoprene, fabric layer, then natural rubber double coating; wool insulated foot; felt soles; guaranteed 5 years (pro-rated); sizes: 5-13 and custom fit (women select one size smaller).*
$105-$115 (custom fit—$124.95-$130) Dan, Nor, T&T

Orvis Deluxe Stretch Waders. *Stretch nylon uppers; features to eliminate chafing, seam leaks; lining eliminates clamminess; most expensive waders made; felt soles; sizes: 7-13, reg., short, long.*
$315 ($365 insulated) Orv

Orvis Deluxe Waders. *Neoprene-coated nylon uppers; full rubber boots; felt soled (with or without aluminum studs); sizes: short—7-9, reg.—7-13, long—9-13. (Note: Insulated models also available—see catalog.)*
$167 (add $16 for studs) Orv

Orvis Ladies' Deluxe Waders. *Same features as above; felt soled only; sizes: 6-8 (use regular shoe size).*
$150 Orv

Over-the-Shoe Waders. *Rubber-coated nylon; made to be worn over regular shoes; olive drab; order by shoe size:7-13.*
$95 Tid

Ranger Waders. *3-ply fabric/rubber/fabric tops; natural gum rubber lowers; treated against ozone; insulated or non-insulated; cleat or felt soles; sizes: short—6-9, reg.—6-13, long—9-13, women's—4-9.*
$75-$122.95 (add about $10 for felts or insulated waders) Pen, Kau, Edd, Bud, Sim, Cab, AnW, Dan

Ranger All-Rubber Waders. *Natural gum rubber top to bottom; treated against ozone; cleat or felt soles; sizes: see above.*
$64.95-$94.95 (add about $5 for felts or insulated) Cab, Fly

Ranger Lightwade Waders. *2-ply PVC; nylon lined; pouch; insulated or non-insulated; felt or cleat soles; sizes: 6-13.*
$39.95-$52.70 (add about $5 for insulated or felts) Ram, Cus, Bud

Red Ball Adirondack Waders. *Nylon economy waders; pouch; belt loops; drawstring top; dark brown; sizes: 7-13.*
$28-$40.95 Mer, AnW, Sim

Red Ball Sportster Waders. *2-ply polyester blend/rubber; insulated; brown; sizes: 7-13.*
$55.78 Mer

Red Ball Sportster Felt Sole Waders. *As above with felt soles; non-insulated; sizes: 7-12.*
$69.95 Bud

Red Ball Master Waders. *3-ply nylon/rubber/nylon; insulated; cleat soles; dark brown; sizes: reg.—7-13, tall—10-13.*
$58.95-$88.95 Sim, Ram, Mer, Dun, Dan

Red Ball Master Felt Sole Waders. *3-ply construction as above without insulation; felt soles; dark brown; sizes:*

reg.—7-13, tall—10-13.

$69.95-$88.95 Dun, T&T, Bud

Seaway Coachman Waders. *Economy rubber with fabric lining; pouch; sizes: 7-13.*

$34.95-$37.95 Fol, Cus

Simms Boot-Foot Neoprene Waders. *Neoprene boot-foot waders; lined inside and out for easy entry/exit; sole not described; sizes: XS-XL (plus kings and longs).*

$225 Kau, Hig

Stream Line Boot-Foot Waders. *Neoprene boot-foot waders; ¼" neoprene; wader extends over shoulders, coverall-style; Velcro closures at shoulders; innnovative design; cleat soles; accessory felt-soled overshoe available; dark blue or camo (add $10).*

$220 (shoes $34) Stream Line, Box 3047, Santa Cruz, California 95063

Boot-Foot Hippers

Boot-foot hippers are the most convenient boot for fishing small streams. They go on quick and afford the maximum in comfort. I use them about 75% of the time, in spite of the fact it seems fashionable to wade around in 6" of water wearing chest waders.

I've had some miserable times with rubber boots, especially before I gave up on the $12.95 specials at the local discount store. Even when I began buying "good" brands, I had some trouble. One pair lasted about a half

season and disintegrated (or, as we say in the business, "blew up"). I'm sure they came from very old stock.

Anyway, I've used Ranger full-rubber hip boots for about five years (and that was only the first pair). They finally weather-checked, but I could have gotten another year or two out of them if I'd stored them between fishing trips instead of leaving them in my trunk. Now I have some new Rangers with the fancy (and more comfortable) fabric uppers.

The hip boots are listed in alphabetical order.

Hodgman Rod and Reel. *Rubber surface; fabric lining; cleat sole; sizes: 6-13.*

$41.95-$45.45 Cus, Fol

Hodgman Rod and Reel Insulated. *Same as above but insulated; wool lined foot and ankle; sizes: 7-13.*

$48.95-$51.95 Cus, Fol

Hodgman Wadewell. *3-ply fabric/rubber/fabric; treated for ozone deterioration; made in Orient; sizes: 9-12.*

$44.95 AnJ

Hodgman Wadewell Felt Soles. *Top-of-the-line Hodgman; felt sole; sizes: 7-13.*

$75.95-$79.20 Mur, Dan

Hodgman Brighton Ladies Hippers. *3-ply nylon/rubber/ nylon uppers; felt sole; sizes: 7-9.*

$73.50 Bud

LaCrosse Hip Boots. *Ozone-resistant full-rubber; steel shank; cleat soles:insulated or non-insulated; olive drab; fabric lining; sizes: 5-13.*

$47.50 (add $10 for insulated) Dun

Marathon Hip Boots. *Inside coating of neoprene, fabric layer, then natural rubber double coating; insulated foot, wool; felt soles; guaranteed 5 years (pro-rated); sizes: 5-13.*

$99-$110 T&T, Nor

Ranger Hip Boots. *Rubber; treated for ultraviolet and ozone protection; non-insulated; cleat sole; sizes: men's—6-13, women's—4-11, child's—4-6.*

$35.95-$59.95 (less for child's, sometimes more for women's) Cus, AnW, Ram, Sim, Cab, Fly

Ranger Hip Boots. *Same as above but insulated with wool fleece; sizes: 8-13.*

$47.50-$67.95 AnW, Sim, Fly

Ranger Hip Boots. *Same as above but non-insulated with felt soles; sizes: 7-13.*

$48.60 Sim

Ranger Hip Boots. *Rubber lower, triple layer fabric/rubber/fabric upper; non-insulated with felt soles or insulated with cleat soles; sizes: men's—6-13, women's—4-9.*

$55.80-$81.95 Cab, Cus, Bud, Sim, Edd, Orv, Dan, Kau

Ranger Lightwade. *Molded PVC; nylon lined; reinforced heels, toes, ankles, shanks; cleat sole or felt sole; sizes: 6-13.*

$37.65-$41.30 Cus, Bud

Red Ball Master. *3-ply upper; one-piece boot; cleat soles; sizes: 7-13.*

$46 AnW

Red Ball Adirondack. *Economy boot with fabric supported upper; molded lower; cleat soles; sizes: 8-12.*
$25-$26.30 AnW, Sim
Seaway Coachman. *Economy hip boot; insulated; vulcanized rubber; fabric lining; sizes: 7-13.*
$27.50-$29.90 Cus, Fol
Servus Northerner Hippers. *Full rubber; cleat soles; sizes: men's—7-13, women's—5-9.*
$37.95 Pen
Servus Northerner Felt Sole Hippers.
As above but with felts; sizes: men's—7-13, women's—n/a.
$42.95 Pen
Youth Hip Boots. *Cut for the youngster in your fishing life; ozone resistant; insulated; cleat soles; olive drab; sizes: 3-6 (26 ½" height).*
$54.95 Dun
Youth Hip Boots. *As above except non-insulated; sizes: 2-6 (22" height).*
$36 Dun

STOCKING-FOOT WADING SYSTEMS

This is where it's at in waders these days. Stocking-foot waders have many advantages, including greater comfort, more versatility, and longer life expectancy. In general, they're sexier than boot-foot waders.

Most of the waders listed here are relatively new on the market. Only Seal-Dri, a latex stocking-foot wader, has been around for a long time. Seal-Dri waders are still favored by those who want stocking-foot waders with the greatest puncture resistance and more insulation value. Seal-Dri offers an extra heavy-grade now.

The wader that started the stocking-foot craze is, in my mind, the Red Ball Flyweight. These waterproofed nylon waders are extremely light, yet they are tough enough to stand up to "regular" usage. I've had a pair for four or five years and still haven't punctured them. I have taken care to keep my wading socks and shoes clean to avoid unnecessary wear in the wader foot, but that's been my only maintenance. These waders fold up into an incredibly small package, and at 14 oz., they can be packed into those back country lakes and streams. They feature an inflatable air chamber which will help keep out water and provide some buoyancy in case of a dunking.

The lightweights offer no insulation against the cold of the river. I'd recommend long johns or some other clothing to protect against the chill. I use a pair of warm-up pants that can be slipped on over my pants and can be easily removed for greater comfort after the fishing is over.

River Systems has their own lightweight nylon wader, the Feather River, which weighs slightly more than the Flyweights. Feather River waders use belt loops rather than an inflatable air chamber, such as the Flyweight's (which nobody I know uses).

James-Scott (J-S) nearly doubled the thickness of the nylon material typically used in stocking-foot waders in order to create the Bulletproof waders. That doubled the weight and the cost, but the waders are popular with those leery of the extreme lightweight of the other waders.

J-S and Simms popularized the next refinement in wading systems, neoprene waders. These feature nylon-coated, closed-cell neoprene. Neoprene has insulation and comfort advantages over nylon. There are many features you'll appreciate only after using neoprene waders. If you take a dunk, for instance, the tight-fitting neoprene waders will snug even tighter against your body, thus keeping out most of the water. The material is easily repaired with neoprene cement, and the waders can still be worn with small holes in them since the material tends to close in on itself even when punctured.

J-S offers three models: the original chest wader, a waist-high wader, and a lined version of the chest wader. The lining lessens the difficulty of putting on the neoprene waders. Unlined models must be rolled on.

Simms also offers a lined version of the neoprene wader. In addition, they have created a boot-foot wader in neoprene, for those people who prefer that style of wader.

Stocking-foot hippers are a recent offering. They're made of the same material as the Red Balls and River Systems waders. They're listed last.

An economy stocking-foot wader worthy of your consideration is Red Ball's Sportster model. It's reasonably tough and very inexpensive. Stay away, however, from the cheap vinyl waders found in discount stores. They can be punctured in a brief encounter with a mosquito.

Stocking-Foot Waders

James-Scott Bulletproof Waders. *430 denier nylon, 2-4 times thicker than conventional lightweights; 40 oz. total; built-in wading sock and cuff; wading belt, suspenders included; brown; sizes: S-XL.*
$100 Kau, Pen, Ram, Hun, Fly, Orv, Nat
James-Scott "Original" Boot-Sock Waders. *Neoprene for increased durability and comfort; very stretchy for freedom of movement; warmer than conventional stocking-foot waders; built-in gravel cuff, suspenders, and quick-release buckles; drawstring top; can be rolled down to waist level; sizes: S-XL or custom fit.*
$125 ($135 larger sizes; add $30-$40 for custom fit) Pen, Hun, Fly, Orv, Nat, AnJ, Bob, Ram, T&T
James-Scott Waist High Waders. *As above but only waist high; no suspenders or straps needed; will take care of 90% of wading situations; sizes: S-XL.*
$110 Dun
James-Scott Lined Boot-Sock Waders. *As above with nylon stretch fabric bonded to both sides for easy/on, easy/off; slightly less elastic; sizes: S-XL.*
$165 ($175 larger sizes; add $30-$40 for custom fit) T&T, Fly, Bob, Bud

James-Scott Boot-Sock Waders

JOBE Waders. *Neoprene, ⅛" thick; lined; padded straps; gravel guards; sizes: S-XL.*
119.95 Pen

Red Ball Sportster Waders. *Economical stocking-foot wader; nylon; brown; sizes: XS-XL.*
$17.95-$24.30 Mer, Cus, H&H, Fly, Dan

Red Ball Flyweight Master S/T Waders. *Lightweight 220 denier nylon; 14 oz. total; inflatable air chamber at top snugs wader to body and provides flotation; sizes: XS-XL.*
$49.95-$73.80 Pen, Mer, Kau, Orv, Dan, Bud, Ram, Cab, Fly, H&H, LLB, Bob, Sim, Cus, Hun, Dun

River Systems Feather River Waders, *Lightweight 220 denier nylon; 20 oz. total; fold to 9"x12"; belt loops for 1½" belt; drawstring top; sizes: XXS-XL.*
$49.98-$69.95 Pen, AnJ, Fly

Seal Dri Latex Waders. *Latex rubber; one piece so no seams to leak; stretches; front pouch; suspenders and patch kit included; sizes: S-XL.*
$39.95-$71.49 Mur, Dan, Kau, Bob, Fly, Let, Edd, Cus, Hig, EJH, Pen, Cab, Bud, H&H, Dal, Orv

Seal Dri Extra Heavy Latex Waders. *Heavy latex rubber, 50% thicker, 35% more puncture resistant, 13% more tear strength than regular Seal Dri waders; sizes: S-XL.*
$56.95-$89 H&H, Pen, Kau, Hig, Bud, Edd, Dan, Fly, Cus, Cab, Bob, EJH

Simms Lined Neoprene Waders. *Neoprene lined inside and out with nylon for easy entry/exit; sizes: XS-XL (plus kings and longs).*
$149.95-$180 Hig, Kau, Cab

Stocking-Foot Hippers

Red Ball Master S/T Hippers. *Lightweight nylon hip boots; sizes: S-XL.*
$28.50-$41.75 Cab, Dun, Pen, Dan, H&H, Orv, Bud, Cus

River Systems Feather River Hippers. *Lightweight nylon; 220 denier; 12 oz. total; Velcro cinch straps at top; 9"x12" travel bag; sizes: S-XL.*
$35-$57.95 Fly, Pen, EJH, Ram

Wading Shoes

Wading shoes are used over stocking-foot waders and hippers. Before you gape at the $100 shoes here, remember that there are still many of the fly fishing unwashed who use tennis shoes and have just as much fun. Felt soles are difficult to find on tennies, however, and by the time you buy felt soles, glue them on, and figure that the tennies aren't going to outlast the soles, you're better off with a regular wading shoe.

I think any of these shoes would be a good investment. The River Systems and the Red Ball Master are of one price and quality range. The others are in another range.

In buying, you want your shoe to be comfortable first. Aesthetics can follow afterwards someplace. Most of the shoes here can be counted on to give you good service in spite of what they're put through.

The only thing left for wading shoe designers to develop is a better lacing system. Shoes with laces are a pain, especially when the laces are wet. Shoes with Velcro closures catch weeds and fly lines and sometimes come undone because of that. The current Velcro "laces" are close-but-no-gold-star. The new Orvis Lightweight Wading Shoes may be even closer. They feature speed lacing (with eyelets like little D-rings) so the entire boot can be tightened from the top. They utilize plastic cord clamps (like those used on sleeping bag stuff sacks) in place of knots. An innovative system that might just answer all the complaints.

The shoes are listed in alphabetical order. Please note that some brands are ordered in street shoe sizes, others one size larger. Women have a wider variety of ordering instructions to follow. To further complicate matters, catalogs don't always agree on how to order. The industry needs to standardize this system, but in the meantime, it's wise to try on wading shoes before buying.

Danner River Gripper Shoe. *Nylon mesh uppers reinforced with silicone-treated roughout leather; felt soles; sizes: D-width—6-14; EE-width—7-12; women's B-width—4-10 (men order one size larger than street shoe size; women order regular size).*
$78.95-$99.95 Fly, Dan, Nor, Kau, Cus, Bud

Gary Borger Ultimate Wading Shoe. *7" man-made "leather" tops; triple thickness felt soles; padded collar; hard plastic toe; sizes: 6-14 (men order one size larger than street shoe size; women order regular size).*
$49.95-$77.50 Dan, Kau, Bud, Pen, AnJ, Dal, LLB, Bob, Mur, Ram, Fly, Cus, Cab, Hun, H&H, Orv (studded soles also)
Gary Borger Ultimate Wading Shoe. *As above but with Velcro "laces"; sizes: 6-13.*
$85 Orv (studded soles also, add $7.50)
James-Scott Wading Shoe. *Man-made "leather"; 8" tops; hard toe; felt soles; pull-on loop; sizes: 6-12 and extra wide 13-14 (men order one size larger than street*

shoe; women order one size smaller).
$65-$67.50 T&T, Hig, Bob
Orvis Lightweight Wading Shoe. *Man-made leather uppers; reinforced toe (in the style of Out West shoes listed below); felt soles (studs available—add $5); speed laces with "B-locks" so no knots needed; sizes: 6-13, EE (order one size larger than street shoe).*
$57.50 Orv

Red Ball Master Wading Shoe. *Nylon uppers with rigid toe and heel; felt soles; vents; sizes: 6-13 (men order same size as street shoe; women order two sizes smaller).*
$37.95-$59.95 Hig, Cab, Dal, Pen, Mer, Dun, Ste, Bob, Bud

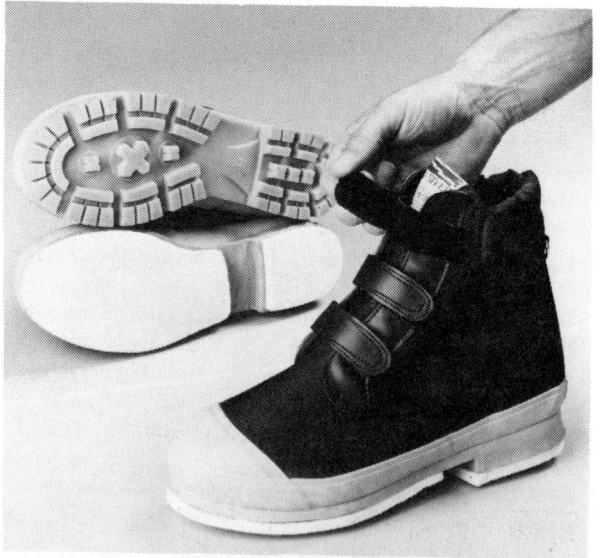

River Systems Out West (Wind River) Wading Shoe. *Velcro "lacing"; brown nylon uppers with yellow toes; steel shank; felt soles; padded ankle tops; D-ring for pulling on; sizes: men's—6-14, women's—5-7 (although some catalogs recommend same size fit, most recommend ½-1 size larger than street shoe size).*
$34.50-$52.95 Pen, H&H, Dan, T&T, Cus, AnJ, Cab, Let, Fly, EJH, Sim, Bud, Dal, Edd, Ram

Russell Wading Shoe. *Heel and toe reinforced with heavy leather; felt soles; sizes: 6-12 (use street shoe size).*
$99.95-$109.95 Cus, AnR, Dan

Socks and Cuffs

With the popularity of stocking-foot waders has come a number of accessories for between foot and wader and between wader and shoe. Many of these are very useful; some are rather faddish. You can decide which is which.

One item that's important is some kind of gravel guard. These come in two styles: the gaiter and the sock with fold-down cuff. Either will keep grit from getting into your shoe which is both a discomfort and a point of wear on your waders.

We'll start with the socks for inside the wader, then catch the gravel guard and special outer "socks". The products are listed in random order.

Inside Socks

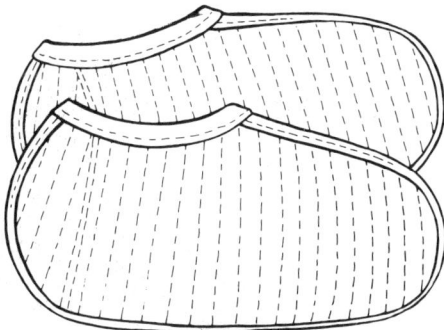

Red Ball Bama Sokkets. *Outer layer of cotton tricot; inner layer of acrylic fiber; helps keep feet dry inside waders; elastic top, reinforced heel; sizes 6-13.*
$5.95-$10.30 H&H, Pen, Mer, Sim, T&T, Dal, Bud, Cus
Bristol Bay wading socks. *Nylon pile in "bootie" style; knit ankles; sizes: S-XL.*
$8.95 Pen
River Systems Inside Sock. *Nylon-pile fleece lining; sizes: XS-XL.*
$6.75-$8 Cus, H&H

Lectra Sock. *Warm feet at last; battery pack goes on belt or in wader pouch; sizes: S-L.*
$12.35 Cus
Barbour Fishing Socks. *Heavy marl knit, 75% wool, 25% nylon; knee-length with turnover tops; good for extra warmth in smaller streams; sizes: M(8-9), L(10-12).*
$9.95-$16.95 Ram, Pen

Outside Socks and Gravel Guards

Simms Gravel Guard. *Nylon gaiter fits around wading shoe top; black; 6".*
$11-$13 Ram, Pen, Hig, Bob, Bud, Kau, Fly

Simms Wader Sox. *Nylon and neoprene sock to replace wool socks; worn between wader and shoe; split upper for easy on/easy off; blue; sizes: S-L.*
$24.95-$30 Pen, Kau
Dan Bailey Wading Sock. *Neoprene; 10" high; shaped like foot for comfort and no seam under foot; for between wader and shoe; brown; sizes: XS(5-6), S(7-8), M(8-9), ML(9-10), L(10-11), XL(11-13), XXL(13-15).*
$23.95 Dan, Bud
James-Scott Boot-Socks. *Nylon-faced neoprene; for all stocking-foot waders; worn between wader and shoe; cuff feature keeps out gravel; good insulation factor; stretches for easy on/easy off; sizes: S(6-7 ½), M(8-9 ½), L(10-11 ½), XL(12-13 ½).*
$30.30-$35 Pen, Cus, Fly, Dan, Hun, Bud, Orv, Hig, Dun, Kau, Bob, Ram

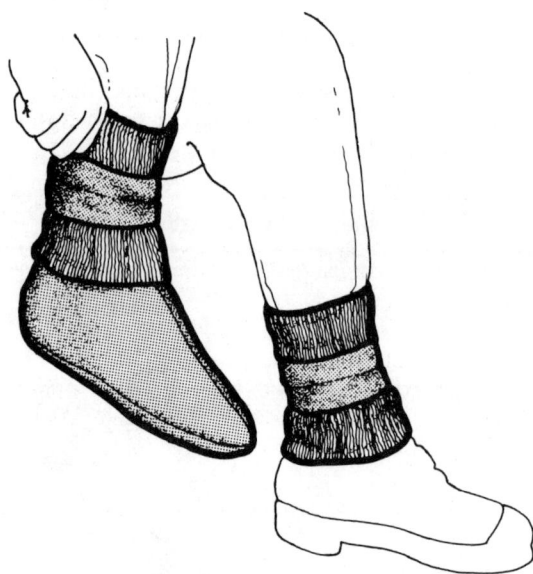

River Systems Wader-Gaiters. *Inner top of ribbed nylon for snug fit; outer cuff of neoprene as gravel guard; worn between wader and shoe; 100% fleece sock; sizes: XS(5 ½-6 ½), S(7-8), M(8 ½-10), L(10 ½-12), XL(12 ½-14).* $12.15-$18.95 Cab, EJH, T&T, Pen, Cus, Ram, Bud, AnR, H&H, LLB, Dan, Fly, Let, Sim

WADING ACCESSORIES

Wader Repair Kits

Today it's not enough just to order a repair kit. You must match the kit to the material. Rubber requires patches. Nylon can take a self-adhesive tape. Neoprene requires a special cement.

I have to take time to praise one product listed here. Sportsman's Goop is wonderful stuff. I've used it to repair huge tears in rubber waders. It will dry well enough to use in 20-30 minutes. It will work on nearly anything. A wonderful product.

There's no particular order to these.

Vinyl repair kit. *42 sq. in. vinyl and cement.*
$2.20 Dan
Conventional rubber patch kit. *Patching material and glue.*
$.85-$.95 H&H, Cus
Red Ball Flyweight Wader Repair Kit. *Special patching material for Flyweights; in convenient packet for vest or wader pocket.*
$1.50-$3.95 Pen, Mer, Cus, Ram, H&H, Bob, Kau, Fly, T&T
Red Ball Master and Sportster Repair Kit. *Patches, 1 oz. tube of cement.*
$2 Mer
Hodgman Universal Kit. *For cloth and rubber; includes cement, cloth and rubber patching material, instructions.*
$3.95-$4.55 Cus, Fol

Compleat Angler Super Kit. *Silicone adhesive, nylon fabric for patches, abrasive paper, brush, instructions.*
$3.25-$4.25 Cus, Mur, T&T, Dan, Sim, Bud, Dal, Ram
Ranger Wader Patch. *For nylon and canvas, with cement.*
$4.25-$4.95 Cus, AnW, Fly, Kau
Seal Dri Patch Kit. *For Seal Dri's latex waders.*
$1.30-$2 Bob, Mur, Dan, Bud, Fly
Magic Patch. *Just heat with match and wipe on area to be patched.*
$2 Mur, Dan
Sportsman's Goop. *An amazing patch; remains flexible after "setting"; use on any material; repairs punctures and tears; waders can be used after 20-30 min. but best patch comes from overnight set; 4.5 oz. tube.*
$2.75-$4 Cus, Bud, Fly, Fol, Mur, Kau, Dan, Bob, H&H, Ram, Ste, Mer, AnR, T&T, Ran
James-Scott Neoprene Repair Kit. *Tube of neoprene cement and instructions.*
$2.95 Fly, Bob
Aqua Seal. *Tube of glue for neoprene waders; 24-hour dry; 1.5 oz.*
$4.95 Kau
Fast Cure. *To be mixed with Aqua Seal above for 2-4 hour dry; 4 oz.*
$4.95 Kau
Ripair Tape. *Self-adhesive tape; waterproof; rip-stop nylon; will repair Flyweights, also good for nylon tents, stuff bags, etc.; 3"x36".*
$1.45 Bud

Replacement Felt Soles and Laces

If you buy a good wader or wading shoe, it will outlast its felt sole. Replacement soles help you get the most out of your waders.

To add new soles, the bottoms of your boots must be clean and dry. A layer of cement is applied to them and to the replacement soles (which you've trimmed to size) before joining. Allowing the glue to set overnight will do the trick.

In buying felt soles, there are a few things to consider. Polypropylene soles are the least expensive but generally do not wear as well as nylon. Nylon wears better than wool but does not grip as well. Woven soles are better than pressed soles, both for grip and wear. Many people, incidentally, use indoor/outdoor carpeting as replacement sole material. Some of it's a good grade of woven nylon that wears well and is real pretty. Some of it will fall apart in two trips. Since you can't tell the difference easily, I'd stay with the replacement soles listed here.

You'll also find cement for soles and replacement wading shoe laces here. Barge Cement, incidentally, makes a good patch for many waders, as well as being the standard waterproof cement for soles. Replacement soles are listed in random order.

Jim Bowes' Boot Grippers. *Needlepunch polypropylene soles; sole and heel separate; completely waterproof; resistant to abrasion.*
$5.40-$7.95 Pen, H&H, EJH, Fol
Wadersafe Resole Kit. *Polypropylene soles; waterproof; one-piece sole; sizes: S(6-9), L(10-13).*
$6.95-$6.99 Dal, Bud
Sportsman's Non-Slip Felt Soles. *Wool felt; one-piece; includes cement; indicate boot size.*
$9.95 Ran
River Systems Felt Sole Kit. *⅜" nylon felt; soles with separate heels; specially designed for RS wading shoes; sizes: 6-7, 8-9, 10-11, 12-13, 14.*
$8.98-$10.95 Pen, Fly, AnJ
Compleat Angler Felt Sole Kit. *Woven nylon felt for greater wear; includes waterproof cement; sizes: S(up to 9), L(10-13).*
$7.80-$12.50 EJH, Pen, Dan, Ram, Bud, Cus, Sim, Orv, Cab, Hun, H&H

Accessory Soles

Accessory soles are designed for special wading conditions. They add versatility to your wading system. There are wading sandals with felt soles to go over waders that have cleat soles. For extremely slick conditions, Korkers, Stream Cleats, or boot chains may be needed. A shop near where you've fallen in for the third time will probably know which add-on works best in that stream.

Korkers. *Full-length sandal with aluminum studs; recommended for weedy streams, ice; replacement studs available; S(to shoe size 9), M(to 11 ½), L(to 13).*
$34.25-$41.50 Mer, Dun, Dal, T&T, Fly, Ram, Dal, Pen
Stream Cleats. *Aluminum bars attached to rubber overshoe; slips over wader without need for straps; sizes (non-insulated boots): S(6-7), M(8-9), L(10-11), XL(12-13), Giant(14-15).*
$32.70-$39.50 Dan, Kau, Bud, Cus, Hun, Fly, Hig, Mur, Orv, AnR

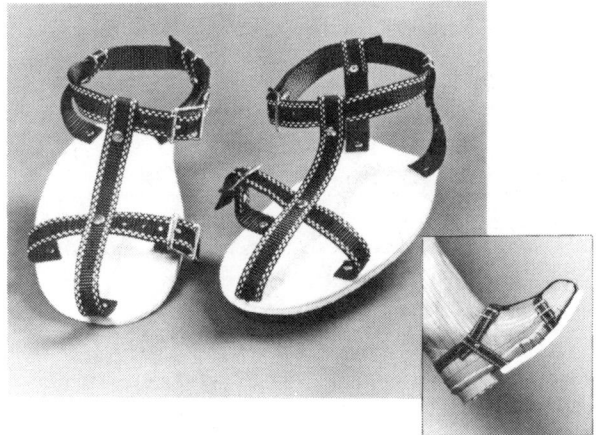

Compleat Angler Premium Felt Sole Kit. *Same as above but with additional heel material; one size.*
$11.95-$13.75 EJH, T&T
Ranger Felt Sole Kit. *Thick felt soles; includes adhesive.*
$8.25-$11.95 Cus, Fly, Kau
Borger Ultimate Felt Soles. *Triple thick nylon/poly to be sewn or glued to wading shoe; sizes: indicate shoe size.*
$7.95 Fly
Custom Non-Slip Grippers. *Sole and heel felt; includes cement, applicator, instructions.*
$5.70 Cus
Borger/Danner Replacement Laces. *Woven nylon; 58".*
$.99 Fly
Compleat Angler Waterproof Cement. *100 ml tube with instructions for applying felt or carpet.*
$2.50-$3 Pen, Ram, Sim
Barge Cement. *2 oz. tube; waterproof cement for felt soles, repairs, other uses.*
$1.90-$2.95 Dan, Pen, Mur, H&H, T&T, Bud
Barge Cement. *8 oz. can with applicator brush.*
$4.95-$5.50 T&T, Bob, Bud, Fly, Dan, Kau

Compleat Angler Wading Sandal. *Woven polyester felt; nylon straps with metal buckles; riveted construction; toe strap adjustable; one size fits 7-13.*
$16.95 Pen
Sampo Rock Huggers. *Felt soles; nylon straps; leather inner sole.*
$29.22 Mer
Stream Grip Sandal.
Felt soles rubber sandal; strap adjustment; sizes: S(6-7),M(8-9),L(10-11),XL(12-14).
$23.95 Bud

Boot Chains. *Small chains that fit over boot much like a sandal does and work like tire chains; sizes: S(6-9), L(10-12).*
$14.55-$15.55 Cus, Dan

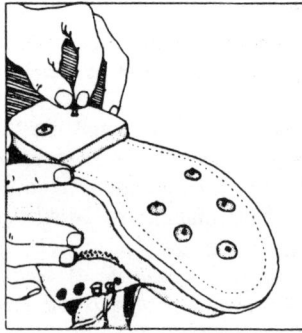

Kleet Feet. *Aluminum rivets to be added to felt soles; drill holes using enclosed depth-guaged drill bit, then hammer rivets in; placement pattern and 14 studs included.*
$10.95-$12.95 Pen, Kau, Dal, Ram, Bud, Hig, T&T
Dri-But. *Sprinkle-on grit; can be used on felt or rubber soles; adhesive, brushes, grit included.*
$16.95 AnJ
Reef Walkers. *Polyester booties with felt bottoms; designed for canoeists and kayakers but has applications for fly fishermen; sizes: M(8-9), L(9 ½-10 ½), XL(11-12), use street shoe size.*
$17.50-$17.95 T&T, Ram

Wading Jackets

There are a lot of rain jackets out there, but these few are advertised as being designed specifically for fly fishing and wading.

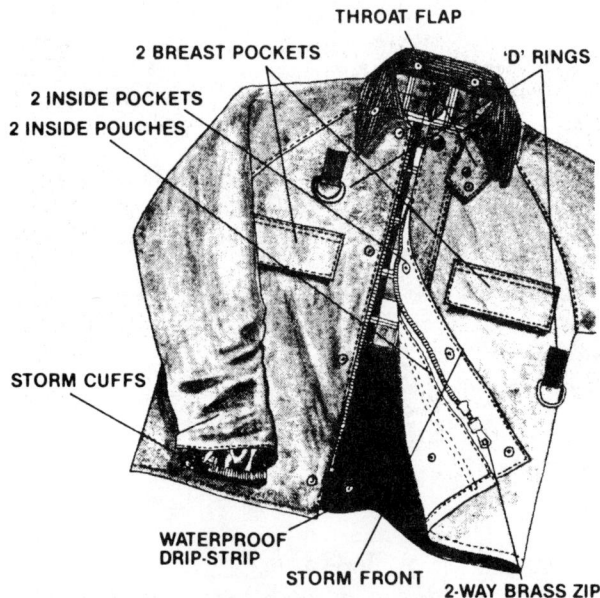

Barbour Spey Wading Jacket. *Egyptian cotton with cotton tartan lining; needs occasional dressing to retain waterproofness; two pockets; brass two-way zipper; D-rings; throat flap, storm cuffs, optional draw string*

hood; length—22"-23"; dark green; S-XL.
jacket—$99.95-$119.95; hood—$16.95-$25.50 Pen, Ram, T&T, Don

Courtesy of The Fly Shop

Columbia Rain River Gore-Tex Wading Jacket. *Gore-Tex waterproof, yet breathable, material; vest access pockets; velcro cuffs; hood; tan; S-XXXL.*
S-XL—$80-$124.95; XXL-XXXL—$88-$110 Mer, Fly, Hig, Pen, H&H, Bud, Kau, Orv, Tid, Dun, Ram, Sim
Gore-Tex Shorty Jacket. *Breathable, waterproof Gore-Tex; cut for over vest; two large pockets, one small; elastic cuffs; elastic bottom with drawstring; hood; olive drab; seam sealer recommended for really nasty weather; sizes: S-XL.*
$69.95-$79.95 Dan, Ste, Bud
T&T Gore-Tex Wading Jacket. *Breathable, waterproof; shorty for use with waders; two pockets; five D-rings; tan; sizes: S-XXL.*
$119.50 T&T
Marathon Wading Jacket. *Rubberized coating over 70 denier nylon; 6 oz. total; marine green; S(36-38), M(40-42), L(44-46), XL(48-50), XXL(52-54), XXXL(even bigger); order one size larger than regular coat size.*
$32.95-$36 Pen, T&T, Bob, Dan, Bud
James-Scott Vest Pocket Rain Jacket. *Urethane-coated nylon; hood stuffs into collar; whole jacket stuffs into its own pocket; small enough to fit in vest pocket; size: L.*
$35 Nat

Wading Staffs

A wading staff can be a real lifesaver. Unfortunately, lots of us don't carry one. Maybe we're all too macho, but probably it's because we don't need a staff that often.

The wooden and bamboo staffs are the strongest and prettiest, but they are cumbersome and attract fly lines like I attract biting insects. The collapsible staffs are handy in their belt holsters. They're not as sturdy as the wood ones, but if used carefully, they'll do the job. Best of all, you're more likely to carry one of them on the stream. The sections are held together with a shock cord. A quick flick will straighten and connect them to form the staff.

The staffs differ in length, grip, and color. The collapsible staffs vary in folded length. The shorter lengths are more convenient but be sure to order a staff that's long enough for you.

Incidentally, a ski pole makes a dandy staff if you remove the basket. The bamboo poles for cross country skiing are particularly attractive as a fishing accessory.

The collapsible staffs are listed first, followed by the hardwood staffs. Good wading!

Folstaf Wading Staff. *Collapsible black aluminum with elastic shock cord for instant opening; ½" diameter; spring-slip case for belt or pocket; sizes: 45", 54".*
45"—$25.95; 54"—$28.95 Kau
Super Folstaf Wading Staff. *As above but ¾" diameter and leather belt holster; sizes: 50", 60".*
50"—$29.10-$42.50; 60"—$39.95-$46.50 Kau, Orv, 50" only—Dan, Cus, Hig, Bud
Lew Childre Staff. *Fold-up aluminum with elastic shock cord for quick assembly; two sizes: 45" (12" collapsed) and 54" (14").*
45"—$27.95; 54"—$44.95 Pen
North Fork Wading Staff. *Fold-up aluminum; elastic shock cord for instant opening; three sections; molded rubber grip with web wrist strap; black; 48" or 56"; optional holster.*
48"—$26.95; 56"—$28.95 (holster—$6.95) Nor
Kustin Folding Staff. *Fold-up aluminum with shock cords for quick opening; cork grip; longer sections for greater strength; size: 60" (20" collapsed).*
$24.95 Fly
Clemens Wading Staff. *59" fold-up metal; tungsten carbide tip; 9½" handle with wrist loop; assembles by a pull on the locking line (not elastic); includes 24" lanyard.*
$59.95 Dal
Red Oak Staff. *With rope handle, lanyard, and French clip.*
$14.30 Mer
Hardwood Wading Staffs. *A variety of woods, mostly ash; usually with lanyard; about 52".*
$21.50-$24 T&T, Let, Pen, Orv
Impregnated Bamboo Staff. *Non-slip grip, lanyard; aluminum tip.*
$85 T&T

Wading Belts

Wading belts serve one important purpose. In a quick dunk, they help keep water from pouring in over your waders.

There can come a situation, however, when the quick dunk becomes a bit more than that. In such a crisis, you may feel better swimming without your waders. Then your belt must come off quickly. So shop for a good belt that will hold the water out but has a quick-release buckle to help you get out if you need to.

All the belts here have some kind of one-hand release. Most are plastic buckles that are squeezed for release. The Great Escape Works belt has a Velcro pull tab for an extra fast release. The Red Ball belt also features a Velcro closure.

Other considerations are fairly minor. Get a belt that doesn't leave a lot of extra material hanging out to catch fly lines. Most of the belts are nylon and can be trimmed and heat-sealed to size. The Compleat Angler's belt is elastic and is designed to leave no loose ends.

I'm prejudiced against bright colors. If you concur, then you'll want a dark or neutral color.

The belts are listed in no particular order. Sizes and colors are listed when they were available.

James-Scott "Can't Lose" Wader Belt. *Nylon with quick-release buckle; leash to attach to wader.*
$6.95 Pen
River Systems Rogue Wading Belt. *1 ½" polypropylene web; floats; quick-release buckle; size: 52" (can be trimmed to fit).*
$3.95-$6.95 Pen, H&H, Cus, Fly

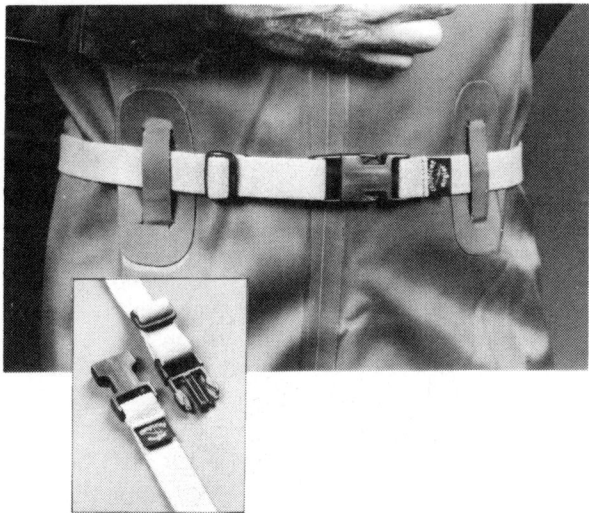

Compleat Angler Belt. *Heavy elastic; no loose end at adjustment; quick-release buckle; tan.*
$4.40-$6.95 Cus, Ram, Dan, Bud, Sim
Ranger Quick Release Belt. *1 ½" black nylon web; quick-release buckle.*
$4.40-$4.95 Cus, AnW, Kau

Bob Jacklin's Yellowstone Belt. *Cotton web; one-hand buckle release; black; sizes: reg.—44", XL—52".*
$2.85-$3.50 Cus, Bob, Fly, Bud, Dan, Hig
Red Ball Sportsman's Belt. *Elastic webbing; Velcro closure; brown.*
$5.95-$6 Mer, Dun

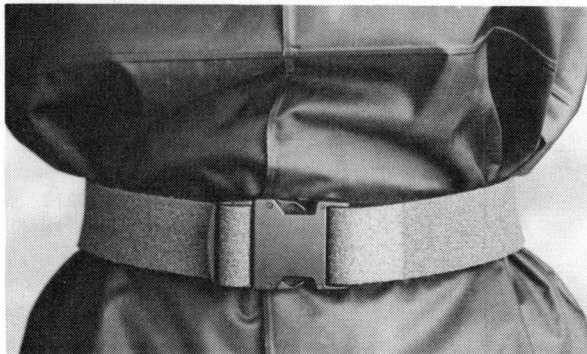

Simms Wade Safe Belt. *Stretch nylon; quick-release buckle; blue; sizes to 46", larger on request.*
$9.95-$12 Pen, Kau, or direct from Simms
Great Escape Wader Belt. *1" webbing; simple D-ring buckles; quick release Velcro tab makes "great escape" easy and quick; 54", can be trimmed.*
$6.95 (+ $.75 shipping) Great Escape Works, 1995 McKinzie Dr., Idaho Falls, Idaho 83401.
North Fork Clipper Belt. *1" nylon; quick-release buckle; black, green, khaki, burgundy.*
$4.95 Nor
Marathon Wading Belt. *1 ½" elastic webbing; round metal buckle, dull finish; olive.*
$6 Bob

Wader Suspenders

"I just got these chest waders, but they keep falling down. Is there anything I can do about that?"

You'd be surprised how often shop keepers hear that question. The answer, of course, is suspenders.

Like wading belts, there isn't a lot to say about suspenders. They have to fit properly. The wider models (2") will carry the weight a bit better. It helps if they're elastic since some room for movement is needed even when the suspenders are fitted correctly.

The fittings and the color should be neutral. Shiny metal and bright colors are best left to suspenders used for dancing.

Two suspenders deserve comment. The River Systems braces have a snap to release them from the waders. Considering the time spent fiddling with the leather tongs, this is a desirable feature. It will also keep the button holes in the leather from wearing.

The other suspender needs comment because it is decidedly different from the others. The North Fork suspender uses "grippers" much like conventional pants suspenders. (You remember those, don't you?). North Fork sends along material to be sewn in as reinforcement on "delicate" wader materials (Flyweights, certainly, neoprenes, maybe). I don't see any particular advantage to this system unless your buttons are missing. In that case, see the listing for replacement buttons in this section.

I suppose you may also be interested in the hip boot suspenders listed here. They are a pretty unusual item, but if hip boots get you down in the pants, they're the ticket. Hip boot straps are also listed here.

There is no significance to the order here. It's not alphabetical because, being an "R", I never thought that was a fair system.

River Systems Out West Suspenders. *H-back design; sizes: reg.—up to 6', XL—over 6'.*
$8-$12.50 Cus, Fly, H&H, Let, Mur
Compleat Angler Suspender. *H-back; adjusts front and back; elastic webbing; rubber sleeves keep leather straps fastened; non-glare fittings; tan.*
$8.80-$15.95 Cus, Bud, Dan, Ram, Sim
Ranger Wader Suspenders. *H-back.*
$6.30-$7.95 Kau, Cus, Fly, AnW
Quality Wader Suspenders. *H-back; leather button-ons; olive green or brown; 1 ½" wide strap or 2".*
1 ½"—$5.46-$6.50; 2"—$6.70-$7.95 Cus, Dan
Red Ball Suspenders. *H-back; adjustable elastic; one size fits all.*
$7.50-$8.98 Mer, Pen

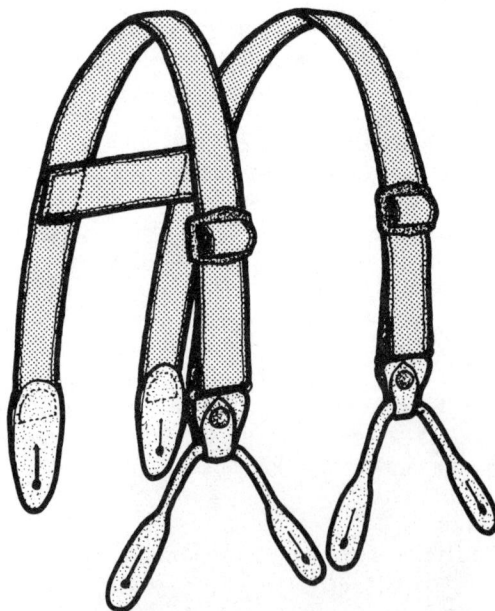

River Systems Green River Suspenders. *H-back; black metal parts for no glare; smaller button holes for snug fit to waders; can be detached from waders by snap; length: 52" but can be cut to fit.*
$9.95 Pen

Orvis Suspenders. *1 ½" webbing; H-back; black fabric, black leather loops; sizes: to 6', over 6'.*
$12.50 Orv, Bob

North Fork Suspenders. *Nylon-coated neoprene and polypropylene webbing; Y-back; 1 ½"; uses plastic grippers much like old-fashioned suspenders; "delicate" wader material requires sewing webbing at contact point; green or tan.*
$11.95 Nor

Hodgman Suspenders. *H-type; 2" wide elastic, leather fasteners.*
$11.95 Nat, AnW

Marathon Ruff 'N Ready Suspenders. *H-back; 1 ½".*
$4.95-$7.95 Cab, T&T, Dal, Bob

Economy Suspenders. *Y-back; nylon; adjustable.*
$2.75-$2.95 Ram, Cor

Hip Boot Suspenders. *Fit over shoulders; won't tug at pants like conventional boot straps.*
$5.95 Pen

Hip Boot Straps. *Replacement straps; nylon web.*
$2.20-$3.50 Pen, T&T, Cus, Dal, Sim, Bud

Ranger Hip Boot Straps. *Replacement rubber straps.*
$1.95-$3.50 Fly, Cus, Kau

Suspender buttons. *Replacement buttons for waders; push through wader and snap together; another nifty item that will save the day sometime; package of four.*
$1.25 Bud

Wader Bags

Most of these duffles for carrying waders feature mesh openings to allow air drying. Individual features are explained in the listings.

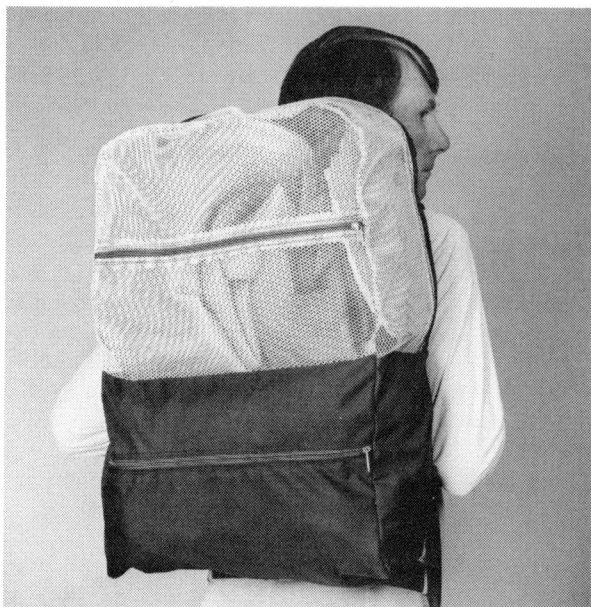

Compleat Angler Wader Pack. *Cordura nylon; mesh upper panel; padded straps convert bag to backpack.*
$39.95 new product, try local fly shop

Wader Duffle. *One large compartment plus two outside pockets; 25"x12 ½"x11"; outer fabric 8 oz. parapec; inside lined with 4 oz. nylon; ends and bottom padded; removable waterproof bag for wet items; rust or forest green.*
$56.95-$57 RLW, Bud

Jumbo Wader Gear Bag. *One large compartment for waders plus two zippered outside pockets for extras; 18"x14"x12".*
$29.95 Pen

River Systems Wader Gear Bag. *Leakproof cordura; three compartments; top mesh panels for air drying; 16"x7"x12".*
$19.94-$26.95 Ram, Pen, T&T, Dal, AnJ, Dan

Wader Bag. *Two compartments for waders, shoes; one inside pocket for socks; mesh top; waterproof bottom; carry strap; green.*
$24.95-$27 Orv, Kau

Tidewater Specialties Wader Bag. *Zips open to lie flat on floor or ground; take waders off right into bag; saves wear and tear on stocking-foot waders; med. for hip boots, large for waders.*
med.—$45, large—$49 Tid

Boot Hangers

I'll just tell you what I know. The U-shaped boot hangers that hang on your closet rod are a pain to use—two hands aren't enough. The handiest of the hangers listed here is the Sportsman's Boot Hanger. It attaches to the wall and your boot heels slip, one-handed, right in. It's worth the extra money in saved frustration.

Hardy Wader Clasps. *Tongs grab boot, grip by tension from chain hung on nail.*
$9.95 Dun

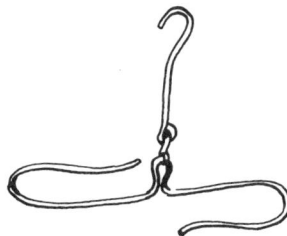

Seaway Boot Hangers. *Double-U to hang in closet.*
$.85-$1.25 Cus, Cor, T&T, Dan, Fol

Sportsman's Boot Hanger. *Wall mount; convenient.*
$2.50-$4.25 Cus, Fly, Ran, Dan, Bud, Kau

Boot Drying Devices

These are popular in areas of the country with high humidity. If you fish every day on a vacation, the portable units can save trouble if you take a spill.

As an alternative, newspapers crumpled up and jammed in a wet boot will help dry it. Change the paper every hour or so until they come out dry.

Dryer Stand. *Stand holds both hippers and waders depending on extensions used; boots slip over drying unit and hang upside down for maximum drying.*
$45 Dun

Ronning Dryer Inserts. *Electric "feet" slip into boots; 8 watts; AC or DC outlets; fits sizes 7 and larger.*
$18.95-$21.95 Dun, Dan

Undies for Waders

Special underwear for wading? Sure. Everything about fly fishermen (and women), from top to bottom and from inside out, is special. Actually, wading is a rather special physical activity, and certain materials, namely polypropylene, are better for use under waders since they don't absorb water. Read on, there are some intriguing outfits here.

Farmer John Wading Suit. *Pile liner in coverall style; suspenders, stirrups included; full access zipper from chest to tailbone for easy-on/easy-off, etc.; from Patagonia Sportswear; navy blue; sizes: S-XL.*
$68.50 T&T

Stream Designs Pile Waderall. *Pile liner in coverall style; suspenders included; leg zippers; full access zipper; navy blue; sizes: S-XL.*
$49.95 Ram

Thinsulate Underwear. *Thinsulate layer between nylon taffeta; jacket and bottoms; tan; sizes: S-XXL.*
$46 jacket; $38.50 bottoms Dun

Polar Fleece Bibs. *Pile liner similar to Stream Designs above; sizes: S-XL.*
$60 Kau

James-Scott Polypropylene Long Johns. *Polypropylene wicks body moisture better than wool or cotton; quality material without the itch of inexpensive polypro; navy blue; sizes: XS-XL. (Note: Tops and bottoms sold separately.*
$24.95 each Fly

Fleece-Lined Polypropylene Long Johns. *As above except American made and fleece lined for softer feel; 100% polypro; navy blue; sizes: S-XL. (Note: Tops and bottoms sold separately.)*
$17.95 tops; $15.95 bottoms Dun

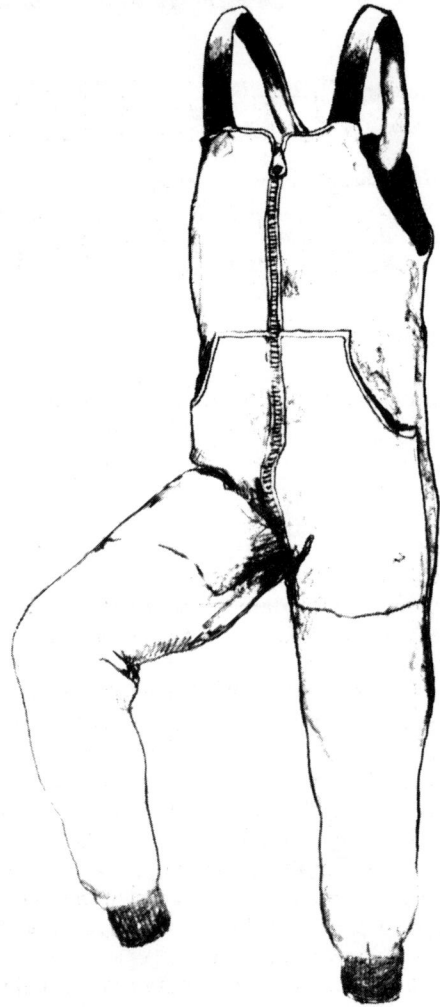

Mark Fiberpile Overalls. *Similar to other pile bibs; navy blue; sizes: S-XL.*
$69.95 Fly

Patagonia Polypropylene Expedition Weight Underwear. *Polypropylene with brushed lining; zip-neck top; elastic waistband, cuffs, and fly; sizes: S-XL.*
Top—$36.95; bottom—$32.95 Kau

North Fork 3-in-1 Pants. *Inner layer polypropylene, middle layer Thinsulate, outer layer polypro; full-length side zippers; sizes: S-XL.*
$39.95 Nor

North Fork Poly-Wool Interlock Long Johns. *Polypropylene inner layer, wool-polypro outer layer; men's and women's sizes. (Note: Tops and bottoms sold separately.)*
$18.95 each Nor

6. Vests and Streamside Equipment

DEVELOPED IN THE 1930s by Lee Wulff, the fishing vest has become the trademark of the fly fisherman. Chest waders, landing net, and fly rod complete the uniform. In such garb, he or she is readily recognized by other members of the subculture.

The popularity of the vest is easily understood. The fly fisherman is an active angler, always on the move. At the same time, he "needs" a lot of equipment. He also wades a lot, and this fact alone makes the spin fisherman's tackle box unworkable.

The shoulder bags favored by fly fishermen before the advent of vests seem a poor second choice, although Lee Wulff can tell you that it took a long time for vests to be accepted. There are now fishing bags as useful (or more useful) than vests (namely Wood River Fly Fishing Bags), but they have the same problems of acceptance that vests did originally. Fly fishermen are a fickle group.

If a fly fisherman were to decide that a fishing bag was the best equipment carrier for him, it would be difficult to switch. As a member of a subculture, identity is very important, and it rests initially with the uniform (including the graphite rod, now). It takes a very confident fly fisherman to buck the tide in any form, let alone the most obvious. Part of the purpose of this book is to introduce you to new products and open your fly fishing horizons a bit, so I've written about fishing bags, specifically the Wood River bags, in a separate section in this chapter.

Do you really need a vest? The "need" for a vest has been created by the enormous amount of gear we feel obliged to carry around with us. A lot of that gear comes in the form of fly boxes stuffed with patterns we might need to match the hatch. Add to that extra spools of fly lines that will enable us to fish each kind of pattern to scientific perfection.

Then there are the wonders of modern chemistry. We need chemicals to float our dries, to sink our leaders, to clean our fly lines, and to repel bugs from our persons.

Add to that the gadgets and assorted paraphernalia that allow us to be efficient and up-to-date in our pursuit of fish: leader straighteners, blood-knot tiers, tape measures, surgical forceps, insect seines, stomach pumps, and the like.

Carrying all that equipment meets some real needs streamside, but mostly it meets a psychological need. It scares us to think we might face a situation in which we didn't have the right fly or the correct equipment. Our insecurities are lessened by a vest full of gear.

To get things in perspective, let's again reduce our equipment needs to a minimum as we did in Chapter 1. Most anglers fish only a handful of streams regularly. On these "home" streams, they can comfortably predict what fly patterns they'll need. One fly box carefully packed with the appropriate flies will suffice.

Add to that a pin-on retractor with clippers and forceps attached. Toss in a spool or two of terminal leader material, an extra complete leader, some fly floatant, and you have all the catch-and-release angler needs. All of it will fit in your pockets.

Still there are times when a vest is best. I require a vest or other equipment carrier when I fish new waters or waters I fish too infrequently to know what flies I'll need. I also like a vest or bag when I'm going to be a distance from my car. I carry a raincoat, water bottle, and my lunch on those occasions.

I've compromised between the minimum approach and the bulging vest over the years. In my car trunk is a duffle bag which carries everything I anticipate needing. I couldn't tell you how many fly boxes, extra reels, and assorted gadgets there are in the bag. I also have a vest (and now a Wood River bag) with minimum gear in it. On each fishing trip, I rummage through my tackle bag and add to my vest or bag only those things I need for that day's fishing.

After a few trips using this system, I made very few errors of omission and carried few unnecessary items. My neck muscles appreciate the light weight, while my psychological needs are still taken care of.

What to look for in a vest. What we all want to know about a new vest is how many pockets it has. Pockets are a matter of status, I suppose, but you might catch more fish if you have fewer pockets to be disorganized in, since you would find your fly boxes faster and get back to the water sooner. Besides the number of pockets, you should consider how those pockets are closed, the vest's special pockets, the comfort, the color of the vest, and the quality of the vest.

Let's start by not overbuying. If you need the 35 pockets in an Orvis Super Tac-L-Pac or the 34 pockets of Columbia Sportswear's Yellowstone, certainly you should get one of those vests. If you don't need that many pockets but purchase a big-capacity vest anyway, you'll just end up buying enough equipment (most of it unnecessary) to fill the rest up. And then, because you own all that stuff, you'll end up carrying it. It will be heavy, and it will detract from your day astream.

The last vest I lived in for a number of years had 18 pockets, and I never filled them up with entirely useful equipment. That vest, incidentally, is one of the reasons I wrote this book. When it finally gave way, I wanted another one just like it and couldn't find one. It was not a name brand (World Famous was the brand and not a description), but I'd only paid $17.95 for it (less than $1/pocket), and it wore well. I wanted another one. Unfortunately, I still haven't found it. (Maybe someone out there will tell me where I can find one.)

The typical fly fisherman can use about 15-20 pockets in his or her vest. That number of pockets is bound to be translated into enough big pockets for fly boxes, a back pocket for a raincoat, and enough inside pockets for all the gadgets. A beginning fly fisherman needs fewer pockets, maybe 10-12.

The next consideration is how those pockets close. I like zippers on all the big pockets. I don't trust Velcro tabs when it comes to pockets for fly boxes, because I often fail to close them properly. I do, however, prefer Velcro for all the smaller pockets containing frequently used items, because Velcro can be opened and closed easily with one hand. Snaps are the worst, not because they don't hold well, but because they almost always require two hands to close unless the pocket is full.

My preference is for the back pocket to close with a zipper. I dislike the open pouches, although they're more convenient for coats and the like. The potential for gear to fall out makes me nervous when I'm swinging the vest on and off. Some vests have both an open pouch and a zippered back pocket.

Special pockets are nifty, and if you carry forceps (you should), a stream thermometer, or spools of leader material, look for a vest with pockets for those items. On the other hand, there's no reason to pay for a vest with tippet-spool pockets if you use, for instance, a Dennison Leader Dispenser.

Comfort is a very important consideration. With the weight you'll be carrying on your shoulders, make sure the vest feels good there. You should really try on vests with weight in them, as you would a backpack. When loaded, many of them weight as much as a backpack anyway. If you get neck aches and headaches from the weight of the vest, as I do, you may wish to consider a fishing bag instead. The only vest manufacturer that I know of who is attempting to make some improvements in the load-carrying characteristics of the common vest is Fothergill Designs. The knit collar is elastic and distributes the weight better. It would be interesting to give the job of designing a fishing vest over to some backpack builder to see what he'd come up with.

The last consideration, and an important one, is color. A vest must be a subdued color. Not only is white, for instance, bright and easily seen by trout, it also sets up a contrasting pattern with other clothing (unless, heaven forbid, it's white, too), and trout have proven to be sensitive to that. Tan, dark brown, green, and camo are good colors for vests. So, too, are any of the dark grays and blues offered these days.

You should also check a vest by inspecting the material and the stitching. It's like buying a suit (only more important). Most vests wear out in two places. One is the zippers (which can be and ought to be replaced if the vest is in good shape otherwise), and the other is the material on the inside at your belt line. That area has the most weight in it, moves the most, and rubs against your belt.

You can judge the quality of vests reasonably well by the price, if you can separate out all the features for a comparison. Many of the big-name vest manufacturers offer some type of economy vest that represents quality with less features, and you should consider one of them if price is a major consideration.

And price should be a consideration. You can spend over $90 for a vest these days, and you can still spend under $20 for one. There's a lot of shopping to be done. There is one feature I wouldn't pay the extra bucks for and that's a Gore-Tex yoke. Gore-Tex, as you probably know, is that remarkable material that keeps out rain but still "breathes" body moisture out. It's expensive stuff. A yoke of the material will surely keep rain off your shoulders (big deal). It will also cause the rain to run down on your vest and soak your chest instead. If it's raining that hard, put on a raincoat. If it's not, let your shoulders get damp. The extra money for this feature is ill spent, I think.

There are a lot of fine vests out there, and the choice of one should be a matter of personal needs and taste, as much as anything. I caution you only to make the decision based on function, not the status afforded by a large number of pockets.

Some notable vests. There are many fine traditional vests from companies of longstanding reputation, Columbia Sportswear, Cortland, Stream Designs, Orvis, and Thomas & Thomas, among others. Newer offerings come from the Wulffs, Fothergill Designs, and Simms.

Among the listings are some vests worthy of mention. Let's start with Fothergill Designs, since their vests are relatively new and gaining popularity rapidly. Chuck Fothergill, best known for his expertise in nymphing, developed the line of vests. They are high quality, expensive vests with some unusual features.

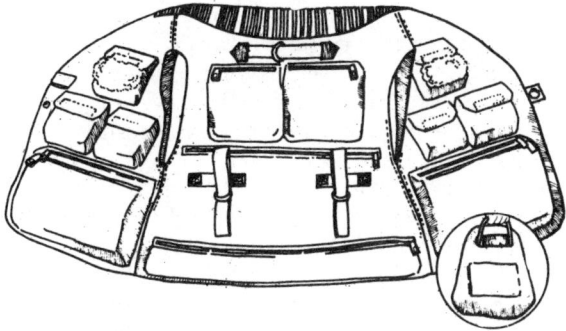

As already mentioned, the vests have a knit collar for comfort. The elastic in the knit absorbs some of the pressure of the weight of the vest and equipment. Beyond this functional improvement on the traditional vest are some extra goodies. Most notable is the self-contained carry bag. Hidden in a long, narrow pocket on the back of the vest is an attached carry bag. Simply pull it out and stuff the vest into it and carry away. Very clever and a great help in storing the vest while traveling.

I also like the straps below the main back pocket and above the carry bag pocket. These allow you to carry a pack rod in its tube on your back. The vests are altogether practical and represent a significant improvement in vest design. If you're in the market for a high quality vest, check out the Fothergill Designs vests.

If you're really into wearing your vest on the way to those high altitude streams, you may appreciate the Simms Guide Vest. It has an attachment to carry a special day pack on the back. If you keep the weight low, this system is better than carrying a traditional day pack over your vest. If you can't keep the weight low, however, the strain on your shoulders might be a disadvantage. The pack hooks on to the yoke of the vest, and the weight would pull directly down on your shoulders without the benefit of padded straps.

Another interesting departure from traditional vests are the Angler's Junction Solution Vest and the Thomas & Thomas Add-A-Pak. These are full-feature vests with a removable lower section. The removal of the lower sections makes them shorty vests suitable for deep wading. You could use one of them like I use my duffle bag. Put all the regular stuff for the home streams in the shorty vest and leave the lower section loaded for other occasions.

There's a considerable difference in price between these two vests with the T&T vest being more expensive.

However, the Angler's Junction vest is made by a company whose products are generally moderately priced, and its lower section is made up of only the front pockets. The lower section on the T&T vest goes full around and adds another back pocket. It is zippered on. With the difference in price and features, you have a fair choice if you'd like a shorty vest with regular vest capabilities. Either choice is less money than buying both a regular vest and a shorty.

Courtesy of The Fly Shop

Columbia Sportswear's Furnace Creek Vest also warrants comment. It's designed for hot weather use. The material is nylon mesh for maximum air flow. It looks like the material used in some athletic jerseys, so if you're into fantasies you can imagine yourself a member of the Olympic fly fishing team. Columbia's Steelheader Vest leans toward the opposite climatic condition by providing hand pockets within the vest construction.

Another vest with a unique feature is the Teeny Vest, designed by Jim Teeny. It's traditional except for a concealed hood. If your hat permits its usage, this would be a neat accessory on windy, rainy, or cold days.

Lists of special vests. If you're looking for a vest for a special use, you'll find it easier to locate models for comparison from these lists.

Youth Vests. Alexander's Child's Vest, Orvis Children's and Ladies' Vest, Saf-T-Bak Youth Vest, and Thomas & Thomas Child Value Vest.

Economy Vests (about $30 and under). Columbia Sportswear Deschutes, Furnace Creek, and Skykomish Vests, Orvis Simplicity Vest, all Saf-T-Bak vests, Sportflite Economy Vest, Stream Designs The First Vest, THE Fisherman and Fisherman II Vests, Thomas & Thomas Adult Value Vest, and U.S. Line Vest.

Shorty Vests. Angler's Junction Solution Vest, Columbia Sportswear Kalama II Vest, Fothergill Designs Shorty Vest, L.L. Bean Shorty Vest, Orvis Super Wading Tac-L-Pac, Saf-T-Bak Shorty Vest, Simms Master Vest, Stream Designs The Ultimate Vest, THE Deluxe Shorty Vest, and Thomas & Thomas Add-A-Pak Vest.

Women's Vests. Columbia Sportswear Gallatin Vest, L.L. Bean Basic Vest, L.L. Bean Deluxe Vest, Maggie Merriman Vest, Orvis Children's and Ladies' Vest, and Joan Wulff Vest.

Courtesy of The Fly Shop

Columbia's Gallatin Vest

and so it becomes a matter of taste. In fact, if she made one with a handsome trout fly pattern in brown, I might be tempted.

It's simply time to offer more items for women with some consideration for the difference between men and women (be they in taste or physique) but without consideration for stereotypes.

VESTS

Traditional Vests

The vests are listed here alphabetically. In several cases, the number and size of pockets were not specified by the catalogs, and I had to guess. For those you'll find descriptions such as "15 pockets or more".

Vests for women. And while we're on the subject of women's vests, let's send some kudos and crunches to the manufacturers. First, there are a lot of women fly fishermen now, and if my fly fishing classes are any indication, there are many more to come. They deserve the attention of vest makers now and soon their numbers will warrant it from a marketing standpoint.

Some good things are happening for women. There are three vests specifically designed for women: Gallatin from Columbia Sportswear, Maggie Merriman's vest, and Joan Wulff's vest. Hooray for them.

Then there's Orvis. They slough off small women into the child's vest category. But even though they make no other offering to women in their own line of vests, they at least offer the Gallatin. Thomas & Thomas, in one of their infrequent shortcomings, offers no vest either in women's sizes or designed for women. Stream Designs does no better.

Worse than omission is Simms offering of their Master Vest in the small size in lilac "for the ladies". It might be pretty, guys, but lilac isn't a color for a vest. Bright colors don't make for sneaking up on trout.

One might argue that I should mention the color of Maggie Merriman's vest, too, since it has a pretty print lining (with flowers on it). But the color is on the inside,

Alexander's Child's Vest. *4 pockets—2 large belly, 2 med. upper; tan; sizes: 14, 16.*
$22 Let

Alexander's Turkey Creek Vest. *15 pockets—2 large belly, 2 med., 2 small upper, 1 back, 8 inside; 2 D-rings; rod holder; sizes: S-XXL.*
$32.50 (XXL—$35.90) Sim

Angler's Junction Solution Vest. *13 or more pockets—4 large, 2 med., 1 back in main, top section; 2 large, 4 med. in detachable lower section; can be worn as shorty with lower pockets removed; lower pocket sections are in front only, unlike Thomas & Thomas Add-A-Pak (listed below); made by Sportflite; sizes: M-XL.*
$59.95 AnJ

Columbia Sportswear Deschutes. *13 pockets—2 large, 4 med. belly; 2 med., 2 small upper, 1 back, 2 inside; back pouch; tan; sizes: S-XXXL.*
$30-$39.95 ($33.50-$45.95 XXL +) AnW, Cab, Mer, Kau, Ste, Cus, H&H, Pen

Columbia Sportswear Furnace Creek. *7 pockets—2 large belly, 2 med., 2 small upper, 1 back; back pouch; nylon mesh material for hot weather; 100% polyester mesh except 6 front nylon-coated pockets; green; sizes: S-XL.*
$24-$33.95 Cus, H&H, Ram, Let, Fly, Hig, Mer

Columbia Sportswear Gallatin. *19 pockets—4 large belly, 3 med. upper, 1 back, several inside; back pocket zippered; tippet pockets inside; designed for women; D-ring; slate blue or tan; sizes: XS-L.*
$39.95-$55.50 Pen, Orv, Bud

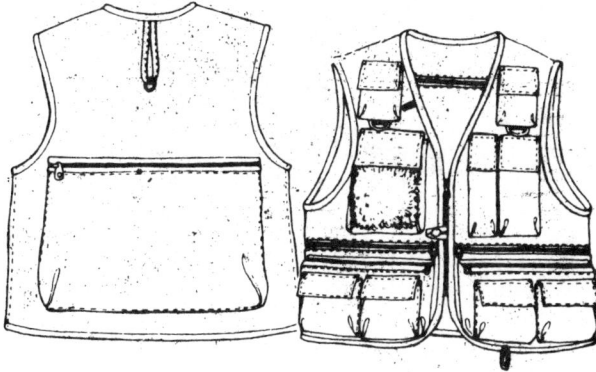

Courtesy of Bob Jacklin

Columbia Sportswear Henry's Fork II. *25 pockets—4 large, 4 med. belly, 3 med., 2 small upper, 1 back, inside pockets; front pockets double-stitched for durability; zippered back pocket; 2 D-rings; tan; sizes: XS-XL.*
$44.50-$59.95 AnW, Cab, Bob, Cus, Dun, Fly, Hig, Mer, Bud, H&H, Let, Kau, Pen, Spo

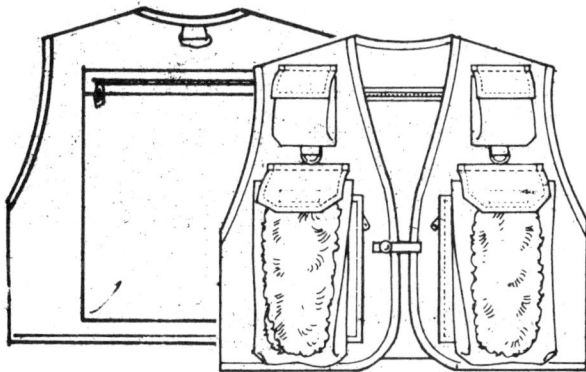

Courtesy of Bob Jacklin

Columbia Sportswear Kalama II. *18 pockets—4 large belly, 2 med. upper, 1 back, others; back pouch zippered; shorty vest for wading, tubing; green; sizes: S-XL.*
$35-$45.50 AnW, H&H, Bob, Ste, Fly, Kau, Hig, Mer
Columbia Sportswear McKenzie. *11 pockets—4 large belly, 2 med., 2 small upper; 2 large inside; back pocket; sizes: S-XL.*
$29.95-$37.95 Pen, Fly
Columbia Sportswear Skykomish. *7 pockets—1 large, 2 med. belly, 2 med. upper, 1 inside, 1 back; large pocket zippered, others on front Velcro; back pouch; economical vest made from end runs (you remember those from football—they work just fine); tan; sizes: XXS-XL.*
$20-$27 Bud, Mer, H&H, Bob

Courtesy of The Fly Shop

Columbia Sportswear North Umpqua II. *14 pockets—6 fairly large belly, 2 med., 2 small upper, 2 inside, 2 back; most pockets zippered; back pouch and zippered pocket; 65/35 poly/cotton; tan; sizes: S-XXXL.*
$37.25-$52 H&H, Bud, Mer, Hig, Fly

Columbia Sportswear Steelheader. *14 pockets—2 large, 4 med. belly, 2 large, 2 small upper, 1 special forceps, 1 back, 2 special hand-warming pockets; designed for cold weather steelheading; large zipper pulls; special forceps pocket with Velcro close; heavy 10.8 oz. duck; 2 D-rings; sizes: S-XXXL.*
$44.55 (XXL, XXXL—$47.80) Mer

Columbia Sportswear Yellowstone. *34 pockets—6 belly, 4 upper, others; special pockets for spare spools, forceps, etc.; reinforced neck; Gore-Tex yoke; tan; sizes: S-XL.*
$60.25-$82.50 Pen, H&H, Bud, Cus, AnW, Ram, Mer

Cortland Deluxe Vest. *16 pockets; 100% cotton; sizes: S-XL.*
$38 C&C, Edd, Tac, Fly

OUTSIDE

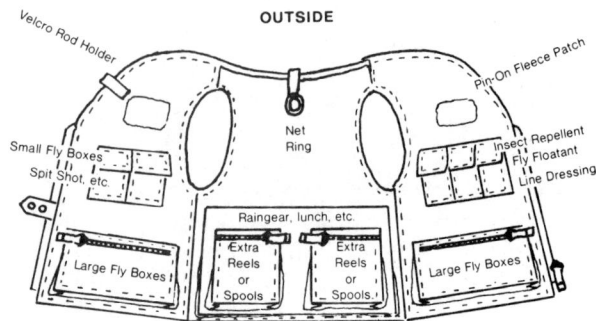

Dale Clemens Tackle Organizer. *20 pockets—2 large belly, 2 med., 3 small upper, 1 large, 2 med. back, 10 inside; 100% cotton; pockets for sunglasses, leaders, etc.; sizes: S-XL.*
$42.95 Dal

Dan Bailey Fishing Vest. *9 or more pockets—2 large, 4 small belly, 2 med., 2 small upper, 1 back; D-ring; basic vest; light tan (nearly white); sizes: S-XL.*
$40 Dal

Fothergill Designs Vest. *15 pockets—4 large belly, 6 small upper; 1 large, 2 med. back; 2 inside; back pockets zippered; nylon knit collar for load-bearing and comfort; self-contained carry bag; tote straps on back for coat, pack rod, thermos; sizes: S-XL.*
$85-$92 Bob, Tid

Fothergill Designs Shorty. *13 or more pockets—2 large, 4 med. belly; 2 med. upper; 1 large, 2 med. back; similar to vest above in other features; tan; sizes: S-XL.*
$83 Fly

L.L. Bean Basic. *10 pockets—2 large belly, 2 med., 2 small upper, 1 back, others; rod holder; tan or sage green; sizes: men's—S (34-36), M (38-40), L (42-44), XL (46-48); women's—S (6-8), M (10-12), L (14-16). (Note: Women's sizes not listed in current catalog.)*
$39.50 LLB

L.L. Bean Shorty. *14 pockets—4 large belly, 2 med., 2 small upper, 1 back, 5 inside; D-ring; rod holder; 4" shorter than standard; tan or sage green; sizes: men's as above.*
$51.50 LLB

Maggie Merriman Vest. *10 pockets—4 large belly, 2 upper, 1 inside, 1 back, others; back pocket zippered; designed for women; tan with print lining and zippers; sizes: ladies' S,M,L.*
$55-$60 Bud, Bob, Fly, Pen

Orvis Children's and Ladies' Vest. *7 pockets—2 large belly, 2 med., 2 small upper, 1 back; Velcro closures; 65/35 poly/cotton; sized for children and women who can wear children's sizes; tan; sizes: S(12), M(14), L(16).*
$34.50 Orv

Orvis Simplicity. *6 pockets—2 large belly, 2 med., 1 small upper, 1 back; back pouch has snap closure; two large front pockets zippered, others snap closure; light tan (bordering on white); sizes: S(36-38), M(40-42), L(44-46), XL(48-50).*
$18.50 Orv, Let

Orvis Tac-L-Pac. *20 pockets—3 large belly, 1 med., 3 small upper, others inside and on back; large pockets zippered, others Velcro; 60/40 poly/cotton; tan; sizes: same as Simplicity plus XS(32-34).*
$59.50 Orv

Orvis Super Tac-L-Pac. *35 pockets—4 large, 4 med. belly, 2 large, 1 med., 3 small upper, 1 large, 2 med. back, more inside; closures on med. and small pockets mainly Velcro, others zippered; zippered back pocket; 60/40 poly cotton; tan; sizes: S(36-38), M(40-42), L(44-46), XL(46-48), XXL(48-50).*
$76.50 Orv

Orvis Super Wading Tac-L-Pac. *29 pockets—as above without 2 small upper; short for wading; tan; sizes: same as Super Tac-L-Pac.*
$69.50 Orv

Saf-T-Bak Value. *7 pockets—2 large belly, 2 small upper, 2 inside, 1 back; D-rings; tan; sizes: S-XXL.*
$14.75 Sim

Saf-T-Bak Deluxe. *12 pockets—2 large, 4 med. belly, 2 med., 2 small upper, 1 rear, 1 apron front; economy vest made in USA; 3 D-rings; cotton/poly blend; light tan; sizes: S-XL.*
$24.30-$26.95 Sim, Pen

Saf-T-Bak Shorty. *9 pockets—2 large belly, 2 med., 2 small upper, 2 inside, 1 back; 3 D-rings; short vest for wading; sizes: S-XXL.*
$19.55 Sim

Saf-T-Bak Youth. *7 pockets—2 large belly, 2 med. upper, 2 inside, 1 back; rod holder; 2 D-rings; tan; sizes: S-L.*
$16.95 Pen

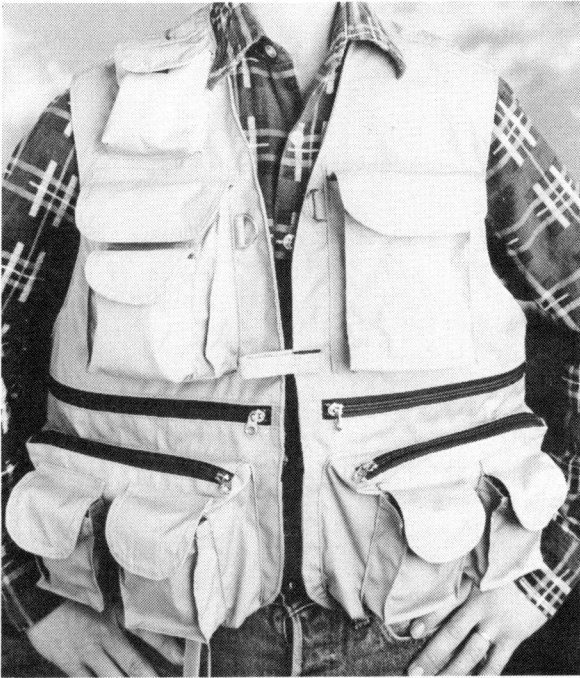

Simms Guide Vest. *14 + pockets—4 large, 4 small belly, 2 med., 2 small upper, 1 back, others inside; 2 D-rings; will carry optional day pack (see below); open-bottom retractor "pocket"; tan or gray; sizes: S-XL.*

Simms Master Vest. *11 + pockets—2 large, 4 small belly, 2 med., 1 small upper, 1 back, others inside; shorty vest; 2 D-rings; tan or gray—additionally "lilac" in small "for the ladies"; sizes: S-XL. (Note: Lilac or any other light, bright color is not good for a fishing vest whether you're a lady or not.)*
$65 Kau, Hig

Simms Detachable Day Pack. *A small day pack attachable to Guide vest above; navy blue.*
$25 Hig, Kau

Sportflite Deluxe. *13 pockets—2 large, 4 small belly, 2 med., 2 small upper, 2 inside, 1 back; 2 D-rings; rod holder; tan; sizes: S-XL.*
$34.95 Tac
Sportflite Economy. *8 pockets—4 large belly, 2 med. upper, 2 inside; rod holder; 2 D-rings; tan; sizes: S-XL.*
$29.95 Tac

Sportflite Premium. *12 pockets—4 large belly, 3 med., 2 small upper, 2 inside, 1 back; thermometer and scissor holders; back pocket detachable; 1 D-ring; rod holder; tan; sizes: S-XL.*
$44.95 Tac

Stream Designs The Classic. *25 pockets—4 large, 4 med. belly, 2 med., 2 small upper, 2 back, 9 inside; forceps holster; rod holder; back pouch and zippered back pocket; 83/17 poly/cotton; 2 D-rings and net ring; tan; sizes: S-XXL.*
$64.95-$72.95 Pen, Bud, Don, Kau, Hig, Hun, Mer
Stream Designs The First. *8 pockets—2 large belly, 2 med., 2 small upper, 1 inside, 1 back; 83/17 poly/cotton; 2 D-rings; back pouch; tan; sizes: S-XL.*
$28.75 direct from Stream Designs, 123 Sylvan Avenue, Newark, New Jersey 07104 (201) 481-6074

Courtesy of The Fly Shop

Stream Designs The Spring Creek. *16 pockets—3 large, 2 med. belly, 2 med. upper, 2 back, 8 inside; forceps holster; zippered back pocket and open pouch; rod holder; 2 D-rings and net ring; double yoke; 83/17 poly/cotton; tan; sizes: S-XL.*
$49.95-$62.50 Don, Fly, Kau, Bud, Ram, Hun, Mer

Stream Designs The Ultimate. *16 pockets—2 large, 4 med. belly, 2 med., 2 small upper, 4 inside, 1 back; shorty vest for wading; forceps holster; rod holder; 2 D-rings and net ring; double yoke; 83/17 poly/cotton; tan; sizes: S-XXL.*
$54.95-$68.95 Pen, Ram, Bud, Mer, Hun, Kau, Fly, Don
Stream Stalker. *12 or more pockets; camouflage material; 50/50 poly/cotton; D-rings; sizes: S-XL.*
$80-$85 Fly, Nor
Teeny Vest. *13 or more pockets—2 large, 4 med. belly, 2 med. upper, 1 back, others inside; concealed hood; sizes: S-XL.*
$69.95 Ste
"THE" Deluxe. *14 pockets—2 large, 2 med. belly, 2 med., 2 small upper, 5 inside, 1 back; poly-cotton blend; tan; sizes: S-XL.*
$34.95-$59.95 Cus, Dan
"THE" Deluxe Shorty. *12 pockets—as above except no med. upper pockets; short for wading; sizes: S-XL.*
$42-$57.95 Cus, Dan

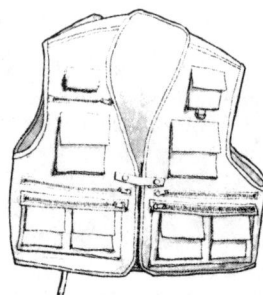

"THE" Fisherman. *15 pockets—11 front, 1 back; 100% cotton; sizes: S-XL.*
$23.35-$34.99 Cus, Dan
"THE" Fisherman II. *Economy vest; zippered back pocket; D-rings; sizes: S-XL.*
$18.80-$25.95 Cus, Dan

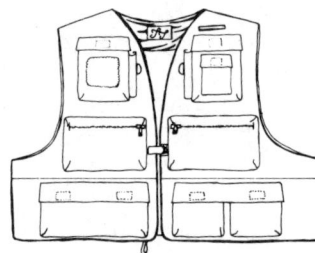

Thomas & Thomas Add-A-Pak Vest. *22 pockets with lower section attached; 16 pockets as shorty vest; combination vest with shorty main section and lower section zippered on/off; dark brown; sizes: S (36-38), M (40-42), L (44-46), XL (48-50).*
$95 T&T
T&T Classic. *15 pockets—2 large belly, 2 med., 2 small uppper, 1 back, 8 inside; rod holder; 2 D-rings; zippered back pocket; dark brown; sizes: see above.*
$49.50 T&T
T&T Adult Value Vest. *7 pockets—2 large, 2 med. belly, 2 small upper, 1 back; economy vest; 2 D-rings; sizes: see above.*
$23.50 T&T
T&T Child Value Vest. *5 pockets—4 front, 1 back; economy vest; D-ring; sizes: XXS (boy's 14, men's 32), XS (16, 34).*
$19.50 T&T
U.S. Line Vest. *11 pockets; heavy poplin; sizes: S-XL.*
$19.50 Edd
Wulff vests, Joan Wulff Vest. *9 or more pockets—2 large, 4 med. belly, 2 med. upper; 1 back; back pocket zippered; cut for women; 65/35 poly/cotton; rod holder; decorative silkscreened Royal Wulff; tan with green trim; sizes: P(6-8), S(10), M(12), L(14).*
$59.95 Wul
Wulff vests, Lee Wulff Vest. *17 pockets—3 large, 1 med. belly, 1 med., 4 small upper, 1 back, others; D-rings; rod holder; decorative silkscreened Royal Wulff; tan with green trim; M-XXL.*
$59.95 Wul

Flotation Vests

This is a brief listing of flotation vests designed with the fisherman in mind. If you swim as well as I do, then you may find yourself in need of a flotation vest. Such a lifesaving device may be required by law in some waters when you're canoeing or floating a river, or it may simply be smart. Some of you out there using old innertubes with duct tape seats for float tubes would be well-advised to wear a flotation vest.

These vests not only contain flotation material or are inflatable, they also have pockets like a regular fly fishing vest. Frankly, I've never used mine in place of a vest. I've always worn it over my vest or tossed my vest in the bottom of the canoe. However, I think I look better in my fisherman's flotation vest than in a regular orange or yellow vest, so I wear it more often.

The standard flotation vests have closed-cell foam to provide buoyancy. They are bulky but cheap and efficient. The inflatable vests rely on a CO2 cartridge to fill them. They are also inflatable by mouth, but I can't see anyone blowing up one of those things while bobbing down the Yellowstone River, so the cartridges had better work. I'd recommend investing in a test cartridge, too, so you can try out the system before you need it. You'll also find an inflatable jacket listed here that uses the same system.

Coleman Sportsman Flotation Vest. *Sizes: M-XL.*
$25.10 Sim
Souci Vest. *4 pockets; urethane-coated nylon; aquafoam flotation; USCG approved; sizes: S-XL.*
$32.95 Cus
Sportsman's Vest. *2 pockets; urethane-coated polyester; aquafoam flotation; USCG approved; sizes: one size for chest 30"-52".*
$22.70 Cus
Stearns Flotation Vest. *3 pockets; USCG approved; D-rings; sizes: S-XXL.*
$29.95 AnJ
Stearns Flotation Vest. *4 pockets; USCG approved; D-rings; sizes: S-XXL.*
$23.95-$39.95 AnJ, Fol (also Youth vest—$20.95)
Stearns Inflatable Jacket. *7 pockets—4 front, 1 back, 2 hand pockets; cotton/poly; CO2 cartridge inflates jacket at a pull; D-ring; tan; sizes: S-XL.*
$143.95 Dan
Stearns Inflatable Vest. *6 pockets; CO2 cartridge inflates vest at a pull; extra cartridges available at about $2 from most sources; inflatable by mouth (available anytime); tan; sizes: S-XL.*
$79.95-$99.95 Kau, Dan, Cab, Cus
Youth Flotation Vest. *4 pockets; Etha foam insert will support 50-90 pound youngsters; good for anytime child is near water.*
$24.95 Dun

VEST ALTERNATIVES

For many of us, a vest is not quite right. For me, it was the neck muscles that, in part, convinced me. With a fully-loaded vest, I began to suffer after an hour or so. Two or three hours into the day I would develop an outstanding headache. I like to fish more than three hours, so I'm using a Wood River bag now (described in a separate article later in this section), as an alternative. I use the waist strap option to put the weight where backpacking has taught me it belongs. Although I'm really still trying it out, the Wood River Bag has been impressive. There are reasonable alternatives to the vest.

The lady fly fisher in my life uses a Wood River bag all the time. She got hers first, being less tied to tradition than I (although fishing bags are the most traditional equipment carrier). She had the same trouble with a vest that I had.

Others may have less pressing reasons to try an alternative to the vest. For one thing, they may simply be free of the need to be part of the group. That freedom provides them the opportunity to choose how they want to haul their tackle. That kind of freedom to be different is difficult to develop in this sport.

In any case, there are alternatives out there. The first group I've called Halter Vests. They are abbreviated vests that are carried by straps over the shoulder and around the chest. There is typically a set of pockets in front and in back. They are lighter than conventional vests and are cooler and less cumbersome. Since they ride high, they can be used while deep-wading without changing vests.

Halter Vests

Angler's Chest Pack. *Pockets front and back with shoulder and chest straps; 6 pockets—2 large, 3 med. front, 1 large back; urethane-coated nylon; fastens by D-rings and snaps; dark brown; one size fits all.*
$38.29-$49.50 Orv, Let, Dal
Handy Andy Wader Pack. *Similar in configuration to Tackle-Tote (below) but vinyl.*
$19.95 Dal
James-Scott Non-Vest. *Set of front and back pockets held in place by straps over shoulders and around chest; at least 11 pockets—3 med., 4 small front, 1 large, 3 med. back; fastens by quick-release buckles; tan; one size fits all.*
$65 Pen

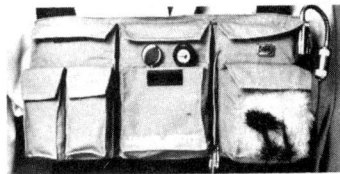

James-Scott Steelheader's Vest. *The front half of the Non-Vest with X-back suspenders; designed to eliminate places where line can catch; tan; one size fits all.*
$39.95 direct from James-Scott, 356 Hillcrest, El Segundo, California 90245 (800) 624-9245, CA—(800) 831-5257

Tackle-Tote. *Pockets front and back; shoulder and chest straps; 7 pockets—1 large, 1 med., 1 small front, 1 large, 2 med., 1 small back; Cordura nylon; fastens by D-rings and snaps; green; one size fits all.*
$29.95 Pen

Thomas & Thomas Angler's Pack. *8 pockets—7 front, 1 back; similar to Tackle-Tote above; 4 D-rings; pockets for thermometer, light; urethane-coated nylon; dark brown; one size fits all.*
$36.50 T&T

Chest Fly Boxes

The second type of vest alternative is really an extended fly box and is often carried in addition to a vest. These "chest fly boxes" have carrying systems similar to the halter vests, with straps over the shoulders and around the chest.

The boxes are rigid material, either aluminum or plastic. The boxes open away from the angler's chest, displaying trays with flies in compartments or on foam. There are attachments for Flex-Lites and floatant on the Richardson box, allowing it to substitute for a lightly outfitted vest. The others will force you to use pockets for some equipment if you don't use a vest with them.

These chest boxes are very popular in the East but seldom seen on western waters (at least in Colorado, Wyoming, and Montana).

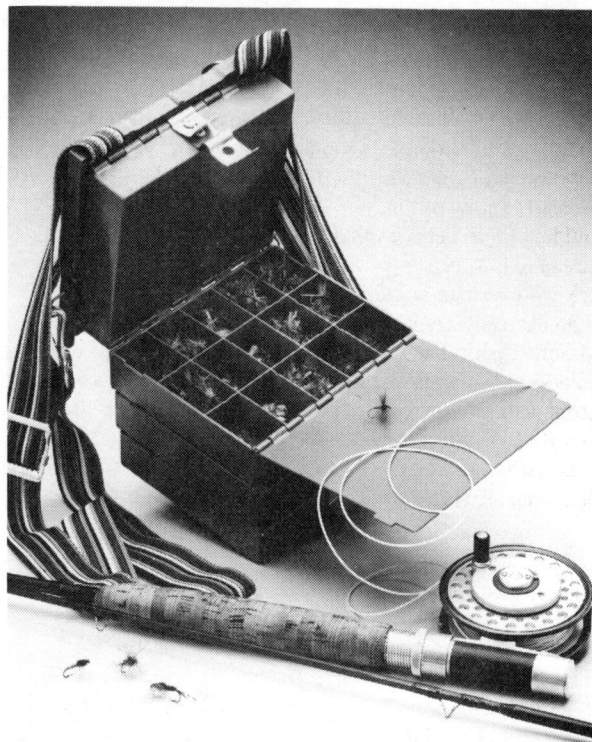

Down's Fly Box

1¼" deep); more trays can be added; all trays have covers and are independently accessible; attachments for dry fly spray and Flex-Lite; aluminum finish or wood grain;

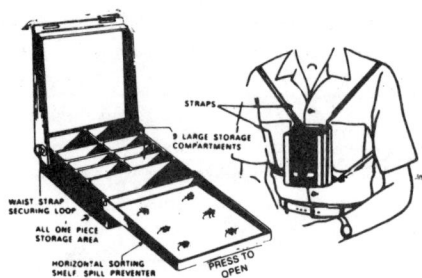

Cortland Tak-Pak. *Chest fly box; polyurethane and polypropylene plastics; 9 comp. tray plus foam-lined sorting shelf; neck and waist strap harness.*
$11.95-$14.95 Ram, Hig, Mer, Bud

Down's Fly Box. *High impact styrene; stainless steel hinge pins, snaps, and harness hook-ups; 3 box styles—8 comp., 15 comp., and open; boxes can be stacked on in any combination; lightweight; green.*
$26.95 ($5 each additional tray) Pen or direct from Down's Fly Box, 97 Eck Circle, Williamsport, Pennsylvania 17701 (717) 326-2497

Richardson Chest Fly Box. *6¼"x5⅜"x2⅞"; aluminum box with riveted joints; shoulder straps and harness; three trays standard—1 with leader pouch and three pads for nymphs, 2 with 16 comp. fly boxes (one ¾" deep, one*

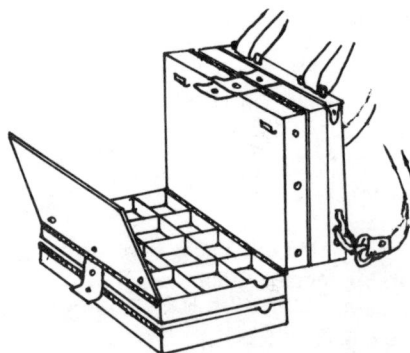

weighs 23 oz. with straps; recognized standard in chest fly boxes; 30-day return policy.
3 tray—$95; 4 tray—$112.95 Let or direct from Richardson Chest Fly Box, Osceola Mills, Pennsylvania 16666 (814) 339-6512

Miscellaneous Carrying Systems

Next we have some miscellaneous equipment carrying systems. Included here are two very attractive "waist vests", one by Sportflite and the other from Thomas & Thomas. They'll be very comfortable to carry with the weight on your waist and should be considered by anyone who shares my trouble with weight carried by the shoulders. I've used a fanny pack for camera gear for years, and it works very well, so these waist vests should work well for the angler.

The other system here is the North Fork Pack-Vest and Soft Tackle Bag. The Pack-Vest is a day pack with pockets on the waist band. Again, the weight will be on your hips for more comfort, but this system offers limited accessiblity to gear pockets. The Soft Tackle Bag, which can be added to the Pack-Vest, gives additional access. It attaches at chest level.

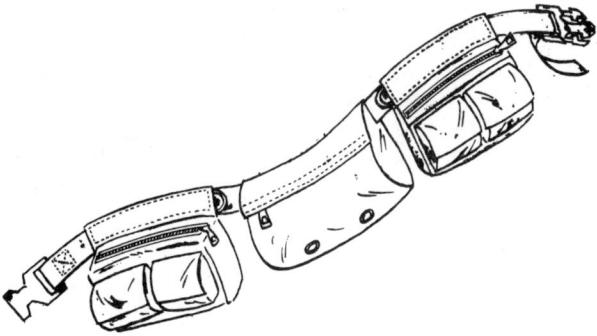

Sportflite Waist Pack. *7 pockets; fanny pack style; quick-release buckle; webbed belt; poly/cotton blend; tan or camo; sizes: S/M, L/XL.*
$19.95-$22.95 Tac, AnJ

North Fork Pack-Vest. *A day pack with accessory pockets for fly fishing; two side panels attach for front access, each has large zippered pocket and large pocket with Velcro closure; snap hooks for attachment of Soft Tackle Box listed next.*
$39.95 Nor

North Fork Soft Tackle Box. *Cordura nylon cover; internal fly book of open-cell foam with closed-cell protective walls; streamer book; pocket for accessories; 2 D-rings for attachment to North Fork Pack-Vest; forest green and tan.*
$19.95-$23.95 Nor, Pen, Let

Thomas & Thomas "Vest-on-a-Belt". *9 pockets; two side bags, one back bag; quick-release buckle; urethane-coated nylon; dark brown; fully adjustable for waist or chest; bags movable for versatility; an interesting alternative to the vest; see Sportflite Waist Pack for comparison, although it's smaller with less durable fabric.*
$32.50 T&T

Fishing Shirts and Jackets

The next vest alternative is really an extension of the vest. Fishing shirts and jackets offer few, if any, advantages over the vest for carrying equipment. Since you can't take off the shirts (in good taste), they are particularly difficult for me to imagine using like a vest. Carrying all that weight streamside is one thing, but carrying it everywhere or unloading it frequently seems foolish. The shirts are handsome, and as a fashionable thing to wear around the cabin, I think they're great. The fishing jackets amount to a vest with long sleeves.

Deschutes Fishing Jacket. *22 pockets including 3 sleeve pockets; vest with long sleeves; tan; sizes: S-XL.*
$53 Let

Hal Janssen Fishing Shirt. *5 pockets—4 front, 1 sleeve; shirt-style vest (or vest-style shirt); short or long sleeves; D-rings; cotton polyester; sizes: S(34-36), M(36-40), L(40-44), XL(46-48).*
$44.95 Fly

THE Fishing Shirt. *5 pockets; long sleeves; poly/cotton blend; tan; sizes: S-XL.*
$19.95 Dan

von Schlegell Fishing Shirt. *6 pockets; large back pocket; 100% cotton; long sleeves; sizes: S-XL.*
$32 Dan

Fishing Bags

The final alternative to vests is the fishing bag. There's really only one functional bag on the market, the Wood River Fly Fishing Bag. The Barbour bags are handsome and appeal to some sense of tradition, but they are impractical as equipment carriers. Access is limited, and the closures are cumbersome.

The Wood River bag is treated in a separate article below, since it's so different.

Barbour Tarras. *Cotton duck bonded with rubber; single pocket with waterproof lining; 2 outside pockets; buckle and strap closure; leather and brass trim; shoulder strap.* $67.50 Don

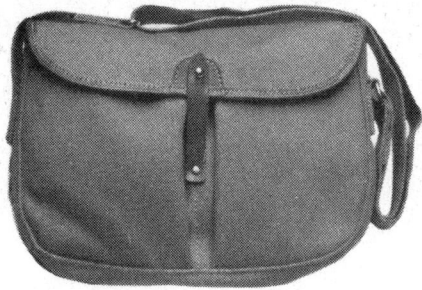

Barbour Glenzier. *Materials similar to Tarras; single pocket; 2 outside pockets; removable waterproof liner.* $51.50 Don

Barbour Tweed. *Materials similar to other Barbour bags; large size, 23"; removable fish liner.* $97.50 T&T

Wood River Fly Fishing Bags. *Nylon pack cloth with rigid inserts; pockets inside for boxes, paraphernalia; outside pockets for forceps, Flex-Lite, fly dope, bug juice, etc.; raincoat pouch below; rod holder on top; straps adjust for over-shoulder, around-waist, or chest-high carrying; a remarkably versatile system; tan, black, brown, brown camo, green camo; sizes: from 8"x5"x6" to 14"x7"x7". (Note: See article and full list of sizes below.)* $62.50-$79 (depending on size and accessories) AnJ or direct from Wood River Bags, Box 804, Santa Ana, California 92702 (714) 966-0609

Wood River Fly Fishing Bags

Like the many people who browse through ads in fly fishing magazines with as much enthusiasm as they read the articles, I'd seen the drawing of a Wood River bag and read the accompanying copy. But even though I had a good reason to consider a fishing bag to replace the headaches accompanying my use of a vest, it just didn't register.

To be honest, I put the Wood River bag in the same category as the Richardson Chest Fly Box. It must be, I thought, an equipment carrier of regional interest. The chest fly box is popular in the East; the bag was popular someplace else, like California. I'd never seen one in use

in Colorado or Montana, so I didn't think about it for myself. That was silly.

In fact, I probably still wouldn't know anything about the bags had not Peter Ross, the man behind the bag, sent me a sample bag to try out. I gave the sample bag to the lady I mentioned earlier. As you may recall, she was suffering the same maladies associated with having a lost of weight on the shoulders.

To make a longer story shorter, that bag was so well-engineered and so efficient at carrying equipment in a comfortable fashion that I ordered one for myself. So, I'm writing this to introduce you to Wood River bags because they are great tackle carriers, great enough for me to buy one (and I'm generally a miser).

As Peter will tell you (over and over if you give him the chance), fishing bags are the traditional tackle carriers for fly fishermen. Vests are a relatively new addition. However, his bags are as different from the old bags as vests are.

Wood River bags are cut from nylon pack cloth, a very durable material. The material is supported by internal styrene inserts so that the shape of the bag is retained. These inserts can be removed to allow the bag to be folded flat for travel if necessary. As it is, the bag is much easier to pack in the car than a vest.

Beyond the quality of the material and the construction of the bag, it is simply a marvelously well-engineered piece of equipment. On that basis alone, it's worthy of description here.

Take the strap system, for example. The straps come in four sections, joined as necessary with large areas of Velcro. With two sections in place, the bag fits comfortably around the waist. This is the way I wear mine. The weight is where it belongs—on the hips. With three sections, the bag can be worn over the shoulder, like a creel. An optional shoulder pad with drying patch adds comfort. Finally, with all four sections in place, the bag can be worn chest high for wading, so there's no need to have two carriers, one regular and one short for wading.

The carrying system is very flexible. With the waist straps or shoulder straps, you can carry the bag at your side or behind you. In position behind you, the bag is completely out of the way and very comfortable. It can be easily swung around front for fly changes.

With the bag in front, it's easy to locate everything since the top, when open, reveals all the pockets. The rigid box provides a working area, too, and rod holders on top of the bag will give you both hands free for knot tying. There is even an accomodation for fly tying from the box. A pocket will hold your vise securely upright, and you can work directly over the box without fear of dropping materials or finished flies. I can't think of any better set-up for streamside tiers. You can even tie in mid-stream if you need to keep your place in line (Henry's Fork Green Drake fishermen, take note).

To make up for the lack a big back pocket for raincoat and what-have-you, Peter has built a pouch under the bag. A raincoat or sweater can be pushed through the end openings and secured with Velcro straps. It doesn't provide quite the capacity of a vest's back pocket, but I think the total capacity of my Trout bag comes close to that of my vest. I can carry my usual equipment (remember, though, that I go rather light), my lunch, and my camera with one extra lens inside the bag. My raincoat or sweater (or both if the sweater is lightweight) goes in the pouch. It's crowded with everything in there, but it still works well.

Just a note on carrying a camera. I had previously carried a waterproof fanny pack for camera gear, in addition to my vest. Knowing what happens to cameras and film when they get wet, I have refused to carry such equipment around my neck or in my vest. The Wood River bag is ideal for camera equipment since the material is water repellent. The bags will even float (at least for a little while) if dropped or if you go in, further protecting the equipment inside.

Accessories available for the bags include the shoulder pad, a creel (which Peter recommends for extra storage or use as a nymph net), pack rod straps, and a Velcro net release. This last option is another example of Peter's innovative design. Your net is clipped onto a D-ring attached to a square of Velcro. The mating section of Velcro is attached to a strap or the bag. When you need the net, a quick yank frees it from the strap. No more messing around with those damn French clips.

There is also a way to attach the bag to the gunwales of a canoe or boat, so that you can work directly from it and still wear a flotation vest. Goodbye to wet vests from the bottom of the boat.

There are more features, too many for the space available here, but I hope this has served to get a quality product to your attention better than it has gotten there before. I like well-designed equipment that is constructed with real care, and so I like Wood River bags. Mostly I simply enjoy fishing with one. With the bag on my waist and behind me, I am unencumbered and free to enjoy my day astream. I haven't found any negative things.

The only hurdle to owning and using the Wood River bag is psychological/social. You'll be out of uniform, at least until a number of fly fishermen start using the bags. I'd just as soon get rid of the uniform idea, anyway, and get back to judging a fly fisherman by his or her ability on the stream instead of the number of pockets in the vest or the brand name of the waders.

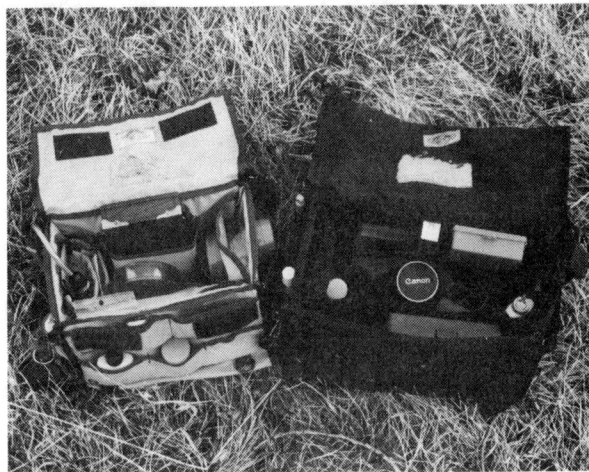

Here are the models. You'll have a little trouble translating these into your fishing needs if you've only owned a vest. The Salmon is about the smallest model I'd recommend if you carry the usual amount of stuff. It will be a little tight with lunch, etc., but it's very nice for chest wading. I bought the Trout for the extra capacity I need for my camera, and it's been more than enough to hold everything I require. Whatever model you choose, Peter will let you exchange it if you're not happy with it. He'll even let you change your mind on colors if you wish. The colors available are tan, brown, black, brown camo, and green camo.

(Note: An economy model is in the works. Watch for it from L.L. Bean, perhaps. All models are available in their showroom in Maine, incidentally. Angler's Junction carries the Trout model in their catalog.)

The bags are listed from the largest to the smallest.

Excursion Model. *14"x7"x7"; 26 pockets; inside pockets for fly boxes, tying tools, plus center open area; outside pockets for tippet spools, forceps, sunglasses, leader wallet, Flex-Lite, floatant, etc.; inside fly patch; weighs 23 oz.*
$79

Trout Model. *12"x7"x7"; 21 pockets; features similar to Excursion; weighs 20 oz.*
$72.50

Salmon Classsic Model. *10"x6 1/2"x6 1/2"; 17 pockets; see features above; box pockets cut larger; weighs 15 oz.*
$77.50

Salmon Model. *Same size as Salmon Classic; a good bag for the trout fisherman in spite of the name; weighs 15 oz.*
$67.50

Saltwater Model. *Same size as Salmon Classic; 11 pockets; special features for the saltwater fisherman; weighs 15 oz.*
$69.50
Little Trout Model. *10"x5 ½"x6"; 13 pockets; similar features to Excursion but fewer for smaller size; weighs 12 oz.*
$65
Ultra Light. *8"x5"x6"; a small bag for the backpacker or light traveler.*
$62.50

To order or for further information, write: Wood River Fly Fishing Bags, Box 804, Santa Ana, California 92702 (714) 966-0609. Peter will gladly help with your choice of bag and accessories.

FLY BOXES AND WALLETS

There are over 175 fly boxes and streamer wallets listed here, so you should be able to find the one that's just right for you and your collection of flies. The trouble is in determining which of the many choices is just right.

You might begin your search based on material used in the boxes. Most listed here are a variety of plastic. Your other choice (omitting leather streamer wallets and handmade wooden boxes for the time being) is aluminum.

The plastic boxes are inexpensive and fairly durable. Most have transparent lids which allow you to go through a number of boxes without opening each one. The plastic boxes will eventually become scratched to some extent depending on how you care for them, and the latches may wear. Plastic boxes with metal hinges or metal hinge pins will last much longer than those with plastic hinges. Overall, you can expect to get your money's worth from

any of the boxes here. DeWitt, Bonnand, Myran, and Flambeau are the major manufacturers of plastic boxes.

The aluminum boxes are even more durable. You'll probably be able to pass them down. The offerings in aluminum boxes are more complete since all the possibilities available in plastic boxes are there plus metal clips for wet flies and nymphs. Perrine and Wheatley are the major aluminum box manufacturers.

You must also consider the type of flies you'll be storing in the box you buy. Wet flies, streamers, and nymphs supposedly do not require as much protection as dry flies since their hackle does not have to stand straight and true. They are often carried on individual metal clips, fastened in flat foam, or dropped onto a magnetic floor. The system of describing metal clips may be confusing at first. A "5-point clip" simply has five fairly large clips. A 7-point clip has seven smaller clips. Occasionally, you'll find a reference to "large 7-point" clips, and that will mean that there are seven clips more the size of regular 5-point clips.

Streamers are often carried in "wallets", which are also listed here. Generally, wallets have fleece lining, and the streamers are simply hooked into it. No protection is given hackle, but streamer hackle is pulled back by the current anyway.

Dry flies get more attention since their hackle must be protected. The basic dry fly box has open compartments into which a number of dries are placed. If the compartments are not overloaded, they work fine. Other systems have been designed to hold dries upright and away from the box or other flies. Angled foam strips are one popular method. Flies are hooked into the foam so that hackles are unmolested. Magnetic bars are used in a Bonnand box (#275) in much the same fashion as the angled foam, and Wheatley's # 4601 uses slit rubber bars for the same protection. Perrine and Martin have systems of individual, "stand-up" clips for dries that do the same thing.

If you do salmon, bass, or saltwater fishing, you'll need a box with larger compartments or bigger clips. Look for larger boxes with fewer compartments and depths of 1 ½"-2". For wet flies, look for 5-point clips.

On the other hand, if you carry a lot of small dry fly patterns for selective trout, look for a box with a lot of small compartments. Small dries (#18 and smaller) are difficult to place into and retrieve from the angled foam or individual clip boxes. An 18 compartment box, for instance, will let you organize a lot of patterns and sizes in one box.

Whatever your choice, you should select a box in person, if possible, especially a plastic one. There is a lot of variation in fit in the plastic boxes, and you'll want to get the one with the best closure. Fly boxes should latch well, certainly, but they should also open easily. If it takes a yank to open the lid, expect to create an artificial hatch when opening the box filled with flies.

Some fly boxes of note. There are a few boxes of special interest. The most envied box, and the most expensive, is the Wheatley #1609. It's an aluminum box with 32 individual compartments, 16 each on both the bottom and the "lid". Each compartment has its own spring-loaded lid. If you've ever tried to fish a fly out of an open compartment box in a gale or ever dropped an open fly box in the river, you already know the advantages here. Wheatley offers several other similar boxes in smaller sizes. Average price for the #1609 is about $95, although Hook & Hackle and Merrick's offer it for considerably less.

At the other end of the spectrum, the Bonnand #283 is a plastic box with 10 compartments, each with individual lids. This won't have quite the standing streamside as the Wheatley box, but it only costs about $9.

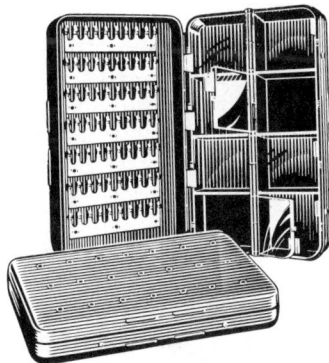

And in the middle of the spectrum is Perrine's #100. It has eight compartments with individual lids on one side and 70 wet fly clips on the other side. Average retail is about $14, and like the other Perrine boxes, it's available from many companies.

Wheatley makes boxes with swing leaves. These add extra capacity to the usually empty center of a wet fly box. They can be worth the extra investment if this additional capacity eliminates the need for another box.

My fly box system. Old hands can skip this section. You've already developed your own system for carrying flies, and all you'll want to do is argue. But the beginner may be overcome with all the choices. He can read on.

First, I have what I call a working box. It's a Scientific Anglers box, size medium. In it, I can carry all the types of flies and all the common patterns I need on my home streams. One side of the box is angled foam for dries in sizes 12-18. The other side of the box is flat foam, and there I hook wet flies, nymphs, and a few streamers. I like the latch system on the S/A box. Similar boxes are available from Perrine, Wheatley, and Fly-Rite.

I also carry a smaller box made by Myran (#1452) for midges and small dries. It has six open compartments. This is a rather recent acquisition replacing a Fly-Rite Pocket Pak which I outgrew. I like the transparent box a little better, too.

I use a Fly-Rite Streamer Fly box for the collection of Little Brown Trout streamers and Muddlers I carry. It has two sides of flat foam. I used to carry an open compartment box, but I found it difficult to pull out the streamer I wanted. Not only are the streamers better displayed and therefore easier to find, I think they're better protected hooked upright in the foam. I use barbless hooks, but I haven't had any problems with flies coming loose. The foam, angled or flat, will last longer with barbless hooks (and so will the fish you release). Similar boxes are available from Perrine, Scientific Anglers, and Wheatley.

My collection of nymphs is also carried in a flat-foam box. It's a Perrine box that I converted years ago before foam was available in ready-made boxes. I had more flies than the clips would hold so I glued some patches of foam inside both lids. I punched holes in the foam to match the existing ventilation system, and the box has served me well. It's a small box, probably a #60. Perrine now makes a box (#67) in that size with foam strips one side and flat foam on the other. Wheatley's #1401EF is the same size and has flat foam both sides, but no catalog carries it. Larger boxes with flat foam are available from both companies and from Fly-Rite.

Finally, I carry a wooden fly box made for me by Wayne Albaugh of Maryland. It's a handsome addition to my fishing bag, and I carry my special dry flies in it. These include my match-the-hatch patterns and a few pretty attractors.

I own other boxes which are really storage boxes. I have a couple of Flambeau Mighty Tuff boxes for wets and large nymphs. They've been good boxes although they're a bit scratched up now. My next purchase will be a DeWitt #1085C which I'll use for bass poppers. The four compartments are 2" deep, perfect for the hairy bass bugs.

As you can see, I have a bit of everything. Everything except a Wheatley #1609. Oh well, maybe someone I know will read this and get me one for Christmas.

Boxes and wallets listed here. The fly boxes are listed in alphabetical order by brand name and then by size within the product line. The size of the box follows the model number. I've given the number of compartments where applicable, but that may not always help since some are of unequal size. Where they were available and space permitted, I've included diagrams or other illustrations of the boxes.

The streamer wallets are listed last. Many anglers still prefer to carry streamers, nymphs, and wets in wallets, and there are a considerable number to choose from.

Fly Boxes

Adventurer

Adventurer boxes are molded from acrylonitrile plastic. They have plastic hinges and a friction closure.

#210. *7"x3 ¼"x1 ¼"; 9 comp.*
$1.50 Cus
#215. *Same as #210 but with 5 comp.*
$1.50 Cus
#220. *4 ⅝"x3"x1 ⅛"; 6 comp.*
$1.10 Cus
#221. *Same as #220 but with 4 comp.*
$1.10 Cus

Bonnand

These come from the French company that in 1910 first introduced the plastic bobber. They have friction closures. Materials vary as described.

#271. *3.5"x2.5"x.75"; polystyrene; transparent lid; brass hinge; 4 streamer comp.*
$2-$2.51 Mur, Hun, Mer

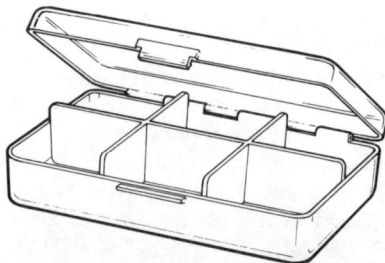

#272. *Same as #271 but with 6 comp.*
$2-$2.51 Cus, Bud, LLB, Hun, Dan, Mer

#273. *Same as #271 but with clips for 27 flies.*
$5-$6.68 Mer, Hun
#274. *Same as #271 but with magnetic floor.*
$7.52 Mer
#280. *5.75"x3.5"x1.25"; polypropylene; transparent lid; brass hinge pin; pale green; 5 streamer comp.*
$9.19 Mer
#281. *Same as #280 but with 6 comp.*
$9.19 Mer
#282. *Same as #1280 but with 10 comp.*
$9.19 Mer
#283. *Same as #282 but compartments have individual lids.*
$9.19 Mer
#275. *5.9"x3.7"x1.2"; molded ABS plastic; transparent pale green; brass hinge pin; three 5.5" magnetic bars.*
$9.19-$9.95 Cus, Dan, Mer
#285. *Same size as #275 but with 5 streamer comp.; transparent top and bottom.*
$5.95-$7.50 Pen, Orv, Mer, Hun
#286. *Same as #285 but with 6 comp.*
$5.98-$6.68 Mer, Hun
#287. *Same as #285 but with 10 comp.*
$5.75-$7.95 Pen, Orv, LLB, Fly, Hun, Mer
#231. *6.56"x4.06"x1.15"; molded ABS plastic; transparent pale green; brass hinge pin; 5 streamer comp.*
$6.75-$9 Mer, LLB, Fly, Orv
#232. *Same as #231 but with 6 comp.*
$8.35 Mer
#233. *Same as #231 but with 15 comp.*
$6.75-$9 LLB, Mer, Orv, Pen

Cortland

Cortland's boxes are molded Tenite plastic. The green liner on the bottom and the metal hinges are the trademarks of their boxes.

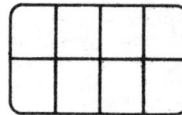
002

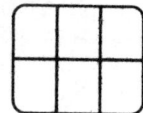
032

#002. *5 5/16"x3 7/16"x1 ⅛"; 8 comp.*
$5.80-$5.95 Fly, Hig, Mer, Pen, Edd, Bud, Tac
#003. *Same as #002 but ⅞" deep and 10 comp.*
$7.10 Edd, Bud, Hig, Mer
#004. *Same as #002 but with ripple foam insert.*
$7.40 Bud, Mer
#032. *4 3/16"x3"x1 ⅛"; 6 comp.*
$5.40-$5.50 Edd, Tac, Fly, Hig, Mer, Bud, Pen
#064. *7 ⅜"x4 5/16"x1 7/16"; 10 comp.*
$7.10-$7.25 Pen, Tac, Edd, Bud, Mer, Fly, Hig
#353. *12 ¾"x6 ⅜"x1 7/16"; 12 comp.*
$17.35-$17.95 Hig, Fly, Mer, Bud, Edd

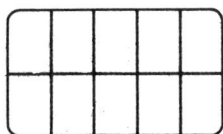
064

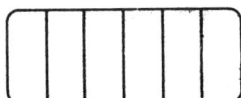
734

#734. *7 1/2"x3 1/4"x15/16"; 6 streamer comp.*
$6.40-$6.50 Fly, Tac, Hig, Mer, Bud, Edd
#735. *Same as #734 but with 14 comp.*
$7.40-$7.50 Bud, Tac, Edd, Mer, Fly, Hig

DeWitt Lite-Tuff

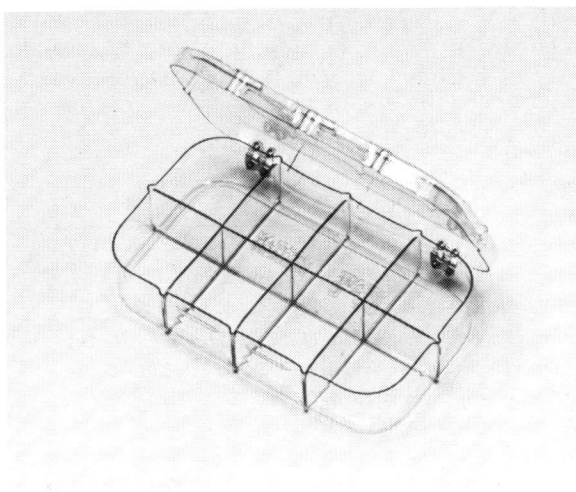

Formed from clear butyrate plastic with stainless steel hinges riveted on, DeWitt boxes have clear tops and bottoms. They have friction closures. The boxes are guaranteed for 1 year. They are made in the USA.

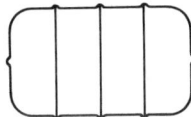

#1020A. *5 11/16"x3 1/4"x7/8"; 8 comp.*
$3.65-$5.87 H&H, Cus, AnR, Dal, EJH, Mur, Hun, Dan
#1020C. *Same as #1020A but with 4 comp.*
$5.25 Dan
#1020T. *Same as #1020A but with 6 comp. of differing sizes.*
$6.25 AnR, EJH, Hun
#1022A. *Same as #1020A but with 6 comp.*
$5.25 AnR
#1022C. *Same as #1020A but with 3 comp.*
$5 AnR
#1023A. *4"x2 13/16"x15/16"; 6 comp.*
$3.30-$5.75 H&H, Cus, AnR, Wul, EJH, Mur, Dal, Hun, Dan
#1023C. *Same as #1023A but with 3 comp.*
$4.50-$5.25 Hun, Dan, AnR
#31024A. *5 11/16" x3 1/4" x1 1/2"; 6 comp.*
$5.75 AnR

#1024C. *Same as #1024A but with 3 comp.*
$5-$5.75 Hun, AnR
#1024R. *5 1/4"x3 1/2"x1 1/2"; 6 comp.*
$6 Hun

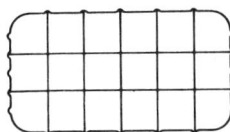

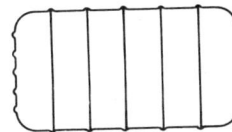

#1026A. *8"x4 1/16"x1 3/16"; 18 comp.*
$5-$7.99 Dal, Hun, EJH, Dan, AnR, Wul, Cus, H&H
#1026B. *Same as #1026A but with 12 comp.*
$5-$7.50 H&H, AnR, Cus, EJH, Mur, Dan
#1026C. *Same as #1026A but with 6 comp.*
$7.15-$7.25 Dan, AnR

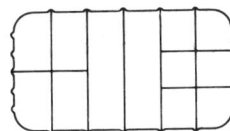

#1026R. *Same as #1026A but with 12 unequal comp.*
$7.15 Dan

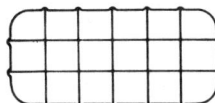

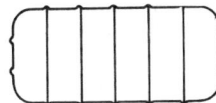

#1043A. *7 1/2"x3 1/4"x3/4"; 18 comp.*
$5-$7.38 Cus, AnR, Dal, Dan
#1043C. *Same as #1043A but with 6 comp.*
$5.75-$6.75 AnR, Mur, Hun
#1045A. *5 3/8"x4 1/16"x1 3/16"; 12 comp.*
$5.50-$6.75 AnR, Wul
#1045C. *Same as #1045A but with 4 comp.*
$5.25-$5.75 Hun, AnR
#1046B. *7 1/8"x4 1/16"x1 3/16"; 10 comp.*
$6.75 AnR
#1080B. *8 1/4"x6 3/4"x1 1/2"; 6 comp.*
$11 Hun
#1080S. *Same as #1080B but with 4 comp.*
$12.50 Hun
#1083A. *9"x4"x1 7/16"; 8 comp.*
$8.50-$10 AnR, Hun
#1083C. *Same as #1083A but with 4 comp.*
$8-$9.25 Hun, AnR
#1085A. *9"x4"x2"; 8 comp.*
$11.25 AnR
#1085C. *Same as #1085A but with 4 comp.*
$8.75 Hun
Vel Foam. *Velvet-covered foam inserts with bars to hold flies; salmon-colored bottom and insert; transparent lid; brass hinges; 3 sizes.*
S—$3.95; M—$4.95; L—$5.95 EJH, Pen, Wul

Flambeau Mighty Tuff

Made of crushproof plastic, Mighty Tuff boxes have metal hinges and friction closure.

#5126. *7 ¼"x4 ¼"x1 ⅛"; 16 small, 1 large comp.*
$3.55-$4.25 Hig, Dal, Dan, Cus, Bob
#5127. *Same as above but with 6 small, 3 large, 2 long comp.*
$3.55-$4.25 Dal, Dan, Hig, Cus, Bob

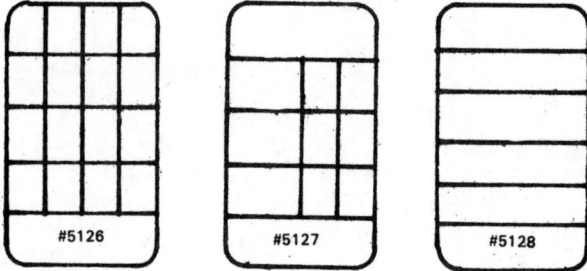

#5126   #5127   #5128

#5128. *Same as above but with 6 long comp.*
$3.55-$4.25 Bob, Cus, Dan, Dal, Hig
#5204. *4 ½"x2 ¾"x1 ⅛"; 4 comp.*
$2.49-$2.95 Bob, Cus, Hig, Dal, Dan
#5206. *Same as #5204 but with 6 comp.*
$2.49-$2.95 Cus, Hig, Bob, Dal, Dan
#5129. *12 ¼"x6 ⅛"x1 ½"; 24 comp.; storage box.*
$7.95 Bob

Fly-Rite

These polypropylene boxes have friction closure and feature foam inserts. The bright blue, orange, yellow colors of the Fly-Rite boxes are distinctive. The boxes utilize plastic hinges.

Ripple Foam Fly Box. *5 ¾"x3 ½"x1"; one side ripple foam, other flat.*
$6.49-$8.95 Edd, TCr, T&T, FlR, Let, Kau, Dal, Dan
Streamer Fly Box. *Both sides flat.*
$6.95-$7.50 FlR, Let
Pocket Pack Fly Box. *3 ⅜"x2 ¼"x¾"; 6 comp.*
$1.50 FlR, TCr, Let
Replacement inserts. *Ripple foam and flat foam inserts; 5 ½"x3 ¼"; self-adhesive backing.*
ripple—$3.85-$4.50; flat—$1.50 TCr, T&T, FlR

Martin

Martin's aluminum box is ventilated and has unique individual, stainless steel "stand-up" clips for flies.

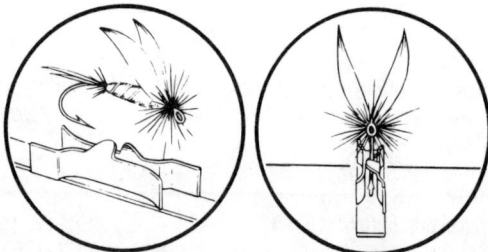

Fly Safe. *6 ¼"x4"x1 ⅛"; clips for 72 flies in sizes 16-1/0.*
$11.45 Sim

Midge Boxes

These two boxes are small (midge size). No manufacturers are given.

Midge Fly Boxes. *3 ½"x2 ¼"x¾"; plastic; transparent lids; vest pocket size; 4 or 6 comp.*
4—$1.95; 6—$2.25 T&T

Mini-Fly Box. *Plastic; folds together; individual lids; can hook on vest; 2 ⅞"x1 ½"x1"; 6 comp.*
$.98-$1.50 Orv, Pen, Bob, Ste, Dal

Myran

Myran fly boxes are tough molded MBS plastic with transparent/translucent tops and bottoms. They have friction closure and brass hinge pins. The ant trademark on top seems entirely appropriate to fly fishing. Myran boxes are made in Sweden.

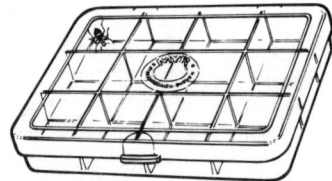

#1451. *4.25"x3.25"x.63"; 12 comp.*
$3.50-$4 Ram, Pen, Orv, T&T, Mer
#1452. *Same as #1451 but with 6 comp.*
$3.50-$4 Pen, Mer, T&T, Orv, Ram
#1471. *4.25"x3.25"x1"; 5 comp.*
$3.76 Mer
#1472. *Same as #1471 but with 4 comp.*
$3.50-$3.76 T&T, Mer

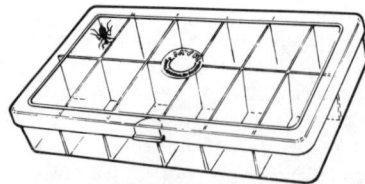

#1691. *6"x3.5"x1"; 12 comp.*
$5-$5.98 T&T, Mer, Pen
#1692. *6.5"x3.75"x1"; 5 streamer comp.*
$5.85 Mer

North Fork

These wallet-style, nylon-covered books are included here because closed-cell "walls" form a box-like protection for hackles (but with this system, the bottoms of the hackles still suffer). One side of the wallet has walls, the other is flat for streamers/wets.

Fly Book. *About the size of a fat checkbook (which is difficult for some of us to imagine); no sizes given in present catalog.*
$5.95-$6.95 Nor, Pen, Tac, Let
Fly Pocket. *An abbreviated version of Fly Book that will fit in shirt pocket.*
$4.95 Nor, Pen, Tac, Let

Orvis, Thomas & Thomas, and Kaufmann

These boxes may or may not be from the same manufacturer. It seems likely they are, and it's probably Dewitt. They are plastic with metal hinges. The box is tan with a transparent lid. The company name is carried on top. Stated sizes vary slightly. Model names are listed for boxes offered by Orvis. T&T's boxes have only model numbers, and Kaufmann's model numbers include letters. The same size box may be offered by all three companies, but it will be listed only once here.

Bass/Saltwater. *4"x9"x1 ⅞"; 5 comp.*
$10 Orv
Salmon Dry. *4"x9"x1 7/16"; 8 comp.*
$10 Orv
Slim 6, #437C. *3 ¼"x7 ½"x⅞"; 6 comp.*
$6-$7.50 Orv, Let, Kau

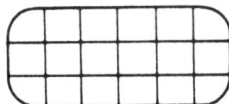

Slim 1, #187, #437A. *Same size as Slim 6 but with 18 comp.*
$6.75-$8 Orv, T&T, Ste, Let, Kau

Shorty 12. *4 ¼"x5 ⅜"x1 ¼"; 12 comp.*
$6.50-$6.75 Orv, Let
Shorty 10. *Same size as Shorty 12 but with 10 comp.*
$6.25-$6.75 Orv, Ste, Let

Midge, #64, #23R. *4 ¼"x3"x1 ⅛"; 6 comp.*
$5-$5.50 Orv, T&T, Ste, Kau
#23C. *Same as midge but with 3 comp.*
$5.25 Kau
Medium 8, #86, #20A. *5 11/16"x3 ¼"x⅞"; 8 comp.*
$5.65-$6.25 T&T, Orv, Kau
#20T. *Same size as Medium 8 but with 6 comp.*
$6 Kau
Medium 4, #20C. *Same size as Medium 8 but with 4 comp.*
$5.65-$6 Orv, Kau
Big 18, #188, #26A. *4 ¼"x8 ¼"x1 ¼"; 18 comp.*
$7.35-$8 Orv, T&T, Kau, Let
#26B. *Same size as Big 18 but with 12 comp.*
$7.95 Kau
Big 6, #26C. *Same size as Big 18 but with 6 comp.*
$7.25-$7.95 Orv, Kau
#88. *8 ¼"x6 ¾"x2"; 8 comp.*
$14 T&T

Perrine

Perrines are the most popular fly boxes in America. They are American-made aluminum boxes with a variety of fly holders.

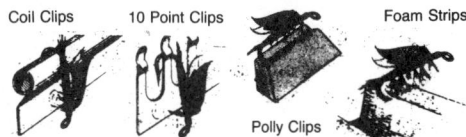

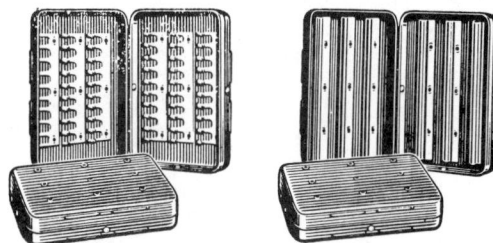

#60. *2 3/"x3 ¾"x⅞"; 6 10-point clips.*
$3-$5.20 Most catalogs
#66. *Same as #60 but with coil clips.*
$3.10-$5.40 Most catalogs
#67. *2 ¾"x3 ¾"x1 ⅛"; foam strips/flat pad.*
$3.80-$6.55 Many catalogs
#68. *Same as #67 but with "Polly Clips" for 44 flies.*
$3.40-$5.90 Sim, Tac, Bud, Ran, AnW, Cus, Dan, Mer, H&H, T&T

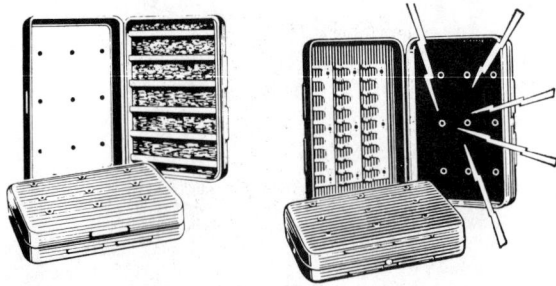

#69. *Same as #67 but magnetic insert and 3 10-point clips.*
$4-$6.80 Cab, Ree, Mer, Kau, Hig, Dal, Dan, Bud, AnW, Cus, H&H, Bob, Sim, Edd
#90. *3 ¾"x6"x⅞"; 14 10-point clips for 140 flies.*
$4.45-$7.70 Many catalogs

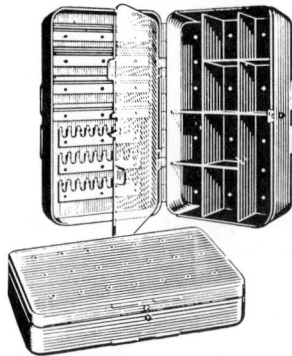

#91. *3 ¾"x6"x1 ½"; 10 comp. with single lid and 4 coil clips plus 3 10-point clips.*
$5.55-$8.20 Kau, EJH, Dan, Mer, Fol, Pen, Tac, Bud, Bob, Sim, Egg, Edd, H&H, Cab, Cus
#92. *Same as # 90 but with 14 coil clips for 140-200 flies.*
$4.55-$6.95 Cus, T&T, Bob, Sim, Tac, EJH, Dan, Mer, Bud, H&H

#95. *3¾"x6"x1¼"; 16 5-point clips for 80 salmon flies.*
$6.35-$9.95 Many catalogs
#96. *Same as #95 but with 14 10-point clips for 140 flies.*
$4.65-$6.60 Edd, Ram, H&H, Mer, Fol, EJH, Dal, Cab, Tac, Sim
#97. *Same as #95 but with 14 coil clips for 140-200 flies.*
$4.55-$8.15 Many catalogs
#99. *Same as #95 but with 6 coil clips, 1 large coil clip,*

and 5 compartments ("for lures") with single lid.
$5.40-$9.20 H&H, EJH, Mer, Dal, Hig, Ree, Dan, Sim, Cus, Bob, Bud
#101. *Same as #95 but with magnetic insert and 4 coil clips with 3 10-point clips.*
$6-$10.25 H&H, Cab, Ree, Fol, Dan, Mer, Kau, Dal, Cus, Pen, Bob, Bud, Sim, Edd
#107. *Same as #95 but with foam strips and foam pad.*
$5.70-$9.90 Many catalogs
#108. *Same as #95 but with flat foam both sides; designed by Bob Jacklin.*
$7.95 Bob

#98. *3 ¾"x6"x1 ⅜"; Polly Clips for 100 flies.*
$5.48-$9.50 Many catalogs
#100. *Same as #98 but with 7 10-point clips and 8 comp. with individual lids.*
$9.75-$16.85 Many catalogs

Plano

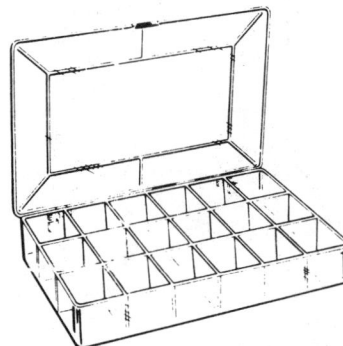

These translucent styrene plastic boxes have plastic hinges and a friction closure.

#3612. *11"x7 ¼"x1 ¾"; 6 long, 6 small comp.*
$3.10 Fol
#3618. *Same size as above but with 18 comp.*
$3.10 Fol
#3448-4. *4 ⅝"x2 ⅞"x1"; 4 comp.*
$.95 Fol
#3449-5. *6 ½"x3 ¾"x1 ⅛"; 5 long comp.*
$1.15 Fol

#3449-7. *Same size as #3449-5 but with 3 long, 4 small comp.*
$1.15 Fol
#3450-6. *8 ¼"x4 ¼"x1 ⅜"; 6 comp.*
$1.70 Fol

Rotary Fly Boxes

Circular boxes with transparent tops that rotate to open fly compartment.

Rotary boxes. *Variety of sizes; clip for attaching to vest.*
$2.05-$4.25 Ste, Dal, Dan

Scientific Anglers

The distinctive gray plastic S/A box has a friction closure (solid latching) and foam insert, either flat or ripple (angled ridges to protect hackle).

Small. *3 ½"x2 ½"x1"; both sides flat.*
$2.95-$5 Pen, Sim, Ram, Mer, Kau, Dan, Fly, Hun, AnJ, Bob, Cor, Tid, Bud, Cus, H&H

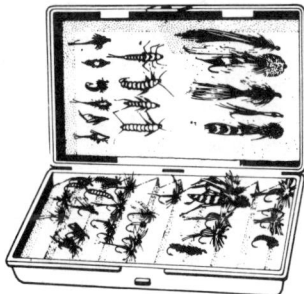

Medium. *5 ¾"x3 9/16"x15/16"; either two flat inserts or one flat, one ripple.*
$5.25-$9 Many catalogs
Large. *8 ⅜"x4 ½"x1 ⅜"; same options as Medium.*
$6.45-$11 Many catalogs

Wheatley

These are the boxes of status from England. The best known and most coveted models have compartments with individual lids. The boxes are aluminum with a variety of inserts.

#1301. *3 ½"x2 ⅜"x¾"; 3 small 7-point clips and 3 10-point clips; 51 flies.*
$12.06-$18 AnR, Wul, Mer, Hun, Kau

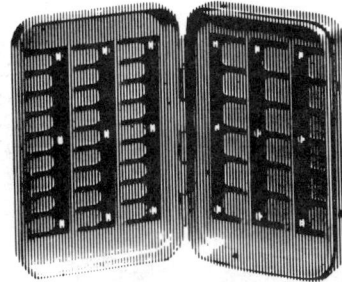

#2301. *Same as #1301 but ventilated.*
$9.38-$10 Mer, T&T
#2303. *Same as #1301 but magnetic insert and 3 10-point clips.*
$9.38-$12.75 Orv, T&T, Mer
#1401. *4 ¾"x3 ½"x⅞"; 5 small 7-point clips and 5 10-point clips.*
$14.74-$19.95 AnR, Mer, Kau, Hun
#1401EF. *Same as #1401 but with Etha Foam inserts instead of clips.*
N/A Ask your local dealer
#1402EF. *Same as #1401EF but with swing-leaf.*
N/A Ask your local dealer
#1601. *6"x3 ½"x⅞"; 7 small 7-point clips and 7 10-point clips; 119 flies.*
$18.76-$20 Mer, Hun, AnR
#1631. *Same as #1601 but with 7 small 7-point clips and 5 large 7-point clips for larger flies; 84 flies.*
$18.76 Mer
#1641. *Same as #1601 but with 10 large 7-point clips; 70 flies.*
$18.76-$20 Hun, Mer
#1651. *Same as # 1601 but with 4 5-point clips and 5 large 7-point clips; 55 flies.*
$18.76-$23.95 Kau, Hun, Mer
#1661. *Same as #1601 but with 8 5-point clips; 40 flies.*
$18.76-$23.95 Mer, Fly
#1671. *Same as #1601 but with 4 5-point clips and 7 small 7-point clips; 69 flies.*
$18.76-$23.95 Fly, Mer, Tid
#2601. *6"x3 ½"x1 ⅛"; 14 10-point clips; 140 flies.*
$14.74-$19.95 T&T, Kau, Mer
#2603. *Same as #2601 but with magnetic insert and 7 10-point clips.*
$14.74-$16 Mer, Orv, T&T
#1602. *Same as #2601 but with swing-leaf for extra capacity; 14 small 7-point clips and 14 10-point clips; 238 flies.*
$22.65-$33.95 H&H, Cus, T&T, Ram, Let, Kau, Mer, Hun, AnR, Pen, Orv
#1632. *Same as #2601 but with swing-leaf; 8 5-point clips and 10 large 7-point clips; 110 flies.*
$22.65-$35.95 Pen, H&H, Orv, AnR, T&T, Kau, Fly, Hun, Mer
#1642. *Same as #2601 but with swing-leaf; 16 5-point clips for 80 large flies.*
$25.46-$31.95 AnR, Fly, Hun, Mer, T&T

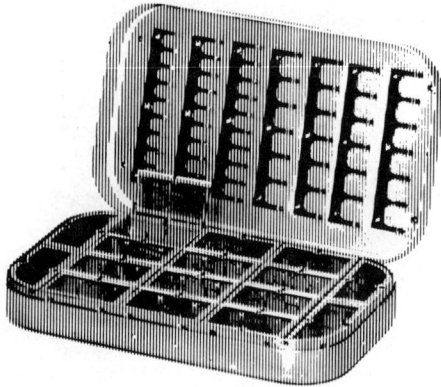

#1607. *Same as #2601 but with 16 comp. (ind. lids), 4 small 7-point clips, and 3 10-point clips.*
$40-$62 Ram, Dun, Let, Fly, T&T, Cus, Dan, Mer, Orv, H&H, Bud, Pen
#1607F. *Same as #1607 but with foam pad instead of clips.*
$44.22-$60 Bud, T&T, Cus, Orv, Mer, Dan
#4607F. *Same as #1607F but with black finish.*
$48.24-$60 Pen, Mer, Kau, Wul, T&T (engraving available)
#1608. *Same as #2601 but with 10 comp. (6 large, 4 small with ind. lids), 4 small 7-point clips, and 3 10-point clips.*
$46.90-$64 AnR, Bud, Kau, Hun, Mer
#1608F. *Same as #1608 but with foam pad instead of clips.*
$45.56-$62 Mer, Bud, Dan
#1609. *6"x3 ½"x1 ½"; 32 comp. with individual lids.*
$73.15-$110 Let, Fly, Kau, Hun, Dan, T&T, H&H, AnR, Cus, Orv, Mer, Pen, Bud
#4601. *6"x3 ½"x1 ⅛"; 10 slit bars of non-absorbent rubber; 120 flies; black finish.*
$14.74-$22 Orv, Tid, Mer, Pen, T&T, Kau
#4600. *Same as #4601 but with Etha Foam inserts instead of rubber bars.*
$17.15-$19 Orv, T&T, Dun
#1302. *3 ½"x2 ⅜"x1"; with swing-leaf; 6 small 7-point clips and 6 10-point clips; 102 flies.*
$14.65-$22 H&H, Pen, AnR, Hun, T&T, Orv, Cus, Ram, Bud
#1307. *Same as #1302 but with 6 comp.(individual lids), 2 small 7-point clips, and 1 10-point clip.*
$27.95-$42 H&H, Cus, Orv, Bud, T&T, Fly, Kau, Dan, Dun, Mer
#1307F. *Same as #1307 but with foam pad instead of clips.*
$29.48-$40 Mer, Dan, Cus, Bud
#1402. *4 ¾"x3 ½"x1"; with swing-leaf; 10 small 7-point clips and 10 10-point clips; 170 flies.*
$21-$30 Ram, AnR, Kau, Hun, Mer
#1407. *Same as #1402 but with 12 comp. (individual lids), 3 small 7-point clips, and 2 10-point clips.*
$34.80-$52 Orv, Bud, Dan, Pen, Tid, Kau, Ram, H&H, Fly, Mer, Cus

#1407F. *Same as #1407 but with foam pad instead of clips.*
$37.56-$50 Mer, Bud
Replacement Etha Foam Pads. *Adhesive-backed replacement pads; 4"x3 ½" or 6"x3 ½".*
$1.50 T&T

Handmade Wooden Fly Boxes

A few catalogs offer wooden fly boxes. These are wonderful to own, as are most wooden things. Aesthetics are the main basis of choice here although the box ought to be functional, too.

Wooden fly boxes. *Specifics vary; check catalogs for details.*
$29.95-$39.95 Bud, Blu, Nor

Streamer Wallets and Fly Books

A variety of styles and brands of streamer books or wallets are listed here. All fold flat to hold streamers, wets, nymphs or whatever fly you think doesn't need the protection of a standard box.

Barbour Canvas Fly Wallet. *Cotton duck trimmed with leather; fleece lining; brass snap.*
$14.95 Don
Barbour Leather Fly Wallet. *Fleece lining; leather cover; brass zipper.*
$18.95 Don
Common Sense Fly Book (#1670). *Similar to Cortland Streamer Fly Book below.*
$7.50-$8.55 Cus, Sim, Edd, Mer
Common Sense Combination Fly and Tackle Book (#1734). *6 ½"x3 ½"; covered in cowhide; pockets of heavy duck; 2 leaves with springs and clips for snelled wet flies; 2 drying pads; 2 parchment envelopes; 4 pockets for tackle; just like Grandad's fly book.*
$9.30-$10.65 Sim, Cus

Common Sense Standard Size Snelled Fly Book (#1525). *2 leaves with springs and clips; 2 drying pads; 2 envelopes; imitation leather cover.*
$6.23-$6.25 Sim, Mer

Common Sense Loose Leaf Fly Book (#1823). *7"x4 ¼"; 6 felt leaves on loose-leaf style rings; 2 fleece pockets on inside covers; cowhide cover; additional leaves available (fleece—$3.15/ea.; felt—$1.50/ea.).*
$11.18-$14.50 Ree, Hun, Mer, Sim
Common Sense Wet and Dry Fly Book (#1890). *6 ¼"x4"x1 ½"; 4 envelopes; 2 drying pads; I wouldn't use this for dries, in spite of its name.*
$13.35-$14.05 Sim, Cus, Mer
Common Sense Streamer Book (# 1736). *4 felt pads; 1 pocket; imitation leather.*
$6.45-$7.05 Mer, Sim

Common Sense Practical Fly Book (#1727). *7"x3 ½"; 6 envelopes; 2 drying pads; cowhide cover; 2 pockets.*
$7.65-$7.85 Sim, Cus
Common Sense Carry-All Fly Book (#1856). *4 ¾"x4"x1 ½"; fleece lining; felt pad; pocket; cowhide cover.*
$9.35 Mer
Common Sense Two Envelope Fly Book (#1760). *6 ½"x3 ½"; 2 env. of tag cloth with transparent fronts; felt pad; imitation leather cover.*
$4.35 Mer
Common Sense Six Envelope Fly Book (#1801). *8"x4 ½"; 6 env. with transparent fronts; 4 full-size, 3 small canvas pockets; 2 felt pads; leather strap closure; brown cowhide cover.*
$14.10 Mer
Common Sense Leader/Fly Book (#1827). *6 ½"x4"; 6 env.; 2 felt pads; 2 leader pockets; brown cowhide cover.*
$9.23 Mer
Common Sense Deluxe Fly Book (#1201). *6 ½"x2 ½"; 2 celluloid leaves; for 48 flies; brown cowhide cover.*
$7.95 Mer
Common Sense Streamer Fly Book (#1661). *6"x2 ½"; 2 fleece pockets; snap closure.*
$6.60 Mer
Common Sense Zippered Fly Book (#1669, #1674). *6"x3 ½" or 9"x3 ½"; fleece lining; brown vinyl cover.*
S—$6.60; L—$7.05 Mer
Common Sense Zippered Leather Fly Book (#1670, #1675). *6"x3 ½" or 9"x3 ½"; fleece lining; brown cowhide cover.*
S—$8.18; L—$9.08 Mer

Cortland Leather Fly Book. *6"x6" open; 3"x6" folded; fleece lining; snap closure.*
$12.95 Tac
Cortland Streamer Fly Book. *7"x4" folded; fleece lining; zippered.*
$12-$14.95 Tac, Hig
Cortland Roll-Up Book. *6"x6" open; fleece lining; snap closure.*
$9.95-$11.75 Tac, Edd
Dart Leather Fly Wallet. *Suede leather cover with synthetic fleece lining; sizes. 4"x6", 4"x7 ½".*
small—$3.80; large—$4.45 Sim
Leather Streamer Book. *3"x6" folded; 6"x6" open; leader comp.; fleece lining; leather cover; no brand name.*
$5.60-$7.80 H&H, Cus, Pen, Mer, Dal
Large Leather Streamer Book. *8"x12" open; leader comp.; fleece pages; leather cover; no brand name.*
$12.35-$17.35 Cus, H&H, Mer
Leather Fly Book. *Leather covered; fleece lining; zippered; variety of sizes; no brand names on these.*
$7.95-$14.50 T&T, Orv, Let, Fly, Kau, Dan

North Fork Streamer Book. *6 leafs of open cell foam; nylon outside; loop for attaching to vest; Velcro closure; green and tan.*
$4.75-$5.25 Nor, Pen, Let
North Fork Streamer Pocket. *Smaller version of Streamer Book.*
$3.75-$4.95 Nor, Pen, Let
Rangeley Wool Fly Book. *7"x3 ½"; outside canvas; fleece lining; pockets; snap closure.*
$5.75-$8.50 Ran, Let
River Systems McCloud Streamer Wallet. *5 ½"x4"; 6 leaves of foam; nylon cover; forest green and black.*
$6.90-$9.95 Pen, Cus, Ram

RELATED EQUIPMENT

Landing Nets and Tailers

A landing net is not a truly essential piece of equipment for most of us. A fish that's to be kept (very few, I hope) could be beached. Fish that will be released can be unhooked by hand.

Still, people who are killing fish use a net to make sure the fish don't get away, and catch-and-release anglers use nets to shorten the playing time, thus reducing the stress on the fish and increasing its chances for survival after release.

Aside from their utility, landing nets are often beautiful additions to our equipment collections. You can begin to feel the same way about your Brodin net as you do about your Kusse bamboo rod.

Cascade Lakes nets are the most common brand available. They are handsome and well-made. For a step beyond the ordinary, consider a Brodin or Gayewski net. The Brodin net is exquisite, and you can add your name or initials on an ivory inlay. You can even have an original scrimshaw work added to the net featuring your favorite fly pattern and trout.

Orvis offers the unusual Catch-N-Release net. It features a rectangular net with a shallow bag to facilitate the quick release of fish. If played too long, fish may die as a result.

If you work a lot of brushy country or simply like to be unencumbered, consider a fold-up net. These nets have spring steel bows that twist up and are held by a plastic or leather holster on your belt. Pulling them out of the holster springs them open.

I've also included a couple of aluminum nets that I could be sure had good bags on them. You should never use a net with a hard nylon bag. That stuff is a fish killer. It will remove the protective slime from a trout and possibly some of its scales. If you have one, throw it away or replace the bag with a cotton or soft nylon one.

Net kits are also listed here for those who like to do their own finishing. You'll need to do the finish work, string the bag, and attach a D-ring or French clip. Those nasty clips are listed here, too. They're supposed to open with one hand, but every one of them I've had has been difficult. The metal is too slick and the spring too tight. It's one of those contraptions that could use some new engineering.

Also included are salmon tailers. When the fish are too big for a net, these are the answer. Simply slip the noose around the tail of the fish, pull tight, and lift the fish.

Whatever device you use to get that fish in hand, remember the thrill of catching it and let it go to fight again, maybe at the end of your own line.

Hardwood Frame Nets

Bauman nets. *2-ply and 3-ply frames, walnut, cherry, or mahogany with ash; handles of those woods plus rosewood, zebra, koa, walnut burl; wood inlays available (add $10); personalization in gold script (add $2.50); sizes: Brook Trout (19" with 7"x12" bow, 17" bag), Rainbow (21" with 7 ½"x13 ½" bow, 19" bag), Brown Trout (20" with 8"x13" bow, 19" bag), Cutthroat (22 ½" with 9"x14 ½" bow, 19" bag).*
Brook—$30-$35; Rainbow—$40; Brown—$40; Cutthroat—$45 Harry Bauman, 5324 N. 62nd Street, Milwaukee, Wisconsin 53218 (414) 463-5333

Brodin Nets. *3-ply bow lamination, walnut/ash/walnut or rosewood/ash/rosewood; contrasting handles of walnut, cherry, Hawaiian koa, bubinga, vermilion, zebrawood, or East Indian rosewood; a very classy net;*

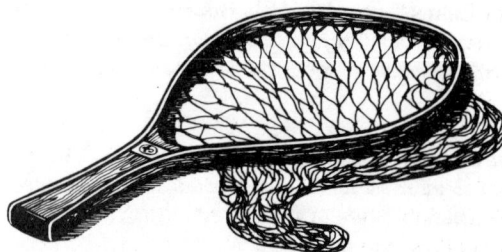

available with ivory inlay for name (add about $10) or original art scrimshaw (add about $60); sizes: Trout (21" with 9"x13" bow, 24" bag), Cutthroat (22" with 10"x15" bow, 24" bag), Steelhead (26" with 13"x18" bow, 30" bag).
Trout—$38-$40; Cutthroat—$41; Steelhead—$44-$49 Fly, RLW, Hig, AnJ, Bud, or direct from Brodin Landing Nets, Box 269, Belgrade, Montana 59714 (406) 388-1604

Cascade Lakes Teardrop Nets. *2-ply ash frame with contrasting handle of cherry, mahogany, or walnut; made in USA; sizes: 18 ½" (11 ½"x6" bow, 7" handle, 17" bag), 21" (13 ½"x7 ½" bow, 7 ½" handle, 19" bag), 23" (15 ½"x8 ½" bow, 7 ½" handle, 21" bag).*
18"—$13.35-$42.85; 21"—$13.85-$45.85; 23"—$14.65-$48.85 Pen, AnR, Kau, Tid, Cab, LLB, Cus, Sim (Sim had incredibly low prices in 1984, but check first, might have been a mistake), or direct from Cascade Lakes Tackle, Box 147, Ballston Lake, New York 12019 (518) 399-3945

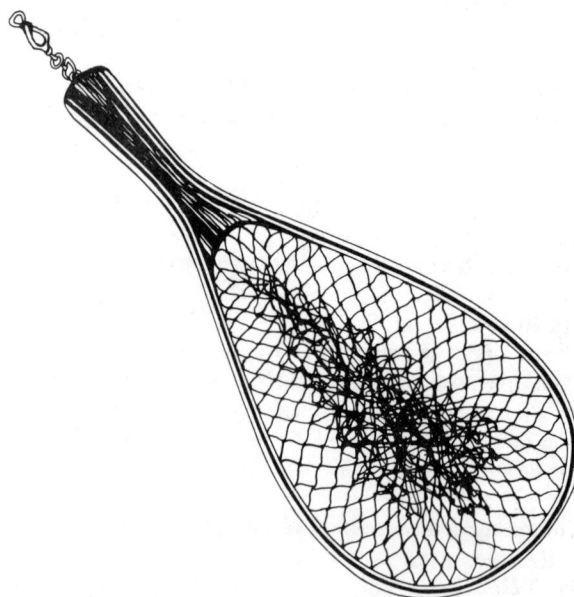

Cascade Lakes Deluxe Nets. *Ash-mahogany-ash frame with cherry or mahogany handles; sizes: 21" (13 ½"x9" bow, 7 ½" handle, 19" bag), 24" (16"x10" bow, 8" handle, 21" bag).*
21"—$28.98-$30.06; 24"—$29.98-$31.73 Pen, Mer

Cascade Lakes Columbia Nets. *Economy net; teardrop shape; sizes: 17", 19", 21". (Note: Only the 21" is in current catalogs.)*
$16.98 Pen
Cortland Small Stream Net. *Hand-rubbed hardwoods; soft net bag; sizes: 16", 20", 22".*
16"—$23.95; 20"—$45; 22"—n.a. Bud, Dun
Egger's Backpacking Net. *Ash/walnut frames with cherry handles; narrower bow for ease in carrying; weighs 6 oz.; size: 18 ½" (11 ½"x6" bow, 17" bag).*
$28 Egg
Gayewski Presentation Net. *Full cherry or walnut; gun-stock finish; tapered cotton net; size: 20".*
cherry—$40-$50; walnut—$50-$60 Bob, Wul, Dan
Gayewski Standard Trout Net. *Ash and mahogany; size: 20".*
$29.95 Bob
Gayewski Old Timer Net. *Similar to Standard but narrower.*
$29.95 Bob
Gayewski Shorty Net. *A shorter version of the Standard.*
$24.95 Bob
Gayewski Madison Net. *Larger version of Standard; size: 23" with 24" bag.*
$29.95 Bob
L.L. Bean Canoe Net. *Ash and mahogany; standard teardrop shape; extra long handle; from Cascade Lakes; size: 30".*
$36.50 LLB
Orvis Battenkill Nets. *Cherry-laminated ash bow with walnut handle; cotton bag; sizes: 14" (9 ½"x6" bow, 17" bag), 18" (11 ½"x6 ½" bow, 17" bag), 20" (12 ¼"x7 ¾" bow, 19" bag), 22" (14 ¼"x8 ½" bow, 21" bag).*
14"—$41; 18"—$43.50; 20"—$46.50; 22"—$49.50 Orv
Orvis Catch-N-Release Net. *Same materials as other Orvis nets; distinctive rectangular frame and shallow, flat-bottomed net allow easy release of fish; size: 21" (8" bag).*
$52.50 Orv
Store brand wood nets. *A variety of woods and sizes; consult individual catalogs for details.*
$14.95-$29.95 Ram, H&H, FlR, Let, Dal, Mur, Dan, AnJ, Mer
Thomas & Thomas Nets. *2-ply ash bows with mahogany handle; nylon bags; sizes: 18" (11 ½"x6" bow, 19" bag), 20" (13 ½"x7 ½" bow, 19" bag), 22" (15 ½"x8 ½" bow, 19" bag).*
$31.50 T&T
Thomas & Thomas Custom Nets. *3-ply oak and mahogany; sizes: 17", 20".*
$85 T&T

Aluminum Frame Nets

Aluminum nets. *Brown anodized aluminum frame; brown rubber handle; dark tan cotton bag; 7"x13" bow; with 36" elastic cord.*
$7.50 FlR

Jacklin's Econo-Net. *All aluminum (except the bag, of course); 18" white mesh of soft nylon; ½" mesh.*
$5.95 Bob

Fold-Up Nets

Cabela's Folding Net. *Folds into leather belt pouch with snap closure over handle; lanyard attached; open length—19", folded—11 ½"; bow—13 ½", bag—19 ½"; weight—10 oz.*
$9.95 Cab
Insta-Net. *Folds into 5 ½" square vinyl pouch which attaches to belt; spring steel hoop; cotton net; 15"x11"; bag—18" deep.*
$10.95-$13.95 Cus, Dan, Fly, Kau, EJH, Hig, Dal, Mur, Pen, Bud, T&T
Deluxe Insta-Net. *Similar to regular Insta-Net but with leather case.*
$12.95-$17.95 Kau, Dan, Pen, Cus, Bud
Pragleria Folding Net. *Net extractor built into handle; case.*
$23.95 Pen

Net Kits

Cascade Lakes Nets. *Ready to finish and string netting; sizes: 18 ½", 21", 23" (see Cascade Lakes Teardrop Nets above).*
18 ½"—$17.95-$27.25; 21"—$18.50-$28; 23"—$18.95-$29 AnR, Fly, Mer
Egger's Backpacking Net. *Glued; needs finishing and net work; sizes: 18 ½" (11 ½"x6" bow), 21" (13 ½"x7 ½" bow).*
small—$18.50; large—$19.50 Egg
Gayewski Nets. *Ash and mahogany; sizes: standard and Madison (listed above).*
$18 Bob
Thomas & Thomas Nets. *Ash and mahogany; sizes: see T&T nets (listed above).*
$21.50 T&T

Replacement Bags

Cascade Lakes Bags. *Order proper size for frame (see nets above).*
$5.98-$9.95 Pen, AnR, Fly, Kau
Insta-Net Bags. *Cotton.*
$2.95-$3.95 EJH, Pen
Soft Nylon Bag. *Replacement bags; sizes: 24" deep (with ¾" mesh), 22" (1" mesh).*
24"—$5.95-$6.95; 22"—$3.95 Bob, Dan, Mer
T&T Replacement Bag. *19" deep; "fits any frame".*
$7 T&T

Net Accessories

French clips and swivels. *The less-than-ideal way to attach net to D-ring on vest.*
$1.47-$3.09 Cus, Pen, Ram, T&T, Bob, Bud, Dan, Mer

Salmon Tailers

Salmon Tailer. *Brass and stainless steel; rubber handle; steel wire bow; nylon wrist thong; with brass clip for attaching to vest.*
$59.75-$60 T&T, Hun
Hardy Telescopic Fish Tailer. *Aluminum alloy; wire bow; sliding brass ring; nylon wrist thong; 32" closed, 40" open.*
$53 Mer

Miscellaneous Streamside Equipment

Included here are various pieces of equipment you can't live without on the stream. How would you ever fill your vest if you tried to live without them?

Stream Thermometers

I carry a stream thermometer, but I never rush down to the water at the beginning of a day's fishing and check the temperature to determine if I should be fishing. What I have done is started fishing with dries, without success, taken the water temperature, and used it as an excuse. So, I guess, a stream thermometer is important.

The water temperature determines how active the fish will be. I do use my thermometer a lot in the spring to judge what type of flies to use in our streams as they begin to warm up. I also use it to check lake temperatures to determine whether the fish will be active.

The prime temperature range for trout is 45-75 degrees with the most active feeding at 55-65 degrees. Warmwater fishing can be monitored in your local area by taking water temperatures as springtime weather warms the water. As temperatures increases, watch for spawning activity and keep notes on your fishing success.

If you keep good books on insect hatches, temperature is one of the variables you should be recording, along with time of day, time of year, your bio-rhythms, and weather conditions.

The best of the basic stream thermometers is the metal dial-face type. It works fast and is unbreakable. Although not a dial-face type, the most handsome is Hardy's brass-cased thermometer. The most unusual is, by far, the wristwatch thermometer from North Fork.

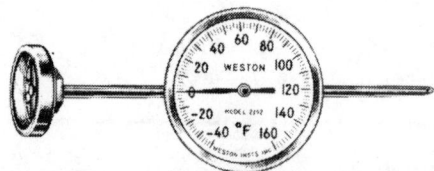

Metal Dial Stem Thermometer. *Steel stem with dial display; plastic sheath with pen clip; 1 deg. increments.*
$17.50-$17.95 Pen, T&T

Deptherm. *Measures depth and temperature; helpful for boaters and floaters; 20-120 deg.*
$3.50-$5.98 Pen, Tid, Cab, Cus, Ran
Economy Stream Thermometer. *Molded plastic case with pen clip; no details.*
$1.95-$3.95 Cus, H&H, T&T, Mur, Hun
Hardy Pocket Thermometer. *Brass case over glass tube; 5 ¼"; ring-top for lanyard; very handsome.*
$18-$19.95 Dun, Hun

Metal-Cased Glass Thermometer. *Glass encased in metal; pen clip; 6 ½" long; available in Celsius or Fahrenheit (most catalogs carry F. only).*
$8.95-$11.95 T&T, Orv, Bud, AnR, Ste, LLB, Let, Fly, Kau, Hig, Dal, EJH, Hun

North Fork Fly Fisherman's Watch (and thermometer). *Simply dip your wrist into the water and get an instantaneous reading of temperature; certainly our most unusual thermometer and the only one with stop watch, alarm, and calendar; made by Casio.*
$49.95 Nor

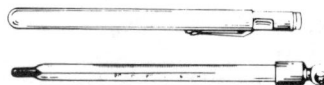

Taylor Stream Thermometer. *Glass in plastic tube with pen clip; -40 to 120 deg.; 2 deg. increments.*
$7.95-$9.95 Pen, Dan, AnJ, Bud, Wul
Taylor Dial Thermometer. *Plastic with dial reading.*
$10.95 Bud

Creels

If it weren't for the fact that I know a lot of people who carry their beer in creels, I might not have included them. I wouldn't want to encourage too much harvesting of one of our great natural resources—trout.

But here they are, from the Articreel to the old-fashioned willow creel. Use them wisely, my friends.

Articreel 100. *10 ½"x14"x4"; heavy canvas "desert bag";*

cools by evaporation; one main compartment; lined, waterproof inside bag.
$13.85-$22 H&H, Cab, Kau, Dan, Orv, Pen, Ram, Sim, Cus

Articreel 200. *Same as 100 but with zippered gear pocket.*
$16.35-$26 Cab, Ram, Cus, Sim, Kau, Dan, H&H, Orv, T&T

Articreel 300. *Similar to 200 but larger; 10 ½"x18"x4".*
$18.90-$30 Pen, H&H, Orv, Cab, Cus, Dan, Sim

Articreel detachable. *For use with Orvis Tak-L-Pak vests.*
$18.55 Orv

Articreel Tackle Pouch. *7"x12"; snaps on creels.*
$5.75-$8.50 Ram, Cus, Cab, H&H, Pen, T&T, Sim, Dal, Dan, Kau

Cold Creel. *A number of brand names use "cold creel" or a variation; most are a canvas material; for additional features see specific catalogs.*
$9.05-$17.55 (depending on size and brand name) Cus, Tac, Sim, Mer

Minum River Creel. *Creel plus 5 pockets; form-fitting; nylon pack cloth and vinyl construction.*
$26.95 Ste

North Fork Coldwater Creel. *Mesh lower, Cordura upper; Velcro closures; with shoulder strap and wader belt.*
$26.95-$27.95 Nor, Pen

Orvis Creel/Tackle Bag. *Urethane-coated nylon; 2 large comp. inside, 1 large, 1 med. outside; worn over shoulder or around waist.*
$16.75 Orv

Rattan, wicker, and willow creels. *A number of these "old-fashioned" creels are offered, mostly without brand*

names; consult catalogs for details.
$8.25-$36.50 (depending on features) Cab, Cus, T&T, Orv, AnW, Sim, Tid, Dun, Kau, Mer, LLB

Sportflite Creel. *Mesh canvas and nylon; nylon leg shield; 2 D-rings; adjustable strap; brown.*
$12.95-$14.95 Tac, AnJ

Forceps and Pliers

Even with the barbless hooks I hope you'll be using, flies are often difficult to dislodge from a fish's mouth. Surgical forceps are a great tool for reaching into those mouths and retrieving a $1.25 fly. Keep them on a retractor or in a special pocket for easy access. You can even lock the jaws of the forcep on a pocket flap, preferably inside your vest or bag where they won't glitter too much.

The decision between straight and curved jaws is a matter of personal choice, I think. I've used both. The curved jaws give you a little better view of what you're doing. With the straight jaws you don't need to worry about picking up the forceps with the curved jaws pointing the wrong direction for easy removal of the fly.

If you've never used forceps, try them. You'll never go without.

The pliers listed here are useful for a number of streamside duties. The most important use is bending down hook barbs.

Curved jaws forceps. *Of varying sizes; locking jaws.*
$4.90-$6.50 Pen, H&H, Bud, Don, Fly, Hig, Dal, Hun, Wul, Bob, Cab, Orv, Cus, Tac, FlR

Straight jaws forceps. *Of varying sizes; locking jaws.*
$4.95-$7.50 Many catalogs

Large bent forceps. *Offset for better view of operation.*
$4.95 Cab

Angler's Pal Pliers. *Pliers, split shot crimper, scissors.*
$3.95-$4.50 Pen, H&H, Sim, Ram

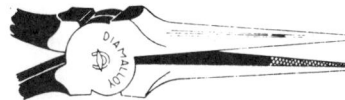

Diamaloy Miniature Pliers. *4" long; plastic-coated handles; needle nose; spring keeps jaws open.*
$11.45 Dan

Needle-nosed pliers. *4"-6"; stainless steel.*
$4.50-$6.98 H&H, Cus, T&T, Bud, Fly, Dan, Hig

Cuda scissor-pliers. *5 ½"; stainless steel.*
$12.95-$14.95 Kau, Orv

Scissor-pliers. *Stainless steel.*
$4.40-$5.95 Orv, Fly, Dal, Egg, Let, LLB, Cus, Dan

Fly Patches

Fly patches can be attached to your vest or fishing bag to provide a place to dry out flies before returning them to their boxes. The wool hat band serves the same purpose.

Among the furry patches, wool holds flies best. The lower-priced imitation fur is generally not a good fly holder. It will be a more expensive patch after a few flies fall off.

The other options utilizing sponge or foam are heralded as improvements over wool, and you may wish to try them. Wheatley's Keeper with a magnetic strip is an interesting variation.

Tote-A-Lure. *Leather-backed sponge; 3" diameter; tie-tack attachment.*
$2.50 T&T
Vest patches. *Wool; about 3"x3"; with pin.*
$.60-$2.50 H&H, Fly, Kau, Mer, Hig, Cus, Pen, Dal, Mur, Dan, Hun, T&T, Bud
Clip-On Fly Patch. *Shearling on leather with suspender-type clip.*
$2.95 Pen
Vest patches. *Sponges; for Wulff vests; with Velcro.*
$1 Wul
Wheatley Pin-On Fly Keepers. *2"x2"; leather with choice of wool or magnetic strip; with pin.*
$6 T&T

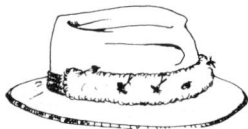

Hat bands. *Wool, elastic back.*
$2.95-$4.25 Many catalogs
Visor band. *Wool; fits over bill of cap.*
$3.95 Pen

Retractors

These handy little devices keep often-used equipment like forceps and clippers close at hand and easily accessible. They commonly have a nylon cord, spring-loaded in a metal or plastic case. They are pinned on your vest at a convenient place, preferably inside where they won't reflect light.

Bigger retractors are used for nets. Some of them can be clipped on your belt, although that's a terrible place to hang a net if you have to do any walking through timber.

Cortland Retrieve-It Jr.. *14" nylon cord; with metal clip.*
$5-$5.95 Pen, Tac, Edd, Mer

Cortland Retrieve-It Sr.. *24" chain; metal ring; belt clip.*
$6.45-$7.70 Bud, Tac, Fly, Mer
Hardy Keeper. *Nylon cord; metal clip.*
$7.25 Dun
Little Pal Retractor. *Nylon cord; metal clip.*
$2.50-$3.15 H&H, Cus
Big Pal Retractor. *24" nylon cord; metal clip.*
$3.45-$3.95 Ram, Mur, Sim, H&H, Cus

Lights

A hatch cannot be met without the ability to tie on new flies, and as darkness approaches, a light becomes essential. The most popular of these lights for fly fishermen is the Flex-Lite. It features a flexible neck that can direct the beam where it's needed. An adjustable-beam model is now available. It provides a concentrated beam used for tying on flies and a broader beam used for walking out.

Bite lites are also popular. They are turned on by applying pressure to the sides of their soft plastic case. You can use the light by squeezing it between your teeth, leaving both hands free.

The Lens-Lite offers a third option. It hangs around your neck. The light shines directly away from you and a magnifying lens folds out to aid in tying on the fly.

I've included the Panasonic Head Lamp because I use a light similar to it, and it's proved very satisfactory for both tying on flies and walking out. The Johnny Stewart light is a natural extension of this just for people who need a searchlight to get back home, included here just for fun.

Remember to keep any light pointed away from the fish. Simply turning your back to the feeding fish will do the trick, and that will also help you calm down enough to tie a good, fast knot.

Flex-Lite. *5 ½" anodized aluminum case; 3 ¾" gooseneck; takes 2 AA.*
$8.95-$12.95 Many catalogs
Adjustable Beam Flex-Lite. *As above but beam can be adjusted for concentrated or broad beam.*
$11.95-$17.75 Orv, Tid, Cus, Tac, Let, Kau, Hig, Dan, Ram, Pen, H&H
Plastic flexible-neck light. *Similar to Flex-Light but plastic case and oversize clip.*
$4.85-$9.50 AnW, Sim, Wul, EJH, AnJ

Berkley Clip-On Lite. *Rectangular light with bracket to clip on cap visor or pocket.*
$3.25-$5.20 Cus, AnW, Bob, Dan, Fol
Bite Lite. *Let's give all these lights this name even though I think they're officially "Glo-Worm" lights; in any case, they're all made by the same people; 2"x1"x¾" and only ½ oz.; turns on by pressure applied to case, so if you don't drool a lot, you can hold one in your mouth while you use two hands to tie on a fly; pretty nifty.*
$2.50-$3.75 Orv, Ram, Hig, Fly, Let
Fisherman's Lens-Lite. *2"x2" plastic case; with magnifying lens; hangs around neck; 2 C batteries.*
$11.50-$14 Orv, Let, Kau, Dan (from whom you can get extra magnifying lenses)
Johnny Stewart's Search 1 Helmet Spotlight. *Hard hat with headlamp for those after-dark anglers who can't find their cars; complete with quick-release light brackets, rechargeable battery, adjustable beam; this could be the ultimate (but mostly it's here just for fun).*
$83.65 Fol
Panasonic Head Lamp. *Self-contained so no wires; adjustable, elastic head band; takes 4 AA.*
$14.95 Ram
Tekna Micro-Lite. *1,600 candlepower; traditional flashlight; 3 ½" long; uses 2 N batteries.*
$5.50-$6 T&T, Bud
Tekna-Lite. *1,600 candlepower; flashlight; 5 ½" long; uses 2 AA batteries.*
$9 T&T

Micro Lith Lite. *Krypton bulb; 1,400 candlepower; flashlight; 4" long; 1.5 oz.; waterproof; lens doubles as magnifier, fire starter; includes 3 volt lithium battery.*
$19.95-$20 Orv, Bud

Tapes and Scales

Now, here's some equipment you don't want, at least not if your imagination is better than reality (and whose isn't?). A measuring tape will trip you up nine times out of nine. I'm waiting for a fisherman's tape with 2" long "inches" so it's at least close to what I think a fish measures.

Scales are rather esoteric things for me. Unless I can find one that weighs up to 1 ½ pounds in quarter ounce increments, it won't be of much use to me. However, for

the big timers, a scale is important. I'd use one if I didn't have such an ability to accurately guess the weight of fish.

Incidentally, there is a right and wrong way to measure and weigh trout.

If you're likely to be measuring your trout, have the tape ready, preferably on a retractor. Don't keep the fish under stress any longer than necessary (and measuring isn't necessary to begin with). If possible, measure the fish on its side in the water or in your net. Laying it on a bed of wet grass is okay. Be sure your tape is dry before returning it to its spool. For a quick measure, hold the fish up to your rod or net and mark the spot. Measure the distance after the fish has been released.

There's only one correct way to weigh a fish...in the net. Never hang a fish from the scale. Just weigh the net and fish and subtract the weight of the net later.

The Chatillion scales are the top line. They are made of brass and come in a variety of ranges (except 1 ½ lb., ¼ oz.). They are the most accurate scale here. The Zebco De-Liar provides little accuracy since the scale runs to eight pounds but is only about 2" long.

Chatillion Spring Balances. *Brass (and beautiful); easily adjustable to zero; a variety of scales and increments available: 4 lb. (1 oz. increments); 6 lb. (1 oz.); 10 lb. (4 oz.); 15 lb. (4 oz.); 30 lb. (8 oz.); 50 lb. (8 oz.).*
$22.95-$39 (depending on scale size as well as catalog) Cus, Cab, Ram, Orv, Fly, Pen, Kau, Hun, Dan, Bud
Mariner Scale. *Plastic case; dial face (looks like a grocery store scale); with 40" tape; 16 lb. or 50 lb.*
$6.70-$9.95 Sim, AnJ

Zebco De-Liar. *24" tape and spring scale to 8 lb.*
$2.10-$3.75 Cus, Sim, Ran, Mur
Zebco De-Liar for bigger liars. *40" tape and spring scale to 28 lb.*
$2.35-$4.75 Ran, Fol, Sim
Store brand tapes. *A variety of measuring tapes, all in small plastic spools; retractable metal measures; key chain; usually 36"; with store logo.*
$2.50-$3.50 Fly, Hig, Pen

Hook Sharpeners

It's after you've missed three strikes in a row when you know you've set the hook properly that you finally check your hook point and find it lacking in sharpness. You can change flies, if you have another of the same pattern, or you can touch up the point with a sharpener. This is an essential tool, really, but one that is often under-used because many of the sharpeners are difficult to handle with the tiny hooks used by fly fishermen. You may need to try several out before you find one that works easily for you and will be one that you'll use every time you ought to.

Bear Stone hook hone. *Grooved stone.*
$1.15 Sim

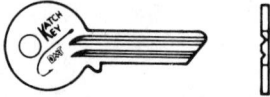

DMT Katch Key. *600 mesh diamond on milled grooves, one large, one small; all on a key that can be attached to vest.*
$5-$6.45 Ram, Cus, Nor, Dan

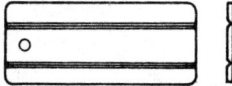

DMT Sharpie. *600 mesh diamond on milled grooves; flat area for small hooks; hole for attaching to vest.*
$8.95-$9.95 Ram, AnJ, Dan
DMT Flyfishing Sharpie. *As above but with flexible magnetic strap that attaches to vest and holds Sharpie and hooks.*
$12.95 AnJ
Everkeen stone. *Larger stone that will do knives as well as hooks; 3 ¼".*
$1 AnW

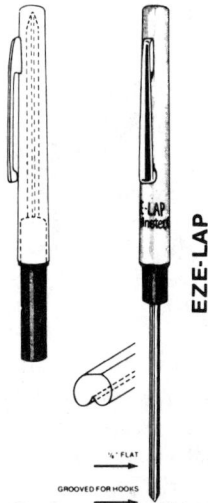

EZE-Lap Pocket Sharpener. *Flat area with groove; hook is moved up and down in groove to sharpen; pocket clip; opens like fountain pen; 5 ½" with sharpener in cap.*
$4.40-$6.65 LLB, Dan, Orv, Pen, Kau, Bud, Hun, Dal, Cus, Ste, Fly

Filex hook file. *Flexible like emory board; dual grit for small or large hooks; 3"x1"x1/16".*
$1 T&T
Hardee hook file. *Metal file in form similar to points file (that's automobile talk); 5 ¼".*
$1-$1.60 AnW, T&T
Hy-Point Power Hook Sharpener. *Battery operated sharpener; uses AA battery; 5 ½", so small enough for vest pocket.*
$9.95-$11.50 Kau, Fly, Tid, AnJ, Cab, Bud

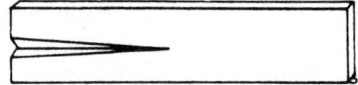

Jero's hook hone. *Flat stone with triangular groove.*
$1.75 Sim
Pal hook hone. *Sharpening stone with groove for hooks.*
$1.90-$2.50 H&H, Mur, Cus
Pal hook hone. *Sharpening stone as above but with retractor.*
$3.50 Sim
Sharpoint hook hone. *Triangular stone with groove; 2¼".*
$1-$3.25 AnW, T&T

Water Purifier

This is neither an odd nor an end, it's a water purifier. Considering that the water is not safe to drink 99 44/100% of the time, either this little device or a water bottle (or beer can, I suppose) should be with you if you're going to be out and away very long. This is lighter than a water bottle. It's a big straw with filters in the center. The filters stop microorganisms as well as sediment. They will clog before the system loses its effectiveness. One straw should last a season, depending on how clear the water is. (More on water purification in Chapter 11.)

Pocket Purifier. *A large "straw" with purifying elements inside; fits easily into vest or bag.*
$9.95 Ram

7. Flies

ORDERING FLIES THROUGH the mail is another game of chance for fly fishermen. Buying flies without inspecting them first requires confidence in the supplier, and it's still risky. In short, flies are another item best purchased from your local fly shop.

However, if you don't have the luxury (that's right, a local fly shop is a luxury) of buying in person or if you need special patterns for a trip, there are some things you can do to cut down on the risks you're taking.

First, deal only with a fly-fishing-only catalog or one with a strong fly fishing reputation. This is your best insurance against poor flies. It takes a practiced and caring eye to tell a good fly from a second-rate one. Retailers without that expertise are likely to carry flies that represent the best deal, rather than the best flies.

Second, buy American when possible. I drive a foreign car, so don't think I'm blindly patriotic about American-made products. With trout flies, however, there's reason to buy from American producers. It's simply another insurance policy when you can't buy in person. I've seen a lot of terrible foreign representations of trout flies. Some of them are only suggestive of the original patterns. There are, on the other hand, good foreign-tied flies offered by reputable companies, so you can't put on blinders.

American-tied flies vary in quality, of course, and you must be able to judge them. Still, they are generally better than flies that come from tiers who probably have no idea what the flies are used for.

Finally, check the flies you receive for quality. Check the hooks to be sure they are sharp and the shanks straight. A bent shank shows that the hook has been abused in the vise; it may break or bend further. Look at the wings to make sure they are straight on the body. Wings would be a quality control person's nightmare, and consistently straight and true wings are one mark of a good tier.

The tails should be compact and should lie in a straight line with the shank. On a dry fly, they should be roughly equal to the length of the hook. Hackle must also be proportioned to the hook (about 1½ times the gap for standard dries) and must be of good quality. Heads must be finished properly with cement, and the head is the only part of the fly that should have cement on it. Color seems to be a problem with foreign flies. Make sure the flies you receive are true to the original pattern in color and materials.

A computerized fly pattern file. The age of computers has arrived at the doorstep of fly fishing. Paul and Jeanne Giauque of Nymphs and Other Things (see catalog listed later in this chapter for address) have developed a computerized listing of fly patterns with over 12,500 references.

The flies are listed by name, type, and scientific name, and give a text where the pattern is discussed. The Giauques have worked from a personal library of 130 books to do this. Here's a sample listing:

Light Hendrickson
Nymph
Ephemerella rotunda
Mayflies, The Angler, and The Trout
Fred Arbona, Jr.

The flies are sorted into 13 categories, similar to what I've used in this chapter, and if you're interested only in flies for shad, for instance, you can order a "sub-set". Present costs for an entire run (at 33 references a page, that's six pounds of paper) is $32 plus shipping. If you prefer the convenience of 3"x5" cards, that can be arranged for about $200 more. Other options are available.

Serious tiers, fishing clubs, researchers, and fly shops may find this service valuable. As one of the first attempts to make the computer work for the fly fisherman, it's of interest to us all.

Catalog companies that carry flies. You'll find most of the catalogs that are in the rest of the book listed in this chapter as sources for flies. The descriptions of those catalogs in a later chapter will give you an idea of how strong their fly selection is and how well illustrated the flies are.

There are some folks who specialize in flies with few other supplies in their offerings. I'll briefly describe these companies here, and if there's a three-letter code next to the company name, I've included it as a sources for flies.

Aqua Flies, Inc.
Box 1091
Cambridge, Maryland 21613

Aqua Flies is relatively new on the fly fishing scene. They offer a selection of "America's Favorite Flies" at reasonable prices. Write for a full listing.

Fly of the Month (FOM)
86 Huntville Road
Katonah, New York 10536
(914) 232-8744

Every month, members of the Fly of the Month Club can look forward to receiving a small package in the mail. In it, they'll find a fly, background information on it, and tips on how and when to fish it.

In addition, they receive discount prices on flies and selected equipment. All this for one buck a month or $10 a year.

Jack Montague
5304 Lipizzan Trail
Punta Gorda, Florida 33950
(813) 639-4007

Jack Montague, wood carver extraordinaire (see Chapter 12), also offers a complete line of flies, including salmon, steelhead, and saltwater flies. The saltwater selection is extensive. Jack studied under Harry and Elsie Darbee and ties "in the Catskill tradition". Jack's carvings are meticulously done, and that makes a good recommendation for his fly tying. Write for his catalog, especially if you're interested in saltwater flies.

Jim O'Brien
Box 222
Phelps, New York 14532
(315) 331-0224

Jim specializes in hairwing salmon flies, salmon dry flies, and trolling streamers. Inquiries will bring a price list and sample fly. Jim also does custom framing of flies or photos and fly. A photo of a big trout can feature the fly that caught it in shadow-box format.

John Betts (Joh)
1452 South Elizabeth
Denver, Colorado 80210
(303) 722-7052

John Betts is the synthetic materials man. His flies are tied almost entirely with man-made materials right down to the hackle, which is a blend of crinkled polyester and polypropylene. Although the traditionalist won't be convinced, there are advantages to the use of these materials, including their durability and flotation characteristics.

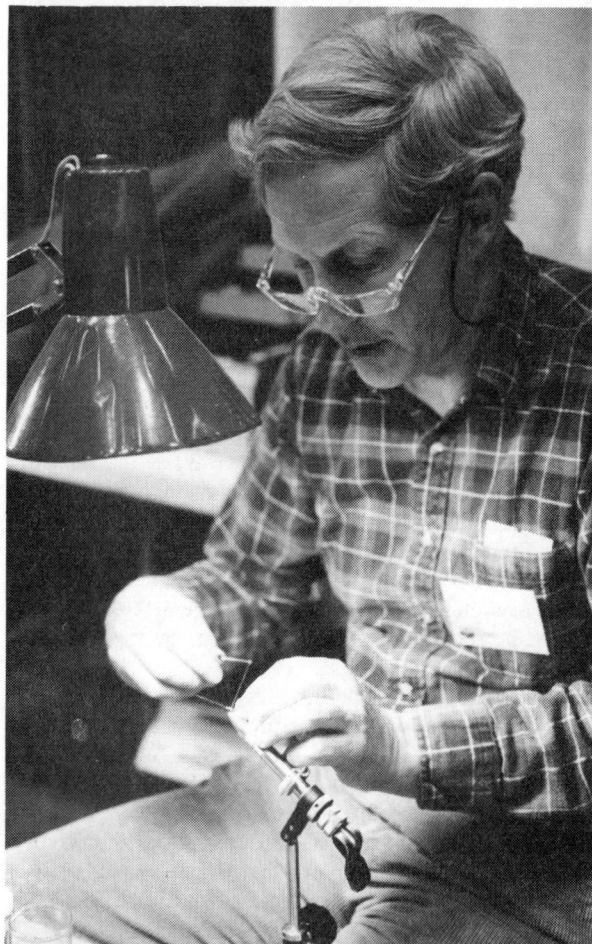

Even the traditionalist will be impressed by the quality of John's flies. They are well designed and well tied. If you're interested in innovative techniques and unusual flies, you should try a John Bett's artificial artificial.

John ties all his own flies, including some ties not available elsewhere. Notable is the upside-down style (USD). The hook rides up and parachute-style hackle rides flat on the water. The tail is allowed to follow the bend of the hook and, thus, rides cocked upward in a fashion imitating the natural mayfly.

John also has such unusual ideas as fly rod "plugs" and floating wooly buggers with detachable diving planes. He's wading in uncharted waters, but his progress is fascinating.

Included in John's newsletter/catalog are the synthetic materials he uses and books on his techniques. If you order a sample of flies from John, I recommend that it include a detached body fly, a legged pattern, an USD (described above), a funnel dun, and a bass frog. You (and hopefully the fish) will find them intriguing.

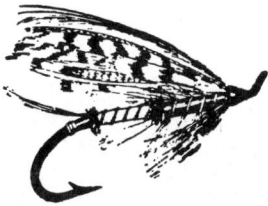

Maxwell MacPherson, Jr. (Max)
10 Hillside
Bristol, New Hampshire 03222
(603) 744-3313

Max MacPherson was an apprentice salmon fly tier under Alex Simpson of Aberdeen, Scotland. His studies went on for five years before he could be considered an expert. If the salmon flies in his catalog are any indication, Max is not just an expert, he's a master.

I've been in awe of this man's tying ever since receiving his catalog. Salmon flies are impressive anyway, but these flies are exceptionally beautiful and, for a change, the photographs of them are excellent. There are 17 pages of full-color, close-up photos of salmon flies in the catalog. That makes it expensive to produce, and that's why it costs $3 (as of this writing).

But the cost should mean nothing to the salmon fisherman, who will gain access to unusual patterns, or to the tier, who will order inspiring samples with which to compare his own work, or to the collector, who will find authentic patterns tied with original materials.

Among the collector's pieces in the catalog I received are the Horse Leech Fly, the first salmon fly to receive a name (sometime in the 17th century), and blind-eye salmon flies with silkworm gut eyes. Max can also handle special orders for authentic flies tied with original materials. Some of these sell for $35 or more. (Low water and other patterns are, however, competitively priced.)

For salmon flies, Max MacPherson is The Source.

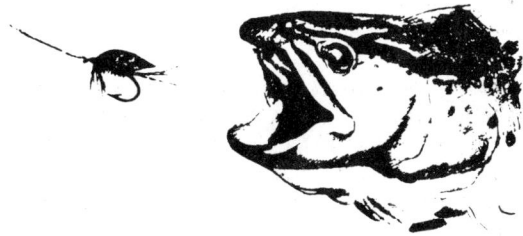

Monty Montplaisir (Mon)
Box 212
Colebrook, New Hampshire 03576
(603) 237-4979

Monty Montplaisir offers traditional patterns and specialty patterns of his own design. The latter include the Montville Special (from the Henryville Special), the Montberg (from the Hornberg), and the Montabou Smelt (from the real thing).

Monty's patterns are intriguing. The man has good credentials, too. For one thing, he's been a columnist for *Fly Tyer Magazine*. He ties all the flies himself, so you can be assured of consistent quality.

NORM'S STONE FLY NYMPHS
U.S. PATENT NO. D264,490

Norman Anderson Quality Flies
15151 S.E. Royer Road
Clackamas, Oregon 97015

Norm Anderson is best known for Norm's Stonefly, a very life-like nymph pattern. That fly is featured in several catalogs, and it's one of the few that isn't copied. If it says Norm's Stonefly, it comes from Norm Anderson.

Write for Norm's pattern list. He also supplies latex strips and other materials.

Nymphs and Other Things
Box 453
East Windsor, Connecticut 06088
(203) 623-9525

Paul and Jeanne Giauque offer custom-tied flies and commercial tying services. They also offer a computerized fly pattern file that's described in the introduction.

Teeny Nymphs
Box 970
Gresham, Oregon 97030

Although Jim Teeny's catalog offers a number of fly fishing items, including his vests and nymph lines, he is best known for the Teeny Nymph, a patented pattern not found in other catalogs.

The nymphs are fairly simple flies tied with pheasant tail dyed in a variety of colors. And there are lots of big fish pictured in the brochure to back up their effectiveness.

Flies listed here. I've done something a bit different in this section of the book. I've listed all the sources for each fly pattern, no matter how many there are. I've done this in order to provide the novice or the traveler an indication of which flies are the most popular across the country and in specific regions. The premise is that companies don't carry products that move slowly and that patterns that sell well must be good producers. Hence, patterns with a lot of sources are the best producers.

Of course, there are a lot of exceptions. The Elk Hair Caddis is an excellent producer in the West, especially in the Rockies. It won't have as many sources as say the Light Cahill which is popular across the country, but it will be listed in some variation in every western catalog. To make good use of this section in creating fly selections for yourself, you'll have to become familiar with where the catalog companies are located. Their addresses are given in Chapter 14.

In this way, you can use this section to plan a fishing trip to a distant location. I hope to go steelhead fishing one of these years, for instance, and I can find the most popular patterns by looking here. I'll especially be interested in the ones offered by the three or four catalogs located in the Northwest.

You may pick up this book in a few years and see some patterns that are no longer available. Every year new patterns show up in magazine articles and are then offered by several catalogs. Some of them become popular and join the list of common flies. Others are only passing fancies that didn't work out for the average angler.

Just for fun, I went through the completed lists and picked out the top five or so patterns based on the number of sources for them. You can decide from this list whether the system has credibility. The number of sources for each pattern is given in parentheses.

Dry Flies: 1. Royal Wulff (28); 2. Adams (27); 3, 4. Humpy and Light Cahill (26); 5. Gray Wulff (25); 6-8. Quill Gordon, March Brown, Dark Cahill (24).

Terrestrials: 1. Black Ant (23); 2, 3. Cinnamon Ant and Letort Cricket (17); 4. Letort Hopper (16); 5. Joe's Hopper (15); 6. Dave's Hopper (13).

Wet Flies: 1. Wooly Worm (22); 2. Black Gnat (21); 3. Quill Gordon (20); 4. Dark Cahill (19); 5, 6. Light Cahill and Coachman (18).

Nymphs: 1. Zug Bug (24); 2. Montana (23); 3. March Brown (21); 4. Gold-Ribbed Hare's Ear (19); 5. Tellico (17).

Soft Hackles: 1. Partridge and Orange (9); 2. Partridge and Yellow (8); 3. Pheasant Tail (6).

Emergers: 1. LaFontaine Emergent Sparkle Pupa (6); 2. Mayfly Emerger (4); 3-5. Yellow, Olive, and Brown Floating Nymphs (3).

Spinners: 1. Trico (9); 2. Olive (7); 3. Rusty (5).

Midges: 1. Black (16); 2. Cream (15); 3. Olive (12); 4, 5. Adams and Brown (10).

Streamers: 1. Muddler Minnow (24); 2, 3. Marabou Muddler and Mickey Finn (21); 4, 5. Matukas and Black-Nosed Dace (18); 6. Gray Ghost (17).

Bass Flies: 1. Hair Popper (9); 2. Hair Mouse (8); 3, 4. Hair Frog and Dave's Eelworm (7); 5, 6. Dave's Near Nuff Frog and Harewater Pup (6).

Saltwater Flies: 1. Lefty's Deceivers (9); 2. Horror (7); 3, 4. Snapping Shrimp and Brooks Blondes (6); 5. Bonefish Fly (5).

Steelhead Flies: 1, 2. Skunk and Skykomish Sunrise (15); 3, 4. Babine Special and Fall Favorite (11) 5, 6, 7. Polar Shrimp, Thor, and Royal Coachman (9).

Salmon Flies: 1. Rusty Rat (16); 2. Cosseboom (13); 3. Silver Rat (12); 4, 5. Black Rat and Black Bear (11); 6. Hairy Mary (10).

I hope you'll find this section interesting and useful (especially because it took a long time to do). I haven't listed prices for each pattern. You'll find a brief summary of prices for each type of fly in the introduction to the lists. Don't shop for the cheapest fly, shop for the best.

The flies have been listed by category: dry flies, terrestrials, wet flies, soft hackles, nymphs, streamers, midges, emergers, spinners, steelhead flies, salmon flies, bass flies, and saltwater flies. I've also listed flies of mainly regional interest, such as New England's tandem streamers, in a separate section. You may wish to argue about some of the placements—one man's wet fly is another's nymph—but I think you'll find your favorite fly in a reasonable category.

DARK SPRUCE
LIGHT SPRUCE

Illustrations in the listings have been provided courtesy of Bob Jacklin's Fly Shop, West Yellowstone, Montana.

DRY FLIES

This is where the romance and glory are. Dry fly fishing is considered the height of the art (although I wonder if nymph fishing, for instance, isn't more difficult), and some anglers won't fish unless they can use dries. That purist attitude means that for a good portion of the year those anglers must have other hobbies.

Nevertheless, there is something very special about seeing a trout come to a well-presented dry. In terms of fly selection and presentation, dry fly fishing is often more challenging and, therefore, more rewarding than other types of fly fishing. Whatever the allure, dry fly fishing is what most of us think about when we say fly fishing.

Dry flies can be roughly divided into three categories: imitative patterns, suggestive patterns, and attractors. Imitative patterns are designed to match the hatch of a particular insect, the Green Drake, for example. Suggestive patterns, such as the Adams, don't imitate any particular insect, but they suggest something very edible to trout. The Royal Coachman and other attractors don't even suggest an insect, but they are bright and/or bushy and get the trout's attention.

The highest camp is to find trout feeding on a particular insect, match that insect with an appropriate pattern, present the fly with delicacy and authenticity, and catch fish. I've read somewhere that the biggest difference between fly fishermen and other anglers is that fly fishermen know why they're catching fish. That's never more true than in the situation I've just described.

So, to the purist, the real purist, even suggestive patterns, let alone attractors, are not to his liking since he'll never know exactly why the trout took the fly.

Here are some popular patterns in each category:

leaves mayflies, caddis, and stoneflies. In the listing, I've tried to get all the caddis patterns together under that name. I've done the same with stoneflies, although some of the stonefly patterns are called "salmon flies" in Montana due to a geographical aberration of the name. (Stoneflies used to be called "willow flies" here in Colorado before all the "foreign" entomologists moved in.)

Mayfly patterns have had to go in the pot with the rest of the fixings. Many of the remaining patterns are done with a mayfly silhouette. Bivisibles and spiders are two exceptions. And if you think I erred by not putting spiders in with the terrestrials, don't embarrass yourself by writing me a letter. Spiders represent a tying style, not the actual bug. (Whew, I almost called a spider an insect, and that would surely have gotten me some letters.)

Flies listed here are tied in the traditional manner unless specified otherwise. Other tying styles include parachute, no-hackle, Iwamasa dun, and extended bodies, among others. If the word following the lead word in the listing is capitalized, it's part of the name of the fly, as in "Hopper, Joe's". Otherwise, it indicates a tying style, as in "Gray Fox, thorax". (The exception is Iwamasa dun, as in "Black Gnat, Iwamasa dun", which is capitalized because it's the proper name of the man who developed the style)

There is some duplication of patterns under different names. Some catalogs insist upon using the Latin which leaves the beginners out (and some of us more advanced fly fishermen who never liked foreign language in school), and that causes duplication with the common names. Other flies have several names, evidently. I've simply used the catalog listing in all cases.

In this section of the book, I haven't included prices for each fly. They're fairly consistent. The range is $.95-$1.50 with some of the larger or more intricate patterns as high as $2. The average for an American-tied dry fly is about $1.30. Imports averaged about $1.

Imitative	Suggestive	Attractor
Blue Dun	Adams	Humpy
Blue-Winged Olive	Black Gnat	Irresistible
Brown Drake	Bivisible	Royal Caddis
Green Drake	H&L Variant	McGinty
Henrickson	Haystack	Queen of the Waters
Cahill	Mosquito	Professor
Pale Evening Dun	Leadwing Coachman	Parmachene Belle
Quill Gordon	Rio Grande King	Royal Wulff
King's River Caddis	Brown Spider	Silver Doctor
Bird's Stonefly	Tan Variant	Pink Lady

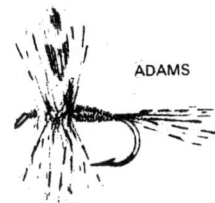

ADAMS

The distinction between categories is not always clear, and I'm sure I've given you something to argue about with this list. I'm still wondering myself where the Renegade goes, suggestive or attractor.

We might also divide our list further into the major food categories. With terrestrials and midges already separated and streamers taking care of baitfish, that

Adams. #10-20
Hig, Let, Bud, Mur, H&H, Orv, AnJ, Bob, Blu, Big, Cus, Pen, Edd, Nor, Hun, Ste, Joh, FOM, Mon, Don, Kau, Cab, Ran, T&T, Dan, Mer, Fly
Adams Caddis. #14
Mer
Adams Irresistible. #8-16
Cus, Pen, Edd, Nor, Hig, AnR, Ran, T&T, Fly

Adams Variant. #10-18
Cus
Adams Wulff. #10-18
Cus
Adams, Delaware. #12-16
AnR
Adams, Female. #10-20
Hig, Cab, Dan, Mer, Bud, Hun,
FOM, Cus, Pen, AnR, Blu, Big, Kau
Adams, Female, parachute. #12-16
Pen
Adams, Green. #12-14
Mer
Adams, hairwing. #10
Mer
Adams, parachute. #10-18
Orv, Bob, Blu, Mer, Cus, Pen, Nor,
Bud, Joh, Mon, Let, Hig, Big, Kau,
Cab, T&T, Dan
Adams, paradun. #12-18
Kau
Adams, spentwing. #10-20
Bud, Don, Blu, Dan, Cus, Edd
Adams, thorax. #12-18
Mon, Orv, Big, Nor
Adams, upside-down. #12-16
Joh
Adams, Wide Wing. #12-18
Big
Adams, Yellow. #10-20
Let, Don, Pen, Edd
Badger Variant. #14-16
Bud
Baetis, Iwamasa dun. # 20
Kau
Baetis, parachute. #16-20
Bob
Beaverkill. #12-16
Egg, Ran
Bi-Fly. #6-14
Let, Dan
Bivisible, Badger. #10-16
Ran, Dan, Hun, Cus, Nor
Bivisible, Black. #10-16
Bud, Dan, Mer, Edd, Nor, Hun, Don,
AnJ, Big, Kau, Cab
Bivisible, Brown. #10-16
Cus, Ran, Pen, Hig, Let, Bud, Edd,
Orv, AnJ, H&H, Nor, Hun, FOM,
Don, Mon, AnR, Big, Cab, T&T, Dan,
Mer
Bivisible, Ginger. #10-18
FOM, Dan, Cus, Edd, Bud, Don,
AnJ, Kau
Bivisible, Gray. #10-16
Kau, Dan, Pen, Don, Edd, Nor
Bivisible, Grizzly. #10-16
Dan, AnJ, Let

Black Gnat. #10-20
AnJ, Orv, Let, Bud, H&H, AnR,
Bob, Cus, Pen, Edd, Nor, Hun, Ste,
Don, Blu, Big, Mon, Kau, Cab, T&T,
Dan, Mer, Fly
Black Gnat, Iwamasa dun. #14-20
Hig
Black Gnat, parachute. #14-18
Mon, Let, T&T, Mer, Nor, Orv
Black Gnat, Wide Wing. # 12-14
Big
Black Quill. #10-20
Blu, Joh, Bud
Blue Dun. #12-20
Big, Blu, Mon, Don, FOM, Joh, Cus,
Orv, AnJ, Pen, Edd, Nor, H&H,
Bud, Let, Bob, Kau, Cab, Ran, T&T,
Dan, Mer
Blue Dun Irresistible. #8-12
Cab, T&T
Blue Dun, Iwamasa dun. #10-22
Hig, Blu

Blue Dun, parachute. #10-18
Blu, Bob, Hig, Bud, Joh, Kau, Dan,
Mer
Blue Dun, thorax. #16-18
Edd
Blue Dun, Wide Wing. #12-18
Big
Blue Quill. #10-20
Mur, Joh, Dan, Cus, Kau, Big, Edd,
Nor, H&H, Don, Bud, Let, T&T, Blu,
Bob, AnR
Blue Quill, parachute. #12-16
Bob
Blue Quill, Wide Wing. #12-16
Big
Blue Upright. #8-16
Ste
Blue-Winged Olive. #10-20
Cus, Pen, Let, Bud, Orv, AnR, Mur,
H&H, Hun, Joh, Edd, Nor, FOM,
Don, Mon, Bob, Big, Cab, T&T, Dan,
Mer, Fly
**Blue-Winged Olive, Eastern,
Iwamasa dun.** #18
T&T
Blue-Winged Olive, Iwamasa dun.
#10-22
Str, Blu, Kau, T&T

Blue-Winged Olive, parachute.
#12-18
Joh, Big, T&T, Mer
Blue-Winged Olive, paradun.
#14-20
Let
Blue-Winged Olive, thorax. #14-20
Nor, Hig, Orv, Bud, Mon, Big
Blue-Winged Olive, Wide Wing.
#12-18
Big
Brown Drake. #10-12
Blu, Kau, Pen, Joh
Brown Drake, extended body. #8-12
Bob, Kau, Bud, Hig, Str
Brown Drake, Iwamasa dun. #8-12
Kau, Blu
Brown Drake, no-hackle. #8-12
Blu
Brown Drake, parachute. #10-14
Blu, Joh
Brown Drake, paradrake. #10-12
Blu, Kau, Fly
Brown Drake, thorax. #10-14
Blu, Nor
Brown Hackle Peacock. #10-20
Bud, Ste, Dan, Blu, Cab, Ran, Cus
Brown Hackle Yellow. #10-20
Bud, Blu
Brown Variant. #10-18
Cus, Let
Caddis, Adams. #14
Mer
Caddis, Antron. #14-20
Blu
Caddis, Bucktail. #4-20
Blu, Big, Let, Bud, Str, Ste, Kau,
Cab, Dan
Caddis, Chuck. #12-18
Edd

COLORADO KING

Caddis, Colorado King. #12-14
Bob
Caddis, Delta Wing. #14
Mer
Caddis, Eagle's. #12-20
Blu
Caddis, Elk Hair. #10-18
Dan, Mer, Fly, Hig, Bud, Mur, H&H,
Hun, Ste, Mon, Cus, T&T
Caddis, Fluttering. #10-20
Dan, Nor, Mer, Cus, H&H, Bud, Let,
Hig, Blu, Kau

Caddis, Genetic. #14-18
Hig

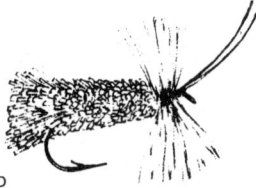

GODDARD
CADDIS

Caddis, Goddard. #8-18
Bob, T&T, Bud, Dan, Fly, Blu, Kau,
Cab
Caddis, Hemmingway. #12-18
Kau
Caddis, Henryville Special. #10-20
Mer, Cus, Edd, Egg, Let, Bud,
H&H, Hun, Mon, Cab, Kau, Big,
Nor, Blu, Bob, AnR, T&T, Dan, AnJ,
Orv
Caddis, King's River. #10-20
Dan, Mer, Cus, Edd, Orv, Blu, Big,
Kau, Cab
Caddis, LaFontaine's Dancing.
#12-16
Mon, Bud, Kau, Mer
Caddis, Little Black. #14-18
Bob
Caddis, Little Brown. #12-18
Blu, Bud
Caddis, Micro. #20
Str
Caddis, Mink Wing. #12
Mer
Caddis, October. #8
Fly
Caddis, Pheasant. #12-16
Blu
Caddis, Royal. #10-18
Blu
Caddis, Spentwing Partridge.
#14-20
Kau
Caddis, Tent Wing. #10-18
Dan, Cus, Nor
Caddis, Tied Down. #8-12
Ste, Kau
Caddis, Troth Elk Hair. #10-18
Dan
Caddis, Vermont. #12-20
AnR
Caddis, Wharry. #10-16
Dan
Caddis-Hopper, Eddie's. #14
Edd
Cahill, Dark. #10-20
Ran, Kau, Big, Blu, Cus, Hig, Let,
Bud, H&H, Hun, Pen, Edd, Nor, Joh,

FOM, Don, Mon, Bob, AnR, AnJ,
Orv, T&T, Dan, Mer
Cahill, Dark, parachute. #14
Let
Cahill, Dark, thorax. #12-16
Edd
Cahill, Lemon. #10-18
Mer, Let

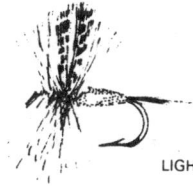

LIGHT CAHILL

Cahill, Light. #10-20
Cus, Pen, Mon, Don, FOM, Joh, Edd,
Nor, Orv, Hun, AnR, Bob, Blu,
H&H, Mur, Bud, Let, Egg, Hig, Big,
Kau, Cab, Ran, T&T, Dan, Mer, Fly
Cahill, Light, fanwing. #8-14
Dan
Cahill, Light, parachute. #10-18
Dan, Mer, Pen, Nor, Orv, Let, Bud,
Mon, Bob, Blu, Big, Kau, Cab, T&T
Cahill, Light, paradun. #12-16
Let
Cahill, Light, thorax. #12-20
Hig, Mon, Edd, Nor, Orv, Big
Cahill Quill. #10-20
Bud, Blu
Cahill Quill, Light. #10-20
Dan
Callibaetis, Iwamasa dun. #16
Str
Callibaetis, thorax. #16-20
T&T, Kau
CFK Tan Dun, Wide Wing. #12-18
Big
Coachman. #10-20
Mer, Cus, Pen, Edd, Bud, Joh, Don,
Blu, Ran, Dan
Coachman Trude. #6-16
Dan, Mur, Joh, Hig
Coachman, parachute. #12-14
T&T
Coffin Fly. #12-14
Hun
Compara-Dun. #16-22
Dan
Cowdung. #10-20
Bud, Don, Dan, Ran, Mer, Cus, Edd
Cream Drake. #10-12
Joh
Cream Variant. #12-18
Cus, Pen, Edd, Nor, Let, H&H, Bud,

Mon, Orv, AnR, Big, T&T, Mer
Damselfly. #6-10
Dan
Dark Montreal. #12-16
Ran
Dragonfly. #6-10
Dan
Dun Parachute. #12-18
Cab, T&T
Dun Variant. #10-18
Mer, Cus, Mon, Hun, Edd, Nor, Bud,
Let, Orv, AnR, T&T
Elkwing Paradun. #16-20
Fly
Float-N-Fool, parachute. #14-18
Kau
Ginger Quill. #10-20
AnR, Blu, Big, Let, Bud, H&H, Mer,
Cus, Pen, Edd, Hun, Joh, Don, Mon,
Kau, Cab, Ran, AnJ, Orv, T&T, Dan
Ginger Quill, fanwing. #8-14
Dan
Ginger Quill, Iwamasa dun. #12-18
Hig
Ginger Quill, Wide Wing. #12-14
Big
Gold-Ribbed Hare's Ear Dry.
#10-14
Cus
Gray Drake, extended body. #8-12
Hig
Gray Fox. #10-18
Cus, Orv, Pen, Edd, Mur, H&H, Joh,
Nor, AnR, Big, Kau, T&T, Mer, Let,
FOM, Don, Mon
Gray Fox Variant. #10-16
Cus, Pen, Edd, Nor, Let, H&H, Hun,
Mon, Orv, AnR, Big, T&T, Mer
Gray Fox, paradun. #12-16
Let
Gray Fox, thorax. #12-14
Edd, Orv
Gray Hackle. #14-16
Ran, Nor
Gray Hackle Peacock. #10-20
Blu, Cab, Bud, Ste, Dan, Cus
Gray Hackle Red. #10-20
Bud, Blu
Gray Hackle Yellow. #10-20
Cab, Bud, FOM, Blu, Dan, Fly, Cus
Gray Parachute. #14-18
Joh, Kau
Gray Quill. #12-16
Pen
Gray Trude. #12-16
Hig
Gray/Yellow, no-hackle. #16-20
Bud

Green Drake. #6-12
Blu, Kau, Ran, Mer, Pen, Edd, Bud, H&H, Joh
Green Drake Wulff. #8-14
Bob, Orv, Dan, Nor

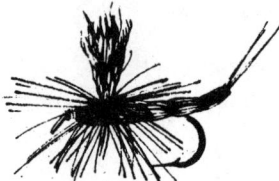

GREEN DRAKE — EXTENDED

Green Drake, extended body. #10-12
Bob, Str, Bud, Hig
Green Drake, fanwing. #12-16
Ran
Green Drake, Iwamasa dun, extended body. #6-12
Kau, Blu, Ran, T&T
Green Drake, no-hackle. #6-12
Blu, Edd
Green Drake, parachute. #10-14
Joh, Blu
Green Drake, paradrake. #8-12
Blu, Kau, Dan, Fly, Let, Bud
Green Drake, thorax. #10-14
Nor, Blu, Orv, Bud
Green Drake, Western. #6-12
H&H, Big, Cus
Green Drake, Western, Iwamasa dun. #10
T&T
Green Drake, Western, thorax. #10-12
Orv
Grizzly King. #10-14
Edd, Don
Grizzly Variant. #12-18
Let
Gulper Special. #14-18
Mer, Blu, Kau

HAIR WING VARIANT

H&L Variant. #8-18
Bud, Hig, Dan, Orv, Mer, Cus, Pen, Bob, Blu, Big, Kau, Cab

Hare's Ear Dry. #10-20
Ran, Let, Dan
Haystack. #12
Cus
Hendrickson. #12-16
Bob, Hun
Hendrickson, Dark. #10-20
Orv, AnJ, AnR, Blu, Big, Hig, Let, Bud, Mur, Cus, Pen, Edd, Nor, Kau, Cab, Ran, T&T, Dan, H&H, Joh, FOM, Don, Mon
Hendrickson, Flick. #12-16
Edd, Don
Hendrickson, Iwamasa dun. #14
Str, T&T
Hendrickson, Light. #10-20
Cus, Pen, Edd, Nor, AnJ, AnR, Ran, Blu, Big, Kau, Cab, T&T, Dan, Mer, Hig, Mon, Don, Let, Bud, H&H, Joh
Hendrickson, Light, paradun. #12-14
Let
Hendrickson, parachute. #14
Let
Hendrickson, thorax. #12-16
Mon, Orv, Edd, Nor
Hexagenia, paradun. #6
Fly
Hexagenia, Iwamasa dun, extended body. #4
T&T
Hornberg Dry. #8-16
Cus, Edd, Ran

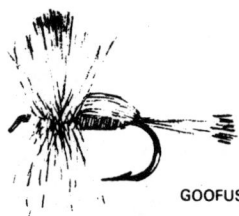

GOOFUS

Humpy. #8-18
Cus, Edd, Mon, Don, Pen, Nor, Orv, Joh, Ste, Hun, Ran, Cab, AnJ, Bob, Blu, H&H, Mur, Big, Kau, Hig, Bud, Let, T&T, Dan, Mer, Fly
Humpy, Elk Hair. #10-14
AnR, Hig, Hun
Humpy, Poly. #18-22
Blu, Bud, Mon
Iron Blue Dun. #10-20
Blu, Dan, Bud
Irresistible. #8-16
Hig, Let, Cus, Pen, Edd, Nor, Kau, Ran, Blu, Bob, AnR, Bud, Mur, H&H, Don, AnJ, Orv, Dan, Mer

Irresistible, Adams. #8-16
Cus, Pen, Edd, Nor, Don, Ste, Hig, H&H, Hun, AnR, Ran, T&T, Fly
Irresistible, Black. #10-14
Pen, Don, Edd
Irresistible, Blue Dun. #8-12
Cab, T&T
Irresistible, Parmachene Belle. #8-14
Ran
Irresistible, Rat-Faced. #8-14
Cab, Ran, Hig
Irresistible, White. #10-12
Let, H&H
Isonychia. #10-14
Joh
Isonychia Dun, Iwamasa dun, extended body. #8
Str
Kolzer Firefly. #8-16
Dan
Lady Beaverkill. #12-16
Ran, H&H
Leadwing Coachman. #10-20
Mer, Blu, Ran, Bud
Little Brown Quill. #20
Str
Little Marryat. #14-16
AnR
Loopwing Paradun. #12-18
Mer, Fly
Mahogany Dun, Iwamasa dun. #14
Kau
Mahogany Dun, thorax. #16-18
T&T, Kau
Mallard Quill. #12-16
Pen
March Brown. #10-20
Hun, Cus, Pen, Edd, Joh, FOM, Don, Nor, Ran, Cab, Mon, Kau, H&H, Mur, Bud, Let, Big, Bob, Orv, AnJ, AnR, T&T, Dan, Mer
March Brown, Iwamasa dun, extended body. #12
Str, Hig, T&T
March Brown, parachute. #10-14
Big
March Brown, paradun. #10-14
Let
March Brown, thorax. #10-14
Edd, Nor, Orv
Mayfly, Brown. #10-16
Orv, H&H, Nor
Mayfly, Brown, thorax. #12-18
Orv
Mayfly, Cream. #10-16
Cus

Mayfly, Ginger. #12-14
Cus
Mayfly, no-hackle. #12-20
Kau, Blu, Joh
Mayfly, Olive, parachute. #14-18
Kau
Mayfly, Olive, paradun. #14-18
Kau, Hig
Mayfly, Slate/Olive, thorax. #14-20
T&T
McGinty. #10-20
Dan, Ran, Don, Bud, Mer, Edd
Meloche. #10-20
Dan
Mosquito. #10-20
Cus, Pen, FOM, Don, Edd, Nor, Ste,
Hun, H&H, Orv, AnJ, AnR, Bob,
Bud, Hig, Blu, Big, Cab, Ran, Dan,
Mer, Fly
Mosquito, California. #12-18
Kau
Mr. Rapidan Dry. #12-16
Mur
Olive Dun. #10-20
Dan, Edd, Bud, Don, Blu, Kau, Ran
Olive Dun, thorax. #14-20
Kau, Dan
Olive Quill. #10-20
Bud, Don, Dan, Edd, Blu, Kau
Orange Asher. #14
Cus
Pale Evening Dun, Wide Wing.
#12-18
Big
Pale Morning Dun. #10-20
Dan, AnJ, Blu, Kau, Bud, Cab
Pale Morning Dun, Iwamasa dun.
#14-18
Str, T&T, Kau
Pale Morning Dun, paradun. #16-20
Hig
Pale Morning Dun, thorax. #16-20
Orv, Kau, Hig, Bud, T&T
Pale Morning Dun, Wide Wing.
#12-18
Big
Pale Sulphur. #14-18
Nor
Pale Sulphur, thorax. #16-18
Hig
Pale Watery Dun. #12-16
Pen, Don, Edd
Parmachene Belle. #12-16
Ran
Pink Lady. #10-20
Ran, Bud, Don, Mer, Edd
Professor. #12-16
Ran, Mer

Queen of the Waters. #12-16
Cus, Ran
Quill Gordon. #10-20
Cab, Cus, FOM, Don, Mon, Pen,
Edd, Nor, Orv, AnR, Bob, Big, Kau,
Let, Hig, Bud, Mur, H&H, Hun, Joh,
Ran, T&T, Dan, Mer
Quill Gordon, fanwing. #8-14
Dan
Quill Gordon, Iwamasa dun,
extended body. #14
Str, T&T
Quill Gordon, thorax. #12-16
Edd
Rat-Faced McDougal. #8-16
T&T, Mer, Bud, Edd, Nor, Orv, AnJ,
AnR
Red Quill. #10-20
Cus, Hig, Pen, Let, Edd, Bud, H&H,
Joh, Hun, Nor, Orv, AnR, Blu, Mon,
Don, Big, Kau, Cab, Ran, T&T, Dan,
Mer
Red Quill, thorax. #12-16
Edd, Nor
Renegade. #10-20
Dan, Cus, Ste, H&H, Pen, Nor, Orv,
AnJ, Bud, Hig, Big, Kau, Cab
Renegade, double. #10-14
Cus
Rio Grande King. #10-20
Bud, Dan, Cus
Rio Grande King, parachute.
#10-18
Dan, Bud
Rio Grande Trude. #6-16
Hig, Dan, Fly
Royal Coachman. #10-20
Pen, Don, Edd, Nor, Orv, AnJ, AnR,
Blu, Big, Cus, Let, Bud, H&H, Hun,
Ste, Joh, FOM, Kau, Cab, Ran, T&T,
Dan, Mer
Royal Coachman, fanwing. #8-18
Dan, Nor, Orv, AnR, Ran
Royal Coachman, Iwamasa dun.
#12-18
Hig
Royal Coachman, parachute.
#10-18
Dan, Mer, Pen, Nor, Orv, Blu, Hig,
Bud

ROYAL HUMPY

Royal Humpy. #8-18
Mer, Fly, Bud, Mur, H&H, Cus, Pen,
Cab, Kau, Big, Bob, AnJ, Orv, T&T,
Dan
Royal Trude. #6-16
Dan, Fly, Bud, Hig, Blu, Kau
Salmon Fly, Elk Hair. #4-8
Dan
Salmon Fly, Henry's Fork. #6-8
Orv, Cab

JACKLIN'S SALMON FLY

Salmon Fly, Jacklin's. #4
Bob
Salmon Fly, Muddled. #2-4
Fly
Silver Doctor. #12-16
Ran
Slate/Tan, no-hackle. #16-20
Bud
Sofa Pillow. #4-10
Dan, Ste, Pen, Nor

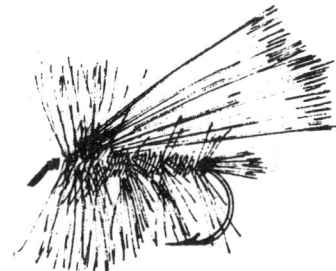

ELK HAIR SOFA PILLOW

Sofa Pillow, Elk Hair. #2-8
Bob, Bud
Sofa Pillow, Improved. #2-10
Orv, Kau, Cab, T&T, Fly
Sofa Pillow, Super. #4-8
Bud
Spider, Badger. #12-18
Edd, Bud, Mer, Blu
Spider, Black. #12-18
Edd, Mer, Bud
Spider, Blue Dun. #12-18
Edd
Spider, Brown. #12-18
Edd, Mer
Spider, deer hair. #18-20
Fly

Spider, Furnace. #12-18
Edd
Spider, Ginger. #10-20
Bud
Spruce Fly. #10-20
Bud
Stimulator. #8-16
Kau
Stonefly, Big Golden Spent. #4
Str

BIRD'S STONE

Stonefly, Bird's. #4-14
Bob, Blu, Dan, Edd
Stonefly, Early Brown. #12
Str

FLUTTERING STONE

Stonefly, Fluttering. #2-10
Bob, Blu, Big, Bud, Ste
Stonefly, Golden. #8-10
Cab, Orv, Nor
Stonefly, Henry's Fork Golden.
#8-10
Cab

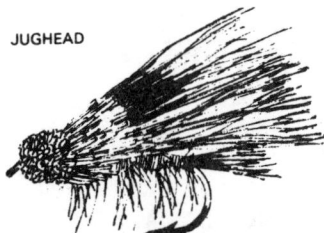

JUGHEAD

Stonefly, Jughead. #6
Bob
Stonefly, K's Butt. #2-4
Blu
Stonefly, Light. #10-14
Cus
Stonefly, Little Yellow. #12-14
Fly, Str, Edd
Stonefly, Low Floater. #2-6
Bud
Stonefly, Muddled Golden. #6-8
Fly
Stonefly, Parks. #4-8
Hig

Stonefly, The Surface. #4-8
Wul
Stonefly, Tiny Winter. #18
Edd
Sulphur Dun. #12-18
AnR, Mer, Pen, Let, Mur, Joh
Sulphur Dun, Iwamasa dun. #16
Str
Sulphur Dun, thorax. #14-18
Edd
Sulphur, Female. #14-18
Let
Sulphur, paradun. #14-18
Let
Sundance Special. #8-16
Dan
Tan Variant. #10-18
Cus
Tiny Brown Quill, Iwamasa dun.
#20
T&T
Tri-Color. #12-16
Nor
Trico. #24-26
Joh, Edd
Trico, Iwamasa dun. #20
T&T
Trico, thorax. #20-24
Orv, Mon
Tupps Indispensable. #10-20
Dan, Bud, Mer
Variant, Dark. #10-20
Hig, Hun
Variant, Light. #10-20
Hig, Hun
Whitcraft. #10-20
Bud

White Miller. #10-20
Mer, Cus, Edd, Nor, Bud, Joh, Don,
Ran, Dan
White Moth. #12
Mer
White Tip Montreal. #12-16
Ran
White/Black, thorax. #18
Kau, T&T
Wulff, Adams. #10-18
Cus

Wulff, Ausable. #8-18
Orv, Mer, Pen, Hig, H&H, Don, Mon,
Edd, Nor, AnR, Blu, Kau, Cab, T&T
Wulff, Black. #8-18
Dan, Pen, Edd, Nor, Let, Bud, Don,
AnJ, Ran
Wulff, Blonde. #8-18
Kau, T&T, Let, Dan, Cus, FOM,
Bud, Nor, Cab, Big, Blu, AnJ

Wulff, Brown. #8-18
Ran, Hig, Let, Don, Bob, Dan, Edd
Wulff, Coachman. #8-14
Edd, Don
Wulff, Gray. #8-18
Wul, Cus, Pen, Let, Hig, Edd, Nor,
Orv, Bud, H&H, AnJ, AnR, Hun,
FOM, Don, Mon, Bob, Blu, Big, Kau,
Cab, Ran, T&T, Dan, Fly

GREEN DRAKE
— WULFF

Wulff, Green Drake. #8-14
Orv, Bob, Nor
Wulff, Grizzly. #8-18
Wul, Fly, Let, Pen, Hig, Edd, Bud,
H&H, Hun, Nor, Orv, Blu, Big,
FOM, Mon, Don, Kau, Cab, Ran,
T&T, Dan, Mer, Cus
Wulff, Grizzly King. #8-14
Ran
Wulff Irresistible. #8-16
T&T, Cab, Kau
Wulff, Kennebago. #8-14
Ran
Wulff, Montreal. #8-14
Ran
Wulff, Parmachene. #8-14
Ran
Wulff, Pink Lady. #8-14
Ran
Wulff, Powder Puff. #8-14
Ran
Wulff, Red. #10-18
Nor

ROYAL WULFF

Wulff, Royal. #8-18
Wul, Hig, Cus, Pen, Edd, Mon, Don,
FOM, Joh, Nor, Blu, Big, Kau, Cab,
Hun, H&H, Mur, Bud, Let, Ran,
Bob, AnR, AnJ, Orv, T&T, Dan,
Mer, Fly
Wulff, Welch. #8-14
Ran

Wulff, White. #8-18
Wul, H&H, Hun, Joh, Don, Cus, Pen, Edd, Nor, Cab, Ran, Kau, Big, Bob, Let, Hig, AnR, AnJ, Orv, T&T, Dan,

Mer
Yellow Drake. #10-12
Joh
Yellow Drake, Iwamasa dun,

extended body. #12
T&T
Yellow May. #12-16
Ran

TERRESTRIALS

The creepy crawlies from Mother Earth often tumble or fly ill-advisedly into trout streams, there to be gobbled by hungry fish. This works out to the advantage of the fish and the angler, but not the bug.

Many of the patterns here are traditional, but a few are fairly new and worthy of note. The McMurray Ant patterns are constructed of balsa wood in two sections. The wood is secured to the hook and painted to match the insect of the day. (Yellow Jacket is my favorite color, but I don't know how well fish take it.)

Corkers are also made of a buoyant material and are quite unlike traditional flies. Thomas & Thomas offer a full selection of body styles (two-door, four-door, etc.) and colors.

Hoppers have come a long way in recent years. Dave Whitlock and other inventive tiers have turned their talents on this important late-summer trout food. The old Joe's Hopper still has its following, but some of the new patterns look like they're ready to jump out of the fly box. (I carry mine in a jar with holes in the lid.)

Terrestrials are always worth a try, and often they are better

producers than any other type of fly when there is no hatch. That's most of the time, incidentally. In some areas of the country, Pennsylvania in particular, terrestrials are the favored type of fly. The Letort Hopper and Cricket were born of the necessity to please finicky spring creek trout with landborn insect imitations.

Prices range from about a dollar to $1.50 with the average price about $1.25. Some of the intricate hopper patterns are more.

Ant, Black. #10-24
Let, Bud, Mur, H&H, Hun, Orv, Bob, Blu, Big, Cus, Pen, Edd, Nor, Str, Don, Mon, Kau, Cab, Ran, T&T, Dan, Mer, Fly
Ant, Black Flying. #10-24
Mer, Let, Bud, Hun, Fly, Edd, Nor, Big, Blu, Kau, Cab, Dan

ANTS

Ant, Brown. #10-12
Ran
Ant, Brown Flying. #12-18
Kau, Nor
Ant, Cinnamon. #12-24
Mer, Big, Blu, Pen, Edd, Nor, Let, Bud, Mur, Hun, Mon, Bob, Orv, T&T, Cab, Kau, Dan
Ant, Cinnamon Flying. #14-24
Big, Let
Ant, Dave's Red. #14-16
Fly
Ant, deer hair. #14-22
Blu
Ant, Red. #10-20
Dan, Cus, H&H, Str

Ant, Red and Black. #12
Edd
Ant, Red Flying. #14-18
Nor
Ant, Rod's. #16-20
Hun
Beetle, Black. #10-18
Orv, AnR, Hig, Dan, Pen, Edd, Nor, Bud, Mon, Blu, Big, Kau, T&T
Beetle, Bronze. #12-16
Pen
Beetle, Crowe. #14-20
Kau, Cab, Mer, Nor, Mur, Let
Beetle, Dave's Black. #14-16
Fly, Cab
Beetle, Dekon. #14-18
Hun
Beetle, Ron's. #14-18
Orv
Corkers, Ant. #16
T&T
Corkers, Bee. #10
T&T
Corkers, Black Beetle. #12
T&T
Corkers, Black Cricket. #12
T&T
Corkers, Caddis. #12
T&T
Corkers, Green Inchworm. #12
T&T

Corkers, Hopper. #12
T&T
Corkers, Japanese Beetle. #12
T&T
Corkers, Lady Bug. #16
T&T
Corkers, Leaf Hopper. #12
T&T
Corkers, Transistors. #16
T&T
Cricket, Dave's. #6-14
T&T, Kau, Cab
Cricket, Jay-Dave's. #6-8
Hig

LETORT CRICKET

Cricket, Letort. #10-18
Let, Mer, Pen, Edd, Nor, Orv, AnJ, AnR, Hig, H&H, Hun, Mon, Bob, Blu, Big, Kau, Dan
Cricket, Rod's. #14-16
Hun
Cricket, Shenk's. #10-16
Mur
Green Caterpillar. #12
Mer

Green Leaf Hopper. #20
Mer, Edd
Hopper, Baby. #14
Cus

BOB'S HOPPER

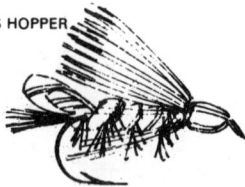

Hopper, Bob's. #6-12
Bob
Hopper, Bullethead. #6-12
Big
Hopper, Dan's Deer. #6-12
Dan

DAVE'S HOPPER

Hopper, Dave's. #4-14
T&T, Mer, Fly, Bob, Blu, Mur, H&H,
Bud, Hig, Kau, Cab, Orv, AnJ
Hopper, deer hair. #8-14
Nor
Hopper, Elk Hair. #6-14
Nor, Bud, Mon
Hopper, Gartside Pheasant. #6-12
Blu, Big, Bud
Hopper, Henry's Fork. #6-14
Kau, Bud, Str
Hopper, Jay-Dave's. #6-12
Hig

JOE'S HOPPER

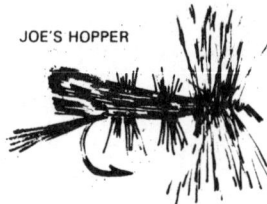

Hopper, Joe's. #4-14
Dan, Mer, Cab, Kau, Big, Cus, Edd,
Blu, Bob, AnJ, T&T, Hig, Bud, Mur,
Ste
Hopper, John's Elk Hair. #4-12
Dan
Hopper, Legged. #8-14
Hun

LETORT HOPPER

Hopper, Letort. #28-16
Let, Dan, Mer, Pen, Edd, Kau, Orv,
Hig, Bud, Mur, Hun, Mon, AnR, Bob,
Blu, Big
Hopper, Muddler. #6-10
Big, Ran
Hopper, Rod's. #14-16
Hun
Hopper, Yellowstone. #6-14
Dan
Hopper-Caddis, Eddie's. #14
Edd
Inchworm. #12-16
T&T, Mer, Cus, Orv, Let, H&H,
Hun, Mon, Kau, Nor

Inchworm, Dave's. #12
Cab
Jassid. #16-22
T&T, Hun, Dan, AnR, Kau
June Bug. #12
T&T
McMurray Ant, Black. #12-22
AnR, Mer, Mur, Hun, Let, Hig
McMurray Ant, Black Beetle. #14
Mer
McMurray Ant, Cinnamon. #12-22
Mur, Let, Hig, AnR, Mer
McMurray Ant, Cricket. #12
Mer
McMurray Ant, Flying Black. #16
Mer
McMurray Ant, Flying Cinammon.
#16
Mer
McMurray Ant, Green Leaf Hopper.
#18
Mer
McMurray Ant, Hopper. #12
Mer
McMurray Ant, Japanese Beetle.
#14
Mer
McMurray Ant, Lady Bug. # 16
Mer
McMurray Ant, Red Head Ant. # 16
Mer
McMurray Ant, Yellow Jacket.
#12-16
Let, Mer

WET FLIES

Wet flies are not in vogue, at least in print. Nobody seems to be writing much about the truth and beauty of wet fly fishing. Nevertheless, there are lots of regular people out on the streams cleaning up with wet Leadwing Coachmans and Black Gnats. Writers don't always have their fingers on the pulse of American fly fishermen.

As a youngster, I watched the old-timers on the Poudre and the Big Thompson Rivers with their elderly Montagues, working downstream, catching trout, and relaxing. I still occasionally see one of these wet fly fishermen with their three-fly rigs, but more and more they are replaced with the upstream, graphite-rod, match-the-hatchers, myself among them. We modern fishermen, I think, move faster, cast more often, are less aware of our surroundings, and frown more while we're fishing than the old-timers.

Thinking about it now, I'm wondering if I even have a slow, gentle rod suitable for throwing the wet fly rig with its droppers. I was taught to fly fish with wets, to work cautiously, slowly downstream, to give the trout several chances to take my Renegade or Royal Coachman or Brown Hackle Yellow. I think I'd like to try it all again. Sometimes the intensity of dry fly fishing and the science of it all just isn't what I'm looking for streamside.

If you feel the same way, you may want to try wet fly fishing with a three-fly rig. Put a bright attractor on the bottom and add two, more sensible dropper flies. Or does the attractor go on the top? My memory fails me . . . must be too full of Latin names. Try the rig both ways.

Prices for wet flies are slightly lower than those for dries. They range from $.80-$1.20, with a few companies charging as much as $1.50 on particular patterns. The average price is about $1.10.

Adams. #6-16
Dan, Mer, Pen, Nor, Blu, Bud, FOM, T&T

Alder. #8-16
Mer, Pen, Edd, Nor, Orv, AnR, Big, Let, Don

Alexandria. #6-16
Big, Bud

Ant, Black. #6-14
Blu, Dan, Edd

Ant, Red. #6-14
Dan, Blu, Bud

April Gray. #12
Mer

Black Gnat. #6-16
Cus, Pen, FOM, Don, Mon, Orv, AnR, Bob, Blu, Edd, Nor, Cab, Ran, Let, Bud, Mur, H&H, Hun, T&T, Dan, Mer

Blue Dun. #6-14
Orv, AnR, Blu, Cus, Pen, Edd, Nor, Ran, Bud, H&H, FOM, Don, Mon, T&T, Mer

Blue Professor. #10-14
Hun

Blue Quill. #6-16
Let, Orv, Bud, Cus, Pen, Edd, Nor, H&H, Don

Blue-Winged Olive. #10-16
FOM, Orv, AnR, Mer, Pen, Nor

Brown Bear. #6-10
Bud

Brown Bomber. #4-12
Dan

Brown Hackle. #8-16
Ran, Mur, H&H, Don, Mer, Cus, Edd

Brown Hackle Peacock. #6-14
Blu, Bud

Brown Hackle Yellow. #6-14
Bud, Blu

Butcher. #10-12
Bob

Cahill, Dark. #6-16
Pen, Cus, Orv, AnR, Bob, Big, Cab, Edd, Nor, Ran, Let, Bud, T&T, Dan, Mer, H&H, Hun, Don, Mon

Cahill, Light. #6-16
Cus, Pen, Edd, Nor, Orv, Bob, Cab, Ran, Let, Bud, Mur, H&H, Hun, Mon, FOM, Don, T&T, Mer

California Coachman. #8-12
Nor

Captain. #6-16
Pen, Bud

Cardinal. #8-12
Nor

Carey Special. #6-14
Mer, Kau, Cab, Ste, Dan

Coachman. #6-16
Mon, Don, FOM, H&H, Mur, Cus, Pen, Edd, Nor, Bud, Let, Ran, Cab, AnR, Orv, T&T, Dan, Mer

Colorado Caddis. #12-16
AnJ, Cus

Cowdung. #6-16
Big, AnR, Orv, Cus, Pen, Edd, Nor, Ran, Bud, H&H, Don, Dan, Mer

Dark Montreal. #8-12
Ran

Dark Spruce. #8
Mer

Don's Fore and Aft. #14
Pen

Dr. Grantham. #6-12
Ran

Early Brown Stone. #10-12
AnR

Fizzle. #6-10
Bud

Ginger Quill. #6-16
Dan, Mer, Let, Bud, FOM, Mon, Pen, Nor, Ran, Big, Blu, AnR, Orv, T&T

Gold-Ribbed Hare's Ear. #8-16
Mer, Cus, Pen, Edd, Nor, H&H, Hun, Don, Mon, Mur, Let, Big, AnR, Orv

Gray Hackle. #8-16
Hun, Ran, Don, Mer, Edd, Nor

Gray Hackle Peacock. #6-16
T&T, Blu, Let, Bud, Cus

Gray Hackle Red. #6-14
Bud

Gray Hackle Yellow. #6-16
Dan, Cus, Bud, Blu

Grizzly King. #6-14
Bob, Bud, Ran, Don, AnR, Cus, Edd, Nor

Hare's Ear. #6-14
T&T, Dan, Bob, Blu, Cab, Bud

Heim's Hellgrammite. #6-10
Pen

Hendrickson, Dark. #10-16
Don, Cus, Pen, Edd, Nor, Mon, FOM, Hun, T&T, Mer, H&H, Let, Ran, Big, AnR, Orv

Hendrickson, Light. #10-16
T&T, Mer, Pen, Nor, AnR, Big, Ran

Hornberg. #8-12
Nor, Let, H&H, Orv

Iron Blue Dun. #12-14
Mer, Pen

Kelso. #10-14
Pen, Nor

King of the Waters. #6-14
Bob, Bud

Lady Beaverkill. #12
Mer

Lady Mite. #6-12
Bud, Dan

Leadwing Coachman. #6-16
Edd, Cus, Pen, Hun, Don, Mon, Nor, Bud, Let, Blu, AnR, Orv, T&T, Dan, Mer

March Brown. #6-16
Bob, AnR, Blu, Big, Cus, Pen, Edd, Nor, Cab, Ran, Let, Hun, FOM, Don, T&T, Mer

March Brown, American. #6-14
Dan, Blu

McGinty. #6-16
Dan, Mer, Cus, Nor, H&H, Bud, Ran, Cab, Big, Blu, T&T

Montreal. #8-14
Orv, H&H, Don, Cus, Edd, Nor

Mormon Girl. #6-14
Bud, Bob

Mosquito. #6-14
Dan, Mer, Pen, Blu, Ran, Bud, FOM

Mr. Mite. #6-12
Dan

Olive Quill. #6-14
Blu

Orange Fishhawk. #10-14
Mer, Let

Pale Evening Dun. #12-16
Don, H&H, Orv, Mer, Cus, Pen, Edd

Parmachene Belle. #f8-14
T&T, Nor, Cab, Ran, Hun, Bob, AnR, Orv

Pheasant Tail. #12-14
Nor

Picket Pin. #8-14
Hun, Let, Don, AnR, Orv, Mer, Pen, Edd, Nor

Pink Lady. #12-14
H&H

Professor. #6-16
Mer, Pen, Edd, Nor, T&T, Dan, Don, Mon, Ran, Big, Bob, AnR, Orv

Queen of the Waters. #6-14
Bob, Ran, Bud, Nor

Quill Gordon. #6-16
Orv, Cus, Pen, Edd, Nor, Big, Ran, Let, Bud, Mur, H&H, Mon, Don, FOM, Hun, Blu, Bob, AnR, T&T, Mer

Red Quill. #10-16
Pen, Let, Nor

Renegade. #6-14
Dan, Mer, Bud, Blu, Bob

Rio Grande King. #6-14
AnJ, Bob, Blu, Bud, Dan, Cus, Pen

Rockworm. #6-10
Bud
Royal Coachman. #6-16
Hun, Cus, Pen, FOM, Don, Bud,
Edd, Nor, T&T, Dan, Mer, Let, Ran,
Cab, AnR, Orv
Sandy Mite. #6-12
Dan, Bud
Silver Doctor. #6-12
Nor, Bob, Ran
Spruce. #12

Mer
Trout Fin. #8-10
AnR
Uncle Phil. #6-10
Pen
Western Bee. #6-14
Blu, Bud
White Miller. #8-14
Edd, Bud, Ran, Blu, Bob
White Tip Montreal. #8-12
Ran

Wickham's Fancy. #10-12
Bob, Edd
Wonderbug. # 12-16
Cus
Wooly Worm. #2-14
Bud, Cus, Mon, Hun, H&H, Pen,
Edd, T&T, Orv, AnR, Nor, Mur,
Egg, AnJ, Blu, Big, Kau, Cab, Ran,
Hig, Let, Dan, Mer
Yellow-Bodied Grayback. #6-12
Dan

SOFT HACKLES

With the popularization by author Sylvester Nemes, soft hackles have won a place in the hearts and fly boxes of fly fishermen. They are really a type of wet fly and should probably be with them, but I think they are distinctive enough to be separated.

These are about the only wet flies in common usage (at least in print). You don't hear much about the old traditional wet flies. You probably don't have a Cowdung in your box right now. But these are excellent flies, and there is reason to add them to your wet fly collection.

The hackle on these patterns is their most significant feature. Partridge and other very limp feathers are used. These give the fly a lot of life-like movement under the water, and that's makes them attractive to trout and other fish. Give them a try.

Prices range from $.85-$1.25 with the average about a buck.

Grouse and Brown. #8-10
Cus
Grouse and Green. #12-14
Cus
Grouse and Orange. #10-16
Cus, Edd
Grouse and Tan. #12
Cus
Grouse and Yellow. #12-14
Cus
Iron Blue Dun. #10-16
Edd
Light Brown Caddis Spider. #10-16
Edd
March Brown Spider. #8-16
Dan, Edd

Partridge and Black. #10-16
Kau
Partridge and Brown. #8-14
Cus
Partridge and Claret. #12
Cus
Partridge and Flourescent Green.
#10-14   Hig
Partridge and Hare's Ear. #10-16
Kau
Partridge and Olive. #10-16
Kau, T&T
Partridge and Orange. #6-16
Blu, Big, Kau, Hig, Bud, T&T, Dan,
Cus, Edd

Partridge and Purple. #6-16
Blu
Partridge and Yellow. #8-16
Bud, Hig, Kau, Big, T&T, Dan, Cus,
Edd
Pheasant Tail. #6-16
Hig, Bud, Blu, T&T, Dan, Edd
Pink Indispensable. #6-16
Blu
Snipe and Purple. #10-16
T&T, Edd
Starling and Herl. #10-16
T&T, Edd
Tup's Indispensable. #6-16
Blu, T&T, Edd

NYMPHS

The nymphal forms of aquatic insects are always available to trout and other fish. Only at times of heavy surface activity will the good nymph fisherman find himself in second place to the dry fly user.

So why don't we use nymphs all the time? Well, most of us don't think nymph fishing is as much fun as other kinds of fly fishing. Casting weighted flies and sink-tip lines is neither graceful nor relaxing. Working a run can often seem a lot like working.

However, there is a kind of special anticipation found only in nymphing. If an indicator is used, a lot of time is spent watching it drift downstream. The hook must be set at every hesitation. When it is finally met by the reply of a trout, it's exciting and worth the work.

Part of the excitement may come from the fact that the angler has no idea of the size of the fish he's just taken a strike from. More large trout are taken on nymphs than any other type of fly except perhaps streamers. If you don't usually fish nymphs, try a day on your local stream with nymphs. A whole day. You may be surprised at the size of trout your stream holds.

In my part of the woods, there's very little surface activity in winter, and nymph fishing is one of the best ways to take trout. The year around angler must learn nymph fishing.

There aren't as many nymph patterns as there are dry fly patterns, and fish seem to be less selective when feeding on nymphs than they do when surface feeding. There may be several reasons for that. The light may not be as good, for one thing, but that's hardly a satisfactory explanation for every situation.

One thing is for sure. Fish will inspect many things by

mouthing them, and there are lots of things drifting to a fish below the surface. Any juicy-looking thing is likely to be taken, at least momentarily. Fish do the same when surface feeding, but they are more cautious. All fish have a built-in fear of being near the surface, so they're already nervous. Therefore, they're more careful in what they take. In the secure depths, they take things more freely.

Whatever the reason, many nymph patterns are suggestive. The Gold-Ribbed Hare's Ear, for instance, is basically a roll of fur with a little flash added. It has the look of a real nymph, but it doesn't imitate any natural in particular. Other nymphs are designed to imitate one insect. They're useful when you know a stream well enough to know what insects are in it and which of them may be active.

Interestingly, there are very few attractor nymphs. Since attractor dry flies work so well, this seems odd to me. Maybe someone who thinks more like a trout than I can will enlighten me.

I've separated out the nymphs designed to imitate caddis nymphs and those designed to imitate stonefly nymphs, and they are listed after the general list. Among the remaining flies, there are certainly some that should probably go in these categories, but their names don't give that indication. The rest of the list, then, includes mayfly nymphs, suggestive nymphs, and odds and ends, such as cress bugs and shrimp patterns.

Prices for nymphs range from $.80-$1.40, with some of the more complex patterns costing more. The average is around $1.20.

A. P. Nymphs. #8-18
Mer, Fly, Orv, Bob, Cab, Let, Bud, Nor

Amherst Pheasant Tail. #14-16
Hun

Assam Dragon. #4-6
Bud

Atherton. # 10-16
Edd

Baetis. #16
Edd

Beaver. #10-14
T&T, Kau, H&H, Mer, Cus, Orv, Hun, FOM, Don, Mon, Edd

Big Ugly. #4-6
Hun

Big Wooly. #2-8
Bob

Bird's Nest. #8-10
Fly

Bird's Trout Fly Nymph. #4-10
Dan

Bitch Creek. #2-18
AnJ, Bud, T&T, Dan, Mer, Hig, Kau, Big, Blu, Bob, Orv, Cus

Black Creeper. #8-14
Mer, Cus, Ran

Black Drake Nymph. #12-20
Dan

Black Latex. #10-12
Pen

Black Nymph. #10-16
Blu, T&T, Nor

Black Quill. #8-16
Edd, Nor

Blue Dun. #14
Cus

Blue Quill. #8-18
Edd, Nor, Mur

Blue-Winged Olive. #10-18
Cus, Pen, AnR, Orv, Edd, Nor, Let, Mur, H&H, Don, Mon

Bomber. #8-12
Mer, Fly, Nor, Hun

Breadcrust. #8-16
Dan, Ran, AnR, Big, Orv, Cus, Edd, Nor, Let, H&H, Mon, Don

Brown Drake. #8-12
Dan, Pen, Blu

C.K. Nymph. #12-14
Mur

Carrot Nymph. #10-14
Edd, Don

Casual Dress. #2-14
Dan, Fly, Kau, Hig, Mur, Nor

Cate's Turkey. #14
Kau

Catskill Courier. #10-12
Edd

Copper Nymph. #14-20
AnJ, Dan

Crayfish. #6
Kau

Cream Nymph. #10-16
Nor, AnR

Cream Variant. #10-12
Nor

Cress Bug. #10-18
Let, Mur, AnR, Edd

Damsel Fly Nymph. #6-10
Hig, Bud, Blu, Mur, Str, Dan, Mer, Nor

Dan's Mayfly Nymph. #10-16
Dan

Dark Hendrickson Nymph. #10-16
Mer, Mur, H&H, Big, Cus, Pen, Edd, Nor

Dave's Damsel Nymph. #8-12
Cab, Kau, T&T, Mer, Fly

Dave's Dragonfly. #4-8
Cab, Fly

Dave's Hellgrammite. #4-8
T&T

Dave's Shrimp. #6-14
T&T, Kau, Cab, Fly

Dave's Softshell Crayfish. #1/0-8
Cab, T&T

Dragonfly Nymph. #4-10
Mer, Kau, Mur

Dun Variant. #10-14
Edd, Hun, Don

Ed Burke Nymph. #12-16
Dan

Ed's Brown Fork Tail. #4-10
Dan

El Lobo Nymph. #8-12
Dan

FA Ostrich Nymph. #14-16
Str

FA Ostrich Nymph, extended body.
#6-14
Str

Fledermaus. #4-12
Dan, Hig, Hun, Don, Mer, Edd

Flick's March Brown. #12-14
Hun

Furry Foam Damsel. #10
Big

Gartside Evening Star. #8-14
Blu

Gartside Sparrow. #8-14
Blu

Gartside Yum-Yum. #4-6
Blu

Ginger Quill. #10-14
Pen, AnJ

GIRDLE BUG

Girdle Bug. #2-10
Dan, Mer, Fly, Bob, Blu, Kau, Hig,
Cus, Pen
Gold Latex. #10-12
Pen

HARE'S EAR

Gold-Ribbed Hare's Ear Nymph.
#8-18
Cus, Orv, AnJ, AnR, Bob, Blu, Kau,
Cab, Hig, Let, Pen, Edd, Nor, Bud,
Mur, Egg, T&T, Dan, Mer, Fly
Golden Quill. #8-12
Let
Grannom Pupa. #12-16
H&H, Cus, Nor
Gray Fox. #10-14
Don, Edd
Gray Nymph. #6-18
Dan, Mer, Orv, AnJ, AnR, Kau, Let,
H&H, FOM, Mon, Don, Cus, Edd,
Nor
Gray Rat. #10-14
Ran
Green Drake. #8-14
Cus, Pen, Edd, Nor, Orv, Bob, Blu,
Kau, Bud, Don, Dan, Fly
Half Back. #6-10
Cus, Hig, Ste
Hellgrammite. #4-10
Dan, Hig, Mer
Hendrickson. #12-16
T&T, Mon, Don, Hun, Let, Ran,
AnR, Orv
Hexagenia Nymph. #8
Mer
Isonychia. #10-14
Hun, Don, Edd
Jennings Nymph. #8-12
Nor
Kaufmann Hare's Ear #8-16
Kau
Kelso #10-12
Pen
Lake Dragon. #4-12
Kau
Leadwing Coachman. #8-14
T&T, Edd, Nor, Let, Don, AnR
Light Cahill. #10-16
Mer, T&T, Orv, Big, Kau, Let, Mur,
H&H, Hun, Mon, Cus, Pen, Edd, Nor
Light Hendrickson. #10
Mer
Mahogany. #8-16
Nor

Marabou Damsel. #10-12
Kau
Marabou Nymph. #8-14
Bud, Orv, Nor

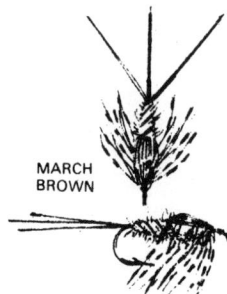

MARCH
BROWN

March Brown. #10-18
Pen, Mer, Cus, Mon, Ste, Hun, H&H,
Mur, Let, Hig, Ran, Cab, Edd, Kau,
Big, Bob, AnR, AnJ, Orv, T&T, Dan
Mar-Lin (scented body). #4
Ste
Martinez Black. #8-14
Fly, Ran, Kau, Hig, Edd
Martinez Mayfly. #12-14
Bud
Matt's Fur. #4-16
Blu, Edd, Kau, Hig, Ste
May Nymph. #8-18
Dan, Cus
Miracle Nymph. #14-18
Dan
Mosquito Larvae. #14-20
Mer, Big, H&H, Don, Cab, Kau, Cus,
Edd
Mossback. #4-12
Dan
Mountain Damsel. #10-12
Kau
Mr. Q.T.. #6-10
Cus
Murray's Hellgrammite. #4-12
Mur
Muskrat. #8-18
Ste, T&T, Mer, Don, H&H, Let, Hig,
Cus, Pen, Edd, Nor, Ran, Big, AnR
Olive Drake Nymph. #12-20
Dan, AnR
Olive Dun. #10-16
T&T, Blu, H&H, Don, Edd
Otter. #8-16
Dan, Don, Ste, H&H, Bud, Let, Big,
AnR, Mer, Cus, Edd, Nor
Pale Evening Dun. #16
Don, Edd
Pheasant Tail. #8-20
Mur, Hun, T&T, Dan, Let, Kau, Big,
Blu, Bob, Fly, Pen

Pheasant Tail Damsel. #10-12
Big
Prince. #8-14
Mon, H&H, Hun, Orv, Big, Kau,
Mer, Fly, Nor
Quill Gordon. #10-16
Mur, FOM, Don, Cus, Pen, Edd, Nor,
Hun, H&H, Orv
Quill Nymph. #14-20
Dan
Rabbit Fur Nymph. #8-14
Bud
Rockworm. #12
Mer
Rubber Legs. #2-6
Kau, Bud
Sawyer Goose Quill. #14-16
Hun
Scuds. #10-20
Dan, Orv, AnR, Big, Kau, Hig, Str,
Edd
Seaweed Crawfish. #8-12
Mer
Shrimp. #4-18
Blu, Bud, Let, Mur, Ste, Dan, Mer
Simulator. #4-12
Kau
Small Dun Variant. #14-16
Edd, Nor
Soufal. #2-4
Bud
Sow Bug. #10-18
Cus, Ste, Bud, Blu
Squirrel Hair. #10-14
Hun
Stenomena. #10-14
Don, Edd
Stickworm. #10
Cus
Sulphur Nymph. #12-18
Mer, Let, Mur, Don, Edd
Tan Drake Nymph. #12-20
Dan
Teeny Nymph. #2-14
Ste
Tellico. #8-18
Cus, Pen, Edd, Nor, Mon, Don,
FOM, H&H, Let, Cab, Kau, Big,
AnJ, Orv, T&T, Dan, Mer
Timberline. #10-16
Kau
Tino (scented body). #10-14
Ste
Trico Nymph. #24
Edd
Trueblood Shrimp. #10-16
Kau, Ran, T&T, Mer

Water Bug. #10-14
Ran
Western Green Drake. #10-12
Big
Wiggle Nymphs, Hexagenia, Damselfly. #6-10
Dan, Mer
Yuk Bug. #2-6
Bob, Kau
Zug Bug. #8-18
Ran, Cus, Hig, Let, Mon, Don, FOM, Ste, Hun, H&H, Pen, Edd, Nor, Cab, Kau, Big, Blu, Bob, AnR, AnJ, Orv, T&T, Mer, Fly

Caddis Nymphs

Caddis Creeper. #10-14
Ran
Caddis Larva. #10-18
Str, Don, H&H, Hun, Hig, Kau, Big, Cus, Pen, Edd, Nor, Dan, Mer
Caddis Pupa. #10-18
Big, AnR, AnJ, Cus, Nor, Pen, Kau, Cab, Let, Mur, Hun, Str
Case Caddis. #6-16
T&T, Ste, Mer, Nor
Colorado Caddis. #12
Cus
Cro Caddis. #8-10
Fly
Gill-Ribbed Caddis Larva. #8-18
Bud, Dan, Edd
Great Brown Sedge. #8-12
H&H, Nor
Humped Caddis Larva. #12-20
Blu
LaFontaine Caddis Larva. #10-16
Kau, T&T, Mer, Fly
LaFontaine Deep Sparkle Pupa. #12-18
T&T, Cab, Hig, Bud, Kau, Blu, Mer
LaFontaine Diving Caddis. #12
Mer
Latex Caddis Larva. #12-18
Mer, Cus, Let, Ran, Bud, Ste, Pen, Edd
Latex Caddis Pupa. #8-16
Kau
Little Sand Sedge. #14-16
Nor, Mur, H&H
Micro Caddis Pupa. #18-22
Kau
Olive Sedge. #14-16
H&H, Cus, Nor
Peeking Caddis. #10-14
Bud

Philo Caddis Pupa. #12-16
Bud, Blu
Skunk Hair Caddis. #6-8
Bud
Speckled Sedge. #14-16
Nor, H&H
Trueblood's Caddis. #12-14
Don, Edd

Stonefly Nymphs

A.G. Curved Giant Stonefly. #2-4
Big
Bird's Stonefly. #4-10
Dan, Mer, Hig
Black Stonefly. #2-12
Hun, Mer, Pen, Bud, Let, Big, Orv, Edd, Nor
Box Canyon Stonefly. #2-8
Hig
Brad's Salmonfly. #2-6
Fly

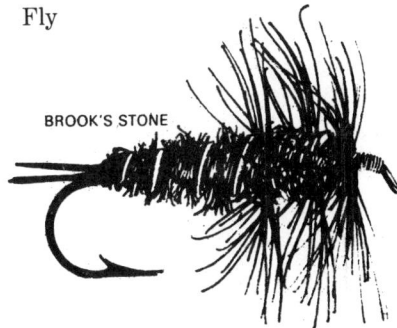
BROOK'S STONE

Brooks Stonefly Nymph. #2-8
Mur, Bud, Kau, Big, Blu, Bob, Dan
Brownstone. #6-10
Bud
Dave's Stonefly. #2-12
Cab, T&T
Drifting Stone. #2-8
Bob, Bud
Early Black Stonefly. #10-14
AnR, T&T, H&H, Don, Edd, Nor
Early Brown Stonefly. #10-16
Str, T&T, H&H, AnR, Mer, Nor
Emerging Stonefly. #8-12
AnJ
Flick's Stonefly. #10-12
Edd
Furry Foam Grove's Stonefly. #2-4
Big
George's Brown Stonefly Nymph. #4-14
Bud, Dan
Golden Stonefly. #4-14
Dan, Fly, Ran, Str, Hun, Hig, Let, H&H, Nor
Kaufmann Dark Stone. #2-4
Fly

Kaufmann Stone. #2-12
Kau
Latex Stonefly. #10-18
Cus, Pen
Light Stonefly. #10-12
Pen
Little Stonefly. #10-14
Edd, H&H, Blu, AnR, Nor

MONTANA

Montana Nymph. #2-12
Orv, AnJ, AnR, Bob, Blu, Big, Kau, Cab, Hig, Cus, Pen, Edd, Nor, Let, Bud, H&H, Hun, Ste, Don, Mon, T&T, Dan, Mer
Norm's Stone. #4-6
Ste
Perla Stonefly. #8-12
Pen, H&H, Nor
Stone Rubber Legs. #4
Bud
Stonefly. #4-18
Dan, Mer, Cus, Edd, Mur, Str, Bud, Let, Hig, Ran, Big, Bob, Orv
Swannundaze Stonefly. #2-14
Blu, Nor
Ted's Stonefly. #6-12
Mer, Orv, AnR, Kau, Let, H&H, Don, Mon, Edd, Nor
Troth Stonefly. #2-6
Pen, Blu

DRIFTING STONE

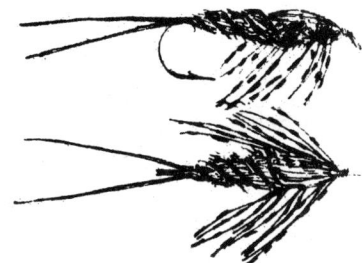

STREAMERS

Few of us fish streamers as often as we should. We seem to reserve them for the big rivers and the big fish. I wonder, however, if we might not take more big fish from the neighborhood stream if we fished it thoroughly with a streamer. Might be an interesting experiment.

I became convinced about streamers one evening in Yellowstone National Park. I'd just met Bob Lewis who was guiding for Bob Jacklin then and most likely still is. I gave his partner a trip back to their car, and Bob gave me a tip in return. The trip was short, the tip was good, and that's probably the last time I'll get the better of Bob in a trade.

Anyway, Bob told me to go to a particular spot in a river I'd fished a few times. He gave me specific instructions: go at dusk, use a Black Wooly Bugger and a stout leader, cast into the pool I'd find there, and watch out. Now, I was skeptical, having followed many a wild trout chase to no avail. The river he sent me to had not been good to me. I'd caught fish, but most were about as long as the streamer I'd now be using.

It only took two casts to find out that Bob Lewis knew of which he spoke. On the second cast (the first good one), I took a 17" brown. I was amazed. My dry flies during the day were attracting 5" trout, but the streamer at dusk . . . I took two more big fellas in next 20 minutes

of fishing before dark and bear-fright set in. It was almost too easy.

Enough story telling. Go fish with streamers and get your own stories.

Typical streamer patterns range in price from $.95-$1.75 with the average being about $1.50. Some patterns, such as sculpins, require more time and materials. They may cost up to $4. Dave Whitlock's patterns are also more expensive, ranging from about $2 to $2.50. They are listed here under the prefix "Dave's" although you may also find them under Whitlock's or Whit's in the catalogs.

Streamers, more than any other type of fly, seem to be divided into eastern and western patterns. A western angler might not be able to pick a Col. Bates out of a line up, and an eastern angler might be offended by a Zonker. I think you'll see what I mean based upon your own geographical prejudice and on which catalogs offer which patterns. However, on any given day, as they say, any streamer may catch fish in any stream.

I've grouped some of the patterns together. This makes it convenient to see what leech patterns there are on the market, but it may mean you miss a streamer you're looking for in its regular alphabetical order. Keep looking. If you like streamers and enjoy unusual patterns, try the catalog from Eddie's Flies. They seem to have more streamers than anyone and many of them are exclusive patterns.

Aztec. #4-10
Let
Badger. #4-8
AnR
Ballou Special. #2-10
Hun, Edd
Barnes Special. #2-12
AnR, Ran, Hun, Edd
Black and White. #6-12
Ran
Black Ghost. #2-10
Mer, Pen, Nor, Edd, AnR, Big, Ran, Let, H&H, Hun, Mon, Orv, T&T, Dan
Black Ghost Marabou. #2-12
Edd, Ran
Black-Nosed Dace. #2-14
Cus, Pen, Don, Hun, H&H, Mur, Edd, Nor, Let, Ran, Cab, Kau, Big, AnR, Orv, T&T, Dan, Mer
Bloody Butcher. #6-10
Cus
Blue and White. #6-12
Big
Brown Bear. #8-10
Mer
Brown Ghost. #2-6
Don
Cains River. #2-10
Don

Cardinelle. #6-10
Mer, AnR
Chief Needahbeh. #2-10
Edd
Chub Streamer. #2-6
Blu
Col. Bates. #2-10
Edd
Dave's Golden Shiner Prismatic. #2-6
Cab, T&T
Dave's Shad Prismatic. #2-6
T&T, Cab, Mur
Dave's Silver Shiner Prismatic. #2-6
Cab, T&T
Dusty Streamer. #2-10
Don
Edson Tiger, Dark. #2-12
Mer, Edd, Ran, AnR, Hun
Edson Tiger, Light. #2-12
Dan, AnR, Ran, Hun, Edd
Erskine. #2-10
Edd
Frank Smith Special. #6-12
Ran
Frenchman's Delight. #4-12
Edd
Frost Rainbow-Alewive. #6-10
Ran

Golden Darter. #4-10
Mer, H&H, Nor
Golden Head. #2-10
Edd
Golden Rogan. #2-4
Don
Golden Witch. #2-10
Edd
Gov. Aiken. #2-12
Big, Ran, Edd
Grand Lake Special. #2-10
Edd
Gray Ghost. #2-14
Mer, Cus, Nor, Edd, AnR, Big, Kau, Cab, Ran, Let, Mur, H&H, Hun, Don, Orv, T&T, Dan
Gray Ghost Marabou. #2-12
Ran, Edd
Gray Tiger. #6-12
Ran
Green Ghost. #2-12
AnR, Big, Ran, Hun, Mer, Edd
Green King. #2-10
Edd
Grizzly Bear. #8-10
Pen
Grizzly King. #2-12
Edd, Ran
Hornberg. #4-16
Hun, H&H, Ran, Kau, AnR, T&T,

Dan, Mer, Edd
Hurricane. #2-10
Edd
Jane Craig. #2-12
Edd, Ran
Janssen Baby Bass. #1-4
Cab
Janssen Baby Brook. #4-8
Cab, Fly
Janssen Baby Brown. #4-10
Cab
Janssen Baby Rainbow. #4-8
Fly, Cab
Janssen Olive Back Shad. #1-10
Cab
Janssen Threadfin Shad. #1-8
Orv, Cab, Fly
Jay's Grizzly Minnow. #2-10
Hig
Lady Ghost. #2-10
Edd
Leech, Davis. #6-8
Fly
Leech, Flashabou. #3/0
Big
Leech, Fur. #4-8
Mur

JACKLIN'S LEECH

Leech, Jacklin's. #8-12
Bob
Leech, Marabou. #2-6
Orv, Blu, Kau, Cab, Hig Leech,
Matuka Marabou. #2-4
Fly
Leech, Mohair. #4
Pen
Leech, Stripper. #2-8
Big
Leech, Wooly. #8
Kau
Liggett's Special. #2-10
Edd
Little Brook Trout. #2-12
Big, Kau, Mer, Pen, Edd, Nor, AnR,
Let, Dan
Little Brown Trout. #2-12
Dan, AnR, Big, Mer, Cus, Pen, Edd,
Kau, Let
Little Catfish. #2-10
Edd
Little Rainbow Trout. #2-12
Cus, Pen, Edd, Nor, AnR, Big, Kau,
Let, Dan, Mer

Llama. #4-8
AnR
Lucky Lady. #2-10
Edd
Male Dace. #2-10
Dan
Mansfield. #6-12
Ran
Marabou. #6-10
Mur, H&H, Let, Ran, Big, Ran,
AnR, Cus, Pen
Marabou Bullethead. #2-6
Blu
Marabou Mini-Jig
Hig
Marion Marabou. #1-6
Dan
Matuka. #2-12
Mer, Fly, Pen, Nor, AnR, Blu, Kau,
Cab, Hig, Let, Bud, Mur, H&H, Hun,
Don, Orv, T&T, Dan
Maynard's Marvel. #2-4
Hun
Mickey Finn. #2-14
Cus, Pen, Edd, Nor, AnR, Blu, Big,
Kau, Cab, Ran, Let, Bud, Mur,
H&H, Hun, Mon, Don, Orv, T&T,
Dan, Mer
Miss Sharon. #2-10
Edd
Missoulian Spook. #2-8
Bud, Mer
Monty's Fur Bullhead. #6-8
Mon
Moose River. #2-10
Edd

MUDDLER

Muddler, Minnow. #1-16
Cus, AnJ, AnR, Bob, Blu, Big, Pen,
Edd, Nor, Kau, Cab, Ran, Hig, Egg,
Let, Bud, Orv, T&T, Dan, Fly, Mer,
Mon, Hun, H&H, Mur
Muddler, Brookie. #2-10
Edd
Muddler, Carzy. #6
Big
Muddler, Dragonfly Nymph. #2-12
Edd
Muddler, Flashabou. #1/0-6
Cab, Kau, Big

Muddler, Hornberg. #8-12
Edd
Muddler, Kiwi. #4-6
Big

MARIBOU MUDDLER

Muddler, Marabou. #1-12
Fly, Pen, Edd, Nor, Mon, Hun,
H&H, Mur, Bud, Let, Hig, Cab, Kau,
Big, Blu, Bob, AnR, Orv, T&T, Dan,
Mer
Muddler, Marabou, Varicolored.
#1/0-6
Kau, Bud, Blu
Muddler, Mini-Jig
Hig
Muddler, Monty's Fur #6-8
Mon
Muddler, Trout Fin. #2-10
Edd
Muddler, Zebra. #2-10
Edd
Mylar Integration. #2-10
Dan
Mylar Mickey Finn. #2-10
Dan
Mylar Silver Doctor. #2-10
Dan
Mylar, Brown, Green, and White.
#2-10
Dan
Nine-Three. #2-12
Ran, Hun, Big, AnR, T&T, Mer, Edd
Parmachene Belle. #2-12
Edd, Ran
Pink Lady. #2-12
Ran, Edd
Platte River (aka Bighorn) Special.
#2-12
Cus, Bob, Big, Bud
Professor. #6-12
Ran
Queen Bee. #2-10
Edd
Rabbit Fly. #2-6
Bud
Rabbit Streamer. #2-12
Big, Ran, Edd

Red Gray Ghost. #2-12
Ran, Hun, AnR
Red-Belly Dace. #4-12
Edd
Rogan Royal Gray Ghost. #2-4
Don
Royal Coachman. #2-12
Pen, Edd, Nor, Cus, Big, Kau, Ran,
Hig, Let, Bud, H&H, Orv, T&T,
Dan, Mer
Sculpin. #2-14
Cus, Hig, Big, Hun
Sculpin, Bighorn. #1-2
Bud
Sculpin, Blue Ribbon. #1/0-6
Blu, Bud
Sculpin, Dave's. #1/0-8
T&T, Kau, Cab, Mur, Nor, Mer
Sculpin, Matuka. #1/0-6
T&T, Orv, AnR, Kau, Mon, Nor, Fly
Sculpin, Matuka Marabou. #2-4
Fly
Sculpin, Partridge. #1/0-6
Kau
Sculpin, Pheasant. #1/0-8
Blu
Sculpin, Shenk's. #4-8
Let, Mur
Sculpin, Woolhead. #3/0
Bud
Sen. Muskie. #2-10
Edd
Shenk's White Streamer. #4-6
Mur
Silver Darter. #6-10
H&H, Mer, Nor
Silver Doctor. #2-12
Mer, Edd
Silver Minnow. #8-10
Mer, Cus
Smelt, Andy's. #6-12
Ran
Smelt, Blue. #2-12
Ran, Edd

Smelt, Earl's Gray. #2-10
Edd
Smelt, Eddie's Ripogenus. #2-10
Edd
Smelt, Frost Blue. #4-12
Ran
Smelt, Joe's. #2-10
Edd
Smelt, Kennebago. #2-10
Edd
Smelt, Magog. #2-10
Edd
Smelt, Montabou. #6-8
Mon
Smelt, Penhead. #10
Mer
Smelt, Purple. #10
Mer
Smelt, Thunder Creek. #6-8
Hun
Smelt, Winnipesaukee. #2-8
Hun
Spencer Bay Special. #2-10
Edd
Spruce, Dark. #1-10
Dan, Mer, Pen, Bob, Blu, Big, Kau,
Hig, Let, Bud, Mur
Spruce, Light. #1-10
Mer, Cus, Pen, Nor, Don, Bud, Let,
Hig, Kau, Big, Blu, Bob, AnR, Dan
Spuddler. #1/0-14
Blu, Kau, Hig, Bud, Mur, Dan, Mer,
Cus
Squirrel Tail. #8-12
Ran, Orv, Mer, Edd
Streaker. #2-10
Edd
Supervisor. #2-12
Mer, Edd, AnR, Hun, Don, Ran, Big
Thunder Creek, Black-Nosed Dace.
#4-8
Orv, Mer, AnR, Hun
Thunder Creek, Golden Shiner.
#4-8

Hun, AnR, Orv, Mer
Thunder Creek, Mickey Finn. #6-8
AnR
Thunder Creek, Rainbow Trout.
#6-8
Mer
Thunder Creek, Red Fin Shiner.
#4-8
AnR, Orv
Thunder Creek, Silver Shiner. #4-8
Orv, Mer, AnR
Thunder Creek, Smelt. #6-8
Hun
Tom's Special A.A.. #2-10
Edd
Tri-Color. #2-12
Ran, Edd
Troth Bullhead. #3/0-6
Blu, Kau, Bud
Trout Fin. #8-12
Edd, Ran
Warden's Worry. #4-12
Ran, Edd
Waterman's Silver Outcast. #4-6
Mur
Whitefish Streamer. #2-6
Blu
Wooly Bugger. #2-10
Fly, Cus, Orv, Bob, Blu, Big, Kau,
Pen, Nor, Hig, Let, Bud, Mur, Hun,
T&T, Dan, Mer
Wooly Worm Mini-Jig
Hig
Yellow Perch. #2-10
Blu, Bud, Big, Mer, Edd
York's Kennebago. #4-12
Ran
Zonker. #2-8
Fly, Bud, Mur, Hig, Kau, Big, Bob,
AnR

MIDGES

Midges or Chironomid are an interesting trout food. So miniscule are they that it's a wonder that a trout would go out of its way to munch one. But I guess we humans will eat chocolate chips when no chocolate chip cookies are available.

Trout feed on midges under two common situations. In winter and early spring, there are no other insects as active as midges. They represent a major source of food. At other times of the year, there may be so many midges hatching that scooping them up by the mouthful becomes possible, and trout will feed on them.

I've seen this latter phenomenon happen on the Firehole in mid-summer. The Tiny Whites, as I call them, hatch so thickly that trout line up, cafeteria style, with their snouts out of the water, letting the current deliver dinner to them. If you can get your fly on the assembly line, you can do well, very well.

Midge fishing is tough. It requires fine leaders, fine presentation, and fine eyesight. It's often rewarding, however, and sometimes it's the only thing that will work.

Prices for midges range from $.90-$1.40.

Adams Midge. #18-28
Cus, Pen, Edd, Nor, Hig, H&H, Mon,
T&T, Mer, Fly
Black Gnat Midge. #20-24
H&H, Mer, Cus
Black Midge. #20-28
Cus, Pen, Orv, AnJ, Blu, Edd, Nor,
Cab, Hig, Let, H&H, Hun, Mon,
T&T, Mer, Fly
Blue Dun Midge. #18-28
Orv, Cab, Hig, Mon, T&T, Mer
Blue Quill Midge. #20-22
Edd
Blue-Winged Olive Midge. #20-24
Edd
Brown Midge. #16-28
Cus, Pen, Edd, Nor, Hig, Bud, H&H,
T&T, Dan, Mer
Caenis. #20-26
Let, H&H, Hun, Mon, Cus, Nor
Cinnamon Midge. #20
Mer
Coachman Midge. #18

Mer
Cream Midge. #16-28
Orv, AnJ, Blu, Fly, Cus, Edd, Nor,
Cab, Let, Bud, H&H, Hun, Mon,
T&T, Mer
Dark Cahill Midge. #20
Mer
Dun Midge. #20-24
Cus, H&H
Ginger Midge. #20d-24
Cus, H&H
Ginger Quill Midge. #18
Mer
Golden Midge. #18-22
Hig
Gray Hackle Peacock. #20-28
Let
Gray Midge. #16-24
Dan, Mer, Pen, AnJ, Blu, Hig, Bud,
Hun, Mon
Green Midge. #10-14
Ran
Grizzly Midge. #16-22
Dan, Mer

Light Cahill Midge. #18-24
Mer, Pen
Midge Nymph. #12-26
Kau, Let, Bud, Dan
Midge Pupa. #14-26
T&T, Dan, Pen, Edd, Big, Kau, Let,
Bud
Mosquito Midge. #20-24
Mer, Hun
No Name Midge. #20-28
Let
Olive Midge. #20-28
Mer, Cus, Pen, Edd, Orv, AnJ, Blu,
Cab, Bud, H&H, Mon, T&T
Red Midge. #16-20
Blu
Sulphur Dun Midge. #18
Mer
Tan Midge. #20
Mer
Yellow Midge. #20
Mer

EMERGERS

No matter what game you're playing, if it's a good one, it will have many levels to it. Fly fishing is a good one, and one of the "levels" that many fly fishermen have recently discovered is the surface film, that place in the water where all sorts of wonderful things happen.

Among those things happening in the film is the hatching of stream-born insects, particularly mayflies, caddis, and midges. In the transformation from nymph/pupa to adult, insects are very easy targets for trout. Precious seconds go by as nymphal husks are split to reveal flying insects, and in that time span, those emerging insects are helpless. Trout love it.

Emerger patterns are simply nymphs with some protuberance representative of wings unfolding. The protuberance may be a simple ball of polypropylene or a pair of hackle tips. The fly is tied to float, but it floats low since it generally has no supporting hackle.

This can be a killer fly when the hatch is on. Since emergers are easier targets than adult insects, this fly is often the choice of the trout (and the experienced angler).

There's not much romance here. The flies are simple, as are their names. Nobody's name is associated with particular patterns, with one exception. Gary LaFontaine's caddis emerger is one of the most popular flies here.

Color and size are the critical choices, as they are in other fly selections. You'd do well to have a wide selection for those times when fish are rising to the hatch but traditional dries don't seem to work.

Prices for emergers range from $.82-$1.65 with the average price about $1.20.

Black Floating Nymph. #14-18
Kau
Blue-Winged Olive, cutwing. #14
Str
Brown Drake Emerger. #10-14
Blu
Brown Drake, cutwing. #8
Str
Brown Floating Nymph. #14-18
Hig, Bud, Kau
Chironomid (midge) Emerger.
#16-20
Orv
Cream Floating Nymph. #14-16
Nor

Green Drake Cripples. #12
Mer
Gray Floating Nymph. #14-16
Kau, Nor
Green Drake. #10-14
Blu
Hendrickson. #12-16
Edd
Hendrickson, cutwing. #14
Str
LaFontaine Emergent Sparkle Pupa. #12-16
Blu, Kau, Cab, Hig, T&T, Fly
Loop Wing Emerger. #14-20
Dan

Mayfly Emerger . #10-18
Blu, Bud, Orv, FOM
Mosquito Emerger. #14-18
Kau, Orv
Mr. Rapidan Emerger . #10-14
Mur
Olive Floating Nymph. #14-18
Hig, Bud, Nor
Orange Caddis Emerger. #8
Fly
Paranymph . #16-18
Mer, Fly
Slate/Brown Floating Nymph.
#10-22
Edd, Let

Slate/Olive Floating Nymph. #18-24
Let, Edd
Slate/Tan Floating Nymph. #8-12
Edd, Let
Slate/Yellow Floating Nymph.
#14-18
Let
Sparkle Dun. #10-20
Blu

Sparkle Floating Nymph. #10-20
Blu
Tan Floating Nymph. #14-18
Bud
Timberline Emerger. #12-16
Kau
W.B. Caddis Emerger. #8-20
Edd
Western Green Drake, cutwing. #10

Str
Western Pale Morning Dun,
cutwing. #14-16
Str
Yellow Floating Nymph. #14-18
Hig, Kau, Nor
Yellow/Brown Floating Nymph.
#16-22
Edd

SPINNERS

Spinners represent mayflies in their final form as food for trout. After hatching, molting, and mating, mayflies often die over the water. They fall to the surface, their wings outstretched. This spent-wing profile is what the spinner (not to be confused with the Mepps variety) imitates.

SPINNERS

Spinners are often a good choice when mayfly mating swarms are over the water. They seem to work best late in the day or early in the morning. The riseform associated with spinner falls is more subtle than the often splashy rise to adults; the fish are in no hurry to get to the inactive spinners. When the fish are sipping, try a spinner.

These patterns are very simple—a tail, a body and the wings. Wings are tied with several materials, and each material has its following. Most common is polypropylene yarn. The material floats well, and the pattern of the individual fibers on the water suggests the veining in mayfly wings.

Hackle wings are made from hackle fibers pulled from the hackle stem and bunched together. Hen-winged spinners have relatively wide, round hackle tips which suggest the natural insect's wing. Iwamasa style wings utilize cut or burnt wings.

In rough water, deer hair is a good material. Outline is not as important, and the added flotation will help keep the fly on the surface. None of the flies listed here were described as having hair wings.

I've assumed the spinners have poly wings, unless the catalog listed them as having one of the other styles. Prices range from $.92-$1.50. The average price is about $1.20.

Amber Spinner. #8-18
Edd
Black Spinner. #16-22
T&T, Dan, Fly
Brown Drake Spinner, Iwamasa
style, extended body. #8
T&T
Brown Drake Spinner. #12-14
Nor
Brown Spinner. #14-20
Bud, AnR
Callibaetis Spinner, hackle wing.
#16
Orv
Callibaetis Spinner, hen wing.
#14-16
Kau
Callibaetis Spinner. # 16
Mon
Callibaetis Spinner, Iwamasa style.
#16
Kau, Str
Cream Spinner. #8-26
AnR, Let, T&T, Edd

Dun/Brown Spinner, hen wing.
#14-18
T&T, Hig, Kau
Dun/Cream Spinner, hen wing.
#14-18
T&T, Kau, Hig
Gray Spinner. #16-22
Dan, Let
Green Drake Spinner, hackle wing.
#10
Orv
Green Drake Spinner, Iwamasa
style, extended body. #6
T&T
Green Drake Spinner. #12-14
Nor
Hen Wing Spinners. #14-18
T&T
Hexagenia Spinner, Iwamasa style,
extended body. #4
T&T
Loopwing Spinner. #12
Mer
Mahogany Spinner, hackle wing.

#10-18
Let, Orv
Olive Quill Spinner. #16-18
Fly
Olive Spinner. #8-28
Blu, Bud, Let, Mon, T&T, Dan, Edd
Pale Olive Spinner, hackle wing.
#16-18
Orv
Pale Sulphur Spinner, hackle wing.
#16
Orv
Partridge Spinner, hen wing.
#16-18
Kau, T&T
Reddish Brown Spinner. #8-22
T&T, Edd
Rusty Brown Spinner. #16-20
Fly
Rusty Spinner, hackle wing. #14-20
Orv
Rusty Spinner, hen wing. #18-20
Kau
Rusty Spinner. #14-22

Dan, Nor, Mon, Let, AnR
Rusty Spinner, Iwamasa style.
#14-18
Str, Kau
Slate/Olive Spinner, hen wing.
#16-20
T&T, Kau
Speckled Spinner. #16-18
Nor
Sulphur Spinner. #16-18

AnR
Tan Spinner. #8-22
Let, Dan
Trico Spinner, hackle wing. #20-24
Let, Orv
Trico Spinner. #18-26
AnR, Blu, Bud, Mur, Mon, Orv, Let, Mer, Edd
Trico Spinner, Iwamasa style. #20
Str, Kau

White/Black Spinner, hackle wing.
#20-24
Orv
White/Black Spinner, hen wing.
#18-22
Hig, Kau, T&T
White/Yellow Spinner, hen wing.
#18-20
T&T

STEELHEAD FLIES

Steelhead fishing is something like a Western rendition of salmon fishing. Most of the flies are wet flies with only a few dry patterns. The flies are generally colorful, as are salmon flies.

A list of steelhead flies can be divided into summer flies and winter flies. I don't have the experience to do that, but here's Stewart Custom Tackle's division.

Summer patterns: Mack's Canyon, Dark Mack's, Stewart, Skunk, Juicy Bug, Del Cooper, Dr. Spratley, Purple Peril, Buck Coachman.

Winter patterns: Fall Favorite, Sandy Favorite, Marmot Special, Skykomish Sunrise, Polar Shrimp, Orange Shrimp, Babine Special, Orange Comet, Steelhead Shrimp, Pink Lady.

Prices range from $.82-$1.85, but the extremes are uncommon. Most steelhead flies cost between $1.25 and $1.50. Many catalogs offer steelhead flies, but Kaufmann's, Blue Ribbon Flies, and Stewart have the most patterns and the most unusual patterns. The list is divided here into wet flies and dry flies.

Steelhead Wet Flies

Babine Special. #1-8
Blu, Big, Kau, Dan, Mer, Fly, Edd, Bud, Ste, Don, T&T
Badger Hackle Peacock. #2-10
Blu
Battle Creek Special. #2-8
Fly
Black Bastard. #1-8
Dan
Black Prince. #2-8
Edd, Blu, Don, Kau, Nor
Black Wooly Worm. #2-6
Kau
Boss. #2-8
T&T, Fly, Blu, Kau
Brad's Brat. #2-8
T&T, Don, Blu, Kau, Edd
Bright Roe. #2-8
Blu, Kau
Brindle Bug. #2-10
Edd, Kau, Blu, Don
Buck Coachman. #2-6
Ste
Burlap. #2-10
Fly, Bud, Kau, Blu
Coachman. #2-10
Blu
Coal Car. #6
Kau
Comet. #1-8
H&H, Ste, Dan, Cus, Kau, Blu

Cowichan. #6-8
Dan
Dark Gordon. #1-8
Dan
Dark Mack's. #2-6
Ste
Dark Montreal. #2-6
Bud
Dead Chicken. #2-10
Blu
Dean River Special. #2-8
Blu
Del Cooper. #2-6
Ste
Deschutes Demon. #4
Mer
Doctor Rex. #4
Mer
Dr. Sprately. #2-6
Ste
Fall Favorite. #1-8
Mer, Fly, Cus, Edd, Ste, H&H, Don, Kau, Blu, T&T, Dan
Flat Car. #6
Kau
Freight Train. #2-8
Kau, Blu
Hex Nymph. #2-10
Blu
Juicy Bug. #2-12
Ste, Kau
Kispiox. #2-8

Kau, Blu
Lady Coachman. #2-10
Blu
Mack's Canyon. #2-8
Ste, Blu, Kau, T&T
Marabou. #2-6
Kau
Marabou Egg Sack. #2-10
Blu, Bud
Marmot Special. #2-6
Ste
McLeod Ugly. #1-10
Dan, Blu, Bud
Mossback. #4-8
Fly
Muddler Minnow. #2-10
Big, Blu, Kau, Cab, Don, Edd
October Caddis. #2-8
Don, Edd
Orange Demon. #1-8
H&H, Dan, Cus
Orange Shrimp. #2-6
Ste
Pink Lady. #2-6
Ste
Polar Shrimp. #1/0-8
T&T, Dan, Fly, Edd, Blu, Cab, Kau, Ste, Don
Princeton Tiger. #2-8
Cus, H&H
Purple Peril. #2-8
Mer, Edd, Big, Ste, Kau, Don, Blu

Red Ant. #6
Kau
Royal Coachman. #1-10
T&T, Dan, Blu, Kau, Cab, H&H,
Don, Cus, Edd
Sandy Favorite. #2-6
Ste
Silver Comet. #4-6
Big, Fly
Silver Hilton. #2-8
Blu, Big, Kau, Don, Mer, Fly, Edd
Single Egg. #2-10
T&T, Blu, Big, Kau, Mer, Fly
Skunk. #1-10
Fly, Cus, Nor, Edd, Blu, Big, Kau,
Cab, Bud, H&H, Ste, Don, T&T,
Dan, Mer
Skunk, Green Butt. #1/0-8
T&T, Mer, Cab, Don, Kau, Fly
Skunk, Red Butt. #2-6
Kau
Skykomish Sunrise. #12-10
Ste, Don, H&H, Fly, Cus, Nor, Edd,
Bud, Cab, Kau, Big, Flu, T&T, Dan,
Mer
Spring Nymph. #4-6
Mer

Spring Wiggler. #2-10
Blu, Mer
Spruce. #2-8
Blu, Kau, Don, Edd
Steelhead Shrimp. #2-6
Ste
Stewart. #2-6
Ste
Stilliguamish. #2-8
Edd, Don, Kau, Blu
Thor. #2-8
Mer, Fly, Edd, Nor, Blu, Big, Kau
don, T&T
Two Egg. #2-10
Blu, Bud, Mer
Umpqua Special #2-8
T&T, Mer, Cus, Nor, H&H, Cab,
Kau, Blu
Winter's Hope. #3/0
Kau

Grizzly Wulff, #4-8
T&T
Goddard Caddis. #4-8
T&T
Grease Liner. #4-8
Kau, T&T
Humpy. #4-8
Kau, T&T
Irresistible. #4-8
T&T, Kau
Muddler, low water. #4-8
T&T
Royal Humpy. #4-8
T&T
Royal Wulff. #4-8
Kau, T&T
Steelhead Bee. #6
Kau
Steelhead Caddis. #6
Kau

Steelhead Dry Flies

Black Wulff. #4-8
Kau, T&T
Bomber. #4-6
T&T, Kau

SALMON FLIES

Salmon flies are a bit out of my league, there being few salmon in Fish Creek. Tying them is also out of my league. So, if my brief introduction seems elementary, that's because it is.

Traditional salmon flies are fished wet. The prettiest ones are featherwing or feather-and-hair mixed wings. Many fishermen prefer the more durable, less expensive hairwing flies. Often the flies will be offered in either single hook or double hook. Low water flies are tied half-shank on single hooks. Dry flies are also used for Atlantic salmon. Most of these patterns are large renditions of flies you may recognize, such as the Wulff series.

Unfortunately, many of the catalogs don't bother to tell whether their salmon flies are featherwings or hairwings. Many patterns are one or the other, but several are tied either way. For the beginning salmon fisherman, this is unfortunately confusing. For the purposes of dividing up the list, I've assumed the flies are hairwings unless described otherwise. The list is divided into three categories: featherwing and mixed wing, hairwing, and salmon dry flies.

In this section, I've included prices for each fly. You'll find some astounding ranges, partly because I may have misclassified some flies and partly because there's a great deal of difference between a high quality salmon fly tied to original specifications with original materials and a production fly tied for expediency. Blind eye flies, for instance, are tied to authentic specifications on eyeless hooks common to previous times. They are offered by Max MacPherson (see introduction to this chapter) whose catalog you need if you are interested in salmon flies. Other catalogs of interest are Donegal's, Hunter's, and Eddie's.

Featherwing and Mixed-Wing Salmon Flies

Akroyd. #5/0-2/0
$10 Max
Alexandra. #5/0-1/0
$8 Max
Autumn Creeper. #5/0-2/0
$10 Max
Badger. #5/0-1/0
$8 Max

Baron. #7/0-4
$8-$15 Max, Don
Benchill. #5/0-4
$8-$11 Max
Berrington's Favorite. #5/0-1/0
$8 Max
Black Doctor. #7/0-4
$8-$15 Don, Max
Black Doctor, blind eye. #4/0
$15 Max

Black Dog, blind eye. #4/0
$15 Max
Black Dose. #5/0-10
$3.50-$11 Let, Pen, Edd, Max, Hun,
T&T, Dan
Black Fairy. #1-12
$2.20-$3 Let, Edd
Black Labrador. #2/0-8
$2.75-$3.25 Hun
Black Ranger. #7/0-4

$8-$15 Don, Max
Black Spean, low water. #1/0-4
$2.50 Max
Blue and Yellow Wasp, low water.
#1/0-4
$2.50 Max
Blue Charm. #5/0-12
$1.75-$11 Max, Ran, Orv, Dan, Pen,
Edd
Blue Charm, low water. #1/0-4
$2.50 Max
Blue Doctor. #5/0-4
$8-$11 Max
Bumbee. #5/0-1/0
$8 Max
Candlestick Maker. #5/0-1/0
$8 Max
Carron. #5/0-2/0
$10 Max
Childers. #7/0-4
$8-$15 Don, Max
Claret Alder, low water. #1/0-4
$2.50 Max
Crimson Glory. #5/0-4
$8-$11 Max
Dreadnought. #5/0-1/0
$8 Max
Durham Ranger. #7/0-4
$8-$15 Max, Don
Dusty Miller. #7/0-12
$2-$15 Don, Max, Pen, Edd
Eden Bulldog, blind eye. #4/0
$15 Max
Gordon. #7/0-4
$8-$15 Don, Max
Green Highlander. #7/0-8
$3.50-$15 Max, Pen, Edd, Hun, Don,
Orv, T&T, Dan
Green Highlander, blind eye. #4/0
$15 Max
Green Queen. #5/0-1/0
$8 Max
Horse Leech Fly. #4/0
$20 Max
Jimmie. #5/0-1/0
$8 Max
Jimmie, low water. #1/0-4
$2.50 Max
Jock Scott. #7/0-8
$2.75-$15 Max, Pen, Edd, Don, Hun,
Let, T&T, Dan
Jock Scott, blind eye. #4/0
$15 Max
Jockie. #5/0-1/0
$8 Max
Joe Brady. #5/0-1/0
$8 Max

Kate. #5/0-4
$8-$11 Max
Kate, blind eye. #4/0
$15 Max
Lady Amherst. #7/0-8
$2.50-$15 T&T, Edd, Don
Lady Caroline. #5/0-2/0
$10 Max
Lady Grace. #5/0-1/0
$8 Max
Logie. #5/0-12
$2.20-$8 Max, Edd
Logie, low water. #1/0-4
$2.50 Max
Mar Lodge. #7/0-8
$2.75-$15 Edd, Don
Mar Lodge, blind eye. #4/0
$15 Max
Miss Amherst. #5/0-4
$8-$11 Max
Moonlight. #5/0-2/0
$10 Max
Muddler. #6/0-10
$1.85-$3.65 Hun, AnR, Orv, Edd
Nighthawk. #5/0-1/0
$8 Max
Orange Parson. #7/0-8
$2.75-$15 Don, Edd
Oriole. #1-12
$2.20-$2.45 Edd
Salmon Hornberg. #6
$3 Orv
Salscraggie, blind eye. #4/0
$15 Max
Sherbrook. #5/0-4
$8-$11 Max
Silver and Blue. #1-12
$2.20-$2.45 Edd
Silver Blue, low water. #1/0-4
$2.50 Max
Silver Doctor. #7/0-8
$3.50-$15 Max, Pen, Edd, Don, Hun,
T&T, Dan
Silver Gray. #7/0-12
$2.20-$15 Max, Don, Pen, Edd
Silver Gray, blind eye. #4/0
$15 Max
Silver Ranger. #7/0-1
$12-$15 Don
Silver Wilkinson. #7/0-4
$8-$15 Max, Don
Sir Richard. #7/0-4
$8-$15 Max, Don
Skirrow's Fancy. #5/0-1/0
$8 Max
Sweep. #5/0-8
$2-$8 Max, Let, Orv, Pen, Edd

Teal and Red, low water. #1/0-4
$2.50 Max
Thunder and Lightning. #2-8
$2-$4 T&T, Mer, Pen, Let, Don, Edd
Thunder and Lightning, low water.
#1/0-4
$2.50 Max
Toppy. #5/0-1/0
$8 Max
Torrish. #7/0-4
$8-$15 Max, Don
Torrish, blind eye. #4/0
$15 Max
White Wings, low water. #1/0-4
$2.50 Max

Hairwing Salmon Flies

Black Ant
$2.50 Wul
**Black Bear, Red, Green (most
popular), Orange Butt.** #6/0-10
$1.75-$3.65 Max, AnR, Blu, Orv,
Pen, Edd, Ran, Let, Hun, Don, Mon
Black Conrad. #3-10
$2 Pen
Black Cosseboom. #2-8
$2.25-$2.95 Don
Black Doctor.
$2.95 Blu
Black Dose. #2/0-8
$1.80-$3.65 Max, Orv, Cus, H&H,
Mer, AnR
Black Fitchtail. #6/0-10
$1.85-$3.25 T&T, Edd, Hun, Don
Black Ranger. #6/0-10
$1.85-$2.15 Edd
Black Rat. #6/0-10
$1.80-$3.65 AnR, Blu, T&T, Mer,
Cus, Edd, H&H, Hun, Don, Mon, Orv
Black Sheep. #4-8
$4 Orv
Blue Charm. #6/0-10
$1.85-$3.80 AnR, T&T, Mer, Max,
Edd, Blu, Let, Hun, Max
Blue Colburn. #2-6
$1.75 Ran
Blue Doctor. #6/0-10
$1.85-$3 Max, Edd
Blue Rat. #2-8
$1.75-$3.50 Ran, Hun, Don, AnR
Blue Sapphire #2-8
$2.25-$2.95 Don
Blue Squirrel Hitch Fly. #4-6
$2.50 Wul
Brown Fairly. #3-10
$2-$3 Let, Pen

Cains River Special.
$2.95 Blu
Colburn Special. #6/0-10
$1.85-$3.50 Edd, Blu, Hun, AnR
Conrad.
$2.65 Blu
Copper Killer. #6/0-10
$1.85-$3.50 T&T, Hun, Don, Edd,
Blu, AnR
Cosseboom. #6/0-10
$1.85-$3.65 Mon, Don, Hun, Dan,
Mer, Pen, Edd, Max, AnR, Blu, Let,
Orv, T&T
Crosfield. #2-8
$2.25-$3 Max, Don
Dragon Fly.
$2.50 Wul
Dunc's Special.
$2.95 Blu
Durham Ranger. #6/0-10
$1.85-$2.15 Edd
Dusty Miller. #1/0-8
$2.25-$3.65 Hun, Don, Orv, Mer
Englehardt Special. #2-8
$3-$3.50 AnR
Garry (Yellow Dog). #2/0-8
$2.25-$3.25 Hun, Don, Max
General Practitioner. #1/0-6
$3.25-$4 Hun, T&T
Gold Rat. #2-8
$2.25-$2.95 Don
Gray Rat. #6/0-10
$1.85-$3.50 Blu, AnR, Don, Mer, Edd
Green Butt. #1/0-8
$2.25-$4 Don, T&T
Green Colburn. #2-6
$1.75 Ran
Green Colburn Red Butt. #2-6
$1.75 Ran
Green Cosseboom. #1/0-6
$1.75-$4 Ran, T&T
Green Highlander. #2/0-8
$1.85-$3.50 AnR, Max, Cus, Blu
H&H, Mer
Green Rat. #2-8
$2.25-$2.95 Don
Grizzly King. #6/0-10
$1.85-$3 Blu, Max, Don, Edd
Hairy Mary. #6/0-10
$1.75-$4 Let, Ran, Orv, T&T, Edd,
Max, AnR, Hun, Don, Mon
Herb Johnson Bucktail. #2-4
$2.25 Edd
Hopper.
$2.50 Wul
Hot Orange. #6/0-10
$1.85-$3.65 Mon, AnR, Orv, Mer,
Edd

Ingalls Butterfly. #6/0-10
$1.85-$3.50 Orv, T&T, Pen, Edd,
AnR, Blu, Let, Hun, Don
Jock Scott. #4-8
$1.80-$3.65 AnR, Mer, Cus, H&H,
Orv
Laxa Blue. #2-10
$2.75-$3.50 Hun
Mickey Finn. #6/0-10
$1.85-$3.50 AnR, Edd
Miramichi Cosseboom.
$2.95 Blu
Miramichi Squirrel. #6/0-10
$1.85-$2.15 Edd
Monkey Amherst. #2-8
$2.25-$2.95 Don
Moth.
$2.50 Wul
Nighthawk. #2-8
$3-$3.50 AnR
Onset. #2-8
$2.25-$2.95 Don
Orange Blossom. #6/0-10
$1.85-$3.50 Blu, Don, Hun, Max,
AnR, Edd
Orange Blossom Special.
$2.95 Blu
Orange Charm. #6/0-10
$1.85-$3.50 AnR, Hun, Edd
Orange Colburn. #2-6
$1.75 Ran
Orange Cosseboom. #6/0-10
$1.85-$2.15 Edd
Pass Lake. #2/0-8
$3 Max
Professor. #6/0-10
$1.85-$2.15 Edd
Rat. #6/0-10
$1.85-$2.15 Edd
Ray's Red. #6/0-10
$1.85-$2.15 Edd
Red Abbey. #6/0-10
$1.85-$3.50 Edd, Blu, Don, AnR, Max
Red Butt. #1/0-8
$2.25-$4 T&T, Don
Red Squirrel Hitch Fly. #4-6
$2.50 Wul
Roger's Fancy. #6/0-10
$1.75-$3.50 Ran, Hun, AnR, Edd
Ruelland Special. #2-8
$2.25-$2.95 Don
Rusty Rat. #6/0-10
$1.75-$4 H&H, Mer, Max, Cus, Pen,
Edd, Hun, Don, Mon, Orv, T&T,
Dan, Let, Ran, Blu, AnR
Silver Blue Hitch Fly. #4-6
$2.50 Wul
Silver Cosseboom. #2-8

$2.95-$3.50 AnR, Blu
Silver Doctor. #2/0-8
$1.85-$3.65 AnR, Orv, Max, Cus,
Blu, Mer, H&H
Silver Downeaster. #6/0-10
$1.85-$3.50 Blu, AnR, Edd
Silver Ranger. #6/0-10
$1.85-$2.15 Edd
Silver Rat. #6/0-10
$1.85-$3.65 Dan, Mer, Pen, Edd,
Mon, Don, Max, Hun, Blu, AnR, Orv,
T&T
Single. #4-8
$3 Let
Stoat Tail. #2-8
$2.25-$2.95 Don
The Haggis Hitch Fly. #4-6
$2.50 Wul
Tube Fly, Blue Charm. #6-10
$3 Orv
Undertaker. #2-8
$2.65-$3.50 Blu, AnR
Yellow Cosseboom. #6/0-10
$1.85-$3.50 AnR, Edd

Salmon Dries

Adams Irresistible. #4-8
$1.75-$1.95 Edd
Badger Bivisible. #4-8
$1.75-$1.95 Edd
Black Wulff. #2-8
$1.50-$2.95 Don, T&T, Edd
Bomber. #1-10
$1.50-$3 Don, T&T, Pen, Edd, AnR,
Let, Hun
Brown Bivisible. #4-8
$1.75-$1.95 Edd
Brown Wulff. #4-8
$1.75-$1.95 Edd
Buc Bug. #4-8
$1.75-$3 Orv, AnR, Hun, Pen, Edd
Coachman. #4-8
$1.75-$1.95 Edd
Cosseboom. #4-8
$1.75-$1.95 Edd
Gray Wulff. #3-8
$2-$3 Wul, Hun, Orv, Pen, Let, AnR
Grease Liner. #4-8
$1.50 T&T
Grizzly Wulff. #4-8
$1.50-$3 Hun, Wul, T&T, Edd
Humpy. #4-8
$1.50 T&T
Irresistible. #2-8
$1.50-$3 Don, Orv, T&T, Edd, AnR
MacIntosh. #4-8
$1.65-$2.50 Edd, Hun, AnR

Matane Special. #4-8
$2.50 AnR
Orange Cosseboom. #4-8
$1.75-$1.95 Edd
Peppermint Stick. #2-6
$2.50 AnR
Rat-Faced McDougal. #2-8

$1.75-$2.95 Hun, AnR, Don, Edd
Royal Humpy. #4-8
$1.50 T&T
Royal Wulff. #3-8
$1.50-$3 Wul, Orv, T&T, Pen, Let,
AnR, Hun
Salmon Skater. #4-8

$1.75-$1.95 Edd
Silver Gray. #4-8
$1.75-$1.95 Edd
White Wulff. #2-10
$1.75-$3 Wul, Orv, Pen, Edd, Hun,
Don, Let, AnR

BASS BUGS, POPPERS, AND FLIES

Bass flies are the comedians of the fishing world. The more outrageous their costume, the better they seem to catch bass, and therefore, the more entertaining they are to the angler.

Although there are some variations of flies for trout, most of these patterns have been developed just for bass. Currently foremost among the pattern originators is Dave Whitlock, whose distinctive genius for knowing what bass will take is apparent in items such as the

Big Sky's Wooly Bass Bugger

Harewater Pup, Gerbubble Hair Bug, and 'Lectric Leech. Catalogs list his patterns with the prefix "Whit's" or "Whitlock's" or, as I've chosen to do, "Dave's".

Many catalog companies carry bass patterns. Among them you'll find Murray's to have some off-beat bugs. Harry Murray lives on the Shenandoah River, so he has lots of opportunity to work on smallmouth. Doug Brewer at Big Sky is also coming up with some good-looking flies. A bassman would do well to get those two catalogs.

If you haven't tried bass fishing with a fly rod, you're missing lots of fun. For me, the sullen bulge of a charging bass is one of the most exciting moments in fishing. Combine that charge with the topwater clobbering of a floating bug... it will take your breath away.

However, trout fishermen sometimes fail to do well at bass fishing. Bass operate differently than trout and that requires the angler to approach the sport in a manner quite unlike his approach to trout fishing. For one thing, there's nothing very subtle about plopping a big, noisy hair mouse near a moss bed. It goes against the idea of careful presentation so deeply ingrained in the trout fisherman's mind.

Placing the fly and working it requires the same amount of thought as it does in trout fishing. But the angler needs to take a different tack. This is not the place to explain all that (and right now, for me, it's too intuitive to explain very well), but my message is that you should try bass fishing with a fly rod and be ready to shed the assumptions you hold from trout fishing.

Alder Wet. #2-4
$.95 Pen
Bass Caddis Bucktail. #8
$1.65 Mur
Bass Golden Stone. #6
$1.65 Mur
Bass Improved Sofa Pillow #6
$1.65 Mur
Bass King Popper. #1/0,2
$1.20-$1.75 Mur
Big Bass Damsel. #3/0
$2 Big
Black Gnat Wet. #2-4
$.95 Pen
Blue Dun Wet. #2-4
$.95 Pen
Bluegill Bug Poppers, cork. #4-12
$.98-$1.50 Kau, Cab, H&H, Orv

Bomber. #1-2
$2.50 Edd
Crayfish. #2-8
$1.50-$2.25 Mur, H&H, Big, Orv
Dahlberg Diver. #1/0-4
$2.09-$2.75 Kau, Cab, Mur, Orv
Dark Cahill Wet. #2-4
$.95 Pen
Dave's 'Lectric Leech. #1/0-8
$1.89-$2.50 Kau, Cab, Fly
Dave's Black Ann Yellow. #2-6
$2.09-$2.50 Cab, Fly
Dave's Chamois Leech. #2-6
$1.89-$2.50 Fly, Cab, Kau
Dave's Cottonmouth Snakey. #3/0
$2.50 T&T
Dave's Crayfish. #1/0-8
$2.50-$2.95 Fly, Kau

Dave's Damsel Dragon. #6-10
$2.09-$2.95 Kau, Cab, Fly
Dave's Dragonsel Moth. #6
$2.50 Edd
Dave's Eelworm. #3/0-4
$2-$2.50 Kau, Cab, Hig, AnR, Big, T&T, Edd
Dave's Gerbubble Hair Bug. #2-6
$2.25-$4.25 Mur, Hun, T&T, Edd
Dave's Golden Shiner Prismatic Streamer. #2-6
$2.09-$2.50 Cab, T&T
Dave's Harewater Pup. #1/0-4
$2.09-$2.95 Orv, T&T, Fly, Mur, Cab, Kau
Dave's Most Whit Hair Bugs. #2-10
$2.50-$2.75 Kau, T&T, Edd
Dave's Mouserat. #2-6

$2.09-$2.95 T&T, Mur, Cab, Kau, Fly
Dave's Near Nuff Frog. #2-10
$2.09-$4.25 Mur, Hig, Cab, T&T, Edd, Fly
Dave's Porky's Pet. #2-10
$2.09-$2.75 Cab, T&T, Edd, Fly
Dave's Shad Prismatic Streamer. #2-6
$2.09-$2.50 T&T, Cab
Dave's Silver Shiner Prismatic Streamer. #2-6
$2.09-$2.50 Cab, T&T
Dave's Snakey. #3/0-2
$2.50 T&T, Kau
Dave's Wiggleleg Frog. #2-6
$2.09-$3.50 Kau, Cab, T&T, Fly
Dave's Wuldbee. #2-6
$2.75 T&T
Devil Bug. #4,10
$1.95 Mur
Devil Mouse. #4
$1.95 Mur
Feather Eel. #1/0-4
$2.35 Hun
Flashabou Girdle Bass Bugger. #2-6
$2 Big
Flashabou Wooly Bass Bugger. #2-6
$2 Big
Floating Muddler. #1/0-4
$1.05-$2.75 Orv, Kau, Cab
Florida Muddler. #4/0
$1.50-$2.75 H&H, Orv

Gaine's Diving Demon. #2-6
$1.30-$1.75 Edd, Mur

Gaine's Froggie Popper. #2-4
$1.35-$1.75 Mur, Edd

Gaine's Minnow Popper. #1/0-6
$1.25-$1.75 Edd, Mur
Gaines Bee. #8
$1.75 Mur
Gaines Lightning Bug. #10
$1.75 Mur
Gaines Old Joe. #4,8
$1.75 Mur
Gaines Pan Pop Rubber Legs. #8
$1.75 Mur
Gallasch Crawl'N Twitch Popper. #4,8
$1.75 Mur
Gallasch Pop'N Crawl Popper. #1,4
$1.75 Mur
Gallasch Spouter Bug. #1
$2.75 Mur
Giant Shimmy Leech. #3/0
$2.75 Big
Girdle Bass Bugger. #2-6
$2 Big
H.G. Tappley Bass Bug. #6-8
$2.25 Mur
Hair Frog. #1/0-6
$2.25-$4.25 Hig, H&H, Hun, Don, AnR, Big, Orv
Hair Moth. #2
$1.85-$2.25 Edd, Don
Hair Mouse. #2-6
$1.85-$4.25 Big, Orv, Cus, Edd, Hig, H&H, Hun, Don
Hair Popper. #3/0-6
$1.90-$4 AnR, Orv, Dan, Cus, Edd, Don, Hun, H&H, Hig
Hairy Hank. #4
$1.85 Edd
Hairy Mary. #4
$1.85 Edd
Hare's Ear Wet. #2-4
$.95 Pen
Humpback Leech. #6
$2 Big
James Wood Bucktail. #2-4
$1.35 Mur
Joe's Bass Hopper. #3/0
$2 Big
Keel Hair Bug. #4
$2.75 Orv
Keel Popper, cork. #2
$2.75 Orv

Kicker Frog. #1/0-4
$2.25-$2.75 H&H, Orv
Leadwing Coachman Wet. #2-4
$.95 Pen
Lefty's Flashabou Bass Streamer. #4-8
$1.50 Mur
Light Cahill Wet. #2-4
$.95 Pen
Marabou Leech. #1/0-4
$2.25-$2.75 Hig, Hun, AnR, Orv
Minnow Popper. #1/0-2
$1.10-$1.50 Orv, Cab
Murray's Flying Hair Moth. #4-6
$2.50 Mur
Murray's Homely Hair Mouse. #4-6
$2.50 Mur
Murray's Krazy Kicker. #4-6
$2.50 Mur
Murray's Shenandoah Hair Popper. #6-10
$2.50 Mur
Peeper Popper. #8
$1.50 Orv
Popping Frog. #2
$1.50-$1.80 Orv, H&H
Prismatic Golden Shiner. #3/0
$2.50 Big
Prismatic Muddler. #1/0-4
$2.50 Kau
Prismatic Shad. #3/0
$2.50 Big
Prismatic Streamer. #1/0-6
$2.15-$2.25 Kau, Hun, Edd
Professor Wet. #2-4
$.95 Pen
Pusher Bug. #1/0
$2.25 H&H
Royal Coachman Wet. #2-4
$.95 Pen
Rubber Legs . #8-12
$.71-$1.15 Hig, Cab, Kau
Rubber-Tailed Bass Bugger. #6
$2 Big
Rube Wood Wet. #2-4
$.95 Pen
Sneaky Pete. #4-10
$1.50-$1.75 Mur, Orv
Tandem Muddler. #4
$2 Big
Walt's Cork Bass Popper. #2-10
$1.60 Mur
Wave Muddler. #2-4
$2 Big
Wooly Bass Bugger. #6
$2 Big
Wooly Leech. #1/0-4
$2.25 Kau

SALTWATER FLIES

I can tell the difference between freshwater and saltwater, and I could probably guess from looking at the flies listed here that they aren't intended for trout in the St. Vrain or bluegill in Sawhill Ponds. Otherwise, I'm rather limited, having never angled for sea fish. I hesitate to base anything on what I've read about the sport. As

a writer, I know better.

One thing I can observe is that there seems to be a large price spread for the same fly, more so here than in any other category except salmon flies. It's not uncommon to find a dollar's difference in prices and a few high prices are double that of the low price. With that in mind, I've elected to include the prices for each fly.

Bend Back. #2/0
$1.70-$2 T&T, Kau, Blu
Black Mylar. #6
$1.75 Kau
Blue Death. #4/0
$1.65 Blu
Bonefish Crab. #1
$1.95 Orv
Bonefish Fly. #2-6
$1.15-$1.95 Orv, Dan, H&H, Kau, Blu
Bonefish Fly, Frankie-Belle. #2-8
$1.20-$1.85 Kau, H&H, Don
Bonefish Special. #2-6
$1.30-$2 Orv, T&T, Hig, Kau, Blu
Bonefish Special, Chico's. #4
$1.95 Fly
Brook's Blondes. #3/0-4
$1.20-$2.25 Edd, AnR, Don, Blu, Kau, H&H
Chinese Claw. #4/0
$1.40-$2.65 H&H, Blu, Orv
Chocolate Candy Fly. #4
$1.67 Wul
Cockroach. #1/0-4/0
$1.30-$2.75 T&T, Fly, Kau, Hig
Crab, Blue. #4
$2.75 Fly
Crab, Bonefish. #1
$1.95 Orv
Crab, Dave's Saltwater. #3/0-4
$2.09-$2.95 T&T, Fly, Cab, Kau
Crab, Salty. #1/0
$2.65 Orv
Crazy Charlie. #2-6
$1.20-$1.95 Orv, Hig
Finger Mullet. #3/0-1/0
$2.65 Orv
Galli-Nipper. #2-8
$1.85 Don
Glass Minnow. #1/0-4
$1.70-$2.75 Kau, Blu, Orv, Fly
Gold Cup. #4/0
$1.65 Blu
Golden Claw. #3/0
$1.20-$1.30 Hig
Golden Mantis. #4
$1.45 Blu

Green Mantis. #2-6
$1.15-$1.45 Dan, Blu
Hagen Sands. #2-8
$1.85 Don
Horror. #2-8
$1.20-$2 Don, H&H, Kau, Orv, T&T, Fly, Blu
Lee Cuddy. #2-6
$1.10-$1.20 Hig
Lefty's Deceivers. #4/0-4
$1.30-$2.75 AnR, Orv, Fly, T&T, Blu, Kau, Hig, H&H, Don
Lime Candy Fly. #4
$1.67 Wul
Marabou Deceivers. #4/0-2
$1.95-$2.50 Don
Mini Puff (PF). #4
$1.95 Fly
Nantucket Sand Eel. #3/0-1/0
$1.25 Edd
Nasty Charlie. #4
$1.95 Fly
Needle Fish. #3/0
$2.65 Orv
Peppermint Candy Fly. #4
$1.67 Wul
Permit Fly. #1
$1.95 Orv
Pink Fluff. #4/0
$1.40-$2.65 Blu, H&H, Orv
Pinkie-Belle. #4
$1.45 Blu
Poppers. #2/0
$2 Edd
Roughneck. #2-6
$1.10-$1.20 Hig
Sailfish. #4/0
$2.50-$3 Fly, Kau
Sailfish Streamer. #4/0
$3-$3.25 Kau, Blu
Sal-Mul Mac. #3/0
$2-$2.50 Blu, Kau
Salty Diver. #1/0
$2.65 Orv
Sea Arrow Squid. #3/0
$2.50 Kau
Sea Ducer. #2/0
$2-$2.75 T&T, Fly, Blu, Kau

Shrimp Fly. #2-8
$1.85 Don
Shrimp, Crackling. #2-6
$1.10-$1.20 Hig
Shrimp, Dave's Saltwater. #1/0-8
$2.09-$2.95 Cab, Kau, T&T, Fly
Shrimp, Gold and Brown. #4
$2 T&T
Shrimp, Grass. #4
$1.45 Blu
Shrimp, Mono. #2-6
$1.15 Dan
Shrimp, Pink. #2-6
$1.45 Blu
Shrimp, Pink Swimming. #2-6
$1.15-$1.95 H&H, Kau, Orv, Dan
Shrimp, Snapping. #2-6
$1.15-$2 Orv, T&T, Kau, Blu, Dan, Fly
Shrimp, Snapping, Banded. #2-6
$1.15-$1.95 Dan, Fly
Silverside. #2-4
$2.65 Orv
Skipping Bug Popper. #2/0
$2.65 Orv
Tarpon Fly, Apte. #3/0-4/0
$1.49-$2.65 Blu, H&H, Kau, Orv
Tarpon Fly, Black and Orange. #3/0
$2 Kau
Tarpon Fly, Blue Grizzly. #4/0
$2.75 T&T
Tarpon Fly, Chase. #4/0
$1.40-$1.65 H&H, Blu
Tarpon Fly, Chico's Shallow Water. #4/0
$2.50 Fly
Tarpon Fly, Grizzly and Black. #5/0-2/0
$1.20-$1.30 Hig
Tarpon Fly, Grizzly and Red. #5/0-2/0
$1.20-$1.30 Hig
Tarpon Fly, Key. #4/0
$2.65 Orv
Tarpon Fly, Orange and Grizzly. #5/0-1/0
$1.80-$2.75 Kau, Don, T&T, Dan
Tarpon Fly, Orange and Yellow.

#5/0-1/0
$1.80-$1.85 Dan, Don
Tarpon Fly, Red and White.
#5/0-1/0
$1.80 Dan

Tarpon Fly, Red and Yellow.
#5/0-1/0
$1.80 Dan
Whistler. #3/0-1/0
$1.85-$2.50 Don, Kau

Whistler, Deep Water. #3/0
$2.50 Fly
Yucatan Special. #4
$1.95 Fly

REGIONAL FLY PATTERNS

The flies listed here are patterns or tying styles you may not recognize, unless you live in a region in which one of them was developed. Tandem streamers, for instance, were developed in New England, particularly in Maine, for trolling in the deep lakes there. They may work as well in a Wyoming lake, perhaps, but you're not likely to find one in a Wyoming fly shop.

My interest in regional patterns began in the Yellow Breeches Fly Shop in Pennsylvania. I found a whole tray of Honey Bugs, fished with them in nearby Falling Spring, and caught trout. I'd seen no fly like them in Colorado, and it was a fascinating experience. (Honey Bugs are not listed here, but you'll find a kit for tying them in the fly tying chapter.)

There are only a few patterns here. You'll find most regional flies in the shops around the country, not in catalogs. Stop in those shops during your travels, take some regionals home, and try them out. You may be surprised.

I've listed the type of fly, the region, and the prices for these flies.

Tandem Streamers

Ballou Special. #4 Region: New England.
$2 Edd
Barnes Special. #4-12 Region: New England.
$2-$2.50 Ran, Hun, Edd
Black Ghost. #2-12 Region: New England.
$1.95-$2.50 Mer, AnR, Ran, Hun, Edd
Black Ghost Marabou. #4 Region: New England.
$2 Edd
Black Russian. #4 Region: New England.
$2.50-$3 Sim
Black-Nosed Dace. #4 Region: New England.
$1.95 Mer
Blue and White. #4 Region: New England.
$2.50-$3 Sim
Blue Smelt. #4-12 Region: New England.
$2 Ran, Edd
Chief Needahbeh #4 Region: New England.
$2 Edd
Col. Bates. #4 Region: New England.
$2 Edd
Dark Edson Tiger. #4 Region: New England.
$2 Edd
Earl's Gray Smelt. #4 Region: New England.

$2 Edd
Eddie's Ripogenus Smelt. #4 Region: New England.
$2 Edd
Erskine. #4 Region: New England.
$2 Edd
Frost Blue Smelt. #4-12 Region: New England.
$2 Ran
Golden Head. #4 Region: New England.
$2 Edd
Golden Witch. #4 Region: New England.
$2 Edd
Gov. Aiken. #4-12 Region: New England.
$2 Big, Ran, Edd
Grand Lake Special. #4 Region: New England.
$2 Edd
Gray Ghost. #2-12 Region: New England.
$1.95-$2.50 Hun, Big, Ran, AnR, Mer, Edd
Gray Ghost Marabou. #4-12 Region: New England.
$2 Ran, Edd
Green Ghost. #2-12 Region: New England.
$1.95-$2.50 AnR, Big, Ran, Hun, Mer, Edd
Green King. #4 Region: New England.
$2 Edd
Grizzly King. #4 Region: New

England.
$2 Edd
Hurricane. #4 Region: New England.
$2 Edd
Jane Craig. #4-12 Region: New England.
$2 Ran, Edd
Joe's Smelt. #4 Region: New England.
$2 Edd
Kennebago Smelt. #4 Region: New England.
$2 Edd
Lady Ghost. #4 Region: New England.
$2 Edd
Lake George Ghost. #4 Region: New England.
$2.50-$3 Sim
Liggett's Special. #4 Region: New England.
$2 Edd
Light Edson Tiger. #4 Region: New England.
$2 Edd
Lithuanian Prince. #4 Region: New England.
$2.50-$3 Sim
Lucky Lady. #4 Region: New England.
$2 Edd
Magog Smelt. #4 Region: New England.
$2 Edd

Marabou. #4-12 Region: New England.
$2 Ran, Edd

Mickey Finn. #2-12 Region: New England.
$1.95-$2.50 Mer, Edd, AnR, Ran, Hun

Miss Sharon. #4 Region: New England.
$2 Edd

Moose River. #4 Region: New England.
$2 Edd

Muddler Minnow. #4 Region: New England.
$2 Edd

Nine-Three. #2-12 Region: New England.
$2-$2.50 Big, AnR, Ran, Hun, Edd

Orange Blossom. #4 Region: New England.
$2.50-$3 Sim

Parmachene Belle. #4-12 Region: New England.
$2 Ran, Edd

Pink Lady. #4-12 Region: New England.
$2 Ran, Edd

Queen Bee. #4 Region: New England.
$2 Edd

Red and White. #4-12 Region: New England.
$2 Edd, Ran

Red Gray Ghost. #2-12 Region: New England.

$2-$2.50 Ran, AnR, Hun

Royal Coachman. #4 Region: New England.
$2 Edd

Screw Driver. #4 Region: New England.
$2.50-$3 Sim

Sen. Muskie. #4 Region: New England.
$2 Edd

Silver Fizz. #4 Region: New England.
$2.50-$3 Sim

Spencer Bay Special. #4 Region: New England.
$2 Edd

Streaker. #4 Region: New England.
$2 Edd

Supervisor. #2-12 Region: New England.
$1.95-$2.50 Hun, Big, Ran, AnR, Mer, Edd

Tom's Special A.A.. #4 Region: New England.
$2 Edd

Tri-Color. #4-12 Region: New England.
$2 Ran, Edd

Winnipesaukee Smelt. #6-8 Region: New England.
$2.50 Hun

Yellow Perch. #4 Region: New England.
$2 Big, Edd

York's Kennebago . #4-12 Region: New England.
$2 Ran

Other Regional Patterns

Coho Streamer. #2 Region: Alaska.
$1.25 Fly

Devil Bug Dry Fly. #8-14 Region: Maine.
$.85 Edd

Doc Sprately Wet Fly. #6-10 Region: Northwest.
$1.25 Kau

Doodle Bug Dry Fly. #8-12 Region: Maine.
$.75 Ran

Iliamna Pinky Wet Fly. #8 Region: Alaska.
$.90 Fly

Iliaska Black Muddler. #4 Region: Alaska.
$1.50 Bud

Karluk Flash Fly Wet. #2 Region: Alaska.
$1.25 Fly

Slim Jims Emergers. #10-14 Region: Northern Maine.
$1.20 Edd

TDC Nymph. #10-14 Region: Northwest.
$1.25 Kau

White Fly Spinner. #12-14 Region: Pennsylvania (Yellow Breeches).
$1.20 Let

RELATED ACCESSORIES

Floatants and Fly Dryers

Dry flies won't float for long unless they're treated with something to make the materials waterproof. Silicone is the primary chemical in most floatants, although you'll still find a few anglers mixing gasoline and paraffin for a homemade remedy.

Floatant comes in three forms: paste, liquid, or aerosol spray. The paste comes in a tub or squeeze bottle. It's rubbed between the fingers to liquefy it before appplication. The liquid type is typically sold in an hourglass-shaped bottle. The fly is placed in the empty top, the cap replaced, and the bottle inverted to soak the fly. The aerosol is, well, aerosol.

Floatant can also be rubbed on leader to help control the depth at which sub-surface flies ride. This works well when midge pupas are the trout's target. You can "grease" the leader to within six inches of the fly, and because the fly is unweighted and light, the floating leader will keep it within a few inches of the surface, right where the fish are feeding.

Even treated flies finally sink after all those trout pull them under. When they do, you don't have to change flies. You can dry your fly, re-treat it, and fish on. The fly dryers, as I call them, are powders that pull the moisture out of the fly material.

Cortland's Dry-Ur-Fly was the first such product I used. It comes in an open-mouthed container. You simply place your soaked fly in the container, cup your palm over it, and shake. The wet powder needs to be flicked off, and then the fly can be re-treated. The powder itself is used over and over again. Newer products use flip-top containers with small openings. Their instructions suggest that you put the powder in your hand and roll the fly in it, then discard the powder. I suggest you get an empty 35mm film canister and put the powder in it.

Then use it like the Cortland product. (Or just buy the Cortland product.)

You sometimes need one more bit of chemistry, this one to sink leader material or flies. Although there are two schools of thought here, most anglers want their dry fly leaders to sink. This eliminates the crease on the surface caused by the leader resting on the water. That crease throws a shadow that can spook fish. Again, there's a home remedy, streamside mud rubbed into the leader, but modern chemistry also has an answer.

I don't know why this chemical isn't called sinkant, but in the fly shop, you should ask for leader sink. Because these products are more often used for leaders than flies, they're listed in the chapter on fly lines. But the product can be used on flies that don't sink as they're supposed to, because of the materials used. An unweighted Muddler Minnow, for instance, can be fished on the surface or underwater, but its deer hair head is very buoyant. Leader sink will supposedly help sink it. (In reality, it's better to carry weighted and unweighted Muddlers and switch flies.)

Fly floatants

Blip Paste-Kote. *Paste in tub.*
$1.25-$1.60 T&T, Cus, Pen, Dan
Cortland Dab. *Paste in tub.*
$2-$2.25 Mer, Hig, Bob, Bud, Fly
Cortland Dry Fly Spray. *Aerosol.*
$2.25-$2.50 AnR, Pen, Kau, Bud, Edd, Fly, Bob, Mer, Hig, T&T
Dave's Bug Flote. *Paste in squeeze bottle with flip top.*
$2.50 Fly, Mer, Hig
Dilly Wax. *Paste in tube.*
$2 FlR, Mer
Dry Fly Aero-Spray. *Aerosol.*
$2.99 Dal
Float. *Paste in tub.*
$1.65 Dal

Float-Kote. *Aerosol, from Superior Fly Products.*
$2.95-$3.95 AnJ, Pen, Dan, Bud
Floto. *Liquid, by Weber.*
$1.20-$1.75 Edd, Fol, AnW, Cus
Flyta. *Liquid, non-silicone.*
$1.50-$2.50 T&T, Egg, Cus, Bud, H&H

Free-Float. *Paste in tub.*
$2.50 Dan, Hig, Bud

Garcia Dry Fly Dressing. *Liquid in hourglass bottle.*
$1.85-$2.39 Sim, Pen
Gerhke's Gink. *Paste in squeeze bottle with flip top.*
$1.90-$3 Bob, Mur, Hig, Edd, Pen, Cus, Dal, Bud, H&H, Big, Fly, Dan, T&T
Gudebrod Dry Fly Dressing. *Liquid silicone.*
$1.29 Tac
Hi'N'DRi. *Paste.*
$1.15-$1.50 Mur, H&H, Cus
Kaufmann's Float High. *Paste in tub.*
$1.75 Kau
Mountain Cork. *Paste.*
$1.40 Cus
Mucilin. *Liquid in flat bottle with brush top, without silicone.*
$1.85-$2.25 Dan, Kau, EJH, Bob
Mucilin. *Liquid with silicone.*
$2-$2.25 Bob, Dan, Kau
Mucilin paste. *Without silicone.*
$1.60-$2 Mur, Bob, Dan, Kau, Ste, Pen
Mucilin. *Paste with silicone added.*
$1.85-$2.25 EJH, Bob, Dan, Kau
Murray's Floatant. *Liquid.*
$1.50 Mur
Nufly-Kote. *Liquid for use on new flies.*
$2.75-$3.25 T&T, Hig, Orv, Pen, Ste
Optima. *Paste in tub; tub attaches to watch band.*
$2.25 Dan
Orvis Silicone Fly Dressing. *Silicone gel in flip-top container.*
$1.75 Orv
Orvis Super Float. *Liquid.*
$3 Orv, Let

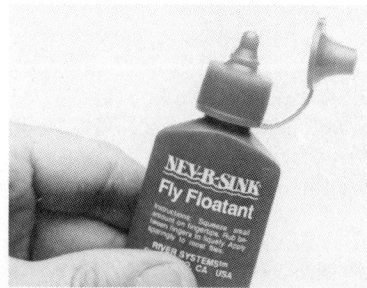

River Systems Nev-R-Sink. *Paste in tub form or squeeze bottle.*
$1.75-$1.98 Pen, Sim, Ram, Edd

Seidel "700". *Aerosol spray, environmentally safe.*
$2.85-$3.50 Edd, Cus, H&H, EJH, Sim, Fly
Seidel "700". *Atomizer bottle.*
$2.35-$2.85 Fol, H&H, Cus
Silicote. *Liquid in hourglass bottle.*
$2.50 Dan

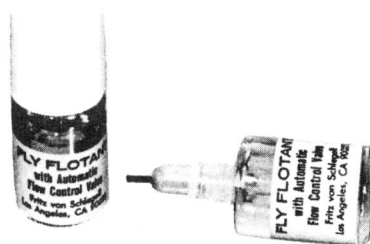

Simms Fly Rise. *Paste in tub.*
$2 Pen
Simms Fly Rise. *Liquid in special dauber applicator.*
$2.50-$3 Pen, Hig

Til-Tip (sometimes called von Schlegell floatant).
Liquid in bottle, with brush top.
$2.20-$2.50 T&T, Dan, Cus
Top-Fly. *Liquid, from National Feather-Craft.*
$2.50-$3 AnR, T&T, Hun, Nat
Top-Fly. *Paste.*
$1.50-$1.95 Hun, Nat

Fly Dryers

Cortland Dry-Ur-Fly. *Powder in open-mouth container.*
$2-$2.25 Bob, Hig, T&T, Mer, AnR, Kau, Bud, Pen
Dry-Kote. *Powder in flip-top container with small opening.*
$2.49-$2.95 Pen, Orv, Ste, AnJ, Dan
Fli-Restore. *Powder in plastic vial.*
$1.50 Edd

River Systems Nev-R-Sink Drying Crystals. *Powder in open-mouth container.*
$1.95 Ram

Seidel "800". *Powder in flip-top container with small opening; silicone floatant added.*
$2.50-$3.59 Hun, EJH, Cus, Fly, Sim, Dal, H&H

Simms Fly Drier. *Powder in flip-top container with small opening.*
$2.50 Hig

Super Dry Fly. *Powder in tub.*
$2.95 Pen

Other Accessories

Ty-Rite Fish Hook Holder. *Like a small ballpoint pen, with hook to hold flies while attaching to leader.*
$2.95 Dan, Bud

Fly pen. *Ballpoint pen converted for use in tying flies to leaders; stainless steel loop is pushed out of pen, holds flies while tying knot.*
$3 T&T

Bottle Holder. *Holder for 1 oz. bottles, clips to vest.*
$3.25-$3.65 T&T, Orv

Flip lens. *3x magnifiying lens that attaches to glasses, flips out of way when not in use.*
$14-$15.95 Orv, Kau, Hun

Eyeglass loupe. *3x circular lens; attaches to glasses; flips out of way.*
$14 Fly

Flip Focal. *1¾x or 2¼x lens; attaches to hat brim with tie tack; flips out of way after fly is tied on.*
$10.50-$11.95 Let, Fly, T&T, Pen, Nor, Bob

Aids for Matching the Hatch

One of the best things about fly fishing is that it combines art and science in equal measure.

The art comes in the presentation of the fly and in some kind of creative intuition about what will make up that perfect combination needed to take trout. Art is part of the creation of flies at the tier's table.

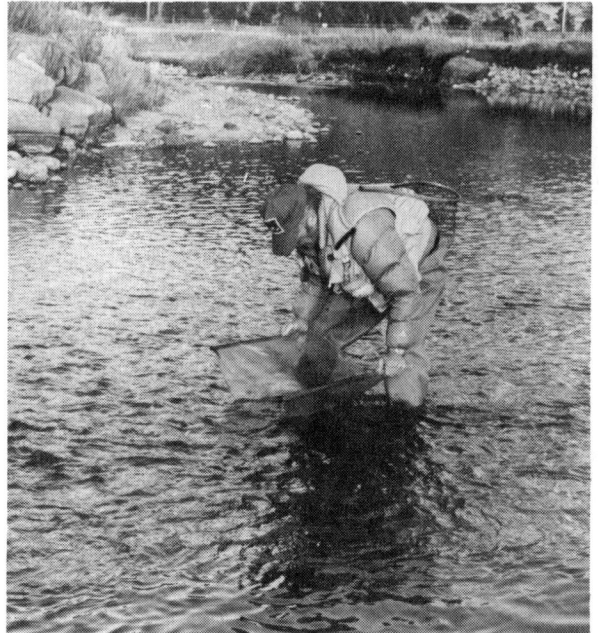

Science has a part in the physics of the sport, in casting dynamics, and in leader energy curves. But mostly, science comes in the study of the fish, especially the study of what fish eat. Entomology can become as much a part of the sport as casting. Indeed, some fly fishermen spend as much time with their noses in the water as they do standing and casting.

I began this section by stating that fly fishing combines art and science in equal measure, and it should. He who leans one way or t'other too far misses the maximum gain from the sport. Without art, the stream becomes only another of life's laboratories. Without science, a full understanding and, therefore, a full appreciation of what's happening is impossible.

Most beginners, I've found, rely on art alone. They can't tell a mayfly from a grasshopper, for instance. In the case of rank beginners, art translates roughly as luck. When an angler finally discovers the science of it all, another plateau is passed and the world is, once again, enlarged.

Some budding scientist/anglers, on the other hand, spend too much time plucking mayflies from their butterfly nets. They think they know why they're not catching more fish—they didn't bring along an exact imitation of the *Ephemerella maximus*. I think they're not catching fish because they don't keep their flies in the water.

As for me, I lived without science longer than most. Just fished my Humpy morning to night. But those times when fish were rising, but not to my fly, finally got to me. I wanted to know why. The rejection was too much for my fragile angler's ego. A bit of bug learning went a long way toward fixing the predicament.

An angler's study of entomology gives him or her a knowledge of trout food, and that allows him to match his offering to whatever is on the water. This has come to be called "matching the hatch", thanks to Ernie Schwiebert and his landmark book of that title.

There are other books besides Schwiebert's that can help in that initial hurdle of understanding. Art Flick's *Streamside Guide* and Dave Hughes' and Rick Hafele's *Complete Book of Western Hatches* come to mind, but there are many others. Entire books have now been written on every major type of trout food. You'll find an extensive list in the chapter on books.

Once you've decided to do a little streamside science, it becomes a fascinating part of the sport. Soon, you'll need some scientific "instruments", things like seines and pocket magnifiers and stomach pumps. That's what this section is all about.

If you really get interested in entomology, this list won't satisfy you. When that happens, I recommend the catalog from Bio Quip. It is full of interesting devices for collecting, preserving, and studying insects. The most practical of them for the fly fisherman is the pocket net. It folds up in the fashion of the Insta-Net landing net. Unfolded, it makes a 12" aerial net, and you can save your fishing hat for its intended purpose.

You'll also find "kick" nets (for the collection of nymphs), field collecting bags, specimen jars, and whatever else you may need. There's even a "Mobile Interceptor Trap" that mounts on top of your pick-up so you can collect mayfly samples on your way to the river.

Bio Quip has a lot of books, some of which are of interest to the angler. A 330 page book on the mayflies of North America is one example. It's interesting to note that a couple of our "angling" books made it into this scientists' catalog. Arbona's mayfly book and the stonefly book by Arbona, Swisher, and Richards are nestled right in there with *The American Cockroach*. There's even a book

entitled *Entertaining with Insects*, which is, of course, a cookbook.

For a full listing of entomological supplies, write Bio Quip, Box 61, Santa Monica, California 90406 or call (213) 322-6636.

(Owners of catalog companies would do well to take a look at this catalog, too. The main part of the catalog has been printed in quantity, enough to supply demand for two years, and a "tip in" has been added in the center with current prices. It's a bit inconvenient to use, although this one's organized beautifully, but it saves a lot of printing money which could be passed on to customers and company alike.)

Insect Seines and Nets

Alexander nymph net. *Ultra-fine nylon mesh; fits over regular landing net; folds up very small; for catching water- and air-borne insects.*
$4.95-$5.95 Fly, Pen, T&T, Kau, Dal
Bio Quip pocket nymph. *Described above; fold-up aerial net.*
$8 Bio Quip (see address above)
Bio Quip "kick" net. *For underwater insects; square, 36" each side.*
$29.50 Bio Quip (see address above)
Bio Quip Mobile Interceptor Trap. *Just in case you're curious after reading the introduction to this section.*
$285 Bio Quip (see address above)
Cascade Lakes insect net. *Fine nylon mesh with hardwood handles; 6"x13"; rolls up.*
$4.84-$5.95 Mer, Pen, Kau

Minnow net. *The pet store's helper; have to be a good aim to snare a floating mayfly in fast water.*
$.45-$.49 Sim, Hig

Match the Hatch Accessories

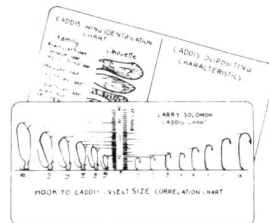

Caddis Fly Chart. *Plastic card with identification information for caddis, with hook sizes according to wing sizes; by Larry Solomon.*
$1.95 T&T

Spin-a-Fly. *Streamside plastic dial with information aiding in insect identification, size, hatch activity, water type.*
$4.95-$4.99 T&T, Mer, Dal

Loupe. *Eyepiece like jewelers use; 2 ½ x; for observation of insects found in water.*
$2.50 T&T
Pocket magnifier. *5x-9x lens in lightweight case; sets up in correct focal length.*
$9-$13.95 Pen, Bud
Pocket magnifier. *Nickel-plated case, swing-out lens; 10x.*
$6 T&T
Pocket lens. *Plastic lens the size of a credit card; 5x.*
$2 John Betts (address in chapter introduction)
Stomach pump. *Only for the die-hard match-the-hatch, catch-and-release angler; beats killing the fish to find out what it's been eating, but not by much; too much trauma involved for angler and fish to use this unless you're desperate.*
$3.35-$4.95 T&T, Dan, Mer, FlR, Fly, H&H

8. Fly Tying

FLY TYING IS A hobby within a hobby, and there are many fly fishermen who take up tying only to find out they like it better than fishing. The sport reverses on them, and they end up fishing in order to use up the supplies of the flies they've stockpiled. For most of us, however, tying is an enjoyable adjunct to the sport. It fills the hours away from the stream with an activity important to our success as fly fishermen.

Most people begin tying in order to save money, although the initial investment may mean a year or two will pass before that happens. Those same people stay with tying, even when they become rich and famous, simply because it's relaxing and fun.

There are two, more compelling reasons to take up tying and stay with it. One is the satisfaction of catching fish on flies you've tied yourself. It makes the act of fly fishing somehow more complete. After tying for several years, I can't imagine fishing with someone else's flies; it just wouldn't mean the same to me. This feeling is difficult to describe to a non-tier.

Simply said, the connection is complete between angler and fish when the fly comes from the angler's own hands.

The other compelling reason for tying is a matter of control. Because you can tie flies exactly in the manner you wish, you have choices the angler who buys ready-made flies does not have. You can create a fly in precisely the form you believe will catch fish, the most fish and the biggest fish. This is another thing that's difficult to describe to the non-tier. He can choose between flies in the trays at the shop, but the choices are very limited compared to the choices available to the tier at his desk. The boundaries of those choices change as the tier gains experience, and a good tier finds only expanding boundaries, seemingly without limits. It's an adventure to sit down at the tying desk, and not an hour goes by without some experimentation that may lead to The Perfect Fly.

Perhaps you're considering learning to tie flies but feel that it's too difficult. I teach fly tying, and every class includes someone who thinks he'll never be able to tie a fly. Has trouble with shoelaces, let alone flies. Every one of those people has left the class a competent fly tier. It's not a difficult activity, although it is close work requiring patience. But if a person fails to like tying, it's almost always his temperament, not his ability, that is the deciding factor.

If all this is enough to make you want to start tying, take a class. The money is well spent, for tying is frustrating to learn without help. There are beginner's books and video tapes on the market, and some of them are good. But nothing will get you started as well as a class. It's comforting, too, to see how poorly your fellow beginners are doing. The most inspirational moment in my classes has been when I've showed the students my first fly. All of them feel better about their own efforts, so bad is that fly.

Beginners will find the number of items listed here boggling. Let's make it simple. As a beginner, you need a vise, a bobbin, a pair of scissors, hackle pliers, a whip finisher, and materials. You can get along without the other tools or make your own for a while. Supplies and materials you should have include cement, thread, hooks, a neck or two, some dubbing, and any other materials the flies you wish to tie require.

The initial investment will go something like this:

Vise—about $20-$35	Thread—$1
Bobbin—$4-$6	Hooks—$5/100
Scissors—$5-$8	Neck—$8-$10
Hackle pliers—$3-$5	Dubbing—about $5
Whip finisher—$5	Other materials—$5
Cement—$1.50	Total—$62.50-$86.50

That means you'll have to tie between 50 and 70 flies to break even on the initial investment. Add $40-$50 for lessons, and you've got some tying ahead of you. And this is a very skin-and-bones budget. Within two fishing seasons, however, you'll be even, and from then on, your flies will cost you very little except your time. And time spent at the tying desk is recreational.

But, again, I don't want to dwell on economics. Fly tying will add to your overall appreciation of fly fishing. What's a better investment than that?

I've listed the tools first in this chapter, followed by the hackle, dubbing, and hooks. We'll begin with the tool that is most important to your success as a tier, the vise.

FLY TYING TOOLS

Fly Tying Vises

The fly tying vise has one function—to hold the hook securely while you're attaching feathers and other things to it. For this, you'll pay anything from about $15 to over $150, depending on your needs, your involvement in tying, and your mood.

Remember that some people (notably Lee Wulff) don't use a vise at all. They hold the hooks and all in their hands. I don't know anyone coordinated enough to tie flies that way, but it's done. And I suppose a Vise-Grip taped to a table would do the job, but there's no convenience and even less art in this kind of a system. So, a vise is considered essential.

The most common type of vise uses the collet-and-sleeve system. Tapered jaws are pulled into the sleeve, forcing them closed. A lever on a cam is often used to pull the jaws into the sleeve. Another common system is a threaded hand nut or T-handle which pulls the jaws in as it is tightened. Some vises use a threaded sleeve which compresses the jaws as it's tightened. The Regal Vise is one notable exception to the common closure system. Its jaws are closed and must be opened by a lever.

Attached to the vise head, which includes the jaws and their closure system, is the vise shaft. In most vises, this is simply a straight steel rod about ⅜" in diameter. A special C-clamp slides on this shaft, and the clamp attaches to the tying table. On some less expensive vises, the C-clamp is cast as an integral part of the shaft, and the height of the vise is not adjustable.

An alternative to the C-clamp is the pedestal base. This is a heavy base into which the shaft is secured to provide the necessary stability during tying. Pedestal bases have the advantage of not requiring a table, but they have little, if any, height adjustment.

The basic vise, then, uses the collet-and-sleeve system to tighten the jaws. The jaws are held at a fixed angle. The straight shaft fits into a C-clamp, and its position on the shaft is movable to allow height adjustment. Other features on vises are considered options, and there's where the extra cost comes in.

The first option you may wish to have is an adjustment for the tilt of the jaws. Being able to change the angle of tilt can aid in attaching some materials and can also simply add to the tier's comfort. The adjustment is made, typically, by loosening a nut at the junction of the jaws and shaft. A tool is usually required for this change.

The second option is rotation of the jaws within the sleeve. This allows the hook to be turned upside down. Salmon fly tiers relish this option since so many materials are placed under the hook. It also allows inspection of the dreaded Other Side of the fly, which many of us ignore out of simple fear of what it looks like. Lacquering is made easier with this option, too.

A final option for adjustment of jaws is a side-to-side movement. Again, this allows inspection of the Other Side. On most vises, this adjustment can be made simply by loosening the lock nut holding the shaft to the clamp or pedestal and turning the whole vise. Some vise heads are designed to move in this way as an extra convenience.

Here's a list of the vises that have these options.

Tilt option: Benchmark, CarterCraft, Futura, Helux 350, HMH, Price, Regal, Renzetti, Thompson Ultra, and Xuron.

Rotation option: Benchmark, CarterCraft, Futura, HMH, Orvis, Price, Reed's, Regal Rotating, Renzetti Presentation, Thompson 360, and Universal.

Side-to-side option: Price, Regal (with adaptor), Renzetti Presentation, and Xuron.

For the beginner. The beginner at fly tying will likely find the list of choices bewildering. There are so many vises available, even in the beginner's price range, that decisions are difficult. This is, however, one area in fly fishing that has an industry standard that is appropriate to beginner and experienced tier alike. That standard is the Thompson A vise.

The Thompson A is offered by more companies, by far, than any other vise. It's been fancied up by its parent company and copied by many other companies, but it remains the most popular of the vises and perhaps the most practical.

The Thompson A was the first collet-and-sleeve vise. Its basic design hasn't changed over the years. The quality of the workmanship and materials is excellent for its price, about $30.

A beginner may be attracted by the lower-cost imported copies of the Thompson vise. They can be purchased for about half as much. Some of these imports are real dogs, but some of them can be a suitable alternative for the tier on a budget. Look for a vise with well-fitting jaws and good overall finish.

Even if you get a good imported vise, there are usually two problems with them. The first is the quality of the steel in the jaws. The jaws will wear faster than those of the Thompson. When they do wear, however, they can often be replaced with standard Thompson jaws. The other common problem is with the casting of the C-clamp. I've seen these clamps crack and break simply under the pressure of being attached to a table.

In answer to the imports, Thompson has created the Patriot vise, a vise that's similar to the A. As such, it's a superior choice to the Thompson B, their former beginner's vise. At about $18, the Patriot should provide an attractive alternative to those people who feel they need to save the bucks.

The purchase of a vise is not the best place in fly tying for a beginner to save money, since the vise is central to success.

Other vises of good reputation in the beginner's price range include the Crest vises, the Helux vises, and the Orvis Simplicity. Some of the other inexpensive vises listed here may be entirely adequate, but I'm not familiar with them.

I have, incidentally, omitted a number of vises that I feel are just too limited to be of use. Almost all of them are imports from India. Most of them have poor jaws closure and poor workmanship.

Fly Tying Vises

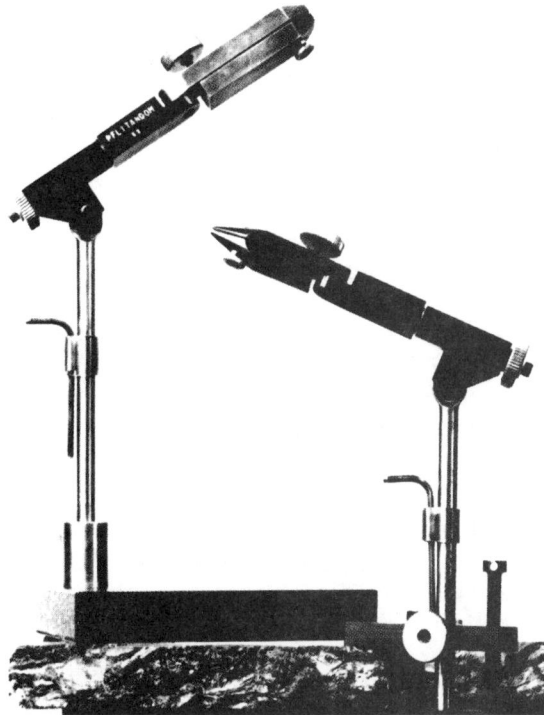

CarterCraft Pocket Vise. *Similar in style to Pfli-tandom but without all the adjustment features.*
$49.95 CarterCraft (see address above)

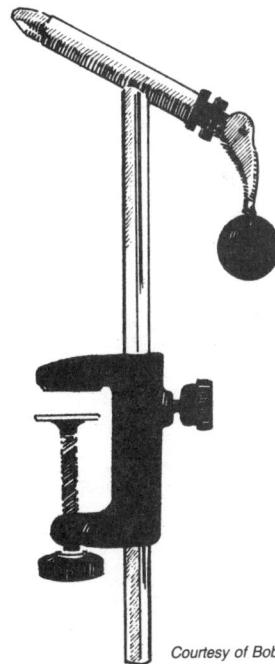

Courtesy of Bob Jacklin

Benchmark Vise. *Collet with threaded hand nut close; fully machined parts; rotates 360 degrees; angle fully adjustable; non-glare finish on vise, chrome on shaft; narrow jaws.*
$69.95 Bul

CarterCraft Pfli-tandom Vise. *Jaws tighten in parallel movement with hex wrench; rotates, tilts, fully adjustable; an interesting design, very flexible in use; folds up to fit easily in vest pocket or tying kit; three jaw sizes available; wood, pedestal, or "Anyplace"-type base; lifetime guarantee.*
$99.50-$112.50 (depending on base) CarterCraft Sales, 5510 Dean Court S.E., Salem, Oregon 97301 (503) 390-0199

Crest Supreme (#300). *Collet with lever-and-cam close; hard plastic ball on end of lever; non-glare finish; for hooks #2-#32; C-clamp; optional jaws; adjustable height; lifetime guarantee against defects.*
$24.95-$31.95 AnJ, Bud, EJH, Tac, Hun, Bob, Mer, Tid, Fly

Crest Custom (#200). *Collet with threaded "T"-handle close; non-glare finish; C-clamp; adjustable height; lifetime guarantee against defects.*
$21.76-$26.95 Fly, Bud, Mer, Tac

Crest Custom S/S (#400). *Similar to #200 but with slotted jaws for hooks from #2-6/0.*
$26.95 Fly

Crest Vise (#100). *Collet with threaded handle close; non-glare finish; economy vise; C-clamp cast with vise shaft, so not adjustable.*
$16.50-$19.95 Mer, Tac

Futura Vise. *Collet with threaded locking nut close; tilts and rotates; stainless steel; height adjustable; "Anyplace"-type clamp fits any size table.*
$29.95 Cab

Helux Model 350. *Collet with lever-and-cam close; collet has tilt adjustment and locking Allen bolt; non-glare finish; height adjustable; C-clamp.*
$34.95 Tac

Helux Model 250. *Similar to Model 350 but without tilt feature.*
$25.95 Tac

Helux Model 100. *Collet with threaded "T"-handle close; height adjustable; C-clamp.*
$21.95-$26.95 Tac, Nat

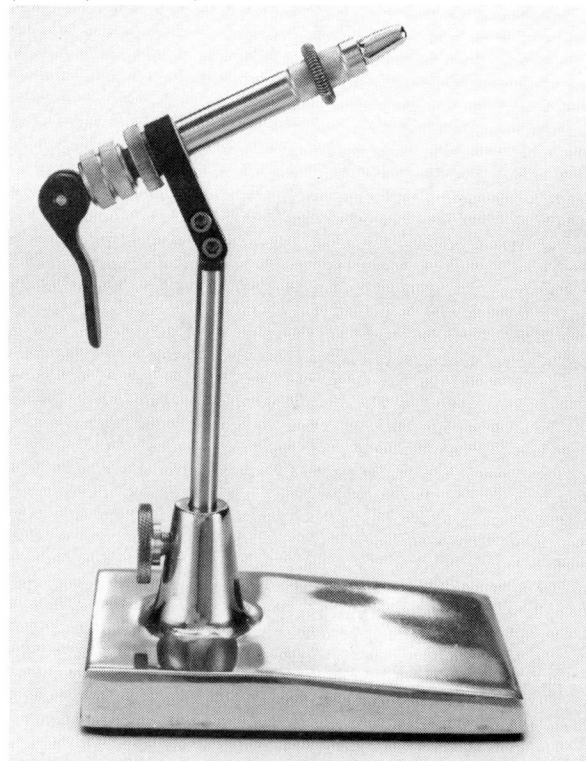

HMH Vise. *Collet with lever-and-cam close; all parts in vise itself are machined; angle adjustable; full rotation; with two jaws, Magnum for 6/0-#16 and Midge for #12-#32; optional jaws available; C-clamp (2½") or pedestal base (4½ lb.); lifetime guarantee against defects.*
C-clamp—$155-$157.50; pedestal—$184-$185; both—$215
Mer, Hig, Nat, Fly, Don, Hun, Fre

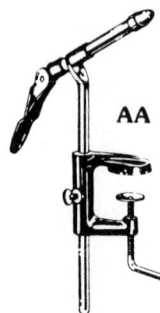

Import AA. *A Thompson "A" copy made in India; although a reasonable facsimile, you get what you pay for; expect jaws to wear faster and cast base to be more fragile; a generic name for vises sold under a variety of brand names including FTM, Sunrise, and Hank Roberts.*
$9.95-$18 Many catalogs

Master Vise. *Collet with lever-and-cam close; 360 degree rotation; two jaws included; angled jaws; non-glare finish; height adjustable; C-clamp.*
$24.95 Cab

Orvis Fly Tying Vise. *Collet with lever-and-cam close; jaws hold #2-#28 hooks; rotates 360 degrees with locking capability throughout rotation; jaws can be locked in regular or inverted position; non-glare black finish; height adjustable to 8" above table; C-clamp; replacement parts available.*
$67.50 Orv, Fly, Bud, Let, Hig, Ste

Orvis Simplicity Vise. *Similar to Orvis vise above but with stationary jaws.*
$36 Orv

Price Vise. *Collet with threaded hand nut close; fully adjustable to raise and lower fly, swivel toward tier, angle up and down, rotate 360 degrees; jaws hold flies from*

5/0-#28; black finish; adjustable height; C-clamp adjustable to 3¾" with holes for use with Price Lamp and Magnifier (listed separately); lifetime guarantee.
$99.95 Kau, Nat, Fly, Mur, Edd

Price Jr. Vise. *Simpler model of Price Vise; jaws do not rotate or swivel.*
$49.95 Nat, Kau

Price Jr. Travel Vise. *Take-down version of Price Jr.; fits in 5"x7" fleece-lined wallet.*
$59.95 Kau

Reed's Super Vise. *Collet with lever-and-cam close; full rotation with release of lock nut; non-glare finish; angled jaws; standard and super jaws included; C-clamp; height adjustable.*
$38.25 Ree

Reed's Fly Tying Vise. *Collet with threaded handle close; one-piece construction; economy vise; C-clamp; height adjustable.*
$17.50 Ree

Regal Vise. *Jaws sprung shut, opened by lever for hook insertion; takes hooks from 6/0-#32; tilts 180 degrees up and down; larger hooks held in place by unique "pocket"; height adjustable; C-clamp or pedestal base; lifetime guarantee.*
C-clamp—$69-$89; pedestal—$89-$99 Edd, Kau, T&T, Dan, Fly, Hig, Bud, Blu

Regal Rotating Vise. *Same as regular Regal but with full rotation possible; available in C-clamp or pedestal.*
C-clamp—$105; pedestal—$125 Bud, T&T

Regal Vise Neck Adaptor. *A 2-minute conversion allows movement of the vise jaws side to side as well as up and down.*
$7.50 T&T

Renzetti Master Vise. *Collet with threaded close; curved stem can be adjusted to any angle at juncture with pedestal base; fine jaws for hooks #2-#20; optional jaws; stainless steel, brass, and aluminum construction; a quality vise of unusual design; C-clamp or pedestal base.*
pedestal—$71.95; clamp—$67.15 Dal

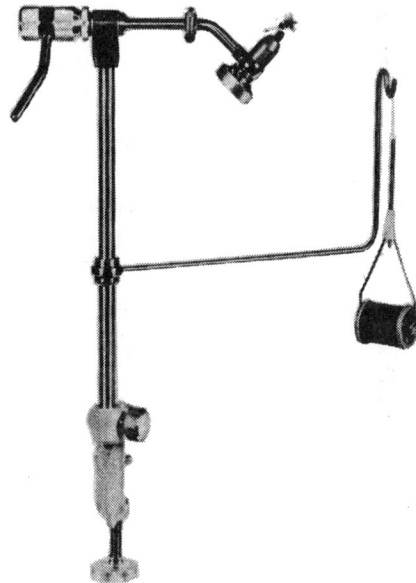

Renzetti Presentation Vise. *Collet with threaded lock nut close; arm holding jaws rotates on ball bearings; extremely close tolerances in the machining of parts; two jaws—standard (#2-#20) and midge (#16-#28); stainless steel, brass, and aluminum; C-clamp or adjustable pedestal base.*
pedestal—$145.18; clamp—$138.99 Dal

Streamside Vise. *A small vise that can be held in hand or screwed into downed tree or wooden post streamside; finger loop and screw attachment included.*
$4.95-$7.50 EJH, Dal, Let

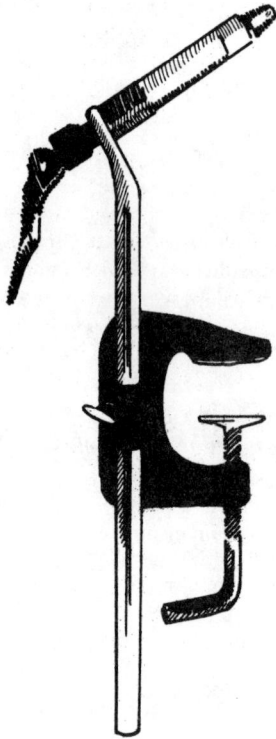

Courtesy of Bob Jacklin

Thompson "A". *The standard in the field; the original collet vise; lever-and-cam close; optional jaws; available in black finish as "Pro" model (add about $3); adjustable height; C-clamp.*
$23.90-$36 Sim, Mer, Kau, Pen, Cor, Ree, Dal, Let, Hun, Mur, Don, Cab, Hig, Spo, Ran, EJH, Egg, Tac, Blu, H&H, Bud, T&T, Edd, Dan, AnR, Fly, Bob
Thompson "B". *Collet same size as "A"; tightened by threaded hand nut; 9" cast aluminum stand with integral C-clamp; an economy vise.*
$18.60-$29.75 Sim, Tac, Ran, Mer, Let
Thompson "C". *Similar to "B" but collet horizontal and shorter.*
$25 Let

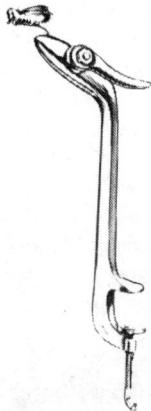

Thompson "F". *Jaws capable of wider opening than standard vises; non-standard lever close; cast aluminum*

stand with integral C-clamp; an economy, special purpose vise.
$13.25-$16.81 Don, Sim, Mer, Cor, Ree, Dal, EJH
Thompson Patriot Vise. *Heralded as America's answer to the cheap imports; collet with lever-and-cam close; non-glare finish; adjustable height; C-clamp.*
$15.50-$22.95 H&H, T&T, Cor, Ran

Courtesy of Bob Jacklin

Thompson Pro II. *A Thompson "A" in a weighted pedestal base; non-glare finish; optional jaws.*
$40.05-$65 H&H, Mer, Tac, T&T, Dan, Fly, Cor, Let, Sim, Bob, Kau, Edd, Hig, Cab, Spo
Thompson Three-Sixty. *Similar to "A" but with 360 degree rotation; no need to loosen screws or levers for rotation; uses two adjustable Delcrin washers for tension; accepts "A" accessories; pedestal base.*
$47.25-$69.95 H&H, Pen, Mer, Tac, EJH, T&T, Spo, Dan

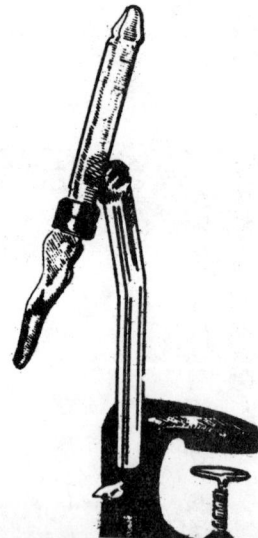

Thompson Ultra. *Similar to "A" in design but with fully adjustable collet angle; adjusts with screw; can be used horizontally or vertically; adjustable height; C-clamp.*
$26-$39.25 Many catalogs

Universal #2 Rotating Vise. *Small vise with rotating capabilities; bobbin holder included.*
$22.50 Ran
Veniard Cranbrook. *Collet with lever-and-cam close; hooks up to 3/0; adjustable height; C-clamp.*
$24 Let
Veniard Ingram. *Similar to Cranbrook but with threaded lock nut close.*
$24 Let
Veniard Croydon Hand Vise. *The original after which the Streamside Vise (listed above) is patterned; made in England; small vise with finger loop.*
$10.95 Let
Waite Forward. *Patterned after Price Vise (and advertised as being identical).*
$49.95 Waite Forward, 2922 N.E. Waller, Bend, Oregon 97701 (503) 388-1185
Xuron Vise. *A modernistic-looking vise, certainly the most striking design among the vises; straight jaws with lever close; for hooks from 5/0-#28; available with ball joint base for more adjustment possibilities; vise shaft bent for more freedom of movement while tying; can be used left- or right-handed; chromed but optional black finish for head or base or both; C-clamp or pedestal; an interesting alternative to the traditional vise; lifetime guarantee.*
C-clamp—$49.95-$51.20; C-clamp rotary—$64-$66; pedestal—$78.40; pedestal rotary—$92-$98 Mer, AnR, Edd, Don

Electric Fly Tying Vise

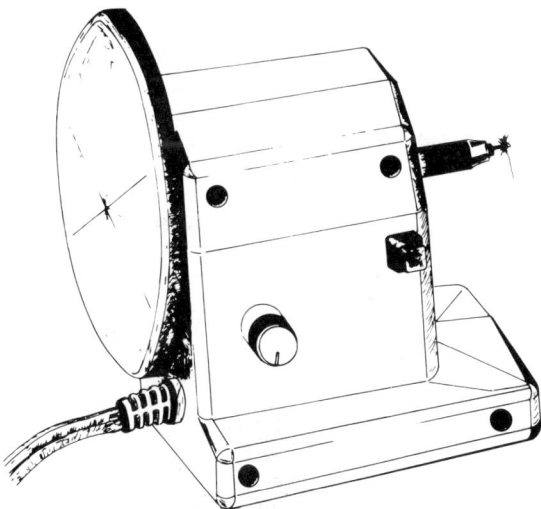

DIMENSIONS:
7½" High   8" Long   5" Wide
Design is protected by Registration #8417975.

The industrial revolution has finally arrived in fly tying. Recently introduced, the Electrical Fly Tying Vise from Pollard Enterprises is advertised as being "for the fly fisherman who thinks he has everything".

The collett sticks straight out from the quality plastic case that houses the motor. A computer chip controls the variable speed motor. The vise is well designed and manufactured.

If you already tie, the vise will force you to reverse your tying habits. You know the old saying abut the difference between stream and lake fishing. In a stream, the water moves and the fish stay in one place. In a lake, the fish move and the water stays in one place. In regular tying, the bobbin rotates and the hook stays in one place. In electric tying, the hook rotates and the bobbin stays in one place.

You can order the Electrical Fly Tying Vise for $160 from Pollard Enterprises, Box 4915, Boise, Idaho 83711. Visa and Mastercard are welcome.

Optional Bases and Clamps

A number of optional holders for the vise standard (shaft) are available. The pedestal base is the most common option, and three are offered here.

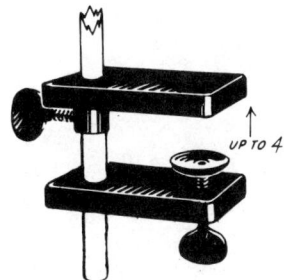

An interesting alternative to the traditional C-clamp is the Anyplace Base. By dividing the C-clamp into two separate parts, this device allows the attachment of a vise to surfaces as thick as four inches. It's great for the camping fly tier who has to deal with Forest Service picnic tables, which were definitely not designed with the fly tier in mind.

Finally, you may find the Vise Stand Adaptor helpful. This L-shaped rod fits into the standard C-clamp and takes the vise shaft on the other end. The rod will allow an additional 4½" of height adjustment and will also allow the vise to be swung away from the tying table.

Anyplace Base. *A two-section C-clamp; each section secures to the typical ³⁄₈" vise standard with thumb screws; will allow vise placement on thick tables to 4" (like the picnic tables in Yellowstone National Park).*
$6.58-$8.25 Kau, Tac, Tid, Fre, AnJ, Bud, Mer
Benchmark C-Clamp. *For standard ³⁄₈" shafts; machined parts.*
$14.95 Bul
Crest Pedestal Base. *Pedestal base; rubber pad on bottom; takes down for easy transport; accepts ³⁄₈" vise shaft.*
$15-$18.95 Bud, Mer, Fly, Tac

Reed's Deluxe Pedestal Base. *All metal; blued, lacquered finish; will hold vise shaft horizontally or vertically.*
$13.95 Ree

Thompson Conversion Base. *Pedestal base; accepts Thompson vises and others with shafts up to ⅜"; steel with rubber pads on bottom.*
$25.95-$36.95 Cor, Cab, Mer, T&T, Kau, EJH, H&H, Spo

Vise Stand Adaptor. *An L-shaped rod that fits in vise C-clamp and takes vise shaft; raises or lowers vise as much as 4½"; a nifty idea if you can't ever get the right height.*
$14.95 Hun

Material Clips

Material clips are used to hold tying materials out of the way while other materials are attached or worked with. The simplest clip is a coil spring that is hooked over the vise's collet sleeve. The other common clip is a stamped metal sleeve that slips over the collet sleeve and sticks up above it. I happen to prefer the simple coil spring. It will hold several materials at once, slides easily up and down the sleeve, and is less obtrusive.

HMH Material Clip. *Stainless steel wire; fits ½"-⅝" collet sleeves.*
$.60 Hun

Spring clip. *A spring hooked together and pushed over collet sleeve; simple and does the job.*
$.25-$1.50 Bud, Tac, Dan, T&T, Edd, Kau, Mur, Dal, Fly, H&H, Hig, Let, EJH, Ste, AnR

Sunrise Material Clip. *Stamped metal clip; slips over collet sleeve and sticks up to hold materials.*
$.75-$1.49 Sim, Dan, Spo, Egg, EJH, Tac, Ste

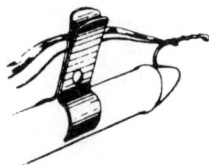

Thompson Material Clip. *Similar to Sunrise above; blued.*
$1.70-$2 Kau, Dal, H&H, Hig, Blu, T&T, Let, Edd, Ree

Bobbin Rests and Other Tools

Bobbin rests are designed to hold the bobbin away from the vise and in a stationary position. This not only keeps it out of the way, it also keeps the bobbin from spinning. The other tools here are specialized devices, one for holding parachute-style wings upright while the fly is completed and the other to aid in building extended bodies.

Lempke-Cordes Fly Body Extender. *Post-and-pulley system holds extended body during tying.*
$29.95 Fre

Parachute Tool. *The "gallows" tool; attaches to any vise shaft; holds parachute wing upright during tying.*
$4.25 Let

Renzetti Bobbin Cradle. *Heavy wire rest attaches to vise shaft and extends beyond jaws to hold bobbin.*
$12.39 Dal

Thompson Bobbin Rest. *Wire rest extends beyond tip of jaws to hold bobbin and thread stationary during tying.*
$5.95-$8.10 Sim, Kau, Tac, EJH, Mer, Hig

Optional Jaws

Optional jaws are necessary with most vises to hold the full range of hook sizes you may use. The list below should allow you to select jaws appropriate to your needs.

Midge Head. *A small accessory midge jaw; flat metal butt fits into regular vise and is clamped there; the midge jaws hold okay although they wear quickly; expect some trouble getting head to hold in regular vise.*
$3.80-$6.95 H&H, Edd, Kau, Dan, Let, Dal, EJH

Crest Midge or Saltwater Jaws. *Replacement jaws for small and large flies; sold separately.*
$7.95-$8.50 Tid, Bud

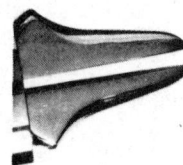

Trout Jaws   Restricted Jaws

HMH Trout Jaws. *For #2-#22 flies.*
$18.45 Mer, Hun, Fre

HMH Restricted Jaws. *For #18-#32 flies.*
$18.45-$18.50 Mer, Don, Hun, Fre

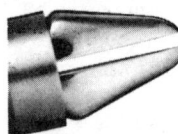

Midge Jaws   Magnum Jaws

HMH Midge Jaws. *For #12-#32 flies.*
$18.45-$18.50 Hun, Don, Mer

HMH Magnum Jaws. *For 6/0-#16 flies.*
$18.45-$18.50 Mer, Don

Renzetti Magnum Jaws. *For hooks to 5/0.*
$9.55 Dal

Renzetti Midge Jaws. *For #16-#28 flies.*
$8.50 Dal

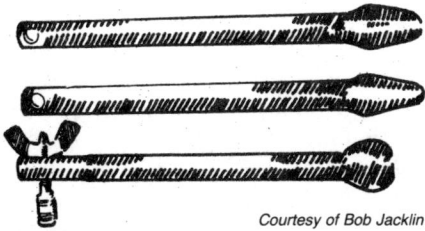

Courtesy of Bob Jacklin

Thompson Midge Jaws. *For #18-#22 flies.*
$6.95-$12 Most catalogs
Thompson Super Jaws. *For 1/0-6/0 flies.*
$6.95-$13 Many catalogs
Thompson Standard Jaws. *Replacement jaws.*
$8.50-$11.25 Edd, Dan, Cor, Hig, Bob, Fly
Thompson Replacement Parts. *All parts on Thompson A are available.*
Varies with part Kau

Fly Tying Lights

A tying lamp will improve your flies—more light, more precision. There are several here specifically designed for tying. These include the Price, Orvis, Magni-Tyer, and the Moffat lamps. All of them are small and positioned by goosenecks. The Moffat must be permanently attached or used with an optional C-clamp; the Magni-Tyer uses a C-clamp. The others attach to the vise shaft.

The Vise-Lite is a travel lamp based on the design of the Flex-Lite. A very nifty idea for camping tiers.

The other lamps have been adopted from other uses. The Luxo Lamp is a regular swing-arm lamp, as is the Magna Lux (which has a magnifying lens). The fluorescent magnifying lamp is used at drafting tables, in art departments, and at electronic repair desks. As adopted tools, they're great.

I used a regular swing-arm lamp for years. The one I bought cost $14.95 and uses a poorly designed C-clamp that drives me nuts. Once the set-up is done, the lamp is fine. You can pick one up at your local discount store. I recently replaced that light with one that has a magnifier, somewhat similar to the Magna Lux. It uses a standard incandescent bulb rather than the circular fluorescent bulb, and although the first one I had melted under the heat of the 60 watt bulb it said I could use, the second one (courtesy of the retailer) with a 40 watt bulb has been a pleasure to use. I guess the best thing was that it only cost about $25.

So, if you don't care about portability, you can get a satisfactory inexpensive lamp or lamp/magnifier locally. It seems to me that all the lamps here, except the Vise-Lite and perhaps the Magna Lux, are too expensive. Someone should be able to make a small, convenient lamp for less money.

Fluorescent magnifying lamp. *Swing-arm lamp with circular fluorescent light (which means no hot lamp in your face); 5" lens; extra outlet on clamp base.*
$79.95 Cab

Luxo Lamp. *Swing-arm lamp; spring-loaded, fully adjustable arms; pedestal base (hooray, no cheap C-clamp to hassle with); heat sink shade.*
$59.95 Kau
Magna Lux Magnifier Light. *Swing-arm lamp and magnifier; 3¾" ground-glass lens with light source directly next to it; spring-loaded arms for fully adjustable 39" reach; 3x power; 40W bulb included; 4-way clamp.*
$44.95 Kau
Magni-Tyer. *Separate goosenecks (10") for lamp and magnifier; mounted on 8" stem which attaches to table with C-clamp; lots of clearance; 25W bulb; 5" plastic lens comes with protective flannel bag (all plastic lenses must be treated carefully during cleaning or scratches will result).*
$63-$70 Mer, Fly, Tid, Fre
Moffat Lamp. *Flexible neck; plastic shade; 100 watt capacity; must be mounted with "quick coupler" (included) or special C-clamp ($11.90); optional magnifier (listed below).*
$49.95 AnJ
Orvis Vise Lamp. *A small high-intensity lamp with gooseneck; attaches to ⅜" or ⁷⁄₁₆" vise shaft; optional magnifier (listed below).*
$59.50 Orv
Price Lamp with Magnifier. *Flexible neck; fits Price vises; small magnifying lens attached.*
$69.95 Kau, Fly
Vise-Lite. *9" gooseneck Flex-Lite; attaches to vise shaft; adjustable beam; great for camp tying; battery operated.*
$16.95-$19.95 Cab, Hun, T&T, Kau

Fly Tying Magnifiers

Magnifiers are a great help to many of us and a necessity for some of us. Whatever magnifying system you select, be sure to try it out first. You'll need to make sure you won't get eyestrain from it, and need to see how much working room there is behind the lens.

Some of the lamps listed above also come with magnifying lenses, and you may wish to consider one of them.

Fly Tying Glasses. *Half-frame eyeglasses; look through for magnifying or over for regular vision without having to remove glasses; 2x.*
$7-$8.95 Cab, LLB
Moffat Magnifier. *Flexible neck; 4" ground glass lens; 2x power; must be mounted with "quick coupler" (included) or special C-clamp ($11.90).*
$34.50 AnJ
Optipack Magnifier. *Small, portable lens; with fold-up case; attaches to collet sleeve of vise. (Note: I don't think this would be satisfactory for continued use while tying, but you could use it for selected fine work.)*
$7.50 EJH
Orvis Magnifier. *Option for Orvis Vise Lamp (listed above); attaches to vise shaft.*
$30 Orv

Bobbins

Bobbins hold spools of thread and other tying materials. Generally they dispense the material through a stainless steel tube. The most common form uses a spring-steel frame to hold the spool of material. Tension can be adjusted by bending the steel wire. The Thompson Jiffy Bobbin uses a wing nut for tension adjustment, and the Chase Bobbin can be tightened or loosened with a screw adjustment.

There are many fine tools here, but a few are worthy of special mention. For beauty, try the Thompson bobbin made of mesquite wood. Thompson offers a full set of these tools. The Dorin bobbins feed thread through a hole near the end of the bobbin tube, thus eliminating the need for bobbin threader and cleaner. That's a definite improvement. This same improvement is evident in the Spring Bob, which has a very short tube. The springiness of the resulting lever action also aids in protecting the thread from breakage.

Brass Thumb Bobbin. *Spring steel bobbin with enlarged brass center section for thumb.*
$4.25-$5 FlR, Dal

Chase Bobbin. *Case extends from tube around spool giving larger hand hold; short tube; requires coin to exchange spools; spool tension fully adjustable.*
$4.25-$6.45 Sim, TCR, Ran, Dan, Mer, Let, Ree, Edd

Crest Custom Bobbin #4. *Spring steel with hardened chrome tube and brass spool arms; hard plastic spool ears; 4½".*
$2.95-$3.72 AnJ, Mer

Crest Custom Bobbin #5. *Similar to #4 but longer; 5½".*
$3.72 Mer

Crest Custom Bobbin #6. *Similar to #4 but shorter.*
$3.72-$3.95 AnJ, Mer

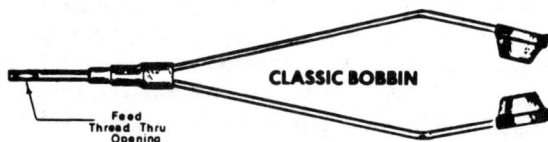

CLASSIC BOBBIN

Feed Thread Thru Opening

Dorin Classic Bobbin. *Stainless steel tube and frame; brass spool ears; thread feeds through hole in side of tube eliminating need for bobbin threader; for 3/0 and smaller threads; 3¾".*
$4.75-$5.25 Bob, Mer, T&T

Dorin Dual Bobbin. *Stainless steel tube and frame; brass spool ears; thread feeding system as above; small tube extension fits in end to convert for smaller flies; 4⅛".*
$4.75-$5.75 Bud, T&T, Mer

Dorin Maxi Bobbin. *Stainless steel tube and frame; brass spool ears; thread feeding system as above; for heavier threads, A-3/0; 4".*
$4.95-$5.25 T&T, Mer

Matarelli Bobbin. *Hard-chrome nickel tube and stainless steel frame; brass spool ears; made in USA; available in regular (3½") or long (4½").*

$4.20-$5.95 Kau, H&H, Let, Fly, Edd, Bob, Hig, Bud, Hun, Dan, Tac, AnR, Blu, Mur

Matarelli Floss Bobbin. *Same as regular bobbin but with flared tube for handling fine thread and floss; available in regular or long.*
$4.20-$5.95 Kau, Mur, AnR, Tac, Bud, Hig, H&H, Hun, Don, Blu, Dan

Matarelli Midge Bobbin. *Same configuration as regular bobbin but sprung tightly for sewing machine bobbins; 3".*
$4.20-$5.95 (thread bobbins $.50 each-$.75/3—Kau, Hig) Blu, Don, Dan, Fly, Hig, Kau, Bud, Hun, H&H, Let, Tac, AnR

Matarelli Travel Bobbin. *Tube big enough to take regular thread but uses sewing machine bobbins like Midge model.*
$5 Hun

R.C. Rumpf Bobbin. *Spring steel with chrome tube; 4¼"; flare-tube available.*
$2.85 Sim

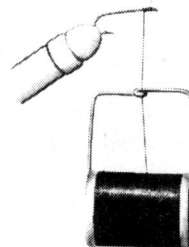

Reed Bobbette. *Very simple bobbin; one-piece wire with center loop for thread or floss.*
$.55 Ree

Renzetti Midge Bobbin. *Stainless steel frame and tube; brass spool ears; 3⅜".*
$5.18-$5.95 Dal, AnR, T&T, Mer, Blu

Renzetti Streamer Bobbin. *As above but larger for 6/0 and heavier threads; 4⅜".*
$5.36-$6.10 Mer, T&T, Dal

Renzetti Material Bobbin. *Stainless steel frame and tube; plastic spool ears; designed to handle lead wire and tinsels; 3¼".*
$4.75-$5.50 AnR, T&T, Mer

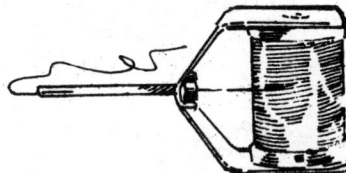

Courtesy of Bob Jacklin

Renzetti Floss Bobbin. *Stainless steel frame and flared tube; plastic spool ears; for floss, obviously; 3¾".*
$4.28-$4.95 Blu, Mer, Dal, T&T

S&M Bobbin. *An economy bobbin; flat metal spool holder; full adjustment on thread tension; short (1¼") and long (2") tubes available.*
$2.20-$4 Bob, Sim, Let, Edd, Ran, H&H, Mer

S&M Material Bobbin. *A holder for spools of floss and other bulky materials; no tube; ½" or 1" width.*
$.75-$1.25 Mer, EJH, Bob, Edd

Spring-Bob. *Stainless steel frame and tube; tube very short for easy threading; designed to be springy in use to protect threads; a very interesting innovation.*
$6.95 Fly
Sunrise Wire Bobbin. *Stainless steel frame and tube; brass spool ears.*
$2.95-$4 Edd, Dan, Fol, Let

Thompson Jiffy Bobbin. *Snap arbor; tension adjustable with wing nut; sizes: 2½", 4".*
$4.73-$6 H&H, Mer, Ree, EJH, Tac, Cab, Spo
Thompson Spring Wire Bobbin. *Stainless steel frame and tube; tube offset to allow direct feed from spool to tube.*
$4.73-$7.50 Mer, Cor, Let, Edd
Thompson Classic Wood Bobbin. *Open-frame style turned from mesquite; uses sewing machine bobbins; same tool as featured in the Thompson tool kits.*
$15.38-$18 Mer, Hig
Veniard Spigot Bobbin. *Stainless steel frame and tube; brass spool ears.*
$4 Let

Bobbin Threaders

Bobbin threaders and cleaners can save you from getting red in the face. Without the use of the threader, the only way to thread a bobbin is to suck the thread through the tube. This technique can lead to hyperventilation, especially if you haven't used a bobbin cleaner to ream the tube. Considering the cheapness of this tool, everyone should have one of these on their tying table.

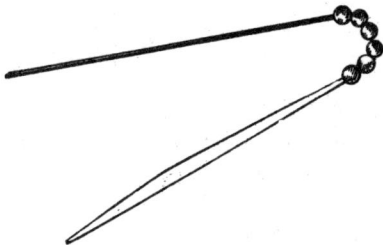

Crest Bobbin Threader/Cleaner. *One end is looped for threading bobbin, other straight for cleaning tube; bead chain "handle" in between.*
$1.62-$1.95 Mer, Fly

Dorin Bobbin Threader. *No details.*
$1.75 Mer
Matarelli Bobbin Threader/Cleaner. *Similar in style to Crest Threader/Cleaner above.*
$2.10-$3.25 Kau, Blu, Dan, Bob, Let, Mur, AnR, Hig, Tac, H&H, Hun (midge size too)
Renzetti Midge Bobbin Threader/Cleaner. *Wire loop one end; cleaning needle other end.*
$4.28-4.95 Blu, Dal, Mer, T&T, AnR, Tac, Let

Renzetti Streamer Bobbin Threader. *Wire loop and metal handle; for larger bobbins.*
$2.25-$2.50 Mer, T&T
Renzetti Streamer Bobbin Cleaner. *Metal shaft for insertion in tube of larger bobbins.*
$2.25-$2.50 T&T, Mer
S&M Bobbin Threader. *Wire loop with brightly colored plastic bulb for handle.*
$.75-$.80 Mer, Bob, Edd
Thompson Bobbin Threader/Reamer. *Wire loop.*
$3.21 Mer
Threader/Cleaner. *Similar to Matarelli but with brass "handle" instead of beads.*
$2.50-$5.25 FlR, Orv, Edd
Universal Bobbin Threader. *Fine wire loop with fluorescent pink handle (for easy finding).*
$1.25 Ran

Bodkins

Bodkins are simply needles with handles. They're used for applying small droplets of cement to heads of small flies, for cleaning hook eyes, for teasing dubbing, and for separating quills. Some of these tools have half-hitch tools as part of the handle, a convenient arrangement, although other sizes of half-hitch tools (listed separately) will be needed for extremely small or large hooks.

Cane-Handled Bodkin. *Handle of rejected rod sections; as Hunter's catalog says, they may not have made great rods, but they make great bodkin handles.*
$2.50-$3.50 T&T, Hun
Crest Half-Hitch Bodkin. *Bodkin attached to brass half-hitch tool.*
$2.22-$2.50 AnJ, Mer, Fly
Dorin Bodkin. *Stainless steel needle in white plastic handle; small and regular.*
small—$1.75; reg.—$1.90 Mer
Renzetti Bodkin. *Brass hex handle.*
$2.50-$2.70 Hun, AnR, Let

Sunrise Small Bodkin. *Aluminum handle.*
$.85-$1.25 Let, Dan
Sunrise Bodkin. *Aluminum handle; with half-hitch tool.*
$1.35-$1.75 Fol, Dan, Let, Egg
Thompson Bodkin. *Heavy, knurled handle with hexagonal end; 4¼".*
$2.54-$4.75 Mer, Let, Dan, Cor, EJH, Edd, Don, Kau, Bud, Dal, H&H
Universal Half-Hitch Bodkin. *Steel needle with molded plastic half-hitch tool.*
$3.15 Sim

Dubbing Tools

There are two types of tools for dubbing. One is a needle with serrations. Some companies call these needles "teasers". The serrations allow you to "pick out" dubbing material already placed on the hook, thus creating a fuzzier fly. The other tool is a hook to help control a dubbing loop. Dubbing is placed in a loop of thread, spun tight to create a "chenille", then wound on the hook. A dubbing hook makes this operation more convenient. Some people use a hackle plier as a weight on the dubbing loop instead of a dubbing hook, but the plier will not open the loop for inserting material the way a good dubbing tool will. This is a secondary purchase for the tier on a budget, but once you've used one, you'll never understand how you got along without it.

One tool here is rather unusual and requires some explanation. The Multus Dubber is a machine for mass producing dubbing threads. Sections of thread are held in place on the face of the machine, and a crank twists the dubbed thread. The completed thread is placed on cards and stored in the bottom of the Dubber.

Some of the other inventive devices here sound like good ideas for the tier, but I haven't had the opportunity to try them. The thrill of exploration will have to be yours for now.

Andra Dubbing Teaser. *Dubbing hook one end, teasing needle with serrations on other.*
$3.75 Dan
Cal Bird's Dubbing Tools. *Set of 3 wires bent to different shapes; covers all dubbing needs, including spinning the dubbing, wrapping the dubbing on hook, and reinforcing herl and dubbing with thread.*
$7.95-$14.95 Kau, Dan
Crest Half-Hitch Dubbing Tool. *Wire bent to facilitate the twisting of dubbing materials; attached to half-hitch tool.*
$2.22-$2.75 Mer, AnJ, Fly
Donegal's Dubbing Needle. *Stainless steel needle on wood handle; handle turned on lathe in very attractive patterns; a nice addition to the tying table.*
$4.50 Don
Dubbing Needle. *Long hexagonal brass handle with needle.*
$2.65-$2.95 Orv, T&T

Dubbing Teaser. *Brass handle with dubbing hook on one end and barbed needle for teasing on other.*
$3.05-$4.85 Bud, T&T, H&H, Orv
Dubbing Twister. *1 oz. hex base; brass stem; stainless steel hook; heavy base makes this a quick twister.*
$2.95 Hun, T&T
Hellekson Dubbing Needle. *Brass and stainless steel; needle with half-hitch tool.*
$2.95 Nat
Matarelli Dubbing Loop Twister. *3-in-1 tool for dubbing; dubbing hook and twister one end, bodkin other end.*
$2.10-$3.25 H&H, Kau, Hig
Matarelli Shepherd's Hook. *A simple wire hook with bodkin on one end and dubbing hook on other.*
$2.10-$2.19 Hun, Tac, AnR

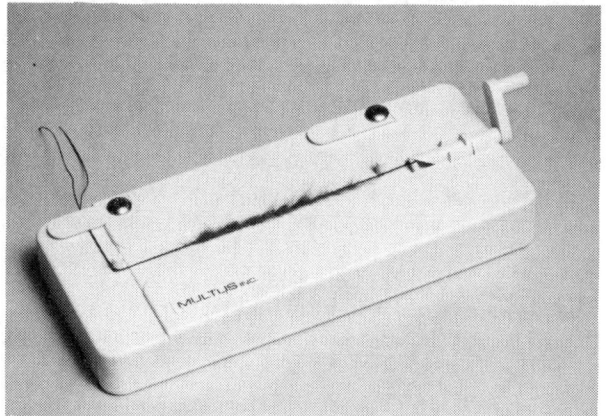

Multus Fur Dubber. *For preparing quantities of dubbing; run thread through crank to tab and back, lay dubbing on thread, use crank to wind tight; dubbed threads can be stored on slotted cards in compartment underneath.*
$9.50-$13.95 Pen, H&H, Bud, Orv, T&T
Renzetti Dubbing Needle. *Long metal handle with dubbing needle attached; brass and stainless steel; 6½".*
$2.39-$2.95 Mer, Blu, Tac, Dal, Let
Renzetti Dubbing Twister. *Wire twister on metal handle; brass and stainless steel.*
$2.39-$2.75 Tac, Mer, Dal
Renzetti Twister and Teaser. *Combination tool with wire twister and special dubbing teaser with fine serrations; brass and stainless steel.*
$3.75-$4.75 Mer, Hig, AnR, Edd, Dal, Tac
Renzetti Teaser Baby. *A small needle with serrated edge for teasing fur and hair.*
$1.13 Mer
Sunrise Dubbing Twister. *Hook on one end, finger loop other end.*
$1.85 Let
Sunrise Dubbing Twister and Bodkin. *"W"-shaped hook and bodkin.*
$1.85 Let

Thompson Dubbing Twister. *Heavy handle with short wire twister attached.*
$3.21 Mer
Veniard Dubbing Needle. *Knurled, aluminum handle.*
$1.75 Let
"W" Dubbing Twister. *Stainless steel wire bent in form of "W" to hold dubbing loop open while applying material.*
$2.25 Tac
Wood Handle Dubbing Teaser. *Metal pick on wood handle.*
$2 Bob

Hackle Gauges

Hackle gauges are handy little items, especially for the beginner or for the pro with limited ability to judge spacial relations. They allow you to judge hackle size "on the hoof", that is, while the hackles are still on the neck. Some people can judge hackle size accurately without a tool. Others have a pile of ill-selected hackles at the end of every tying session.

This tool can be very useful if you're inclined to speed up your tying by sorting feathers. The Du Bois tool has a circular gauge. The hackle is turned in a circle and placed on the gauge. The Sturgis tool is a tapered gauge. The hackle is spread and the tool placed underneath it. The distance from feather shaft to hackle edge is compared to the markings on the tool. The Du Bois tool also has a number of other gauges to help in judging proportions and other measuring needs.

Du Bois Fly Tier's Gauge. *Measures hackle, wings, tails, shank length, hook gape; printed on aluminum scale; 1½"x8".*
$3 Hun, Let

Sturgis Hackle Gauge. *Tapered celluloid gauge with widths marked to correspond to hackle sizes.*
$1.02-$1.95 Kau, EJH, Don, Ran, Tac, T&T, Dal, Mer, Spo, Blu, Hun

Hackle Guards

Hackle guards keep the hackle out of the way while the fly head is being finished. Both of these tools work the same way, although they're quite different in appearance. A hole with a split extending from it to the edge of the tool allows the guard to be placed over the hook eye with the thread left in front. The guard pushes the hackles back out of the way while the head is finished and cemented. These tools help beginner's with what seems an impossible task, but most experienced tiers have learned some magic to cope with the problem.

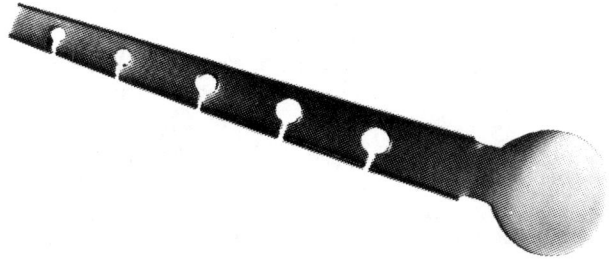

One-Piece Hackle Guard. *5 holes for small to large hooks.*
$1.50-$2.75 Fly, Fre, Kau

Thompson Hackle Guards. *Set of 3 guards of different sizes.*
$2.95-$4.75 Many catalogs

Hackle Pliers

Hackle pliers get more attention from tiers than any other tool except scissors. Hackle pliers are used to grasp the hackle while it's being turned onto the hook. This critical stage of tying must be done without glitches, and a good tool is essential.

The traditional hackle plier is the English-style tool. Heavy gauge steel wire is wound in a circle with the two ends protruding to one side. Jaws are formed on these ends, and these jaws are forced to meet. The tension of the coiled steel wire creates the grabbing power of the pliers. Squeezing opens the jaws and allows the hackle tip or butt to be placed between them. The circle of wire is then used as a finger loop for the winding.

Other pliers are made of flat metal, but all of them rely on the same idea. Perhaps the most controversial part of the selection of pliers is the construction of the jaws. On many of the English pliers, one or both jaws are corrugated. Other pliers use rubber pads, again on one or both jaws, which will distribute the tension on the hackle stems and reduce breakage. They don't hold as well, in return.

Dorin's "J" Pliers use an unusual departure from the standard form of jaws. One end of the pliers is coated with soft plastic; the other end is a bare metal hook. They hold extremely well, but it's difficult to insert the hackle tip into the opening. I haven't had the opportunity to try Dorin's Teardrop Pliers, but they are reputed to have very good holding qualities while still being easy to open and insert materials into.

The one other plier of note is the EZ Mini-Hook, which isn't a plier at all. It works in the fashion of plastic bobbers. A metal hook is pushed down, and the hackle tip is inserted into the opening. The spring is then released, and the hook retracts into a hole, closing the opening. Spring tension holds the hackle in place.

You'll probably have to do some experimenting to come up with the hackle pliers that work best for you. Since they are important to your success as a tier, you should not hesitate to spend the money on a good tool here.

Artery Clamp "Pliers". *We're borrowing from the medical profession again; these clamps are reputed to have a very secure grip (and well they should); 3 sizes.*
$3.35 Dan
Brass Hackle Pliers. *Traditional design in brass; fine, tapered nose.*
$3.25 Dal
Crest Standard Pliers (#70). *Flat high-carbon steel; long, narrow jaws for small hackles.*
$2.22 Mer
Crest Hackle Pliers (#80). *Both jaws corrugated; flat high-carbon steel; rubber grips.*
$2.50-$2.95 AnJ, Mer, Bob
Crest Sure-Grip Hackle Pliers (#90). *Traditional English pliers; stainless steel; jaws corrugated.*
$3.72-$3.95 Mer, AnJ
Danville Herb Howard Hackle Pliers. *Stainless steel; available in fine, medium, or large with long, tapered nose or regular nose; one side corrugated, other side smooth.*
$1.90-$3.25 Tac, Kau, Sim, H&H, Dal, Edd
Dorin "J" Pliers. *Spring steel; straight end covered in soft plastic; other end a stainless steel hook; hackle placed between metal part and plastic-covered end; new design.*
$2.25-$2.50 Bob, Fre, Bud, Mer, Dan

Dorin Teardrop Pliers. *Simple teardrop design; black finish; sizes: midge (2½") and standard (3").*
2½"—$2.45-$3.50; 3"—$3.95-$4.25 Tac, H&H, Dal, AnR, Mer, Bud, Kau, Orv, Ste, Fre, T&T

English Hackle Pliers. *It's difficult to tell, usually, whether "English" pliers are made in England or Japan or India since the name is used for a style of pliers as well as the origin of pliers; these are from Bob Jacklin's catalog, and Bob not only says they're from England, he says they're the finest quality pliers he's used; Bob ties a lot of flies, so we'll believe him; midge and standard.*
$4-$4.95 Bob

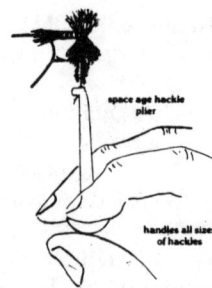

E-Z Mini Hook. *Not a pliers at all but a spring-loaded clip to hold hackle stem, floss, or other materials; some people swear by them, others at them; plastic case.*
$1.49-$2.50 Ran, Ste, T&T, Edd, Kau, Hig, Tac, Blu, Orv, H&H, EJH, Bud, Nat, AnR
Pro Hackle Pliers. *Spring wire with flat grips for ease in opening and closing; 2½" and 3".*
$3.25-$3.50 Tac
R.C. Rumpf Hackle Pliers. *Stainless steel in traditional English style; corrugated jaws; sizes: small and medium. (Note: These pliers are "chemically passivated" before shipping which is really nice if you don't want your pliers to be too active while you're trying to tie.)*
$2.30 Sim
Sunrise English-Style Pliers. *Stainless steel.*
$1.75 Let
Sunrise Hackle Pliers. *Long-nosed pliers; stainless steel.*
$1.75-$2.80 Let, Don, Sim, Fol
Sunrise Midge Pliers. *A small pliers for work with smaller hackles.*
$1.70-$2.80 Fol, Let, Sim, Don

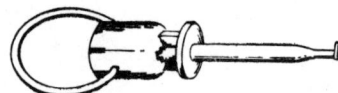

Sunrise Ezee Hackle Pliers. *Similar to E-Z Mini Pliers but with finger ring.*
$1.60-$1.95 Sim, Dan

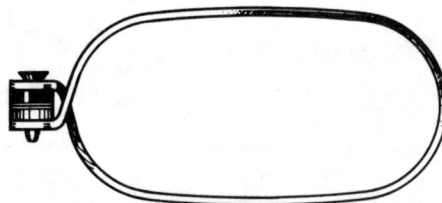

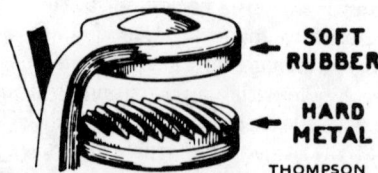

Thompson Duplex Pliers. *Flat spring steel; black finish; one jaw soft rubber, one corrugated metal.*
$2.65-$4.25 Many catalogs

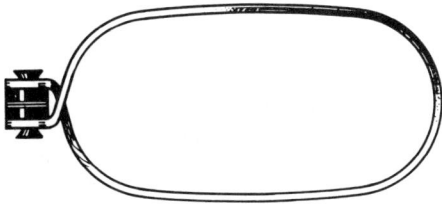

Courtesy of Reed's

Thompson Non-Skid Pliers. *Rubber pads both jaws.*
$2.03-$4 Cab, Let, H&H, Bob, Dan, Don, Mer, Mur, Edd,
Cor, Ree, Dal, EJH, Spo
Thompson Replacement Pads. *Pads for pliers described above.*
$.25 EJH

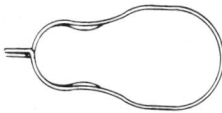

Thompson Midget Pliers. *Flat spring steel; small size.*
$2-$3 EJH, Sim, Edd, Dan, Ran, Mer, Blu, Hig
Thompson English Pliers. *Traditional style; metal jaws.*
$2.03-$7.50 Sim, Mer, Edd, Blu, Ran, EJH
Veniard Hackle Pliers. *Traditional style and actually made in England; 3 sizes (you know what they are).*
$2.10-$2.50 Let

Hair Flairing Tools

Only one tool here. It looks like an overdeveloped dubbing twister, and to tell you the truth, I don't know how it works. Anything that might help in spinning deer hair is worth a try.

Kaufmann's Hair-Flair. *Aids in flairing deer hair for muddlers, bass bugs, and the like.*
$6.95 Kau

Hair Stackers and Packers

Hair stackers allow the tier to even the ends of deer hair and other hair used for wings and tails. There is no good way to make the ends even without a tool, in spite of what you may read about tamping hair on your palm or wherever. Some people use expended rifle cartridges, others cut down chapstick tubes, but every tier I know uses some device to make those wings look pretty. If you've been fighting deer hair wings, try a stacker.

There are two types of stackers. One has a long body and center tube. With the two parts together, hair is placed in the tube, and the tool is tapped on the table. The tool is then held at just the right angle (this is the tricky part, folks), and the body is removed from the tube. (If you remove the tube from the body, the hair will stay in the body of the tool.) The tips of the hair are

left protruding from the tube and can be removed. The length of the hair is not important with this type of stacker, but developing the right touch is.

The second style has a short body and long tube. With the tube in the body, the hair is inserted and the tool tapped as with the first style. Then the tube is lifted away from the body, and the hair is picked up by the butts. The length of the hair must match the length of the stacker's body with this type of tool. And we're still waiting for a company to come up with a short enough body for all our tying needs.

An inexpensive alternative is the S&M Hair Evener, a sheet metal trough into which hair can be placed, tapped even, and picked back out. Developing a knack for removing the stacked hair without disturbing it is the key here.

Hair packers are somewhat similar in appearance to half-hitch tools. They are used to tamp spun deer hair bodies. Compressing the spun hair makes for tighter bodies and heads. Packers are listed first.

Hair Packers

A-Y Hair Packer. *3 sizes of aluminum tools for packing deer hair after it's spun on hook.*
$7.95 Hun
Hair Compressor. *Hair packing tool; one end for large hooks, the other for small.*
$3.95 Nat
S&V Hair Packer. *Brass tool for packing hair after spinning; handles hooks #1-16; instructions.*
$5.95 Mer, Fly, AnR

Hair Stackers

Classic Stacker. *Turned from solid rosewood; stained and polished; in traditional form; functional and beautiful; some made domestically, some imported from India.*
$2.95-$9.95 AnR, Hun, Fly, Cab
Crest Hair Stacker. *Brass with chromed tube.*
$3.72 Mer

Courtesy of The Fly Shop

Gausdal Small Hair Stacker. *Finely-finished stacker with knurled grip; chrome finish; flared opening.*
$5.50-$6.95 Kau, AnR, Fly

Gausdal Medium Hair Stacker. *Same as small version; of course, it's larger.*
$6.50 AnR

Gausdal Large Hair Stacker. *Same as small version; of course, it's even larger than the medium.*
$7.50-$7.95 AnR, Kau

Hellekson Hair Stacker. *Small size.*
$5 Nat

Renzetti Pro-Stack Double Stacker. *Both sides of center section open; one side has small tube, other large tube; aluminum center section, brass tubes.*
$6.60-$10.50 H&H, T&T, Let, Mer, Tac, Ste, Blu, Orv, Kau, Dal

Renzetti Midge Pro-Stack. *A small stacker; chromed.*
$5.85-$6.66 Dal, Mer, Tac, T&T

Renzetti Standard Pro-Stack. *Regular size; chromed.*
$5.85-$6.66 T&T, Mer, Tac, Dal

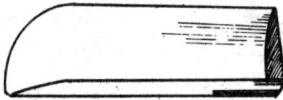

S&M Hair Evener. *Inexpensive alternative to hair stackers; stamped metal "half-tube", open on one side.*
$1.50-$2 Bud, Mer, Mur, Dan, Bob Thompson Hair

Thompson Hair Stacker. *Standard aluminum hair stacker.*
$4.40 Mer

Thompson Wood Hair Stacker. *Turned from mesquite, a dramatically grained wood.*
$9.58-$11.95 Mer, Hig

Courtesy of E. J. Hille

Three-in-One Stacker. *Tube and 3 knurled cups for different size hair; one of those nifty ideas.*
$3-$4.95 EJH, Don, Let

Half-Hitch Tools

These ingenious tools will help you tie the half-hitch knot. Although I know many tiers who use these tools regularly, the half-hitch happens to be one knot I can tie easily by hand, so I don't own one. They are all of the same style, a hexagonally-shaped rod with a round, tapered end with a hole in it. The hole slips over the hook as part of the transaction of thread from tool to hook. Half-hitch knots are used to secure thread along the way so that materials already secured are not disturbed by the following tying operations. They are not suitable for finishing the head of a fly. For that, you need the whip finish knot. Of course, there's a tool for that, too.

Crest Half-Hitch Tool. *Hexagonally-shaped brass tool; ends have different sizes holes for small and large flies.*
$2.22-$2.50 AnJ, Mer

Half-Hitch Tool Set. *Hexagonal-shaped tools; three sizes for all hooks.*
$1.50-$3.25 EJH, Kau, Don, Let, Tac, Dan

Renzetti Half-Hitch Tool. *Hexagonally-shaped brass tool with two different end sizes; 3".*
$2.25-$2.70 Hun, Let, Mer, AnR, T&T, Dal

Sunrise Half-Hitch Tool. *Similar to above tools but made of aluminum; two sizes: extra fine/fine and medium/large.*
$2.25-$2.35 Fol, Sim

Scissors and Other Cutting Tools

Scissors get a lot of attention from tiers. They're used extensively during the tying operation, and very fine work is required of them. It's difficult to buy scissors, because brand names have not become well established in the market. Most of the scissors come from India (Sunrise being the most common brand). Scissors from Europe are of higher quality and higher price. American scissors, such as the Thompson Supreme, fall in the middle price range. Surgical scissors, the real things with gold-plated handles and all, are the most expensive scissors. Whether they're worth the $50 price tag is up to you.

In buying scissors, you'll need to pay attention to two or three main features. The points are the most important part of the scissors for the tier. They should be fine and should cut to the end. It's preferable to try out several pairs in the fly shop. You can "sight" them to see the fit of the blades, and it doesn't hurt to cut paper with them to make sure they cut down to the point. Most tiers prefer straight points, but curved scissors are also available.

Since the preferred way of using scissors is to carry them in hand during the tying operation, it's important to get scissors with comfortable finger loops. Length comes into play here, too, since the scissors that are too short will puncture the tier's hand and those that are too long will be in the way all the time.

There are a few scissors that are not typical. Spring scissors do not have finger loops, and they are sprung open for convenience. Dorin's Nippers have open points but add a finger loop to the tool, thus making it possible to carry them in-hand during tying. Dorin's tools are among the most inventive in the industry, and you might give them a try if you have trouble holding traditional scissors in your hand.

Several scissors are designed for the heavier jobs a tier faces, particularly cutting deer hair. Nothing seems to dull scissors more quickly. The most common scissors for that purpose are the Wiss Quick-Clips, which someone rescued from the anonymity of fabric stores years ago. They have replaceable blades, and they work well for deer hair. Other shears for heavy hair use the traditional scissors style.

Other speciality tools here are the wing cutters. These tools are used to cut hackle and body feathers in the shape of mayfly wings. In the age of wing burners, these may not be around much longer. X-Acto knives are also listed. They're useful for a number of trimming, skinning, and dividing tasks.

Wish I could make some specific recommendations, but I've used only one pair of scissors for my tying in the last four years. They're Sunrise scissors, and they've worked well. Only recently have they begun to loose their edge. I've backed them up over the years with Wiss Quick-Clips for the tougher hairs, and that may have helped prolong their lifespan. I think there are a number of adequate scissors out there, if you can pick out the individual pair yourself.

Most catalogs offers scissors, but many of them do not give brand names. As in the other sections of the book, these are not listed.

Crest 4" Scissors. *Straight blade; large finger holes; fine points.*
$4.95 AnJ
Curved-End Scissors. *Curved tips for those tiers with that preference; a variety of sizes.*
$3.79-$8.50 EJH, Cab, Bud, Don, Ran, T&T, Tac, Ree, Egg
Deer Hair Shears. *Polished, ice-tempered stainless steel; one blade is serrated to hold coarse hair during cut; a special scissors for the tier who does a lot of work with coarse hair.*
$15.75-$25.75 Hun, AnR
Dorin Nippers. *Small scissors with adjustable ring that fits middle finger; rests against upper side of index finger; easily held during tying.*
$8.95-$10.49 Kau, Mer, Tac, T&T, Dal
Fiskars Clipper. *Rubber-coated handle with finger loop, on the idea of the Wiss Quick Clips; stainless steel blades.*
$3.95 Cab
Fiskars Scissors. *Stainless steel; fine points; rubber-coated handles; 4". (Note: Ed Story of National Feather-crafters says you need to get the Fly Tye Model; his are, Cabela's are not specified.)*
$5.95-$8.75 Nat, Cab

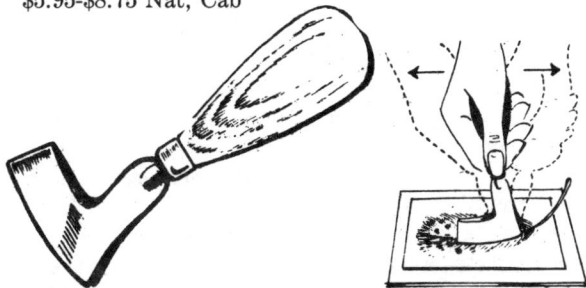

Hille's Wing Cutter. *Wood handle and specially curved blade for trimming hackle to wing shape; cut wings resemble hackle-tip wings; includes cutting board and instructions.*
$7.95 EJH

Hille's Miniature Snips. *One-piece snips with hollow ground steel cutting edges; self-opening; like simplified Wiss Quick-Clips; 4" with 1¾" blade.*
$2.95 EJH
Large-Thumb Hole Scissors. *Extra large thumb hole for ease in carrying scissors in-hand while tying; 3½".*
$12 Ran
Orvis Scissors. *Long points; fairly large finger holes; 3½".*
$14.25 Orv, Ste

Reed's Hackle Trimmer. *Holds razor blades upright for use in trimming hackles down in size evenly; although most tiers prefer their hackle "natural" for dries and wets, this could be useful in preparing hackle for grasshopper legs, for wings, and for nymph palmering.*
$9.50 Ree
Rodmaker's Quick Snips. *Similar to Wiss Quick-Clips (listed below) but with case of nickel-plated steel.*
$13.59 Dal
Snippers. *Similar to Wiss Quick-Clips (listed below); plastic handles hold steel blades; for the tough job of cutting deer hair.*
$4 FlR
Spring-Loaded Scissors. *Regular scissors with spring-loaded opening feature; stays open, ready for use; 4½".*
$5.95 Cab
Spring scissors. *No finger holes; curved handles hold blades apart, ready for use.*
$7.95-$9.95 Dal, Tac
Spring scissors from T&T. *Slightly different style than regular spring scissors; surgical grade stainless steel; very fine points; straight or offset blades.*
$14.95 T&T

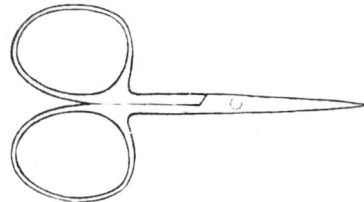

Sunrise Scissors. *Imported scissors; straight or curved blades; 3" or 3½".*
$4-$5.50 Edd, Sim, Dan, Let
Sunrise Solingen Scissors. *Heavy duty scissors with large finger holes; 3½".*
$4-$4.95 Let, Don
Surgeon's scissors. *The real thing; tungsten-carbide blades blended into the stainless steel handles which are gold-plated; these are cosmetic seconds (reducing their*

cost tremendously without affecting their performance); available either straight or semi-curved; serrated edges available.
Straight—$47; semi-curved—$42-$45; serrated edges—$49.50 Hun, AnR

Thompson Supreme Scissors. *Ice-tempered steel blade; microscopic serrated edge; open loop finger holes are adjustable; 3½".*
$14.95-$22.50 Kau, Edd, T&T, Dan, Mer, Bud, Ste, Cor, EJH, Hig, Orv
Thompson Midge Scissors. *Stainless steel; 2¾".*
$13.50-$14 Blu, Mer
Thompson Large Loop Scissors. *Stainless steel; fine points; large finger loops; 3¾".*
$15-$16 Mer, Blu
Ultra Midge Scissors. *Stainless steel; fine points; large finger holes; 2½".*
$15.75 T&T
Veniard Scissors. *Large finger holes; fine points; straight or curved points.*
Straight—$9; curved—$9.50 Let
West German Scissors. *Another quality scissors from Hunter's catalog; hardened stainless steel; fine points; adjustable finger loops; refurbishing service; 4"; straight or semi-curved.*
Straight—$17.50; semi-curved—$18.50 Hun

Wiss Quick-Clips. *Plastic handles hold replaceable steel blades; fits in hand well while tying; excellent for clipped deer hair bodies.*
$7.50-$8.50 Hig, Mur, AnR, Bud (or your local fabric store)
Wiss Quick-Clips Blades. *Replacement blades for Wiss scissors.*
$3.50 Hig
X-Acto Knife. *Aluminum handle with replaceable steel blade.*
$1.29 (blades—$.95/5) Tac
X-Acto Knife Set. *3 knives and 14 assorted blades in wood chest.*
$10.95 Tac

Tweezers

Tweezers are just handy to have around to pick up hooks and other small things. I like the curved points because they'll sit on the tying table ready for use and I can see what I'm after better. This is definitely a secondary tool and one you can pick up at the drugstore.

Sunrise Tweezers. *Standard steel tweezers for every kind of extricating; straight or curved.*
$1.98-$3.30 Let, Fol

Tweezerman Tweezers. *The ultimate in tweezers; made in Europe of hardened stainless steel; 3 styles: fine point, slanted, double slant.*
$13 (or $33 the set of 3) Hun
Vise Tweezers. *Open when squeezed, closed when released; straight point; 4½".*
$2.50-$2.95 T&T, Nat
Xuron Tweezers. *Stainless steel; tapered shanks, beveled edges; fine points; made in Switzerland; 4¾".*
$8.95-$9.95 AnR, Don
Xuron Curved Tweezers. *As above but with very fine curved points.*
$9.45 Don

Whip Finishers

Although many tiers consider this tool to be pocket fluff, I don't. Of course, I never learned to tie the whip finish knot by hand. The whip finisher holds the thread against the hook while wraps are laid over it. Wrapped over itself, the thread forms a smooth and secure head for the fly.

The traditional whip finisher is a difficult tool to learn. Beginners get very frustrated by it and often give up and substitute the half-hitch (not a recommended practice). I've had more success in my tying classes with the Matarelli whip finisher. It's an entirely different approach to the problem of tying the knot and one that's simpler to learn. In addition, I think the tool allows more control and is more versatile. It can lay a whip finish anywhere on the hook, and it can be used left- or right-handed. (Note: In the lists of traditional whip finisher, Charlie's Whipper and the Thompson R/L are designed for lefties.)

There are places for economy in tying tools, but this is not one of those places. Inexpensive whip finishers have inexpensive spring steel which gives up its spring very easily. We've gone through a number of them in our classes trying to help beginners economize, and we've finally quit. It's false economy. The tool is used on every fly, and you should spend some money on it, whether you get the traditional style or the Matarelli.

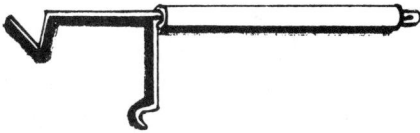

Charlie's Whipper. *A modification of the traditional style that allows right- or left-handed use; brass and stainless steel.*
$4.50 T&T
Crest Whip Finisher. *The traditional model; long size.*
$3.94-$3.95 Mer, AnJ

Matarelli Whip Finisher. *The only alternative to the traditional tool; easier to learn and more control; can be used left- or right-handed; can place a knot anywhere on hook shank; after years of using the other style, I've converted.*
$4.20-$5.95 Many catalogs
Renzetti Whip Finisher. *Extra long handle with small finisher; half-hitch tool other end.*
$5.50-$5.75 AnR, Hun, Let, T&T, Tac
Sunrise Large Whip Finisher. *Traditional model, similar to Crest model.*
$2.50-$4.20 Sim, Fol, Let, Dan
Sunrise Small Whip Finisher. *Traditional model but smaller.*
$2.25-$3.40 Fol, Sim
Thompson Whip Finisher. *Traditional model; sizes: standard (hooks #10 and larger) and small (#10 and smaller).*
$4.73-$7.50 H&H, Kau, Don, Hun, Dan, Let, Blu, Hig, Ran, EJH (left-hand model also), Bud, Mer, Edd
Thompson R/L Whip Finisher. *Traditional model but can be used either right or left handed.*
$4.73-$6.30 Mer, Hig, T&T, Tac, Cor, Dal, EJH

Tool Sets

Most of these collections of tying tools are aimed at the beginner who has no idea what to buy. Experienced tiers have their tools and already know which among them are useless.

There are some items of interest to the experienced tier, among them the Thompson tool sets. They may represent a step up for someone who's looking to class up his or her act. The mesquite tools are particularly

attractive. Old pros may also be interested in the empty Thompson tool case offered by Merrick's. I was happy to find it, since I've wanted to put my tools in a case ever since I saw the Thompson sets. Finally, Egger's offers a streamside tool set, including hand vise, that will allow you to go afield with a separate set of tools.

And now for the beginners waiting anxiously to find out if they should buy a kit . . . probably not. First, almost without exception, the brands of the tools included in these kits are not given in the catalogs. I don't think you should ever buy a fly tying tool, or anything else in fly fishing, without knowing who makes it (even if you wouldn't know a good brand from a bad one). Second, you don't need all the tools in most of these sets to start tying, and in some cases, you need some tools that are not included.

All you will be doing here is letting someone else do your shopping for you. If you know absolutely nothing about tying tools, even after reading the introduction to this chapter, and if you trust the company offering the tool set and if you can save some money by buying all the tools at once, fine.

Beginner's Tool Kit. *Bobbin, pliers, scissors, half-hitch bodkin, Thompson Patriot Vise.*
$32.95 H&H
Clemen's Deluxe Tool Kit. *Scissors, bobbin, whip finisher, small and large hackle pliers, half-hitch tools, bobbin threader, and dubbing needle; in plush-lined black leather case with brass zipper.*
$24.95 Dal
Crest Tool Set. *Bobbin, bobbin threader, half-hitch tool, half-hitch/fur tool, half-hitch bodkin, half-hitch dubbing tool, hair stacker, 4" scissors, Sure-Grip hackle pliers; in soft, roll-up case.*
$24.95-$29.95 Bud, AnJ, Tid, Mer, Fly

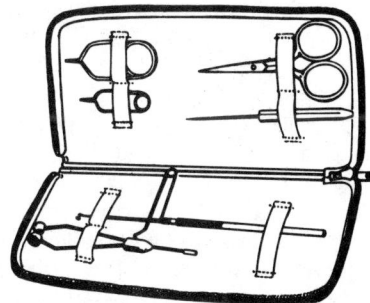

Egger's Kit. *Pliers, scissors, bodkin, whip finisher, bobbin; in velvet-lined leather case.*
$16.95 Egg
Hunter's Tool Set. *Thompson A, Matarelli whip finisher, bobbin, and bobbin threader, $15 scissors, pliers, material clip, thread.*
$55.95 Hun
Letort Beginner's Kit. *Import AA, Chase bobbin, whip finisher, scissors; Du Bois gauge, half-hitch tool, hackle pliers.*
$30 Let

Master Tool Kit. *Smaller version of Streamside Tying Kit below but without vise, dubbing twister, and tweezers; in brown leather case with velvet lining and zipper closure; 4¼"x8½".*
$23.50 Egg

Professional Tool Kit. *Thompson A Vise, bobbin, bodkin, scissors, pliers.*
$32.95-$43.95 H&H, Kau

Streamside Tying Kit. *Streamside vise, hackle pliers, whip finisher, bobbin threader, half-hitch tools, bodkin, scissors, bobbin, tweezers, dubbing twister; in black leather case with velvet lining and zipper closure; 5"x9½".*
$27.50 Egg

Tackle-Craft Took Kit. *Eight common tools in velvet-lined, fitted case.*
$18.50 TCr

Thompson Chrome and Brass Tool Kit. *Scissors, pliers, dubbing needle, bobbin threader, hair stacker, whip finisher, bobbin; in padded, zippered leatherette case; 4"x7"; a handsome kit.*
$52.50-$62.95 Mer, EJH

Thompson Mesquite and Brass Tool Kit. *Same tool selection as above but bobbin and hair stacker of mesquite; very nice stuff.*
$68.63-$82.95 Mer, T&T, EJH

Thompson Tool Case. *The empty case for the kits above; ideal for those of us who like the kits but already have the tools.*
$15 Mer

Fly Tying Kits

Like the tool sets, these collections of tools and materials are mostly aimed at the beginner. There are a few exceptions that might interest the more experienced tier. There's Dave Whitlock's Bass Fly Tying Kit, which includes materials and instructions for flies that are probably not for the beginner. Donegal's offers another kit for the experienced tier, this one for salmon flies. It contains enough materials for two flies (plus flub ups), and that's enough to get you hooked on the art. (Note: I tried to come up with something other than "hooked" for that last sentence, but I failed. "Addicted" was too close to the truth, and "mesmerized" was too long a word.) Murray's Hellgrammite Kit may also be of interest.

Buying a beginner's tying kit is something I can't recommend. Although many of these kits have excellent materials and good tools, you won't learn fly tying just by buying a kit. That much I can guarantee. Some of them have instructions, it's true, and you may tough it out and learn from them, but even the best of the books written for the beginner are difficult to learn from. The other thing I can guarantee is that you'll have unused materials from your kit that you'll pass on when you pass away. I have materials from my Hank Roberts kit from 1958. You just don't end up tying everything the people who assemble kits think you should.

I'd recommend that you buy the tools you need and a few materials for the flies you want to start tying and spend the rest of your money on fly tying lessons. You can add tools and materials as need requires and skill permits. If you do buy a beginner's kit, get one from one of the shops specializing in fly fishing. The folks doing the tool and material selection are experts, and their choices are probably sound.

Dan Bailey's All-Around Fly Tying Kit. *Materials, tools separate; no list of materials; tools include Thompson A, Matarelli bobbin, hackle pliers, scissors, bodkin.*
Materials—$50; tools—$48.65 Dan

Dave Whitlock's Bass Fly Tying Kit. *Materials, formulas, diagrams, for Whitlock's Top-to-Bottom warmwater flies.*
$50 Hig, Kau, Mer

Donegal's Salmon Fly Kits. *Kits for individual patterns for those tiers who would like to try a salmon fly; each kit contains enough materials for two flies; hair wing patterns include Blue Rat, Cosseboom, 5 others; feather wing patterns include Jock Scott, Green Highlander, 4 others; instructions.*
Hairwing—$3; featherwing—$4.95 Don

Fly Shop Beginner's Kit. *Tools, materials, hooks, cement; with Crest Custom Vise.*
$64.95 Fly

Hank Roberts Standard Intermediate Kit. *Comes with hooks, materials. (Note: I don't consider the vise in this kit to be adequate, even for a beginner.)*
$24.50-$24.95 Fol, Sim

Hank Roberts Deluxe Intermediate Kit. *More materials than Standard kit; vise is slightly better but still inadequate.*
$44.25-$44.75 Sim, Fol

Hank Roberts Pro Fly Tying Kit. *More materials than Deluxe kit; contains a Sunrise "AA" vise, an adequate tool.*
$65.40 Fol

High Country Flies Kit. *Tools and materials; with Thompson A vise.*
$74.95 Hig

Letort Fly Tying Kits. *Kits for dries, wets and nymphs, streamers; materials fully listed.*
$14.25-$30.75 Let

Murray's Hellgrammite Kit. *Materials, hooks for "a whole season's supply"; instruction sheet; sample fly.*
$10.95 Mur

Orvis Fly Tying Kit. *Tools and materials for tying streamers, wets, dries, and nymphs; with Orvis Simplicity Vise, Eric Leiser beginner's fly tying booklet, and even a wing burner.*
$78.50 Orv

Practical Western Fly Tying Kit. *Tools and materials in plastic tackle box carrier; with Crest Supreme Vise, Matarelli bobbin.*
$84.95 Bud

Rangeley Region Beginner's Kit. *Materials, tools, instructions (and a free lesson if you can go to the shop); Thompson Patriot Vise; includes Dick Stewart's "Universal Fly Tying Guide".*
$46.95 Ran

Steelhead Tying Kit. *Materials to tie about 50 patterns.*
$22.95 Kau

Stewart Custom Tackle Beginner's Kit. *Materials (completely listed in catalog), tools, instructions; Import AA vise.*
$39.95 Ste

No-name kits. *A variety of unspecified tools and materials assembled by individual companies as starter kits for beginners.*
$10-$79.95 AnJ, Mer, Dun, Cor, Ree (includes bass bug kit), EJH (includes cork body kit), Mur (includes bass bug kit), Cab (includes bass bug kit)

Head Cement and Applicators

There are many good cements. I've been satisfied with every kind I've tried. A regular clear lacquer or a head cement will work to finish the heads on all but the bigger flies where a heavier cement will give a high gloss in one coat. For years, I used fingernail polish, which is just a high grade enamel or lacquer, and liked it. It even came in a bottle with a brush applicator. (I didn't like buying it, however—too many funny looks.)

I've switched over to the thinner cements now because I like the applicator from Universal Vise (listed below) for cementing heads. Its fine point allows me to direct the cement where I want it. It's a very practical and inexpensive applicator. There is some seepage of cement from tube as air returns to the squeeze bottle after use, but it's only a slight inconvenience. Because very little air gets in the container, I haven't found it necessary to keep thinner on hand, either.

The thin cement I use now (a local brand I couldn't find in the catalogs) saturates the thread better, but it also tends to bleed into the materials if you're not careful in application. Tiers are always after the perfect head cement consistency, and that's why thinners are available for most cements.

A vinyl cement is preferred where flexibility is important. Tiers use it to coat quill wings, for instance. Dave's Flexament is a product developed specifically for its flexibility.

Applicator jar. *Glass bottle with plastic cap; brass handle with needle in cap; from Crest or Renzetti.*
$2.45-$3.85 AnJ, Bud, Orv, AnR, Tac, Hun, T&T, Kau, Cab, Ste, H&H, Let, Mer, Fly, Dal, Egg, EJH

Universal Vise Cement Applicator. *Plastic squeeze bottle with needle-nose tube; self-cleaning; an excellent applicator, especially when tying small flies.*
$1-$2 Ran, EJH, H&H, Egg, Edd

Colored lacquer. *Seals and waterproofs; colors: clear, yellow, white, red, black.*
$.90-$1.75 (thinner—$.55-$1.50) Kau, Ran, Edd, Mer, H&H (plus dark brown and green), Ree (plus blue, gray, chartreuse, purple, green, orange, pearlescent), EJH (plus brown, green, gray, and quart sizes), T&T

Crest Head Cement. *Quick-drying, penetrating.*
$1.75 (thinner—$1.75) Fly

Dave's Flexament. *Developed by Dave Whitlock for flexibility.*
$1.95 (thinner—$1.25) Hig, Mer

Fli-Bond Cement. *Clear or black.*
$1.60 Mer

Fluorescent colored lacquer. *Seals and waterproofs; colors: fl. red, pink, yellow, green, orange, and non-fl. white primer.*
$1.10-$1.75 (thinner—$.55-$1.50) Mer, T&T, Ree (plus blue), EJH, Edd

Fly-Tite Cement. *A non-toxic cement made of "all natural ingredients"; can be thinned with denatured alcohol; 2 oz. bottle.*
$1.95 FlR

Gudebrod Head Cement. *Clear liquid.*
$1.39-$1.74 Tac, Sim, Ran, Dal

National Feathercraft Head Cement. *Ed Story recommends it and that's usually good enough.*
$1.85-$1.95 (thinner—$1-$1.45) Nat, Hun

Price's Angler's Corner Head Cement. *High gloss cement and thinner; several companies suggest this runs pretty thick, so purchase thinner with it.*
$1.75-$2.50 (thinner—$1.50-$2) Edd, AnR, T&T, Kau, Ste, Bud, Hun, Tac, Fly

Streamside Anglers Head Cement. *In 1 oz. jar.*
$1.50 (thinner—$1.50) Hig

Thompson Head Cement. *Built-in brush applicator.*
$3.76-$3.95 Mer, Tac

Tiltip Head Cement Formula 251. *Cement in unique applicator bottle; brush in top; from von Schlegell.*
$2.50 Bud, Dan, T&T

Total Coat Head Finish. *Covers head to smooth finish.*
$4.95 Kau
Veniard Cellire Varnish. *A celluloid varnish favored by English salmon fly tiers; colors: clear, red, black, yellow, red.*
$1.50-$2 (thinner—$1.25-$1.50) Hun, AnR
Wapsi Vinyl Cement. *Flexible cement; 1 oz.*
$1.20 (thinner—$1.10) Hig
Weber Head Cement. *Clear liquid; 1 oz.*
$1.20-$1.95 AnW, Fol, Ran, Edd

Tying Wax

Wax is used to coat tying thread so that dubbing material will stick to it. Some people use waxed thread, but many of the best tiers use regular thread and apply wax only where they need it. This has the advantages of not clogging up bobbin tubes with wax and of leaving the thread free to absorb cement.

Of the waxes I've tried, I like the Overton's Wonder Wax the best. Its consistency works best for me. The cake waxes and beeswax (not included here) are too hard. Thompson's wax is too soft. So you see we can get into the same trouble with consistency of the material here as with cements.

Incidentally, chapstick or saliva are considered adequate substitutes for wax. John Betts, the synthetic materials proponent, uses cross country ski wax. It's available in many consistencies—start out with red.

Dilly Wax. *Supplied in squeeze tube.*
$2.95 Let

Overton's Wonder-Wax. *Good wax, not too soft, not too hard; in plastic case with threaded bottom for dispensing; a several year's supply.*
$2.50-$3.50 Most catalogs
Thompson Dubbing Wax. *A very soft wax in chapstick-style container.*
$2-$3 H&H, Mer, Blu, Mur, EJH, Edd, Tac
Thompson Wax. *The old standard in 1 oz. tin.*
$2.69 Dal

Wing Burners

A relatively recent addition to the tier's arsenal of tools, wing burners make very realistic wings from hackle and body feathers and from synthetic material. You simply select the correct style and size of burner, center the feather in it, squeeze the feather in the tool, and use a match (if you can light one with one hand) or lighter to burn off all the material sticking out of the burner. Voila. The perfect imitation wing.

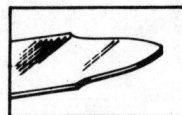
MAY FLY

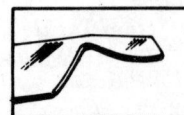
CADDIS

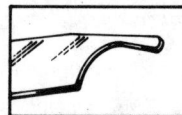
JUNGLE COCK

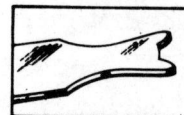
NYMPH

The most complete set of burners comes from Renzetti. They produce burners for everything, including jungle cock imitations.

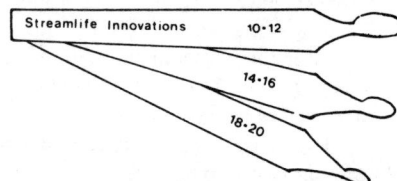

Iwamasa Mayfly Wing Burners. *For mayfly wings; sizes: #10/#12, #14/#16, #18/#20.*
$3.40-$3.95 each; $9-$10.50 set Kau, T&T, Blu

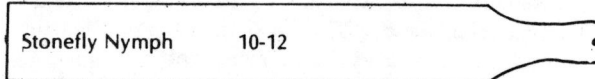

Renzetti Mayfly/Stonefly Nymph Case Burners. *For case feathers on nymphs; sizes: fine(#12-# 16), small(#10-#12), medium(#8-#10), large(#4-#6).*
$2.35-$3.75 each; $12.50-$13.30 set H&H, Orv, Kau, Hun, Mer, Dal, Edd, Let, AnR, T&T, Tac

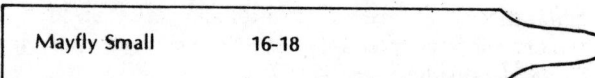

Renzetti Mayfly Wing Burners. *For mayfly wings; sizes: fine(#18-#22), small(#14-#18), medium(#10-#14), large(#6-#10).*
$2.35-$3.75 each; $9.95-$12.95 set Kau, Tac, Orv, AnR, Hun, Edd, Dal, Mer, T&T, H&H, Hig, Let

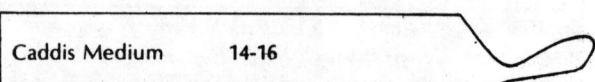

Renzetti Caddisfly Wing Burners. *For caddis wings; sizes: fine(#18-#20), small(#16-#18), medium(#14-#16), large(#10-#14).*
$2.35-$3.75 each; $12.50-$13 set Kau, AnR, H&H, Hun, Orv, Dal, T&T, Mer, Tac

Jungle Cock Medium — Streamer

Renzetti Jungle Cock Eye Burners. *For jungle cock imitations; sizes: small (jassids), medium (streamers), large (big streamers), extra large (salmon flies).*
$3.06-$3.45 each; $12.50 set Mer, T&T, Tac, Let, Dal
Shoup's Wing Things. *Set of 8 burners for all types of cases and wings; spring steel; Teflon-coated; hook sizes #4-#18; instructions.*
$13.50 (set) Hun, Let, T&T
Sunrise Angle Mayfly Wing Burners. *Set of 4.*
$7.95-$9.95 Edd, Cab
Sunrise Angle Stonefly Case Wing Burners. *Set of 4.*
$7.95-$9.95 Cab, Edd

Miscellaneous Tools and Other Neat Things

Here are all the odds and ends again, lumped together for your enjoyment. Scalpels, blenders, and moustache combs . . . the catalog companies have them all.

Flat-jawed pliers. *Stainless steel; 4"; for debarbing hooks.*
$4.50-$7.95 Orv, Bud, H&H, Dan, T&T, Dal, Mur
German Silver Scalpel. *Steel handle with replaceable blades; millimeter ruler on side of case.*
$5.99 (blades—$.59) Dal
Lance. *Razor sharp lance for trimming.*
$2.55-$2.95 Kau, Fol, Tac
Mini Fur Blender. *Small electric blender for hair and fur.*
$19.35-$23.95 H&H, Kau, Fly
Miracle Mill Blender. *Similar to above; guaranteed 1 year.*
$23.50-$23.95 T&T, Fre
Tier's Pumice Stone. *A pumice (which admittedly you can get in the drugstore) for keeping the rough spots off finger tips for ease in tying.*
$1.50 Hun
Tuffilm. *A clear plastic fixative in aerosol can; use on quills to keep them from fraying and on deer hair bass bugs to aid in flotation; 4¾ oz.*
$3.25-$4.95 AnR, Bud, Hun, Nat
Aztec comb. *Fine-toothed aluminum comb for dolling up Aztec streamers.*
$1.50 Let
Hoffritz Underfur Comb. *A tiny aluminum comb to clean underfur from guard hairs; in a plastic case; looks like a moustache comb to me; 2½".*
$2.50-$2.75 Hun, Hig
Waste-Trol. *Metal frame with nylon bag; clamps to table or attaches to vise; sizes: 8"x13¾" and 6"x8"; for catching tying trash so you don't catch hell.*
$10.95-$17.95 Many catalogs
Waste-Trol Pedestal Base Adaptor. *For use with vises using pedestal bases.*
$4.39-$5.40 Cab, Hig

FLY TYING MATERIALS

Threads

Tying thread ensures the essential contact between materials and hook. In a sense, it's a tool, and as such, it engenders fear, loathing, and great pleasure in the craftsmen who use it. Fear comes from the use of a new, untested thread, loathing from an inferior thread that breaks mid-fly, and pleasure from the old familiar thread that is reliable and just the right color.

Thread was exclusively silk way back when, and some tiers still insist on using silk thread. Nylon thread has generally replaced silk, being preferred for its superior strength, especially in very small diameters. Still, everyone ought to try a spool of silk thread just for the experience.

The diameter of tying threads is indicated by 0s (commonly spoken of as "oughts", as in "three-ought thread") with 6/0, for instance, being finer than 3/0. Those two sizes are particularly useful. The heavier 3/0 thread is used for bigger flies and is acceptable for hook sizes as small as #16. The finer 6/0 thread is used for smaller flies, where the compact thread windings are necessary. (However, I know a number of tiers, myself included, who use 6/0 on all but streamers and large flies requiring heavy materials.)

A heavier thread, such as an 0 or an A (a common thread size for rod building), is used for spinning deer hair bodies on poppers. The pressure that must be exerted on the thread as it bites into the deer hair can break finer threads. At the other extreme, very small flies, #20 and smaller, will look better tied with a thread even finer than 6/0. In the listings, you'll find "midge" threads, including Danville's Spiderweb, with stated sizes of 8/0-18/0.

You must also decide whether to use unwaxed or waxed thread. Wax helps the thread adhere to the materials and the hook during tying. It's considered necessary only when dubbing. Using a thread that's pre-waxed is convenient, but that's its only advantage. Its greatest disadvantage is that the wax comes off the thread during tying and clogs up the bobbin tube. Many experienced tiers prefer unwaxed thread. Not only does it not leave a waxy build-up in the bobbin, it also "takes" cement better, producing flies with more durable heads. Those people who use unwaxed thread add wax to their thread during dubbing. I prefer this system myself.

I've omitted all threads without brand names or a very specific description. Nobody should buy "nylon thread" from a catalog when they can buy a brand name they know somewhere else.

Betterbug thread. *For spinning hair; no size given; colors: yellow, olive.*
$1.25 Bob
Danville Flymaster waxed thread. *6/0, 7/0; 50-200 yds.; colors: black, white, gray, pale yellow, coffee, cream,*

buttercup yellow, red, orange, burnt orange, hot orange, brown, mahogany, olive, fl. red, lt. olive, lt. brown, buff, tobacco brown, chartreuse, claret, wine.
$.35-$1.20 (depending on size of spool as well as source) Many catalogs
Danville nylon thread. *2/0-6/0; 50 yds.; colors: black, white, red, yellow, orange, brown, gray, blue, green, coffee, beige, dk. brown.*
$.47 Mer
Danville Spiderweb. *Equivalent to 8/0; 100 yds.; white, but can be colored with markers. (Note: Others listed under midge thread may be Danville thread.)*
$.43-$.45 Mer, H&H
Midge thread. *8/0, 14/0, 18/0, 20/0 (depending on the catalog's description); fine strand nylon; clear/white (can be colored with markers).*
$.50-$.99 Let, Bud, Bob, Kau, Edd, Don, Fly, Dal, T&T, Hun, AnR
Floss thread. *1-strand; waxed; a little confusing whether this should go in the floss or thread, but it's often described as "flat thread"; a very strong thread for spinning hair; 100 yds.; colors: black, white, red, yellow, orange, gray, fl. red, fl. white, fl. yellow, fl. orange, fl. green, fl. pink, fl. blue.*
$.50-$.95 Tac, AnR, Hig, Kau, Bob, Dal

Monocord. *3/0, A, B; waxed or unwaxed available; 50-200 yds.; most, if not all, of this is made by Danville; colors: white, black, red, yellow, gray, orange, brown, blue, green, dk. gray, olive, worm green, warm green, primrose, silver gray, burnt orange, tobacco brown, beige, charcoal, maize.*
$.35-$1.19 (depending on size of spool as well as source) Most catalogs
Nymo. *3/0 or A; a strong thread with some of the characteristics of floss; spreads out on the hook to give very smooth body; 100 yds.; colors: white, black, red, brown, dk. brown, ginger, lt. tan, tan gray, dk. gray, dun, moss green, lt. green, blue, yellow.*
$.70-$.99 Don, Fly
Silk thread. *2/0, 3/0, 4/0, 5/0, 6/0; 50 yds.; colors: black, white.*
$.58-$.80 Don, TCr, Dan, EJH, Ran, Edd, Mer, Kau
Silk thread (other colors). *2/0; 50 yds.; colors: black, white, brown, beige, lt. blue, dk. green, maroon, orange, yellow.*
$.58-$.75 Mer, EJH, Edd
Silk thread. *Size A; 50 yds.; colors: red, black.*
$.75 Ran
Super K thread. *Aka Super Thread; a Kevlar thread; about 3/0 but much stronger; 50-100 yds.; colors: cream,*

olive, orange, yellow, green, brown, lt.gray, dk. gray.
$1.25-$1.50 Hun, Dal, Nat, Orv

Floss

Floss is used as a body material and as ribbing on other body materials. Like thread, it was exclusively silk in former times. Now it is largely created from rayon. Most floss has four strands. These may be used together for a complete body or may be separated for ribbing or for bodies on small flies.

So infrequently is the brand name of floss given that I've included those without identification even though it's against my better judgment. Most are probably from Danville.

Acetate floss. *1-strand; for hard-shelled bodies, such as ants; wrap floss body and apply acetate to "melt" body; colors: black, yellow, red, scarlet, brown, pink, peacock green, cream, pale yellow, ginger, silver gray, wine, dk. red, apple green, soldier blue, burnt orange, worm green, chartreuse, kelly green. (See also: plastic floss and Solu-Floss.)*
$.30-$.50 Kau, TCr, Fly, Spo, Mer
Floss. *2-strand or 4-strand; 10 yds.; colors: white, black, kelly green, moss green, dk. brown, tobacco brown, scarlet, yellow, claret, buttercup yellow, orange, rust, pink, dk. olive, olive, lilac, lt. blue, green highlander, pale blue, burnt orange, blue, silver doctor blue, brown, lt. brown, seal brown, buff, cream, dk. gray, lt. gray, bright green, peacock green, apple green, forest green, insect green, moss green, wine, chartreuse, lavender, golden olive, green olive, bright orange, coral, blue dun, lt. green, purple, dk. red, tan, golden yellow, pale yellow, ginger, gold.*
$.30-$.55 Most catalogs
Fluorescent floss. *1-strand, 2-strand, or 4-strand; for steelhead and saltwater flies; fl. colors: neon red, saturn yellow, orange, signal green, fire orange, white, blue, shrimp orange, lime green, shell pink.*
$.27-$.75 Many catalogs
Pearsall's Gossamer Floss. *Pure silk; see Pearsall's Stout Floss for bad news about availability; colors: wine, yellow, orange, green, pink, brown, black.*
$.95 Blu
Pearsall's Marabou Floss. *Pure silk; no longer made; colors: wine, yellow, orange, green, pink, black.*
$.95 Blu
Pearsall's Stout Floss. *Pure silk made in England; a traditional favorite of salmon fly tiers, this floss is no longer made; supplies are so limited, this may no longer be in catalogs; 20 meters; colors: cosseboom, lt. olive, olive, lemon yellow, yellow, golden yellow, white, black, lt. blue, laxa blue, claret, brown, blue rat blue.*
$3.25-$3.50 Hun, AnR
Plastic floss. *1-strand; will soften with solvent to make hard shell bodies; can be flattened while soft; black, lt.*

blue, brown, lt. brown, buff, cream, claret, dk. gray, lt. gray, bright green, insect green, olive, dk. olive, golden olive, green olive, orange, bright orange, pink, dk. red, scarlet, tan, bright yellow, golden yellow, pale yellow, white. (See also: acetate floss and Solu-Floss.)
$.35 EJH

Plastic floss solvent. *For "melting" plastic floss; 1 oz.*
$.70 EJH

Silk floss. *Silk for those traditionalists; 20-50 yds.; colors: black, lemon yellow, rusty rat gold, hot orange, silver doctor blue, red, brown, blue dun, claret, gray, lt.olive, med. olive, dk. olive, orange, insect green, med. green, dk. green, blue, dk. yellow, pink, cream, tan, white.*
$.35-$1.80 Hun, Ree, Ran

Solu-Floss. *Heavy floss; for use with solvent to create hard shell and flattened bodies; colors: black, white, cream, tan, yellow, dk. yellow, red, blue dun, lt. blue, insect green, lt.green, med. green, orange, hot orange, lt. olive, med. olive, dk. olive, claret, brown. (See also: acetate floss, plastic floss.)*
$.50 Ree

Solu-Floss solvent. *Solvent for Solu-Floss; 1, 2 oz.*
$.90-$1.25 Ree

Hackle

Let's see how normal your background as a fly tier and buyer of hackle is. Answer the following true/false questions:

1. When you started tying, you were astounded that someone would charge $5 for a bunch of chicken feathers. *T/ F*

2. You had a neighbor, a friend, or a friend of a friend who owned chickens (or you went looking for such a person), and you asked him to give you the feathers from a chicken that was to be slaughtered. *T/F*

3. The resulting bloody mess of feathers (sometimes on the skin and sometimes loose in a brown paper bag) convinced you that $5 was not too much to pay for a neck. *T/F*

4. Having decided to buy a cheap neck, you bought brown and tied every pattern with brown hackle. *T/F*

5. Because you wanted to tie an Adams, you went looking for something called grizzly hackle (which you initially thought came from a bear), and when you found out the cheapest of those was $15, you bought a variant or cree or chinchilla and called it good. *T/F*

6. You accidentally wondered into a real fly shop one day and saw a Metz #1 grizzly. By this time, you recognized a good neck when you saw one, and you got so excited you took it up to the counter without looking at the price. After the initial shock, you mumbled something about forgetting your checkbook and left with the same astonishment you felt about the $5 neck but 10 times stronger. *T/F*

7. You decided you had to have a Metz neck. You asked for one for Christmas, but everybody thought you were kidding. ("$50 for a bunch of chicken feathers? Come on, what do you really want?") *T/F*

8. In desperation, you sold your '48 Studebaker (the clutch was out anyway) and added that to all the money you'd saved from the paper route (no dates for six months), and you bought a Metz #1 grizzly. *T/F*

9. You were convinced that you caught more fish on flies tied with Metz hackle. *T/F*

10. You now own four expensive necks (grizzly, brown, ginger, and blue dun) and are looking at a black, but you can't understand how anyone could think of spending $120 for a jungle cock skin. *T/F*

If you answered "true" to six of the questions, you're pretty normal, eight and you have nothing to worry about, and 10 "true" answers makes you part of the crowd.

In any case, most of us started our hackle buying with something called an India neck. It wasn't too long before we wanted better feathers and colors that weren't available in the imports, namely grizzly. Maybe we bought a Spencer or other domestic grizzly in the meantime, but once we'd seen a Metz neck we wanted one.

Most of us waited for that Metz neck until we couldn't stand it any longer, until our flies deserved the best (at least in our eyes), until we'd saved up for it, or until someone finally couldn't stand listening to us any longer and gave us one for Christmas.

(The latter occasion is the most remarkable, and if you have someone in your life who will chalk over $30-$50 for a bunch of chicken feathers in the name of love and charity, take care of him or her.)

In the eyes of the uninitiated, that's all that Metz neck is . . . a bunch of chicken feathers. But dare not say that to a fly tier. To him or her, it is the ultimate in hackle, and hackle is at the heart of a well-tied fly, especially a dry fly. And, as with anything that's at the heart of something, there is some mystique involved in the ownership of a fine neck.

Perhaps the non-tier or the beginner can understand the pleasure of owning a Metz or Hoffman or Colorado Quality Hackle neck, but it's unlikely. That secret pleasure is shared only by those who tie and have gone through all the steps that it takes to bring a tier to the best.

Selecting a neck. Beginners have a lot of trouble picking out a good neck. Although most of us can tell the difference between a dry fly hackle and a chicken feather taken from a pillow, there are many subtleties between an average dry fly hackle and an exquisite one. I can't explain all those subtleties here, partly because I know them only on some kind of subliminal level. I can, however, tell you how to get into the ball park.

First, when you buy hackle, it's for a specific type of fly. A Metz hackle on a wet fly would be a waste of the hackle and would not be as effective as a cheap wet fly hackle. For wet flies, streamers, and nymphs, hackle should be soft and webby. It needs to flow with the movement of the current and the fly. You'll find hen necks listed in this chapter. They are inexpensive and entirely appropriate for use on wet flies.

Hen necks have feathers with rounded tips and lots of web. The web is the soft material next to the feather shaft. If you hold any hackle feather up to the light, you can see the web. It's the darker area close to the shaft. It usually forms an inverted "V" with the narrow point toward the tip of the feather. On wet fly hackles, it covers most of the feather. On good quality dry fly hackle, it's restricted to a small area near the shaft end.

Dry fly necks have feathers with sharply pointed tips and very little web. The feathers are narrow, and the individual barbules are stiff. This stiffness allows the hackle to hold the dry fly up, on top of the water. Suppliers don't grade wet fly hackles. Perhaps they should. They do grade dry fly hackles, and quality varies.

If you buy Metz or one of the other top brands, your grading is done for you, but you can still go through a group of Metz necks and find differences that give you a choice. In that case, the differences may be in shade or in the size of the neck rather than the quality of the hackle. (Word has it that Buck Metz grades every Metz neck, and this personal attention gives the necks exceptional consistency.) On the other hand, if you buy less expensive necks, grading is spotty at best.

So let's assume that as a beginner you're looking at a number of imported necks and trying to pick out the best dry fly neck. First, check the sheen on the necks. Good quality necks have a glossy appearance. Unfortunately, this can be imitated with a coat of wax. If the necks have been waxed, the sheen will be unnaturally consistent throughout the necks, and you'll probably be able to feel the waxy build-up. No, this doesn't necessarily mean the necks are bad, but it's good that you're suspicious.

Next, look at the tips of the feathers. They should be pointed, not round. Pull a feather gently up. (It doesn't do to be pulling feathers off necks you haven't purchased.) The feather should be fairly consistent in width throughout its length. If it's size 12 at the bottom and size 18 at the top, what size is it?

Finally, look at the web (as described above). A dry fly hackle will have little web. Since all feathers have some web, this is a matter of comparison. Take a look at a Metz before you judge an imported neck and you'll know what qualities you're looking for.

Once you've rounded up two or three necks that are the right color and that you've graded as the top, you can find the one that's the best bargain for you. Bend the neck slightly so that the feathers stand up. Find the size 12 hackles. (I know that's difficult for a beginner, but for the purposes of comparison, it doesn't matter whether you pick a size 14 or a size 10.) Now, compare the number of feathers of that size and smaller on each of the necks you have in hand. The one with the most feathers of size

12 and smaller is the most useable and the best buy.

If all this seems too much, go to a reputable fly shop, tell the clerk you want an inexpensive brown neck, and ask him to pick out the one he'd choose for himself. After he's made the selection, ask him to show you how he chose. At least you'll know enough from the explanation here to know if you are in a reputable fly shop.

Hackle colors, a dictionary. There are many different colors and patterns in natural chicken feathers, and the descriptions of them make up a language all its own, as a beginning tier is quick to learn. The standard colors—brown, white, cream, and black—are part of everyday language, but those are about the only terms in common with the rest of English. Here's a brief dictionary of color descriptions with definitions using regular English.

Badger: white or cream with black center near shaft; sometimes referred to as silver badger; if main color is tan or golden, referred to as golden badger.

Blue dun: rich gray with bluish tone; lightest shade often referred to as pale watery dun or some variation; with rust overtones referred to as rusty blue dun; dk. blue dun with bronze cast referred to as bronze blue dun.

Chinchilla: cream to gray background with indistinct, darker barring; looks like an undeveloped grizzly.

Cree: white and ginger background with indistinct gray barring; tri-colored in appearance.

Coachman brown: a very dark brown, bordering on black.

Dun: rich gray; if grizzly pattern is present, then referred to as dun grizzly.

Furnace: light to dark brown with black center near shaft.

Ginger: light colors ranging from straw (lt. ginger) to reddish-golden tan; with indistinct brown barring referred to as ginger variant.

Grizzly: white background with distinct black barring.

Sandy dun: ginger with dun overtones or vice versa; also called honey dun.

Variant: patterned dark on lighter color, as in ginger variant or cream variant; pattern usually indistinct; optionally, any neck of a weird pattern or color that doesn't fit into other category.

White splashed: predominantly white with irregular "flecks" of brown; if pattern is reversed, referred to as brown splashed.

This is not a complete list, but from it, you can probably piece together what most "variant" descriptions mean.

Dry Fly Hackle

Why not start at the top! The so-called genetic hackles come from chickens bred for the job. These are the best science can provide, hackle developed for sheen, stiffness, length of feather, lack of web, and number of feathers.

These chickens are raised in protected environments. Try to get a ticket to the Metz grounds, and you'll see what I mean. Not only are the chickens protected from outside sources of disease, they are also individually housed at some of the "factories" in order to protect them from each other. In short, every effort is made to produce a perfect neck.

There are a limited number of producers of genetic hackles, and although their necks vary in quality, all are considered superior to the imported necks which come from "regular" chickens.

Most of these necks are graded 1-3, with #1 necks the best. Generally, #2 necks have feathers of a quality equal to that of #1 necks, but they contain fewer feathers or they may have some slight damage. Necks graded #3 have feathers of less quality. It's my feeling that #2 necks provide the best bargain for the serious tier on a budget.

Metz Necks

As you can tell, I'm a Metz fan. They are prime necks. It's not easy to explain how hackle can incite feelings of devotion, but Metz necks can. The feathers are long, web-free, and just the right stiffness. (Yes, I think dry fly hackle can be too stiff.) The necks are full, almost puffy, with feathers.

These necks are expensive, certainly, but you get your money's worth. Demand for them is greater than the supply, especially in some colors. I've known shops to keep phone lists for the day the necks come in.

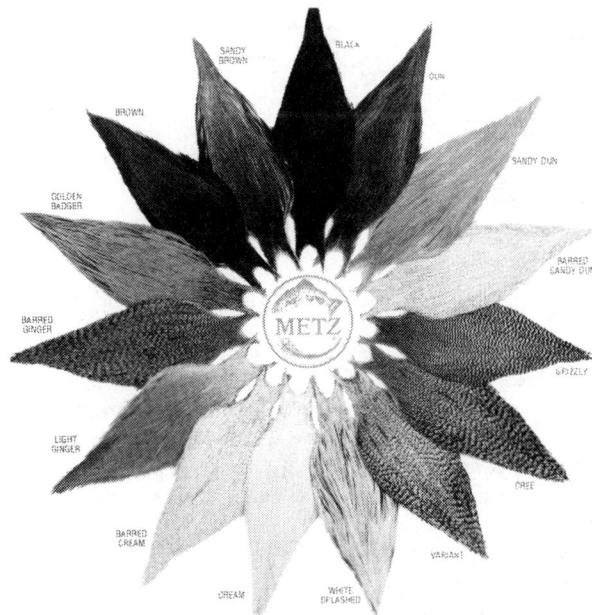

Colors: golden badger, barred badger, light ginger, barred cream, cream, white splashed, variant, cree, grizzly, sandy dun, barred sandy dun, dun, black, sandy brown, brown, dyed coachman brown (#2 only).

Metz #1
$39.85-$49.75 Many catalogs
Metz #2
$28.20-$35.50 Many catalogs
Metz #3
$15.45-$19 Many catalogs
Dyed Metz. *Blue Ribbon Flies offers #2 and #3 grizzly necks dyed olive, yellow, green, dun, brown, and coachman brown.*
#2—$40.50; #3—$22.45 Blu

Colorado Quality Hackle

The new kid on the block comes from just down the road a piece from me. Colorado Quality Hackle has entered the market in direct competition to Metz. Indeed, the prices of the two brands are almost identical, by design I'm sure. The folks at CQH want the buyer to know that they think they've got as good a product as Metz. In some regards, they do.

The best of the CQH necks are, indeed, comparable to Metz necks. The differences are subtle, and the choice rests with the preferences of the individual tier. However, the CQH necks do not have the consistency, especially of color but also in number of feathers, that Metz does. Probably the difference rests in the number of years that their genetic work has been going on. Oddly enough, the biggest color problem appears to be with the brown necks, which I would have guessed to be the easiest to develop. Many of the CQH #2 brown feathers have a black center, much like a furnace hackle.

For mail order, then, I'd stick with Metz, but if you can go into a shop and inspect both necks, then the choice is yours. Because CQH offers several colors not available from Metz, the choice may be easy. In any case, I'm glad there is some competition in the top of the market. That's good for everybody.

Colors: white, cream, watery blue dun, lt. blue dun, med. blue dun, dk. blue dun, rusty blue dun, bronze blue dun, dun grizzly, grizzly, ginger variant, cree, ginger, brown, furnace, black.

CQH #1
$39.95-$47.95 Bob, T&T, AnR, Hig, Mer
CQH #2
$29.95-$39.95 Mer, AnR, T&T, Bob, Hig

Hoffman's

Henry Hoffman produces one kind of hackle, grizzly, and he calls his product, appropriately, Super Grizzly. These are exquisite feathers, long and stiff. The necks appear smaller than Metz and CQH necks, but I believe they contain as many, or more, feathers. I still remember the day my friend bought a Super Grizzly. An onlooker would have thought he was showing off a new pet—he couldn't help petting it as he held it. He didn't let me touch it for two weeks.

Hoffman necks are not as accessible as Metz necks, and you're not likely to find one in your local shop. If you're finicky about your griz and, for some reason, are unhappy with the other grizzly necks, try a Hoffman Super Grizzly. The people at Kaufmann's Streamborn say that if you can find a better grizzly, they'll eat it. I guess they haven't been taken up on the offer since a picture of the event would surely have made the press. They also offer a full refund if you're not happy with the neck. I'm certain the other companies would offer the same refund for the necks since demand exceeds supply.

Hoffman's Super Grizzly #1
$52-$55 Kau, Bud, Blu, Dan, Bob
Hoffman's Super Grizzly #2
$35-$37.75 Blu, Dan, Bud, Kau
Dyed Hoffman's. *Dyed in a variety of colors, including med. and dk. brown, lt. and med. ginger, olive, lt. and med. dun, cree, and black.*
#1—$57-$65; #2—$41.25-$42.50; (#3—$35 Kau only) Kau, Blu, Bud

---

Other Domestic Necks

All of the necks listed here are genetically developed to some extent. In a few cases, it may be seat-of-the-pants genetics, but all these birds are raised with hackle in mind. You may recognize some names, like Spencer, as long-time regional favorites.

These necks generally fit in some place between the name-brand necks and the imports, both in quality and price. They can provide a reasonable alternative to the more expensive necks, and some of them may be nearly as good. Except as noted, I haven't seen any of these necks, so you're on your own.

Al's #1 and #2. *A grizzly neck; #1 necks available dyed in olive, blue dun, brown, and ginger.*
#1—$30; #2—$23.33; #1 dyed—$32.50 Mer
Hebert Genetic Hackle. *In three grades; offered by Hunter's, a respected material supplier; they make a case for these hackles based on the idea that they're raised*

outdoors where the sunshine can improve feather gloss, the cold weather can increase the number of feathers, and exercise can make the hackles stiffer and longer; colors: straw, lt., and dk. ginger; brown; coachman brown; cream; golden, dun, and silver badger; cree; lt., med., dk., iron, honey, watery, blue, and grizzly dun; black; chinchilla; brown splashed cream; white-laced brown.
$17.50-$39.50 Hun
Spencer Hackle. *Long known in the Rocky Mountain states for economical grizzly hackle, these necks are quite good in their top grade; although the catalog listing is a bit confusing, Bud Lilly also offers other colors, apparently from Spencer, and dyed colors, definitely from Spencer; colors: grizzly, brown, ginger, cream; grizzly dyed the following colors: black, blue dun, yellow, lt. and dk. olive.*
#1—$24.95-$29.95; #1 dyed—$31.95; #2—$19.95-$22.50; #2 dyed—$23.95; #3—$14.95-$15.95; #3 dyed—$16.50 Bud, Hig
T.H. Genetic Hackle. *Offered only by High Country Flies and listed right next to the Metz and CQH; some unusual colors; colors: badger, honey dun, pale cream dun, brown cream, furnace, lt. and med. blue dun.*
#1—$46.50; #2—$36.50; #3—$26.50 Hig

Courtesy of Bob Jacklin

Unnamed domestic necks. *These range from probable road kills to $59 neck and saddle combinations; rather chancy shopping here unless you're buying from a firm you know, trust, and can return goods to; colors: grizzly, bleached grizzly, ginger, dun, white, cream, black, badger; grizzly dyed the following colors: olive, red, yellow, blue, orange, brown, and dun.*
$7-$59 Natural colors—Edd, Nat, Fly, Dan, Don, Bob, Orv, EJH, Mur, Dal, Ree, Hun, Kau, Dal, Fly; dyed—Nat, Dan, Fly, Orv, Kau

Imported Necks

I won't argue that these are good beginner's necks nor that you can occasionally find a really good neck among them. I will say that you get what you pay for. In this case, you'll get shorter feathers with more web and fewer feathers per neck. In many cases, you'll need two or more of the feathers to tie a fully hackled dry fly. Often there are few, if any, usable feathers smaller than size 16.

Like nearly everyone else, I started tying with India necks. There are some situations where I can see value in them, and I still buy one now and again. One of these situations is the fly pattern that calls for an unusual color. These are usually patterns I'm experimenting with or that I use only infrequently, and I want to get by cheap. India necks, carefully selected, are the ticket. And sometimes I just can't resist the unique color combination of some of these necks. They look pretty in my tying kit, even if I seldom find a use for them. (I do have some pretty wild looking streamers.)

Imported necks. *Most from India; colors: all the standard colors, many of the non-standard colors, and some dyed necks.*
$4.95-$22 (Note: I told you there were some really good India necks out there, and the high price confirms that.)
Let, Spo, Bob, Edd, AnR, Tac, Mur, Dal, Ree, Hig, Mer, H&H, Bud, Egg, Kau, Orv

Wet Fly Hackle

The hackle listed here is soft and webby. That makes it ideal for underwater flies where the action of the feather adds to the fly's attractiveness to trout. Many of these hackles come from hen birds. The hen necks are listed first, since they are the most common source of wet fly hackle. Following that listing are other sources for hackle material, most notably birds of the grouse family. You'll find a remarkable variety of those birds, mostly thanks to Blue Ribbon Flies. It's unlikely that you'll find a pattern that calls for California Quail (although you've likely heard of California nymphs), but you may find a use for the feathers on some wonderful pattern of your own invention.

Wet Fly Necks

Chinese necks. *Extremely soft with heavy webbing; ideal for Matukas and palmered body hackle on flies such as the Wooly Worm and Wooly Bugger; colors: all your favorites plus oddities such as red variant, black variant, and dun variant; also dyed colors, including olive cree, hot orange, magenta, purple, orange and olive variant and others.*
$2.25-$6.50 Hun, Nat, Edd, T&T, AnR
Hen necks. *Most of these are imports, but unlike the India necks listed above, the feathers are rounded and soft; suitable for wet flies and nymphs; colors: all the regular colors plus speckled brown, partridge, grouse, and other irregulars; dyed colors also available.*
$1.50-$3.95 Don, Tac, Edd, Fly, Nat, Bob, EJH, Mur, Hig, Blu, Mer, Hun, H&H, Kau, Orv
Metz hen necks. *Although not the "better half" of the Metz line, these hen necks are consistent in coloration and structure as are the famous dry fly hackles; graded #1 and #2; often sold in "sets" which include neck and back; colors: most of the colors offered in Metz dry fly hackle.*
$6.75-$13.25 Mer, Blu, H&H, Tac, Let

Grouse and Partridge Feathers

Blue Grouse. *Predominantly blue/gray feathers on the male, brown mottled on the female; from the "fool hen" of the Rockies and Pacific Northwest (which is more sportingly hunted with slingshots than guns); full skin.*
$6.95 Blu
Bobwhite. *The common quail of the plains and Southeast; brown and white coloration; body feathers.*
$1 Blu
Brown spotted snipe. *Yes, Virginia, there really are snipe, but no, Virginia, I don't know what flies they're used for, so this placement in the hackle section is a guess; full skin.*
$9.95-$15 Mer, Blu
California Quail. *The state bird; feathers of many colors including blue, gray, brown, white, black; full skin.*
$5.50 Blu
Chukar. *A European partridge introduced in the West; variety of colors including gold, brown, gray; some feathers barred; loose feathers and wings (with shoulder feathers recommended by Ed Story of National Feathercrafters for soft hackles).*
$.60-$1 Nat, Mer
Cortniex Quail. *Unless this is the Corturnix Quail of Hawaii, I'm lost; maybe it comes from Mexico; let's just leave it as a mystery bird—our world needs more mysteries, you know; full skin.*
$5.50 Blu
English grouse. *Don't know if this is a specific bird or just a nice way to say grouse feathers like the old timers used; brown/black.*
$1-$1.25 Don, T&T
Grouse. *A generic term for any mottled gray/brown feather not identified before it was plucked; loose feathers or skin.*
Loose feathers—$.50-$.85; skin—$9.95-$14.95 EJH, Tac, Fly, H&H
Hungarian Partridge. *Since this is often used as hackle for the Soft Hackle flies and other wet fly patterns, I'll include it here; these feathers are generally sold loose in zip-lock bags, but full skins are also available; color: natural grays and browns.*
Loose feathers—$.69-$2.75; full skins—$6.95-$12.95
Feathers—T&T, Nat, Mur, Blu, Mer, Egg; skins—Blu, Big, Bob

Mearn's Quail. *Aka Harlequin Quail, aka Fool's Quail; found in southern states bordering Mexico; colors predominantly brown; full skin.*
$9.95 Blu

Partridge. *Another generic term, probably the same item as Hungarian partridge listed above; also available dyed olive or brown from The Fly Shop; loose feathers or skin offered.*
Feathers—$.50-$1.75; skin—$11.95 Many catalogs (Tac, Fly for skins)

Ruffed Grouse. *A common grouse (unless you're hunting it) of the northern Rockies and eastern mountains; brown and white; full skin.*
$3.95-$6.95 Nat, Blu

Sage Grouse. *A large grouse of the West; predominatly white/cream with brown and gray; full skin.*
$6.95-$8.95 Blu

Sharptail Grouse. *A brown and white bird of the northern Rockies; full skin.*
$8.95 Blu

Spruce Grouse. *Found in the northern Rockies and Canada; gray, black, and brown; full skin.*
$7.95 Blu

Starling rump. *Great stuff for soft hackles and you're doing a service to native birds threatened by this illegal immigrant (brought to the U.S. by some freak who wanted all the birds mentioned in Shakespeare plays to frolic around his new home in America).*
$.60 Nat

Streamer Hackle

Streamer feathers are used not only for regular hackle, but also for beards and wings. A prime streamer feather is longer and narrower than a hen neck feather, although those feathers are preferred for some ties, such as the Matuka streamer. I've listed saddle hackle and streamer necks here.

Saddles come from the back of the chicken. They have large feathers. Most of them are natural colors. Streamer necks are full necks with larger feathers than regular dry fly or wet fly necks. Most of them are domestic white necks dyed astounding colors.

Saddles

Al's #1 saddles. *Domestic hackle; color: grizzly.*
$7.50 Mer

Colorado Quality Hackle saddles. *Genetic hackle; colors: see CQH's dry fly hackle listing above.*
$7.95-$10.95 T&T, Hig

Domestic grizzly saddles. *Unnamed saddles; colors: grizzly, bleached grizzly; also grizzly dyed in the following colors—brown-olive, blue, pale olive, rust, dun, purple, green, orange, red, yellow, brown, and olive.*
$3.25-$12 AnR, Fly, Bob, Don, Let, Ste, Hun, Kau

Hen saddles. *Softer, more rounded than saddles from cocks; colors: black, gray, brown, ginger, mottled tan,* mottled brown, mottled cream, chinchilla; also dyed red, yellow, blue.
$2.50-$3.95 Kau, Dal, Tac, Egg, Hig, Mer, Bud

Hoffman's #1, #2, #3 saddles. *Graded saddles from Hoffman Super Grizzly capes; colors: grizzly and, from Blue Ribbon Flies, #2 and #3 grizzly dyed olive, green, brown, coachman brown, dun, and pale yellow.*
#1—$20-$22; #2—$12-$13.35; #3—$8 Kau, Dan, Blu, Bud

India saddles. *Saddles from the imported necks; colors: grizzly, brown, black, gray, tan/white, badger, cream, cree, ginger, ginger variant, furnace.*
$2.50-$3.95 EJH, Fly, AnR, Spo, Orv, Hun, H&H, Kau

Metz #1, #2 saddles. *Graded saddles from Metz capes; colors: see Metz dry fly hackle listing.*
#1—$7.50-$9.25; #2—$3.99-$4.50 Bob, Tac, Dan, Let, Cab, Edd, Mur, Dal, Hig, Mer, H&H, Kau, Bud, Blu

Saddle hackle. *Generic saddles; many are white chickens dyed; colors: brown, black, olive, badger, ginger, white, red, yellow, green, blue dun, purple, blue, pink, magenta, dk. green, claret, hot orange, gray, cream, furnace, red variant, ginger variant.*
$2.29-$10 Ste, Don, Edd, Cab, AnR, Mur, Dal

Spencer #1, #2, #3 saddles. *From the Spencer hackle farm; colors: grizzly and, from High Country Flies, grizzly dyed olive, yellow, brown, and, from Bud Lilly's, brown, ginger, cream.*
#1 grizzly—$7.95-$8.95; #2 grizzly—$3.95-$5.95; #3 grizzly—$2.95; #1 dyed—$9.95; #2 dyed—$6.75; #3 dyed—n/a; #1 colors—$4.95; #2 colors—$2.95; #3 colors—$1.95 Hig, Bud, Big

T.H. saddles. *Domestic saddles; colors: badger, brown, blue dun, ginger.*
$8.75 Hig

Streamer Necks

Streamer necks. *Generic streamer necks; most are white necks dyed wild and crazy colors for steelhead flies; colors: black, white, hot yellow, yellow, hot orange, hot pink, olive, red, hot green, fiery brown, blue, silver blue, claret, green, magenta, lt.dun, med. dun, dk. dun, fl. blue, fl. red, orange, purple, brown olive, insect green, kingfisher blue, lime, brown, badger, ginger, furnace, cree, maroon.*
$3.39-$7.95 Many catalogs

Quills and Wings

Most of the feathers listed here are used for tying wings and wing cases. Quill wings, favored for some wet flies and traditional dry flies, generally come from primary and secondary flight feathers of ducks and other birds. Feathers from bird wings are referred to as quills. These feathers are usually sold in pairs, one feather from the right wing and one from the left, so that the curve of the wing on either side of the fly matches.

Rolled wings generally come from the barred flank feathers of ducks. Body feathers from other birds are sometimes used, and you can take a look at the full skins of birds, listed in other sections of this chapter, for sources of unusual wing material.

Some of the materials here are substitutes for feathers no longer available. Substitutes are indicated by "(sub.)" following the name of the feather. Thus, "Blue heron (sub.)" is not a blue heron feather; it is a substitute feather dyed to represent a blue heron feather. Generally, trout and salmon will not snub a fly tied with a substitute; only finicky fly tiers do that.

As a reminder, I haven't listed all sources. There are simply too many to make a full list feasible or useful. Instead, if a material has less than 15 sources, the sources are listed. If there are over 15, the sources are listed as "many catalogs". "Most catalogs" means over 20 sources.

Quills

Courtesy of Bob Jacklin

Bustard quill (Florican). *Used in salmon flies; a hard-to-find feather.*
$5-$15 a pair Don, Blu, Mer, AnR
Speckled bustard (sub.). *A turkey feather that mimics this now-unavailable feather called for in many traditional salmon fly patterns.*
$2.50 a pair Don
Duck quills. *Less coarse than goose quills, therefore more suitable for dry flies and small wets; natural colors are gray and white, other colors dyed; colors: gray, white, red, black, yellow, olive, brown, blue, orange, green, dun, claret; sold by the matched pair or sets of matched pairs.*
$.35-$2 Most catalogs
Goose quills. *Suitable for larger wet flies and for streamers; fairly coarse material, difficult to work with on small flies; colors: natural gray and white, dyed orange, red, yellow, black, brown, green, blue, dun, olive, claret.*
$.35-$1.10 Most catalogs
Holland goose. *Brown goose quill; for the Prince nymph.*
$.39 Nat
Speckled hen quills. *Brown on tan/cream, a popular winging material.*
$.50-$1 Hig, H&H, Hun, Ste, Fly, AnR, Kau, Orv
Swan Nazurias. *Called for in salmon fly patterns; substituted for with goose; colors: white, scarlet, yellow.*
$.25 Ran

Turkey quills. *A material used frequently on patterns such as muddlers and grasshoppers; some colors difficult to find (see Foto-Feathers below); colors: bronze, bleached bronze, mottled brown, white, gray, gold, brown, olive, amber, orange, red, yellow, blue, green, black, dun, maroon.*
$.35-$3.95 Many catalogs
Horan's Mottled Turkey. *Turkeys raised for the tier; the Metz of the future in turkey quills?*
$3 Dan

Foto-Feathers. *White turkey feathers with photo-reproduced patterns imitating hard-to-find natural turkey quills; colors: mottled brown turkey, yellow hopper (olive yellow and brown), King's River Caddis (tan and brown), nymph wingcase (brown and ebony brown).*
$1.35-$1.95 Dan, Fre, Don, Fly, T&T, Mur, Kau, H&H

Full Wings and Less Common Quills

Blue Jay wings. *Blue with black barring.*
$4.50-$4.75 Blu, Mer
Bobwhite wings. *Brown wings, small.*
$.50 Nat
Capercailzie wings. *These might really be Capercaillie, a European grouse with charcoal plumage and brown wings; catalogs and other materials references vary in spelling (and none include the Latin name); brown speckled.*
$5.50 Mer
Golden plover wings. *Light brown.*
$1.85-$2 Blu, Mer

Courtesy of Bob Jacklin

Grouse wings. *Med. brown.*
$.85-$2 EJH, Dal, Ree, TCr, Tac
Guinea hen wings. *Gray.*
$.25-$1.85 EJH, Let, Don, Edd, AnR, Ree, Mer, Hun, H&H, Kau
Macaw wings. *Blue one side, yellow other.*
$1.50 Ree
Mallard wings. *Natural gray with a variety of dyed colors available.*
$.30-$1.50 Most catalogs
Moorhen wings. *Slate gray.*
$.80-$.90 EJH, Tac
Partridge wings. *Gray/brown.*
$.75-$2.75 Tac, Don, Let, Mer, EJH
Peacock wings. *Natural brown.*
$1-$1.50 Don, Bob, AnR
Ring-necked Pheasant wings (cock). *Gray/brown with subtle barring.*
$.75-$1.50 Ran, TCr, Mur, EJH, Let, Tac, Blu, Mer
Ring-necked Pheasant wings (hen). *Gray/brown. (Note: Other pheasant wings are listed in the section on pheasants.)*
$.75-$1.70 Let, Don, Fly, Nat
Rook wings. *Black. (Note: Rook is British for raven.)*
$1.25 EJH
Ruffed grouse wings. *Natural.*
$1-$1.25 Mur, Nat
Starling wings. *Gray/black.*
$.50 Nat, EJH
Teal wings. *Black and white barred.*
$.30-$2.75 Many catalogs
Turkey wings. *Natural gray and mottled.*
$1-$3 Bud, Egg, Nat, Mur
Woodcock wings. *Brown.*
$4 Mer
Wood duck wings. *Brown/gray*
$.65-$.75 EJH, Edd
Yanosh (Bali Duck). *Useful as streamer wings; long, like a saddle hackle; closely barred like mallard flank;*

great minnow imitations possible from the real thing.
$2 Let

Flank and Other Body Feathers

Gadwall flank. *Natural brown.*
$1.25-$3.50 Blu, Nat
English teal flank. *Beats me what an "English" teal is—European bird books list a duck simply called Teal (the old world species of the Green-Winged Teal); but we're dealing with fly tiers, not bird watchers, so we just have to take our chances sometimes.*
$1.40 Blu
Hooded Merganser flank. *Gray/brown.*
$1.25 Blu
Mallard breast. *Deep reddish brown.*
$.50 Hig, Nat
Mallard flank. *A common substitute for Wood Duck and teal flank; natural gray barred; also dyed to imitate Wood Duck; other colors: pale olive, green, yellow, bronze, dun.*
$.50-$3.95 Most catalogs
Pintail flank. *Barring more distinct and finer than mallard.*
$1-$1.75 Let, Don, Tac
Teal flank. *Guess it doesn't matter which teal this comes from, although it's probably the Green-Winged Teal; fine black and white barring.*
$.30-$2.75 Many catalogs
Wigeon flank. *Brown/gray barring.*
$.60-$1.25 Blu, Nat
Wood Duck breast. *White (and wine-colored feathers from Nat)*
$.35-$.95 EJH, Dal, Edd, Nat
Wood Duck body feathers. *All the feathers from 2 birds; plucked by hunters and bagged.*
$12 Nat
Wood Duck flank. *The most highly sought after flank feather for traditional dry fly wings; the black/white barred feather is often replaced by the more common, less expensive mallard flank; the lemon feather is sometimes replaced by a dyed mallard flank feather but it's just not the same.*
$.20-$4.50 Many catalogs
Wood Duck skin. *This should hold you for awhile.*
$16.95-$29 Ste, Kau, Edd, Blu, EJH, Tac

Pheasants

There are such a variety of feathers on our common Ring-necked Pheasant that the possibilities for their use are limited only by the tier's imagination. To top it off, the number of other pheasant skins available can stress even the best of those imaginations.

Some of the feathers from the birds listed here are commonly used in many flies. Golden Pheasant tippet is one example. These gold/orange feathers with a black tip are used as tails on patterns such as the Royal Coachman and Rio Grande King. Golden Pheasant tails, as well as

Ring-necked Pheasant tails, are used for the Pheasant Tail nymph and for Teeny Nymphs.

Other pheasant feathers are required for salmon flies, and still others are used on grasshopper and streamer patterns. In all, pheasant feathers are a rich source of unusually patterned and colored materials.

Argus Pheasant. *The largest of the pheasants world-wide, over 6' long (4' of which is tail); native to Malaya, Sumatra, and Borneo; named for the mythical Argus with a hundred eyes; tail and wing feathers are the most useful; spots with brilliant centers in intricate pattern.* Tails—$3.50; wing quills—$1.50 Tails—AnR; wing quills—Nat, Ree

Golden Pheasant. *A native of China and Tibet; crest of golden feathers; orange/gold tippets with black border; tails a mottled golden brown.*
Body feathers. *Natural red, yellow, green.*
$.50-$2.45 EJH, Ree, Don, Tac
Cape. *Neck and crest.*
$6.95-$10.95 Many catalogs
Crest. *Long, curved feathers.*
$3.95-$4.25 Kau, EJH, Dal, Edd, AnR, Ree, Hig, Hun
Center tails. *The longer tail feathers.*
$1-$6.50 Don, Bob, Tac, Edd, AnR, Ste, Let, Hig
Side tails. *Shorter, narrower, for smaller nymphs.*
$3-$4.50 Let, AnR
Complete tails. *Center and side tails.*
$3.50-$5.25 Mer, Blu, Hun, TCr
Skin. *Including head.*
$8.95-$45.95 (Note: More expensive models include tail.)
Ste, Don, Tac, Cab, AnR, Let, EJH, Blu, TCr, Mer, Hun, Kau, Orv
Skin. *Without head.*
$7.50-$9.50 EJH, Hun, H&H, T&T, AnR
Tippets. *By the package.*
$.60-$4 Many catalogs

Lady Amherst's Pheasant. *Sometimes called simply Amherst Pheasant (but not by gentlemen); introduced into England by, you guessed it, Lady Amherst; red crest, silver collar with black bars, green back, rest white; wings black and white.*
Body feathers. *Green, yellow.*
$.95-$1 Ree, EJH
Cape. *Crest and tippets.*
$5-$18 Many catalogs
Crest. *Red feathers by the package.*
$.50-$.95 Tac, Edd
Center tails. *Longer feathers.*
$22.50-$27.50 AnR, Don, Hun, EJH, Blu
Side tails. *Shorter feathers.*
$9.50-$9.75 Hun, AnR
Skin. *Some include tail, others don't.*
$16.75-$69.95 Mer, Kau, TCr, Let, Don, AnR
Tippets. *Per package.*
$.50-$3 Dan, Ste, Don, Edd, Fly, Spo, Tac, Kau, EJH,

Dal, Ree, Mer, H&H, Ran
Dyed tippets. *Green, dun, red, yellow.*
$1.75 EJH
Wing. *Black and white primaries, iridescent green shoulder.*
$2.50 Tac

Reeve's Pheasant. *Named for Englishman who brought it from China in early 1800s; white head, golden neck, mottled yellow, white, black, brown body feathers; silver/black tail.*
Tail. *Silver/black pattern.*
$3.70 Let
Skin. *Some with, some without tail.*
$17.95-$32 Mer, Don, Tac

Ring-necked Pheasant. *Many hunters who associate this bird with Kansas and other places in the heartland of America may feel uneasy to learn that it's an import with probable origins in the southern Soviet Union; many colors available, including the "church window" feathers of the back.*
Rump. *For the Carey Special and other flies, by the package or full patch.*
$.60-$5.95 Ste, Don, Tac, Fly, Blu, Kau
Dyed rump. *Black, olive, yellow, brown.*
$.75-$.95 Fly, Kau, Blu
Tail. *Complete tail.*
$2.50-$4.95 Kau, Ste, EJH, Tac, TCr, Fly, Mur, Blu
Tail. *Complete, dyed orange, black, olive, green, yellow, red, purple.*
$3.95 Blu
Tail. *Individual tail feathers.*
$.35-$1.25 Most catalogs
Tail. *Individual feathers dyed dun, green, yellow, red, ginger, hot pink, flame orange, insect green, black, antique gold.*
$.80-$3 Ste, Mer, Fly
Skin. *Complete.*
$5.95-$14 Many catalogs
Skin. *Dyed orange, black, olive, green, yellow, red, purple.*
$11.95 Blu
Hen tail. *Less defined pattern.*
$.75-$1.95 Bud, Let, Don, Tac, T&T, Ree
Hen skin. *Mottled brown.*
$5.95-$10 Blu, AnR

Silver Pheasant. *Aka Zebra Pheasant; black crest, silver back with zigzag black bars, breast black with some iridescence.*
Body feathers and tippets. *Silver white with black V-shaped barring.*
$.60-$3.25 Dan, Ran, H&H, Dal, EJH, Let, Tac, Don, Edd, Fly, Ree, T&T, AnR, TCr
Skin. *Complete, less tail.*
$24-$38 Ran, TCr, Ree, Don, Edd, AnR, Mer, Hun, H&H, Kau

Wing quills. *Black and white, by package or complete.*
$.35-$12 EJH, Ree, TCR, Ran, Mer, Tac, Edd, H&H, Ran

Tetras Pheasant. *Couldn't find a thing about this one, another mystery bird; complete tail.*
$4.80 Mer

Some Other Common Feathers

These are the miscellaneous feathers all experienced tiers will recognize. The odd feathers are listed in the next section.

Goose biots. *Or stripped goose; the leading (shorter) side of goose quills; perfect for tails and feelers on stonefly nymphs and other buggy flies; colors: natural gray, white; also dyed black, brown, olive, amber, rust orange, dun, yellow, red.*
$.50-$2.95 Ste, Mur, Hig, Hun, Kau, Bob, Tac, Fly, Nat, Orv

Goose shoulders. *Nazurias (or nasurias or nashurias . . . fly tiers are terrible spellers); soft, longer (4"-6") feathers with curved fibers from sides and shoulders of goose; used for wings on larger flies; particularly useful as swan substitute in salmon flies; colors: black, white, blue, claret, green, orange, red, yellow, brown, olive, gray, lt. blue, dk. green.*
$.45-$2 Edd, Don, Let, Tac, AnR, EJH, Dal, Nat, Ree, Mer, Hun, Kau

Goose shoulders. *Cussettes; shorter than and not as soft as nazurias; colors: gray, white, black, blue, green, orange, red, yellow.*
$.50 EJH

Grizzly marabou. *Body feathers from grizzly chickens; soft fibers have plenty of action underwater; for beards, hackle, wings; colors: natural grizzly; also dyed brown, tan, olive, yellow, orange, dun, red.*
$.50-$4 Edd, Tac, Fly, AnR, Nat, Don, Mur, Mer, Hig, Kau

Grizzly tabs. *Top half of necks; for wings on Adams and other patterns; some use in hackling but mostly this will save your best necks for hackles; to size 18.*
$7.50 AnR

Guinea hen body feathers. *From those naked-headed farm birds (you've seen them run over on the road out front of the farm house); originally from Africa now domesticated for their tasty eggs and flesh that is reputed to have a taste like pheasant; black feathers with white spots; sometimes used as jungle cock substitute but feathers from pheasant, starling, or the plastic replicas are probably better; colors: natural; also dyed blue, orange, olive, yellow, red, brown.*
$.45-$3.25 Most catalogs

Guinea skin. *Full skin.*
$5.50-$14.95 Blu, Big

Jungle cock neck. *Embargoed and nearly impossible (there was a black market in this material) to get until domestic birds became available; beautiful feathers with the famous "eyes" called for in so many salmon fly and streamer patterns.*
$120-$125 (about the same as previous black market price but legal and not damaging to the wild populations) Let, T&T

Jungle hen skin. *Haven't seen one of these, so not much to report.*
$25 T&T

Mallard flight feathers. *Blue with white tip; used on McGinty salmon fly and Western Bee as winging material.*
$.25-$.55 Ree, EJH, H&H, Mer

Mallard drake skin. *Flanks, breast, wings.*
$6.50-$11.95 TCr, Kau, Tac

Mallard hen skin. *Mottled brown overall.*
$3-$5.55 EJH, TCr

Mallard hen body feathers. *Mottled brown.*
$.60-$1.50 Hig, Nat, Tac, EJH

Mallard shoulder feathers. *Natural bronze color.*
$.40-$2.50 T&T, H&H, Nat, AnR

Marabou. *Rightfully from the Marabou or Adjutant Stork of Africa and southeast Asia; given the military name from its stiff strut, just in case you're curious; protected partly because the tail feathers are favored in India as decorative attachments; the term now refers to any soft body feather of like nature, often those from domestic turkeys; soft fibers, very lively underwater; absolutely the best streamer wing material; colors: white; also dyed gray, orange, purple, cerise, pink, green, hot white, hot lime, hot yellow, hot orange, hot green, hot red, hot pink, hot blue, hot fire orange, black, red, yellow, blue, blue dun, olive, brown, dk. olive, lt. brown, lt. olive, chartreuse, wine, bronze, dk. brown, cream, insect green, gold, ginger, and probably others.*
$.40-$2.50 Most catalogs

Ostrich. *From the great flightless desert bird of Africa; herl used as ribbing and collars; colors: gray, black, yellow, orange, brown, white, dk. gray, olive, green, olive brown, red, purple, cream, blue, lime, tan.*
$.40-$2 Most catalogs

Peacock. *The famous fly tying feathers from the Peafowl come from the eyed tail coverts of the cock bird; individual barbs extending from main shaft are used in a number of ways, including herl bodies, stripped herl bodies, and fancies in streamer wings; swords are separate feathers with short, intensely iridescent green fibers used for tails; body feathers are used for beards and hackle on wet flies.*

Peacock body feathers. *Beards and wet fly hackle.*
$.45-$1.95 Ree, EJH, Tac, Don

Peacock eyed tails. *Full tail feathers (actually tail coverts) with eyes in place; natural color.*
$.23-$2.75 AnR, TCr, T&T, Edd, Bob, Don, Ste, Tac

Peacock eyed tails. *Bleached, stripped, dyed red, yellow, green, claret, blue dun, olive, black, orange, blue, ginger, brown.*
$.60-$.65 Don, EJH

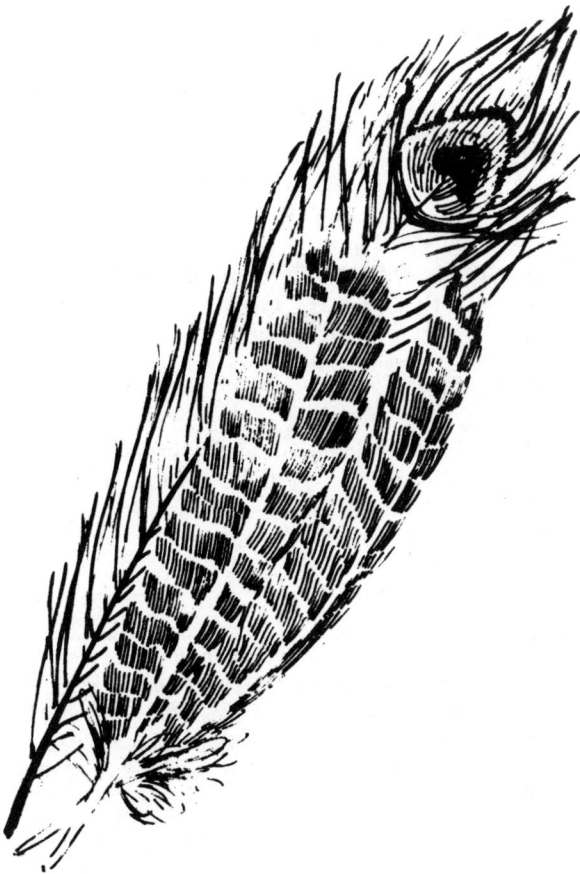

Courtesy of Bob Jacklin

Peacock eyes. *Protectors of wildlife, relax—these are the "eyes" from the tail and not eyeballs or anything gross; barbs from the eyes make the best stripped quill bodies; natural color.*
$.15-$1 Hig, Blu, Mer, Fly
Peacock eyes. *Dyed dun, olive, yellow, red.*
$.90 Mer
Peacock herl. *The fibers from the tail coverts; iridescent green; among the body materials most attractive to trout.*
$.50-$2.75 Most catalogs
Peacock sword. *Feather with bright fibers.*
$.20-$2.50 Most catalogs

Turkey tails. *Expensive and difficult to find in some colors; colors listed separately to aid in finding the specific one you've been longing for.*
Black.
$1.50-$3 Let, Don, AnR
Blue dun.
$1.50-$2.75 Hun, Let, AnR
Cinnamon.
$.75-$3.25 Tac, AnR, Hun, EJH, Don, Let
Mottled brown.
$.75-$2.75 Edd, Fly, T&T, Nat, AnR, Tac, Bob, Let, Dan, EJH, Hun, Kau

Mottled gray.
$3 Don
White.
$.75-$1.25 Hun, EJH, Let
White-tipped.
$.75-$1.50 Ran, Blu, Mer, Hun, H&H, Ree, Kau, Let, Don, Tac

White duck body feathers. *For fan-wing patterns.*
$.45-$.75 Ree, Don, Edd

Oddsities and Endsities, Hard-to-Find Feathers

Many of these unusual feathers are called for in salmon fly patterns. Others are feathers you may have used with success on local patterns or that may have worked as a substitute for an inaccessible feather. Little explanation of the uses of each feather is offered here, since I don't know many of the uses and there are too many materials to research every one of them this time around. Maybe next time. My guess is that if something in this section catches your eye, you already know its intended purpose.

Black Heron quills (sub.). *If Donegal's is satisfied with this substitute, the salmon probably will be too.*
$1.50 Don
Blue Heron quills (sub.). *No legal authentic feathers available.*
$.75 Dal
Blue Jay (sub.). *Another feather called for in salmon fly patterns. (Note: Blue Jay wings listed under the section on wings.)*
$2.95 Don
Canvasback speculum. *The colorful portion of the trailing edges of the flight feathers.*
$1 Nat
Capercailzie tails. *From the European grouse. (Note: Wings are listed in that section.)*
$4.75 Mer
Cock of the Rock (sub.). *Dyed orange substitute.*
$2.50-$4.50 Hun, Don, AnR
Condor quill (sub.). *Popular for quill bodies, stripped of the flue or with it for furry bodies; natural gray or dyed olive, red, amber (from Don).*
$.60-$2.95 EJH, Don
Crimson Glory set. *Golden Pheasant crest dyed hot orange with tippets dyed bright red, for the Crimson Glory pattern.*
$8 Hun
Emu plumes. *Compares to ostrich but quill is stronger allowing its use in quill bodies.*
$.25 EJH
Indian Crow (sub.). *Feathers dyed reddish orange to imitate natural for salmon fly patterns.*
$2.80-$4.50 Hun, Don, AnR
Kingfisher feathers (sub.). *For salmon flies.*
$1 Edd

Kingfisher skins. *For salmon flies.*
$4.95-$18 Don, Tac, AnR, Ree, Mer, EJH, Edd
Macaw tail (sub.). *Substitute for those wonderful feathers from the Central and South American parrot; these are dyed either blue or orange/red unlike the natural which has both colors.*
$2.50 Hun
Macaw tail. *Pairs; red or blue/gold (different color each side); commonly used for horns on salmon flies.*
$2.95-$3.50 Don, AnR
Macaw center tail. *Complete tail section.*
$20 Don
Macaw body feathers. *Red, blue, yellow.*
$.95 Ree
Pintail speculum. *Metallic brown with white tip; called for in Joe's Smelt and other patterns.*
$2.75 AnR
Starling back and flank. *Heavily spotted for use as substitute jungle cock.*
$.60 Nat
Starling skins. *The full skin, most useful in winter plumage which is heavily spotted. (Note: Rump and wing feathers listed in other sections.)*
$1.25-$3.95 Nat, Blu, Ran, Hig, Let, EJH, Don, Tac
Stripped red quill. *Quills of the appropriate color already stripped and ready for use . . . the ultimate in convenience.*
$2.25 AnR
Toucan (sub.). *Necks dyed to imitate the original; golden orange or yellow.*
$3.75 AnR
Turkey marabou and body feathers. *Natural colors.*
$1 Orv, Blu
Turkey round wings. *Short wing feathers; colors: gray, white, green, yellow, blue, red, brown, black, olive, orange.*
$.70-$.75 Mer, Fly
Turkey shorts. *Soft fibers for wet fly and nymph wings; natural and bleached (from Nat only).*
$1-$2 Nat, Hun, Don, AnR
Turkey skirt feathers. *From the wild turkey; finely textured; used for cases on small nymphs.*
$.75 Nat

Hair and Fur

The materials listed here all come from animal skins through the generosity of trappers, hunters, and people who pick up road kills. I thought I might divide the list up into two categories, hair and fur, but then I got confused. Bucktail is definitely hair, and seal is definitely fur. But what of hare's mask or mink that has fur with guard hairs, both useful in tying?

Then I thought I might make it simpler by dividing the list by the uses of the materials, but there's some overlap there, too. In short, the simplest way to do this is to list all the natural hair and fur in alphabetical order and give you a few hints about common uses. I've also listed the general color of the material when I was familiar with it or when it was given in the catalogs, but you'll find some gaps that I hope you'll be able to fill with your own knowledge or with the help of a good materials reference.

Again, the prices are listed here only as a general guideline. The sizes of the hide patches vary and are generally not listed in the catalogs. Ordering from catalogs that don't list sizes is kind of like ordering a new Chevrolet but not knowing whether you're getting a Chevette or a Caprice. Fortunately, most of the catalogs give you a fair amount for the price (which is considerably less than the price of a Chevy). A 2"x2" piece is minimum in my mind unless specified as less for exotic furs.

This alphabetical listing, incidentally, is something catalog compilers might try. It's less creative than some of their systems, but I'd rather spend my time tying flies than looking through catalogs in search of a particular item.

A.B. Natural. *Antron blended with natural furs; each packet comes with a pamphlet listing colors, common names, Latin names, and suggested patterns; colors: lt. fox belly/yellow, buff fox/yellow and olive, cream red fox/yellow, pink fox/yellow, buff fox, pink fox, mahogany brown, muskrat, olive, brown olive, creamy white, English hare. (See also: Hare-Tron Dubbin.)*
$1.45 Dal
African Goat. *A highly translucent dubbing used as a seal substitute; easily dyed; this is a trademark product which means it will be consistent between catalog companies; colors: natural cream, white, black, lt. olive, olive, dk. olive, golden olive, brown olive, amber, hot orange, burnt orange, brown, dk. brown, fiery brown, mahogany, lt. dun, dun, dk. dun, blue dun, green, insect green, lt. yellow, yellow, scarlet, lt. blue, purple, claret. (See also: angoran goat, seal, seal sub.)*
$.60-$1 Orv, Mer, AnR, Hig, Hun, Kau
African goat skin. *A small skin with short white hair; for parachute wings up to size 14.*
$3 Bob
Alpaca. *A long-fibered wool.*
$1 Blu
American opossum. *(Note the correct spelling, catalog folks) the American rendition of one of the most popular dubbing materials, Australian opossum; light gray, thick and glossy; takes dye well.*
$.50-$1 Hig, Ran, Don, Bob
Angora. *A long, soft rabbit fur; excellent dubbing; colors: cream, white, black, lt. gray, dk. gray, brown, dk. brown, seal brown, mink brown, fiery brown, rust, cinnamon, tan, buff, lt. dun, dk. dun, green, insect green, olive, gold olive, pale yellow, yellow, amber, orange, burnt orange, claret, red, dk. red, pink, dk. pink, lt. blue. (See also: rabbit, Hareline Dubbin.)*
$.60-$.90 Ran, Let, Edd, Mer, Dan, Mur, EJH

Angoran goat. *May be the same material as African Goat, above; considered a seal substitute, glossy and translucent; colors: white, cream, black, ginger, brown, dk. brown, mahogany, fiery brown, green, insect green, highlander green, lt. olive, olive, dk. olive, brown olive, lt. yellow, yellow, amber, orange, burnt orange, hot orange, lt. dun, dun, dk. dun, red, claret, shrimp, blue, purple.*
$.95-$1 Ste, Fly

Antelope. *A fairly coarse hair, hollow; spins well; tan or white.*
$.40-$1.25 Many catalogs

Antelope. *Dyed orange, black, red, yellow, dun.*
$1-$1.25 Blu, Fre

Artic fox. *Long-fibered and soft; cream/white.*
$.50-$1.50 Let, Edd

Australian opossum. *A natural dry fly dubbing, highly favored; colors: natural lt., dk. gray/buff, bleached white, dyed black, insect green, olive, golden olive, rusty brown, dk. brown, yellow, red, orange, claret.*
$.30-$1.39 Most catalogs

Badger. *Underfur creamy; guard hairs white-tipped with black bar beneath; used for hair wings and body dubbing.*
$.40-$1.39 Most catalogs

Badger. *Dyed red, blue, yellow, hot orange, green.*
$1.50 Hun

Badger tail. *Tan.*
$1.75 Tac

Beaver. *Suitable for nymph bodies; colors: natural brown to gray.*
$.30-$1.39 Most catalogs

Beaver. *Bleached white, cream, dyed black, brown, olive, blue dun, amber, yellow, orange, rust, claret, violet, insect green.*
$.30-$1.39 Don, Ree, Bob, Tac, Fly, Blu, Hun, Mer

Big horn sheep. *Coarse gray hair.*
$1.25 Mur

Black bear. *Natural blacks and browns; some catalogs call this brown bear, but unless it comes from Alaska, it's just brown hair from the black bear.*
$.40-$1.75 Many catalogs

Black fox. *Long-fibered black fur.*
$.50 Ran

Black squirrel tail. *Soft, silky fur; natural black.*
$1.95-$3.95 Hun, H&H, AnR

Bobcat body fur. *Natural gray/brown.*
$.75-$1 Tac, Let

Bobcat tails. *Natural colors.*
$1.50 Nat

Bucktail. *One of the most popular and useful materials; used for wings, tails, spun hair bodies; colors: natural white, dyed black, gray, brown, green, lt. olive, dk. olive, red, pink, magenta, yellow, orange, lavender, purple, blue, dk. blue, turquoise, fl. chartreuse, fl. green, fl. yellow, fl. orange, fl. red, fl. white, fl. blue, fl. pink. (See also: goat.)*
$2-$4.75 Most catalogs

Calf body hair. *A very fine, straight, short hair; ideally suited for small hair wing patterns; white or black.*
$1.25-$2.95 Mur, Hig, Blu, Orv, Fly

Calf tails. *Aka kip tails, impala tails; a crinkly hair of medium to fine texture used commonly for hair wings; colors: natural white, dyed black, gray, brown, tan, olive, red, pink, rust, claret, magenta, yellow, orange, blue, lt. blue, purple, green, fl. orange, fl. yellow, fl. chartreuse, fl. green, fl. pink, fl. blue, fl. white, fl. red.*
$.75-$2.19 Most catalogs

Camel. *Don't ask me what fly you'd use this for, but you'd probably walk a mile to get one if the fish were rising to it; tan.*
$1 Blu

Caribou. *A coarse gray hair; suitable for spun hair bodies.*
$.40-$1 Many catalogs

Chinchilla. *Very soft gray fur.*
$.40-$.75 Don, Tac, Fly, EJH, Mer, Kau

Chinese boar. *Hard bristles for tails, legs, feelers; strong fibers; lighter colors translucent; natural colors black, gray, white, dk. ginger, lt. ginger in each package.*
$1-$1.25 Tac, Edd, Fly, T&T, Mur, Hig, Mer, H&H, Ran, Kau

Coyote. *Natural browns and grays.*
$.40-$.75 Dan, Tac, Edd, Fly, Mur, Blu, Mer, Bud

Deer. *An indispensable material; in fine textures makes terrific hair wings; in coarse textures spins well for bass bug bodies; (note: catalog companies would do well to grade their deer hair for wings or for spinning); colors: natural gray, bleached white, dyed black, brown, dk. brown, fiery brown, golden brown, rust, red, blue, purple, olive, dk. olive, golden olive, creamy yellow, yellow, orange, gold, rusty orange, dun, chartreuse, fl. yellow, fl. red. (See also: mule deer, whitetail deer.)*
$.40-$2.19 Most catalogs

Deer foreleg. *Shorter hair of different texture.*
$1.75 Mur

Deer masks. *Variety of textures, lengths, and colors of deer hair; usually good texture for caddis wings, para-duns.*
$1-$7.50 Let, Fly, AnR

Eastern pine squirrel tails. *Barred color; called for in Blue Charm salmon fly pattern and streamer patterns.*
$.60-$1.95 Don, Hun, Nat, AnR

Eastern pine squirrel hide. *Quarter hides in limited supplies.*
$1.50 Nat

Elk. *Originally an alternative to deer, now considered superior in some aspects; less hollow, so may float better than deer which absorbs water; finer texture than most deer; natural colors favored for some caddis patterns; colors: natural browns and tans, dyed brown, black, gray, olive, orange, yellow, blue dun, red, blue, green.*
$.50-$1.50 Many catalogs

Elk hock. *Darker colors.*
$.50-$.75 Big, Hig

Elk mane. *Longer hair.*
$.75 Tac, Fly

Elk masks. *Darker colors, some with reddish tints.*
$6 Big

Ermine. *The winter form of the weasel; white. (See also: weasel.)*
$.75 Kau

Fisher tails. *Black.*
$3.95 Tac

Fitch fur. *Aka ferret; soft, cream-colored fur.*
$.45-$.75 Dan, Don, Edd, Fly, EJH, Mur, Blu

Fitch tail. *Cream and brown.*
$1-$1.25 Don, Tac, Edd, T&T, AnR

Fox squirrel blend. *Reddish brown fur, clipped and packaged.*
$1.25 Dal, T&T

Fox squirrel fur. *Reddish brown fur on the hide.*
$.75-$1.50 Mur, Blu, Hun, Nat

Fox squirrel fur. *Dyed olive, brown, black, bright green, orange, amber, dun.*
$1 Blu

Fox squirrel tails. *Reddish brown.*
$.50-$1.79 Many catalogs (and from road kills in your own home town)

Goat. *Aka capras; long, white guard hairs with silky underfur; J. Edson Leonard calls this superior to bucktail for wings, more durable and economical.*
$.50-$1.25 Tac, AnR, Edd, Let, Ran, Mer

Gray fox fur. *Natural gray.*
$.50-$2.75 Many catalogs

Gray fox masks. *Hair fine enough for small salmon flies.*
$6.50 AnR

Gray fox tails. *Natural gray, long hair.*
$3.50-$9 Don, Tac, Edd, AnR, EJH, Mer, Hun

Gray squirrel blend. *Natural gray fur, cut and packaged.*
$1.25 Dal, T&T

Gray squirrel fur. *Gray fur on the hide.*
$.75-$1.50 Mur, Nat

Gray squirrel tails. *Natural gray/white.*
$.69-$1.79 Most catalogs

Gray squirrel tails. *Dyed gold, green, orange, red, yellow, olive, black, purple, fl. blue.*
$.80-$3.95 Orv, Ran, Mer, EJH, Nat, Kau, Hun, Don, Tac, Edd, Fly, AnR

Groundhog. *Natural browns. (See also: woodchuck.)*
$.75 Nat

Groundhog tails. *Natural browns.*
$1.50 Nat

Hare's ear blend. *Hare's ear cut and packaged; colors: natural brown, dk. natural brown, white, olive, ginger, brown, brown olive, dk. olive, lt. dun, black, gold, orange.*
$.75-$1.45 Dal, Bud, Nat, T&T

Hare's mask. *Full masks for the Hare's Ear nymph*
$.79-$3.15 Most catalogs

Hare's mask. *Dyed dun, gold, black, olive, dk. olive, brown, dk. brown, rusty brown, golden olive, orange, cream, yellow, gray.*
$.79-$3.15 Tac, Fly, Nat, AnR, Edd, Orv, Kau, Mer, Hun, Bud

Hare-Tron Dubbin. *Rabbit with Antron added for sparkle; ideal for LaFontaine patterns and all nymphs; soft fur that dubs very nicely; colors exceptionally pure; a fine product from Bob Borden in Washington state; a brand name product so you can be assured of consistency; colors: lt. cahill, March brown, gray, golden brown, lt. olive brown, dk. dun, black, pale yellow, yellow, golden stone, olive, creamy gray, olive dun, caddis green, pale olive, dk. brown, burnt orange, ginger, dk. olive, seal brown, lt. gray, cinnamon caddis, olive tan, olive brown.*
$.90-$1.45 Hig, H&H, Dan, Fly, Kau, Nat (as Fur-Glo Tron), Orv (as Antron/Hare Blend)

Hare-Line Dubbin. *Another product from Bob Borden; pure rabbit fur dyed an amazing number of colors; colors are exceptionally pure; some guard hairs in all blends but can be removed for dry fly bodies; some nymph blends have all guard hairs left in; these two products are a pleasure to use for dubbed bodies; colors: lt. cahill, hare's ear, dk. hare's ear, olive hare's ear, yellow, caddis green, brown, lt. gray, chocolate brown, March brown, black, olive, orange, green damselfly, stonefly, gray, pale yellow, lt. olive, rusty orange, red, rust, dk. dun, bright yellow, insect green, hot orange, cinnamon caddis, dk. olive, amber, antique gold, olive dun, olive brown, olive tan, purple, seal brown, peacock, white, cream, golden brown, dk. olive brown, creamy olive brown, sand, tan/yellow, ginger, creamy gray, dirty yellow, fl. orange, fl. coral, fl. yellow, fl. pink, fl. lime green, fl. royal coachman red.*
$.90-$1.50 H&H, TCr, AnJ, Dan, Fly, Kau, Orv (as Spectrablend)

Horse hair. *Variety of colors.*
$.60-$1 Mur, Let

Lynx. *Natural grays and browns.*
$1 Blu

Lynx tails. *Natural grays and browns.*
$1.49-$2.50 Mur, Mer, Tac, Nat

Marten. *Natural brown.*
$.60-$.75 Mer, Tac, Fly, Blu

Marten skin. *The whole thing.*

$35-$40 Blu

Marten tails. *Natural brown.*

$4.95 Tac

Masterblend. *A blend of natural furs; although many catalogs offer natural fur blends, this one, Natureblend, and T&T Redi-Fur are the only ones marketed under a brand name; colors: lt. fox belly, white, pink fox, stonefly yellow, basic olive, cream red fox, red fox, beaver, mink, black rabbit/brown wool/mink, rabbit/red fox, muskrat, black, primrose, sulfur, amber, pale olive, golden olive, English hare's ear, sandy fox, Australian opossum, iron blue dun, white.*

$1.45 Dal

Mink. *A fine underfur with guard hairs; natural dk. brown.*

$.40-$1.50 Let, Don, Spo, Edd, T&T, Dan, Tac, EJH, Mur, Blu, Mer, H&H, Ran

Mink tails. *Natural white/cream, dk. brown, black, tan, gray/dun, ginger.*

$.89-$3.99 Many catalogs

Mohlon yarn. *This is probably mohair and nylon; a very fuzzy yarn; colors: cream, yellow, hot pink, olive, lt. gray, wine, white, rust, mint green, dk. olive, black, brown, lt. olive, orange, chocolate brown, hot orange, kelly green, dk. gold, red, sand, lt. yellow, lavender, purple.*

$.40-$.75 Tac, Edd, Fly, Mur, Mer, Kau

Mole skins. *From the underworld comes this fur in natural colors and dyed wine, olive green.*

$.50-$1.05 Don, Dan, Tac, Fly, Nat, Kau, EJH, Ree, Hig, Blu, Mer, H&H

Monga Ring-Tail tail. *Of the same consistency and about the same size as squirrel tail; alternating bands of white and black; probably from the Ring-Tail Cat of Central America and extreme southern U.S.; not a Coatimundi tail, as some catalogs suggest, unless it's 2' long and as thick as a dog's tail.*

$1-$2 Many catalogs

Monga Ring-Tail tail. *Dyed red, yellow, green.*

$1.75-$2 Tac, Edd

Moose body hair. *Dark brown hair; fairly long and used commonly for tails on dry flies; the stiffness of the relatively fine hair makes it ideal.*

$.50-$1.39 Most catalogs

Moose body hair. *Bleached for use on lighter patterns.*

$1-$1.25 Mer, Fly

Moose mane. *Longer, somewhat coarser than body hair; used as tailing material, ribbing, and by itself as body material, as in the Mosquito; individual hairs range in color from white to dk. brown and any piece of hide usually includes a mixture of colors.*

$.50-$1.39 Most catalogs

Moose mane. *Dyed yellow, green, orange, brown, gold.*

$1-$1.25 Bud, Blu

Mountain goat. *Natural white.*

$.75-$1.25 Hig, Blu

Mule deer. *In my part of the country, this is what you get when you buy "deer"; mostly grays and tans with white tips; it might be nice if every catalog specified which kind of deer they carried. (See also: deer, whitetail deer.)*

$.80-$1.25 Let, Bob, AnR, Hig, Blu, Hun

Muskrat. *Fine gray underfur, one of the easiest to dub; brown guard hairs are easy to remove for dry flies or are left in for nymphs; called for in one of America's favorite patterns, the Michigan Caddis, aka Adams.*

$.30-$1.39 Most catalogs

Muskrat. *Bleached cream, dyed brown, black; and from Blue Ribbon Flies, dyed "any color".*

$.30-$1.39 Edd, Nat, Blu

Muskrat skin. *For the Adams devotee, a few years' supply.*

$3.95 Tac

Natureblend. *A blend of "100% natural furs", unspecified but most likely rabbit; a number of colors dyed for specific imitations; I've listed what I think is the most common pattern or insect for each color, but up to five are given; colors: Pale Watery Dun, Female Green Drake, Dark Green Drake, Pale Evening Spinner, Male Green Drake, Adams, Lt. Cahill, Blue-Winged Olive, Caenis, Lt. Hendrickson, Gray Fox, Hare's Ear. (See also: Masterblend, T&T Redi-Fur.)*

$1.45 Dal, T&T

Norwegian black bear. *Never have seen one, myself; natural color.*

$.55 Hun

Nutria. *From those muskrat-like critters of the South; reddish brown.*

$.40-$.65 Hig, Don, Edd, Blu, H&H, Bud

Otter. *Natural colors ranging from beige to dk. brown.*

$.30-$1.50 Many catalogs

Peccary. *From the wild pigs of the South; stiff hairs, 3"-4" long; used for tails and bodies; natural colors from variegated cream to dk. brown.*

$.75-$2 Let, Edd, Bob, Tac, T&T, Kau, Hig, AnR, H&H

Polar bear. *The real thing and difficult to come by; for streamers and salmon fly patterns; glossy yellow/cream; had a friend who ended up with about 6 sq. feet of the real thing, and he was the most popular person in our trout club for years.*

$4-$4.95 Don, T&T

Polar bear (sub.). *Much more economical and nearly the same; colors: natural cream, dyed orange, red, blue, green, yellow, black, olive, brown, fl. yellow, fl. orange, fl. pink.*

$.35-$2 Ree, Ran, Don

Porcupine bristles. *Brown with white tip and base; used for tails.*

$.30-$1 Ree, T&T, H&H, Tac, EJH

Porcupine quills. *Hollow; can be used as body by slipping over hook and tying down ends; natural cream.*

$.30-$1 Tac, EJH, Edd, Fly, T&T, Let, Ree, Mer, H&H, Kau

Porcupine quills. *Dyed black, blue, brown, blue dun, olive, red, yellow.*

$.60 Tac

Rabbit. *A favorite for many patterns, especially nymph patterns; colors: white, cream, black, brown, lt. brown, dk. brown, chocolate brown, buff, beige, reddish brown, gray, dun, green, insect green, olive, lt. olive, dk. olive, golden olive, red, pink, salmon pink, amber, yellow, orange, blue. (See also: angora, Hare-line Dubbin.)*
$.30-$1.19 Most catalogs

Rabbit skins. *Full skins; colors: natural gray, white, dyed black, brown, olive, yellow, gold, buff, red, rust, purple, fl. pink, fl. orange, fl. chartreuse.*
$2-$8.95 Tac, Edd, Fly, AnR, Cab, Bob, Don, Nat, Big, Hun, Blu, EJH, Bud, Kau

Rabbit strips. *Narrow strips of rabbit fur cut for use on Zonkers, that wonderfully life-like streamer pattern; colors: white, black, brown, dk. brown, tan, lt. gray, dk. gray, chinchilla, grizzly, olive, olive yellow, yellow, gold, rust.*
$1-$2.95 Dan, Bob, Fly, T&T, Hig, Blu, Bud, Kau, Big

Rabbit tails. *Puffy white, I suspect.*
$.30 Mer

Raccoon body fur. *Mostly gray.*
$.40-$1 Mur, Hig, Bob, Don, Tac, Blu, Mer, H&H, Ran

Raccoon tails. *Long black and white hair.*
$1-$4 Mer, Ran, Don, Tac

Red fox. *A popular fur with reds and creams.*
$.30-$1.50 Many catalogs

Red fox tail. *A bushy tail that will look good on your car antenna if you don't use it for tying.*
$5.95 Tac

Sable tails. *Natural dk. brown.*
$2.49 Tac

Seal. *The natural fur; popular for nymph bodies due to its translucency; colors: natural brown, cream, dyed black, blue dun, olive, yellow, green, scarlet, orange, hot orange, fiery brown, claret, lt. blue, purple.*
$.30-$2.50 Edd, Don, EJH, Bob, AnR, Fly, Ree, H&H, Big, Kau

Seal (sub.). *Very close to real thing and more economical; colors: all of the above plus dk. olive, dk. brown, insect green, maroon, gold, lt. yellow, fl. pink. (See also: African Goat, angoran goat.)*
$.75-$1.75 Kau, Don

Silver fox. *Natural grays.*
$.60 Mer, Tac

Silver fox tails. *Natural grays.*
$14.95 Tac

Silver monkey. *A fine textured hair.*
$.50-$1.50 Hun, AnR, Ran

Skunk. *Natural black and white fur; easily dubbed.*
$.30-$3 H&H, Ran, Dan, Don, Edd

Skunk tails. *Natural black and white/cream.*
$1.25-$2.29 Let, Tac, Edd, T&T, AnR, EJH, Bud, Ran

Snowshoe hare. *If taken in winter, this is a bright white; in summer, colors would be similar to any other wild rabbit; probably a winter hide (that's when most hunting seasons are).*
$1 Blu

Sparkle wool. *Wool with tinsel "spun" in it; very*

popular, according to Ed Story; colors: rust, brown, muskrat, olive, black.*
$.65 Nat

T&T Redi-Fur. *A blend of natural furs; no specifics on type of fur used, except for those indicated by the animal name; colors: white angora, lemon cahill, stonefly yellow, primrose, cream fox, amber, ginger, lt. fox belly, pink fox, red fox, sandy fox, beaver, beaver brown, mink, muskrat, lt. blue dun, blue dun, iron blue dun, hare's ear, yellow olive, tan olive, lt. olive, olive, baetis olive, golden olive, brown olive, gray olive, green olive, olive dun, enough olives to start a deli, insect green, caddis larva green, isonychia claret, black. (See also: Masterblend, Natureblend.)*
$1.45 T&T

Weasel body fur. *Cream. (See also: ermine.)*
$1 Let

Weasel (ermine) tails. *Fiery brown.*
$.50-$.55 EJH, Edd

Weasel tails. *Dyed black.*
$1 Hun

Whitetail deer. *Natural brown. (See also: deer, mule deer.)*
$1-$1.25 Many catalogs

Wolf. *Natural browns, cream; long guard hairs.*
$.60 TCr

Woodchuck. *Natural colors. (See also: groundhog.)*
$.50-$1.50 Let, Don, Tac, Edd, T&T, Kau, Mur, Hig, Blu, Mer, H&H, Ran

Woodchuck tails. *Natural ginger.*
$.75-$1.50 Edd, Nat

Wool. *On the hide; natural cream/yellow and dyed brown, dun, olive, black.*
$1 Blu, Bud

Wool yarn. *Wool for wound bodies; colors: black, white, burnt orange, orange, cream, toast, sounds like breakfast, mustard, claret, olive, now lunch, red, wine, and dinner, pale yellow, yellow, gold, green, pale olive, olive gray, peacock green, insect green, chartreuse, seal brown, med. brown, dk. brown, tan, buff fox, rust, gray, blue, purple, fl. red, fl. yellow, fl. orange, fl. lime, fl. fire orange, fl. white, fl. blue, fl. pink.*
$.25-$.75 Many catalogs

Synthetic Dubbing and Yarns

The materials in this section are all synthetic body materials. Most are dubbing but some yarns are also included.

It didn't take fly tiers long to discover the benefits of using man-made materials in tying. Polypropylene, for instance, is lighter than water and therefore makes an ideal dry fly body. In the proper texture, it dubs easily (although not as well as many natural furs), and it takes a dye well.

By altering the texture of these synthetics, nymph dubbing has also been created. Ultra-Dub is one example. Others imitate natural seal fur.

Antron of carpet fame has come into recent good favor due to its sparkle. The LaFontaine patterns in current fashion make great use of this material to imitate the bubbles carried by nymphs and pupa. Kapok, the material of life preservers, is also used by tiers, mostly as a dry fly material because of its floating ability.

All this is said with the knowledge that if tomorrow a new synthetic were to come on the market that looked just like a quill body and floated like balsa, some people would shun it in favor of natural materials.

The materials are presented in alphabetical order.

Antron. *Pure Antron courtesy of DuPont; in solid colors or blended; best used for nymphs; can also be blended with natural fur to give it that extra sparkle; colors: clear, black, white, cream, lt. yellow, yellow, gold, amber, orange, lt. orange, burnt orange, red, claret, lt. brown, med. brown, dk. brown, gray, lt. green, green, olive, dk. olive; blends: cream/yellow, cream/amber, green/cream, olive/gray, gold/brown, rust/yellow, dk. blue/olive brown, pale yellow/gold, rusty orange/orange, green/bright green, dk. brown/black, dk. brown/gray, olive/bright green, pale yellow/gold.*
$.45-$1.40 Spo, Fly, T&T, Nat, Blu, Kau, Mer, Orv, Dal, Tac (yarn form)

Aztec yarn. *Synthetic yarn for use on Aztec streamer patterns; colors: olive, brown, black, white, gold, orange, lt. gray, dk. gray, cream, brick, blue.*
$.50-$1 Mur, Let

Buggy Nymph. *Translucent, porous nymph material; colors: rust, lava brown, sage brown, black, lt. brown, dk. brown, isonychia, aqua green, mint, silver black, tan, copper, lt. hare's ear, dk. hare's ear, lt. olive, olive, blue dun, spruce, mustard.*
$.75 Fly

Fluorescent nylon yarn. *A synthetic wool dyed fluorescent colors for steelhead and other patterns; colors: fl. yellow, red, green, orange, white, blue, pink.*
$.30-$.40 Edd, Hun, AnR

Fly-Rite. *The most popular synthetic dry fly dubbing; 100% polypropylene; easy to work with; 40 colors; colors: 1. white, 2. black, 3. dk. olive, 4. bright yellow, 5. rust, 6. choc. brown, 7. dk. gray, 8. golden olive, 9. golden yellow, 10. blue-winged olive, 11. orange, 12. cream, 13. grannom green, 14. golden amber, 15. lt. olive, 16. chartreuse, 17. golden brown, 18. rusty orange, 19. lt. tan, 20. dk. tan, 21. lt. gray, 22. cahill tan, 23. olive sulfur, 24. tiny blue-winged olive, 25. cream variant, 26. Adams gray, 27. speckled dun, 28. dk. reddish brown, 29. western olive, 30. March brown, 31. pale morning dun, 32. rusty olive, 33. orange sulfur, 34. quill gordon, 35. inch worm green, 36. ginger cream, 37. gray drake, 38. pale watery yellow, 39. med. brown, 40. caddis pupa green. (See also: Spectrum, Poly Fur.)*
$.65-$1 Let, Tac, Edd, Mur, Fly, T&T, AnR, Mer, EJH, Dan, H&H, Ran, FlR

Kapok. *The life preserver material that, like polypro,*

has a density less than water; white.
$.25-$1 Ree, Let, Edd, Nat

K-Dub. *Synthetic with floatant already applied; colors: black, white, olive, tan, rust, blue dun, gray, yellow, brown, cream, green, dk. olive, sulphur, warm gray, gold, pink gray.*
$.80-$1 Mur, Mer, H&H, T&T, Tac

Poly II. *Polypropylene compressed into sheet form; when torn apart with fingers, resembles regular poly; material can also be cut with scissors into wing shapes; colors: white, dk. olive, cahill cream, dk. cream, creamy orange, creamy pink, black, choc. brown, med. golden yellow, med. gray, dk. gray, mahogany, pale yellow, rust, pale watery olive, nymph, tan, dk. green olive.*
$.55-$.80 FlR, TCr, Dan, Edd, T&T

Poly II Fluorescent. *As above but fluorescent colors; colors: fl. yellow, orange, red, green.*
$.85 FlR, Dan, Tac

Poly Fur. *Another polypropylene dubbing material; colors: white, cream, lt. cahill, beige, black, gray, cream ginger, lt. ginger, fawn fox, cream red fox, pink fox, tan, yellow, stonefly yellow, dirty yellow, amber, golden ginger, creamy orange, primrose, fiery brown, med. brown, choc. brown, dk. brown, mahogany, blackish brown, insect green, grannom green, bronze olive, pale olive, med. olive, med. olive brown, lt. dun, blue dun, dk. gray, brownish gray. (See also: Fly-Rite, Spectrum.)*
$.75-$.90 T&T, Dal

Polypropylene yarn. *Same material as the dubbing but in yarn form; can be separated for smaller flies; can also be used for spinner and mayfly wings (see also: poly wing material in misc. section); colors: white, cream, tan, gray, yellow, choc. brown, black, blue, lt. gray, olive, blue dun, dk. pink, brown, salmon, lt. yellow, gold, insect green, yellow gold, violet, red, green, rose, rust.*
$.25-$.60 Spo, Edd, Tac, Ran, Dan, Bob, Mur, Don, EJH, Bud, Kau, H&H, Hig

Seal substitute. *An unspecified synthetic created to imitate the texture and sparkle of real seal; colors: cream, white, black, gray, red, pink, claret, brown, fiery brown, green, olive, chartreuse, amber, orange, hot orange, rusty orange, yellow, lt. blue, purple. (See also: T&T Seal-Sub.)*
$.60-$.75 Fly, Edd

Sparkle yarn. *Translucent synthetic yarn with lots of sparkle; colors: cream, white, tan, black, gray, lt. yellow, yellow, orange, burnt orange, gold, dk. gold, seal brown, dk. brown, olive, dk. olive, kelly green, worm green, grass green, bronze, rust, purple, brick, blue.*
$.50-$.60 Tac, Bud, T&T, Mur, Nat, Hig, Mer

Spectrum. *Fine denier polypropylene for dry fly bodies; 50 colors; dubs easily; colors: 1. muskrat, 2. lt. caddis green, 3. pale olive, 4. copper, 5. olive, 6. med. dun, 7. yellow/olive, 8. dun/olive, 9. cream/tan, 10. dun/claret, 11. slate/brown, 12. breadcrust orange, 13. brown hare, 14. pale gray, 15. tan/claret, 16. cream/olive, 17. copper/brown, 18. chartreuse, 19. baetis, 20. cream, 21. pale yellow, 22. med. ginger, 23. yellow cream, 24. mahogany, 25. cinnamon, 26. honey, 27. bronze, 28.*

orange, 29. med. gray, 30. gray fox, 31. cahill, 32. dk. olive, 33. pale gray, 34. brown olive, 35. salmon, 36. amber, 37. lt. pink, 38. insect green, 39. sulfur, 40. golden yellow, 41. brown, 42. pink, 43. inch worm, 44. mink, 45. golden tan, 46. red brown, 47. pale dun, 48. March brown, 49. white, 50. black. (See also: Fly-Rite, Poly Fur.)

$.75-$.90 Dan, EJH, Fly, AnR, Bud, Nat, Hig, Hun

T&T Seal-Sub. *A substitute for real seal fur in nymph and pupa patterns; much more economical than seal or its natural fur substitutes; colors: white, cream, black, gray, lt. gray, dk. gray, dk. dun, tan, ginger, brown, lt. brown, dk. brown, fiery brown, red, primrose, yellow, amber, orange, burnt orange, insect green, grannom green, teal green, olive, lt. olive, dk. olive. (See also: seal substitute.)*

$.90 T&T

Ultra Dub. *Originally from Ken Ligas' Creative Anglers; a shaggy, nymph dubbing; colors: 1. black drake, 2. brown drake, 3. caddis green, 4. dk. mahogany, 5. olive brown, 6. cinnamon, 7. leech brown, 8. peacock, 9. damsel brown, 10. yellow, 11. shrimp, 12. black, 13. white, 14. lt. beige, 15. muskrat, 16. March brown, 17. dk. rust, 18. olive, 19. sand, 20. dirty yellow, 21. pale olive, 22. lt. muskrat, 23. gill red, 24. yellow/green, 25. olive green, 26. copper, 27. beaver brown, 28. golden brown, 29. dk. claret, 30. lt. hare's ear, 31. dk. hare's ear, 32. pale sulphur, 33. pink fox, 34. golden olive, 35. med. hare's ear, 36. little yellow stonefly, 37. olive hare's ear, 38. cream fox, 39. pale brown, 40. amber.*

$.65-$1 Edd, Cab, EJH, Dan, T&T, Kau, H&H, Hun, Mer

Unseal Nymph Blends. *Colors blended for specific nymphs; colors: (how's your Latin?) Ephemera Stenonema, Blue-Winged Olive, Green Drake, Epeorus, Paraleptophlebia, Caenis, Baetis, Lt. Ephemerella, Potamanthus, Leptophlebia, sulphur, hellgrammite, pale brown pupa, red pupa, gray caddis pupa, cinnamon sedge, pale olive pupa, Niemeyer Isonychia, Hexagenia, Epeorus Pleuralis, yellow stone, dk. Stenonema, perla, gray olive caddis pupa.*

$.65-$.90 Dal, Let, T&T

Yorkshire Flybody Fur. *A wool-like fur; colors: white, black, pale watery dun, iron blue dun, gray dun, yellow, golden olive, cream green olive, dk. olive, dk. brown, sedge brown.*

$.90 Dan

Yorkshire Dollybody Yarn. *Similar to polypropylene yarn; colors: white, black, orange, lime, pink, yellow, blue, gray.*

$.90 Dan

Miscellaneous Tying Materials

These are not exactly left-overs, just things that didn't fit in the other big categories. And so, you'll find a number of minor categories to wander through.

Body Materials

Burlap. *For the Burlap steelhead pattern and golden stone nymphs; colors: natural tan, amber, brown, olive, bleached white, black.*

$.60-$.75 Mer, Kau, Fly

Chamois. *For use on leech patterns; colors: black, purple, olive, white, dk. gold, brown.*

$1-$1.75 Hig, Cab

Chenille sizes

Fine
Small
Medium
Large

Chenille. *A common material for nymphs, streamers, and other patterns; most made from rayon now, although J. Edson Leonard suggests that silk is the only correct material; colors: white, cream, black, gray, blue gray, dk. gray, brown, lt. brown, dk. brown, seal brown, ginger, tan, coffee, yellow, golden yellow, lt. yellow, amber, orange, burnt orange, lt. orange, lt. olive, med. olive, dk. olive, yellow olive, olive green, green, insect green, lt. green, red, dk. red, claret, pink, blue, purple, dun.*

$.30-$1.29 Most catalogs

Fluorescent chenille. *Same as above, dyed fluorescent colors; colors: fl. white, red, pink, rose, blue, green, fire orange, orange, yellow.*

$.40-$1.29 Many catalogs

Honey Bug chenille. *Special dyes for the Falling Spring special; you may think you could tie a Honey Bug with just any pink chenille, but the fishermen of Pennsylvania would argue with that; colors: black, cream, white, buff, dun, gray, insect green, olive, shrimp, pink, pale yellow.*

$1 EJH, Dal

Sparkle chenille. *Chenille with tinsel interwoven; for wild and crazy Wooly Worms and streamers; colors: white, black, brown, gray, yellow, red, blue, green, tan, pink, dk. brown, ginger, insect green, coffee, orange, dk. olive, fl. yellow, fl. orange, fl. green.*

$.40-$.60 Kau, Dan, Don, Fly, Tac (the widest selection of colors)

Ultra Chenille. *A velour-type chenille; very bushy; colors: white, black, red, pink, wine, claret, yellow, orange, fire orange, rust, blue, purple, insect green, olive, pale olive, dk. olive, golden olive, tan, chocolate, gray, pale yellow, brown, lt. brown, blue gray, lt. gray, dk. gray, green, green olive.*

$.75-$1 Dal, Mer, EJH, Fly

Variegated chenille. *Bi-colored chenille; colors: black/yellow, black/orange, olive/yellow, black/green, black/olive, brown/yellow, black/red, brown/orange, dk. olive/white, yellow/white, white/red, yellow/red, black/white, white/pink, green/yellow, blue/white, fl. chartreuse/white, fl. yellow/black.*

$.40-$.65 Kau, Dan, Tac, Fly, Nat

Glo-Bug yarn. *The fluorescent yarn used for egg patterns; colors: apricot supreme, pink lady, burnt orange, chartreuse, champagne, cherise, cotton candy, cream delight, lt. roe, dk. roe, deep dk. roe, salmon egg, flame, golden nugget, moss, Oregon cheese, peachy king, sunrise yellow, baby pink, egg.*
$2 Nat, Ste, Orv, Fly, AnR, Kau, Hun, Mer

Latex sheets. *Natural rubber to be cut into strips to create segmented nymph and pupae bodies; can be dyed with Pantone markers (listed under dyes and markers); colors: cream, charcoal, dyed olive, orange, yellow.*
$.20-$1.25 Many catalogs

Latex strips. *Pre-cut for your convenience; colors: cream, caddis green, golden yellow, dk. brown, olive, brown, black.*
$1.50 Ste

Leech yarn. *A fairly coarse yarn adopted by fly tiers for leech patterns; colors: black, golden olive, brown/blue, green/purple, ruse, black olive, gray, dk. green, olive.*
$.55-$1 Hig, Bud, Kau

Monofilament, flat. *A wide mono used for ribbing or bodies; clear.*
$.60 T&T

Monofilament, oval. *Another type of mono used mainly for ribbing; colors: clear, black, brown, amber, olive.*
$.50-$.75 Hig, Edd

Plaston. *A plastic, oval strand, 1/32"x1/64"; touted as creating perfect segmented quill bodies but I wonder about its floating ability; colors: white, black, brown, lt. brown, cream, green, red, yellow. (See also: Swannundaze, V-Rib.)*
$.25 EJH

Raffene. *A raffia substitute; colors: black, dk. brown, claret, cream, gold, insect green, olive, orange, yellow, blue, pink, scarlet, tan, silvery white. (See also: raffia, swiss straw.)*
$.50-$.75 Hig, EJH

Raffia. *From the raffia palms of Madagascar; a paper thin, quarter-inch wide material for bodies; somewhat out of vogue now, but very useful for creating thin, segmented bodies much like quill bodies; colors: beige, black, red, claret, yellow, lt. orange, orange, brown, lt. brown, chocolate brown, gray, blue, olive, green. (See also: Raffene, swiss straw.)*
$.30-$.90 Ran, Kau, EJH, Ree, Edd, Ste, Don, Fly

Swannundaze, 1/16". *A hard but flexible nylon strand; the original size; can be wound to create very life-like nymph bodies; sometimes used as ribbing; many colors translucent to add realism; colors: 1. cream, 2. beige, 3. tan, 4. ginger, 5. med. brown, 6. dk. brown, 7. caddis green, 8. olive dun, 9. dk. olive, 10. yellow, 11. orange, 12. pink, 13. silver gray, 14. dk. gray, 15. black, 16. lt. transparent amber, 17. dk. tr. amber, 18. lt. tr. olive, 19. dk. tr. olive, 20. tr. brown, 21. tr. black (smoke), 22.*

clear, 23. med. tr. amber, 24. pale tr. orange. (See also: V-Rib, Plaston.)*
$.50-$.75 Many catalogs

Swannundaze, 1/32". *Same stuff but thinner; colors: clear, lt. transparent amber, dk. tr. amber, lt. tr. olive, dk. tr. olive, tr. brown, tr. black, tr. amber, pale tr. yellow, pale tr. orange.*
$.50-$.75 Dal, Mer, H&H, Kau, Orv, Dan, T&T, AnR

Swannundaze, 3/32". *Same stuff but wider than original; colors: clear, dk. amber, transparent brown, tr. black.*
$.50-$.75 Mer, H&H, AnR, T&T, Dan, Kau

Swiss Straw. *A rayon material in ribbon form; a substitute for raffia; useful as body material and wing cases; colors: white, black, cream, gray, tan, copper, lt. olive, olive, amber, golden amber, yellow, orange, insect green, fiery brown. (See also: Raffene, raffia.)*
$.75-$2.25 Mer, Kau, Nat, Ran, Fly, AnR

V-Rib. *Similar to Swannundaze but more pliable; can be stretched (and therefore made thinner) than standard Swannundaze, but don't know how it compares to new, thinner Swannundaze; all colors translucent; colors: clear, black, red, yellow, amber, orange, green, olive, brown. (See also: Plaston.)*
$.70-$.75 Fly, Mer

Popper Corks, Sponge Bodies, and Other Eccentricities

Betterbugs. *A selection of cork popper bodies pre-mounted on stinger hooks; primed and ready to paint; sizes: #2-#4; shapes: popper, frog, slider; several sets available including $24.95 kit with paint.*
$5.95 for 10 AnR

Bugazote Foam. *A closed-cell foam for floating bugs, hoppers; colors: white, black, red, yellow.*
$.80-$1 Mer, Fly

Furry Foam. *A fuzzy foam used mainly for nymphs bodies; in sheets that may be split, then cut for desired taper; wound on like latex; colors: cream, buff, black, gray, lt. gray, dk. dun, lt. olive, dk. olive, lt. brown, dk. brown, seal brown, burnt orange, lt. orange, green, blue, golden yellow, fl. yellow, fl. red, fl. orange, fl. pink, fl. green.*
$.75-$.85 Big, Edd, Kau, Hig, Mur, Mer, Tac, Fly

Mayfly body material. *A thin sponge with adhesive back; fold around hook and trim; cream.*
$.25 EJH

McMurray Bodies. *Balsa bodies ready to attach to hook; float wonderfully high without a chance of sinking; painted to represent common terrestrials; colors: black ant, cinnamon ant, yellow jacket, lady bug, black beetle, Japanese beetle, leaf hopper.*
$.39-$.75 Let, Nat, Mur, Mer

Nymph pins. *Soft wire pins that can be bent to form flattened nymph bodies; can also be used to create wiggle nymphs.*
$.60-$1.25 Fly, Mer

Nymphforms. *Pre-cut forms for creation of flat-bodies nymphs; unweighted; white.*
$1-$1.75 Orv, Let, Mur, T&T, Tac, Kau, H&H
Nymphforms. *Same form but weighted; black.*
$1.95-$2.65 Bud, Kau, Orv, T&T
Perma-Float Hooks. *Hooks with unsinkable styrofoam bodies molded on; can be trimmed; sizes 6, 10.*
$2.75-$3 per doz. T&T

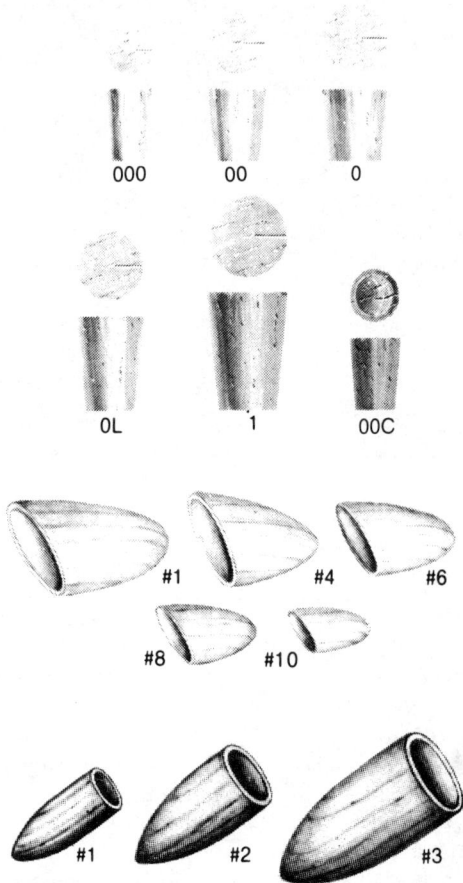

Popper corks. *Available in the following shapes—untapered, tapered, slanted, bullet-head; ready to mount (some require slotting) and paint. (Note: Not all shapes available from all sources.)*
$.70-$3.30 EJH, Ree, Edd, Tac, Don, Kau, H&H, Mer
Popper corks. *On the hook.*
$6.95-$7.95 Dal
Sponge rubber bodies. *This is rather a confusing area; many styles and colors; best look to individual catalogs for help in ordering; sponge rubber bodies can be threaded onto the hook, cemented on, or lashed on with thread (which changes the shape of the body); here are the shapes and corresponding colors, not all available from every catalog: bass bug and panfish bug—black, yellow, red, white, orange, green; inch worm—green; cricket/hopper—black, brown, green, tan, yellow; beetle—black; ant—black, red, brown.*
$.70-$1.25 Fly, Kau, Mer, TCr, Tac, T&T, Nat

Sponge rubber bodies. *Odd shapes and sizes, well-described in catalog; floating or sinking; colors: black, white, gray, red, yellow, orange, green, tan.*
$.35-$.55 EJH

Wing Materials

Hayline Wing Material. *Very light plastic straw-like material; transparent; for spent-wing spinners.*
$.50 Don

Jungle Cock substitute. *Jungle cock eyes photo-reproduced on plastic sheets; improved now to the place that only close inspection can separate them from the real thing (closer inspection than trout or salmon give flies); for most of us, it's this product or a feather substitute.*
$.65-$1.50 Bob, Ran, Orv, Dan, Tac, H&H, Mer, Dal, EJH, Kau
Latex wing cases. *Pre-cut sections of latex for nymph wing cases; colors: brown, black, amber.*
$.60 Blu

Mayfly wing material. *Clear plastic with veined pattern; sheets or pre-cut.*
$.35-$.40 Mer, Tac
Microweb. *Thin sheets of synthetic material; integral pattern that resembles veining; can be colored with Pantone markers (see below); colors: white, cream, gray, black, olive, brown.*
$1.95-$2.95 Dal, Mur, Kau, Bud, Hig, Mer, H&H, Let, Tac, EJH, Fly
Poly Wiggle. *Very long fibers of fine polypropylene for use on streamer wings; lots of action underwater; colors: white, black, pale watery dun, med. gray, tan, chocolate brown, rust brown, western olive, dk. olive, chartreuse, pale yellow, yellow, red, orange, blue, pink.*
$.85-$1.05 FlR, TCr, Dan, Let, Mer, Tac
Poly II. *Die-cut wings from Poly II sheets (see above); six colors in each pack; pre-cut for mayflies or caddis; colors: cream, gray dun, white, dk. cream, lt. gray dun, pale rose dun.*
$2.35-$3.50 T&T
Poly wing material. *A polypropylene yarn suitable for spent-wing spinners, loop-wing emergers, and some upright-wing patterns; the "crinkly" nature of the material gives spinners a very realistic light pattern on the water surface; colors: black, white, cream, tan, pale dun, pale watery dun, dun, iron dun, gray, yellow, gold, primrose, rust, pink, blue, lemon wood duck.*
$.50-$.75 Dal, Orv, Mer, Let, T&T

Wyngs. *Waterproof material; opaque but can be colored with Pantone markers (see below); cut or burned to desired shape; for down-wing and flat-wing patterns.*
$1.75 T&T

Eyes

Bead chain. *Beads connected by wire, i.e. keychain; to be cut into pairs and tied on hook as eyes; gold or silver.*
$.60-$1 Ste, T&T, Tac, Fly, Kau, Mer, Nat, AnR
Doll's eyes. *Clear plastic semi-bubble; black iris; flat back; can be glued on bass bugs, streamers; diameters: 4-10 mm; colors: white, yellow (Mer, Cab, AnR only), sparkle yellow (Mer only).*
$.50-$1.89 Mer, Cab, Fly, AnR, Hig, Hun, Orv, T&T, Ste

Glass eyes. *Pair of eyes connected by wire; can be wound directly on for additional weight or wire snipped short and wound on; sizes: 2-8mm; colors: clear (back can be painted any color), or gold, silver, amber (Fly only).*
$.45-$.75 EJH, Tac, Fly
Optic eyes. *No details on these; colors: gold, silver.*
$.60 Fly

Lead Wire and Ribbing Wire

Lead wire. *Used to weight nymph and streamer hooks before tying on materials; sizes in inches: .011, .015, .020, .025, .030, .035, .040, .045, .057.*
$.50-$2.80 Most catalogs, heavier weights available from Bud, Kau
Lead wire. *Square wire; sizes in inches: .017, .025, .031, .040.*
$.90-$1 Dal, Mer, Nat, T&T
Ribbing wire. *Fine wire for ribbing fly bodies; colors: silver, gold, blue, green, red, copper.*
$.40-$1.25 Many catalogs
Tinsels, Piping, and Braids Chenille tinsel. *Tinsel in*

chenille form; for heavy, full metal bodies; colors: gold, silver.*
$.30-$1 Ree, Hig, Mer, H&H, Kau, Orv, Don, Spo, Tac, EJH, Dan, Edd, T&T
Diamond Braid. *Aka Poly Flash; for streamer, steelhead flies; colors: silver, gold, peacock, green, pearl, purple, copper, blue, red.*
$.75-$1.35 Hun, Kau, Fly, Mer, Mur

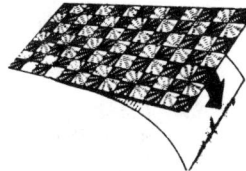

Fishscale Prismatic Sheets. *Prism-patterned plastic used for the sides of saltwater streamers and other flies; colors: silver, gold, red, green, yellow, orange, purple, chartreuse. (See also: prism tape.)*
$1.50 Orv
Ever-Glo Tinsel. *Glow-in-the-dark tinsel; glows for about 1 min. after charge from flashlight; for night flies, obviously; 750 strands; colors: red, orange, yellow, blue, green, white.*
$3.50 Orv
Ever-Glo Braid. *Glow-in-the-dark tubing in same colors as above plus black; 3/16" or 1/4"; 1 yd.*
$1.75 Orv
Flashabou. *That wonderful mylar tinsel in packages of some 2,000 strands; intense colors; stretchable to reduce width so can be used as ribbing on very small flies; accept no substitute, none are as stretchable; I use this for all my tinsel requirements; can be used for tinsel bodies, as ribbing, or to add some flash and color to streamer wings; colors: silver, gold, pearl (my favorite), red, royal blue, kelly green, copper, electric blue, lime green, purple, black, med. blue, fuchsia, yellow, grape, bronze, pink. (See also: Fly Flash.)*
$2.69-$3 Many catalogs
Fly Flash. *A Flashabou-style tinsel; not as stretchable but less expensive; colors: silver, gold, green, red, blue, purple.*
$.65 Spo
Mylar piping. *Aka mylar tubing; mylar braided around a cotton core; originally this was used as decoration on women's clothing (at least some of the colors); remove core, slip over hook, and tie down; makes exceptionally good streamer bodies; colors: silver, gold, pearl (color changes with different underbodies), green, red, blue, yellow, purple, copper.*
$.30-$1.50 Most catalogs
Mylar sheet. *Mylar in sheet form to be cut and trimmed; colors: silver, gold.*
$1.55 Ree
Mylar sheet, Sparkle Brite. *Patterned mylar sheet; colors: silver flake, gold flake, diamond flake.*
$1 Mer, Fly
Mylar tinsel. *Reinforced with thread; colors: silver, gold,*

green, copper, red, blue, purple, bronze, dk. blue.
$.50-$.60 Hun, Orv, AnR

Mylar braid. *A braided mylar useful on steelhead and saltwater flies; used in place of tinsel chenille; colors: silver, gold, red, green, blue.*
$1 Nat, Hun, AnR

Mylar, oval. *An oval tinsel for ribbing; colors: silver, gold.*
$.50-$.70 Hig, Mer, H&H, Don, Edd, Fly, T&T, AnR

Mylar tinsel. *A flat tinsel; color: gold one side, silver other.*
$.45-$.75 Orv, Ste, AnR, Orv, Kau, Ran, Hun, EJH, Mur, Hig, Mer, H&H, Tac, Edd, T&T

Mylar tinsel. *Color as above but different sizes available; sizes in inches: 1/64, 1/32, 3/64, 2/32.*
$.60-$.70 T&T, Fly

Prism tape. *Plastic sheet with pattern, adhesive back; colors: silver, gold, red, yellow, blue. (See also: Fishscale Prismatic Sheets.)*
$1.10-$1.50 Hun, Mer, Hig, Mur, Kau

Sparkle tape. *No details on this but probably similar to prism tape; colors: silver, gold, multi-color.*
$1.10 Mer

Tinsel, embossed. *Pattern embossed on metal tinsel; color: silver, gold, copper (EJH, Don only).*
$.45-$1 Most catalogs

Tinsel, English embossed. *Sorry, I'm not into salmon flies enough to know how the English emboss their tinsel; silver.*
$.90 Don

Tinsel, flat metal. *In sizes narrow, med., and wide; colors: silver, gold, copper (Hun, Don, Edd, AnR only), red (EJH only), blue (EJH only).*
$.40-$1.50 Many catalogs

Tinsel, French lace. *A twisted tinsel; colors: silver, gold.*
$.40-$2.50 Hun, Let, Don, AnR, EJH, Mer, Ran, Orv

Tinsel, iridescent. *An iridescent tinsel.*
$2 Orv

Tinsel, oval. *An oval tinsel for ribbing and bodies; colors: silver, gold, copper (AnR only).*
$.40-$1.95 Most catalogs

Tinsel, round. *Another variation; colors: silver, gold.*
$.50-$2.10 Ree, Hun, Let, AnR

Dyes and Markers

Fly Dyes. *Dyes for tying materials; colors: chocolate brown, wood duck, cinnamon brown, brownish slate, black, lilac blue, bluish slate, turquoise, jungle cock orange and yellow, lemon yellow, brilliant orange, scarlet, cardinal red, slate, olive slate, shrimp pink, salmon egg, chartreuse, dk. olive, insect green, highlander green, fl. red, fl. canary yellow. (See also: Veniard dyes.)*
$3.95-$5.25 Bob, Let

Fly dyeing bleach. *A special bleach to prepare materials for the dye.*
$2 Dal

Fly dyeing wetting agent. *A chemical to help materials take colors better when dyeing.*
$.50 EJH

Veniard Dyes. *A well known dye for tying materials; colors: black, red, green, insect green, highlander green, yellow, bright yellow, lemon yellow, Naples yellow, hot orange, claret, slate dun, blue dun, summer duck, med. olive, golden olive, sherry spinner, crimson, kingfisher blue, teal blue, silver blue, Cambridge blue, purple, magenta, fiery brown, fl. blue, fl. green, fl. yellow, fl. orange, fl. gray, fl. red, fl. white, fl. pink. (See also: Fly Dyes.)*
$2.50-$3.95 Hun, EJH, H&H

Pantone markers. *Waterproof colors in marker form; used to add color to latex bodies and other materials; colors: 353M lt. green, 382M insect green, 380M pale olive, 101M sulphur yellow, 162M creamy pink, 176M pink, 102M lt. yellow, 136M amber yellow, 583M med. olive green, 165M red orange, 104M med. olive, 347M grass green, 124M buff ginger, 154M brown, 180M rust, 119M brown olive, 464M dk. brown, 492M reddish brown, 499M mahogany, M black, 422M med. gray, 413M pale gray, 438M dk. brownish purple, 9M charcoal gray, 150M burnt orange, 115M yellow, 172M red, 471F dk. brown, 457F dk. olive, 424M gray, 123M golden yellow, 109M dk. yellow, 466M lt. tan, 404M dk. gray, 368M kelly green, 365M lt. green.*
$1.25-$1.80 Mer, H&H, T&T, Fly, Let

Miscellaneous Materials

Curon. *Hope you know what this is; 8"x8" square.*
$2.50 Ran

Fishair, 24 denier. *Artificial hair; in 24 denier this is an excellent material for hair wings, very fine; unfortunately this material may not be available for long since demand is low; colors: pearl white, golden yellow, fl. spring green, fl. lavender, fl. hot pink.*
$.89 Tac

Fishair, 50 denier. *Thicker strands; a suitable substitute for bucktail and preferred in some saltwater patterns; easy to work with; fluorescent colors have a lot of snap and act like "light fibers"; colors: "natural" white, black, and brown; polar bear white, mouse gray, squirrel brown, feather red, emerald green, moss green, mustard yellow,*

sky blue, silver blue, peacock blue, royal blue, nugget gold, burgundy, regal purple, fl. yellow, fl. pink, dk. pink, lt. pink, fl. day-glo tangerine, fl. day-glo yellow, fl. day-glo orange, fl. chartreuse, fl. lime green.
$.75-$4.69 Don, Spo, T&T, Cab
Fishair, 70 denier. *A thick artificial hair; colors: see 50 denier list.*
$.95-$4.69 Hun, Kau, Tac, T&T, Cab, AnR
Mean Streak Marker. *Represents the silk anchorline used by some caddis nymphs.*
$2.95 Kau
Microfibetts. *A stiff synthetic fiber suitable for tails; unbreakable; will take dye.*
$1-$1.50 Mer, Orv, H&H, T&T

Rubber hackle. *Sheets of live rubber with slits cut partially through them; can be tied on in a group, then easily separated for hackle effect or separated and tied on as legs; great colors, bass photos jump off the wall chasing after this material; colors: black, white, brown, blue, green, gray, orange, yellow, red, aqua, chartreuse, purple, fl. chartreuse, fl. orange*
$.75-$1.99 Fly, Cab, Spo, Tac, ArR, Hig, Dal, EJH, Orv, Kau, Hun
Rubber legs. *Individual rubber strips; colors: White, Black, Gray, Yellow, Brown.*
$.30-$1.00 Edd, T&T, Bob, Dan, Blu, H&H, Mur, EJH

FLY TYING HOOKS

You need a master's degree in fly fishing to know everything about hooks. Specialized terms run amuck in this part of the sport, and understanding them can be a hobby in itself.

However, there should be no confusion about how much one must know in order to be an accomplished fly tier. Many people only know enough to order "dry fly hooks" or "wet fly hooks", and they are able to tie flies that catch fish.

If you already know the difference between a sproat and a limerick bend, a ball eye and a tapered eye, a 94840 and a 3399, you can skip this section and start ordering hooks. All others, get out your notebooks.

Hook Nomenclature. The accompanying diagram, courtesy of Mustad-Viking, defines the terms used to describe a hook. Most important to the average tier is the shank and the gap.

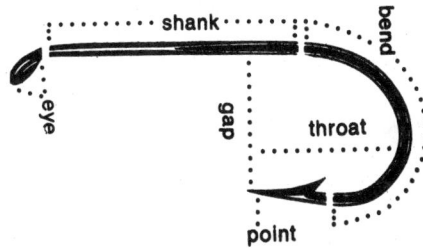

Hook Sizes. Hook sizes relate directly to the hook gap. That's hardly adequate in describing the true size of a hook. An eight extra-long #12 is quite a bit larger than an extra-short #12. The gap on the two hooks, however, should be the same in the same style hook.

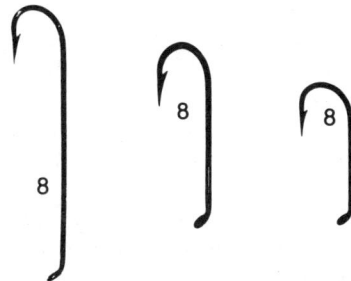

In typical trout and bass fishing, sizes range from #2 to #32, with the larger number denoting the smaller hook. Hook sizes are given in even numbers in this country today. Odd numbered hooks are, I believe, still available in England and in some Mustad styles.

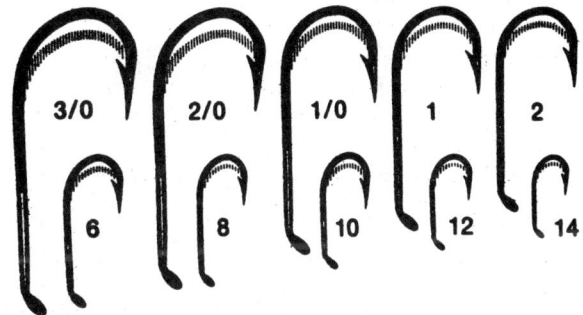

Larger hooks are measured in oughts, as in 3/0. At this end of the spectrum, the higher the number, the larger the hook. Most of these large hooks are for saltwater flies.

Shank Lengths. There is a relatively consistent standard within a manufacturer's line, if not within the industry, for a hook shank of a given size (gap).

A hook with this standard shank is listed without a shank description. Hooks with longer or shorter shanks are listed with a comparison to the standard length. For instance, a #12 hook with a shank standard to a #10 hook is listed as having a two extra-long (2xl) shank (don't forget to count the #11). A #18 4xl, then, has the shank of a standard #14. A #18 2xs (two extra-short) has a shank standard to a #20 hook. At first, this is a confusing system, but it makes much more sense than trying to measure shanks.

Long-shanked hooks are commonly used for streamers and nymphs. Short-shanked hooks are used for spiders and other dry flies.

Hook Wire. Again, there is a standard for the weight of the wire used in hooks. Lighter than standard wire is designated as extra-fine (xf). Heavier wire is listed as extra-strong or extra-stout (xst).

Extra-fine wire is used for dry fly hooks to aid in their floating ability. Extra-strong wire will help sink a wet fly or nymph, and it's stronger.

Hook wire is either round or flat. If flat, it's called forged wire.

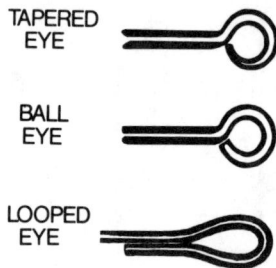

Hook Eyes. There are two parts to the description of a hook eye. One is the style of the eye. There are four typical styles. The ball eye, the tapered eye, and the looped eye are shown in the illustration. The doubled eye, used on double salmon hooks, is an extension of the looped eye.

A second description of the eye relates to whether it continues straight out from the shank (ringed eye), slants up (turned-up eye), or slants toward the gap (turned-down eye). The arguments surrounding hooking efficacy deal in part with the angle of pull effected by the angle of the eye. The physics of it all are best left to those pursuing their master's degrees, but I can give you my subjective opinion. The turned-down eye (tde) has superior hooking properties in my experience, except in the small hook sizes (#20 and smaller). In those sizes, the tde interferes with the hook gap. The turned-up eye (tue) does not hook as well as the ringed eye (re) for me. Perhaps with a different knot than I use, the tue would be just as good, but I've had good experience with the ringed eye in small sizes.

Hook Bend. Here's another area that can elicit hours of debate about hooking qualities. As for me, all these bend styles have been around for years and that's enough to convince me they work. Some of them are more

pleasant to the eye, but that doesn't help them catch more fish.

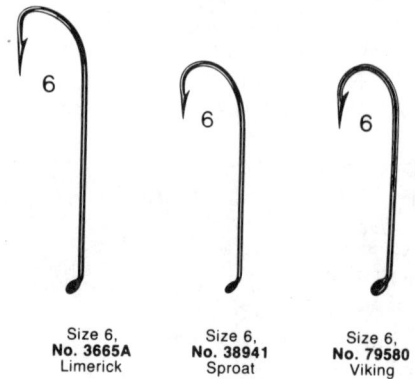

Size 6,
No. 3665A Limerick   Size 6, **No. 38941** Sproat   Size 6, **No. 79580** Viking

All illustrations courtesy of Mustad-Viking

Common hook bend styles include round, sproat, Carlisle, limerick, Aberdeen, Kirby, and O'Shaughnessy. There is also a wide-gap hook and the upside down keel hook.

KIRBED   STRAIGHT   REVERSED

Hooks can also be bent so that the hook point is off center with the shank. A bend in one direction is known as a kirbed hook. If bent away from center in the other direction, it's called a reversed hook.

Another bend you'll find in hooks is a kink. If the kink is in the shank, it's to help secure a popper body. Such a hook is described as kinked, but there's another kind of kink. It's near the point, and it's a replacement for the barb.

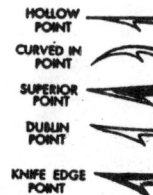

HOLLOW POINT
CURVED IN POINT
SUPERIOR POINT
DUBLIN POINT
KNIFE EDGE POINT

Hook Points. Again, there are several types of hook points. The most common is the hollow (or hollow ground) point. The bottom is straight to the actual point while the top is curved down to the point. A superior point has the opposite pattern.

Hook Finishes. The typical freshwater hook is bronzed. This gives some rust protection but is entirely inadequate for saltwater. Hence, other finishes have been created for saltwater use.

Japanned hooks have a blue-black lacquer finish. They are rust-resistant. Tinned hooks will resist rust indefinitely. Nickel-plated or true nickel hooks are among the best finishes for saltwater. Gold-plated hooks are also used for salmon and saltwater flies. These are more expensive but excellent in resisting rust. Cadmium hooks will last the normal life span of a saltwater fly. They do rust eventually, making them safe for the broken-off fish (and we should always think about those trophies).

Hook Manufacturers. Every fly tier knows Mustad-Viking. They are the largest producers of hooks in the world. The hooks are made in Norway. The quality is high and consistent. They offer a multitude of hook styles. If you can't find the hook you want in the Mustad line, you don't really want it.

Partridge hooks have a long tradition in fly tying, especially among salmon fly tiers. They are made in England. The hooks are very good, but they are considerably more expensive than Mustad.

The dominance of Mustad in the marketplace has only recently been challenged, and that to only a minor extent. The intruding company is VMC, a French hook maker. Tiers who can break away from their favorite Mustad 94840 are finding an alternative in the VMC 9280. It's an impressive hook with an extremely sharp point. Other hook companies are entering the market.

Meanwhile, plodding away in the background is the American hook manufacturer, Eagle Claw. Their share of the market is probably negligible, partly because they don't have a large number of styles for the tier, but mostly because they haven't marketed to the fly fisherman. Can anybody out there tell me the model number of Eagle Claw's dry fly hook? (It's a #59.)

Hooks Listed Here. I've probably missed some in this list of about 115 hook styles, but these are the hooks listed in fly fishing catalogs. There are more styles and certainly more sizes, but we'll stick with these as being the hooks most interesting to fly fishermen.

I've tried to break the hooks down by their typical use for dry flies, wet flies, and so on. There is some overlap, of course, and the distinctions are not always clear.

Unless noted, these hooks are bronzed with a standard-sized, straight shaft of regular-weight wire and a tapered, turned-down eye. Within the categories, hooks are listed alphabetically by manufacturer and in numerical order thereafter according to model number.

For the purposes of organization, 1xl and 2xl hooks are generally considered nymph hooks, while 3xl and longer shanks are considered streamer hooks. Deviations from this exist where manufacturers specify other uses. Hooks with special finishes are considered under saltwater and salmon hooks. Special-use hooks are considered under a separate category.

The prices listed here are for boxes of 100. Prices vary according to source, of course, but they also vary according to size of hook. Nowhere is this more dramatic than in salmon flies where the range of prices may be nearly $50.

I haven't listed all the sources for common hooks. If there were less than 15 sources, they're listed. If there were 15-20, I listed sources as "many catalogs". Over 20 sources, I listed them as "most catalogs".

Abbreviations: xl = extra-long shank; xs = extra-short shank; xf = extra-fine wire; xst = extra-strong (stout) wire; tde = turned-down eye; tue = turned-up eye; re = ringed eye.

Dry Fly Hooks

Eagle Claw #59. *Round bend, fine wire; sizes: 8-18.*
$3.78 Tac
Eagle Claw #60. *Sproat bend, fine wire; sizes: 8-16.*
$3.78 Tac
Eagle Claw #61. *An inexpensive barbless hook; round bend, fine wire; sizes: 6-16.*
$3.78 Tac
Jacklin's dry fly. *A barbless dry fly hook; no details; sizes: 10-18.*
$4 Bob

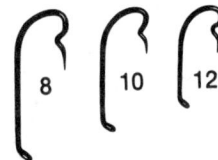

Mustad #3257B. *Barbless with kink; superior point; sproat bend; sizes: 1-16.*
$2.19-$3.75 Bul, Cut, Kau, Ree, Tac, EJH, Mer

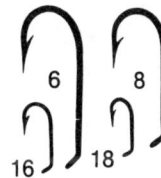

Mustad #7948A. *The standard hook (although you may not recognize its number in light of the popularity of the 94840); slightly shorter and stronger than 94840; round bend; sizes: 2-20.*
$2.66-$4.35 Ree, Blu, Bob, H&H, Cut, Kau, Dan, Dal, Edd, Mer, Fly
Mustad #94833. *Lightweight dry fly hook; round bend, 3xf; sizes: 6-22.*
$2.66-$4.75 Most catalogs
Mustad #94836. *An alternative to the 94840 for those of us who think its shaft is too long in smaller sizes; round bend, 1xs, 1xf; sizes: 10-20.*
$2.66-$3.71 Cut, Mer
Mustad #94838. *A short shank hook for greater hooking capacity for fly size; round bend, 2xs, 1xf; sizes: 8-20.*
$2.66-$4.75 Many catalogs

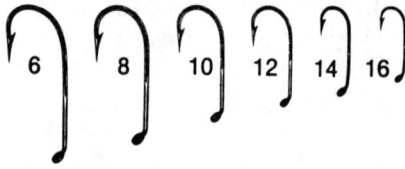

Mustad #94840. *Most popular dry fly hook; round bend, 1xf; sizes: 1/0-28.*
$2.65-$4.85 Most catalogs

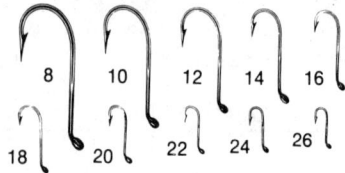

Mustad #94842. *Standard turned-up eye hook; round bend, tue, 1xf; sizes: 1-28.*
$2.65-$5.10 Most catalogs
Mustad #94845. *Barbless equivalent of 94840; round bend, 1xf; sizes: 6-22.*
$3.76-$6.75 Most catalogs
Mustad #94847. *Barbless with kink; round bend, 3xf; sizes: 10, 12; note: couldn't find this in Mustad's catalog. (See also: #3257B.)*
$4.80 Ree

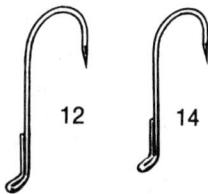

Mustad #94863. *Old-fashioned turned-up eye, barbless; round bend, tue (looped), 1xf; sizes: 12-18.*
$3.06-$5.10 Hig, TCr, Cut, Kau, Hun, Mer, Fly
Partridge B. *English turned-up eye hook; tue; sizes: 10-20.*
$6.45 Blu
Partridge L3A. *The Capt. Hamilton standard dry fly hook; sizes: 8-22.*
$7-$10 Let, Hun, Blu

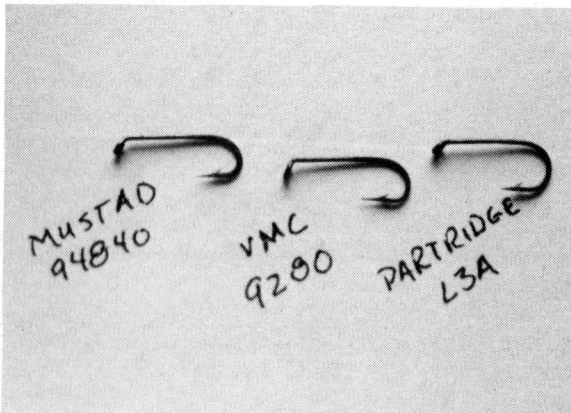

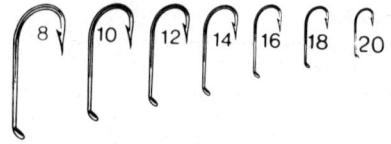

VMC #9280. *Direct competition for Mustad's 94840; modified round bend, xf; sizes: 6-20.*
$3.49-$4 Tac, Bob, EJH

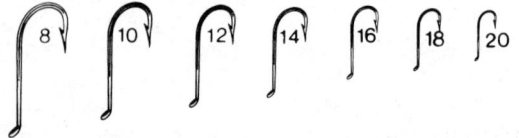

VMC #9281. *Compare with Mustad's 94842; round bend, tue, xf; sizes: 6-20.*
$3.49-$4 EJH, Tac, Bob

VMC #9282. *Compare with Mustad's 94838; modified round bend, 1xs, xf; sizes: 8-18.*
$3.49 Tac

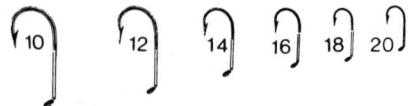

VMC #9288. *Compare with Mustad's 94836; round bend, short point, "short shank", xf; sizes: 6-20.*
$3.49-$3.55 Tac, EJH

VMC #9289. *An turned-up eye, short-shank hook; round bend, tue, short point, xf; sizes: 6-20.*
$3.49-$3.55 EJH, Tac

Spider Hooks

Mustad #9263A. *Gold-plated spider hook; tue; sizes: 10, 12.*
$4.30 Ree
Mustad #9479. *For spider or egg patterns; reversed bend, tde, 5xs, 1xf; sizes: 2-18.*
$2.50-$3.75 Egg, Mer, Fly, Don, Kau, Ree, Cut

Mustad #9523. *Standard spider hook; reversed bend, tue, 5xs, xf; sizes: 2-18.*
$2.50-$4.20 Tac, T&T, H&H, Cut, Kau, Dan, Ste, Bul, Mer, EJH
Mustad #94843. *Light wire spider; tue, 4xs, 3xf; sizes: 6-18.*
$2.66-$5 Cut, Kau

Midge Hooks

Mustad #277. *The ultimate midge hook for when, as the Cutthroat catalog says, you want to impress your few remaining friends; gold-plated; reversed bend, 1xs, flatted eye; size: 32.*
$4.50 Cut
Mustad #540L. *To help work your way down to the 277; gold-plated; round bend, reversed; size: 28.*
$5.75-$5.95 Ree, Kau
Mustad #94859. *The more sensible midge hook; round bend, xf; sizes: 12-28.*
$2.49-$4.95 Many catalogs
Partridge K1A. *The Marinaro midge hook; xf; sizes: 24-28.*
$7.50-$10.65 Hun, Blu, Let

Wet Fly Hooks

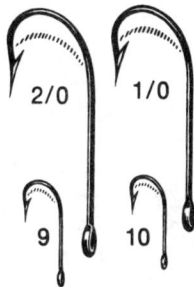

Mustad #3136. *Ringed-eye wet fly or nymph hook; Kirby bend; sizes: 2/0-4.*
$2.15 Ran
Mustad #3399. *Economical wet fly and general purpose hook; sproat bend, tde (ball); sizes: 2/0-16.*
$1.83-$2.95 Spo, Ree, Edd, Mer, EJH, Ste
Mustad #3399A. *Similar to 3399 but with smaller eye; sproat bend, tde (small ball); sizes: 2-18.*
$1.69-$3 Ste, Pen, Mer, Ran, Bud, Bob, Blu, Kau, Dan, Mur, EJH, Cut
Mustad #3399D. *Similar to 3399 but with smaller eye and lighter wire; sproat bend, tde (small ball), 2xf; sizes: 10-16.*
$3-$3.25 Ran, EJH

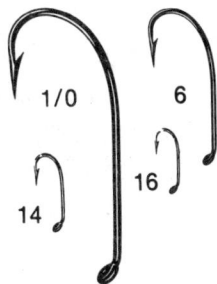

Mustad #3906. *Most popular wet fly hook, tapered eye; sproat bend; sizes: 2-20.*
$2.59-$4.65 Most catalogs

Partridge G3A. *Wet fly hook; sizes: 2-18.*
$8-$8.30 Let, Blu
Partridge L2A. *Capt. Hamilton wet fly hook; sizes: 2-18.*
$8-$10 Blu, Let

Nymph Hooks

Eagle Claw #63. *General nymph hook; round bend, 2xl, xf; sizes: 6-16.*
$3.78 Tac
Mustad #3906B. *Wet fly and nymph hook; sproat bend, 1xl; sizes: 2-20.*
$2.69-$5.35 Most catalogs

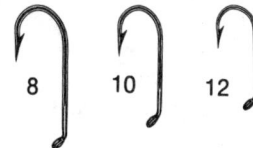

Mustad #7957B. *Wet fly and nymph hook; round bend, 1xl; sizes: 1/0-20.*
$2.76-$5.40 Cab, Egg, T&T, Tac, AnR, Hig, Ree, H&H, Ste, Bul, Spo, Mer, EJH, Don
Mustad #7957BX. *Extra-strong wet fly and nymph hook; round bend, 1xl, 1xst; sizes: 2-18.*
$2.91-$5.60 Bud, Kau, Ste, Cut, Blu, EJH, Fly

Mustad #9671. *A standard nymph hook; round bend, 2xl; sizes: 2-18.*
$2.91-$5.15 Most catalogs
Partridge H1A. *Capt. Hamilton nymph hook; 2½xl; sizes: 2-18.*
$9.65-$10 Blu, Let
Partridge H3ST. *The Draper hook for flat-bodied nymphs; shank has double wire, separated and shaped for nymphs; an outstanding example of creative hook making; 4xl; sizes: 4-16.*
$28.75 Let
Swimming Nymph Hook. *Curved to allow "curler" nymph tie with belly lower than tail and head; sizes: 8-14.*
$11 Orv
VMC #9279. *Standard nymph hook; 2xl; sizes: 2-14.*
$4.50 Bob

Streamer Hooks

Eagle Claw #58. *Standard streamer hook; round bend, 3xl; sizes: 6-16.*
$3.78 Tac

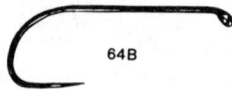

Eagle Claw #64B. *Barbless streamer, wet fly, or steelhead hook; sproat bend, xl; sizes: 8-16.*
$3.18 Tac
Jacklin streamer hook. *Barbless streamer hook; 4xl; sizes: 2-6.*
$3.95-$4 Bob, Bud

Mustad #3191. *A very long-shanked streamer hook with ringed eye that is recommended for Thunder Creek streamers; Carlisle bend, re, xxl; sizes: 2/0-12.*
$1.46-$2.35 Spo, EJH
Mustad #3260B. *A gold-plated streamer hook (for those special occasions); long-shanked; superior point; Aberdeen bend, re, xxl; sizes: 3/0-12.*
$2.49-$4.55 Cab, Ree
Mustad #3261. *Similar to 3260B but for everyday use, i.e. bronzed finish; sizes: 2-10.*
$1.75 Ree
Mustad #3263B. *Similar to 3260B but with fine wire; size: 2.*
$6 Kau

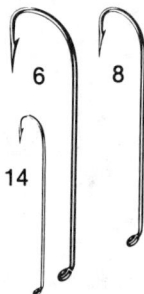

Mustad #3665A. *With the standard streamer bend; limerick bend, ½" longer than regular (note: some catalogs call this 6xl); sizes: 1-16.*
$3.01-$5 Most catalogs
Mustad #3907B. *Not in current catalog; 8xl; sizes: 10,12.*
$3 Ran
Mustad #9575. *Similar to 3665 but with looped eye; sizes: 2-12.*
$3.50-$6.15 Kau, Orv, Ran, H&H, Ree, AnR, Don, Fly, Mer, Tac, Hun, Edd, Bul, Dal, Cab
Mustad #9672. *A favorite streamer and nymph hook; round bend, 3xl; sizes: 2-18.*
$3.28-$5.95 Most catalogs
Mustad #9674. *Similar to 9672 but 4xl; sizes: 1/0-14.*
$3.28-$6.40 Bul, EJH, Dan, Cab, Kau, Cut, H&H, Blu, AnR
Mustad #33960. *Not in current catalog; 4xl, tde; sizes: 2-12.*
$2.60-$3 Dan, Edd, Ran

Mustad #36620. *Similar to 3665A but with ringed eye; limerick bend, re, ½" longer than regular (6xl); sizes: 2-14.*
$2.04-$3.50 H&H, Hun, AnR, Cut, Kau, Dal, EJH, Mer
Mustad #36680. *Similar to 3665A but shorter shank; limerick bend, re, ¼" longer than regular (3xl); sizes: 4-12.*
$3.55-$3.65 EJH, Hun
Mustad #38941. *For streamers and stonefly nymphs; sproat bend, 3xl; sizes: 1-16.*
$2.48-$5.90 Many catalogs
Mustad #79580. *Same style as 9671-9674 but longer shank; round bend, 4xl; sizes: 1-18.*
$3.49-$6.15 Most catalogs
Mustad #79582. *Same style as 79580 but 6xl; sizes: 6-12.*
$3.79-$5.50 Cut, Kau

Mustad #94720. *Very long-shanked streamer hook; round bend, 8xl; sizes: 2-10.*
$3.95-$5.80 Don, Edd, EJH, Mer, Ran, Hun, AnR, Ree, H&H
Partridge. *For trolling streamers in the style of Carrie Stevens; 8xl; sizes: 2/0-5/0.*
$16.50-$19 Hun, AnR
Partridge D4A. *Streamer hook; 4xl, tde; sizes: 6-16.*
$9.05-$11.80 Bob, Blu, Let
VMC #8923. *With the standard streamer bend; limerick bend, re, 2xl; sizes: 2-12.*
$2.25 EJH
VMC #9146. *Ringed-eye streamer hook; Aberdeen bend; re, 3xl; sizes: 4/0-10.*
$2.30 EJH

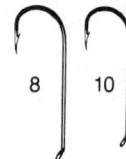

VMC #9148. *Similar to 9146 but with turned-down eye; sizes: 4/0-10.*
$2.30 EJH

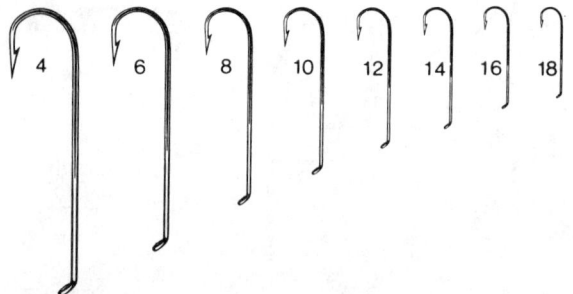

VMC #9283. *Long-shanked streamer hook; round bend, 4xl; sizes: 2-18.*
$3.49-$4.50 Bob, Tac, EJH

Salmon Hooks

Eagle Claw #1197B. *For salmon and steelhead patterns; sproat bend, xl; sizes: 1-8.*
$2.79-$6 Hig, Tac, Kau, Fly

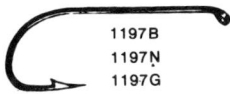

1197B
1197N
1197G

Eagle Claw #1197G. *Similar to 1197B but with gold finish; sizes: 1-8.*
$4.50 Kau

Eagle Claw #1197N. *Similar to 1197B but with nickel finish; sizes: 1-8.*
$3.95-$4 Fly, Kau

Mustad #3406. *Economical salmon or steelhead hook; O'Shaughnessy bend, re; sizes: 2-8.*
$1.92-$3.44 Spo, Cut, Fly

Mustad #3582. *Double hook with ball eye; brazed and bronzed; tde; sizes: 2-12.*
$16 Kau

Mustad #3582C. *Similar to 3582 but turned-up oval eye, brazed with black finish; tue; sizes: 1/0-14.*
$13.79-$25.60 Cut, Ran, Kau, Cab, Mer, Don, Edd, H&H, T&T, Bul

Mustad #3852F. *Similar to 3582 but turned-up tapered eye, brazed with black finish; tue; sizes: 1/0-12.*
$14.15-$22.50 Don, Ree, Dan, EJH

Mustad #3908C. *Nickel-plated salmon hook; sproat bend, tde, xst; sizes: 2-10.*
$3.13-$4.25 Fly, Cut

Mustad #7970. *Salmon hook with ball eye and extra-strong wire; limerick bend, 5xst; sizes: 1-12.*
$3.37-$5.60 T&T, Mer, Fly, Dan, Cut, Kau

Mustad #9049. *Salmon hook with Dublin point, looped oval eye; limerick bend, tue, xf, xl; sizes: 2-12.*
$4.50-$5.50 Kau, Edd, Mer, Hun, AnR, Ran, Don

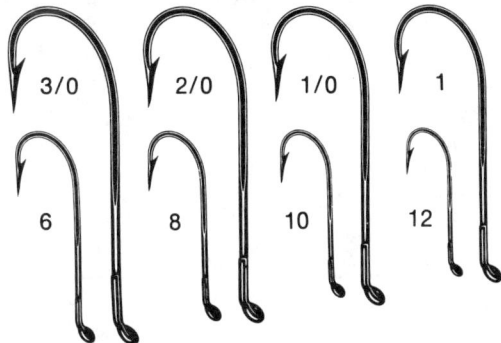

3/0   2/0   1/0   1

6   8   10   12

Mustad #36890. *Called the classic salmon hook; a popular hook similar to 9049 but heavier with black finish; for wet flies; limerick bend, tue; sizes: 6/0-12.*
$3.62-$10.20 Many catalogs

Mustad #90240. *Low water salmon hook with short hollow point; for dries and low water wets; limerick bend, tue (looped), xl, 2xf; sizes: 4-10.*
$2.96-$5.30 Ste, T&T, Mer, AnR, Blu, H&H, Cut, Ran, Kau, Hun, Fly

Partridge M. *Standard salmon single wet fly hook; tue, xst; sizes: 5/0-12.*
$10-$18.50 Hun, Edd, Blu, Kau, Orv, Let, Don

Partridge P. *Brazed double salmon hook similar to Partridge M; sizes: 3/0-12.*
$25-$35.40 Orv, Edd, Let, Don

Partridge N. *Low water single; tue, 2xl; sizes: 10/0-12.*
$10-$19.60 AnR, Blu, Orv, Let, Kau, Don, Edd

Partridge Q. *Low water double similar to Partridge N; brazed; sizes: 3/0-12.*
$25-$35.40 AnR, Orv, Hun, Let, Don

Partridge 01. *Wilson salmon dry fly hooks; a traditional favorite; short point; modified sproat bend, xf; sizes: 2-16.*
$10-$13.40 Blu, Kau, Orv, AnR, Hun, Let, Don

Partridge 01 (dbl). *Wilson double hook similar to Wilson single; sizes: 3/0-12.*
$26.75-$29.75 Hun

Partridge Blind Eye. *The traditional hook without eye; hand-filed Dublin point; extra-nice finish; shank tapered and etched to receive twisted gut or monofilament eye; sizes: 5/0-2/0. (Note: Donegal's carries cat gut leaders for use in constructing traditional salmon flies on blind eye hooks; price: $3.)*
$32-$39.95 Don, Hun

Partridge Presentation Hooks. *Extra-fine finish on large hooks; sizes: 7/0-4/0.*
$20 Don

Sea Trout. *Double hooks for sea run trout or steelhead; bronze or nickel finish; round bend, tde, 2xl; sizes: 6-10.*
$26 Hun

Saltwater Hooks

Eagle Claw #254CAT. *Saltwater hook for wets and streamers; tin-plated for corrosion resistance; O'Shaughnessy bend, re, xst; sizes: 5/0-6.*
$2.19-$8.33 Hig, Dan, Cab

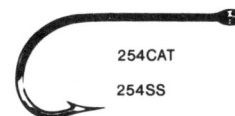

254CAT
254SS

Eagle Claw #254SS. *Same as 254 but stainless steel; sizes: 4/0-6.*
$3.19-$7.75 Cab, Kau

Mustad #1405. *Nickel-plated, xl for pencil poppers; can be used for prismatic baitfish pattern; vertical hump in shank; perfect bend, re, 4xl; sizes: 1/0-2.*
$7.50 Hun

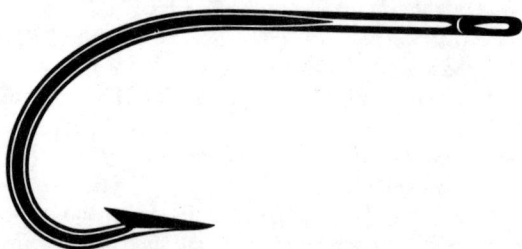

Mustad #3407. *Standard saltwater hook; cadmium-plated and tinned; O'Shaughnessy bend, re; sizes: 8/0-8.*
$1.99-$8.15 AnR, Bul, Edd, Cut, Kau, Dan, Fly, Don
Mustad #3408B. *Similar to 3407 but with turned-down ball eye; sizes: 4/0-4.*
$2.10-$3.29 Cut
Mustad #9082A. *Saltwater popper hook, kinked; sizes: 3/0-1/0.*
$18-$22 AnR
Mustad #9175. *A short-shank saltwater hook, cadmium-plated; O'Shaughnessy bend, re, 3xs, xst; sizes: 6/0-1/0.*
$2.06-$6.50 Cut, Hun
Mustad #9674B. *Nickel-plated streamer hook; round bend, re, 3xl; sizes: 4-6.*
$5.25-$6.50 Hun, Hig
Mustad #34007. *Stainless steel saltwater hook; O'Shaughnessy bend, re; sizes: 10/0-6.*
$3.60-$55.50 (for 10/0) Bul, Don, Dal, Orv, Hun, T&T, Hig, Ree, Blu, H&H, Cut, Kau

Caddis/Bait Hooks

Mustad #37140. *Ringed-eye bait hook for caddis nymph and pupae patterns; wide gap bend, slightly reversed, re; sizes: 2/0-16.*
$1.89-$2.99 Cab, Cut, Dan
Mustad #37160. *Similar to 37140 but with turned-up ball eye; sizes: 3/0-26.*
$1.99-$3.55 Most catalogs
Partridge A. *Offset bend with turned-down eye; sizes: 10-18.*
$6.45-$6.50 Hun, Blu

Partridge K2B. *Yorkshire caddis hook; special bend, tue, 1xl; sizes: 8-16.*
$7.50-$10.65 Let, Hun, Blu
Partridge K4A. *Grub hook; special bend, wide gap, tde; sizes: 8-18.*
$7-$8.50 Blu, Hun

Stinger and Bass Bug Hooks

Mustad #1404. *Humped stinger hook, will take hard-bodied poppers; open bend, wide gap, re, vertical hump, xf; sizes: 1/0-4.*
$7.50 Hun
Mustad #3366. *Economical popper and bass bug hook; sproat bend, re, xl, 1xf; sizes: 6/0-12.*
$1.22-$4.50 Cor, Spo, Hun. Tac, Ree, EJH, Don

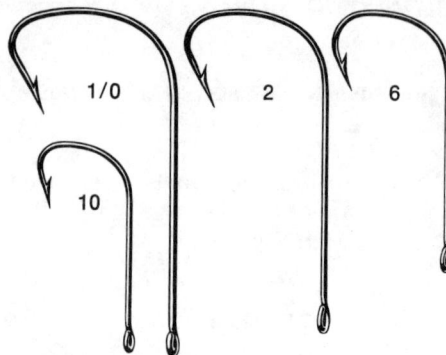

Mustad #37187. *The standard stinger hook for deer hair poppers, straight shank; open bend, re; sizes: 1/0, 2, 6, 10.*
$2.48-$5.90 Most catalogs
Mustad #33900. *Popper hook with standard bend, single kink in shank, superior point; sproat bend, re, 2xl; sizes: 2/0-12.*
$2.30-$3.45 Ree, EJH
Mustad #33903. *Similar to 33900 but with double kink in shank, 3xl; sizes: 1/0-14.*
$1.82-$3.55 Ran, AnR, Ree, H&H, Cut, Kau, Mer, Bul, Cor, Edd, Mur, EJH, Fly, Don

Keel Hooks

Eagle Claw. *Keel hook for streamers and bass bugs used in weedy waters; hook rides up; no other details; sizes: 2-8.*
$3.60 Edd
Mustad # 38972. *New keel hook; sproat bend, re, 1xf; sizes: 14, 16.*
$3.53-$3.65 H&H, Cut
Mustad #79666. *Standard keel hook; sproat bend, re, 6xl; sizes: 4-10.*
$1.72-$4.20 Cab, Mer, H&H, Ree, Cut

Special Hooks

Partridge K3A. *The Swedish dry fly hook mentioned in LaFontaine's writing; kinked in a rather odd fashion; tde, 2xl; sizes: 10-18.*
$10-$11.20 Kau, Blu, Let

Mustad #9174. *Short-shank hook for egg clusters, superior point; O'Shaughnessy bend, re, 3xs, xst; sizes: 2-8.*
$1.82-$3.50 Cut, Kau, Fly, Orv

Mustad #94831. *A lightweight streamer hook suitable for hopper patterns; round bend, 2xl, 2xf; sizes: 4-16.*
$2.91-$5.95 Most catalogs

Hook Extensions

Double Waddington shanks. *Steel wire shank with looped eyes fore and aft; can be used to create tube-fly patterns or wiggle nymphs and other hinged flies; sizes: ¾"-2½".*
$6.50/50 Hun

Slipstream tubes. *Plastic tubes with molded ends to prevent materials from slipping off; sizes: 1", 1½", 2".*
$3.20/10 Hun

Tandem hook wire. *Stainless steel wire for creating tandem hooks; plastic-coated or uncoated.*
$.40-$.50 H&H

FOR THE FLY TYING ROOM

Fly Tying Chests

The items here range from pieces of furniture for your tying den (the one with the cozy fireplace, leather couch, rod rack, and large mounted fish you bought at a garage sale) to suitcase affairs for the traveling tier.

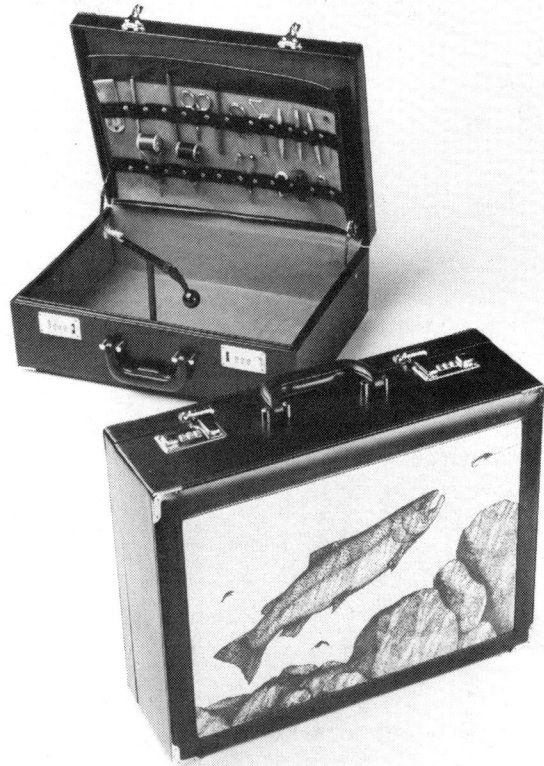

Ausable Attache. *A briefcase-style materials case; brown leatherette with silk-screened print of brown trout one exterior side, rainbow trout other side; with case open, panel displays tools; vise is held by adjustable clamp; combination locks; 17½"x13"x5½".*
$75 Fly, Let

Brittany, The. *Tying chest; hardwood with brass hardware; hanging file system; removable front panel coverts to lap or table top tying surface; double drawers; handsome and well-designed.*
$139.95-$169.95 Fly or direct from Saddle Wood Plaza, 2940 S. 5th, Suite G, Garland, Texas 75041 (214) 271-5618

Hackle Hutch. *Wooden tying chest with carrying handle; opens to make tying desk with "pigeon hole" drawers above; partition keeps materials from moving during transportation; an ingenious traveling-tier's desk; 25½"x15"x11".*
$169.95 Dan

Master Tyer's Chest. *A real piece of furniture that will look nice in the living room and allow you to become part of the family again; 66½" tall; choice of woods; 32 drawers (or to your specifications); it's beautiful, I'm envious.*
$1,870 Hun

Oak Tool Chest. *Oak; seven drawers; steel trim with nickel-chrome finish; interiors felt-lined; steel-plated drawer bottoms; tongue-and-groove joints; two sizes: 16"x12 ¼"x8½" or 20"x12¼"x9½".*
$235-$255 Don

Orvis Fly Tying Desk. *Oak tying stand with formica top; vise stand, thread and head cement holders; 10"x18" work surface; some assembly required (which makes it a great Christmas gift).*
$42.50 Orv

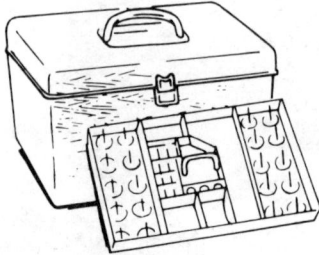

Plastic tying box. *Like sewing box (which it might be); three compartments.*
$12.95 Fly

Portable tying desk. *Wood with formica top; place for vise to be clamped; spool and tool holders; finished desk, kit, or plans; 14"x20".*
Finished—$44.95; kit—$24.95; plans—$3.50 Ste

The Professional. *Large oak chest with handle, hinged in middle; open, it has 24 shelves; 11 plastic boxes included for materials; built-in vise-tool drawer and combination vise-stand/work board; 11"x18"x12". (See also: Traveler's Fly Tying Box.)*
$225 T&T

Traveler's Fly Tying Box. *A wooden chest, hinged in middle; open, it has 11 shelves, eight boxes; includes 8½"x11" tying bench; 12" tall, 9½" wide, each side 6" deep when open; shelves adjustable from 1½"-3". (See also: The Professional.)*
$89.95 Fly

Wood fly tying box. *Opens like briefcase; top and bottom sections separated; three sections top, four bottom; handle doubles as vise stand; 20"x12"x5".*
$49.95 Ste

Stack Packs and Other Storage Ideas

The organization of fly tying materials is a lifelong task. The various containers listed here will perhaps allow time for your other lifelong pursuits, including some fly tying.

Dubbing Pouch. *Dubbing wallet; 40 pockets; covered in simulated rhino hide (the real stuff would be too heavy, I'm sure); 4½"x7½". (See also: Fur File.)*
$6.95 (or $17.50/3) T&T

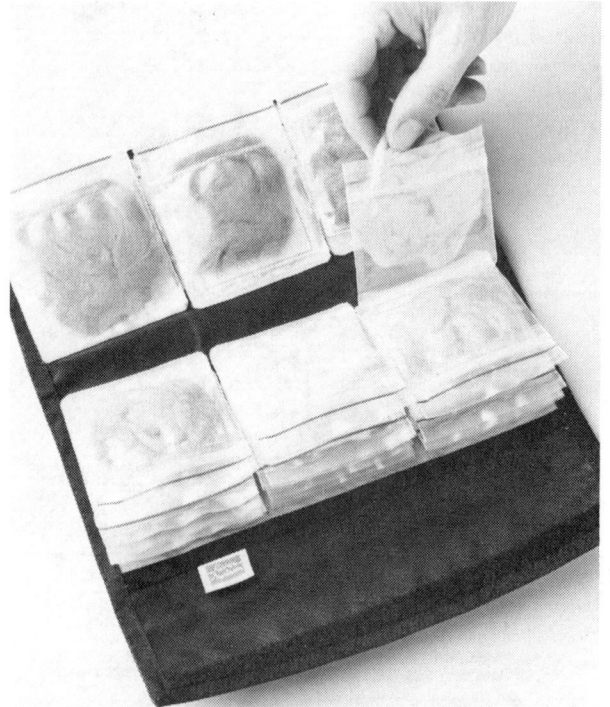

Fur File. *Dubbing wallet; 36 zip-lock compartments; covered in green pack cloth with Velcro close; from River Systems; 4½"x10"x2". (See also: Dubbing Pouch.)*
$11.50-$15.95 Let, H&H

Plastic boxes. *For materials, flies, whatever; variety of sizes.*
$.40-$.95 Hun

Spover Covers. *Plastic covers for thread and floss spools; package of 30.*
$2.95-$3.50 T&T, Fly, Kau

Stack packs. *Six circular plastic containers with connecting threads; really a series of open boxes with one top; diameters: 1⅝", 2", 2¾".*
$1.35-$2.95 Hun, Edd, Dal, AnR, Tac, Kau

Stak Pak. *Not to be confused with circular containers above; plastic boxes with drawers; grooved to stack; 1¾"x1"x½".*
$2/20 T&T

Zip-Lock bags. *Polyethylene plastic with zip-lock closure; sizes in inches: 2x3, 3x4, 3x5, 3x14, 4x3, 4x4, 4x6, 4x8, 5x5, 5x8, 6x9, 6x15, 8x10, 10x10, 9x12, 12x15, others.*
$.25-$3.30/doz. FlR, Ran, Kau, Mur, Hun, Tac, H&H, T&T, TCr, AnR

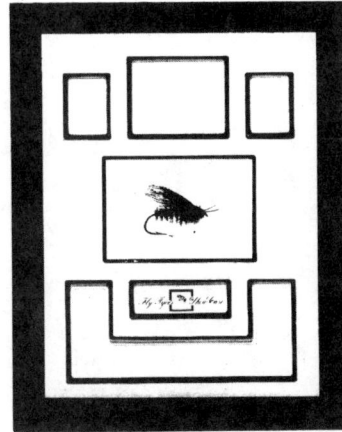

Fly Displays and Other Good Ways to Show Off Your Flies

Shadow boxes and display frames give us the opportunity to show off our tying prowess (or the skills of our friends). The brooch pins listed here can be used as tie tacks, hat pins, or vest decorations.

Brooch pins. *Salmon fly hook with pin; gold-plated, chrome-plated, or black; 1/0, 2/0, 3/0, 6/0 depending on source. (Note: You can get one pre-tied for $6 from Kau.)*
$2.39-$3.95 Dal, Don, Kau
Brooch pins. *Tie tack back; choice of hooks: Partridge low-water salmon, Mustad nymph, wet fly, or streamer; left or right hand; variety of sizes.*
$3.25 Hun
Classic Angling Flies Display Case. *Victorian-style frame; magnetic mounting for seven flies; printed background with antique engraving of fish; 9"x11"x2".*
$22.95 T&T

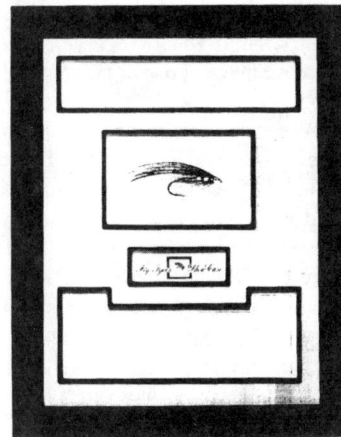

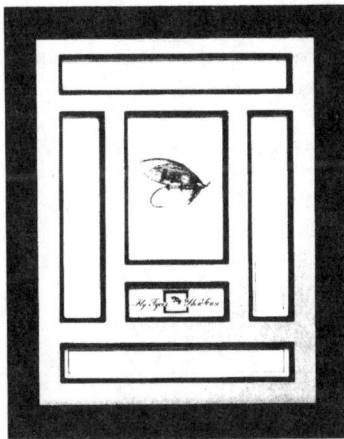

Fly Tyer's Showcase. *Shadow boxes in four styles; mattes, glass, frame, instructions included; 18⅜"x14⅜" and larger.*
$33.95-$49.95 Fly, Kau
Fly Mounting Frame. *Simple frame in shadow box style; 8"x10", 10"x12".*
$15 T&T

9. Floats and Boats

FLY FISHERMEN are willing to fish from anything that floats, including rooftops as flood waters wash their houses downstream. The great diversity of floating devices used by fly fishermen include regular aluminum fishing boats, sea-worthy cabin cruisers, and Lake Powell house boats, none of which are included here.

What is included here are the compleat anglers' favorites, the crafts in which they look best and which suit the sport best. Float tubes, canoes, rubber rafts, drift boats, and Rangeley boats have made the list, and Portaboats are included for the reluctant floater.

Each of these boats has its place and special function in the fly fisherman's life, and there's reason to own one of each, probably. The experience of each is different, too, and some will suit you more than others.

One is decidedly different than the others, the float tube, affectionately called the belly boat. Float tubing is an experience every fly fisherman ought to try. If you'll excuse the expression, it's a kick. Let's begin our exploration of floating devices for fly fishermen with the belly boat.

Float Tubes and Accessories

Float tubes, belly boats, fancy innertubes . . . whatever you call these ingenious flotation devices, they are a wonderful way for a fly fisherman to pursue his sport. I wish I knew who to credit for first putting a seat in an innertube—that kind of creative genius deserves recognition.

Not only is the float tube an excellent way to get to fish, it's just a marvelously fun device. In its basic form, the float tube is simply a truck innertube with a heavy-duty nylon cover to protect it from punctures. If you swim as well as I do, you'll appreciate the fact that most float tube makers have now added a second flotation chamber as a safety feature in case you drive the hook of a #2/0 streamer through the nylon cover.

In more sophisticated float tubes, manufacturers have also increased the size of the cover in the rear. The inflated innertube conforms to the cover, creating more air capacity in the back where most of the angler's weight rides. With the increased buoyancy in the back, the angler sits in a more level and, therefore, more comfortable position.

A seat makes the outfit workable, and swim fins give the ensconced angler mobility. A casting apron keeps slack line from becoming tangled with the tube or with the angler's legs.

In practice, the inflated tube is placed on the ground. The fisherman steps into the leg openings in the seat and pulls the tube up around him or her. Unless the water is warm enough for swim trunks, the float tuber wears chest waders and carries his equipment in a shorty vest, a Wood River or similar fishing bag, or in the pockets found on many float tubes. The wise angler wears long underwear for warmth, at least in trout waters. Swim fins are worn on or in place of wading shoes.

The only other equipment adjustment for float tube fishing is the recommended use of a long rod, 9' or longer. A shorter rod makes it nearly impossible to keep backcasts off the water.

Standing around on dry land holding a float tube around your middle will make you the laughing stock of bait fisherman nearby, but the laughter dies down quickly after the first fish is caught just past their casting range. The intervening time between dry land and fly fishing, however, can be quite entertaining for everyone.

With swim fins on and the float tube blocking the view of your feet, it's difficult to walk forward to the water. It's safer to walk backwards, but you'll have to convince yourself of that since walking backwards is not one of those things we do a lot of. I always feel a bit like I'm in a Monty Python movie as I shuffle backwards in search of the water in an outfit that only someone with a British sense of absurdity could fully appreciate. And I always get too anxious to make my entry into the water and end up sitting down only to find out it's not deep enough to kick out. I try to fake it by digging my feet into the bottom, but often I must stand up again. The resulting wallowing around has its moments.

Once out in the water, however, there is nothing quite like float tube fishing. Its appeal, I think, speaks to the nature of the sport. A float tube fisherman is independent of anyone else. He can go where he pleases without conference, and he doesn't have to coordinate his paddling with someone else who invariably screws up. A float tube is quiet, which suits the sport well, and not too fast in the water, which is also appropriate.

Finally, there is the same sense of immersion (not too deeply felt, I hope) that a fly fisherman gets from wading in a river and feeling part of it. Certainly, he can wade in a lake, but in doing so, he meets only the edge of the water. The total experience is not there. And riding around in a boat on top of the water is not the same at all. With legs dangling into the medium and a close-up view of the water's depth and everything on its surface, the float tuber's experience is more fulfilling that the wader's or boater's.

Like so many things in fly fishing, only the experience itself will teach you what those of us fortunate enough to have tried float tube fishing know to be true.

Float tube safety. Everything I have to tell you is just common sense, but since you, too, are a fly fisherman, your common sense quotient is suspect.

First, you want good, strong material for your float tube's cover. Even with a 10' rod and an excellent backcast, there's still the chance of a puncture from a big hook. And then there's also the chance of meeting a submerged tree limb or whatever. Your only protection is the nylon cover.

In the same vein, you should buy a float tube with a second flotation chamber in case of a "flat". Most models have a backrest with a small innertube in it. This provides comfort and enough flotation for the return to shore. If you're really a poor floater and swimmer, one as poor as myself, you may want to wear an additional life preserver. Something like the inflatable fishing vests listed in the chapter on vests may be subtle enough to protect your ego while it protects your life.

Punctures are rare with a quality float tube, fortunately, but I still wouldn't be without the secondary flotation chamber. Del Canty's float tube is itself an air bladder with two chambers. If you're considering a "self-contained" float tube such as Del's, there must be two or more separate chambers for proper safety.

If a puncture or valve failure puts you in the water, it's imperative that you get out of the tube. The secondary air chamber in the backrest can force your head underwater. A quick-release buckle on the seat will help get you out of the tube or at least turn around in it so you can grasp the backrest-turned-life preserver. No responsible float tube manufacturer produces a tube without the quick-release feature, and all listed here have it.

Finally, you need to protect your body from excessive heat loss. Most float tubing is done in stocking-foot waders which offer little, if any, insulation. Neoprene waders are best here, but you will still be better off with a good set of long handles to keep your lower body warm. In cold water, you can actually lose the ability to move your legs if they're not protected. Comfort suggests the need for long underwear, safety demands it.

Incidentally, I've seen float tubers go down the rivers. In some waters, such as Idaho's Silver Creek, this can hardly be called unsafe. The stream is wide, clear of debris, and slow. In other waters, the Bighorn River in Montana, for instance, the practice of float tubing can hardly be called sane. In that kind of water, the float tube offers no advantage over canoes or drift boats, but it has many drawbacks, including possible loss of life.

An unusual float tube. I must draw your attention to one float tube that's quite out of the ordinary. It's Del Canty's Lunker Hunter. Del Canty is THE lunker hunter, and he developed his float tube to be completely mobile in transit as well as in the water.

The Lunker Hunter uses no innertube. It is the air bladder. Because of that, it's lightweight and rolls up fairly small, making it suitable for backpacking. It inflates at a low pressure which makes it very puncture resistant. Since it can be filled by blowing into the valve, you can keep it afloat even if one of the two large chambers is punctured. Complete loss of pressure in one of the chambers still leaves you with half the tube inflated, which makes it much safer than the float tubes with secondary flotation in the backrest. You can also make pressure adjustments if cold water leaves you feeling low, and that kind of in-water adjustment is not possible with a regular innertube.

If you purchase the bivouac bag with the Lunker Hunter (so that you can spend three days and nights out fishing), you can use it to inflate the tube. You fill the bivouac bag with air by waving it around, trap the air by holding the end of the bag shut, and then squeeze the bag, forcing air into the chambers through a connecting valve. Monty Python again, right? Right. But it works, and it means you don't have to mess with an air pump.

The Lunker Hunter doesn't have a backrest (although you can strap your sleeping bag on the back for the same effect), and it lacks the polish of the fancier makes. It's also yellow. But, it's a nifty idea and it works. You can be in the water catching fish while your partner is still trying to find the air pump in the trunk.

For more information, write Del Canty's Lunker Hunter Systems, Inc., 4039 Hwy. 91, Leadville, Colorado 80461 or call (303) 486-0769. The booklet Del has written about float tubing and trophy fish hunting is viewed as somewhat of a religious testament among true lunker hunters, so be sure to ask for it. You'll love the part about going over the 60' falls in the float tube.

FLOAT TUBES

Prices include innertubes unless otherwise noted.

Browning. *Coated 210 denier nylon; double-stitched; backrest; two pockets; colors: gold on red or brown camo.*
$69.95-$84.50 Cus, Dun, Fol

Bucks Bags. *420 denier, 8 oz. nylon; polyester stitching; backrest holds small innertube; two side pockets set to back and one back pocket in addition to backrest; D-rings; three handles; takes 20" innertube; weights to 280 lbs.; casting apron; colors: beige on green with red back for safety around boaters.*
$124.95 AnJ

Caddis. *Standard model; no-frills tube; no secondary flotation so life jacket necessary; no pockets; six D-rings for attaching equipment; two nylon web handles for easy carrying; takes 16" innertube; size: 40"x40"; colors: green on beige, green camo, brown camo.*
$30.80-$39.95 H&H, Cab, Cus

Courtesy of Bob Jacklin

Caddis. *Deluxe model; 8 oz. nylon fabric; seams triple-stitched with double-strength nylon thread; when inflated back is larger than front so level floating is possible; backrest holds small innertube; two side*

pockets; four D-rings; three web handles; casting apron to keep line out of way; takes 20" innertube; size: 42"x42"; color: beige on brown.
$64-$99.95 H&H, Cab, Bob, Ram, Cus

Custom. *Vinyl-coated nylon; two pockets; four D-rings; no secondary flotation; takes 20" innertube; color: green.*
$72 EJH

Del Canty's Lunker Hunter. *Float tube is its own air chamber, no innertubes; two chambers for safety; can be inflated by mouth or by use of bivouac bag (see article in introduction to this section); no backrest (unless you use your sleeping bag); casting apron; backpacks well; total weight: 3 lbs.; color: yellow.*
About $99.95 Del Canty's Lunker Hunter Systems, Inc., 4039 Hwy. 91, Leadville, Colorado 80461 (303) 486-0769

Fishmaster 250LT. *Canvas covered; two pockets; takes a 20" innertube; no secondary flotation; up to 250 lbs.*
$55.90 Tac

Fishmaster 350LT. *Similar to 250LT but covered in polyester.*
$62.90 Tac

Fishmaster 400LT. *Similar to 350 LT but with larger innertube for weights to 300 lbs.*
$68.90 Tac

Float King. *Nylon covered; more flotation in back for level ride; tall backrest with innertube; two side pockets; three handles; casting apron; eight D-rings; a fairly recent addition to the market, not currently available through catalogs but carried by dealers; write or call Float King for information.*
About $100 Float King, 1008 Vista Ave., Boise, Idaho 83705 (208) 336-5464

JOBE-USA. *Strike model; economy model; 8 oz. ballistic nylon; two side pockets, one back pocket; no secondary flotation; two to three times more flotation in back for level floating.*
$80.55-$89.50 Cus, Hig, Dan

JOBE-USA. *Pro II model; 8 oz. ballistic nylon; more flotation in back for level ride; tall backrest holds small innertube; two side pockets; three web handles; casting apron; Velcro rod holder; for weights to 245 lbs.; colors: beige on blue with orange front and back panels for safety around boaters.*
$84.95-$129.95 Hig, Cus, Orv, Dan, T&T, Pen

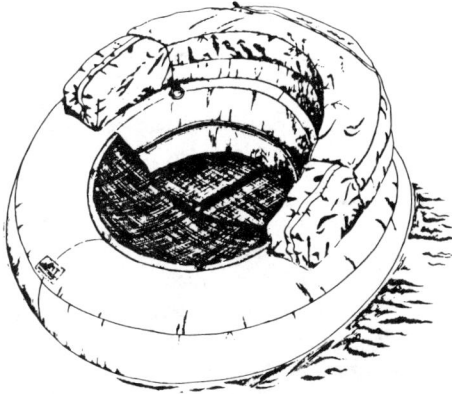

Courtesy of The Fly Shop

Mountain Trader. *Great Lakes model; double-stitched nylon; two side pockets joined to backrest; backrest can take small innertube; colors: green or camoulfage (add $10). (Note: A deep-seat option is available for anglers over 180 lbs. and long-legged people; keeps knees from hitting bottom of tube; add $9.)*
$100 (may not include innertube, can't tell from catalog) Fly

Osprey. *Woven nylon; three snap hooks; takes 10.0"x20" tube (not included); colors: white, green.*
$49.95 (without tube) Cor

Water Bagel. *Urethane-coated nylon pack cloth; backrest holds small innertube; two side pockets; web handles; casting apron; color: brown.*
$125 Don

Float Tube Accessories

The main equipment beyond the tube itself is the set of swim fins you'll need to navigate in the water (albeit backwards). There are many styles in many price categories. For paddling around the bass pond, I think regular old $7.98 swim fins from the local discount store are entirely satisfactory, but for big waters where lots of distance must be covered, larger fins ordinarily used by divers are preferable. They give you an amazing increase in power. And one brand, Force Fins, features up-turned fins that allow you to walk forward.

A second type of fins is commonly called paddle pushers or paddle fins (or some other variation). They have a paddle on each side of the angler's foot. The paddles are hinged. As the angler moves his foot forward, the paddles fold flat. On the backstoke, they lock in the "out" position, creating the power stroke. Paddle fins allow the angler to move forward in the water, but they get mixed reviews from their users. Since they fit over the heel of a wading shoe and do not interfere with walking, they are most advantageous when you must walk a distance to the water or when you're doing wading and floating. However, they are not very efficient at moving the angler, and many catalogs suggest their use only on shallow, smaller lakes where wading and floating may be done in equal share and no great distances need be covered.

Most float tubes are inflated on the spot. It requires a pick-up or station wagon to transport more than one inflated tube conveniently. Inflation can be done with a foot pump or with one of the electrically operated pumps that plug into a cigarette lighter. A pressure gauge is handy, if you can find one that registers low pressure. It takes awhile to get the knack of filling the tube properly. If it's overinflated, the tube rides high and is more susceptible to puncture. If it's underinflated, cold water will further reduce the air pressure, and you could become fly fishing's answer to the low rider.

Incidentally, don't leave your inflated tube sitting in direct sun or in your closed car in the sun. Nobody likes the kind of unpleasant surprise that may follow.

Swim Fins

Force Fins. *Made for float tubers; tips of fins curve upward allowing you to walk forward (which many*

people prefer, as evidenced by any city sidewalk); V-tail design (patterned after the tails of such well-known swimmers as tuna and bonita) for maximum power; padded heel strap; unbreakable urethane plastic; sizes: med./large—7-8; large—9-10; extra large—11-12.
$40-$44.95 Bob, Cus, Dan, T&T, Fly, Ram
Frog Foot Fins. *Lace-up fins; fit over largest wading shoes; sizes: L—8-10; XL—11-13.*
$32.95-$39.95 Kau, Hig

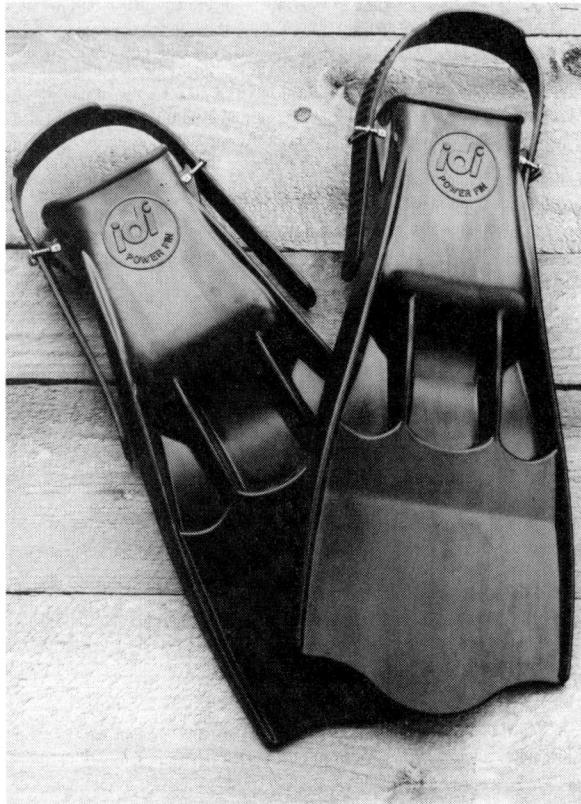

Power Fins. *Oversize swim fins; sizes: reg.—5-9(stocking feet); large—10-11(stocking foot) or 9(boot foot); extra large—12-13(stocking foot) or 12(boot foot).*
$29.95-$39.95 Cab, Kau

Paddle Pushers. *Vertical fins; fold back on forward stroke, fold out for power stroke; easy to walk in; see remarks in introduction to this section; sizes: M/L—7-11(tennis shoes only); L/XL—11-13(tennis shoes or wading shoes).*
$10.75-$13.95 EJH, H&H, Fly, AnJ, Tac, Cus

U.S. Divers Swim Fins. *Rubber; full-foot pocket with soft molded heel; black; order regular shoe size; sizes: med.—6-8; large—9-10; extra large—11-13.*
$39.50 AnJ

Other Accessories

Bucks Bags creel. *Hooks on D-rings and hangs in water.*
$17.95 AnJ
Hard sole booties. *Neoprene bootie to be worn over stocking-foot wader; provides hard sole to protect waders while float tubing; neoprene for warmth; sizes: small—6-7; med.—8-9; large—10-11; extra large—12-13.*
$19.50-$36 LLB (sizes 5-15 available), Kau, Fly, Orv
Mt. Traders suspenders. *1/2" foam padding; adjustable; to hold tube up while walking.*
$19.95 Fly
Float tube suspenders. *No brand name; to hold float tube up while walking to water or while wading shallow areas.*
$13-$18 Kau, EJH
Osprey tackle bag. *For Osprey float tube; attaches to snaps on float tube or belt (included); 9½"x6½"x4".*
$13.95 Cor

And Now a Float Tube Motor

For the ultimate in your float tubing comfort, there's now an electric motor available designed specifically for float tubes. The Water Otter from Rich Manufacturing is almost too good to be true (as is anything that is well designed).

The motor relies on a 12-volt gell cell battery which is recharged with household current. Stated operating time is 4-6 hours of continuous use. The battery is self-contained, eliminating the potential problem of extension wiring. The unit provides thrust enough to power a float tuber of some 300 lbs. at speeds of 5-8 mph.

The motor is housed in a watertight plastic housing. In case you have to dump it, it will float. The Water Otter attaches to any float tube with quick-release straps (included).

The unit is compact, measuring only 9½"x6"x3½". So confident in its reliability is Rick Menard that he offers a five-year warranty on the motor. And a money-back guarantee backs up his certainty that you'll like the Water Otter.

Retail cost will be about $139.95, but think how much fun you'll have. For more information, write Rich Manufacturing, Box 2042, Elko, Nevada 89801. And let me know how it works for you.

Water Otter motor. *An electric motor for your float tube; details in article above.*
About $139.95 Rich Manufacturing (see address above)

BOATS FOR THE FLY FISHERMAN

Two kinds of boats are particularly associated with fly fishing, the canoe and the McKenzie boat. The canoe has a long tradition among eastern fishermen and is a sentimental favorite for a quiet day afloat with fly rod. The McKenzie boat is the standard drift boat for western rivers. It is practical, tough, and a pleasure to fish from.

I've included river rafts here, also. Due to their portability when deflated, rafts are preferred by fly fishermen who travel to their rivers. They are very stable in the water and can be used in much the same way as a McKenzie boat.

Other boats listed here include the Rangeley Boat, a particularly pleasing modification of the canoe that is eminently suited to the fly fisherman, and the Porta-Boat, an interesting solution for those fishermen who don't want to hassle with a boat or raft but always want one when they get to the lake.

Canoes

Canoes have their origins among the American Indians. The birch bark canoe was the common method of travel for Indians of the Northeast. If you respect traditions and those people who maintain them, you'll enjoy reading John McPhee's *The Survival of the Bark Canoe* which you'll find at your library or local bookstore.

If, after reading McPhee's book, you have to have your own birch bark canoe, you can order one built in the strictest tradition of the Malecite Indians and white fur traders who followed them. The canoes range in length from 10' to 37' and in price from over $1,000 to nearly $6,000. Contact Henri Vaillancourt, Mill Street, Greenville, New Hampshire 03048. (Note: This information is quite old and discovered late in my research, so I had no time to verify it. However, if you have a burning desire for a birch bark canoe, it's worth a try.)

For something almost as traditional but perhaps more practical, take a look at the offerings of RKL Boatworks.

These cedar boats are built using the W.E.S.T. system which uses wood sandwiched between layers of epoxy resin and clear fiberglass. The result is a wood boat with complete protection from the elements. Purists may find the plastic-looking finish objectionable. I find it practical. The boats are beautiful in the way only a very practical thing can be. (Old Town, incidentally, also offers wood canoes.)

On the other hand are the canoes built of modern man-made materials, made by such well-known manufacturers as Mad River and Old Town. They utilize materials, ABS plastics and Kevlar for instance, that are amazingly strong and light. Of course, aluminum canoes are also part of the current scene with Grumman being the foremost manufacturer. Their popularity has been somewhat diminished by fiberglass and plastic materials which offer some distinct advantages.

The plastic and Kevlar boats are practically indestructable. Almost every canoe catalog shows one of their canoes trashed on a rock mid-river, usually bent nearly in two. Such mistakes would, of course, be the undoing of an aluminum boat, but the modern materials have memory. A few minutes in the sun and a little help from the canoeist bring them back to their old form. In such cases, gunwales and keelsons will have to replaced, but the accident won't hang you up in the back country someplace.

Finally, after all the high-priced canoes, I must mention the Coleman canoe. It's the Chevrolet among the boats here. I bought mine from a local discount store for about $350, considerably less than any of the other canoes here. It's made of Ram-X, an ultra-high molecular weight polyethylene with specific ultra-violet inhibitors. It's not sexy or even traditional, but it floats. I've used it for trips down the Bighorn with complete confidence. It's stable and fairly light. It does not have the maneuverability of higher priced boats, and it won't please the connoisseur. But if you use a canoe only occasionally or if you have a limited budget, the Coleman is the answer.

Bean's Mad River Canoe. *16' ABS; one of the finest canoes made; ABS Royalex, a vinyl ABS plastic foam laminate; lightweight but very rugged; for white water and open water; specifications: 15" depth at center, 35" beam, 22½" bow height; capacity: 1,100 lbs. with 6" freeboard; weight: 75 lbs.; color: green outside, gray inside.*
$870 LLB

Bean's Mad River Canoe. *17'4" ABS; similar to 16' model; specifications: 15" depth at center, 36" beam, 22½" bow height; capacity: 1,200 lbs. with 6" freeboard; weight: 85 lbs.*
$920 LLB

Bean's Fiberglass Canoe. *16' fiberglass with Kevlar reinforcement; for flat water and moderate white water; specifications same as 16' ABS model above; weight: 68 lbs.*
$815 LLB

Blue Hole Canoes. *Another Royalex canoe (see also: Mad River and Old Town canoes); several models including OCA Whitewater; length: 16'.*
About $700 Blue Hole Canoes, Sunbright, TN 37872

Coleman Canoes. *A number of models built of Ram-X, a plastic material; economical and practical; lengths: 13', 15', 17'; colors: red/orange, green.*
About $400-$500 Local sporting goods dealers, discount stores, or Coleman, 445 N. Minnesota, Wichita, Kansas 67214

Grumman Canoes. *The most popular aluminum canoe in a number of lengths and styles; a durable material unless you wrap it around a rock in mid-stream; noisy, so fly fishermen beware.*
About $500-$800 Local sporting goods dealers and marinas or Grumman Boats, Marathon, New York 13803

Mad River Canoes. *Mad River makes some of the finest canoes in the world; they also make many models, too many to describe here; three are given under Bean's listing, and I've selected one more, made of a different material, for this listing; you should really write for their catalog if you're in the market for the best and most modern in canoes; the Lamoille model is made of Kevlar with Airex foam; Kevlar is one of the best materials around for canoes, light and very strong (and, of course, expensive); a touring canoe over 18' long, the Lamoille weighs only 60 lbs.; specifications: 18'3" in length, 15" depth at center, 32" beam, 19" bow height; capacity: 1,100 lbs. with 6" freeboard; weight: 60 lbs.*
$1,699 Clavey Equipment, 30 Pamaron Way, Novato, California 94947 (415) 883-8826 or Mad River Canoes, Box 610, Waitsfield, Vermont 05673 (802) 496-3127

Old Town Canoes. *Probably the most coveted canoes are from Old Town; wood models of a beauty all their own and canoes of the most modern materials, including ABS Royalex; the Penobscot, for instance, is Royalex, 16'2" and weighs 77 lbs.; if you're in the market for the best, be sure to write for Old Town's catalog.*
Wood—about $1,500-$2,000; plastic—about $900-$1,100
Old Town Canoes, Old Town, Maine 04468

RKL Ugo Solo Canoe. *Made of western red cedar sandwiched with layers of epoxy resin and clear fiberglass; length: 15'; beam: 30"; capacity: 450 lbs.; weight: 40 lbs.*
$1,925 RKL Boatworks, Mt. Desert, Maine 04660

RKL River Canoe. *Same beautiful construction of Ugo Solo Canoe above; length: 17'; beam: 34".*
$1,975 RKL Boatworks (see address above)

RKL Cruiser Canoe. *See above; length: 18'; beam: 34".*
$1,975 RKL Boatworks (see address above)

Rubber Rafts

Rubber rafts are really boats for river rats of a different type than fly fishermen. However, for long trips on rivers with lots of kinds of water, rafts are the best choice for anyone. They hold a lot of gear, and I think they require less expertise than canoes, for instance, to traverse white water and other difficult situations. For fly fishermen traveling with families, there's no safer choice.

Many boats listed here are for two to four people, the size most appropriate for most fly fishermen. However, if eight wasn't enough for you, your family might appreciate a larger model. Some are listed here; for others, contact the manufacturers.

Your choice of a raft certainly centers around size, but there are a lot of other factors to consider. Of primary importance is the material and its coating. The weight of the material gives it tear resistance. The coating makes the material waterproof and gives it protection from abrasion and weathering. The heaviest material you're likely to find in a raft is 48 oz. (ounces per square yard), but for most purposes, 30 oz. will do.

The two most popular coatings are Hypalon and neoprene. Hypalon is considered superior, but it is also more expensive (of course). Both coatings will eventually wear thin. When that happens, the raft can be re-coated by applying a Hypalon or neoprene paint.

Rafts of 13' in length are adequate for two or three people. Greater length is required for trips requiring a bigger payload. Storage space for the deflated raft may also be a consideration for you, although most rafts of equal length roll up about the same.

The bow and stern rise may be something for you to compare, if you can get the figures from the companies. A high bow protects better from spray. Raising the stern increases maneuverability. Raising both bow and stern, a common practice, improves handling and keeps occupants dry, but the decrease in contact with the water can cause control problems when the wind is up.

The raft's features and the accessories available are other considerations. Incidentally, I haven't included the blue-light-specials from the local discount store. They may be fun for family paddling on the farm pond, but nobody should take one of them down the Colorado River.

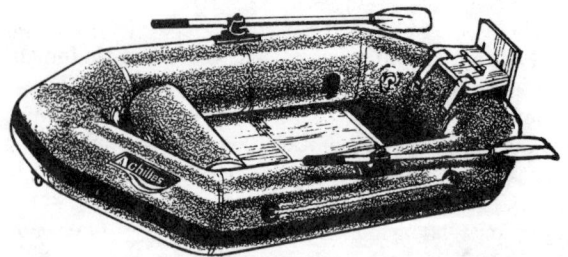

Courtesy of Ramsey Outdoors

Achilles. *Two-person raft; nylon with Hypalon coating outside and neoprene coating inside; stores in small stuff sack; complete with collapsible oars, oarlocks, floor boards, inflatable seat, motor mount, bow line, bellows foot pump, carrying case; capacity: 530 lbs.; weight: 24 lbs.; size: 7'1"x4'; color: red.*
$425-$460 LLB, Ram

Achilles. *Four-person raft; similar to Achilles two-person raft; capacity: 792 lbs.; weight: 31 pounds; size: 9'6"x4'7"; color: red.*
$550-$580 Ram, LLB

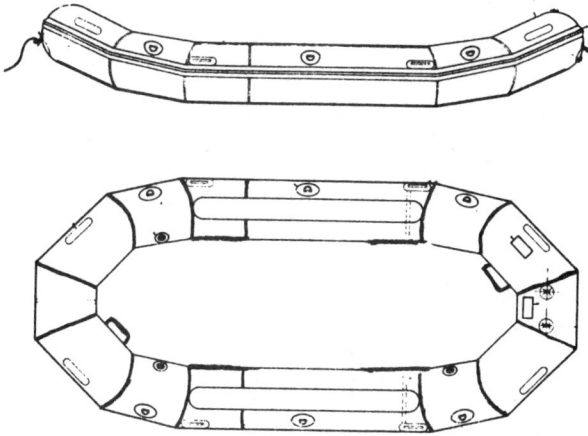

Avon Drifter. *This well-respected British manufacturer offers many raft models; two are designed for fishermen, the Drifter and the Pathmaker; Hypalon-coated nylon both sides; guaranteed for five years; stores in 44"x22"x10" stuff sack; includes foot pump, repair kit, motor mount brackets; length: 12'4"; width: 5'10"; bow/stern lift: 9"; capacity: 1,700 lbs.; weight: 76 lbs.*
$1,420 Clavey Equipment, 30 Pamaron Way, Novato, California 94947 (415) 883-8826
Avon Pathmaker. *Same construction as Avon Drifter; length: 13'; width: 5'10"; bow/stern lift: 9"; capacity: 1,870 lbs.; weight: 85 lbs.*
$1,625 Clavey Equipment (see address above)
Campways 14' and 15' River Rider. *Hypalon-coated rubber; these are big river runners; weights: 14'—93 lbs.; 15'—118 lbs.; sizes: 14'—13'6"x6'8"; 15'—15'x6'10".*
14'—$1,399; 15'—$1,499 Kau
Sea Eagle 8. *30 mil PVC hull; five air chambers; deflated will fit in sleeping bag stuff sack; molded oarlocks and oar clasps; includes pressure gauge, repair kit, instructions; capacity: four adults (950 lbs.); weight: 31 lbs.; size: 9'7"x4'6".*
$159.95-$225 AnW, Cab or Sea Eagle, 104 Arlington Ave., St. James, New York 11780 (516) 724-8900
Sea Eagle 9. *Larger version of Sea Eagle 8; 38 mil hull; five air chambers; capacity: five adults (1,200 lbs.); weight: 43 lbs.; size: 11'x4'8".*
$187.95-$260 Cab, Sea Eagle (see address above)

Drift Boats

The heritage of the famous McKenzie-style drift boats may rest in the bank dories used by the fishermen of New England and later the Pacific Northwest. It was in the Northwest that the boats were transformed into river boats.

Styles evolved on each river, but the McKenzie style emerged as the standard. It has a pointed stern, which the oarsman, situated in the middle of the boat, faces. The bow has been flattened to accept a motor. On many of the big rivers of the Northwest, a drift is followed by a power run back up to the car. But many rivers where drift boats are used are too shallow and rocky to permit use of a motor, and the drift down is followed by a shuttle back up the river by car.

There is one traditional wooden drift boat here, made by Greg Tatman. It's available in kit form, as well as a completed boat.

The other boats are fiberglass, and they come from respected manufacturers who use the best processes and materials. If you order one of their catalogs, you'll find a large selection of drift boats. (This is one of those situations where your world is enlarged. You thought drift boats were only for fly fishermen, and then you find out that only two of 20 models are for fly fishermen.)

The style is different on all the models, depending on what they are designed for. The fly fishing models generally have more room. Seats are designed so that anglers have more mobility within the boat. Most models have single seats fore and aft of the oarsman.

ClackaCraft. *Quality fiberglass construction; guaranteed against defects for one year and against bottom damage for life; a popular drift boat in Montana and the Northwest; many models available in 14' and 16', but two models are made specifically for the fly fisherman, the 16-CF and the 14-CF; lengths: model 16-CF—15'5", model 14-CF—13'6"; weights: 16—270 lbs., 14—190 lbs.; capacities: 16'—755 lbs., 14'—580 lbs.; colors: white, dk. green, lt. green, dk. blue, lt. blue, yellow, black, dk. brown, lt. brown.*
16'—$1,599, 14'—$1,569 ClackaCraft, 16969 S.E. 130th, Clackamas, Oregon 97015 (503) 655-9532

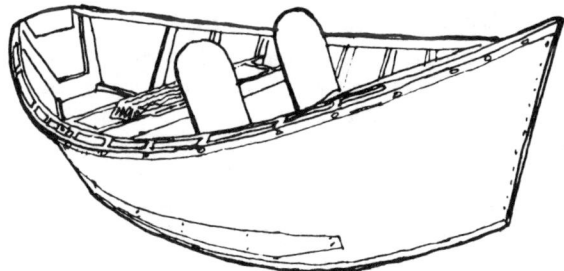

Greg Tatman. *Wooden McKenzie boats available assembled but unfinished, in kit form, or complete; made of fir marine plywood with oak hand rails; the drift boat equivalent of the birch bark canoe, but very practical; sizes: 8' and 10' boats, and 12' pram (flat bow and stern), 14' and 16' drift boats, and 16' high side drift boats; specific kit prices: 8'—$295, 10'—$350, 12'—$395, 14'—$449, 16'—$495, 16'(h.s.)—$575; with hull assembled, prices are $150-$200 more; assembled but unfinished*

boats are $300-$400 more than kits; prices for finished
boats given below.
12'—$995, 14'—$1,095, 16'—$1,295, 16'(h.s.)—$1,395
Greg Tatman Wooden Boats, Box K, Springfield, Oregon
97477 (503) 746-5287 (Note: Dealer list available.)

Lavro. *Lavro makes a number of McKenzie boats, with
two models are designed specifically for fly fishermen;
seating and standing areas provide additional space for
flying arms and piles of fly line; fiberglass throughout
with non-skid surfaces; 24 oz. woven roving is used in
layers, as many as 21 in some boats; hand-laminated for
consistency; one of the favorite boats on the Bighorn and
other Montana rivers; lengths: model 16-RF—16'3",
model 14-RF—13'11"; weights: 16—290 lbs., 14—240 lbs.;
capacities: 16—1,000 lbs., 14—750 lbs.; color: white with
blue interior.*
16-RF—$1,775; 14-RF—$1,475 Lavro, Inc., 16311 177
Ave. S.E., Monroe, Washington 98272 (206) 794-5525

Other Boats

There are only two boats in the "other" category. One
is the Porta-Boat, a fold-up boat, which is included for
those who want the feel of a real boat without the
problems of hauling one.

The other boat is the Rangeley Boat. Unless you live
in Maine, you probably won't recognize this boat. It was
developed by Maine guides, and it amounts to an enlarged
canoe. Somehow, though, it stands apart. I want one. It
would seem to have the advantages of the canoe's
maneuverability and ease of handling with the advantages
of a bigger boat's stability. Most of all, the boats are made
of cedar and are simply beautiful to behold, in the water
or in the garage.

Porta-Boats. *The amazing fold-up boat; included here
since it's an altogether kinky idea; polypropylene; folds
to 4" deep; lengths: 8', 10', 12'; weights: 39-59 lbs.;
capacities: 500-645 lbs.*
8'—$499.95; 10'—$575.95; 12'—$649.95 Fol
RKL Rangeley Boats. *Originally built for Maine guides;
looks like a fat canoe or a skinny row boat (depending,
I suppose, on whether you're an optimist or a pessimist);
stable (you can stand up and cast) yet maneuverable;*

western red cedar sandwiched between layers of epoxy
resin and clear fiberglass; mahogany seats and trim
standard; these are beautiful boats, folks; length: 17';
beam: 49"; midship depth: 15"; bow depth: 26"; weight:
140 lbs.*
$2,700-$3,100 RKL Boatworks, Mt. Desert, Maine 04660

RKL Little Rangeley Boats. *A smaller version of the
Rangeley Boat listed above; length: 14'; beam: 39";
midship depth:12"; bow depth: 23"; weight: 90 lbs.*
$2,300-$2,600 RKL Boatworks (see address above)

Accessories for the Floating Fisherman

Bean's canoe chair. *Aluminum frame with canvas; only
5½" tall; frame designed to fit over keelson.*
$16 LLB
Bean's Moose River paddles. *Straight or bent; these are
some of the prettiest hardwood paddles around;*
$32-$37.50 LLB
Bean's River Duffles. *Waterproof bags for storage of
gear while boating, canoeing, rafting; PVC-coated
Dacron; pliable to -20 degrees; sizes: small—8"x10"x30";
med.—8"x12"x30"; large—13"x16"x32".*
$14.50-$47.50 (depending on size) LLB
Sima Sports Pouch. *Waterproof bag for cameras;
heavy-gauge vinyl; inflatable chamber for flotation and
shock protection; sizes: reg.—14"x12"; large—17"x17".*
$15.95-$21.95 Ram
Wind River float bags. *Waterproof bags for storing
cameras and other gear while floating rivers; PVC
laminated to nylon; padded shoulder straps on larger
models; sizes: small—10"x17"; med.—16"x31"; large—
25"x16"x9"; extra large—43"x16"x9".*
$6.95-$21.95 (depending on size) Ram
Waterproof bag. *Translucent 20 mil vinyl; inflatable air
chambers.*
$29.95 Nor
Universal car top carrier. *For boats, canoes; gutter
clamps; 78" bar.*
$49.95 Ram
Yakima car top carriers. *For boats, canoes, cargo; roof
mounted or gutter clamps; 1" aluminum cross bar, 54",
66", or 74" in width.*
$61.50-$66.75 LLB

10. Rod Building

I N A TYPICAL FLY fisherman's development, rod building comes late, sometime after fly tying and before senility. It's part of the sport that is, unfortunately, skipped over by many fly fishermen, perhaps because they think it's only for those people who can't afford a ready-made rod. Not so.

Like fly tying, rod building adds something special to the sport. Casting a rod you've "built" (more accurately, "assembled") is something like catching fish with flies you've tied, and the pride you'll take in the rod will enhance your appreciation of the entire activity.

Rod building itself is engrossing and recreational. If you do it correctly, it will take all of your concentration, just like fishing for that trout rising in a tough place. You can get so wrapped up (excuse the expression) in rod building that you forget to watch the Super Bowl. At the same time, it's relatively easy to learn and to do well. It's meticulous, time-consuming work, but no extraordinary abilities are required.

It's not possible to give you full instructions on rod building here, nor is it necessary. I built my first rod with only the help provided by the Gudebrod pamphlet on rod wrapping. It costs about a buck. You'll find it listed in the chapter on books. Most fly shops that carry rod building supplies have it, too. If you still feel insecure, you can get full books on the subject. Those by Dale Clemens come to mind. I have two of his books, and they are excellent resources.

If you're ordering your rod building supplies by mail, I'd suggest you deal with one of the catalogs that specialize in those items. Their catalogs are filled with information on rod building, including how to space guides. Don't expect any information with your blank or other supplies, although it's sometimes included. The catalogs from Coren's, Dale Clemens, Pfeiffer's, and Beartooth Rods each have a beginner's section in them that will help you get started. Bullard's International is another excellent source of rod building supplies.

I recommend these catalogs because I know that if you don't know exactly what supplies to order or if you get in trouble while building your rod, you can get expert help by phone. You'll likely get good information from any of the companies referenced in this book, but you can be assured of it through these particular companies.

Just for fun and with the hopes of giving you confidence to build a rod on your own, here are the steps involved:

1. Choose your rod blank and select components to match.
2. Find the spine of the rod and mark it. (Note: Many manufacturers do this for you, but check their work anyway.)
3. Mount and glue the reel seat in line with the spine.
4. Ream the cork handle to fit the blank and glue on.
5. File the feet of the guides so the wrap will be tapered.
6. Tape on guides and tip top, preferably in a straight line and lined up with the reel seat properly.
7. Wrap guides and ferrules. (Caution: Cast no rod before its time; don't flex the joined rod until the ferrules are wrapped.)
8. Coat the threads with color preserver if desired.
9. Coat the threads with one of the finishes designed for that purpose; rotate while drying if necessary.
10. Go fish.

Perhaps the most difficult of all these steps is the first. That's where help from your local shop can be invaluable. Not only will they be able to assist you in components, but they may also stock finished rods for you to try out and to measure for guide placement. Component kits are also available from some companies. They aren't listed here because of space and time limitations and because it's more fun to build a rod using your own handle and reel seat selections.

ROD BLANKS

Choosing your rod blank is just like choosing a finished rod. Refer back to Chapter 2 for ideas on that. You should, by all means, try out a finished rod of the same brand as the blank if possible. Waving a blank is even less helpful than waving a finished rod and may break the blank. Be extra careful in your selection since there is usually no return on a blank you've wrapped.

For the most part, these rods are described in the chapter on rods and require no further explanation. A few brands listed here are only sold as blanks, but I haven't tried many of them out.

For each rod, I've listed the length, the line weights, the diameter of the butt and tip, and the blank's weight. The butt diameter is listed in inches, most often in the form of a decimal (.325, for instance) but sometimes in 64ths of an inch. The tip is always given as a single number which represents 64ths. A 5 is really 5/64 of an inch.

A word of warning. The measurements for many of the rods varied from catalog to catalog. I've used the ones most commonly published or ones from manufacturers' catalogs, but I don't guarantee any of them. Fortunately, butt diameter is not too crucial. Reel seats come in only a couple of inside diameters (I.D). Seats with a 5/8" I.D. will fit rods up to .625"; those with 3/8" I.D. will fit blanks with butts up to .375". Bushings are commonly used to fill the space between blank and seat.

Tip tops, on the other hand, must fit snugly. Again, it's best to deal with your local shop. If you use the mails, deal with one company, order according to their specs, and check the fit right away when you get the rod. If they've bummed it up, raise hell and offer to change companies.

Beartooth Rod Company

Carbonite Graphite Blanks

Length	Line	Price
7½	5/6	$63
8	5/6	$68
8½	5/6	$72
8½	6/7	$72
9	5/6	$75
9	6/7	$75
9	7/8	$75
9	8/9	$75

Bea

Diamondback Graphite Blanks

Length	Line	Tip	Butt	Oz.	Price
7	4/5	4½	.285	.8	$86
7½	4/5	4½	.300	.9	$90
8	5/6	4½	.325	1.3	$96
8½	4/5	4½	.325	1.3	$102
8½	5/6	5	.335	1.3	$102
8½	6/7	5	.350	1.5	$102
8½	7/8	5	.365	1.7	$102
9	3/4	4½	.325	1.3	$106
9	4/5	4½	.335	1.4	$106
9	5/6	5	.350	1.4	$106
9	6/7	5	.365	1.5	$106
9	7/8	5	.375	1.5	$106
9	8/9	5½	.390	1.7	$106
9	9/10	5½	.400	2.1	$106
9	10/11	5½	.410	2.2	$106
9½	5/6	5	.375	1.7	$112

Bea

Diamondback Graphite Travel Rod Blanks

Length	Line	Price
8½	6/7	$122
9	5/6	$120
9	6/7	$120

Bea

Bullard's Dura-Flex Graphite Blanks

Length	Line	Tip	Butt	Oz.	Price
7½	5/6	4½	.315	1¼	$37.50
8	6/7	4½	.290	1 9/16	$39.50
8½	6/7	4½	.361	1⅝	$41.50
9	8/9	4½	.400	2 7/16	$44.50

Bul

Cabela's Rods

Cabela's Fish Eagle Graphite Blanks

Model	Length	Line	Tip	Butt	Oz.	Price
GF703	7	3/4	5	16/64	¾	$31.95
GF704	7	4/5	5	17/64	1	$31.95
GF763	7½	3/4	5	18/64	1	$34.95
GF764	7½	4/5	5	18/64	1⅛	$34.95
GF765	7½	5/6	5	19/64	1¼	$34.95
GF804	8	4/5	5	19/64	1⅛	$36.95
GF805	8	5/6	5	20/64	1½	$36.95
GF806	8	6/7	5	23/64	1⅝	$36.95
GF865	8½	5/6	5	20/64	1½	$38.95
GF866	8½	6/7	5	23/64	1¾	$38.95
GF867	8½	7/8	5	24/64	1⅝	$38.95
GF904	9	4/5	5	24/64	1½	$41.95
GF905	9	5/6	5	25/64	1¾	$41.95
GF906	9	6/7	5	25/64	1⅞	$41.95
GF907	9	7/8	5	25/64	2⅛	$41.95
GF908	9	8/9	5	26/64	2¼	$41.95
GF9011	9	1 1/12	5	31/64	3¾	$49.95
GF966	9½	6/7	5	26/64	1¾	$43.95
GF968	9½	8/9	5	27/64	2⅜	$43.95
GF1008	10	8/9	5	28/64	2½	$46.95
GF1068	10½	8/9	5	29/64	2⅝	$48.95
GF1168	11½	8/9	5	30/64	3⅛	$49.95

Cab

Cabela's Fish Eagle II Graphite Blanks

Model	Length	Line	Tip	Butt	Oz.	Price
704	7	4/5	5		17/65	$45.95
805	8	5/6	5		20/64	$47.95
806	8	6/7	5		23/64	$47.95

Model	Length	Line	Tip	Butt	Price
865	8½	5/6	5	20/64	$50.95
866	8½	6/7	5	23/64	$50.95
906	9	6/7	5	22/64	$54.95
907	9	7/8	5	24/64	$54.95
908	9	8/9	5	26/64	$54.95

Dale Clemens Rods

Custom State of the Art Fiberglass Blanks

Model	Length	Line	Tip	Butt	Oz.	Price
80-71-04	7	4	6	.425	1 3/16	$18.98
80-76-05	7½	4/5	6½	.439	1⅜	$18.98
80-76-06	7½	6	7	.495	1⅜	$20.39
80-81-05	8	4/5	6	.498	1½	$19.59
80-81-06	8	6	6	.525	1½	$20.39
80-86-06	8½	6	6	.505	1⅝	$19.68
80-86-07	8½	7	6	.520	1¾	$20.92
80-91-05	9	5/6	6	.533	2	$20.74
80-91-08	9	8	6	.555	2	$20.91

Custom Builder Graphite Blanks

Model	Length	Line	Tip	Butt	Oz.	Price
83-00-75	7	3/4	4½	.248	¾	$47.52
83-00-01	7	4/5	4½	.264	13/16	$47.52
83-00-76	7½	3/4	4½	.272	⅞	$51.17
83-00-02	7½	4/5	4½	.283	15/16	$51.17
83-00-03	7½	5/6	4½	.283	1	$51.17
83-00-04	8	5/6	4½	.303	1 1/16	$54.83
83-00-05	8	6/7	4½	.345	1 3/16	$54.83
83-00-77	8	4/5	4½	.290	1⅛	$54.83
83-00-78	8½	5/6	4½	.308	1¼	$58.48
83-00-06	8½	6/7	4½	.350	1 3/16	$58.48
83-00-07	8½	7/8	4½	.368	1⅜	$58.48
83-00-83	9	4/5	4½	.368	1⅝	$62.14
83-00-08	9	5/6	4½	.370	1¾	$62.14
83-00-09	9	6/7	4½	.312	1 11/16	$62.14
83-00-10	9	7/8	4½	.323	1 13/16	$62.14
83-00-11	9	8/9	4½	.405	2 1/16	$62.14
83-00-12	9	11/12	5	.478	2 15/16	$75.76
83-00-13	9½	6/7	4½	.400	1 13/16	$65.79
83-00-79	9½	7/8	4½	.410	2¼	$65.79
83-00-14	9½	8/9	4½	.418	2 7/16	$65.79
83-00-80	10	6/7	4½	.400	2¼	$69.45
83-00-15	10	8/9	4½	.430	3 1/16	$69.45
83-00-16	10½	8/9	4½	.458	3¾	$73.10
83-00-95	10½	8/9	4½	.453	3⅞	$86.72
83-00-96	10½	10/11	6	.531	4	$99.97

Custom Builder Boron Blanks

Model	Length	Line	Tip	Butt	Oz.	Price
84-00-01	7½	5/6	4½	.287	1⅛	$94.06
84-00-02	8	4/5	4½	.312	1¼	$95.96
84-00-04	8	5/6	4½	.330	1⅜	$98.80
84-00-05	8½	5/6	5	.358	1⅝	$102.60
84-00-07	8½	6/7	5	.362	1 11/16	$102.60
84-00-08	9	8/9	5½	.375	1¾	$121.60

Custom Builder Fiberglass Travel Rod Blanks

Model	Length	Line	Tip	Butt	Price
PRB-6	6	6/7	6	.530	$27.29
PRB-75	7½	6/7	6	.445	$28.29

Fenwick Rods

Fenwick Feralite Fiberglass Blanks

Model	Length	Line	Tip	Butt	Oz.	Price
FL72-5	6	5	4½	.389	1	$10.30-$16.20
FL84-5	7	5	5	.430	1½	$10.85-$19.30
FL84-6	7	6	5	.445	1¾	$11.69-$17
FL90-5	7½	5	5	.460	1¾	$11.75-$20.90
FL90-6	7½	6	5	.468	1½	$11.05-$19.65
FL96-5	8	5	4½	.487	1½	$11.30-$18.43
FL96-6	8	6	5½	.495	2	$11.75-$20.90
FL96-7	8	7	5½	.502	2¼	$11.75-$20.90
FL102-6	8½	6	5½	.520	1⅜	$12.20-$21.70
FL102-7	8½	7	5	.525	2½	$12.65-$22.50
FL102-8	8½	8	5½	.537	2¾	$13.10-$23.35
FL108-8	9	8	5½	.600	3	$14.39-$21.25
FL108-9	9	9	6	.623	3	$13.30-$21.25
FL108-10	9	10	7½	.572	3	$13.30-$25.45
FL108-12	9	12	8	.748	4¼	$17.20-$26.22
FL114-9	9½	9	6	.575	3	$15.29-$25.45

Many catalogs

Fenwick HMG Graphite Blanks

Model	Length	Line	Tip	Butt	Oz.	Price
GFL75-4	6¼	4	4½	.247	5/8	$42.59-$65.75
GFL84-4	7	4	4½	.286	1	$44.20-$72.35
GFL90-5	7½	5	5	.308	1⅛	$49.85-$81.60
GFL90-6	7½	6	5	.305	1⅛	$49.85-$81.60
GFL96-5	8	5	5	.330	1⅜	$49.85-$81.60
GFL96-6	8	6	5½	.343	1½	$49.85-$81.60
GFL102-6	8½	6	5½	.356	1⅝	$55.45-$90.80
GFL102-7	8½	7	5½	.362	1⅝	$55.45-$90.80
GFL102-8	8½	8	5½	.371	1¾	$55.45-$90.80
GFL108-5	9	5	5	.369	1¾	$55.45-$90.80
GFL108-6	9	6	5½	.376	1¾	$55.45-$90.80
GFL108-7	9	7	5½	.394	1⅞	$55.45-$90.80
GFL108-8	9	8	5½	.404	1⅞	$55.45-$90.80
GFL108-9	9	9	6½	n/a	2½	$85.50 (Edd only)

Model	Length	Line	Tip	Butt	Oz.	Price
GFL108-10	9	10	7	.424	2½	$67.50-$110.50
GFL114-9	9½	9	5½	.435	2½	$63.65-$104.15
GFL120-5	10	5	5½	.389	1⅞	$81.76 (Pfe only)
GFL126-9	10½	9	5½	.450	2½	$83.13 (Dal only)

EJH, Mer, Don, Cab, Cor, Pfe, Tac, Dal, Bul, Spo, H&H, Dan, Kau, Sho, Edd

Fenwick Boron-X Blanks

Model	Length	Line	Tip	Butt	Oz.	Price
XFL90-5	7½	5	4	.294	1⅜	$91.35-$155.50
XFL90-6	7½	6	4	.302	1½	$91.35 $155.50
XFL96-6	8	6	4½	.308	1⅝	$91.35-$155.50
XFL102-5	8½	5	4	.318	2	$91.35-$155.50
XFL102-6	8½	6	4	.316	1⅞	$91.35-$155.50
XFL102-7	8½	7	4½	.332	2	$91.35-$155.50
XFL102-8	8½	8	4½	.340	2	$91.35-$155.50
XFL108-4	9	4	4½	.331	2	$91.35-$155.50
XFL108-5	9	5	5	.335	2	$91.35-$155.50
XFL108-6	9	6	4½	.350	2	$91.35-$155.50
XFL108-8	9	8	5	.364	2¼	$91.35-$155.50
XFL108-10	9	10	5	.380	2½	$96.95-$165
XFL108-12	9	12	5½	.527	3½	$102.80-$134.25
XFL114-9	9½	9	4½	.400	2¾	$96.95-$165
XFL114-10	9½	10	5½	.350	2½	$120.04 (Mer only)

Sho, Mer, H&H, Dal, Don, Pfe, Cab, Tac, Dan, Cor, Bul, Kau

Fenwick Fiberglass Travel Rod Blanks

Model	Length	Line	Tip	Butt	Oz.	Price
FL90-6-4	7½	6	5½	.509	2	$19.10-$33.95
FL102-6-5	8½	6	5½	.542	2⅝	$18.40-$32.75

Many catalogs

J. Kennedy Fisher Rods

Fisher Fiberglass Blanks

Model	Length	Line	Tip	Butt	Price
X2037	7	3	4½	.385	$25.95-$30
X2047	7	4	5	.395	$24-$25.95
X2457	7	4/5	5	.440	$26.72 (Mer only)
X2057	7	5	5	.440	$24-$26.72
X2037½	7½	3	4½	.400	$25.95-$30
X2047½	7½	4	5	.415	$25.95-$30
X2057½	7½	5	5	.460	$25.95-$30
X2048	8	4	5	.460	$25.95 (Kau only)
X2058	8	5	5	.465	$24-$30
X2068	8	6	5	.520	$24-$30
X2678	8	6/7	5½	.520	$28.09 (Mer only)
X2068½	8½	6	5	.535	$24-$26.72
X2078½	8½	7	n/a	n/a	$25.95 (Fly only)
X2678½	8½	6/7	5½	.535	$24-$25.95
X2088½	8½	8	5½	.540	$26-$29.23
X2069	9	6	5	.550	$25.95
X2679	9	6/7	5½	.550	$25.95 (Kau only)
X2079	9	7	n/a	n/a	$25.95 (Fly only)
X2089	9	8	5½	.555	$26-$29.95
X2099	9	9	5½	.560	$26-$26.58
X2109	9	10	5½	.585	$29.95-$30.38

Mur, Kau, Fly, Edd

Fisher Graphite Blanks

Model	Length	Line	Tip	Butt	Oz.	Price
X23390	7½	2/3	5	.225	1	$58.45 (T&T only)
X23490	7½	3/4	5	.250	1	$58.45-$75
X24590	7½	4/5	5	.315	1⅛	$58.45 (T&T only)
X23496	8	3/4	5	16/64	1⅛	$58.45-$70
X24596	8	4/5	5	21/64	1¼	$58.45-$75
X25696	8	5/6	5	22/64	1½	$58.45-$75
X23402	8½	3/4	5	.255	1¼	$58.45-$69.95
X24502	8½	4/5	5	22/64	1⅜	$58.45-$75
X25602	8½	5/6	5	23/64	1⅝	$58.45-$70
X26702	8½	6/7	5	24/64	1⅝	$58.45-$71

Model	Length	Line	Tip	Butt	Price
X27802	8½	7/8	5	24/64 1⅝	$59.15-$63.50
X23408	9	3/4	n/a	n/a	n/a	$69.95 (Fly only)
X24508	9	4/5	5	22/64 1½	$58.45-$70
X25608	9	5/6	5	23/64 1⅝	$58.45-$75
X26708	9	6/7	5	24/64 1⅝	$58.45-$75
X27808	9	7/8	5	25/64 1¾	$58.45-$75
X28908	9	8/9	5	25/64 1⅞	$58.45-$74
X29008	9	9/10	5	25/64 1⅞	$58.45-$70
X21208	9	11/12	5½	35/64 2⅜	$69.10-$90
X22308	9	12/13	5½	36/64 3	$69.80 (Mer only)
X24514	9½	4/5	5	26/64 1⅝	$66.43-$80
X25614	9½	5/6	5	26/64 1¾	$66.43-$80
X26714	9½	6/7	5	26/64 1¾	$65.70-$80
X27814	9½	7/8	5	26/64 2	$65.70-$80
X28914	9½	8/9	5	26/64 2⅛	$65.70-$74.95
X29014	9½	9/10	5	26/64 2⅜	$77.50-$84
X24520	10	4/5	5	27/64 1¾	$66.43-$80
X25620	10	5/6	5	27/64 1⅞	$66.43-$80
X26720	10	6/7	n/a	n/a	n/a	$74.95-$79.95
X27820	10	7/8	5	.405 2	$65.70-$80
X28920	10	8/9	5	n/a	n/a	$74.95-$80
X29020	10	9/10	5	27/64 2⅜	$77.50-$84
X29026	10½	9/10	5	28/64 2⅜	$78.18 (Mer only)

Ran, Mur, T&T, Mer, Kau, Fre, Edd, Fly

Fisher Boron Blanks

Model	Length	Line	Tip	Butt	Oz.	Price
XGB26708	9	6/7	5	.360	1⅝	$88.40-$115
XGB27808	9	7/8	5	.375	1¾	$88.40-$115
XGB28908	9	8/9	5	.375	1⅞	$88.40-$115
XGB28920	10	8/9	5	.405	2⅛	$100-$104.95

Fre, T&T, Mur

Fisher Fiberglass Travel Rod Blanks

Model	Length	Line	Price
X4057	7	5	$39.95
X4057½	7½	5	$39.95
X4068	8	6	$39.95

Fly

Fisher Graphite Travel Rod Blanks

Model	Length	Line	Tip	Price
X45608	9	5/6	5	$90
X46708	9	6/7	5	$90
X47819	9½	7/8	5	$100
X48914	9½	8/9	5	$100
X49104	9½	9/10	5	$100

Kau

G. Loomis Rods

G. Loomis Graphite Blanks

Model	Length	Line	Tip	Butt	Price
F843	7	3/4	4½	.250	$40.95-$48.95
F844	7	4/5	4½	.265	$40.95-$48.95
F903	7½	3/4	4½	.270	$52.95
F904	7½	4/5	4½	.280	$44.10-$52.95
F905	7½	5/6	4½	.285	$44.65-$52.95
F964	8	4/5	4½	.285	$57.95
F965	8	5/6	4½	.305	$47.25-$57.95
F966	8	6/7	4½	.345	$47.85-$57.95
F1025	8½	5/6	4½	.310	$50.95-$63.45
F1026	8½	6/7	4½	.350	$50.40-$80
F1027	8½	7/8	4½	.370	$50.95-$80
F1083	9	3/4	n/a	n/a	$85
F1084	9	4/5	4½	.375	$64.95-$85
F1085	9	5/6	4½	.380	$35.55-$85
F1086	9	6/7	4½	.320	$54.25-$85
F1087	9	7/8	4½	.325	$53.55-$85
F1088	9	8/9	4½	.405	$54.25-$85
F10810	9	10/11	n/a	n/a	$100
F10811	9	11/12	5	.480	$66.95-$85
F1145	9½	5/6	n/a	n/a	$90
F1146	9½	6/7	4½	.400	$56.70-$90
F1147	9½	7/8	4½	.410	$74-$90
F1148	9½	8/9	4½	.420	$56.70-$90
F1149	9½	9/10	n/a	n/a	$95
F1206	10	6/7	4½	.405	$59.95-$95
F1208	10	8/9	4½	.430	$76.50-$95
F1266	10½	6/7	4½	.420	$76.50
F1268	10½	8/9	4½	.450	$63-$76.50
F1388	11½	8/9	4½	.460	$66.15-$76.50

Don, Cor, Bul, Spo, Fly

E.J. Hille Rods

Hille Lamiflex Fiberglass Blanks

Length	Line	Tip	Butt	Oz.	Price
5	5	5	20/64	7/8	$16.35
5½	5	5½	22/64	1	$17.20
6	5	5½	23/64	1	$17.30
6½	5	5½	25/64	1⅜	$18
7	5	5½	26/64	1½	$18.30
7	6	5½	27/64	2	$19.10
7½	5	5½	27/64	1⅝	$19.40
7½	6	6	33/64	1⅝	$20.20
7½	7	5½	29/64	2½	$18.65
8	5	5½	29/64	2⅛	$19.90
8	6	5½	31/64	2¾	$20.90
8	7	5½	36/64	2	$19.65
8	8	5½	36/64	2⅓	$21.80
8½	6	5½	30/64	2⅓	$21.80
8½	6/7	5½	32/64	3	$22.75
8½	7	6	37/64	2⅓	$20.45
9	7	6	36/64	3½	$23.25
9	8	6	39/64	2¾	$20.40
9	8/9	7	41/64	3¾	$21.30
9½	7	6	38/64	3¾	$24.55

EJH

Hille Lamiflex Graphite Blanks

Length	Line	Tip	Butt	Oz.	Price
7	2/3	5	15/64	5/8	$57.25
7	3/4	5	15/64	3/4	$57.25
7	4/5	5	16/64	7/8	$57.25
7½	3/4	5	17/64	15/16	$63.35
7½	4/5	5	17/64	1	$63.35
7½	5/6	5	17/64	1³/₁₆	$63.35
8	4/5	5	18/64	1³/₁₆	$65.45
8	5/6	5	19/64	1⅜	$65.45
8½	5/6	5	19/64	1⁷/₁₆	$69.55
8½	6/7	5	20/64	1⁹/₁₆	$69.55
8½	7/8	5	21/64	1¹⁵/₁₆	$69.55
9	4/5	4½	20/64	1⁹/₁₆	$73.65
9	5/6	4½	20/64	1¹¹/₁₆	$73.65
9	6/7	4½	20/64	1¹³/₁₆	$73.65
9	7/8	5	21/64	1¹⁵/₁₆	$73.65
9	8/9	5	21/64	2³/₁₆	$73.65
9½	4/5	5	21/64	1¹³/₁₆	$77.70
9½	6/7	5	21/64	1¹⁵/₁₆	$77.70
9½	8/9	5	27/64	2⅜	$77.70
10	4/5	5	21/64	1¹⁵/₁₆	$81.80
10	6/7	5	22/64	2¼	$81.80
10	8/9	5	28/64	2⁹/₁₆	$81.80
10½	4/5	5	25/64	1¹⁵/₁₆	$85.90
10½	6/7	5	27/64	2⅛	$85.90
10½	8/9	5	30/64	2⅝	$85.90

EJH

Lamiglas Rods

Lamiglas S-Glass Fiberglass Blanks

Model	Length	Line	Tip	Butt	Oz.	Price
SFL84-4M	7	4	5½	.390	1½	$17.55-$21.95
SFL90-5S	7½	5	5½	.410	1⅝	$18.90-$24.69
SFL90-5/6F	7½	5/6	6	.555	1⅝	$18.90-$23.60
SFL96-6S	8	6	5½	.445	2⅛	$20.90-$25.80

Model	Length	Line	Tip	Butt	Oz.	Price
SFL96-6/7F	8	6/7	5½	.580	2	$20.90-$24.95
SFL102-7S	8½	7	5½	.475	2⁵/₁₆	$21.95-$26.90
SFL102-7/8F	8½	7/8	5½	.590	2⅜	$22.30-$26.30
SFL108-5/6F	9	5/6	5½	.541	2⅛	$24.30
SFL108-8S	9	8	5½	.515	2⁹/₁₆	$24.30-$29.97
SFL108-8/9F	9	8/9	6	.655	2¾	$24.30-$29

Cor, Pfe, Edd, T&T, Sho

Lamiglas Fiberglass Blanks

Model	Length	Line	Tip	Butt	Oz.	Price
FL844	7	4	5½	.400	1½	$18.06
FL905	7½	5	5½	.420	1⅝	$19.24
FL916	7½	6	5½	.420	1⅝	$19
FL966	8	6	5½	.500	2⅞	$19.40
FL1027	8½	7	5½	.535	3⅜	$19.57
CFL102	8½	7	6	.575	2⁵/₁₆	$21.70
FL1089	9	9	6	.610	2¾	$21.40
FL10810	9	10	6	.630	3⅝	$21.73
FL10911	9	11	6	.631	3¾	$23.97

Pfe

Lamiglas Graphite Blanks

Model	Length	Line	Tip	Butt	Oz.	Price
GF84 2/3	7	2/3	4½	.238	1¹/₁₆	$51.80 (Pfe only)
GF84 3/4	7	3/4	4½	.260	1	$33.35-$47.25
GF84 4/5	7	4/5	4½	.278	1¹/₁₆	$33.35-$65.50
GFW844L	7	6/7	5	.342	1¾	$40.50-$53.96
GF90 3/4	7½	3/4	4½	.279	1¹/₁₆	$47.61 (Dal only)
GF90 4/5	7½	4/5	4½	.280	1¼	35.75-$52.15
GF90 5/6	7½	5/6	4½	.315	1¼	$35.70-$69.50
GF96 4/5	8	4/5	4½	.286	1⁹/₁₆	$38.10-$55.20
GF96 5/6	8	5/6	4½	.290	1⁹/₁₆	$38.10-$55.40
GF96 6/7	8	6/7	4½	.360	1⅝	$38.10-$73.95
GF102 5/6	8½	5/6	4½	.317	1½	$40.50-$56.30
GF102 6/7	8½	6/7	4½	.361	1⅝	$40.50-$58.85
GF102 7/8	8½	7/8	4½	.368	2	$40.50-$79.95
GF108 4/5	9	4/5	4½	.335	1⅝	$42.85-$64.45
GF108 5/6	9	5/6	4½	.342	1⅞	$42.85-$64.45
GF108 6/7	9	6/7	4½	.342	1¾	$42.85-$64.45
GF108 7/8	9	7/8	4½	.388	1¹⁵/₁₆	$42.85-$64.45

Model	Length	Line	Tip	Butt	Oz.	Price
GF108 8/9	9	8/9	4½	.400	2⁷⁄₁₆	$42.85-$83.95
GF108 9/10	9	9/10	4½	.409	2⁹⁄₁₆	$42.85-$64.45
GSW108 11/12	9	11/12	5½	.481	3⁷⁄₁₆	$52.40-$120
GSW108 12/13	9	12/13	6	.514	3½	$57.20-$120
GF114 4/5	9½	4/5	4½	.375	2	$45.25-$70.70
GF114 6/7	9½	6/7	4½	.383	2⁷⁄₁₆	$45.25-$67.50
GF114 8/9	9½	8/9	4½	.427	2¾	$45.25-$67.50
GF114 9/10	9½	9/10	4½	.431	2¾	$45.25-$67.50
GF120 4/5	10	4/5	4½	.364	3³⁄₁₆	$47.65-$63.48
GF120 6/7	10	6/7	4½	.393	2⅝	$47.65-$70.55
GF120 8/9	10	8/9	5½	.419	2⅞	$47.65-$70.55
GF120 9/10	10	9/10	5½	.451	3³⁄₁₆	$47.65-$70.55
GF126 4/5	10½	4/5	4½	.376	2¼	$50-$70.87
GF126 6/7	10½	6/7	4½	.407	2⁷⁄₁₆	$50-$70.87
GF126 8/9	10½	8/9	4½	.456	3⅜	$50-$66.66
GF126 9/10	10½	9/10	4½	.465	3⅝	$50 (H&H only)

Sho, Mer, H&H, Tac, Dal, Bul, Pfe, T&T

Lamiglas Boron Blanks

Model	Length	Line	Tip	Butt	Oz.	Price
BF90 5/6	7½	5/6	4¼	.318	1½	$61.95-$79.99
BF96 5/6	8	5/6	4½	.293	1⅝	$66.70-$98.20
BF96 6/7	8	6/7	4½	.363	1¾	$66.70-$86.19
BF102 5/6	8½	5/6	4½	.320	1⁹⁄₁₆	$71.45-$104.30
BF102 6/7	8½	6/7	4½	.364	1¹¹⁄₁₆	$71.45-$104.30
BF102 7/8	8½	7/8	4½	.371	2	$71.45-$104.30
BF108 5/6	9	5/6	4½	.345	1¹⁵⁄₁₆	$76.25-$110.45
BF108 7/8	9	7/8	4½	.391	2⅜	$76.25-$110.80
BF108 8/9	9	8/9	4½	.403	2½	$76.25-$110.80
BF114 6/7	9½	6/7	4½	.386	2½	$80.90-$116.50
BF114 8/9	9½	8/9	4½	.430	2¹³⁄₁₆	$80.90-$117.75

Tac, Bul, Sho, H&H

Lew Childre's SG-Series Graphite Blanks

Model	Length	Line	Tip	Butt	Oz.	Price
SGF842-34	7	3/4	3½	.422	⅞	$35.99
SGF842-45	7	4/5	4	.430	1¹⁄₁₆	$38.65
SGF902-45	7½	4/5	4	.292	1¼	$40.25
SGF962-45	8	4/5	4	.304	1⁷⁄₁₆	$42.75
SGF962-56	8	5/6	5	.319	1⅝	$42.75
SGF962-67	8	6/7	5	.331	1½	$43.95
SGF1022-56	8½	5/6	4	.318	1⅝	$47.29
SGF1022-67	8½	6/7	5	.354	1¹⁵⁄₁₆	$47.29
SGF1022-78	8½	7/8	5	.366	1⅝	$49.99
SGF1082-45	9	4/5	4	.326	1⅞	$49.69
SGF1082-67	9	6/7	4	.390	2³⁄₁₆	$49.69
SGF1082-78	9	7/8	4½	.370	2⅜	$52.35
SGF1082-89	9	8/9	5	.409	3⁵⁄₁₆	$54.59
SGF1082-11	9	11/12	6	.511	2¹⁵⁄₁₆	$68.95
SGF1263-89	10½	8/9	4½	.453	3¾	$71.99
SGF1263-10	10½	10/11	6	.531	n/a	$82.99

Tac

Loomis Composites Rods

Loomis Composites Graphite Blanks

Model	Length	Line	Tip	Butt	Oz.	Price
GFF564	5½	4/5	4½	.250	1	$24.30-$29.16
GF704	7	4/5	4½	.265	¾	$40.05-$48.06
GF764	7½	4/5	4½	.285	⅞	$51.03 (Pfe only)
GF765	7½	5/6	4½	.285	1	$42.55-$51.03
GF805	8	5/6	4½	.295	1¹⁄₁₆	$45.55-$54.63
GF806	8	6/7	4½	.305	1⅛	$50.65-$54.63
GF807	8	7/8	4½	.345	1¼	$54.63 (Pfe only)
GF865	8½	5/6	4½	.310	1¼	$54.75-$59.04
GF866	8½	6/7	4½	.310	1¼	$49.20-$59.04
GF867	8½	7/8	4½	.350	1¼	$54.75-$59.04
GF868	8½	8/9	5	.370	1⅜	$59.04 (Pfe only)
GF905	9	5/6	5	.375	1½	$51.60-$62.10
GF906	9	6/7	5	.375	1⅝	$57.40-$62.10
GF907	9	7/8	5	.315	1¾	$51.60-$62.10
GF908	9	8/9	5	.325	1⅞	$57.60-$62.10
GF909	9	9/10	5	.405	2	$57.60-$62.10
GT9011	9	11/12	5	.480	3	$60-$72
GT9012	9	12/13	5	.495	3¼	$75 (Pfe only)
GF966	9½	6/7	5	.400	1⅜	$55.15-$62.10
GF967	9½	7/8	5	.405	1¾	$57.60-$62.10
GF968	9½	8/9	5	.410	2¼	$55.15-$66.10
GF969	9½	9/10	5	.420	2½	$61.35-$66.10
GF1008	10	8/9	5	.430	2¾	$72.36
GF1068	10½	8/9	5	.450	3	$65.25-$78.30
GF1168	11½	8/9	5	.460	3⅛	$73.15-$87.75

Cor, T&T, Pfe

Loomis Composites Boron Blanks

Model	Length	Line	Tip	Butt	Oz.	Price
BF765	7½	5/6	4	.270	1	$75-$81
BF806	8	6/7	4	.310	1⅛	$77.65-$83.70
BF866	8½	6/7	4	.330	1³⁄₁₆	$80.50-$86.94
BF908	9	8/9	4½	.360	1¾	$83.40-$89.91
BF967	9½	7/8	4½	.410	2⅛	$88.20-$95.04

T&T, Pfe

Orvis Rods

Orvis Graphite Blanks

Model	Length	Line	Tip	Butt	Oz.	Price
Flea	6½	4	n/a	n/a	n/a	$95 (Fly only)
Otter	7	5	4½	.268	1	$105
The Tippet	7½	3	4½	.273	1	$105
Brook Trout	7½	4	4½	.270	1⅛	$105
Trout 7½	7½	6	4½	.283	1⅛	$105
Ultra-Fine	7¾	2	n/a	n/a	n/a	$115
Far-and-Fine	7¾	5	4½	.295	1⅛	$105
7/11	7'11"	4	4½	.290	1¼	$105
Tight Loop 4-pc.	8	4	4½	.310	1⅜	$170
Western	8	4	4½	.295	1½	$105
Trout 8	8	6	4½	.298	1¼	$105
All Rounder	8¼	7	5	.328	1⅜	$115
Henry's Fork	8½	5	4½	.325	1¼	$115
Limestone Special	8½	6	4½	.326	1¼	$115
Powerhouse	8½	8	5	.329	1½	$115
Western	8¾	5	n/a	n/a	n/a	$115
Western	8¾	7	5	.330	1¾	$115
Western	8¾	8	n/a	n/a	n/a	$115
Western	9	4	n/a	n/a	n/a	$115
Zephyr	9	4	5	.312	1½	$125-$140
Performer	9	6	4½	.348	1½	$90-$105
Western	9	6	5	.353	1½	$115
9x9	9	9	6	.372	1⅞	$115
Bonefish	9	9	5½	.372	1⅞	$90 (Kau only)
Shooting Star	9	9	6	.372	1⅞	$115
Spring Creek	9¼	5	4½	.350	1½	$115
Western	9¼	8	n/a	n/a	n/a	$115
Advantage	9⅓	7	5	.364	1⅞	$115
Advantage Plus	9⅓	7	5	.364	1⅞	$115
Osprey	9½	6	5	.338	1¾	$130-$145
Light Salmon	9½	8	6	.378	1⅞	$90-$105
Rivermaster	9½	8	6	.378	1⅞	$115
Western	10	7	5	.403	2⅛	$170
Salmon Rod	10	9	5½	.380	2⅝	$170
Two-Handed Salmon	13½	10	6½	.520	6⅜	$170
Two-Handed Spey	15	11	7	.592	n/a	$210

Orv, Fly, Kau

Orvis Boron Blanks

Model	Length	Line	Tip	Butt	Oz.	Price
Powerflex	8½	6	5	.340	1¾	$215
Powerflex	8½	8	5½	.350	1¾	$150-$196
Powerflex Shooting Star	8½	8	5½	.350	1¾	$150-$165
Powerflex	8¾	7	5	.355	1⅞	$215
Powerflex	9	8	n/a	n/a	n/a	$215
Powerflex	9	9	6	.385	2⅛	$215
Powerflex Light Tarpon	9	10	6	.382	2¼	$195
Powerflex	9¼	8	n/a	n/a	n/a	$196
Powerflex Tournament	9½	12	6	n/a	3⅞	$195

Orv, Kau, Fly

Orvis Bamboo Blanks

Model	Length	Line	Price
MCL Flea	6½	4	$425
MCL 7/3	7	3	$450
MCL Midge	7½	5	$450
7½	7½	6	$450
8	8	6	$475
8	8	7	$475

Orv, Fly

Orvis Graphite Travel Rod Blanks

Model	Length	Line	Tip	Butt	Oz.	Price
Trout 8-3pc.	8	6	4½	.305	1⅜	$115-$135
All Rounder-4pc.	8	7	5	.318	1½	$170
Spring Creek-4pc.	9	5	4½	.348	1¾	$140-$155
9x9-4pc.	9	9	6	.372	1⅞	$192

Orv, Kau, Fly

Walton Powell Rods

Powell "Dry Fly" Graphite Blanks

Model	Length	Line	Price
DF70-1	7	4/5	$70
DF76-1	7½	4/5	$70
DF76-2	7½	5/6	$70
DF80-1	8	4/5	$70
DF80-2	8	5/6	$70
DF83-2	8¼	5/6	$70
DF86-1	8½	4/5	$70
DF86-2	8½	5/6/7	$70
DF90-1	9	4/5	$70
DF90-2L	9	5/6	$70
DF90-2H	9	6/7	$70
DF96-1	9½	4/5/6	$70
DF96-2	9½	6/7/8	$70

Powell Rod Co., Box 3966, Chico, California 95927-3966

Powell "Light Steelhead" Graphite Blanks

Model	Length	Line	Price
LTSH86	8½	7/8	$75
LTSH90	9	7/8	$75
LTSH96	9½	7/8	$75
LTSH100	10	7/8	$75

Powell (see address above)

Powell "Steelhead/Salmon" Graphite Blanks

Model	Length	Line	Price
COHO90L	9	8/9	$85
COHO90	9	9/10	$85
COHO96	9½	9/10	$85
COHO100	10	9/10	$85

Powell (see address above)

Powell "Tarpon" Graphite Blank

Model	Length	Line	Price
Tarpon 90	9	11/12	$125

Powell (see address above)

Powell Graphite Travel Rod Blanks

Model	Length	Line	Price
DF86-4	8½	5/6/7	$125
DF90-4	9	5/6/7	$125
COHO90-4	9	8/9	$135
DF96-4	9½	6/7/8	$130

Powell (see address above)

R.L. Winston Rods

R.L. Winston Fiberglass Blanks

Model	Length	Line	Price
Trout	7	5	$45
Trout	7½	5	$45
Trout	7½	6	$45
Trout	8	5	$45
Trout	8	6	$45
Trout	8	7	$45
Trout	8½	5	$45
Trout	8½	6	$45
Trout	8½	7	$45
Steelhead	8¾	8	$47.50
Trout	9	6	$45
Trout	9	7	$45
Steelhead	9	8	$47.50
Steelhead	9	9	$47.50
Steelhead	9	10	$47.50
Saltwater	9	11	$47.50
Steelhead	9	11	$47.50
Saltwater	9	12	$47.50
Trout	9¼	5	$45

RLW

R.L. Winston Fiberglass Travel Rod Blanks

Model	Length	Line	Price
Trout 3,4pc.	7½	5	$47.50
Trout 3,4pc.	8	5	$47.50
Trout 3,4pc.	8	6	$47.50
Trout 3,4pc.	8½	6	$47.50

RLW

Reed-Flex Rods

Reed-Flex Fiberglass Blanks

Model	Length	Line	Tip	Butt	Oz.	Price
F50L-2	5½	5/6	5½	26/64	1½	$23.90
F55UL-2	6	5/6	5	24/64	1⅙	$18.45
F60LM-2	7½	6/7	6	32/64	2	$23.55
F65L-2	7'8"	6/7	5½	32/64	2⅕	$23
F75M-2	8	7	6	34/64	2½	$29.80
F80H-2	8	7/8	6	33/64	3½	$33.35
F90ML-2	8½	7	6	35/64	2½	$31.80
F85M-2	8½	8/9	6	36/64	3¾	$35.85
F100MH-2	9	9/10	5½	39/64	3¼	$37.75
F105H-2	9	9/10	7	40/64	3¾	$38
F107H-2	10	9	7	42/64	5¾	$33.75

Ree

Reed-Flex Parabolic Fiberglass Blanks

Model	Length	Line	Tip	Butt	Oz.	Price
F56UL-2	7	5	5½	27/64	1¾	$21.25
F57UL-2	7½	5	6	30/64	1⅞	$22
F58UL-2	8	5	6	30/64	2¼	$23

Ree

Reed-Flex Super-G Fiberglass Blanks

Model	Length	Line	Tip	Butt	Oz.	Price
GF55-2	6	5/6	5	24/64	1⅙	$20.60
GF56-2	7	5	5	27/64	1¾	$23.35
GF57L-2	7½	5	6	30/64	1⅞	$24.10
GF60LM-3	7½	6/7	6	32/64	2	$26
GF65L-2	7'8"	6/7	5½	32/64	2	$24
GF58L-2	8	5	6	30/64	2¼	$25.10
GF90ML-2	8½	7/8	6	35/64	2½	$31.10
GF85M-2	8½	8	n/a	n/a	n/a	$34.95
GF100MH-2	9	8/9	6	37/64	3⅔	$40
GF105H-2	9	9/10	7	40/64	3¾	$39.10

Ree

Reed-Flex Graphite Blanks

Model	Length	Line	Tip	Butt	Oz.	Price
GF20490	7½	4	5	21/64	1⅜	$97.75
GF20496	8	4/5	5	22/64	1½	$99.75
GF21008	9	9/10/11	5	25/64	1⅞	$104.65

Ree

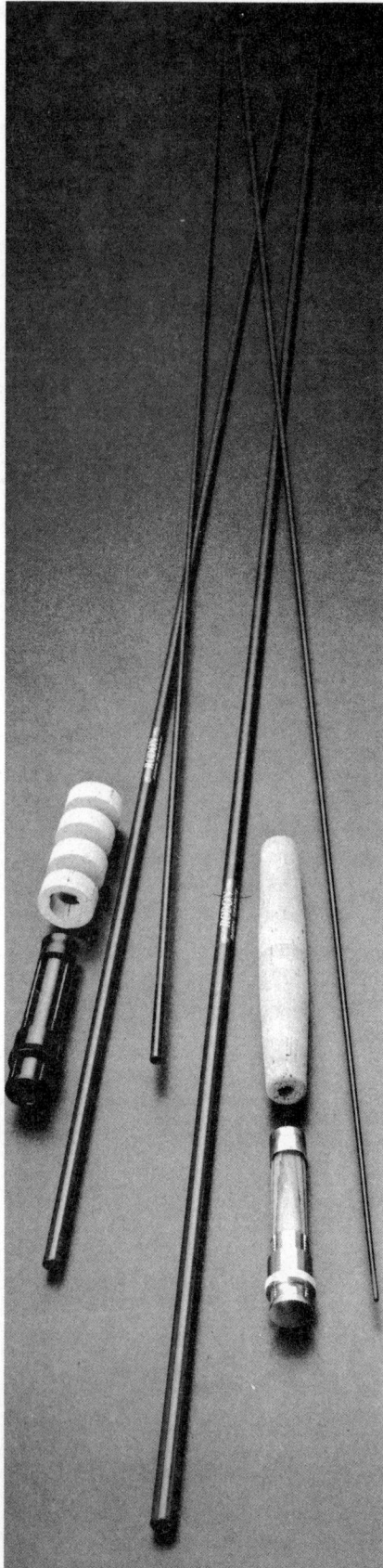

Rodon Rods

Rodon Boron Blanks

Model	Length	Line	Tip	Butt	Oz.	Price
7040	7	4	5	.290	7/8	$109.65-$115
7530	7½	3	4½	.297	1	$111-$111.15
7550	7½	5	5	.305	1⅜	$112.50-$118
8040	8	4	5	.312	1¼	$104-$120
8060	8	6	5	.328	1½	$107-$123
8070	8	7	5½	.335	1⅜	$125 (Don only)
8550	8½	5	5	.328	1½	$110-$126
8570	8½	7	5½	.350	1¾	$120-$142
8580	8½	8	6	.375	2	$145-$151
9060	9	6	5½	.380	1⅞	$115-$132
9070	9	7	6	.396	2⅛	$139-$145
9080	9	8	6½	.406	2½	$139-$158
9570	9½	7	6	.412	2⅜	$150-$156
9590	9½	9	6½	.421	2⅝	$145-$166
9511	9½	11	7	.437	3⅛	$201 (Kau only)
9512	9½	12	7	.437	3⅛	$201-$207
1008	10	8	6½	.421	2⅞	$162-$168
1010	10	10	7	.437	3¼	$174.50 (Don only)
1059	10½	9	7	.445	3⅝	$186.30-$192
1054	10½	14	8	.465	4⅝	$270.75 (Don only)

T&T, Hun, Don, Kau, or Rodon, 123 Sylvan Avenue, Newark, New Jersey 07104 (201) 481-0027

Rodon Boron Three-piece Rod Blanks

Model	Length	Line	Tip	Butt	Oz.	Price
3856	8½	6	5½	.359	2	$174.70 (Don only)
3857	8½	7	6	.365	2⅛	$189.70 (Don only)
3906	9	6	5½	.375	2⅛	$183-$183.60
3908	9	8	6	.421	2½	$203.95 (Don only)
3957	9½	7	6	.406	3	$198-$198.30
3959	9½	9	6½	.437	3⅛	$207-$207.80
3008	10	8	6½	.445	3⅛	$215.30 (Don only)
3010	10	10	7	.468	3⅜	$225.30 (Don only)
3051	10½	11	7	.500	4	$241-$241.75
3201	12	11	7	.578	4⅛	$305-$305.05
3402	14	12	8	.594	6	$409.25 (Don only)
3603	16	13	8	.615	8⅞	$539.70 (Don only)

Kau, Don, or Rodon (see address above)

Rodon Boron Four-Piece Travel Rod Blanks

Model	Length	Line	Tip	Butt	Oz.	Price
4806	8	6	5½	.335	2	$185.10
4857	8½	7	6	.356	2¼	$193.05
4908	9	8	6½	.412	3⅛	$211.50

Don or Rodon (see address above)

Sage Rods

Sage Fiberglass Blanks

Model	Length	Line	Tip	Butt	Oz.	Price
SFL476B	7½	4	5	.490	1¹³/₁₆	23-$29
SFL580B	8	5	5	.540	2⅛	$24-$30

Model	Length	Line	Tip	Butt	Oz.	Price
SFL686B	8½	6	5½	.585	2⁷⁄₁₆	$24-$30
SFL789B	8¾	7	6	.620	2¹⁷⁄₃₂	$26-$33
SFL990B	9	9	7	.650	3⁷⁄₁₆	$30-$38
SFL1290	9	12	n/a	n/a	n/a	$39 (Fly only)

Sho, Kau, Cor, Fly

Sage Fiberglass Travel Rod Blank

Model	Length	Line	Tip	Butt	Oz.	Price
SFS679-3B	7¾	6/7	5	.540	2⅞	$38-$39

Cor, Sho

Sage Graphite Blanks

Model	Length	Line	Tip	Butt	Oz.	Price
GFL470B	7	4	4½	.310	1⅛	$96
GFL476B	7½	4	4½	.330	1³⁄₁₆	$100
GFL576B	7½	5	5	.335	1¼	$100
GFL580B	8	5	5	.355	1⁵⁄₁₆	$103
GFL680B	8	6	5	.365	1⅜	$103
GFL586B	8½	5	5	.360	1⅜	$107
GFL686B	8½	6	5½	.375	1½	$107
GFL786B	8½	7	5½	.385	1¾	$107
GFL886B	8½	8	5½	.400	2	$107
GFL789B	8¾	7	5½	.415	2	$107
GFL490B	9	4	4½	.370	2	$110
GFL590B	9	5	5	.380	2	$110
GFL690B	9	6	5½	.390	1¹³⁄₁₆	$114
GFL790B	9	7	5½	.400	1¹⁵⁄₁₆	$114
GFL890B	9	8	5½	.410	2	$114
GFL891B	9	8	5½	.425	2⅜	$114
GFL896B	9½	8	5½	.420	2³⁄₁₆	$126
GFL996B	9½	9	5½	.435	2⅜	$126
GFL1096B	9½	10	6	.450	2⅝	$126
GFL10106B	10½	10	5	.575	2⅝	$156 (Kau only)

T&T, Kau, Cor, Fly, Sho, Edd

Sage Graphite II Blanks

Model	Length	Line	Tip	Butt	Oz.	Price
GFL480RPB	8	4	4½	.370	1⁵⁄₁₆	$118
GFL686RPB	8½	6	5	.380	1⁹⁄₁₆	$121
GFL590RPB	9	5	4½	.390	1¾	$124
GFL690RPB	9	6	5	.400	1⅞	$128
GFL790RPB	9	7	5	.405	1¹⁵⁄₁₆	$128
GFL890RPB	9	8	5	.410	2	$128
GFL990RPB	9	9	5½	.420	2⅛	$132
GFL1190RPB	9	11	5½	.500	3¼	$158
GFL1290RPB	9	12	6	.520	3½	$162
GFL596RPB	9½	5	5	.415	2	$135
GFL696RPB	9½	6	5	.425	2⅛	$138
GFL796RPB	9½	7	5	.430	2⅜	$138
GFL896RPB	9½	8	5	.435	2½	$138
GFL996RPB	9½	9	5½	.440	2⅝	$142
GFL7100RPB	10	7	5	.475	2⅜	$148

Sho, Fly, Kau, Cor

Sage Three-Piece Graphite Blanks

Model	Length	Line	Tip	Butt	Oz.	Price
GFL589-3B	8¾	5	5	.410	2	$126
GFL693-3B	9¼	6	5	.480	2⅜	$130
GFL796-3B	9½	7	5	.500	2⁷⁄₁₆	$135
GFL699-3B	9¾	6	5	.505	3	$137

Model	Length	Line	Tip	Butt	Oz.	Price
GFL8100-3B	10	8	5	.530	2⁹⁄₁₆	$150
GFL9140-3B	14	9	6	.750	5½	$195
GFL9160-3B	16	9	6	.835	7	$225

Fly, Kau, Cor

Sage Four-Piece Graphite Travel Rod Blanks

Model	Length	Line	Tip	Butt	Oz.	Price
GFL583-4B	8¼	5	5	.410	1¾	$127
GFL783-4B	8¼	7	5	.430	2⅜	$132

Cor, Kau

Scott PowR-Ply Rods

Scott PowR-Ply Graphite Blanks

Model	Length	Line	Price
G75-3	7½	3	$150
G75-4	7½	4	$150-$155
G75-5	7½	5	$150
G80-4	8	4	$150-$155
G80-5	8	5	$150-$155
G80-6	8	6	$150
G85-5	8½	5	$156-$158
G85-6	8½	6	$156-$158
G85-7	8½	7	$168
G90-3	9	3	$156-$158
G90-4	9	4	$156-$158
G90-5	9	5	$156-$158
G90-6	9	6	$156-$158
G90-7	9	7	$165-$168
G90-8	9	8	$168
G95-8	9½	8	$170-$174
G95-9	9½	9	$170-$174
G95-10	9½	10	$173-$177
G100-4	10	4	$162-$167
G100-5	10	5	$162-$167
G100-6	10	6	$165-$174
G100-7	10	7	$170-$174
G100-8	10	8	$170-$174

Mur, Fly, or Scott PowR-Ply, 765 Clementina Street, San Francisco, California 94103 (415) 864-1611

Scott PowR-Ply Graphite Bass Rod Blanks

Model	Length	Line	Price
G85-7B	8½	7/8	$174
G90-7B	9	7/8	$170-$174
G95-8B	9½	8/9	$177

Fly, Mur, or Scott (see address above)

Scott PowR-Ply Three-Piece Graphite Travel Rod Blanks

Model	Length	Line	Price
G70-4/3	6'10"	4	$165
G70-5/3	6'10"	5	$165
670-6/3	6'10"	6	$165
G75-4/3	7'7"	4	$168
G75-5/3	7'7"	5	$168
G95-5/3	9½	5	$220
G95-6/3	9½	6	$227
G95-7/3	9½	7	$227

Mur, Fly, or Scott (see address above)

Scott PowR-Ply Four-Piece Graphite Travel Rod Blanks

Model	Length	Line	Price
G90-5/4	9	5	$195-$220
G90-6/4	9	6	$195-$220
G90-7/4	9	7	$207-$227
G100-7/4	10	7	$233
G100-84	10	8	$233

Fly, Mur, or Scott (see address above)

Shakespeare Fiberglass Blank

Model	Length	Line	Tip	Butt	Oz.	Price
12-0443B	9	10/11	6½	.602	4⅞	$25.80-$42.87

Cor, Pfe

Skyline Graphite Blank

Model	Length	Line	Tip	Butt	Oz.	Price
SKF8007B	8	7	5	.340	1¾	$51.50

Cor

Tackle Shop Rods

Tackle Shop Custom Graphite Blanks

Model	Length	Line	Tip	Butt	Oz.	Price
GF704	7	4/5	4½	.265	¾	$40.85
GF765	7½	5/6	4½	.285	1	$43.39
GF806	8	6/7	4½	.305	1⅛	$46.45
GF807	8	7/8	4½	.345	1¼	$46.45
GF866	8½	6/7	4½	.310	1¼	$50.19
GF867	8½	7/8	4½	.350	1¼	$50.19
GF908	9	8/9	5	.325	1⅞	$52.79
GF909	9	9/10	5	.405	2	$52.79

Tac

Tackle Shop Custom Boron Blanks

Model	Length	Line	Tip	Butt	Oz.	Price
BF765	7½	5/6	4	.270	1	$64.85
BF806	8	6/7	4	.310	1⅛	$66.99
BF866	8½	6/7	4	.330	1³⁄₁₆	$69.55
BF908	9	8/9	4½	.360	1¾	$66.85
BF967	9½	7/8	4½	.410	2⅛	$75.99

Tac

Walt Carpenter Bamboo Blanks

Model	Length	Line	Price
63	6¼	3/4	$225-$295
66	6½	4	$225-$295
70	7	4	$225-$295
73	7¼	4/5	$225-$295
65	7½	5	$225-$295
66	7½	6	$225-$295
806	8	6	$225-$295

Mur

COMPONENTS

Reel Seats

When I'm selecting components for a rod, I spend the most time on the reel seat. The reel seat is important to the appearance of the finished rod, and it's very important to the rod's function.

Basic reel seats are aluminum throughout. Quality and price vary considerably. Finishes on these reel seats are clear aluminum or anodized black or brown. In the listings, all-aluminum reel seats are designated by "body: aluminum". Color is listed with the description of the metal used, as in "metal: clear aluminum". Reel seats built for saltwater and other heavy-duty uses are generally all-aluminum.

Other reel seats use metal "skeletons", usually aluminum or nickel silver, with a different body material. That body material is referred to as an insert, and it is commonly made of cork or wood. The woods used are often exotic, and picking one out is one of the pleasures of rod building. As usual, it's best done in person. If you're ordering from a catalog, it's important to know the woods. A reel seat of zebra wood looks considerably different from one of rosewood.

Reel seats are listed by brand and model. The reel locking feature is listed next. Up-locking is designated by UL, down-locking by DL, and slip rings or slide bands by SR. If more than one code is listed, the reel seat is available in several styles. (For a description of these reel mounting systems, see Chapter 2.) Inside and outside diameters of the reel seats and their lengths are listed when available.

Beartooth USSS, DSS. *UL, DL; metal: clear aluminum; body: walnut, bocote, coco bola, maple.*
$22-$22.50 Bea
Beartooth NSUS, NSDS, NBUS, NBDS. *UL, DL; metal: nickel silver; body: walnut, bocote, coco bola, cherry, maple.*
$22-$32.50 Bea
Beartooth CRN, CRNS, NSB. *SR; metal: nickel silver; body: walnut, bocote, coco bolo, cherry, maple.*
$14-$20 Bea

Benchmark FW-1. *DL; I.D.: .365"; length: 3¾"; metal: clear aluminum; body: rosewood, ebony, zebra wood, burl walnut.*
$39.50-$49.50 Bul

Benchmark FW-2. *DL; I.D.: .300"; length: 3¾"; metal:*

clear aluminum; body: rosewood, ebony, zebra wood, burl walnut.
$39.50-$49.50 Bul

Benchmark FW-3. *SR; I.D.: .325"; length: 3¾"; metal: nickel silver; body: rosewood, ebony, zebra wood, burl walnut.*
$42.50-$52.50 Bul

Benchmark FW-4, FW-7. *UL, DL; I.D.: .610"; length: 3½"; metal: clear aluminum; body: aluminum.*
$24.50-$27.50 Bul

Benchmark FW-5, FW-6. *DL, SR; I.D.: .275"; length: 3⅞"; metal: clear aluminum; body: cork.*
$19.50-$27.50 Bul

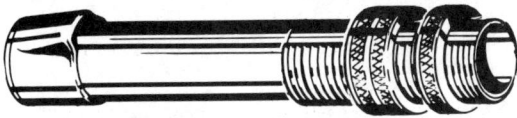

Cal-Air CA-2. *DL; I.D.: 9/16"; length: 3⅞"; metal: black or gold aluminum; body: aluminum.*
$9.25 Bul

Cal-Air CA-3. *DL; I.D.: ⅝"; length: 3⅞"; metal: black or gold aluminum; body: aluminum.*
$9-$9.70 RLW, Bul

Clemens The Limestone. *DL; I.D.: .375"; length: 4"; metal: nickel silver; body: maple, walnut.*
$39.95 Dal

Clemens The R. French. *SR; I.D.: .375"; length: 3¾"; metal: nickel silver; body: walnut.*
$19.95 Dal

Clemens Reel-Lok. *UL, DL; I.D.: .586"; O.D.: .750"; metal: clear or black aluminum; body: chrome.*
$14.45 Dal

Clemens Walnut Reel Seat. *DL; I.D.: .388"; metal: clear or black aluminum; body: walnut.*
$16.95 Dal

Clemens Classic. *SR; I.D.: ⅜"; O.D.: ¾"; length: 3⅜; metal: clear aluminum; body: teak.*
$12.95 Dal

Clemens Elite. *UL; metal: clear aluminum; body: teak (with fighting butt).*
$25.95 Dal

Clemens Fly Reel Seat. *UL, DL; I.D.: .623"; O.D.: .750"; metal: clear or black aluminum; body: aluminum.*
$9.95-$11.49 Dal

Clemens Skeleton Seat. *UL, DL; I.D.: .623"; metal: clear or black aluminum; body: maple, walnut, rosewood, ebony.*
$11.72-$14.80 Dal

Cuddy Double Lock. *DL; I.D.: ⅝"; metal: clear aluminum; body: aluminum.*
$2.50 Dan

Fenwick Salmon/steelhead. *UL, DL; I.D.: .625"; length: 4"; metal: brown or black aluminum; body: aluminum.*
$8.25 H&H

Fuji FPS. *DL; I.D.: ⅝"; length: 4½"; metal: stainless steel; body: graphite-filled nylon, black or woodgrain.*
$4.25-$7.61 EJH, Don, Cab, Sho, Mer, Tac, Pfe, Spo, Cor, H&H, Dal

Ed Gausdal. *UL; length: 3¾"; metal: clear or black aluminum; body: rosewood, mesquite, walnut, coco bola, birch/walnut, bengay, maple.*
$14.95-$16.99 Fly, Pfe

Lakeland. *UL; I.D.: 5/8"; O.D.: 3/4"; length: 4 1/16"; metal: gold and clear aluminum; body: aluminum.*
$1.15-$1.35 Bul, Dal, Sho

Landmark Agatewood Whitewater. *UL; metal: clear or black aluminum; body: rosewood with clear; mesquite with black.*
$23.95 Kau
Landmark Agatewood Clearwater. *UL, DL; metal: clear or black aluminum; body: mesquite, rosewood, chestnut.*
$16.95 Kau
Landmark Agatewood Springwater. *DL, SR; metal: clear or black aluminum; body: rosewood, walnut.*
$12.95 Kau
North Fork. *SR; O.D.: 5/8"; length: 3 1/8"; metal: nickel silver; body: ebony, maple, rosewood, tsuge, sanderwood, briar, tagayasan.*
$31.95 Nor
Orvis Reversed Full Metal. *UL; metal: clear aluminum; body: aluminum.*
$35 Orv
Orvis Western. *UL; metal: satin-finish aluminum; body: cork.*
$20 Orv
Orvis Cork Locking. *UL, DL; metal: clear aluminum; body: cork.*
$16 Orv
Orvis Black Metal. *DL; metal: black aluminum; body: aluminum.*
$10 Orv
Orvis Extended Walnut. *UL; metal: clear aluminum; body: walnut (with extension butt).*
$40 Orv
Orvis Presentation Zebra Wood. *UL; metal: black aluminum; body: zebra.*
$30 Orv
Orvis "125". *UL, DL, SR; metal: nickel silver; body: maple.*
$40-$50 Orv
Orvis Walnut Locking. *UL, DL; metal: clear aluminum; body: walnut.*
$20 Orv, Dan, Kau
Orvis Superfine. *SR; metal: clear aluminum; body: cork.*
$13 Orv
Powell. *UL; I.D.: 5/8"; O.D.: 7/8"; length: 3 1/2"; metal: clear, black, or gold aluminum; body: aluminum.*
$8.50-$12 Kau, Cor, Dan, Fly, Pfe

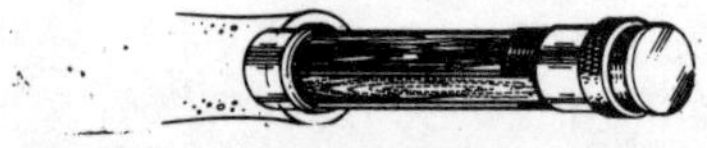

REC NSU, NSD. *UL, DL; I.D.: 5/16"; length: 3 3/4"; metal: nickel silver; body: coco bola, Spanish cedar, walnut, maple.*
$32.50 Tac, Hun

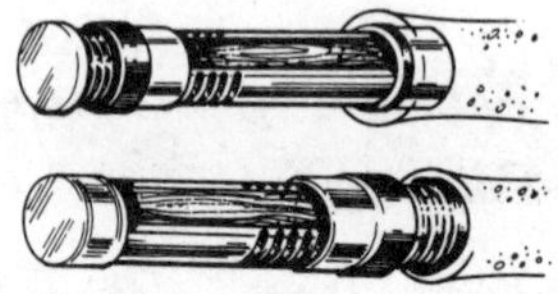

REC USS, DSL. *UL, DL; I.D.: 5/16"; length: 3 1/8"; metal: clear aluminum; body: coco bola, walnut, maple.*
$21 Tac

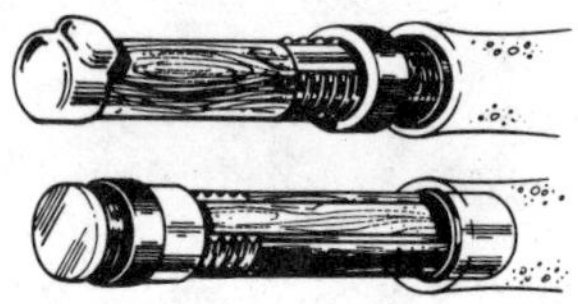

REC USSS, DSS. *UL, DL; I.D.: 5/16"; length: 3 5/8"; metal: clear aluminum; body: coco bola, walnut, maple.*
$24 Tac
REC USSL. *UL; I.D.: 5/16"; length: 3 1/4"; metal: clear aluminum; body: coco bola, walnut, maple.*
$24 Tac
REC NBDN. *SR; length: 3 5/8"; metal: nickel; body: nickel spacer.*
$19.50 Hun
REC CRN. *SR; length: 3 1/2"; metal: nickel; body: coco bola, Spanish cedar, walnut, maple.*
$20 Hun, Tac

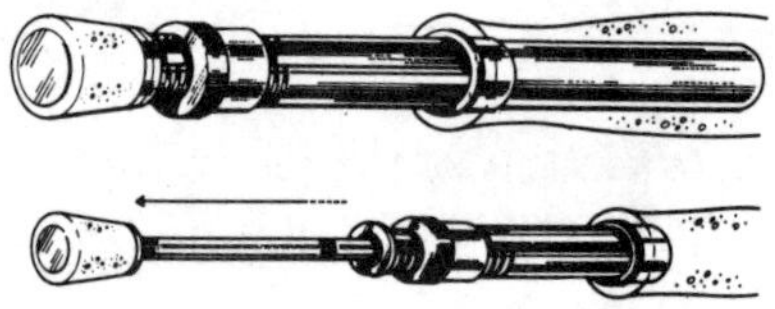

REC REBU. *UL; length: 4 3/8"; metal: clear aluminum; body: aluminum (with fighting butt and cork handle).*
$39.50-$45 Tac, Hun, Bea
Reed's 100. *DL; I.D.: 5/8"; O.D.: 3/8"; length: 3 3/4"; metal: clear aluminum; body: cork, rosewood.*
$8.25-$9.60 Ree
Reed's 300, 350. *DL; I.D.: 5/8"; length: 3 3/4"; metal: brown and gold aluminum; body: aluminum.*
$5.85-$5.96 Ree
Rodon Standard 100. *UL, DL; I.D.: 5/8"; O.D.: 13/16"; length: 4 1/8"; metal: clear, brown, or black aluminum; body: aluminum.*
$9.75-$14.95 Cor, Kau, Don, H&H, Tac, Hun, Edd, Dan, Pfe

Rodon Custom 200. *UL, DL; I.D.: 3/8"; O.D.: .694"; length: 3 3/8"; metal: clear, brown, or black aluminum;*

body: cork, bubinga, chestnut, rosewood, ebony, zebra, walnut, teak.
$10.60-$18.30 EJH, Dan, Fly, Hun, Mur, Kau, Tac, T&T, Pfe, Don

Rodon 308. *SR; I.D.: ¾”; O.D.: ¹³/₁₆”; length: 4”; metal: nickel silver bands, aluminum butt plate; body: cork, flared.*
$10-$15.95 Kau, Don, Dan
Rodon 309. *SR; length: 3½”; metal: nickel silver band and butt plate; body: cork.*
$11.80-$12.95 Hun, Dan, Don, Kau
Rodon Double Lock. *UL, DL; metal: clear, black, or brown aluminum; body: aluminum.*
$10.42-$14.80 EJH, Edd, Kau, Hun, Don, H&H
Sentimentalist. *SR; body: teak.*
$12.95 Fly

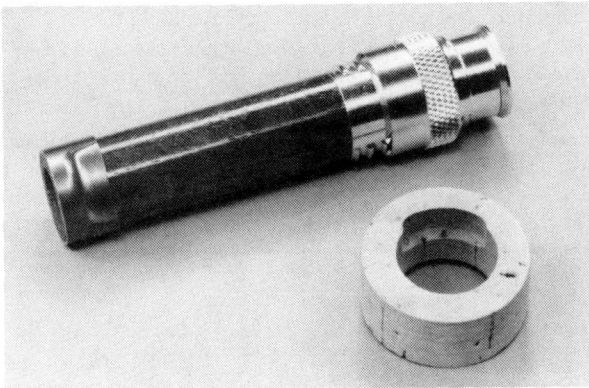

Struble Deluxe. *UL, DL; I.D.: .360”; metal: clear or black aluminum; body: walnut, coco bola, rosewood, teak, zebra.*
$18-$18.90 Sho, Bul

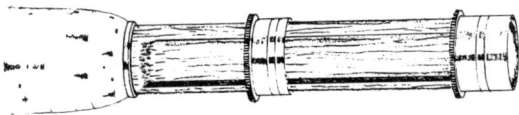

Struble Classic. *SR; I.D.: ⅜”; length: 3¼”; metal: clear or black aluminum; body: teak, cork.*
$10-$10.95 Cor, Sho, Bul

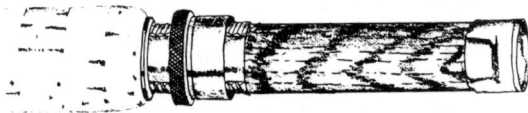

Struble Standard. *UL, DL; I.D.: .360”; metal: clear or black aluminum; body: walnut, rosewood, coco bola, teak, zebra.*
$10.65-$11.30 Bul, Sho

Struble Salt Water. *UL; metal: black aluminum; body: aluminum.*
$25.95 Bul

Struble U-9. *UL; I.D.: .360”; metal: clear aluminum; body: walnut*
$20.35 Bul
T&T Nickel Silver. *UL, DL; I.D.: 5/16”; O.D.: .720”; length: 3¾”; metal: nickel silver; body: black walnut.*
$32 T&T
T&T Nickel Silver. *SR; I.D.: 5/16”; O.D.: .715”; length: 3½”; metal: nickel silver; body: walnut.*
$20 T&T
Varmac Skeleton Seat. *UL, DL; I.D.: ¼-¾”; length: 3”; metal: black or brown aluminum; body: oak, black walnut, cork.*
$2.07-$6.95 EJH, Mer, Cor, Sho, Tac, Pfe, Dal, Edd
Varmac FRSA. *DL; I.D.: .555-.781”; O.D.: 5/8-11/16”; length: 4⅛-4½; metal: black, brown, or gold and brown aluminum; body: aluminum.*
$2.50-$5.50 Mer, Pfe, Tac, Sho, Dal, Ran, Fly, Edd, Kau, H&H, Cor, Egg, Mur, Bul

Extension Butts

Extension (or fighting) butts are used by fly fishermen pursuing big game fish. With the butt in place, the rod can be held against the belly for extra leverage.

Rodon removable plug. *To allow addition of a fighting butt to Rodon reel seats; clear, brown, black.*
$1.30-$1.70 H&H, Kau, Cor, Don, Mer
Cal-Air extension butt. *3”; for Cal-Air CA-3.*
$15 RLW
Powell extension butt. *Black anodized.*
$19.95 Fly
Rodon extension butts. *2½”, 5”; push-in type; for Rodon 100 series reel seats.*
$4.21-$8.45, $4.53-$11.40 Mer, Don, Edd, Kau, Tac, Hun, H&H, Dan
Rodon extension butts. *2½”, 5”; clear, brown, black aluminum or cork insert; for Rodon 200 series reel seats.*
$2.52-$6.25, $2.84-$4.35 H&H, Mer, Don, Hun, Kau, T&T
Benchmark E-1 extension butt. *Cork; for Benchmark FW-4 reel seat.*
$12.50 Bul
Clemens extension butts. *Cork or metal; for Clemens reel seats.*
$8.29-$9.95 Dal

Turning Stock

If you're a master woodworker, you may enjoy turning your own reel seat inserts. Here's the rough stock from which to do that.

Customwood Turning Stock. *18" long; walnut, rosewood, ebony.*
$3.47-$6.99 Dal

Handles

Your choice of handles is very important to the comfort you'll enjoy as you cast your rod. One of the biggest advantages of building your own rod comes from being able to select a favorite grip style from among many choices when a ready-made rod may only offer one or two styles. (For more information on choosing a handle, see Chapter 2.)

Fenwick Hand Hugger Foam. *Half wells; 7¼".*
$1.95 Cab; H&H and Pfe (with reel seat)
Orvis. *Full wells; 7".*
$10 Orv
Orvis. *Reversed half wells; 7".*
$10 Orv
Orvis. *Superfine; 6½".*
$10 Orv
Orvis. *Western.*
$10 Orv
Orvis. *Cigar; 6½".*
$10 Orv

Rodon. *Tapered; I.D.: ⁵⁄₁₆"; 7".*
$3.99-$5.69 Don, Mer, H&H, Tac

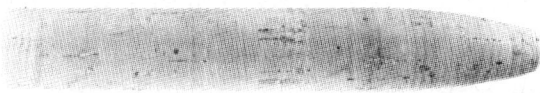

Rodon. *Cigar; I.D.: ⁵⁄₁₆"; 7".*
$3.99-$5.69 Mer, Tac, H&H, Don

Rodon. *Western; I.D.: ⁵⁄₁₆"; 7".*
$3.99-$5.20 H&H, Don, Mer

Rodon. *Full wells; I.D.: ⁵⁄₁₆"; 7".*
$3.99-$5.20 Don, H&H, Mer

Rodon. *Half wells; I.D.: ⁵⁄₁₆"; 7".*
$3.99-$5.20 Mer, Don, H&H

Rodon. *Perfect; I.D.: ⁵⁄₁₆"; 7".*
$3.99-$5.20 Don, Mer, H&H
Store brand or no-name handles. *Perfectionist, Phillipe, Fenwick, cigar, western, full wells, half wells; variety of sizes.*
$1.49-$6.75 Many catalogs

Special Handles and Sealants

If you would like to create a handle from scratch, cork rings and pre-glued cork sticks are available. Once mounted on the blank, they can be turned or worked with rasp and sandpaper to create any size or shape handle you wish.

Cork rings. *O.D.: 1⅛"-1½"; I.D.: ⅛"-½"; ½" thick.*
$.14-$.45 Most catalogs
Burnt cork trim rings. *O.D.: 1⅛"; width: ³⁄₃₂", ³⁄₁₆".*
$.45 Dal
Floret cork rings. *1¼"x³⁄₁₆"; extra-select.*
$.75 Bul
Pre-glued cork sticks. *18", 36" long; ⅜" hole; 1⅛" diameter; ready to turn on lathe.*
$3.50-$3.95, $7.45 Dal, Pfe
Pre-glued cork sticks. *8"; ready to turn on lathe.*
$4 Orv
Clemens Cork Filler Adhesive. *Mix with sanding residue to form paste; apply, dry; fills pits in handle.*
$1.99 Dal
Clemens Cork Sealant. *Penetrant; prolongs life of handles.*
$2.89 Dal
Urethane Cork Sealer. *Seals cork; toughens without changing color or feel.*
$3.75-$4.07 Mer, Ste

Winding Checks

Winding checks are placed on top of the handle to protect the handle and to give a smooth surface to wind against.

Benchmark WC-1, WC-2. *I.D.: .236"-.394"; small and medium widths; nickel silver.*
$3 Bul

Clemens Customwood Hosels. *I.D.: .250", .375";*
walnut, rosewood, ebony; replaces winding check; will
match your reel seat.
$3.99 Dal
Cust-O-Checks. *¼" long; brown, black; I.D.: 16/64"-35/*
64".
$.55 Dal
Fenwick. *I.D.: .200"-.950" (13-48/64"); dark brown.*
$.29-$.49 Cor, Mer, H&H, Pfe, Bul
Nickel silver. *I.D.: .236"-.394" (16-31/64").*
$2.50-$3.50 Hun, T&T, Don, Bea
Rodon. *I.D.: .190"-.850"; black hard rubber.*
$.35-$.60 Mer, Pfe

Rod Guides and Tip Tops

Properly sized and placed guides are essential to the
action of your rod. Their purpose is to control the line
and keep it from slapping on the rod while still allowing
the free flow of line during casting.

There are a number of ways to determine proper size
and placement. The easiest is to use the specifications
gained by holding your blank next to the company's
ready-made rod. This is often possible when dealing with
your local shop. Many of the catalog companies provide
a spacing chart.

If you space your guides using suggested placement or
your best guess, you can judge the proper placement by
attaching the guides with masking tape and running fly
line through them. If they are too far apart, the line will
make a severe angle compared to the arc of the rod as
it's gently bent over. Too many guides can alter the action
of the rod, so use only enough to get a smooth line feed.

There are two general types of rod guides: snake and
ringed. Snake guides are traditional guides made of a
single wire bent to form a loop for the line. Ringed guides
generally combine a circular wire with a center insert of
aluminum oxide, silicone carbide, or other hard material.
Both are combined with ringed stripping guides. (Stripping guides are the larger guides nearest the reel.) Plain
stainless steel stripping guides are out of vogue, but some
rod companies, Deerfield for instance, are going back to
the plain stripping guides because they believe the
ceramic-type inserts are hard on fly lines.

Aetna Foulproof guides might be considered a third
type of guide. They have a double wire loop, which makes
them distinctive in appearance. In function, however,
they are similar to the ringed guides described above.

Fuji introduced single-foot ringed guides a few years
ago. These look nifty and work fine, but their effect on
rod action is still being debated. They are lighter, and
because they have only one foot to wrap, they require
less thread. The weight-savings should make the rod
faster. However, some rod builders argue that more and
longer wraps on a rod will stiffen it, making it faster. It
could be that the two factors here come out about even.
The action of two otherwise identical rods, one with
single-foot guides and the other with traditional guides,

may be indistinguishable. We fly fishermen have been
known to overthink things.

Rod guides do wear out and should be checked often
as a rod "ages". Imperfections and grooves in guides will
destroy fly lines and cost you much more than having
new guides put on. Check guides and tip top by running
a cotton ball over and through them. Tufts of cotton left
on the guides indicate wear. If you don't want to replace
guides yourself, most fly shops offer this service.

The listings for Fuji guides, incidentally, may be a bit
confusing. I put in all the Fuji guides that I found, and
there seems to be quite a bit of overlap between guides
designed for spin fishing and those designed for fly
fishing. Here are the models that Fuji says are for fly
fishing: SG with NSG stripping guides, BZG with
BBNHG stripping guides, BSPHG, SPHG.

Rod Guides

Aetna Foulproof Fly Rod. *Stainless steel loop wire; I.D:*
5/32"-5/16".
$.50-$1 Mer, EJH, Sho, Ree, Dal, Cor
Aetna Foulproof Ultra Light Fly Rod. *Stainless steel*
loop wire; I.D.: 5/32"-⅞".
$.50-$1.55 Mer, Cor, Dal, EJH, Ree, Sho
Custom Ultralight Ceramic. *Single-foot; ceramic guide*
ring.
$.80-$1.08 Dal

Fuji BNHG Hard Speed. *Dbl.-foot; I.D.: 6-16; aluminum*
oxide guide ring, polymer shock ring; black with
luminous ring.
$.52-$1.26 Don, Tac, Pfe, Spo, Fly, Mer, Sho, H&H, Pfe,
EJH, Cor
Fuji BBNHG Hard Speed. *Dbl.-foot, I.D.: 10, 12;*
similar to BNHG but with black frame and ring.
$.62-$1.50 EJH, Mer, Kau, Sho
Fuji NHG Hard Speed. *Dbl.-foot; I.D.: 6-16; similar to*
BHNG but clear frame with black shock ring.
$.42-$1.04 Don, Mer, EJH, Pfe, Sho
Fuji BLVLG Hardloy. *Single-foot; I.D.: 7-16; lighter*
than aluminum oxide; gray ring, no shock ring; black
frame.
$.51-$.89 Mer, Spo, Tac, Don
Fuji LVLG Hardloy. *Single-foot; I.D.: 7-16; similar to*
BLVLG but with clear finish.
$.44-$.85 Spo, Don, Mer

Fuji BSHG Hard Speed. *Triple-braced; I.D.: 6-16; similar to BNHG but triple-braced high frame to reduce line flap.*
$.65-$1.55 Tac, EJH, Ran, Edd, Sho, Pfe, Dan
Fuji SHG Hard Speed. *Triple-braced; I.D.: 6-16; similar to BSHG but clear frame with black shock ring.*
$.43-$1.10 Pfe, EJH, Mer, Tac, Sho

Fuji BSPHG Hard Speed Ultra-Lite. *Single-foot; I.D.: 6-30; aluminum oxide guide ring, polymer shock ring; black finish.*
$.46-$2.48 Bul, Tac, Cor, Sho, Fly, Pfe, Edd, Mer, EJH
Fuji SPHG Hard Speed Ultra-Lite. *Single-foot; I.D.: 6-30; similar to BSPHG but with clear finish.*
$.41-$2.22 Bul, Mer, Pfe, EJH, Cor

Fuji BZG Hard Speed. *Single-foot; I.D.: 6-12; aluminum oxide guide ring; no shock ring; black frame.*
$.70-$1.38 Mer, Kau, Sho, Cor, Pfe, H&H, EJH
Fuji NSG Silicone Carbide. *I.D.: 6-16; silicone carbide guide ring.*
$1.45-$4.26 Mer, Sho, Tac, Don, Pfe, H&H
Fuji SG Silicone Carbide. *Single-foot; I.D.: 5½-10; silicone carbide guide ring.*
$1.55-$3.20 Cor, Dal, H&H, Spo, Don, Sho, Bul, Mer, Pfe

Perfection SSGB. *Stainless steel snake; I.D.: 2/0-9; black finish.*
$.08-$.25 Edd, Kau, T&T, Spo, Sho, Pfe, H&H, Cor, EJH, Mer, Don, Bul, Dal
Perfection SSGP. *Stainless steel snake; I.D.: 2/0-6; clear finish.*
$.08-$.25 Many catalogs
Perfection SSGC. *Stainless steel snake; I.D.: 2/0-9; hard-chrome plated.*
$.20-$.45 Many catalogs

Perfection ACGR, ACS. *Stripping guide; I.D.: 6-12; aluminum-oxide ring, nylon shock ring; chrome or black frame.*
$.85-$2.30 Many catalogs

Perfection WCS. *Stripping guide; I.D.: 8-16; stainless steel, hard-chrome plated.*
$.50-$.95 Tac, Mur, Bul, Pfe, Edd, Spo, Sho
Varmac Aluminum Oxide. *Stripping guide; I.D./size: 8-16; aluminum oxide.*
$1.25 Kau

Tip Tops

Tip tops are the final connection between your rod and your line. They are one of the first guides to show wear, along with the stripping guides.

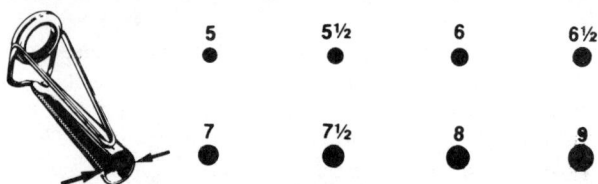

The diameters of the tubes on tip tops are sized for the rod tip in 64ths of an inch. These are commonly stated as a simple number, 4½, for instance. The most common type of tip top is the wire loop model from Perfection. Aetna Foulproof tip tops are made in the style of their guides. No size is listed for Aetna tip tops since they're adjustable for nearly any fly rod. Fuji tip tops match their guides, and the suggested match is given here when available. Fuji lists the following tip tops as being for fly rods: BZT, LST, MHT, BMHT. The size of the tip top's ring is also given when available.

After watching a friend fish for a day on the Bighorn without his tip top, I'd recommend that you carry an extra as well as a stick of ferrule cement in your fishing vest. Rods just don't work very well without a tip top.

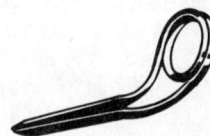

Aetna Foul-Proof. *Adj. diameter; ring size: ³/₁₆"-³/₈"; stainless steel wire.*
$.70-$1 Sho, Ree, Dal, EJH

Custom Ultralight Ceramic. *4½-6; ceramic insert.*
$1.39 Dal

Fuji BLLT Hardloy. *4-6½; aluminum oxide, no shock ring; black finish; use with BLVLG guides.*
$.69-$.89 Don, Spo
Fuji LLT Hardloy. *4-6½; similar to BLLT but with clear finish; use with LVLG guides.*
$.61-$.89 Spo, Don

Fuji BMHT Hard Speed Ultra-Lite. *4½-7½; ring size: 6-8; aluminum oxide, black frame, white ring; use with BNHG, BSPHG, BSHG guides.*
$.88-$1.48 Bul, Edd, Sho, Ran, EJH, Tac, Pfe, Mer, Cor
Fuji MHT Hard Speed Ultra-Lite. *4.5-7.5; ring size: 6-8; similar to BMHT but with clear frame, black ring.*
$.85-$1.32 Cor, Mer, Sho, EJH, Pfe
Fuji BZG Hard Speed. *6-10; ring size: 6-7; aluminum oxide, black frame; use with BSHG, BBNHG guides.*
$.74-$1.20 Bul, Cor

Fuji BZT Hard Speed. *3.5-6; ring size: 6-7; aluminum oxide, black finish; use with BZG guides.*
$1-$1.95 Bul, Mer, Pfe, Sho, Fly, Kau, H&H, EJH, Cab, Dan
Fuji LST Silicone Carbide. *3.5-6; ring size: 7; silicon carbide ring in gunsmoke frame; use with SG guides.*
$1.85-$2.96 Bul, Don, Cor, Spo, Sho, H&H, Mer, Dal, Pfe
Fuji PST Silicone Carbide. *5-7; silicone carbide ring; use with NSG guides.*
$2.09-$3.80 Tac, Spo, Sho, Bul, Pfe
Mildrum Mildarbide Fly Top. *4 ½-8; carboloy.*
$2.05 Cor
Perfection. *4-7; ceramic.*
$1.24-$1.30 EJH, Pfe

Perfection PBF. *4-7; stainless steel loop; black finish.*
$.55-$.99 RLW, Mer, H&H, Bul, Spo, Tac, Cor, Pfe, Kau, Sho, T&T, EJH, Edd, Dal
Perfection PCF. *4-7; stainless steel loop, chrome-plated.*
$.55-$1.40 Ree, RLW, Ran, Sho, Tac, T&T, Pfe, Spo, Fly, Mur, Mer, Cor, Bea, Kau, Fre, H&H, Edd, Don, Dan, EJH, Don, Bul, Dal

Hookkeepers

Hookkeepers are mounted immediately above the handle to give you a convenient place to hang your fly while on the move. The traditional style is simply a wire bent in a square shape. Flies will get their hackles bent if kept in that type of hookkeeper for long.

A bit fancier is the strap-and-ring type. The ring is secured to the blank with the strap. It will move during casting and will pull down close to the rod while in use, thus crushing hackles. Looks great, but not very practical unless it's glued to stand straight out from the rod.

The Fenwick hookkeeper stands off the rod enough to protect hackles, and you should try it if you're concerned about that problem. The dry fly hookkeeper from Dale Clemens will also help protect hackles.

Design-It. *6" material; 14 colors; nylon-covered, tempered wire; you bend to whatever shape you desire.*
$4.95 Dal

Dry fly. *Chrome.*
$.39 Dal

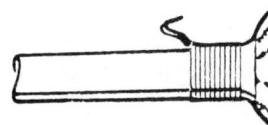

Fenwick. *Black or chrome; bent-back single foot.*
$.16-$.25 Cor, H&H, Spo, Sho, Bul, Mer
Single-foot. *Black, similar to Fenwick.*
$.49 Dal
Strap-and-ring. *Brass.*
$.35 T&T
Strap-and-ring. *Nickel silver.*
$.99-$2.25 Dal, Bea, Don, Bul

Strap-and-ring, stainless steel. *⅝" long; most made by Rodon.*
$1.04-$1.50 Don, T&T, Hun, Pfe, Fly, Mer, Cor, Edd, Kau, Dan,

Traditional loop. *Chrome or black; most made by Perfection.*
$.08-$.35 Many catalogs

Rod Winding Threads

Aside from its use in attaching guides and reinforcing ferrules, rod winding thread is most important as a decoration for your rod.

Your choice of colors shows something about yourself, too. Those who choose blacks and grays probably think Darth Vadir was the hero of *Star Wars*. Reds and yellows show a Type A personality, intense and extremely active streamside and elsewhere. Greens and browns belong to the woodsie group. Someday I'll write a book called *The Psychology of Rod Wrap Colors*.

Mostly choosing thread color is just fun. Many rod builders select a primary color for main wraps and a secondary color for trim wraps. In addition to color, you must also select thread size. Size A thread is the standard for all but the heaviest saltwater and salmon rods. For those heavier rods, you may prefer a size D.

You must also choose between standard thread and NCP (no color preserver required). Standard thread becomes translucent when finish is applied, unless it's first treated with a chemical color preserver. Without color preserver, the color of the blank will affect the final thread color, and with darker threads, the guide feet will show through. Even with color preserver, light colors lose some of their trueness.

NCP thread is opaque. Dale Clemens, in his book *Advanced Custom Rod Building*, recommends that NCP be used for all light colors—white, yellow, light blue and so on. For darker colors, however, he recommends standard thread, since the NCP threads lack "the sparkle and snap" of standard thread colors.

NCP thread, according to Dale, is subject to deterioration if stored in sunlight or under fluorescent light. After treatment with a rod finish, this is no longer a problem, but you should be careful in buying since many shops selling NCP thread may not be aware of the potential for deterioration. Dale also recommends that you take care with all threads to store them in a dust-free location and that, when handling them, you work with clean hands. Oils from your skin will be absorbed by the thread and can affect the final color.

Most threads are sold in 50 or 100 yard spools, but if you do a lot of rod building you may wish to buy in bulk. For cost comparisons, here's the amount you'll get in each thread size if you buy by the ounce: A = 1,200 yards/oz.; D = 575 yards/oz.; E = 400 yards/oz. When more than one spool size is offered, they are separated by a comma in the listings, and respective prices are also separated by a comma. Prices don't vary according to the size of the thread itself.

Danville NCP Standard. *Sizes: A, D; 50 yds.; colors: white, black, red, purple, yellow, gray, dk. brown, lt. brown, lt. blue, dk. blue, burnt orange, maroon, dk. green, green, gold, lt. gray.*
$.60-$.75 Dan, Cor, Bea, Fre
Danville NCP Two Tone. *Size: D; 50 yds.; colors:*

brown/black, yellow/black, white/black, orange/black.
$.60 Cor
Gudebrod Trimar Solids. *Mylar; size: D; 100 yds., 1 oz.; colors: silver, gold.*
$1.02-$1.55, $5.40-$5.95 Mer, Pfe, Tac, Sho, Bul, Cor, Spo, T&T
Gudebrod NCP, Trimar Two-tone Thread. *Mylar; size: C; 100 yds., 1 oz.; colors: black/silver, blue/silver, green/silver, red/silver, brown/silver, white/silver, black/gold, blue/gold, green/gold, red/gold, brown/gold, white/gold.*
$.78-$1.49, $3.17-$4.28 Tac, Mer, Bul, Cab, Dal, Pfe, Sho
Gudebrod NCP Standard. *Sizes: A, C, D; 1 oz.; colors: black, white, blue, sunburst, garnet, goldenrod, orange, dk. blue, rust, blue dun, tan, scarlet, candy apple red, maroon, dk. brown, hot pink, purple, brown, gray, chestnut, dk. green, yellow, green.*
$2.25-$3.15 Mer, Pfe, Cab, Spo, Cor, Sho, Tac, Bul, Dal
Gudebrod Standard. *Sizes: A, D, E; 100 yds., 1 oz.; colors: black, white, blue, sunburst, garnet, goldenrod, orange, dk. blue, rust, blue dun, tan, scarlet, candy apple red, maroon, gold metal, dk. brown, hot pink, purple, brown, gray, chestnut, dk. green, yellow, green, gun metal.*
$.54-$1, $2.34-$3.15 Many catalogs
Gudebrod Space Dyes. *Size: E; 100 yards, 1 oz.; colors: red/white, red/yellow, blue/gold.*
$ .94-$1.15, $3.29-$4.30 Tac, Mer, Cab, Cor, Pfe
Gudebrod Two Tone. *Sizes: A, E; 100 yds., 1 oz.; colors: black/white, black/yellow, black/orange.*
$ .62-$1.39, $2.65-$4.50 Mer, Sho, Dal, Tac, Fly, Pfe, Cab, Cor, T&T
Gudebrod Variegated. *Sizes: A, D, E; 100 yds., 1 oz.; colors: five color.*
$ .75-$1.28, $3.25-$5.30 Mer, Cor, Tac, Cab, Bul, Sho, Pfe
Holland Satin Finish. *Size: S/C; 400 yds.; colors: black, white, orange, yellow, royal blue, med. green, med. brown, med. gray, beige, dk. green, red, lt. purple, lt. gray, dk. brown.*
$2.37-$3.35 Mer, Bul
Holland Astro Nylon. *Nylon and mylar; size: S/C; 1 oz.; colors: black/silver, black/gold, blue/silver, blue/gold, green/silver, green/gold, red/silver, red/gold, brown/silver, brown/gold, white/silver, white/gold.*
$3.95 Bul
Orvis. *Nylon; size: A; 100 yds.; colors: gold, maroon, clear, black, boron blue, green, western red, gray, variegated gold, var. copper, var. gray, Orvis brown.*
$1 Orv
Metallic thread. *Polyester core, metallic outer thread; size: A; 71 yds.; colors: metallic gold, silver, copper, blue, red, green, mauve, brown, aqua, lt. blue, lt. green, rainbow, pearl*
$.99-$1.10 Dal, Cab (gold only), Cor

Weave Patterns

If you've been looking for something distinctive in the

way of decorative wraps, you might want to try weaving. You'll find a book on patterns in the chapter on books or you can buy weave patterns. The following is a sample of the weave patterns available from Dale Clemens.

Weave patterns. *Tarpon, rainbow, brown, bass, mermaid, stonefly nymph.*
$2.49 Dal

ROD BUILDING TOOLS AND CHEMISTRY

Rod Wrapping and Finishing Tools

Devices designed for rod wrapping and rod finishing range from the simple Gudebrod Rod Wrapper, which hangs on your rod and feeds thread while you turn the rod, to complete wrapping stands, which have adjustable-tension thread feeds and drying motors.

You can make an acceptable wrapping stand from a pair of coat hangers, using a heavy book to feed the thread while you turn the rod, but a stand with an adjustable thread feed is much more enjoyable. Thompson makes an inexpensive cast metal model that clamps on the table edge. Its disadvantage is that the rod holders are close together, requiring you to balance the rod manually. If the phone rings, you could be in trouble.

Besides the rod wrapping stands listed here, there are also rod drying stands with motors. These rotate the rod while the finish is drying. That's something the occasional rod builder does by hand, but for the person who builds a lot of rods, this is a necessity. The least expensive of these is the Porta-Turn. It's within the means of most hobbyists.

The items are listed in alphabetical order.

Cabela's Wrapping Stand. *6'; machined aluminum; adjustable thread tension.*
$79.95 Cab
Cabela's Wooden Wrapper. *40"; adjustable thread tension.*
$29.95 Cab
Coren's Finishing Machine. *Low rpm motor with rollers to hold rod.*
$49.50 Cor
Coren's Professional Rod Winder. *10 pound base holds winder steady; takes up to eight 50 yd. spools.*
$65 Cor
Coren's Jr. Rod Winder. *Smaller version of professional model; fits into vise conversion base.*
$27.50 Cor
Cure Master Rod Drying Stand. *Single or three rod models; rod supports with 2 rpm motor.*
Single—$27.99, triple—$69.99 Pfe

Drying motor. *Accessory for stand.*
$6.49-$49.95 Pfe, Dal, Cab, Cor, Bul, Mer, Tac

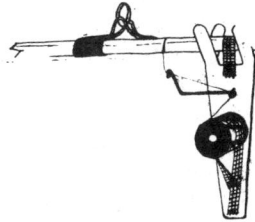

Gudebrod Rod Winder. *Hangs from rod; rod is rotated to wind thread.*
$4.93-$7.99 Pfe, T&T, Sho, Mer, EJH
Hand rod wrapping stands. *Variety of sizes and features, adjustable length, thread tension; can be used with drying motor.*
$34.95-$47.50 Dal, Bul, Orv, Sho, Mer
Port-A-Turn. *Battery-powered motor and rod cradle; turns rod at 2 rpm.*
$19.95-$29.95 H&H, Kau, Sho, Fly
Power Rod Wrapping Machine. *7'-8' board; stand with motor, variable speed foot control; optional drying motor.*
$149.95-$180 Bul, Cor, Mer
Rod bench electrification kit. *Motor, foot pedal, rheostat, wiring, rod holder.*
$34.95 Mer
Rod Builder's Lathe. *Aids in all facets of rod building.*
$249.95-$299 Dal, Pfe
Rod Master. *Variable size; black; rod supports and thread tensioner; clamps on table.*
$59.95 Pfe
Rod Master Jr.. *2', 3'; wood base, supports; adjustable thread tension.*
2'—$34.50; 3'—$39.50 Pfe
Seiders Hand Rod Wrapper. *46"; birch; adjustable length.*
$39.95 Tac

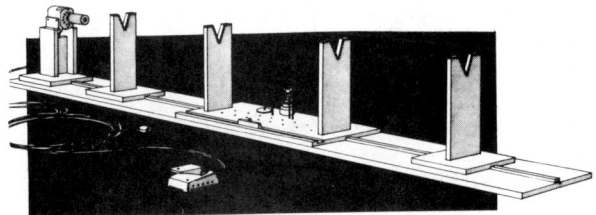

Seiders Power Rod Wrapper. *7'; birch; with motor, foot control.*
$149.95 Tac
Spool-Mate. *Cradle for rod; adjustable thread tension.*
$9.95-$10.95 Cor, Dal, EJH

Thompson Rod Winder. *C-clamp for attaching to table; adjustable thread tension.*
$9.95-$16.50 Spo, Cab, EJH, Edd, Ree, Tac, Mer, Fly, H&H, T&T, Kau, Cor, Dan

Special Aids for Rod Wrapping

The following special tools are designed to help in creating better wraps.

Alcohol lamp. *For burning off loose thread ends.*
$4.85-$5.99 Dal, Sho
Butt Wrap Alignment Tool. *Aids in creating decorative wraps.*
$9.95 Dal
Butt Wrapper. *Brass tool that allows up to nine threads to be wrapped at once.*
$6.89 Dal
Diamond Master. *Aids in creating diamond thread patterns.*
$6.99 Pfe
Wrap Master. *Aids in getting equal wraps.*
$.97 Pfe
Wrap Mate. *Holds loop for wraps out of way.*
$2.29 Pfe

Color Preservers

Color preservers protect the thread from changes in color and translucency due to the effects of rod finishes.

Brilliance. *1 oz., 4 oz.; thin 1:1 for two coats, full strength final coat; water clean-up.*
$1.89, $4.79 Dal

CP-X. *2 oz.-quart; two coats, two hours apart, dry overnight; clean-up with water.*
$1.95-$16.75 Bul
Flex-Coat. *1 oz.-half gallon; two-three coats; water clean-up.*
$1.05-$28.95 Spo, Bul, Fly, Tac, H&H, Don, Pfe, Mer, Dan
Gudebrod. *1 oz., 1 pint; non-blushing; allow 24 hours between coats, use three coats.*
$1.35-$1.99, $8.30-$11.18 Bul, Cor, Spo, Tac, Ran, Pfe, Dal, Mer, T&T, Kau, Mur, H&H, Bea
Reed's. *1 oz.; plastic formula.*
$1.30 Ree
SC-215 Epoxy Coatings Co.. *1 oz., 4 oz.; for use with epoxy thread finishes; water clean-up.*
$1.35-$1.60, $4.50 Sho, T&T
Shoff's. *1 oz., 1 pint.*
$1.35, $6.90 Sho
U-40 Urethane Color Lock. *1 oz.; cleans up with water.*
$2.95-$3.61 Ste, Tac, Mer
Weber. *1 oz.*
$1.75 Edd

Rod Finishes

Finishes are used today mostly to seal and protect the rod wraps. Varnish is the long-time favorite, but it has been surpassed in popularity by epoxy and other finishes.

Cabela's Professional Rod Finish. *.78 oz.; two-part polymer in six individual packets; no measuring needed.*
$3.99 Cab
Crystal Coat. *2 oz., 8 oz.; two-part epoxy finish.*
$4.89, $12.95 Dal
Custom Poly-Build. *2 oz.- quart; two-part polymer finish.*
$4.98-$22.42 Dal
Diamond II Polymer Finish. *2 oz.-gallon; clear two-part epoxy type finish; pot life 20 min.*
$3.75-$40 Bul

Flex Coat Polymer Finish. *2 oz.-gallon; two-part finish with syringes included.*
$3.95-$63.65 Bul, Pfe, Dal, Spo, Mer, Fly, Don, H&H, Tac, Fre, Dan, Cor

G-96 Epoxy Rod Finish. *6 oz.; aerosol spray.*
$3.50 Pfe

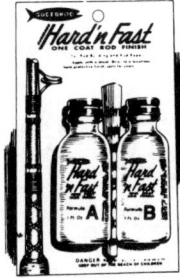

Gudebrod Hard 'N Fast II. *2 oz.; one coat; two-part; sets in two hours, dries overnight.*
$3.95-$5.40 Tac, Cor, Sho, H&H, Mer, Edd
Gudebrod Rod Varnish. *1 oz., 1 pint; clear plastic varnish; tough, shiny finish; replaces spar varnish.*
$1.44-$1.85, $8.50-$9.69 Bul, Bea, H&H, Ran, Mur, Pfe, Kau, Mer, Tac, Spo, Cor, Dal, T&T

Hi-Build/Hi-Gloss. *2½ oz. kit includes color preserver, etc; dries in 45-50 min.; no need to rotate.*
$9.10-$10.50 T&T, Sho
One Coat. *2 oz., 1 qt.; two-part polymer.*
$3.95-$4.75, $19.75 Ran, Sho, Kau
Rodon Epoxy Coating. *2 oz.; two-part finish; with mixing cup, stirrer.*
$5.30-$5.60 Edd, T&T
Shoff's Rod Varnish. *1 oz., 1 pint.*
$1.35, $6.90 Sho
Shoff's Super Skin. *1 oz.; no mixing.*
$3.55 Sho
U-40 Urethane Rod Finish. *1 oz.; flexible, non-yellowing.*
$3.79-$4.51 Tac, Ste, Mer
Weber Rod Varnish. *1 oz.*
$1.75 Edd

Brushes and Brush Cleaners

The following brush cleaners and brushes are designed specifically for rod building products.

Diamond II Brush Cleaner. *2 oz.-4 oz.; solvent for Diamond II, Flexcoat, other polymers.*
$1.50-$2.75 Bul
Flex Coat. *4 oz.; for use with Flex Coat finish.*
$1.90-$2.69 Dal, H&H, Mer, Tac

Gudebrod Cleaning Solvent. *1 oz.; clean-up for varnishes.*
$1.12-$1.59 Dal, Pfe, T&T
S-25 Epoxy Coatings Co.. *4 oz.; use brush in lid to apply finish, return to bottle for cleaning.*
$2.65-$3.25 Sho, Cor, T&T
Urethane Brush Cleaning Solvent. *For use with Urethane Rod Finish and epoxy finishes.*
$3.39 Mer
Flex Coat brushes. *Disposable brushes.*
$.17-$.25 Cor, Dan, Tac, Don, Mer, Fly, Spo

Gudebrod brushes. *2/0-1"; ox hair or Sabeline.*
$1.65-$5.35 Bul, H&H, Sho, Cor, Spo, Tac, T&T, Dal, Mer

Glues and Accessories

Rod Building Glues

Glues are used in rod building to attach the reel seat and the handle to the rod blank. Epoxy is the standard glue for this use.

5 Minute Epoxy. *1 oz.; two-part; dries in five minutes.*
$1.40 T&T
Crystal Clear Epoxy. *4.4 oz.; two-part; dries in 30-60 min.; waterproof.*
$3.95-$4.75 Cab, Kau, T&T, Sho
Devcon 5 Minute Epoxy. *1 oz.; sets in 4.7 minutes.*
$2.80-$4.95 Sho, Fly
Dura-Flex Epoxy. *4 oz.-gallon; waterproof.*
$3.95-$42.50 Bul
Duro Epoxy Cement. *1 oz.; comes in two tubes.*
$1.45-$2.50 Cor, Bul, Pfe
Flex Coat Rod Builder Epoxy. *4 oz., 8 oz.; sets in two hours, dries in 24 hours.*
$3.99-$7.49, $5.90-$7.40 H&H, Pfe, Spo, Tac, Don, Mer
Gudebrod Liquid Rod Cement. *1 oz.; waterproof, cold setting; bonds all rod parts.*
$1.69-$1.99 Edd, Tac, Dal, Spo, Cor, Ran, Pfe, T&T, H&H, Mur
Hunter's Epoxy. *2 oz.; with mixing cup and stirrer.*
$5.10 Hun
PC-7 Epoxy Paste. *2 oz.; for heavy reel seats.*
$2.34 Dal
Rodon Epoxy. *2 oz.; two-part; fast setting (15 min.).*
$5.15 Edd
Urethane Bond. *1 oz.; for mounting seats, grips; expands slightly while curing to fill gaps.*
$2.60-$5.75 Edd, Hun, Ste, Don, Ran, Mer, Sho, T&T, Dal, Kau

Glue Accessories

The following items are designed to make work with epoxy a survivable experience.

Epoxy Thinner. *1 oz., 4 oz.; clean-up for epoxy glues and finishes.*
$1.29, $2.99 Dal
Measuring syringes. *Color-coded syringes for mixing epoxies.*
$.60-$.95 Pfe, Fly, Mer, Tac, Spo, Don, Dal
Medication dispensing cups. *100 cups for mixing epoxies; measurements marked.*
$1.67-$2.99 Bul, Mer, Pfe, Dal
Mix-Alls. *20 cups; 2" diameter, 1¼" deep; for mixing epoxy finishes.*
$1.79 Dal
Mix-Sticks. *4½" stirring sticks for use in mixing epoxies and finishes.*
$.79-$.89 Dal, Pfe

Ferrule Cements

A special cement is used to attach the tip top, but it's not called tip top cement. The name comes from the days when metal ferrules were cemented on rods. Generally the cement comes in stick form. It's heated, applied to the blank, and the tip top is pushed on and aligned. When replacing a tip top, heat it carefully until the cement again softens and then remove the top.

Ferrule Flex. *1 oz., 2 oz.; apply, let dry, heat.*
$1.30, $2.35 Ree
Fuji Hot Melt Glue. *Stick; instant setting.*
$1.20-$1.25 Bul, Cor, Mer
GHQ. *Stick; heat and apply.*
$1.15 Fre
Gudebrod Stick Ferrule Cement. *Stick; plastic resin; flexible, waterproof.*
$.73-$1.50 Cor, Mer, T&T, Bul, Tac, Mur, Dal, H&H, Pfe
Shoff's. *Stick; heat and apply.*
$1 Sho
Weber. *Stick; heat and apply.*
$.90 Edd

Rod Dyes

Tired of the same old boring gray rods? Now you can alter the color of your rod blank before wrapping. See the catalogs for details.

Color Blank. *1 oz.; black, white, yellow, red, med. blue, gold, pearl with Clemens' Crystal Coat.*
$2.49 Dal
Rodcoat. *3 oz.; black, white, red, brown, blue with pump sprayer; refills available.*
$12.45-$13.95 Sho, Dal

Rod Identification

To add that personalized touch to the rod you've built, sign it or add one of the decals listed below. After all, an artist always signs his work.

Custom Rod Decals. *Black, white, blue, red, gold on clear or silver; trim and peel, apply; "Custom Made by . . .".*
$5.99/12 Dal
Heat Embossing Foil. *Silver, gold, metallic copper, blue, red, green, opaque yellow; use with heat embossing pen below.*
$3.95 Dal
Heat Embossing Pen. *With gold foil; heat and write.*
$18.99 Dal
Opaque ink. *White, gold for use with quill-type pen; cover with finish.*
$1.39-$1.49 Dal
Penstix India Ink Pen. *Black; permanent when covered with finish.*
$1.19 Dal
Tac-Type Lettering. *9"x12"; black, white rub-on type; slightly smaller than typewriter; cover with finish.*
$4.80 Bul

Special Tools for the Rod Builder

The tools listed here will help in various rod building tasks.

Clamp Master. *To clamp cork rings while gluing; adjustable 4"-26".*
$8.99 Pfe
Gluing Clamp. *To clamp cork rings while gluing; adjustable to 16".*
$6 Sho
Dial Caliper. *For measuring inside and outside diameters and depth; dial face.*
$13.70-$15.95 Sho, Dal
Vernier Calipers. *For measuring inside and outside diameters and depth.*
$3.95-$7.85 Mer, Dal, Sho
Fractioneer. *6" diameter converts fractions, millimeters, 64ths and other measurements that are so confusing in rod building.*
$1.99 Dal
Guide Placement Aid. *Thin-wall tubing replaces tape in holding guides securely during placement and alignment.*
$1.75 Dal
Mildrum Tip Top Scale. *Measures rod tips (4-10) and tip tops (4-32).*
$3.60-$4.49 Cor, Pfe, Sho

Mitre Master. *To aid in cutting blanks accurately.*
$10.50 Pfe

Push board. *For mounting cork rings; touches only edge of rings.*
$4.39 Dal

Rodmaker's knife. *Two razor-sharp, reversible blades; retractable.*
$1.10 Dal

Smooth Scuff. *Used to dull finish on blanks.*
$.69 Dal

Spine Finder. *Locates rod spine; kit available.*
$49.95; kit—$19.95 Dal

Steel pocket rule. *6" calibrated in 16ths of an inch and millimeters.*
$.99 Dal

Tapered reamers. *For reaming cork handles; three sizes to fit I.D. .300"-.620"; 18".*
$2.94-$3.85 Kau, Dal, Cor

11. Fly Fishing Accessories

I N THIS CHAPTER, you'll find all the items that didn't fit conveniently in other chapters. Some are vital, such as "fishing pillows". Clothing, hats, gloves, and sunglasses take up a large part of the chapter, and these products are ones we use a lot in our adventures.

The offerings of accessories change frequently, so don't expect to find all these items in the catalogs as listed.

CLOTHING FOR FLY FISHERMEN

I've included clothing of specific interest to the fly fisherman. That doesn't mean I've put in the entire contents of the L.L. Bean and Orvis catalogs. They are both filled with fine outdoor clothing, and you can outfit yourself with the best of chinos, guide shirts, and what-have-you from either source.

What I have included are those items that have a fishing theme (such as a shirt with fly embroidered on the pocket) or that are designed primarily for fishing (such as the Columbia up-downer caps). Just circle the items you want for Christmas and give this book to a spouse or friend. Be sure to jot down the correct size in the margin.

You won't find "fishing shirts" in this chapter. Those multiple-pocketed vest-shirts are listed in Chapter 6 with the vests and other equipment carriers.

Belts

Bud Lilly's Trout Belt. *Leather, 1¾" wide; dark mahogany with tasteful trout design and simple brass buckle; sizes: 30"-46".*
$15.95 Bud

Belt Buckles

FFF Commemorative Buckles. *Limited edition (1,000) brass buckles; styles commemorating West Yellowstone or The Federation of Fly Fishers.*
$19.95 Bud

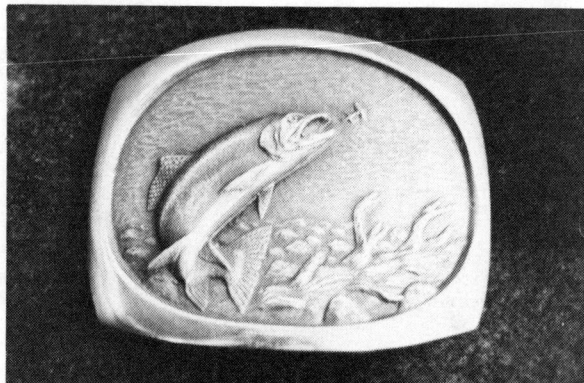

Stephen L. Knight Trout Taking Fly. *Solid bronze, for 1¾" belts.*
$15 T&T

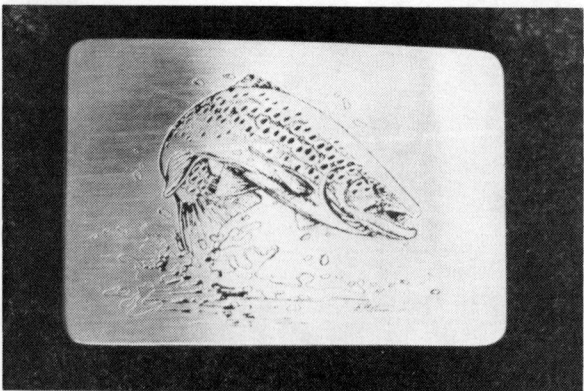

Ampersand Brass Studio Buckles. *Scenes of the Madison, Armstrong Spring Creek, Rising Trout,*

Leaping Trout; beautiful designs by Mike Stidham; 2"x3" or 1⅝"x2½" in size.
$24.50 Bud
Tawdries Buckle. *Bronze rendering of a Dave Whitlock painting; trout taking nymph; 2¾"x2" for belts to 1¾".*
$30 Dan
Chrome Buckle. *Scenes of trout with rock, trout with fly, bass; 2"x3".*
$12.95 Sim
Kenneth Reid's The Stream. *Mountain stream in brass and wood; sizes to fit belt widths ⅞"-1⅝".*
$35 AnJ

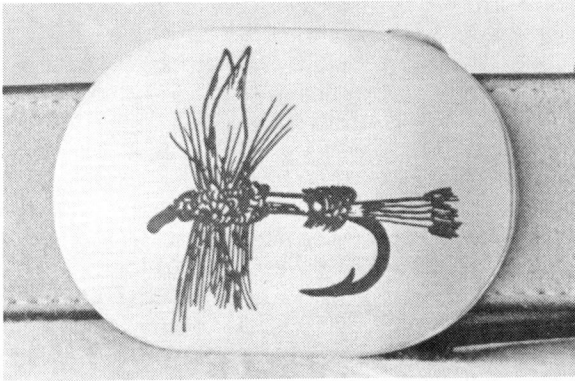

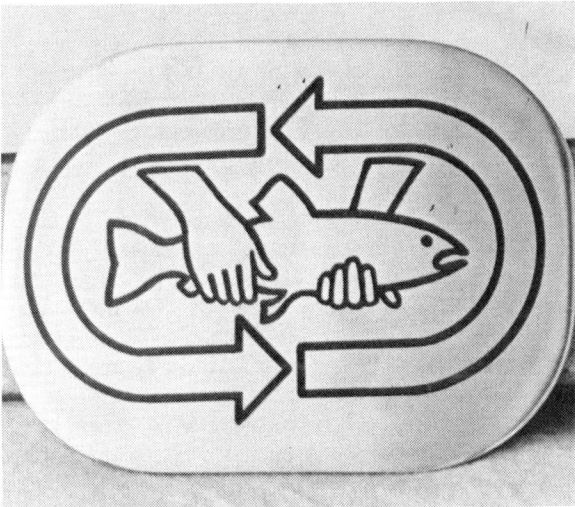

Mains/Favre Buckles. *Variety of styles including catch-and-release symbol, trout fly; in stainless steel; 2"x3" or 2½"x3½".*
$22-$24 Mains/Favre, 3111 S. Valley View Blvd. Suite B-214, Las Vegas, Nevada 89102-7790 (702) 876-6278

Buttons

Scrimshaw Buttons. *Trout fly scrimshaw on buttons that could be used on blazers or other clothing items; set of nine; ⅝".*
$24 Tid

Clothing Items

Trout Bandanas. *Bandanas with trout design; red, blue, brown, green; 24"x24".*
$4-$5.95 Fre, Nor, Hig, T&T, Dan, Bud
Sportsman's Poplin Jacket. *With embroidered fly patterns; tan; sizes: S-XL.*
$229.95 Bud
I.A. White Embroidered Flies. *Patches with embroidered flies, may be sewn on clothing or vest; denim, tan; 3"x3½" or 1½"x2½".*
$15 Bud
Orvis knit shirt. *Short-sleeved sport shirt with dry fly embroidery; yellow, white, navy blue, lt. blue; sizes: S-XL.*
$16.50 Orv
T&T Safari Shirt. *With brook trout embroidery; British tan; sizes: S-XL.*
$34.50 T&T
Oxford Dress Shirts. *With trout embroidery on cuff; blue, yellow; neck sizes: 14½"-17"; sleeve lengths: 32"-35".*
$26.50 Tid
Silk Ties. *With trout pattern; burgundy, navy blue.*
$24 Tid
T-Shirt. *Rising trout and pursuing trout designs; bone; sizes: S-XL.*
$7.95 Mirafiori Ent., 366 N. Log Cabin St., Independence, Oregon 97351
T-Shirt. *"I'd Rather be Fishin'"; yellow, blue, tan; sizes: S-XL.*
$7 Hig
T-Shirt. *"Our land is ¼ land mass, and ¾ water. Therefore, it has been designed for one to spend 75% of all his time FISHING"; yellow, blue, tan; sizes: S-XL.*
$7 Hig
T-Shirt. *"Everyone should believe in something. I believe I'll go fishing. Thoreau"; yellow, blue, tan; sizes: S-XL.*
$7 Hig

T-shirt. *Company logos and slogans; variety of colors and sizes.*
$7-$8 Hig, Mur, T&T, AnJ

T-Shirt. *"Think Trout"; lt. blue; sizes: S-XL.*
$7.95 Ram or Mirafiori Ent. (see address above)

T-Shirt. *"Hooked on Fly Fishing"; navy blue; sizes: S-XL.*
$7.95 T&T, Fly

Gloves

A good pair of gloves is essential to any cold weather angling adventure. Without them, hands become wet and ice up as quickly as rod guides. That's bad. Fly fisherman's gloves should be fingerless in order to manipulate lines, tie on flies, and light a pipe. (Caution: These fingerless gloves should not be worn in general public or the innocent fly fisherman may be confused with a punk rock fan.)

The key to the gloves is the ability of the material they're made of to stay warm when wet. Wool, bunting, and polypropylene have this characteristic. Neoprene, another popular material, is waterproof and provides insulation.

With two exceptions, the gloves here expose all fingers. The mitten/glove from Angler's Junction has a mitten cover that folds back to reveal glove fingers with only the index finger exposed. They are made of acrylic fiber.

The second exception is the Glacier Glove, a neoprene glove designed for fly fishermen. The index finger and thumb are exposed. This is a well-engineered glove. The holes for the exposed fingers are protected from water seepage by foam. Optional finger covers for extremely cold weather are included. The gloves are lined for easy entrance/exit, sometimes a problem with neoprene products. Velcro closures make the wrist fit tight. Without doubt, these are the best gloves for the fly fisherman who does a lot of cold-weather fishing.

Whatever glove you select, beware of frostbite. It's very easy to concentrate so much on your fishing that you forget about your fingers. Loss of sensation is one of the first danger signs, and that means it's time to stop long enough to warm your fingers up thoroughly. The first signs of true frostbite are pain and white patches on the affected areas, and that means it's time to stop for the day. Areas of frostbite may require medical attention, depending on their severity and size, and although it's not likely to happen to even a semi-conscious angler, severe frostbite can require the removal of affected areas. Fingerless gloves may take on a new meaning for anglers who are careless.

And while we're on the subject of cold weather fishing, be sure you're aware of hypothermia, the life-threatening loss of body heat. It can happen even at moderate temperatures when rain, wind, and physical condition work in combination, but it's always a danger when the temperature is low. Any time a person falls in the water, the danger of hypothermia is present.

The best thing is to avoid hypothermia. Dress warmly, preferably in layers that may be adjusted with changes in temperature. Eat well and carry supplemental foods. Fish with a partner—watch him or her for signs of hypothermia and ask for the same regard.

The thing about hypothermia that makes it so dangerous is that it sneaks up on you. One moment you're shivering, and the next thing you know you're in the hospital (if you're lucky). If you stay exposed to the elements after you've felt those first thorough shivers, you're asking for the big ticket for the long ride. Your judgment will soon be affected, so it's vital to act quickly. Don't wait to see if you'll warm up. Contact your fishing partner for help. Stop fishing and get warm. Go back to your car and run the heater, remembering to crack a window for ventilation. Quit fishing for the day and go home to the fireplace.

Backcountry fishing is always more dangerous. If you begin to suffer from hypothermia, you must react quickly. Get help from your friends immediately, get to shelter, eat a candy bar, build a fire, make some hot water for tea or coffee.

Whenever you're fishing with a friend, be aware of hypothermia affecting him or her, as well as yourself. You can tell when someone is cold. Don't let them be tough about it. If their ego is sensitive, claim that you're too cold to keep fishing. Drag them home. One of the first danger signs is shivering. Slurred speech and lack of good judgment follows quickly. You must intervene if your partner shows these more serious signs, since he or she will be unaware of what's happening.

Your main task is to get him warm. This is relatively easy roadside, but in the backcountry, it can be difficult. If you can't build a fire or heat water, make the person get in a sleeping bag and get in with him. Later you can laugh about it, but right then it's got to be done. Get help from other people if possible. Don't be afraid to ask for help. Every competent outdoorsman knows the danger of hypothermia.

Please be careful out there. I don't want to lose any readers. Here's the list of fishing gloves.

Neoprene fingerless gloves. *Lined with nylon for easy-on/easy/off; brown; sizes: S-L.*
$12.95 Dan, Bud

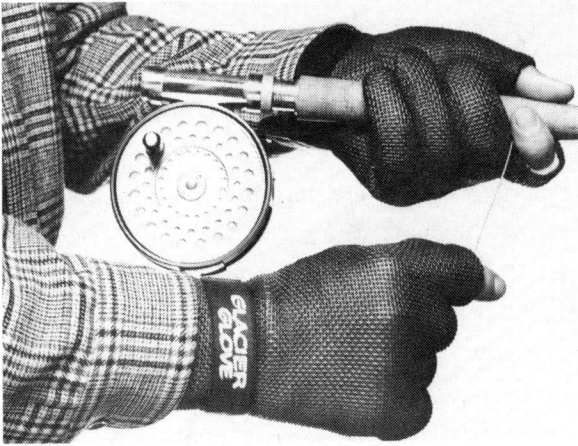

Glacier Gloves. *Neoprene; index finger and thumb exposed; see introduction to this section; sizes: S-XL.*
$39.50-$39.95 Hun, Fly
Columbia Fingerless Gloves. *Wool, retains insulation value when wet; gray; sizes: M,L.*
$13.50 Bud
Wool fingerless gloves. *No brand name; gray; sizes: S-L.*
$8.95-$15.95 Cab, Dun, Tid, Pen, Kau, Fly, Hig, Let, Don

Millar Mitts. *85% wool fingerless gloves; brown; sizes: S-L.*
$16.95-$19.50 Dan, T&T
North Cape Fingerless Gloves. *Wool; gray; sizes: S-L.*
$12.50 Fre
Patagonia Bunting Fingerless Gloves. *Bunting retains insulation value when wet, dries more quickly than wool; navy blue; sizes: S-L.*
$9.95-$12.50 Ram, T&T, Hig, Kau
Bunting Fingerless Gloves. *No brand name; bunting retains insulation while wet and dries quickly; navy blue; sizes: S-L.*
$12.95-$13.95 Pen, Nor
Mitten/fingerless glove. *Mitten folds down to reveal gloves and exposed index finger; acrylic fiber; gray; one size fits all.*
$13.95 AnJ

Polypropylene fingerless gloves. *Won't absorb water; gray; sizes: S-L.*
$8.50 Orv

And to Help Protect You from Hypothermia
This handy little thermometer will hang on your vest and let you know if you should feel hot or cold.

Temperature gauge. *Small thermometer on key chain; 2".*
$1.95 Ram

Hats
Hats serve a number of roles in our fly fishing lives. On the practical side, they protect us from pink dandruff, a malady of the severely sun-burned angler, and they keep hair, sun, and rain out of our eyes so we can see whereat we fish.

Moreover, the choice of a hat is a matter of personal style. Wearing a Columbia Sportswear Gunga Din pith helmet to the stream says something about you. What it says, I'm not sure, but it does make a statement.

Hats are one part of the sport that allows some personal freedom without so much regard to fashion. They are therefore one part of the sport that is simply fun. There are no standards, but there are a few favorites. The Irish tweed hat, the cowboy hat, and the up-downer are probably most popular, but the gimme cap (aka seed cap or corn cap in the Midwest) from the fly shops is edging up there.

Whatever hat you choose, be sure that it's of a neutral color. Your hat is the first highly visible thing that will enter the fish's field of vision. If it's white or any bright color, it may send the fish to the depths.

High Country Caps. *Several mottos to match the T-shirts listed above; green, gold, red, brown, blue; one size fits all.*
$6 Hig
Catch & Release Cap. *Makes your position clear and keeps other anglers from showing you dead fish; tan, gray; one size fits all.*
$7.95 Bud

Fly Shop Caps. *Baseball-style caps with fly shop logos; some in Gore-Tex; variety of colors; one size fits all.*
$5.95-$11.95 Mur, Dan, Hun, Nor, Cab, Bud, Fly

Columbia Gore-Tex Crusher. *A frumpy, roll-up hat with the rain protection of Gore-Tex; green, tan, navy blue; sizes: S-XL.*
$9.95-$15.50 Cab, AnJ, LLB, Ram, Kau, Dun, Bud, Dan, Hig, T&T,
Stetson Angler. *A stylish hat in poplin from the famous cowboy hat maker, but it's pretty bright; lt. tan; sizes: S-XL.*
$12.95 Bud
Stetson Libra. *Herringbone pattern, center crease; tan, gray; sizes: S-XL.*
$24 Bud

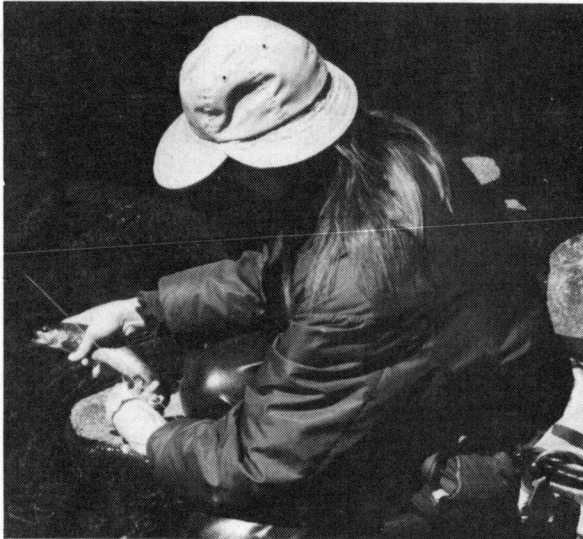

Columbia Up-Downer. *Developed for the bonefish flats, now common in areas far from bonefish; long front brim and fold-down back brim for protection from sun and flies (the ones on the end of your leader); green, tan, navy blue; sizes: S-XL.*
$4.95-$7.95 Cab, Hig, Kau, Dan, Fly

Columbia Gore-Tex Up-Downer. *The bonefish flats hat now in Gore-Tex for rain protection; green, navy blue, tan; sizes: S-XL.*
$9.95-$13.95 Cab, Ram, Hig, AnJ, Dan, Bud

Columbia Mesh Up-Downer. *Mesh top, for hot weather; tan; sizes: S-XL.*
$7.50-$7.95 Fly, Dan, Ram, Kau, Hig
Jones Cap. *The duck hunter's hat with rising trout on front; tan; sizes: S-XL.*
$21.50 Tid
Stetson Suede Hat. *A Safari-hat style, very handsome; tan; no sizes given, so include your hat size.*
$35 Bud
Solar Helmet. *Must be seen to be appreciated, must be appreciated to be worn; a pith helmet with a solar-powered fan imbedded in front (I told you hats were fun); tan; one size fits all.*
$90 Orv
North Cape Folded Hat. *Ragg wool; gray; one size fits all.*
$5.95 Fre
North Cape Visor Hat. *Ragg wool hat with visor; gray; one size fits all.*
$5.95 Fre
Ragg wool crusher. *The crusher style in wool; gray; one size fits all.*
$14.50 T&T
Original Effanem Crusher Hat. *Felt roll-up, sit-on, jam-in-vest-pocket hat; tan, gray; sizes: S-L.*
$8.95 Fre
Orvis Up-Downer. *Up-downer style cap; tan; hat sizes: 6⅞-8.*
$16.75 Orv
Orvis Year-Rounder. *Helmet-style hat with vents; tan; hat sizes: 6⅞-8.*
$22.50 Orv

Columbia Gore-Tex Baseball Cap. *Simple, the hat Mickey Mantle would wear if he were a fly fisherman; navy blue, tan, green; one size fits all.*
$8.95 Ram

Columbia Gunga Din Helmet. *A pith helmet for everyman; tan; one size fits all (although the style doesn't).*
$8.95 Ram

Stetson Cougar. *Felt safari-style hat; brown; sizes: 6⅞-7⅝.*
$39.95 Nor
Stetson Lyle. *Brimmed hat; light tan; sizes: 6⅞-7⅝.*
$19.95 Nor

Columbia Scissor Bill Cap. *The long bill of the up-downer but without the back flap; tan, navy blue; one size fits all.*
$6.25-$6.95 Bob, Ram
Irish knit hat. *The classic Eastern fishing hat; frumpy, fun; assorted tweeds; one size fits all.*
$9.95-$33 Cab, Orv, Let, Kau, Fly
Barbour English Tweed Grouse Hat. *Don't let the name fool you—you can catch trout while wearing this hat; assorted tweeds, no two alike; sizes: M,L*
$20.75 T&T
Guide cap. *In the up-downer style but with shorter front brim and snaps on back brim; brown; sizes: S-XL.*
$11.95 T&T
Bean's Allagash Hat. *A wide-brimmed Australian bush hat with mosquito net, chin strap, and snaps on side to hold brim up; olive green, khaki; hat sizes: 6¾-7¾.*
$32 LLB
Barbour Thornproof Hat. *A basic crusher to match your Spey Wading Jacket; sage; sizes: S-XL.*
$23.95-$27.95 Pen, Tid, T&T
Stetson cowboy hats. *A variety of styles in felt from the famous maker.*
$69.95-$89.95 AnJ

Fashion Accessories

In this part of the list, you'll find a number of pins, money clips, and other accessories to your everyday life that have been designed around a fishing theme. There's even a snuffbox cover (although we know all fly fishermen smoke pipes).

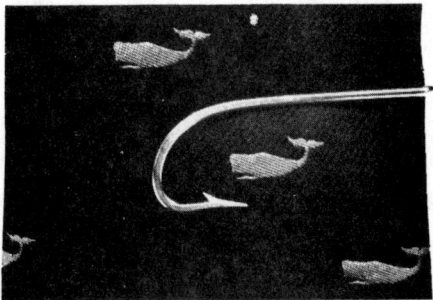

Hook tie bar. *Gold-plated hook designed to slip on tie; elegant and simple.*
$1.34-$3.95 Kau, Dal

Salmon Fly Brooch Pin. *Fully-dressed salmon fly tied on a brooch pin hook; many patterns.*
$6-$24.95 Don, Kau

Feather pins. *Mallard, wood duck, woodcock, turkey, jungle cock feather replicas carved from wood and painted.*
$22.50-$24.95 Don and Wild Wings, Lake City, Minnesota 55401
Trout tie tack. *Leaping trout in gold or silver.*
gold--$119.95; silver—$44.95 Mirafiori Ent. (see address in clothing list)
Tie tack. *Trout or leaping bass by Sid Bell; in gold or silver.*
gold—$190; silver—$21 Tid
Tie tack, pin. *Detailed adult mayfly or caddis or stonefly nymph in sterling silver by Tom Satterthwaite.*
$16.50 Dan

Lighter cover. *Fits Bic lighters; nickel silver with variety of designs including catch-and-release symbol.*
$8 Mains/Favre (see address under belt buckles)

Lighter Cover. *Fits Bic lighters; chrome finish with raised figure of trout.*
$10 Cor

Money clips. *Nickel silver with a variety of designs.*
$8 Mains/Favre (see address under belt buckles)

Snuffbox lids. *Nickel silver with a variety of designs.*
$8 Mains/Favre (see address under belt buckles)
Business card/credit card holders. *Nickel silver with a variety of designs.*
$20 Mains/Favre (see address under belt buckles)

Flask. *Pewter flask engraved with trout one side, fly fisherman other side; 8 oz.*
$29.95 Fly

SUNGLASSES

The most important thing for a pair of fly fisherman's sunglasses to be is polarized. I continue to be surprised at how many people don't know the advantages of polarized lenses, but one streamside comparison between regular sunglasses and polarized ones is all it takes to convince them.

Reduction in glare makes it possible to see the fly on the water and to see into the water. Regular sunglasses reduce total light, but polarized glasses eliminate reflected glare. They are essential, and your fly fishing will improve with them, because you'll be able to see your fly better during the drift and often see the trout coming for the fly.

Until recently, almost all polarized sunglasses had plastic lenses. It wasn't practical to polarize glass. Recent developments have allowed sunglass manufacturers to create glass lenses with the polarizing feature. The less expensive ones use a lamination process with plastic polarized material within glass. Glass lenses, of course, are more resistant to scratching and are more optically perfect (although lamination may negate that factor). They are, however, heavier.

The biggest advantage to the new polarization process for glass is that those people who wear corrective eyeglasses can now have polarized sunglasses without using clip-ons. Even bifocals are available.

Other options available in today's polarized sunglasses are flip-up lenses and photosensitive lenses. Flip-ups allow you to flip the sunglass up and out of the way for tying on flies or for when your fly drifts into shadows. I've gotten used to the flexibility they provide and can't fish without them. Flip-ups are now available in fashion sunglasses made by Foster Grant. They retail for about $10 and are available at many types of retail stores.

Photosensitive lenses become lighter or darker depending on the amount of light available. That feature needs to operate quickly to be of use to the angler, but it has the potential to be very valuable to you depending on the lighting situations you face in your everyday fishing.

You'll also have to decide on lens color. Brown, amber, gray, smoke, green, and yellow lenses are available. Gray and smoke give the truest color renditions. Green and brown are darker lenses. Amber and yellow are considered superior in low-contrast light.

All sunglasses listed here are polarized.

Action Optics Model 1. *Metal frames with photosensitive glass lens; amber, gray.*
$65-$79 Bob, Fly, Dan

Action Optics Model 2. *Nylon frames with photosensitive glass lens; amber, gray.*
$45-$59 Dan, Nor, Fly, Bob
Action Optics. *Prescription lens, regular or bifocal; gray, amber.*
$120, bifocals—$150 Bob
Bill Dance. *Plastic lenses; gray/green.*
$9.95 Cab
Bullard's. *Plastic lenses; brown, smoke.*
$14.50 Bul

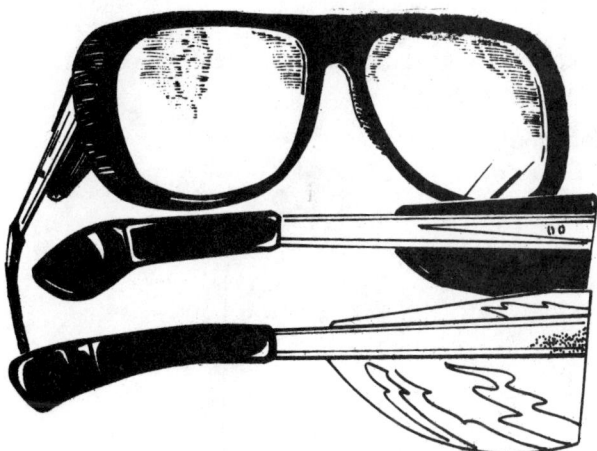

Courtesy of Bob Jacklin

Fisherman's Glasses. *Glass lens with side panels to further reduce light; tan, gray, yellow.*
$8.95-$13.95 Many catalogs

Courtesy of Bob Jacklin

Foster Grant Aqua-Mates. *Flip-ups; available in glass or plastic lenses; amber, gray.*
$7.99-$12.95 Cab, Ram, Bud, Kau, Dal, AnJ, Bob, Ste, Orv, Cus, Let, Dan
Foster Grant Clip-Ons. *Flip-up clip-ons for use over regular glasses; green, gray, brown; sizes: L,XL.*
$5.90-$7.95 Cus, Orv, Dal, Dan, Bud
Foster Grant Wrap-Arounds. *Wrap around lenses to cut out more light; gray, brown.*
$9.95-$11.95 Dan, Cus
Outdoor Optics. *Glass photosensitive lenses; amber, gray.*
$59 T&T
Optix Cormorant. *Special plastic lenses; gray, amber.*
$21.75 Orv
Polafocus. *Polarized top lens with clear, magnifying insert for tying on flies; choice of 1.5x, 2x, 2.5x power; gray.*
$10.95-$25 Cab, Fly, Orv
Polar Eyes. *Glass lenses with a variety of options; prescription lenses available; brown, gray.*
$69; prescription—$100 Polar Eyes, Box 1568, Key Largo, Florida 33037 (305) 451-3776
Reacto-Pol. *Glass photosensitive lenses in wrap-around frame; prescription lenses available; amber.*
$79; prescription—$129 (+ $40 bifocals) Bill Curtis Ent., Box 278, Key Biscayne, Florida 33149

Smith Fisherman's Glasses. *Glass photosensitive lenses, with Croakie; gray, amber.*
$64.95-$65 Hig, Bud, Pen
Teeny Sunglasses. *Regular style glasses; smoke, amber.*
$24.95 Ste
Teeny Locators. *Wrap arounds with limited "window"; amber, smoke.*
$12.50-$14.95 Kau, Nat, Ste
Teeny Locators. *Clip-ons with same features as regular Locators; smoke, amber.*
$12.50-$14.95 Kau, Ste

Sunglass Accessories

Clip-On Case. *Zippered neoprene case can be clipped on vest.*
$5.95 Fly

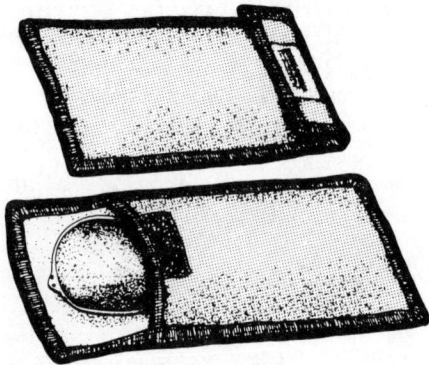

Shade Case. *Foam padded sunglass case, Velcro close, floats; tan.*
$4.50 Pen
Head Huggers. *Holds sunglasses on head.*
$2.95 Ste

Burke Snugger. *Holds sunglasses on head.*
$2.50 Dan
Croakies. *Neoprene band holds sunglasses on head; red, blue, black.*
$2.95-$4.75 Dan, Kau, Tid, Fre, Pen, Bob, Fly, T&T, Hig, Ram, Bud
Spec-Cords. *Soft nylon lanyard hooks to eyeglasses; 23".*
$2.75-$2.95 Bob, Bud

DEALING WITH INSECTS

Insects. We love them when they're mayflies, but we hate them when they're black flies or mosquitos or no-see-'ums. We deal with them chemically (repellents), physically (mosquito nets), or both (Shoo-Bug jacket). And after they wear down our defenses, we use more chemicals to ease our pain.

Repellents utilize a chemical commonly called DEET. The heavier the concentration of DEET, the stronger the repellent. You may also choose a repellent based on its smell. After all, you only want to repel insects. Another consideration is the repellent's form. As a lotion or stick, it is easily and safely applied to the face and hands and can be carried conveniently in a vest pocket. As a spray, it can be sprayed on shirts and pants for added protection. Pump sprays are often small enough to be carried in your vest.

Occasionally, it's not enough to keep bugs from lighting and biting, you must keep them out of your mouth, eyes, and nose. Mosquito head nets are available in two models. I like the Cummings since it provides a hole to stick your pipe out of. Pipe smoke, you know, is an effective insect repellent when the tobacco is cheap enough.

One interesting idea for protection from insects is the Shoo-Bug jacket. It's a mesh jacket and hood that you spray with repellent, stow in a plastic bag for a few hours so that the repellent soaks in, and then wear.

If, in spite of your best efforts, you do get bit, Sting-Eze and After-Bite can help relieve the itching and pain.

Insect bites can be more than irritating, incidentally. One summer in Yellowstone, I got bit by some gremlins the doctor called buffalo gnats. My body reacted unfavorably to the insult, and I had headaches, fever, and the works. It cut into my vacation time. The remedy, incidentally, was an internal antihistamine. Prevention is the only good answer.

Repellents

Ben's 100. *1.25 oz. lotion.*
$2.50-$3.95 Bob, H&H, Fol, Pen
Cutter's. *Lotion.*
$1.79-$3.50 Spo, Fol, Let, T&T
Cutter's. *7 oz. spray.*
$3.95-$4.50 T&T, Let
Cutter's. *Stick.*
$3 Let
Fly-Rite. *1.2 oz. spray pump.*
$3 FlR
Jungle Formula. *2 oz. lotion.*
$3 Orv
Muskol. *1.25 oz. lotion.*
$3.95-$4.50 Ste, Kau, AnW, Fly, Ram, Dan, Pen

Muskol. *6 oz. spray.*
$2.69-$4.50 Cab, Dan, Ram
Repel. *2 oz. lotion.*
$3.95 AnJ
Repel. *4 oz. pump spray.*
$4.95 AnJ
Seidel 400. *Lotion.*
$2.35 H&H

Physical Restraints

Shoo-Bug Jacket. *Mesh jacket; you apply repellent to it; green; sizes: S-XL.*
$26.95-$33 Cab, Ram, Orv
Mosquito head net. *Bucket hat with mesh extending down to the shoulders.*
$4.65-$5 Ste, Orv, Ram, Kau

Cummings insect head net. *Hat with mesh extending down to shoulders; with pipe hole and "window".*
$3.25-$4.95 Cab, Dan, Sim

Last Resorts

After-Bite. *Formula helps relieve itching and pain; in handy "pencil" applicator with foam dabber.*
$2.50-$2.95 AnW, AnJ, T&T
Sting-Eze. *½ oz. in squeeze bottle.*
$2.45 Ram

EQUIPMENT CARRIERS

Tackle Bags

These bags are especially designed to hold the gear a fly fisherman hauls with him or her on trips. You'll find bags for specific equipment, such as waders, in the chapters listing that equipment.

Cabela's Tackle Bag. *Gear bag with pockets designed for the fisherman; tan; 19"x12"x9".*
$29.95 Cab
Orvis Mini-Kit. *Gear bag designed for the fisherman; beige; 15"x6"x6".*
$45.50-$46.25 Orv, Fly, Hun, Let, Dan, Kau, Bud
Orvis Medium Kit Bag. *Next size up; beige; 20"x6"x9".*
$54.50-$55.75 Orv, Kau, Fly, Bud, Hun, Let, Dan

Orvis Jumbo Kit Bag. *The big one; beige; 19 ½"x6"x12".*
$64-$65.25 Orv, Hun, Dan, Fly, Bud, Let, Kau
Dan Bailey's Canvas Tackle Bag. *Large gear bag; dark brown; 22 ½"x9 ½"x7".*
$64.95 Dan

Fanny Packs

I've found these mini-packs to be excellent for carrying my camera gear. The gear is quite heavy and is much more comfortable carried on my waist instead of on my shoulders. In addition, camera gear is much safer streamside in a water-repellent fanny pack.

I use a regular fanny pack like the Deluxe Fanny Pack from Ramsey Outdoor. You can find them at stores that sell outdoor gear. They are less expensive than ones designed for cameras, but you'll have to do some padding and organizing to protect your gear. I'd recommend the packs specifically made for cameras if you can afford one.

Deluxe Fanny Pack. *The basic fanny pack in a variety of colors and camo; 4 ½"deepx14"widex7"tall.*
$11.95 Ram

Camp Trails

Camp Trails Photo Fanny Pack. *Padded, with compartments, film holders; blue; 11 ½"x6"x7 ½".*
$34.95 Ram
Cabela's Camera Fanny Pack. *Fully padded; brown; in two sizes; small—3 ½"x6 ½"x5", large—4"x7 ½"x5 1/5".*
$16.95-$18.95 Cab
Cool-Mesh Fanny Pack. *Cordura nylon; mesh bottom for optional use as a creel; side pockets for fly boxes.*
$19.95 Fly

And a Backpack

L.L. Bean Fisherman's Backpack. *Designed to carry pack rod and gear; green; 20"x12 ¾"x5".*
$39.25 LLB

EVERYTHING ELSE

Drinking Utensils

For the fly fisherman who can't help thinking about fishing water every time he sees liquid, the glassware and coffee cups listed here will aid in the fantasy. There are also some streamside drinking cups, but please use these with caution. I know that what you might drink out of the glassware and coffee cups may be close to poison, but drinking from a stream can really be poison to your system. To be safe, treat your water first.

Orvis glassware. *Trout or trout fly design; set of six; 12 oz. highball, 10 oz. roly poly, or 11 oz. old fashion.*
$39.50-$42.50 Orv
Wheaton glassware. *Gunnar Johnson trout flies, six patterns; 10 oz.*
$6.25-$8 each T&T, Hig
Motion Mug. *A wide-bottomed mug that won't spill on the move; beige/green with rising trout; 4" tall; 16 oz. capacity.*
$7.95 Tid

Trout Coffee Mug. *Mug with trout "sculpture" on outside; brown, beige, gray; 12 oz. capacity.*
$7.95-$8.95 Hig, Fre, T&T or direct from Angler's Expressions, 3951 Hawthorne Way, Boise, Idaho 83703
Fold-Cup. *An ingenious metal cup; folds up flat for easy carrying.*
$2.70 Bud
Collapsible cup. *Plastic; 1" closed, 3" open.*
$1.50 T&T

And to Make Your Streamside Water Potable

Water purifiers are necessary in you drink from most "natural" waters today. Here in the Rockies, it's only been a fairly recent necessity, but now giardia, an intestinal disturbance, is a widespread threat. It's carried by animals, so any watershed can be affected. The disease can be treated, but it's best to avoid it.

Other areas of the country offer no better prospects for a refreshing, carefree streamside sip. Where there are humans or animals upstream (almost everywhere), avoid drinking the water, unless you treat or filter it first.

Potable Aqua. *Water purification tablets.*
$3.95 Ram
Aqua kit. *Plastic water container and tablets to treat 1 qt.*
$7.95 AnJ

Pocket Purifier. *A large "straw" with purifying elements inside; fits easily into vest or bag.*
$9.95 Ram

An Enlightening Item

The Terry Hague lamp features a wood carving of a trout of your choice. It's handsome piece and comes, appropriately, from an art dealer.

Terry Hague Lamp. *Lamp with carved rainbow, brown, or brook; 23 ½" tall.*
$250 Wild Wings (see address under fashion accessories)

And Something to do by the Light of the Lamp

Notecards with fly fishing art on them are a nice way to tell your friend back in New York about the fishing in Jackson Hole. All of these are very nice.

Hugh Mossman. *10 cards with fly fishing watercolor print; 6"x4 ½".*
$8 Dan, T&T, Hig, Bud
Mike Stidham. *Trout prints.*
$4.50 Dan
Francis Davis. *8 cards with trout portraits; 5 ½"x4 ¼".*
$3.50 Wul

Something for the Wall Above the Lamp

The fish "charts" from Windsor Publications are really pieces of art, as well as identification aids. Individual charts are available for western gamefish, trout and salmon, warmwater fish, and fish of the Great Lakes. They also carry duck charts.

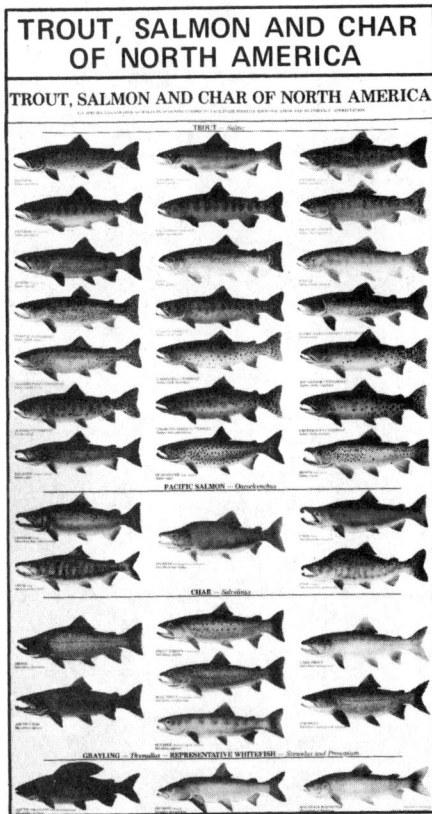

Windsor Fish Charts. *Full-color prints of individual gamefish; 2'x3'.*
$6.50-$7.50 each Tid, AnJ, Nor or direct from Windsor Publications, 2515 Windsor Circle, Eugene, Oregon 97405
(503) 345-1151

More Popular Art

Inside—Trout metal work. *Enameled copper figure of trout; on wood base; 6" tall.*
$20 Tid
Outside—Tire covers. *Covers for the spare; trout design; regular, large.*
$19.95 Cab

Something to Clean Up With After Changing a Tire

Fish, of course, are sensitive to smell, and some species rely almost entirely on their sense of smell to find food. The idea of keeping human smells away from catfish bait, for instance, is a longstanding one.

Now some people are suggesting this is important to trout fishing and even to fly fishing. Two soaps listed here, Cabela's and Pharmacist Formula, are marketed as aids in removing human smells from bait, lures, and flies. Along with the other soap, they also claim to be especially effective at removing the smell of fish from your hands after a day's fishing.

I couldn't say human scents don't repel fish, but most stream fishing is too fast lane for me to think trout take time to sniff before deciding. Lake fishing may be different. Anyway, this is another product you may wish to try for yourself.

Cabela's Fisherman's Soap. *3 oz. bar.*
$2.95/4 Cab
Sportsman's Odor Away Soap. *4 oz. lotion.*
$2.98 Cor
Pharmacist Formula Fisherman's Soap. *1 oz. bar.*
$2.95 Ste

Guide Chairs

I don't know that these are particularly designed for fly fishermen, but they're offered from two of our sources and they're too fancy to take bait fishing. It's difficult to describe these chairs. They come in two parts that, when inserted properly into each other, make a dandy camp/deck chair. Taken apart, the chair is compact and easily stowed in a closet or car trunk. The one I have, from Great Escape Works, is handsome and very comfortable. The engineering is amazing. The chair is attractive and practical. If nothing else, it's a great way to have a half dozen extra chairs in convenient storage for when the guys or gals come over to tell fishing lies.

Caribout chair. *Oak with canvas back; shorter seat than other chair; cobalt, green, navy blue, sand.*
$42.95 Nor (Note: This is not listed in current catalog.)

Outfitter's chair. *Oak with fabric back; long, slightly curved seat; burgundy and other colors; write for details.* $39.95 The Great Escape Works, 1995 McKinzie Drive, Idaho Falls, Idaho 83401 (208) 522-6475

Other Things We Can't Live Without

Fly retriever. *A metal hook with cord attached; put hook on tip top and move to branch that reached out and caught your fly; pull on hook to cut branch; can pay for itself quickly, but you should take care not to damage the trees, too.* $3.50 EJH

Underwater camera housing. *Plastic watertight bag for camera; optically clear window; built-in glove; for those underwater trout shots you could take after falling in or for other, more planned shots; regular—9"x6"x7 ½"; large—10 ½"x10"x7 ¼".* $74.95-$83.95 Cab

Flyshooter. *A rubberband-powered gun that propels a plastic disc; to knock flying insects out of the air; I include this because I heard one of our leading anglers suggest its use, to stun hoppers I believe; a great way to wake up napping fishing partners, too.* $3.95 Ram

Barometer. *Portable, adjusts for altitude up to 5,000'; barometric pressure probably has a lot to do with the* feeding habits of fish and the hatching habits of insects; mostly barometric pressure is a great excuse for a bad day astream; 3 ⅜" diameter, 1 ⅝" deep. $19.95-$24.95 Tid, Dan, Cab

Beverage Belt. *Six insulated pockets for pop or beer cans; easy to pack out the empties, too.* $16.95 Pen

Bootbags. *A bag to be worn over your waders or muddy hiking boots; protects your car interior; neat idea; blue, brown, gray, tan; one size fits all.* $15 AnJ

Dry Fly Sherry. *The ultimate fly fishing accessory. After all, sherry fits our image—fireplace, pipe, and glass of delicate liquid. The perfect present (ation). Each bottle includes a trout fly, safely separated from the sherry.* About $8 From your local liquor store.

Fish pillows. *The best kind of "stuffed" trout; photo-printed and cut to shape of trout; brown, rainbow, or cutthroat.* $26 Nor

Fishing pillows. *Poly/cotton cover; washable; poly fiberfill; 16"x13"; choice of sayings:*

"The people I've met who say they 'used' to fish can never give a good account of why they stopped. Neither can they explain the meaning of their existence."

"If you wish to be happy for one hour, get intoxicated. If you wish to be happy for three days, get married. If you wish to be happy for eight days, kill your pig and eat it. If you wish to be happy forever, learn to fish." $24.50 Orv

12. Books, Magazines and Art

THE VISION OF A fly fisherman curled up in front of a winter's night fire with a fishing book is appropriate to our overall image. Many of the books listed here lend themselves to that idyllic scene, but many are more appropriately read at a table with notepad at hand. They are studious books detailing intricate fly patterns or perhaps the life cycle of the mayfly. Whether your interest lies in entomology or rod building and whether you're a beginner or an expert, there are books for you.

I've divided the list into eight categories to make it easy to find titles in areas of your interest. I hope all the books are in the most appropriate categories. I haven't read them all, you know. The categories are: collecting, entomology, fish, general fly fishing, fly tying, guide books, rod building, and a final section for collected stories and more literary works.

I tried to come up with a recommended reading list, as others have done, but it's impossible for me to be fair. My own prejudices would color the list, and I don't have the wide exposure needed to overcome that.

A quick perusal in your local fly shop goes a long way toward ensuring a wise purchase. The safest categories for your shopping are collecting, where there are few choices, entomology, where almost all the books are well-researched, and literary, where an author must be good to be published. The chanciest categories are general fly fishing, where every topic seems to be worth a cast, and fly tying, where demand has brought an enormous number of books, both good and bad, on the market.

Among all the technical journals and how-to manuals, the more literary works are often lost in the shuffle. It's the same kind of thing that happens streamside—we get so scientific about it all that we sometimes forget to enjoy the experience and learn as much about ourselves as we do about fish and bugs. The literary works are personal anecdotes, the best of which entertain us, certainly, but also teach us something of the human condition, mostly the fly fisherman's condition. And, as any fishing widow or widower can tell you, fly fishermen have a condition that needs understanding.

Our fly fishing world is enriched by the works of authors such as Nick Lyons, Robert Traver, Roderick Haig-Brown, Sparse Grey Hackle, and Ernie Schwiebert, all of whom have spun tales that are more than tales. Hopes for continuation of this heritage of good writing, good humor, and honest insight rest with writers such as Dave Hughes, Steve Raymond, and others, some of whom have yet to make their way up from the magazines. It also rests with readers who must show their appreciation by buying that type of book.

Video tapes may someday replace some of our instructional books, but we'll probably never see a video tape of "The Dancing Fly" or "Fishing Widows". Nor are we likely to see a TV mini-series based on one of the current fly fishing novels, *A River Runs Through It* by Norman MacLean or *The River Why* by David James Duncan. You'll just have to read them.

And read these two works you should. MacLean's novel is wonderful prose and challenges my friend's contention that there is no "literature" in writings about fly fishing. The beginning reads: "In our family, there was no clear line between religion and fly fishing." The end: "Eventually, all things merge into one, and a river runs through it . . . I am haunted by waters."

As for Duncan's novel, it's a love story, a romance novel. The love is split between that for a woman and that for a way of life centered around fly fishing. It depicts the life and times of one Gus Orviston, son of a famous fly-fishing-writer father and a hardy, pants-wearing, bait-fishing mother. Identity, obviously, is an issue for Gus. All this cannot describe how much fun this book is for a fly fisherman. Try it out. (*The River Why*, incidentally, is the Sierra Club's first novel.) Whatever you do, read. The best fishing, as they say, is in print.

For book collectors. Those of us who have been around awhile know that it's best to buy books as they come out.

I've missed a number of books that I didn't buy, that sold out, that weren't reprinted. Now I must haunt dusty book shelves in search of them. When and if I find them, they are usually more expensive than when they were first published. In that regard, fishing books are a good, if minor, investment.

If you've missed a title that you now want or if you're simply looking for an older book for your collection, there are sources for many of those volumes. Garage sales are disappointing places to look for fly fishing books as are most of the used book shops. But here are three excellent sources, all with interesting lists for the collector.

Alec Jackson. Each year Alec Jackson publishes several lists of "Sporting Books for the Discriminating Flyfisherman and Collector". Every list is new and usually contains a special selection of books on a particular subject, such as salmon fishing in Norway or fishing in Scotland. The lists are available in numbered editions for $3 each for the standard catalog or $7.50 for signed catalogs which include a fly tied by Alec. The catalogs contain few recent books, and there are many titles in each listing.

A sample: Phair, Charles. *Atlantic Salmon Fishing.* Foreword by Richard C. Hunt. Illustrated by Ogden M. Pleissner, Robert Nisbet, N.A. and from Photographs, Drawings, and Maps. Folio. pp., xx, 193. Green Cloth, dust jacket (poor), top edge gilt. VERY GOOD. The Derrydale Press, New York, 1937. One of 950. $278.

There are books in every price range, of course, and I consider this listing to be one of your best book hunting sources. Write: Alec Jackson, Box 386, Kenmore, Washington 98028 (206) 488-9806.

The Anglers Art. Another book catalog that concentrates on fly fishing titles comes from The Anglers Art. The catalog will have a new title, probably does already, something like "Books for the Fly Fisherman". It lists current titles as well as out-of-print books, but with fewer really old books than Alec Jackson carries. You'll enjoy the longer descriptions of many of the books, and they will aid in your selection.

A sample: Gingrich, Arnold. *The Joys of Trout,* 1974. 16 pgs. photos. Section on "Fifty Books for a Fly Fisherman". Comments on almost everything having to do with fly fishing for trout: equipment, traditions, techniques, people, organizations, etc. New, $22.50.

You'll also find some angling art here—the issue I have features an Eldridge Hardy print—and a few brief articles about fishing books. Write: The Anglers Art, R.D. 9, Box 204, Carlisle, Pennsylvania 17013 (717) 243-9721.

A Cabinet of Books. Finally, A Cabinet of Books offers "An Interesting Selection for Anglers and Shooters" in their catalog. The catalog contains books on all outdoor topics but concentrates on hunting and fishing. You'll find many interesting angling books in all price ranges, and the search through the rest of the list won't bore you.

A sample: Van Dyke, Henry (Signed by), *Fisherman's Luck.* Scribner's 1899 Special Walton Edition, Ltd #141/150 copies. DeVinne Press. Van Gelder paper. Vellum & boards. 247pp. Special illus-tissue guarded. T. E. G. With an additional Preface & Portrait. VG $150.00.

For their catalog, write A Cabinet of Books, Box 195, Watertown, Connecticut 06795 (203) 274-4825.

Other Book Dealers. The following dealers also handle out-of-print books. Write for listings and catalogs.

Angler's and Shooter's Bookshelf
Goshen, Connecticut 06756

Gary Easterbrook
Box 23898
San Jose, California 95153

Adam's Angling
1170 Keeler Avenue
Berkeley, California 94708

Fur Fin Feather
Box 326
South Holland, Illinois 60473

J.E. Taylor
1451 McMichael Drive
Baton Rouge, Louisiana 70815

Kenneth Anderson
38 Silver Street
Auburn, Massachusetts 01501

The Open Creel
25 Breton Street
Palmer, Massachusetts 01069

The Charles Daly Collection
66 Chilton Street
Cambridge, Massachusetts 02138

Highwood Farms
Box 1246
Traverse City, Michigan 49684

Gunnerman Books
Box 4292
Auburn Heights, Michigan 48057

Pisces and Capricorn Books
514 Linden Avenue
Albion, Michigan 49224

Chestnut Ridge Books
Box 353
Rutherford, New Jersey 07070

Sporting Book Service
Box 18
Rancocas, New Jersey 08073

James Cummins
667 Madison Avenue
New York, New York 10021

Sportsmen's Cabinet
Box 59
Ogdensburg, New York 13669

Morris Heller
Box 529
Monticello, New York 12701

Sportsmen's Encore
342 West 84th Street
New York, New York 10024

The Book House
Box 1284
Chapel Hill, North Carolina 27514

Melvin Marcher
6204 N. Vermont
Oklahoma City, Oklahoma 73112

Rising Trout
Box 1719
Guelph, Ontario, Canada

Any of these companies would probably be glad to help you look for a special book. Write and ask. Meanwhile, here's the list of books currently available from our fly fishing catalogs. Prices will vary considerable when books are available in both hardbound and paper back.

Categories:
   Collecting
   Entomology
   Fish
   Fly fishing, general
   Fly tying
   Guides
   Rod building
   Stories, fiction

Collecting

American Sporting Collectors Handbook, The. *Revised edition. Descriptions, prices, history of bamboo fly rods included along with other sporting gear.*
$16.15 T&T
Fly Reels of the House of Hardy. *By Glenn Stockwell;*

hb; 58 pp. Historical information about Hardy reels, including early photos and advertising pieces.
$16.50-$20 AnR, Hun
Those Old Fishing Reels. *By Albert J. Munger; pb. Dates, history on all types of U.S. reels from early 1800s on. Many photos.*
$10 T&T

Entomology

Aquatic Entomology. *By W. Patrick McCafferty; pb and hb; 400+ pp. Comprehensive aquatic entomology reference book written in language useful to fishermen. Correlates common fly fishing names to scientific names. Over 1,000 illustrations with 124 full color plates of insects. Expensive, but a standard reference book for the serious entomolgist/angler.*
$50-$90 T&T, Cab, Kau, Mur
Aquatic Insects of California. *By Usinger; 508 pp. Technical volume with sophisticated language.*
$35.95 Fly

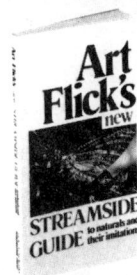

Art Flick's New Streamside Guide. *By Art Flick; pb; 176 pp. An updated edition of the original work that aids in streamside identification of insects and gives matching fly patterns.*
$5.40-$7.95 Most catalogs
Caddis and the Angler, The. *By Larry Solomon and Eric Leiser; hb; 224 pp. The first book devoted to identifying, tying, and fishing the caddis. Many interesting patterns.*
$14.85-$21.95 T&T, Cus, EJH, H&H, Edd, Dal, Dan, Let, AnR, Ran, Hig, Kau, Tac, Spo, Fly

Caddisflies. *By Gary LaFontaine; hb; 336 pp. A fairly new book on one of the trout's main foods, with emergence tables, distribution charts, fishing techniques, and innovative patterns. Patterns from this book are in widespread use now. With 180 line drawings, over 100 photos.*
$16.85-$27.95 Most catalogs

Compara Hatch. *By Al Caucci and Bob Nastasi. Waterproof reference chart to help in identifying major hatches.*
$6.45-$7.95 T&T, Pen, Hig, Dan, Ram, Cus

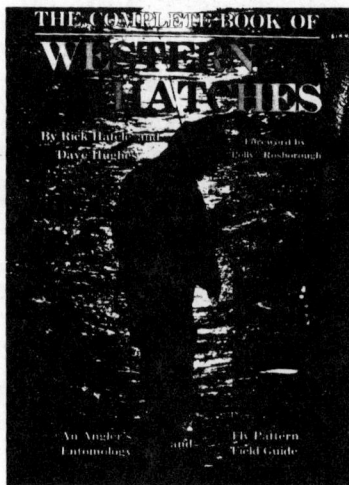

Complete Book of Western Hatches. *By Rick Hafele and Dave Hughes; pb; 223 pp. A resource book for the western angler. Many excellent photos, emergence tables, and patterns to match each form of each insect covered. An extremely practical and informative book for the serious angler.*
$14.20-$18.95 Kau, Fly, Dan, T&T, Cus, Hig, H&H, Bud, Ste, Bob, AnJ

Dave Whitlock's Guide to Aquatic Trout Foods. *By Dave Whitlock; hb; 224 pp. Descriptions and illustrations of all categories of trout food. Tying instructions for author's favorite patterns.*
$16.85-$27.95 Most catalogs

Hatches. *By Al Caucci and Bob Nastasi; hb; 320 pp. Reprint of the popular book on mayfly hatches and patterns to match them. Tying instructions included.*
$24.95-$29.95 T&T, Dan, Fly, Ram, AnJ, EJH, Kau

Instant Mayfly Identification Guide. *By Al Caucci and Bob Nastasi; pb. Entomology translated into simple terms. Illustrated, with 96 color photos. Spiral bound, vest pocket size.*
$7.95-$9.95 Kau, Bud, Don, Pen, Hig, EJH, Ram, Cus

Matching the Hatch. *By Ernest Schwiebert; pb; 220 pp. Paperback edition of the classic work on identifying*
insects and choosing patterns to match them. With color and b&w illustrations by author.
$6.45-$7.95 Dan, Dal, Bob, Cus, T&T, Sim, Kau, Hig, H&H

Mayflies, the Angler, and the Trout. *By Fred Arbona, Jr.; hb; 224 pp. Devoted to identifying and imitating the mayfly hatches of American waters. Over 300 identification drawings and tying sequences.*
$16.85-$27.95 Most catalogs

Meeting and Matching the Hatches. *By Charles Meck; 268 pp. Hatch information on more than eight common insect types with where-and-when information and imitative patterns.*
$11.25-$12.95 T&T, Tac, Let, EJH, Dal

Naturals: a Guide to Food Organisms of Trout. *By Gary Borger; hb; 224 pp. Practical entomology guide devoted to trout food sources, with key to identify insects.*
$13.50-$17.95 Edd, Bud, Let, Hig, Fly, Hun, AnR, T&T, Cus, Dan, Kau, Dal, H&H, Tac

Nymphs. *By Ernest Schwiebert; pb; 368 pp. Comprehensive guide to nymphs including identification, matching patterns, and fishing techniques. Color plates and b&w drawings.*
$12.15-$24.95 Many catalogs

Stoneflies. *By Carl Richards, Doug Swisher, and Fred Arbona, Jr.; hb; 192 pp. Guide to stoneflies and fishing them. Includes entomological information, how to fish stonefly patterns, and new patterns. B&w and color photos.*
$16.85-$27.95 Most catalogs

Stoneflies for the Angler. *By Eric Leiser and Robert H. Boyle; hb; 174 pp. Identification charts, fishing techniques, and tying instructions for stoneflies.*
$15.40-$18.50 Bud, H&H, T&T, Fly, AnR, Kau, Cus, Hig

Trout Flies: Naturals and Imitations. *By Charles M. Wetzel; 160 pp. Reprint of 1955 work which pioneered in the area of hatches and entomology for the fly fisherman.*
$18-$20 T&T, Dan, Hun, Bud, Tac

Fish

Atlantic Salmon, The. *By Lee Wulff; hb; 288 pp. Revised edition of the 1958 classic book on salmon covering all aspects of salmon fishing. With 130 b&w photos and eight pages of color.*
$22.45-$27.95 Wul, Kau, Ram, Tac, Hun, Fly, Dan, Don, AnR, Bud, T&T, Ran, Pen

Fishes of Montana. *By C.J.D. Brown; pb. Covers spawning times, growth rates, feeding habits, and more.*
$9 Dan, Big

Freshwater Wilderness: Yellowstone Fishes and Their World. *By John D. Varley and Paul Schullery; hb and pb. A guide to the fishes of the Yellowstone region, including a description of the waters, the fish that live there, and man's impact. With illustrations by Michael Simon.*
$12.95-$19.95 Dan, Bob, Blu, Bud, Hig

Kamloops. *By Steve Raymond; pb. Angler's study of the Kamloops trout, including history of the area and the trout, patterns, favorite waters, techniques. By one of our best writers.*
$9.95 Ste, Kau

Native Trout of North America. *By Robert H. Smith; hb and pb. All the varieties of trout found in North America and Mexico, with over 40 color photos.*
$15-$28 Kau

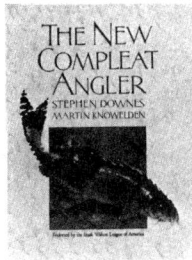

New Compleat Angler, The. *By Stephen Downes; hb. Describes in detail how fish see, including chapters on life histories of various fish with tips on how to catch them.*
$19.95-$24.95 Dan, AnJ, Tid, Don, Fly

Sea Run. *By Les Johnson; hb and pb. Guide to fishing for sea-run cutthroats, including where-to, how-to, and patterns.*
$9.95-$14.95 Ste, Kau

Steelhead. *By Mel Marshall; 186 pp. Reprint. Includes origins and habits of steelhead, all types of fishing techniques, trip planning, recipes.*
$8.85-$10.95 Tac, T&T, Cus

Trout Biology. *By William B. Willers; hb; 206 pp. Characteristics, behavior, life history, food of trout.*
$19.95 Dan, Kau, Bud

Fly Fishing, General

Advanced Fly Fishing. *By Eugene Burns; 288 pp. Modern equipment and techniques.*
$21.95 Tac, Bud

Art and Science of Fly Fishing. *By Lenox Dick. An older book on fly fishing techniques.*
$7.95 Ran

Backpacking for Trout. *By Bill Cairns; hb. Backpacking equipment and techniques for fly and spin fishing.*
$12.60-$16.95 AnJ, Sim

Bass Almanac. *By Lamar Underwood; pb. A collection of facts and information about bass fishing with one section, by Dave Whitlock, devoted to fly fishing for bass.*
$11.65 T&T

Catskill Trout Rivers. *By Austin Francis; hb; 224 pp. Profiles of the famous rivers of southern New York, including the Beaverkill, Willowemoc, Schoharie, and others. Not a guide book as much as historical view of the area's significance to American fly fishing.*
$22.45-$27.95 Let, Ram, T&T, Fly, Blu, Bob, Hun, Pen, Don, Dan, AnR, Kau

Challenge of the Trout, The. *By Gary LaFontaine; 241 pp. Covers the techniques of fly fishing, natural feed, fly patterns, with concentration on western waters.*
$12.95-$13.95 Bud, Fly, AnR, Blu, Dan, Hig, Tac

Common Sense Fly Fishing. *By Ray Ovington; pb. Instructions and illustrations designed to make fly fishing more understandable.*
$8-$8.95 T&T, Tac, AnJ, AnR, Hun

Compleat Angler's Catalog, The. *By Scott Roederer; pb. Listings of nearly every piece of equipment for fly fishermen, with retail sources for them; how-to-buy advice; sections on organizations, publications, and catalog companies; highly recommended, of course.*
Look at cover Johnson Books, 1880 S. 57th Court, Boulder, Colorado 80301

Curtis Creek Manifesto, The. *By Sheridan Anderson; pb. A lighthearted look at the sport of fly fishing with the beginner in mind. Entertaining illustrations.*
$4.50-$5 T&T, Dan, Bud, Fly, Cus, Kau, Bob, Ste, Hig

Fishing Dry Flies for Trout. *By Art Lee; hb; 285 pp. How-to book covering presentation, casting, choosing flies, and so on. Lots of illustrations.*
$12.95-$19.95 Kau, Hun, Fly, T&T, AnR, Cus, Nor

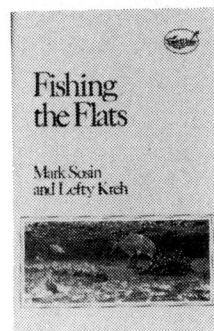

Fishing the Flats. *By Mark Sosin and Lefty Kreh; hb and pb. Detailed instructions on fishing the saltwater flats with all types of tackle.*
$8.95-$16.95 Kau, Hun, Fly, Dan, Don, AnR, Nor

Fishing the High Country. *By Trey Combs. How to fish high lakes and streams, including spin and fly fishing.*
$2.70-$3 T&T, Ste

Fishing the Nymph. *By Jim Quick.*
$7.50 Ran

Float Tubes, Fly Rods, and Other Essays. *By Marv Taylor; pb. Equipment, techniques, and patterns for float-tube fishing.*
$9.86-$10.95 Hig, Fly, Kau, Dal, Dan

Fly Casting from the Beginning. *By Jimmy Green; 80 pp. Basic fly casting instruction.*
$2.50 Fly

Fly Casting with Lefty Kreh. *By Lefty Kreh; pb. Step-by-step photos demonstrating proper casting techniques by a master caster.*
$5.49-$9.95 Cab, T&T, Kau, Cus, Sim

Fly Fisherman's Streamside Handbook, The. *By Craig Woods. A primer for the beginner designed to be carried in a vest pocket for reading during the tough fishing times.*
$8 T&T

Fly Fishing. *By David Lee; hb and pb; 190 pp. Step-by-step approach to fly fishing for beginners.*
$7.15-$16.95 T&T, Tid, Mur, Kau

Fly Fishing. *By Tom McNally. Tackle, casting, and techniques for fresh and saltwater fly fishing.*
$13.45 T&T

Fly Fishing Always.. *hb and pb. Articles by many famous writers, including Lyons, Swisher, Kreh, Brooks, Whitlock, Schwiebert, Wulff, and others. Proceeds from this collection go to benefit the International Fly Fishing Center in West Yellowstone. Hardback edition limited to 1,000 copies.*
$8.95, $35 Angler's Calendar, Route 1, Murtaugh, Idaho 83344

Fly Fishing for Trout: a Guide for the Adult Beginner. *By Richard Talleur; pb; 272 pp. Basic instructions written for the adult novice, with over 200 illustrations.*
$10.10-$16.95 Edd, Tac, Hun, Fly, H&H, Cus, AnR, Ram, Let

Fly Fishing Heresies. *By Leonard Wright. Different approaches to traditional fly fishing problems.*
$5.40 Sim

Fly Fishing in Salt Water. *By Lefty Kreh. A reprint of the original work on saltwater techniques and flies.*
$10.50-$12.95 T&T, Cus, AnR, Hun

Fly Fishing; Simple to Sophisticated. *By Al Kyte. Comprehensive treatment of the sport with the beginner in mind.*
$6.95 Fly

Fly Fishing Still Waters. *By Don Roberts; pb. How to fish lakes and ponds.*
$11 Cus

Fly Fishing Strategy. *By Doug Swisher and Carl Richards; hb; 220 pp. Insights into the sport by two of its most innovative thinkers.*
$10.50-$12.95 Let, Hig, EJH, Cus, Hun, T&T, Dal, Edd, Nor

Flyfishing the High Country. *By John Gierach. A primer on high lakes and streams, with additional chapters on beaver ponds, tackle, prospecting.*
$7.95 Pruett Publishing, 2928 Pearl, Boulder, Colorado 80301

Fly Rod Steelhead. *By Bill Stinson; pb. Techniques for all types of steelheading with a fly rod with illustrations, photos, and color plates.*
$8-$8.95 T&T, Sho, Ste, Fly, Kau

Fresh Water Fish and Fishing. *By Jim Arnosky. Written for starting youngsters out in fishing without the usual emphasis on bait fishing. For ages 8 and up.*
$8 T&T

Greased Line Fishing for Salmon (and Steelhead). *By Jock Scott. Covers the use of the dry fly for salmon and steelhead, with contemporary steelhead patterns added.*
$9.95 Ste, Kau, Hun, Fly

How to Catch Trout Between the Hatches. *By Jerry Meyer; 148 pp. Guide to fishing when no flies are hatching.*
$14.95 Hig

How to Fish from Top to Bottom. *By Sid Gordon.*
$21.95 Bud

How to Take Trout on Wet Flies and Nymphs. *By Ray Ovington. Devoted to fishing with the underwater forms of insects.*
$8.40-$9.95 T&T, Cus, EJH

In the Ring of the Rise. *By Vince Marinaro. In part an expansion of A Modern Dry Fly Code, but much space devoted to rise forms and how to read them. Excellent illustrative photos.*
$10.50-$12.95 Cus, EJH, Mur, AnR, Don, Blu

Joe Humphrey's Trout Tactics. *By Joe Humphrey; pb; 192 pp. Comprehensive guide to trout fishing with sections on finding trout, different fishing situations, each type of fly fishing. Special section on night fishing.*
$11.20-$14.95 Bud, T&T, Cus, Ram, Fly, H&H, AnR, Let, Tac, EJH, Hun, Nor, Dan

Lake Fishing With a Fly. *By Randall Kaufmann and Ronald Cordes; hb and pb; 200 + pp. How-to for lake fly fishermen, including reading lakes, presentation techniques, and food sources. With over 200 illustrations.*
$19.95-$29.95 Kau

Larger Trout for the Western Fly Fisherman. *By Charles Brooks; pb; 224 pp. For the angler seeking large fish by the well-known author from West Yellowstone.*
$9.95-$12.95 Dan, Tac, Fly, AnJ, AnR, Kau, Bud, Ram, Let, Bob, Hun

L.L. Bean Fly Fishing Handbook. *By Dave Whitlock; pb. An instructional book for beginners to the sport. With many illustrations.*
$8.95 Bud, LLB

Lure and Lore of Trout Fishing, The. *By Alvin R. Grove. New edition of 1965 work dealing with all aspects of fly fishing, including trout habits, fly tying, entomology.*
$9.95 Dan, EJH

Masters on the Dry Fly. *Edited by J. Michael Migel. Collection of articles by 16 experts, including Schwiebert, Kreh, and Wulff, on the art of dry fly fishing and entomology.*
$6.95 Edd, Bud

Masters on the Nymph. *Edited by J. Migel and L. Wright; 272 pp. Experts share their nymphing skills, including patterns and techniques. Illustrations by Whitlock.*
$13.45-$16.95 T&T, Hig, Kau, Edd, EJH

McClane's New Standard Fishing Encyclopedia. *By Al McClane; hb; 1,156 pp. Originally published in 1965, now revised and up-dated. Covers so many things I can't list them all—fish species, fly patterns, fishing areas, etc.*
$50 Kau, Bud

Modern Dry Fly Code. *By Vince Marinaro; pb; 307 pp. Reprint of the classic on dry fly fishing, with emphasis on what a trout sees, how it reacts, and proper presentation.*
$9-$12.95 T&T, Let, Pen, Kau, Fly, Blu, EJH, Mur, Dan, AnR

Modern Fly Fishing. *Edited by Larry Solomon. Covers basic tackle, casting, tying, and fly fishing techniques.*
$7.15 T&T

Mountain in the Clouds. *By Bruce Brown; hb. Centered around the Olympic Peninsula and its fish, particularly steelhead and Pacific salmon.*
$12.95 Kau

Nymph Fishing for Larger Trout. *By Charles Brooks; pb. Reprint of Brooks' instruction manual for catching the big fellas.*
$6.05-$10.95 Many catalogs

Nymphing. *By Gary Borger; 223 pp. Basic how-to for nymphing, with information on identifying, tying, and fishing nymphs.*
$11.20-$14.95 T&T, Dan, Dal, Fly, AnR, H&H, Ran, Cus, Edd, Hig, Tac, Spo, Bud, Kau, Hun

Nymphs and the Trout. *By Frank Sawyer.*
$5.95 Ran

Orvis Anthology, The. *Edited by Tom Rosenbauer; hb. Collection of articles and stories from the Orvis writing contest, 1981-1982.*
$16.95 Orv

Orvis Fly Fishing Guide. *By Tom Rosenbauer; pb and hb. Coverage of all aspects of fly fishing, beginning with the basics. With many photos.*
$13.95-$17.95 Orv, Bud

Practical Fishing Knots. *By Mark Sosin and Lefty Kreh; pb; 160 pp. Lots of illustrations to help reader tie many popular knots.*
$4.80-$8.95 Hun, Kau, Cus, Ran, Hig, Tac, Fly, AnR, AnJ, Let, T&T, Cor, Dan, Sim, Bud

Primer of Fly Fishing, A. *By Roderick Haig-Brown. From worms to ethics, encompasses every aspect of fly fishing.*
$8.95-$14.95 Fly, Kau

Selective Trout. *By Doug Swisher and Carl Richards; pb; 224 pp. Techniques for dealing with tough trout*

including matching the hatch. Details on no-hackle flies.
$6.45-$11.95 Many catalogs

Shad Fishing. *By C. Boyd Pfeiffer; 177 pp. All-tackle approach including fly fishing.*
$8.95 Fly

Solunar Tables. *From the work of J. Alden Knight. Originally developed in 1935, this system for predicting feeding times must have some value or it wouldn't be around in the 1980s.*
$1.75-$2 Ran, EJH, Pen

Steelhead Drift Fishing. *By Bill Luch; 94 pp. General book on drift fishing for steelhead, not specific to fly fishing.*
$5.95 Ste, Fly, Sho

Steelhead Fly Fishing and Flies. *By Trey Combs; pb. Comprehensive guide to steelheading, with over 70 photos and 250 patterns.*
$9-$15 Dan, Cus, Sho, Kau, Fly, EJH, H&H, Hun, T&T, Ste, AnR

Stillwater Trout. *Edited by John Merwin; hb. Collection of original work by several authors, covering fishing in lakes and ponds. Excellent book on too-long neglected subject.*
$14.40-$15.95 Edd, Dal, Hun, Blu, Ram

Streamside Flyfisher's Guide. *By Brian Kahn and Max Hale; pb; 120 pp. Streamside reference book with nymph identification, problem solver, personal journal, and gear checklist. Pocket-sized.*
$6.25-$6.95 T&T, Bud, Fly, Hig, Dan

Striped Bass Fishing. *By Frank Woolner and Hal Lyman; hb and pb; 192 pp. Revision of earlier book with maps and charts, how-to.*
$9.95-$18.95 Kau, Tac

Striped Bass on the Fly. *By Russel Chatham; pb. Techniques for taking the striper with fly rod.*
$4.50 Dan

Trout. *By Ray Bergman; hb and pb; 517 pp. Revised and enlarged edition of one of the first modern guides to trout fishing.*
$12.95-$25 Kau, Let, Fly, Ran, Cus, AnR, Hun, EJH, Dan, Edd, Bob, T&T

Trout and the Fly, The. *By Brian Clarke and John Goddard; 192 pp. A new study of fly fishing which challenges old theories with research on trout vision and fly patterns.*
$17.95-$20 Kau, Bud, Dal, Tac, Hun, AnR, Hig, T&T, Dan

Trout and the Stream, The. *By Charles Brooks; pb; 224 pp. A fine book on trout fishing, especially in the West Yellowstone, Montana area. With guide to fishing the author's favorite waters and patterns.*
$9.70-$11.95 Dan, T&T, Bob, Cus, Kau, Fly, Tac, Hun
Trout Fishing and Trout Flies. *By Jim Quick.*
$8.95 Ran
Trout Hunting. *By Frank Woolner. Covers all types of fishing for trout, including bait, spin, fly, ice.*
$12.95 AnJ
Trout Strategies. *By Ernest Schwiebert; pb. Covers matching the hatch, methods of fishing all types of flies, with material drawn from Trout.*
$9.85 T&T
Trout: Tools of the Trade. *By Ernest Schwiebert; pb. Covers fly fishing equipment. Drawn from Trout but up-dated.*
$13.45 T&T
Ultimate Fishing Book, The. *Edited by Eisenberg and Taylor.*
$40 Dan
Wade a Little Deeper, Dear. *By Gwen Cooper and Evelyn Haas; pb. A woman's "guide" to fly fishing.*
$4.45-$4.50 Fly, T&T, Bud, Dan
Western Angler, The. *By Roderick Haig-Brown. From tackle to scenery, one of the books the literate angler should own.*
$10.95 Kau

Fly Tying

American Fly Tyer's Handbook, The. *Edited by Kenneth E. Bay; pb; 132 pp. The favorite fly patterns of 15 of the best tiers with step-by-step instructions on how to tie them. Over 200 photos.*
$13.50-$19.95 T&T, Bud, Hun, H&H, Let, Cus, Dal, Tac
American Nymph Fly Tying Manual. *By Randall Kaufmann; pb; 93 pp. Lists of over 200 nymph patterns with 250 step-by-step photos, with sections on tools and materials.*
$7.45-$10 Kau, Dan, Edd, Fly, H&H, EJH, AnR, Hun, Hig, Ran, Cus, Ste, T&T
Art Flick's Master Fly Tying Guide. *By Art Flick; pb; 220 pp. Nine master tier's show how to tie their most effective patterns. Over 300 photos show tying sequences. With chapter by Whitlock on new materials and tools.*
$7.24-$12.95 Edd, Pen, Spo, Tac, Don, T&T, Mur, Hun, Ran, Kau, H&H, EJH, Cus, Bud
Art of Tying the Wet Fly and Fishing the Flymph, The. *By J. Leisenring and V. Hidy. Out of print, limited supplies. Deals with the Flymph, imitating the transformation stage between nymph and adult.*
$6.95-$12.95 Edd, Kau, EJH
Basic Manual of Fly Tying, The. *By Paul Fling and Don Puterbaugh; pb. An instructional book designed for beginners. With line drawings and some color plates.*
$8-$8.95 T&T, Ran, Edd, Dan, Fly, Bud
Beginning Fly Tyer, The. *By Jim Bainbridge; pb.; 44*

pp. A brief manual to get the beginner started in the right way.
$3.55-$3.95 T&T, Dan
Chauncey Lively's Flybox. *By Chauncey Lively; pb; 96 pp. Forty original patterns with over 300 illustrations on how to tie them.*
$7.95-$9.95 T&T, Edd, Mur, Tac, Let, Dal, AnR, Hun
Complete Book of Fly Tying, The. *By Eric Leiser. An illustrated book for the beginning tier, with photos and with line drawings by Dave Whitlock.*
$13.20-$19.95 Many catalogs
Complete Fly-Tier, The. *By Reuben R. Cross. Instructional book from one of the premier tiers, with most devoted to dry flies. New chapters on salmon flies and tricks of the trade.*
$7.95 Dan, Ree, EJH
Eastern Streamers. *By Dick Frost.*
$3.95 Ran
Essential Fly Tyer, The. *By J. Edson Leonard. More techniques and background on flies from the author of Flies.*
$12.50 Cus
Expert Fly Tying. *By Fling and Puterbaugh; pb. Continuation of the basic manual with more advanced techniques and more difficult patterns.*
$7.95-$8.95 Dan, T&T, Fly, Bud, Bob
Fishing Flies and Fly Tying. *By Bill Blades; 320 pp. A limited edition reprint of a 1951 book, updated by Poul Jorgensen.*
$22.45-$24.95 Dan, Tac, Don, Spo, AnR, T&T, Bud, Hun
Flies. *By J. Edson Leonard; pb; 340 pp. A paperback reprint of a classic tying book. Over 2,000 patterns given, plus information about materials and tying techniques. An excellent reference.*
$13.45-$17.95 Ree, T&T, Ran, EJH, Spo, AnR, Cus
Flies of the Northwest. *By Inland Empire Fly Club; pb. Full color photos of 120 patterns used in the Pacific Northwest, with recipes.*
$8.50 Bud, Kau, Dan

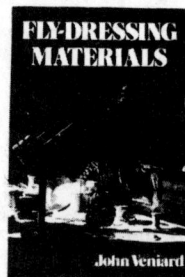

Fly-Dressing Materials. *By John Veniard; 145 pp. Complete treatment of materials and tying techniques.*
$12.50-$13.95 Hun, Fly
Fly Patterns of Alaska. *By the Alaska Flyfishers; pb. Full-color illustrations showing how to tie 137 Alaskan favorites, with additional information on where and how to fish them. Spiral softbound.*
$8.95-$11.95 T&T, Ste, Fly, Kau, H&H

Fly Tyer's Almanac. *Edited by Dave Whitlock and Bob Boyle; pb; 220 pp. Collection of articles about developments in tying and new patterns, with illustrations.*
$8.75-$14.95 Kau, Hun, Dan, H&H, Cus, Tac, AnR

Fly Tyer's Almanac, The Second. *By Dave Whitlock and Bob Boyle; 224 pp. More new flies, materials, and techniques.*
$8.10-$14.95 Hig, Hun, Cus, AnR

Fly-tyer's Color Guide. *By Al Caucci and Bob Nastasi; hb. Color charts, tying instructions, materials, and blending formulas.*
$18.95 AnJ

Fly Tying. *By William Sturgis.*
$8.95 Ran

Fly-Tying. *By Helen Shaw; hb and pb. Reprint of the original work. Tips on tying, with many oversize, well-planned photos.*
$9.95-$19.50 Dan, EJH, Bob, Cus, Cor

Fly Tying, Adventures in Fur, Feathers, and Fun. *By John McKim; pb; 160 pp. Beginning tying instructions accompanied by wonderful line drawings. One of the most enjoyable manuals from which to learn, some techniques for the intermediate tier, too.*
$9.85-$10.95 Dal, Fly, Let, AnR, Blu

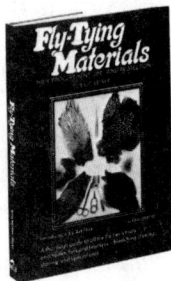

Fly Tying Materials. *By Eric Leiser; pb; 224 pp. Fully illustrated book on materials and their uses. Includes sources and skinning techniques.*
$6.75-$11.95 EJH, Kau, Fly, Let, Hun, Dan, AnJ, Mur, Bud, Tac, H&H, Edd, T&T, Ran, AnR

Fly Tying Techniques. *By Jaqueline Wakeford; hb; 160 pp. More than 400 color photos on fly tying techniques, with sections on tools and materials and a chapter on patterns keyed to techniques.*
$26.95-$29.95 AnR, T&T, Bud, Blu, Hun

Hair Wing Atlantic Salmon Flies. *By Keith Fulsher and Charles Krom; hb and pb; 181 pp. Over 300 patterns with instructions, fishing techniques, and historical information. Over 100 flies in color. Tips for converting featherwings to hairwings.*
$12-$25 T&T, Let, Kau, AnR, Fly, Hun, Don, Edd

Hardy Book of Flies. *Pb; 24pp. Guide to the identification of trout and salmon flies. Full-color plates of 240 flies. Vinyl cover.*
$2.69 Mer

Hooked on Flies. *By William C. Black. "Confessions of a Pattern Inventor". How-to book for the tier who wants*

to experiment with innovative techniques, materials, and patterns.
$13.45 T&T

How to Dress Salmon Flies. *By Pryce-Tannatt.*
$24.95 AnR

How to Make Your Own Lures and Flies. *By Mel Marshall; 192 pp. Step-by-step photos for making lures and flies with a minimun of tools and materials.*
$4.50 Tac, Spo

Lee Wulff on Flies. *By Lee Wulff; hb; 160 pp. Instructions from one of the masters on choosing and tying flies with information about many of the original Wulff patterns.*
$11.20-$15 Wul, T&T, Edd, Tac, AnR, Cus, Let, H&H, Dan, Kau, Bud, Spo, Fly

Master Fly Weaver. *By George Grant; hb. Limited edition, up-dated reprint of original work. Step-by-step techniques.*
$50 Kau, Bud

Mastering the Art of Fly Tying. *By Richard W. Talleur; 224 pp. Complete tying skills course for the beginner and intermediate tier with step-by-step photos.*
$22.45-$24.95 T&T, Dal, AnJ, Fly, Hig, Hun, AnR, Dan, Spo, Tac, Let, Edd

Modern Fly Dressings for the Practical Angler. *By Poul Jorgensen; hb; 240 pp. Tying instructions for the modern styles with over 200 illustrations.*
$14.85-$23.95 Tac, Kau, Dal, AnR, Fly, H&H, EJH, Hun, T&T

Montana Trout Flies. *By George Grant. Limited edition of 1,950 copies. How to tie Montana favorites and how to fish them.*
$50 Bud, Kau

Orvis Fly Pattern Index. *Three-ring binder with 355 full-color photos of all types of flies, with recipes and tying hints. Size: 6½"x8½", lays flat. Two supplements.*
$19.95-$21 Kau, Ste, Let, Hig, AnR, Hun, Fly

Pacific Northwest Fly Patterns. *By Roy Patrick. Flies regionally known in the Northwest.*
$6.95-$7.95 Kau, Fly

Popular Fly Patterns. *By Terry Hellekson; pb and hb; 180 pp. Contains about 800 patterns, mostly from the West, with 200 flies in full color and 400 pen-and-ink drawings.*
$7.13-$15 Kau, Dan, Cus, Hig, Fly, Nat, Cab, TCr, H&H, Mur, Blu, Edd, Pen, EJH, Dal

Poul Jorgensen's Modern Trout Flies. *By Poul Jorgensen. Color guide to up-to-date patterns, photos and recipes for each. Over 300 illustrations.*
$8.75-$12.95 T&T, Mur, Kau, AnR, Ree, Cus, Edd, Bud, EJH, Nor

Practical Flies and Their Construction. *The old manual found in fly tying kits for many years.*
$3.50-$4 Ran, Spo, Egg

Salmon Flies: Their Character, Style, and Dressing. *By Poul Jorgensen; 256 pp. Over 160 salmon flies with detailed information. Over 200 illustrations.*
$14.95-$19.95 Many catalogs

Salmon Fly, The. *By George Kelson; hb; 482 pp. Limited edition reprint of first printing from 1895, with over 300 dressings and eight color plates. Only 2,000.*
$60 Kau, Hun

Saltwater Tying Guide, The. *By Chico Fernandez; pb. How to tie saltwater patterns with FisHair.*
$.50 Tac

Soft-Hackled Fly, The. *By Sylvester Nemes; pb. In-depth look at the soft hackle wet flies.*
$4.95 Dan, EJH, T&T

Soft-Hackled Fly Addict, The. *By Sylvester Nemes; pb; 125 pp. New materials with 90 patterns matched to naturals. Tying instructions and fishing techniques.*
$15.25-$16.95 Kau, Bud, Blu, Let, T&T, Dan, AnR, Fly, Hig

Steelhead Fly Tying Manual. *By Tom Light and Neal Humphrey; pb; 100 pp. List of over 500 patterns. Color plates and over 130 how-to photos on tying 17 steelhead flies.*
$7.45-$9.95 Ste, T&T, Fly, H&H, Hig, Ran

Streamers and Bucktails, The Big Fish Flies. *By Joseph D. Bates, Jr.; hb; 395 pp. Dressings for over 500 streamers with historical information and fishing strategies. As much a promotion and how-to for streamer fishing as a tying book but of great interest to the tier. Excellent reference book.*
$15.25-$16.95 T&T, Let, AnR, Kau, Fly, Ran, Ram, Bud, Edd, Cus, Hun, Let

Techniques of Fly Tying and Trout Fishing. *By George Harvey; pb; 160 pp. Extensive fly tying instructions plus tips for fishing and a pattern dictionary from one of the sport's best teachers.*
$2.95 Dan, T&T, Let, EJH, H&H

Trolling Flies for Trout and Salmon. *By Dick Stewart and Bob Leeman; pb; 122 pp. Many streamer patterns used primarily for anglers in the Northeast where trolling for trout and landlocked salmon is common. Tips including when and where.*
$11.95-$12.95 T&T, Hig, Hun, AnR, Edd, Ran, Ram

Trout and Salmon Fly Index. *By Dick Surette; pb; 143 pp. Over 170 patterns, in full color.*
$11.95-$12.95 Edd, Tac, EJH, AnR

Trout Flies of New Zealand. *By Keith Draper; pb; 180 pp. The most popular patterns in use today with information about where to use the fly.*
$11.95 Kau

Tying and Fishing Terrestrials. *By Gerald Almy; hb; 256 pp. Over 50 new and old terrestrial patterns with step-by-step instructions and illustrations.*
$8.97-$14.95 T&T, Bud, AnR, Dan, Mur, Dal, Fly, EJH, Hig, Tac, H&H, Kau, Let, AnJ, Edd

Tying and Fishing the Fuzzy Nymphs. *By Polly Rosborough; 192 pp. Up-dated version of original book with new patterns.*
$12.75-$16.95 Dan, Cus, Dal, Hun, Kau, AnR, Ran, Bud, Tac, H&H, Fly

Tying and Fishing the Swisher-Richards Flies. *By Doug Swisher and Carl Richards; pb; 48 pp. Patterns*

and tying techniques for the flies created by these well-known innovators.
$6.75-$8.95 Kau, Dan, Hun, H&H, T&T, Dal, Fly, Tac, Let, Cus

Tying and Fishing the Thunder Creek Series. *By Keith Fulsher; 101 pp. How to tie and fish the Thunder Creek streamers.*
$7.95 EJH

Tying and Fishing the West's Best Dry Flies. *By Bob Wilson and Richard Parks; pb; 112 pp. over 200 step-by-step photos for tying the authors' favorite western patterns.*
$7.95-$9.95 H&H, Fly, Bud, T&T, Mur, Ste, Hig, Dan

Tying Bugs and Flies for Bass. *By A. D. Livingston. A nifty little book on bass bugs for the fly fisherman. With good photos of the bugs and instructions for tying and fishing them.*
$8-$10 EJH, AnR

Universal Fly Tying Guide. *By Dick Stewart; pb. Full-color photos of 135 popular patterns, with recipes. Sections on tools and materials.*
$4.45-$7.95 Most catalogs

Veniard Pamphlets. *Pamphlets on a variety of subjects, including dyeing materials, salmon fly patterns, beginners's guide to salmon flies, and tying problems.*
$1-$3 Let

Western Trout Fly Tying Manual, Volume I. *By Jack Dennis; pb; 258 pp. One of the most popular tying manuals, with step-by-step photos for 65 patterns favored by western anglers plus recipes for 242 more. An excellent guide for beginning and intermediate tiers.*
$9.95-$15 Bob, Fly, Nat, Bud, H&H, Cus, Ste, Kau, Dan, Blu

Western Trout Fly Tying Manual, Volume II. *By Jack Dennis; pb; 320 pp. A follow-up to the immensely popular first volume with 50 additional western patterns. Step-by-step photos and instructions.*
$11.85-$17.50 T&T, Kau, Fly, Blu, H&H, Bob, Ste, Cus, Mur, Bud, Dan

What the Trout Said. *By Datus Proper. "About the Design of Trout Flies and Other Mysteries". First book to deal in depth with the relationship between fly design and presentation, from the perspective of the trout and what it sees.*
$16.50-$16.95 Hig, AnR, Dan, Blu, Mur, Bob, Hun, Bud, Ram

Guides

Adirondack Mountains, Sportsman's Map.
$3.50 T&T

Allagash and St. John Map and Guide. *For the wilderness area in Maine, detailed map and information.*
$3.95 Edd

Allagash—The History of a Wilderness River in Maine. *By Lew Dietz. Historical perspective of famous Maine river.*
$5.95 Edd

Anglers Guide to Catskill Trout. *Pathfinder Publications. A guide to the trout streams of New York's Catskill Mountains with state fishing areas, campgrounds, and access points listed.*
$4.45 T&T

Anglers Guide to Pennsylvania Trout. *By John A. Punola. Lists trout streams by county and region with map references, best flies, and catch-and-release sections.*
$4.45 T&T

Angling in New Zealand. *By Keith Draper; hb; 150 pp. How-to for travelers to New Zealand, including all aspects of sport.*
$21.95 Kau

Ausable River Map. *New York's famous river.*
$3.95 Nor

AuSable River Map. *Michigan's river.*
$3.95 Nor

Battenkill River Map.
$3.95 Nor

Baxter State Park and Katahdin Map and Guide. *Roads and trails, with contour lines for this wilderness area in Maine.*
$3.95 Edd

Beaverkill River, Fishing Map. *Two different maps here, I hope.*
$.25-$3.95 T&T, Nor

Bitterroot River Map.
$2.95 Nor

British Columbia Fishing Guide.
$7.95 Nor

Catskill Mountains, Fishing Map
$2 T&T

Catskill Mountains, Sportsman's Map
$2 T&T

Colorado and Wyoming, Tim Kelley's Fishing Guide to. *Edited by Dick Prouty. Brief descriptions of nearly every lake and stream in both states, including Yellowstone National Park. With maps and informative articles. Up-dated every other year.*
$9.95 (+$1.50 shipping) Hart Publications, Box 1917, Denver, CO 80201

Colorado Angling Guide, The. *By Chuck Fothergill and Bob Sterling; pb. Guide to the state's Wild Trout and Gold Medal waters, with descriptions of nearby towns for planning family trips. Many detailed fold-out maps.*
$13.95 (plus $1 postage) Stream Stalker, Box 1010, Aspen, Colorado 81612

Complete Taupo Fishing Guide. *By Peter Gould; hb; 235 pp. Guide to fishing New Zealand from Taupo.*
$20 Kau

Delaware River Map.
$3.95 Nor

50 Trout Ponds in Massachusetts. *By Owen Flynn; pb. Fifty of the state's best with maps, directions, and fishing tips.*
$8 T&T

50 Wisconsin Lake Maps.
$4.95

Fishing Guide to the Delaware River. *Pathfinder Publishing; pb. Details on tributaries, launch areas, canoe rentals, campgrounds with information on trout and shad fishing.*
$4.45 T&T

Fishing in the Florida Keys and Flamingo. *By Stu Apte; pb. Guide to saltwater fishing south of Florida by the originator of many of the most popular saltwater patterns.*
$4.95 Dan

Fishing the Headwaters of the Missouri. *By Norman Strung; pb. Tributaries of the Missouri discussed in detail, including the Madison, Gallatin, Jefferson, Big Hole, and others.*
$6.95-$7.95 Bud, Blu, Nor

Fishing Yellowstone Waters. *By Charles Brooks; pb. Guide to the waters of Yellowstone National Park and surrounding area by one of the most respected angling authors in the region. With photos by Dan Callahan.*
$12.95 Bud, Hig, Nor, Bob

Floater's Guide to Montana, The. *By Hank Fischer; pb; 152 pp. Madison, Yellowstone, and 26 other rivers mapped with commentary for the floater and floating fisherman.*
$6.95 Kau, Bud, Dan, Bob

Fly Fishing in Maine. *By Al Raychard. Guide to the best fishing in Maine, with maps, charts, illustrations.*
$6.95 Edd, Ran

Fly Fishing in New Zealand. *By George Ferris; hb. How-to book covering all aspects of fishing in New Zealand, including entomology, dry fly fishing, night fishing.*
$9.95 Kau

Fly Fishing the Ozarks.
$12.95 Nor

Following the Adams and the Humpy. *By Jane Woolley; pb; 305 pp. "A Guide to Western Stream Fishing for Trout and Salmon". Guide for the coastal states and Colorado, Montana, Wyoming, Idaho, with maps and lodging information.*
$18.95 (+$2 shipping) jw publishing, Box 1093, Palm Desert, California 92261

Guide to Massanutten Mountain. *By J.W. Denton. Hiking trails, trout streams near Virginia's Shenandoah River.*
$5 Mur

Handbook Guides. *Mile-by-mile details of rivers, showing rapids, access points, campsites and giving historical information. Individual guides for Rogue, Middle Fork Salmon, Illinois, John Day, and Deschutes.*
$9.95-$14.95 Kau

Handbook to the Deschutes River Canyon. *By Quinn and King. Designed for river runners but equally practical for other users of the river, including fishermen.*
$11.95 Kau

Living River, The. *By Charles Brooks. More than a guide, a portrait of a river, the Madison. Historical and ecological perspectives of the river. Will teach an*

appreciation of any river.
$15.75-$22.50 T&T, Big, Hig, Bob, Cus, Kau, Bud
Maine Fishing Maps, The Book of. *DeLorme Press.*
*Contains 115 maps of selected lakes and ponds, plus
listing of 1,200 more. Other editions cover streams and
saltwater fishing.*
$8.95 Nor, Edd
Massachusetts Fishing Map
$2 T&T

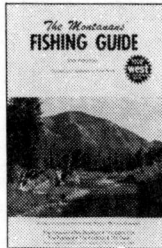

Montanan's Fishing Guide, The. *By Dick Konizeski.
Descriptions of all fishable waters in Montana. In two
volumes, one east of Divide, one west.*
$9.95 (each) Bob, Dan, Nor, Kau, Fly, Blu, Bud
Moosehead Lake Map and Guide. *Roads, trails,
campsites, lakes of the Moosehead area in Maine.*
$3.95 Edd
New Hampshire Trout Ponds, Volume 1. *Northern
Cartographic. Trout ponds of the White Mountains and
the North Country.*
$4.95 T&T, Nor
New Hampshire Trout Ponds, Volume 2. *Northern
Cartographic. Trout ponds and lakes of southern New
Hampshire.*
$4.95 Nor, T&T
**100 Pennsylvania Trout Streams and How to Fish
Them.** *Pb; 54 pp. Chapters on major watersheds written
by fishermen who fish them regularly.*
$5.50 EJH
100 Wisconsin Fishing Trips.
$14.95 Nor
Rivers and Lakes of the North Island. *By George Ferris;
pb; 55 pp. Pocket guide to fishing waters of New Zealand's
North Island.*
$2.95 Kau
Rivers and Lakes of the South Island. *By George Ferris;
pb; 46 pp. Pocket guide to fishing waters of New Zealand's
South Island.*
$2.95 Kau
Sebago Lake Region Map and Guide. *Water depths,
launch sites, navigational aids for Sebago and other lakes
in Maine.*
$3.95 Edd
Shenandoah National Park Map. *Three sections
available: north, central, south.*
$3 (each) Mur
Sierra Trout Guide. *By Ralph Cutter; pb.*
$7.95 Nor

Silver Creek Map.
$3.95 Nor
Smoky Mountains Trout Fishing Guide. *By Don Kirk.*
$7.95 Nor
South Platte River Map.
$3.95 Nor
Steelhead Map of Washington and Oregon. *Shows
winter and summer steelhead runs in rivers of both
states, with monthly catch statistics. Size: 2'x3'.*
$5.35-$5.95 Kau, T&T
Streams of Kentucky.
$9.95 Nor
Trout Fishing the Southern Appalachians.
$6.95 Nor
Trout and Salmon Fishing in Northern New England.
*By Al Raychard. Guide to selected waters in Maine, New
Hampshire, Vermont, Massachusetts.*
$7.95 Edd
Trout Streams in the Catskill Mountains
$2 T&T
Trout Waters in the Adirondack Mountains
$2 T&T
Trout Fishing in New Zealand. *By Rex Forrester; 200
pp. How-to, where-to, when-to book for those dreaming
of a trip to New Zealand, by an experienced guide.*
$14.95 Kau, Fly, Dan
Trout Fishing in North America: Where and When. *By
J.P. Kitching and B.P. Worcester; pb. Lists streams and
lakes with instructions on how to get there and when to
go. Over 1,300 top locations by state. Includes regula-
tions.*
$7.95-$8 T&T, AnR
Vermont Lakes in Depth. *Northern Cartographic.
Collection of depth charts for coldwater lakes. Includes
boat access, bottom profiles, fishing tips, and maps.*
$4.95 T&T, Nor
Vermont Trout Ponds. *Northern Cartographic. Over 150
ponds and lakes with maps.*
$5.95 T&T
Vermont Trout Streams.
$8.95 Nor
Washington State Fishing Guide.
$7.95 Nor
When-Where-How to Fish the Yellowstone Country.
*Large detailed map of Yellowstone area waters; recom-
mended patterns listed.*
$2 Dan
Wyoming Fishing Guide. *By Ken Knapp; pb. Covers all
Wyoming waters and includes maps, guide services, etc.*
$5.95 Dan
Yellowstone Park Map and Guide. *Spiral bound.
Describes all the streams and lakes of the Park.*
$4.25 Bud
Yellowstone Park Map and Guide. *Maps with informa-
tion on camping, fishing, hiking. North edition and
South edition.*
$1.25 (each) Bud

Rod Building

Advanced Custom Rod Building. *By Dale Clemens; hb; 353 pp. Covers every aspect of rod building in depth, including fancy wraps. A standard reference for all rod builders.*
$13.50-$19.95 Many catalogs

Custom Rod Thread Art. *By Dale Clemens. Over 100 thread wrap patterns for rods and other objects with step-by-step instructions.*
$19.76-$21.95 Dal, Cor, Mer, Cab

Decorative Rod Wrapping Guide. *Two books with diagrams and instructions for wrapping flags, diamonds, mazes, and others.*
$2.85-$4.50 (each) Mer, Tac, Bud, Pfe

Do It Yourself Rod Building. *By Bill Stinson; pb. Over 100 photos illustrating rod building for all types of fishing.*
$5.25-$6.95 Ste, Mer, Sho, Kau, H&H, T&T

Fiberglass Rod Making. *By Dale Clemens; hb and pb.; 189 pp. Over 10 years old now but still one of the most popular rod building primers. Full instructions with illustrations on basic techniques suitable to any material but with concentration on fiberglass.*
$6.40-$15.95 Many catalogs

Handcrafting a Graphite Fly Rod. *By Luis Agustin Garcia-Vela; pb. Instructions for building a graphite rod. Spiral bound.*
$6.50 Bud, Dan

How to Build Custom-Made, Handcrafted Fishing Rods. *By John Emery; pb. Booklet on building all types of rods.*
$3.95 Dan

How to Make Bamboo Rods. *By G.W. Barnes; 192 pp. Step-by-step instructions on making cane rods.*
$11.65-$12.95 Hun, T&T, Sho, Tac, Cor

How to Wrap a Rod. *By Gudebrod. Compact guide to wrapping a rod.*
$.85-$2.50 Mer, Sim, Bul, Egg, H&H, Sho, Tac, T&T, Don, Cor, Pfe

Stories, Fiction

Anatomy of a Fisherman. *By Robert Traver; hb and pb;*

117 pp. A distinguished book, honored by fly fishermen since its writing. With photos by Robert Kelley.
$12.95-$16.95 Dan, AnR, Blu, Bud, Fly, Kau

Angler's Astoria, An. *By Dave Hughes; pb. Collection of short works by one of our up-and-coming writers. Insights into fishing experiences in the Northwest that all anglers will appreciate.*
$9.95 Kau

Angler's Coast, The. *By Russell D. Chatham; pb.*
$10 Dan

Bright Waters, Bright Fish. *By Roderick Haig-Brown. The feelings and philosophies of fly fishermen, expressed by one of the great writers.*
$19.95 Kau, Bud

Death of a Riverkeeper. *By Ernest Schwiebert. Collection of short stories by the well-known author. Currently out of print, supplies limited.*
$14.95-$19.95 Bud, Kau, Cus

Fisherman's Fall. *By Roderick Haig-Brown. The angler's excitement for fall fishing, with emphasis on salmon and steelhead.*
$10.95 Kau

Fisherman's Spring. *By Roderick Haig-Brown. The author's fly fishing experiences covering many aspects of the sport.*
$10.95 Kau

Fisherman's Summer. *By Roderick Haig-Brown. Exciting summer fishing experiences centering on the Campbell River.*
$10.95 Kau

Fisherman's Winter. *By Roderick Haig-Brown. A winter trip to the summer waters of Argentina and Chile.*
$10.95 Kau

fish-ing. *By Henry Beard and Roy McKie. Dictionary for constant anglers, weekend waders, and artful bobbers. Good fun.*
$4.95 AnJ

Fishless Days, Angling Nights. *By Sparse Grey Hackle; pb. Collection of anecdotes and fishing stories from one of the country's favorite story tellers.*
$8.95-$9.95 Dan, Tid, Blu, Fly

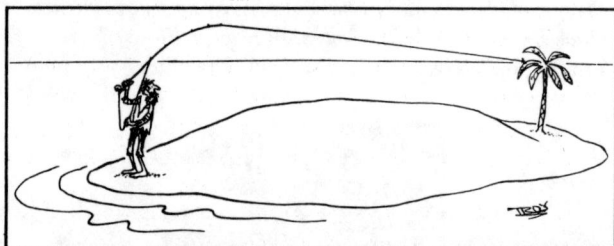

From Fly Fishing #%&!*

Fly Fishing #%&*!. *By John Troy, pb. Cartoons.*
$4.95 Nor

From the World of Roderick Haig-Brown: Writings and Reflections. *By Roderick Haig-Brown. Collected stories and short pieces from one of the masters of fishing literature.*
$9.95-$16.95 Fly, Kau

History of Angling, A. *By Charles Waterman. Covers the development of fishing from prehistoric times to present.*
$15.95-$16.95 Bud, Dan, Mur, Blu

History of Fly Fishing for Trout, The. *By John Waller Hills.*
$8.95 Dan

Master and the Fish, The. *By Roderick Haig-Brown. Describes Haig-Brown's initiation to the Pacific Coast as a young man.*
$7.95-$14.95 Kau, Fly

Remembrances of Rivers Past. *By Ernest Schwiebert. Stories and essays from one of the masters of the sport.*
$13.50 AnR, Blu

Return to the River. *By Roderick Haig-Brown. The spawning run of the chinook salmon detailed in literary fashion.*
$10.95 Kau

River Never Sleeps, A. *By Roderick Haig-Brown. Considered by many to be Haig-Brown's best.*
$9.95-$11.95 Dan, Fly, Blu, Kau, Bud

River Runs Through It, A. *By Norman MacLean. A short novel that has much to say about life as well as about fly fishing, with two other works. A first novel and an excellent work. For the reader/fly fisherman, this and the next book listed are musts.*
$12.50 Dan

River Why, The. *By David James Duncan; hb; 320 pp. Hilarious love story, partly about a woman and partly about fly fishing. The combination makes for great reading. Join Gus Orviston for an irreverent look at our world. High camp, great fun.*
$12.95 Fly, Kau

Seasonable Angler, The. *By Nick Lyons; pb. Collection of stories from one of America's favorite angling authors. Warm insights into the human condition as it pertains to fly fishing.*
$9.95 Nor, Bud

Silent Seasons. *By Russel Chatham.*
$15 Dan

Summer on the Test, A. *By John Walter Hills; pb. Fishing an English chalkstream.*
$9.95 Bud

Trout and Salmon Sport in New Zealand. *Edited by Tony Orman; hb; 190 pp. Stories and articles by New Zealand's most noted writers.*
$18.95 Kau

Trout Madness. *By Robert Traver; hb; 192 pp. Collection of the stories of one of the few authors who manages to find humor in all this; some grand stuff here. Originally published in 1960.*
$9.95-$12.95 Kau, Let, Blu, AnR, Dan

Trout Magic. *By Robert Traver. More from the master story teller. First published in 1974.*
$12.95 AnR, Dan, Kau

Undiscovered Zane Grey Fishing Stories. *By Zane Grey; 200 pp. Recently rediscovered novel and seven short stories from the 1920s, written originally for the Izaak Walton League.*
$16.95-$29.95 Kau, Dan

Waters Swift and Still. *Edited by Craig Woods and David Seybold. A dozen stories by the likes of Traver, Schwiebert, Merwin, Wulff, Waterman, and Lyons.*
$17.95 Dan, AnR, Kau, Blu

Where the Bright Waters Meet. *By Harry Plunkett Greene; pb.*
$9.95 Bud

Year of the Angler, The. *By Steve Raymond; 216 pp. Reprint of original work, a highly respected book. Illustrated by Dave Whitlock.*
$19.95 Kau, Dan

PERIODICALS FOR THE FLY FISHERMAN

If you subscribed to every magazine published for fly fishermen, all you'd have time to do is read, and that wouldn't make you a better angler. In moderation, however, good magazines will keep you posted on the latest and may very well make you a better fly fisherman. They should entertain you as well.

Some of the magazines listed here come as part of membership in an organization. You'll find more information on organizations in a later chapter.

Fly Fisherman Magazine
Box 8200
Harrisburg, Pennsylvania 17105

Issues/year: 6
Subscription: $16.97

This is *the* fly fishing magazine. It has the greatest circulation of any periodical devoted to the sport. It has the best known writers, photographers, and artists. And it has begun to reach a near-perfect balance among all the aspects of the sport.

There was never a time that I can remember when *FFM* was in second place, but there were many times when I, as a young beginner and a western angler, thought it was a disappointing first. It was snobbish and Eastern and purist in the worst sort of way. That's not true now, nor has it been for many years. The magazine has a geographical balance, a species balance, and a balance in all aspects of the sport. I see in the issue before me articles on the San Juan in New Mexico, on Montana's Madison, on three Michigan rivers, and on the Babine in British Columbia. The Babine article speaks of steelhead, the others of trout, and a separate article is about largemouth bass.

There are articles on fly patterns, entomology, equipment, and tackle rigging. In all, the material in the magazine represents the interests of the typical serious fly fisherman. The magazine even has a regular contribution from Nick Lyons to keep us from getting too serious. In short, this is one of the first magazines a budding fly fisherman should subscribe to.

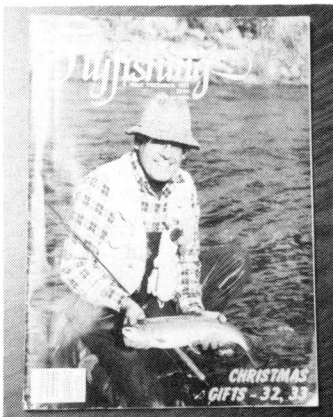

Flyfishing
Box 02112
Portland, Oregon 97202

Issues/year: 6
Subscription: $13.95

Formerly *Fly Fishing the West*, the current magazine has expanded its coverage and shortened its name. The

magazine, in its early days, was roughcut and rather unsophisticated by the standards of the eastern magazines. As such it suited western anglers just fine. They were tired of reading about Theodore Gordon, the Beaverkill, and Light Cahills. They wanted Dan Bailey, the Madison, and Improved Sofa Pillows. *FFW* gave it to them.

Over the years, however, the western angler's sophistication increased. Entomology was no longer a four-letter word (bugs). Armstrong Spring Creek became a mecca. And the magazine recognized these changes and kept up with it. That's a tribute to the leadership of Don Roberts.

Even though you'll find articles about fishing in all parts of the country, *Flyfishing* is still largely a western magazine with western writers. The look of the magazine and its contents are much different than when it began, however. If you haven't read it for a number of years, you should give it another try. The articles are more down to earth than other major fly fishing magazines run, and you'll appreciate its comfortable style and lack of self-consciousness.

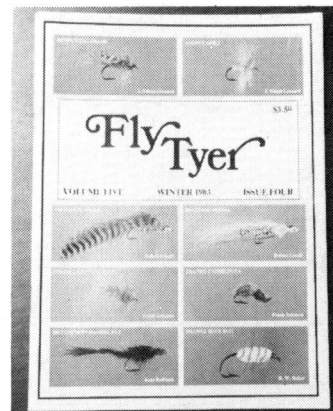

Fly Tyer
Box 1231
North Conway, New Hampshire 03860

Issues/year: 4
Subscription: $13

If you already subscribe to *Fly Tyer*, you must be a serious fly tier. Or, conversely, if you're a serious fly tier, you must subscribe to *Fly Tyer*.

The point is that this is a wonderful publication for tiers. There are many patterns each issue with full tying instructions and good illustrations to back them up. The only color you'll find is on the cover, which is "covered" with photos of each of the featured flies. It's enough to make fingers twitch and eyes squint for anyone who ties, seriously or just for fun.

There are regular columns by such notables as LaFontaine, Borger, Hafele, Hughes, Fling, Puterbaugh, Montplaisir, and others. The mix of tying techniques and entomology is right on, and there's enough about fishing techniques to keep everyone happy. For instance, I got some good tips on fishing soft hackles from LaFontaine's column in the sample issue I have.

Just to give you an idea of the diversity of patterns in each issue, here's a partial list from the sample issue: Cottontail Muddler, Siberian Outpost, Black Shiner, Serpent Fly, Cossell Golden Stone, Hutchinson Damsel Fly, Bleeding Prisma, and Green Despair.

North Fork's Almanac and Advisor
417 Delaware
Kansas City, Missouri 64105

Issues/year: 20
Subscription: $39

North Fork is getting its feet wet in every part of fly fishing right now. This newsletter is an example. It's edited by Tom Meade, a well-known writer, and the advertising touts it as a "personal" newsletter giving "current" fly fishing news.

Since you'll get one just about every other week, the news can be more current than a magazine's. The sample in their latest catalog shows a heavy emphasis on where to fish (without naming specific waters, thank goodness). For instance, there's a brief piece on the arrival of the sea-run cutthroats along the Oregon and Washington coasts and another one about good fishing in the Florida Everglades. It reminds me a bit of "Hunting and Fishing News" but without the hot-spotting and lurid dead fish pictures.

Along with your subscription, you receive a membership number that allows you to call "The Fly Line" and get the names of "local experts" in an area you intend to visit, so that you can contact them when planning your trip. There's also this to mull over: you'll be informed about "special fly fishing areas, many private" that you may fish only by being a member. (Hint: If it's not private, don't pay to fish it.)

Rod and Reel (and Fly-Tackle Dealer)
Box 370
Camden, Maine 04843

Issues/year: 5
Subscription: $12

This is another fine magazine devoted entirely to fly fishing. It was started by John Merwin (*Stillwater Trout*) as a top-quality general fishing magazine. A few years ago the magazine turned fly-fishing-only and kept the high standards of quality.

Like *Fly Fisherman Magazine*, *R&R* attracts top writers, photographers, and artists. The issue I have here has articles by Hughes, Hafele, Wulff, and Traver. Whitlock is often featured, as is Harrison O'Connor, one of my personal favorites.

Rod and Reel doesn't have the history or the circulation of *FFM*, but it's an equal when it comes to quality. In some aspects, quality of photos and photo treatment for instance, *R&R* is better. It gives over more space to equipment and has published several guides to specific kinds of gear. In general, there are also more "soft" pieces dealing with the experience of fly fishing, rather than the hard core where-to, how-to articles.

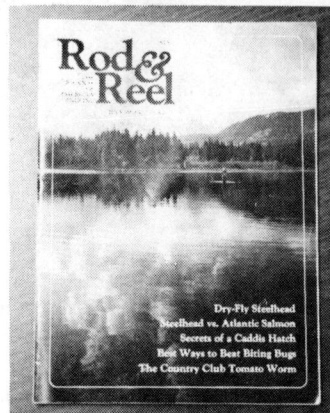

Being the new kid on the block, *R&R* has felt more freedom in running articles that are off-beat, a bit out of the "mainstream", and that's been one of its selling points.

R&R also publishes *Fly-Tackle Dealer*, a quarterly publication for retailers, distributors, and manufacturers of fly fishing equipment. The publication is free to people in the industry and is available by subscription (about $12) to others. It carries articles of interest to the industry, including marketing techniques, reviews of upcoming products, and retail store profiles.

RodCrafters Journal
C.T. Building
Route 2, Box 860-D
Wescosville, Pennsylvania 18106

Issues/year: 6
Subscription: $12 (membership)

RodCrafters Journal brings the know-how of rod builders across the nation together in one magazine. A subscription is included with membership in RodCrafters.

Although the magazine deals with building all types of rods, the fly fisherman will find that most techniques are applicable to his rod building. This is the only magazine devoted to a growing aspect of our sport. Since it comes from Dale Clemens, you can expect expertise in the material covered in the magazine.

Roundtable Magazine
Box 220
Maynard, Massachusetts 01754

Issues/year: 4
Subscription: $15 (membership)

Roundtable Magazine is the official publication of United Fly Tyers, Inc. Like its commercial counterpart, *Fly-Tyer*, it concentrates entirely on fly tying matters.

The sample issues I have include patterns and their background. The historical background, in the hands of some of the writers, is wide-ranging and entirely entertaining. Maxwell MacPherson, for instance, describes the hanging of a distant relative of yesteryear as part of the full explanation of how MacPherson's Rant, a salmon fly, came to be named. Quite a story, but there's quite a story behind many of our flies and it's fascinating to read about them.

Unfortunately, this kind of background material probably wouldn't float in a regular commercial magazine. The audience there is too general. If your interests center around fly tying, this is one of two magazines devoted to tying (see *Fly-Tyer*) that you'll want to try.

In addition to many patterns every issue, you'll find historical pieces, articles on new equipment, and an occasional travel piece that, of course, emphasizes what patterns to take. The overall tone is comfortable; you'll feel as if you're among fly-tying friends.

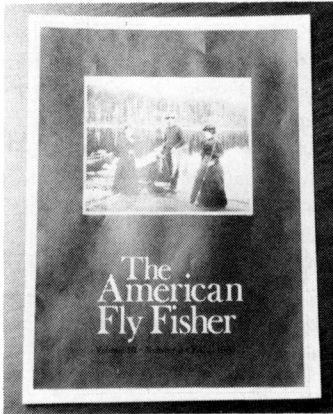

The American Fly Fisher
Manchester, Vermont 05254

Issues/year: 4
Subscription: $20 (membership)

A subscription to *The American Fly Fisher* is included in membership dues to The American Museum of Fly Fishing, housed in Manchester. The magazine features historical articles, photos of antique equipment and flies, and artwork and photos from elderly volumes on the sport.

Interest in the heritage of our sport is not a prerequisite to subscribing to this magazine—you'll develop it from reading the magazine. There is original historical research here and excerpts from long out-of-print books. Lest this sound a bit too much like textbook reading, the articles are written for the popular audience as much as for the scholar. You'll find they are interesting, often entertaining, and always lending of a finer appreciation of where we've been and where we're going.

Some of the most interesting material comes in the form of photos and art from the books in the Museum's outstanding collection. You'll get that rare glimpse of

history frontwards and backwards from these. They can only make you wonder how pictures of us will look to fly fishers of the 21st century.

The Flyfisher
Box 1088
West Yellowstone, Montana 59758

Issues/year: 4
Subscription: $20 (membership)

The Flyfisher is the official publication of the Federation of Fly Fishers. It carries articles on all aspects of fly fishing, including conservation. The magazine is available only through membership in the Federation.

You'll find noted writers and photographers here. This is one of the nicest looking magazines devoted to fly fishing, and because of the limited, selective audience, you can expect articles that are aimed a bit differently than those in the general circulation magazines. If you are a serious fly fisherman with interest in the preservation of the sport and its quarry, you'll enjoy *The Flyfisher*.

Western Hatch Quarterly
1580 S.E. Sherrett
Portland, Oregon 97202

Issues/year: 4
Subscription: $4.95

If, after reading *The Complete Book of Western Hatches*, you had a few questions to ask its authors, this is your chance. Rick Hafele, co-author of the book and editor of this newsletter, has a section devoted to questions from angler/entomologists.

The issue I have talks about how to decide which fly pattern to use when you've collected many different kinds of insects in your samples from a stream. The answer: You ask yourself three questions—1. Which insect is most abundant? 2. Which is most mature? 3. Which is most available? A full explanation follows in the newsletter.

Each issue is centered around the hatches coming up in the next three month period. There is a hatch chart listing common names, distribution, habitat, emergence periods, stages important to imitate, and imitative patterns. Short articles about meeting the hatches with discussions of patterns and techniques are included.

Rick knows of which he speaks, and if you're a western angler hungry for more bug information, this is a good source, especially when you've got a pesky hatch you can't figure out. Can't think of a better person to ask than Rick Hafele.

Other Magazines of Interest

These periodicals are not devoted to fly fishing, but they catch the spirit of the sport, directly through articles about fly fishing and indirectly through coverage of things fly fishermen love, like trout.

Gray's Sporting Journal
Box 2549
South Hamilton, Massachusetts 01982

Issues/year: 4
Subscription: $19.50

Since its inception, *Gray's Sporting Journal* has been heralded as the best-designed and best-written magazine in the country. In its original style, it had issues devoted to separate sports, trout fishing, trophy hunting, and so on. It now melds these in each issue.

But one thing hasn't changed, the devotion to the best writing. This is not how-to material. It's more why-to, a description of the beauty of fine sporting activities and their essence for the sportsman. It's the love of sport, not its mechanics, you'll find in *Gray's*.

Sporting Classics
420 East Genesee Street
Syracuse, New York 13202

Issues/year: 6
Subscription: $18

Sporting Classics covers all aspects of the sporting life. If your interest in fly fishing is nestled in between those for grouse hunting, duck calling, and other fine pursuits, you'll find this high-quality magazine to your liking.

The March/April issue I have concentrates on trout and particularly on fly fishing for them. It contains articles by Schwiebert, Merwin, Schullery, Wulff, Haig-Brown, and others, so you know the best are finding their way into the magazine. If that collection of writers is any indication, other subjects covered by the magazine will be done with class, also.

The art work is outstanding, as are the photos. All in all, it's a pretty package with substance to back it up.

Trout
Box 1944
Washington, D.C. 20013

Issues/year: 4
Subscription: $15 (membership)

Trout, the publication of Trout Unlimited, hit the magazine racks recently, and many people saw it for the first time. In some respects, magazine is devoted to the fish first and the pursuit of fish second.

Not that there aren't plenty of fishing articles in it. There are. And Dave Whitlock holds a tying seminar in each issue. Another regular columnist is Dr. Robert Behnke who knows more about trout than perhaps any other individual. There are regular articles on conservation as well. So, let's say that the magazine is a tribute to trout and other coldwater fishes, a celebration of them.

Take a look at the regular centerfold as further confirmation. The issue I'm looking at now has a pin-up of a rainbow, done by noted artist Mike Stidham. It's gorgeous, and it's going up in my office. There's another piscatorial pictorial in this issue. It's a stunning collection of underwater photos of Atlantic salmon.

Graphically, the magazine is outstanding. The photos are well above average and are used to their best advantage. From that standpoint, *Trout* is the *Audubon* of fishing mags and worth the price of admission.

The magazine is not fly fishing only. In fact, a recent article about the truth and beauty of worm fishing almost caused the magazine's exclusion here. Overlooking such occasional anomalies in the magazine of a conservation organization whose members are mostly fly fishermen, you'll still enjoy the graphics and the information about trout, salmon, and steelhead that you'll find in *Trout*.

CALENDARS AND OTHER PUBLICATIONS

Calendars and fishing diaries are among the more "practical" publications offered to fly fishermen. The calendars and the engagement book listed here are beautiful reminders of our sport for those times when "fluorshine" replaces sunshine and the gurgling of the water cooler makes us turn our heads in search of rising trout only to find settling secretaries. A 9"x12" piece of reality can expand an office immensely.

Fishing diaries allow you to record the details of your fishing trips. These are handy references, especially for the traveling fisherman who fishes a river once or twice a year. The official, organized diaries listed here give you blanks for hatches, patterns used, weather, number and size of fish caught, and other items of interest. Pick out the diary that allows you to record the information you find most useful.

The final entry here is a fly tier's log. It allows you to keep fly tying notes in an orderly fashion. It comes from Rangeley Region Fly Shop.

Calendars

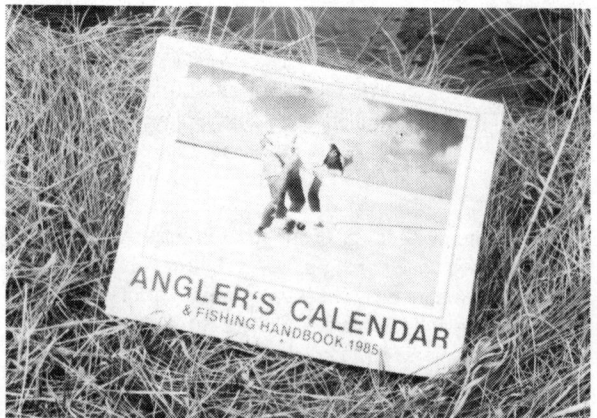

Angler's Calendar and Fishing Handbook
This large (12½" wide x 9½" deep) wall calendar is an standby for many of us. Bobbi Phelps Wolverton has been producing it since 1976 and, in doing so, has brought a

piece of fly fishing and sanity into our dens and offices during those years.

The photos are of fly fishing scenes, fish, and insects, and there is additional information in each calendar, including brief articles about fly fishing. The date blocks on the calendar's face also hold tidbits of timely information, everything from carp spawning (June 7) to the Tiny White Wing Black Hatch in Yellowstone Park (Aug. 6-Oct. 15). A pen and ink drawing of a fly pattern, done by Hal Janssen, is included every month, too.
$6.95 (+ $1.55 postage) The Angler's Calendar, Route 1, Murtaugh, Idaho 83344 (208) 432-6625

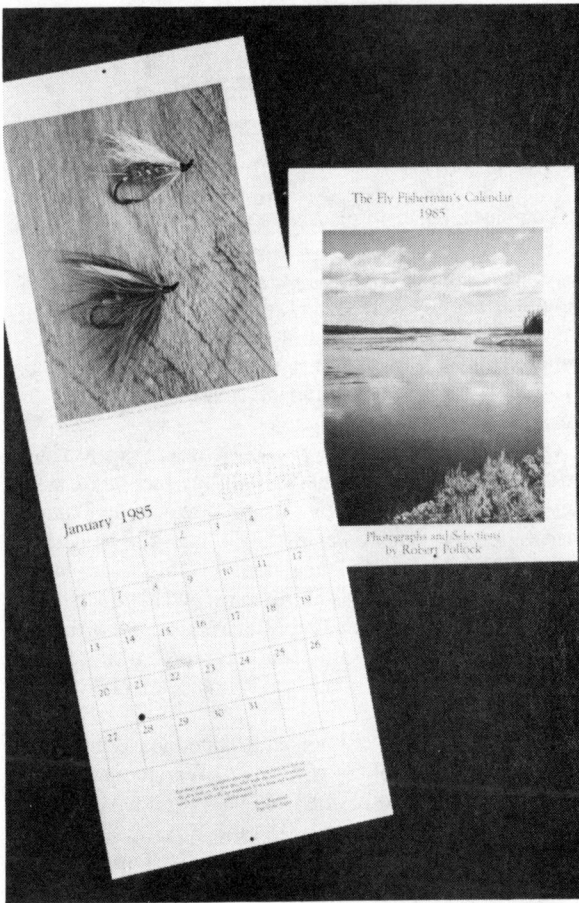

The Fly Fisherman's Calendar

A relatively new entry in this category is Robert Pollock's calendar. It's 9" wide x 12" deep with color photos throughout.

Unlike the Angler's Calendar, which uses the works of many photographers, The Fly Fisherman's Calendar includes only Bob's work. The quality of the photos is excellent, as it should be, for Bob Pollock is an outstanding artist. His works have appeared in *National Wildlife, Natural History, Sierra, Popular Photography,* and other publications.

Among the photos are scenes of rivers, flies, materials, trout, and still lifes. There's even a picture of the Izaak Walton Window from England's Winchester Cathedral in

the calendar I have. Whatever the subject, you'll find each shot interesting, and the variety enlivening. Quotations from several writers are included, to give the mind as well as the eye some refreshment in the heat of battle.

My favorite photos in this calendar are those of rivers without a fisherman in them. Kind of makes me want to take the empty spot.
$7.50 (+ $1.25 postage) Robert Pollock, Ski Road, Allenspark, Colorado 80510 (303) 747-2965

Silver Creek Sportsman's Engagement Calendar

There are 53 color photos, 53 pencil drawings, and 53 quotations from Ernest Hemingway in this desk-top engagement book. Most of the photos are of fly fishing scenes, but there are several duck hunting, camping, and scenery shots as well. All are nicely done. The pencil drawings and quotations are appropriate to the spirit of things. My only criticism is that the locations where the photos were taken are not identified. I'd like to visit some of those places.

Altogether a handsome piece of work and very nice to have on your desk or for use as an engagement calendar or a diary, fishing or otherwise. A portion of the proceeds go to the Nature Conservancy, a wonderful organization that goes around buying nature preserves such as the Sonoita Creek sanctuary, a birding paradise in Arizona, and Silver Creek, a fly fishing paradise in Idaho.
$15 ($45 for leather bound) Nor or direct from Silver Creek, Inc., Box 508, Sun Valley, Idaho 83353 (800) 537-2323

Fishing and Fly Tying Diaries

Fly Fishing Journal

This spiral-bound, paper-covered booklet is small enough to fit in a vest pocket. It opens to a two-page spread of categories with blanks to be filled by the angler. Included in the information is location, weather, time of day, equipment, hatches, patterns used, and results, among others. There are enough pages for 26 entries.
$7.95 Angling Accessories, Box 210209, San Francisco, California 94121-0209

The Fly Fisherman's Log Book

This diary is notebook-style with binder rings. The log book is covered in plastic with a fishing design on the cover. It's small but not small enough to be conveniently carried. Each page has spaces for entries in categories like date, time of day, results, patterns, hatches, weather, water temperature, and others. There is also a section in which maps can be drawn. Refills of 35 pages are available.
$9.60; refills—$3.30 Dan

Fly Tyer's Log Book

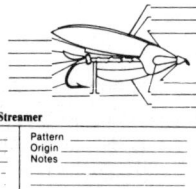

This note-card sized journal has 50 blank pages divided into categories according to pattern types. Just fill in your notes and your memory can relax a bit. Refills of 20 pages are available.
$5; refills—$1.50 Ran

VIDEO TAPES

Now you can bring fly fishing inside with you when the weather's bad and back home with you at the end of your vacation in Montana. Fishing video tapes are here, and they make better use of your television than watching most prime time shows.

Technology comes and goes in fly fishing, but video tapes are probably here to stay. I've watched the people at the fish shows, and they'll spend an hour of their time in front of the tube with a thousand other interesting things going on.

How much you will enjoy and use your fishtape depends on its value as entertainment or educational tool. The best of them will be both fun to watch and informative.

Gary Borger's tapes are both of these. He's a master teacher as well as fly fisherman, and his shows will have lasting value. I haven't previewed other tapes (something you should definitely do if you intend to buy). They may also be good.

The fly tying tapes are a particularly good use of the technology. Close-up photography makes it easy to see the tying techniques. As with all "secondhand" teaching, it's not as effective (nor as much fun) as a good tying class—video tapes don't answer questions very well, and they seldom tell jokes. An advanced techniques tape is bound to come along soon, and I think it will be very effective.

Your local fly shop may have tapes available to rent, or you may be able to catch one at a Trout Unlimited meeting. Some of the catalogs even offer rental. They generally require full payment with a refund coming after the tape is returned. The time periods are necessarily generous, 10-14 days, and the rental fee runs about $10-$15. Those catalogs offering rental service are designated by (r) in the listings.

One company, Video Travel, specializes in tapes. They offer all the tapes listed here, and they have a catalog with over 100 outdoor titles. If you have a particular fascination for video fishing, they'll have the newest releases before the regular catalogs do. They plan a tape based on Joe Humphrey's ESPN show and have a fishing travelogue (called Fly Fishing Video Magazine) with one current title. They also offer rental of tapes. Write: Video Travel, Box 1572, Williamsport, Pennsylvania 17701 (717) 326-6525.

Another company, Salmonoid Productions, offers a fly fishing travelogue on New Zealand. Watch out, though, it may cost you a total of $3,069.95, if you have to go to New Zealand after watching the tape. The tape is called *Waitangirua, a New Zealand Fly Fishing Sampler.* Like all the other tapes, it's available in both VHS and Beta.

Fly Fishing Titles

Anatomy of a Trout Stream. *A close-up study of the environment in which trout live and their requirements for health and happiness, with Rick Hafele (The Complete Book of Western Hatches). A new release that should be very informative. Watch for it in the catalogs.*
N/a Probably the same catalogs as listed below
Fishing the Dry Fly. *60 min. Dry fly skills in riffles, pocket water, pools, and lakes, with Gary Borger (Nymphing and other books). Footage of the Madison, Henry's Fork, Armstrong Spring Creek. Demonstrations of specialized casts, such as the parachute and the*

pendulum. Underwater shots of trout.
$64.95-$80 Bud, Ste, Mer, Fly (r), Nor (r), Cab, Tid, Cus, T&T, Kau (r), Dan, Pen

Fly Fishing for Trout. *60 min. Basic primer on fly fishing, including use of dries, nymphs, and streamers, with Gary Borger. How to read water and select flies based on the hatch.*
$64.95-$80 Dan, Pen, Cus, T&T, Kau (r), Mer, Ste, Fly (r), Nor (r), Tid, Cab, Bud

Fly Fishing with Bob Jacklin—the Wet Fly. *Techniques for fishing the wet fly, nymph, and streamer. Footage of waters near West Yellowstone.*
$59.95 Bob

Fly Fishing with Bob Jacklin—the Dry Fly. *Covers casting, presentation, approach, float and wade fishing.*
$59.95 Bob

Fly Fishing Video Magazine, Issue #1. *60 min. A travelogue for fly fishermen, this one to Lake Illiama in Alaska with Ted Gorken. Fishing for big rainbows and char, with tying instructions for regional flies. Footage of rivers in Bristol Bay area.*
$69.95 Video Travel (see address in introduction)

Hal Janssen's Fly Fishing Secrets I—the Dry Fly. *90 min. Dry fly fishing lessons, including tying instructions, tackle, and streamside entomolgy.*
$62.95-$70 Cab, Kau (r), T&T, Nor (r), Dan, Fly (r), Ste, Bud, Pen, Mer, Cus

Hal Janssen's Fly Fishing Secrets II—the Wet Fly. *90 min. Learn the secrets of tying and fishing underwater forms, including how to impart proper action to the nymph.*
$62.95-$70 Mer, Dan, Bud, Nor (r), Kau (r), Pen, Cus, Fly (r), Cab, T&T, Ste

Hal Janssen's Fly Fishing Secrets III—the Mayfly. *60 min. A video journey to the trout's home. Underwater close-ups of nymphs, dun, and spinner forms as the trout sees them. Tying instructions for imitations of nymph, emerger, adult, and spinner. Footage of Hat Creek, Rising River. (New release; should be available by now in the catalogs.)*
$59.95 Look for it in same catalogs

Fly Casting. *60 min. Casting instructions in three parts, the mechanics, common problems, and advanced*

techniques, with Bruce Bowlen. (New release from Orvis.)
$69.50-$69.95 Orv, Video Travel

How to Tie Dry Flies. *86 min. Concentrates on tying dry flies.*
$69.50 Orv

Nymphing with Gary Borger. *30 min. Expert instruction on nymph fishing from one of the best teachers. Collecting and examining nymphs. Different presentations. Footage of Armstrong Spring Creek.*
$53.95-$60 Fly, (r), Cus, Kau (r), Pen, Dan, T&T, Nor (r), Cab, Tid, Mer, Bud

Tying Trout Flies. *60 min. Close-up photography of tying processes make this an excellent learning tool. Ecology and tying techniques hand-in-hand and a trip to the stream to try out the patterns, with Gary Borger.*
$64.95-$80 Dan, T&T, Tid, Cab, Bud, Fly (r), Nor (r), Mer, Cus, Pen, Kau (r), Ste

Waitangirua, a New Zealand Fly Fishing Sampler. *30 min. Dry fly fishing for 'bows and browns in one of our dream locales.*
$69.95 Salmonoid Productions, 91 Round Hill Rd., Tiburon, California 94920 (415) 435-0306.

Other Titles of Interest

Bass Fishing: Top to Bottom. *60 min. Tutoring by Rick Clunn, winner of bass tournaments. Not a fly fishing tape.*
$59.95-$60 Mer, Kau (r), Nor (r)

Bass in Heavy Cover. *30 min. How to fish for them where they're difficult to catch, with Homer Circle, Al Lindner, and Roland Martin. Not a fly fishing tape (Dave Whitlock, where are you?), but should give some good tips on finding bass and on approach.*
$59.95-$60 Mer, Cab, Kau (r), Nor (r)

Bigmouth. *50 min. Dramatic study of the largemouth bass with exciting underwater photography. Created by Glen Lau, the ultimate bassman. Life history of bass with footage showing habits and including the attempted ingesting of a duckling.*
$79.95-$90 Nor (r), Cab, Kau (r), Mer

Feeding Habits of Bass. *30 min. Lots of underwater footage highlight this study of the feeding habits of bass, with Homer Circle. Why bass hit and how to make them do it.*
$59.95-$60 Kau (r), Mer, Nor (r)

Smallmouth Bass. *30 min. Fishing lakes and rivers for smallmouth, with Homer Circle, Al Lindner, and Glen Lau. Not a fly fishing tape but of interest to those who pursue smallmouth with fly.*
$53.95-$60 Kau (r), Mer, Cab, Nor (r)

Surface Lures and Buzz Baits. *30 min. Top water action with exciting photography. As close to bass fishing with poppers and floating bugs as you can get on tape right now.*
$53.95-$60 Kau (r), Nor (r), Cab, Mer

CASSETTE TAPES

Kap Outdoors is pursuing a noble cause, an oral history of fly fishing utilizing our contemporary experts in the sport. Included in this first series are tapes of conversations with Schwiebert, Wulff, Marinaro, and others. Such informal meetings with the masters allows more personal information than is possible in most of the writing they do. Unfortunately I haven't had the opportunity to listen to these tapes, but they have the potential to be very interesting portraits of the people we respect the most in the sport we enjoy the most.

At present, the following fishing folk have been taped:

Art Flick. *On streamcraft, development of Streamside Guide, fly tying, and fly fishing.*
Charlie Fox. *On terrestrials, stream fishing.*
Poul Jorgensen. *On fly tying, salmon flies, fly fishing.*
Lefty Kreh. *On saltwater fly fishing, tackle, fly casting.*
Vince Marinaro. *On limestone fishing, terrestrials.*
Ernest Schwiebert. *On origins of Matching the Hatch, fly fishing as three dimensional chess.*
Sam Slaymaker. *On simplicity and enjoyment, small streams.*
Joan Wulff. *On casting, wading safety.*
Lee Wulff. *On Atlantic salmon, catch-and-release, boyhood days in Alaska, hair flies.*
1-3 tapes—$12.95 each; 4-6—$11.95 each; 7-9—$10.95 each Pen, T&T, Bob, Kau, Wul, Let

FISHING ART

Many fine artists have turned their talents to fishing subjects, and their work improves our lives away from the stream. The illustrators, painters, photographers, and sculptors bring the trout, insects, equipment, and the stream itself to our books and magazines and into our living rooms.

The closest thing we have now to a major source for fishing art is Wild Wings. Their catalog carries paintings and other flat art, as well as some three dimensional work. Much of the art, however, is on subjects other than fishing (but all of it is on subjects of interest to sportsmen). Founded in 1971, the catalog company has grown into a relatively big business. Circulation of the catalog exceeds 1,000,000.

The prints listed here from Wild Wings are included to give you an idea of what they carry. Since the editions of any one print may sell out quickly, you should write for the catalog. Write: Wild Wings, Lake City, Minnesota 55041. The cost is $2.

The Angler's Art (described in the section on sources for collector's books) carries some art, but not as much as when the company was named. In fact, they're changing their name, and it will soon have more to do with books in order to reflect the contents of their catalog more accurately. There is one print currently listed in The Angler's Art.

Tidewater Specialties offers a limited number of prints, including work by Reneson. The catalog from Bud Lilly's Trout Shop also contains art works. The gallery that is part of that shop in West Yellowstone is a must stop for anglers interested in sporting art.

Other mail order sources concentrate on one artist. Clearwater Publishing, for instance, features the work of Mike Stidham, whose name you may recognize from the work he does for a number of magazines and books. Clearwater currently offers a limited edition of etchings by Mike. For more information, write: Clearwater Publishing, 1646 East First Street, Santa Ana, California 92701 (714) 835-3545.

Jack Montague offers some impressive wood carvings of fish through his mail order company. You can even order them in a species and size to match one you've caught. Write: Jack Montague, 5304 Lipizzan Trail, Punta Gorda, Florida 33950 (813) 639-4007.

Eldridge Hardie's art is available from Hardie-Hill Limited Editions. They publish a nice color brochure on his prints. Eldridge is noted for his underwater scenes of trout on the feed. For his catalog, write: Hardie-Hill Limited Editions, 8118 West Sixty-Ninth Way, Arvada, Colorado 80004 (303) 466-2278.

The work of Dick Leyden is featured in the Donmar Studio catalog. A number of limited edition prints are offered each year. Donmar is most noted for its framing services. Don Leyden is a master at the art, and should you need a special frame for print and flies or whatever, you should consult with Donmar. Write: Donmar Studios,

21 Dorset Lane, Brookfield Ctr., Connecticut 06805 (203) 775-4103.

In addition to the art listed here, there are some "art" items in the chapter on angling accessories. These include belt buckles, lamps, glassware, note cards, and other items that have art work as an integral part of them.

Here are a few examples of the art work available. Sizes were assumed to be the full print size unless specified as image size. Sources in this section refer to the companies described above.

Angler's Decision. *Full-color print by Hugh Mossman; angler on stream; 26"x20½".*
$65 Bud Lilly

Atlantic Salmon Still Life. *Hand-colored print by Dick Leyden; Salmon with rod, reel, and fly wallet; 26"x13"; limited to 200, signed and numbered.*
$125 Donmar

Battenkill Brookie. *Black-and-white print by Dick Leyden; brook trout; 20"x13"; limited to 50, signed and numbered.*
$25 Donmar

Brook Trout. *Hand-colored etching by Mike Stidham; brook trout underwater; 7 ½"x10"; limited to 250 copies.*
$100 Bud Lilly

Brook Trout and Blacknose Dace. *Full-color print by Eldridge Hardie; brook trout turning down on streamer; 18"x13" image; limited to 450 copies, signed and numbered.*
$60 Hardie-Hill

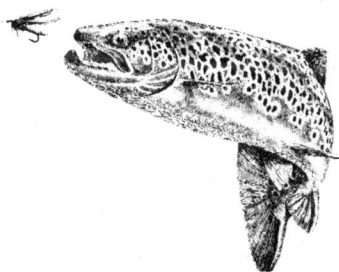

Brown Trout and Spruce Fly. *Hand-colored etching by Mike Stidham; brown trout taking streamer; 7½"x10"; limited to 250 copies.*
$125 Clearwater

Charlie's Friends. *Full-color lithograph by Charles De Feo; rising fish and flies; 10"x13"; limited edition.*
$25 Donmar

Clearwater Rainbow Trout. *Hand-colored etching by Mike Stidham; rainbow turning for angler's nymph; 7½"x10"; limited to 250 copies.*
$125 Clearwater, Bud Lilly

Deepwater Decision. *Full-color print by Rene Harrop; brook trout considering streamer; 24"x17".*
$65 Bud Lilly

End of the Season Brown Trout. *Full-color print by Eldridge Hardie; underwater scene of brown trout feeding; 18"x13" image; limited edition, signed and numbered.*
$100 Hardie-Hill

Leaping Salmon. *Full-color lithograph by John Atherton; salmon rising from water; 23"x17½"; limited to 750 copies.*
$60 Donmar

1983 Minnesota Trout Stamp. *Full-color print with stamp by Edward Philpot; rising brown; 6½"x9"; limited to 1,150 prints, signed and numbered.*
$128.75 Wild Wings

1981 Trout Unlimited Stamp. *Full-color print with stamp by Robert K. Abbett; angler on stream; 14"x21"; limited to 1,700 prints, signed and numbered.*
$200 Wild Wings

1982 Trout Unlimited Stamp. *Full-color print with stamp by John P. Cowan; angler on stream; 14"x21"; limited to 1,150 prints, signed and numbered.*
$140 Wild Wings

1983 Trout Unlimited Stamp. *Full-color print with stamp by Chet Reneson; angler on stream; 14"x21" image; limited to 750 prints, signed and numbered.*
$90 Wild Wings

Reflections. *Full-color lithograph by Charles De Feo; trout leaping over stream; 23"x17½"; limited to 400 copies, signed.*
$50 Donmar

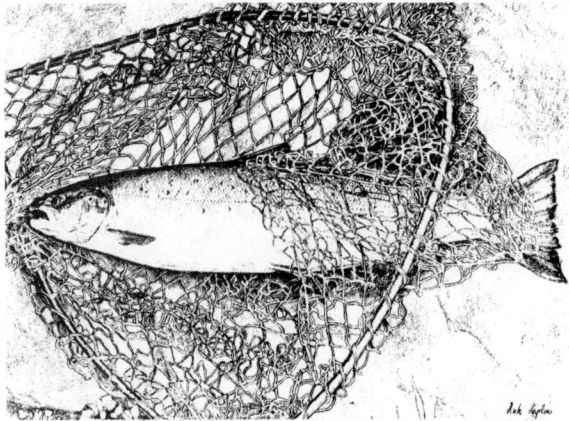

Salmon Soliloquy. *Hand-colored print by Dick Leyden; salmon in net; 13½"x18"; limited to 100, signed and numbered.*
$95 Donmar

Secret Pool. *Full-color print by Chet Reneson; angler on stream; 11"x16"; limited to 500 prints, signed and numbered.*
$50 Wild Wings, Tidewater Specialties

Serenity. *Black-and-white print of pencil sketch; canoe at water's edge; 9½"x12½".*
$20 Donmar

Trout and Flies. *Full-color prints by Eldridge Hardie; brook, cutthroat, rainbow, and brown trout with appropriate flies, individual prints; 22"x17"; limited to 1,500, signed and numbered.*
$30 each Hardie-Hill

Trout and salmon carvings. *Wood carvings by Jack Montague; brook, brown, rainbow, salmon, and special orders; 12"-48".*
$100-$475 Jack Montague

Well Hooked. *Full-color print by Chet Reneson; tarpon angler with fish on; 11"x16"; limited to 500 prints, signed and numbered.*
$40 Wild Wings

Yellowstone Sport Fishes. *A portfolio of 13 prints of the gamefish of Yellowstone National Park; by Michael Simon.*
$7.95 Bud Lilly

13. Organizations

I'M NOT MUCH OF a joiner. I suspect most fly fishermen aren't. The sport attracts the loner, the individualist, the person of a different cut, and often fly fishing is simply best done alone.

However, when I became active in organizations for trout fishermen, particularly fly fishermen, I discovered something—there are a lot of people who share the same outlook on life, the same interests and fanaticisms, and the same concerns for the environment that I do. After years of fishing without that kind of kinship, I was surprised and delighted by it.

Perhaps I grew up in a more sheltered fly fishing world than most people. Here in Colorado in the fifties and sixties, a fly fisherman could go his own way. He could drive an extra mile or two and fish by himself all day long, and that's what I did. My friends liked girls and cars more than trout, a characteristic I didn't fully understand until later, after my formative years, so I fished by myself a lot and it became a habit.

If my interest in fly fishing separated me somewhat from the rest of the world, then joining a trout club made me realize I had company in that separation. If I was a weirdo, then there were a lot of other weirdos, and it wasn't so bad after all. In fact, with company, one can assert that his weirdness is, instead, a strength, a nobility.

I discovered another thing, too. An interest in fly fishing overrides other characteristics, and I found I could get along with anyone, be he carpenter or neurosurgeon (please note that you can tell these two apart by dress, the neurosurgeon being the sloppier of the two). There is little class distinction among fly fishermen, except that determined by skill.

I also found out that I wasn't the world's best fly fisherman (which I could think as long as I fished alone), and the exposure to anglers with more expertise than I had was educational, although a little ego damaging.

And so, the trout club is an educational institution, a model of democracy, and, most importantly, a place where you can feel part of the crowd, albeit a small one. I recommend joining one.

The most common clubs are local chapters of Trout Unlimited or the Federation of Fly Fishers. The common bonds between people in those clubs are a conservation ethic and a love for fishing, particularly trout fishing and often fly fishing. If you share those bonds, you can enjoy and profit from the fellowship of the club, even though you may not be the most proficient fly fisherman.

There are many types of groups you may wish to join, whether they have a local chapter or not. The magazines and newsletters they publish provide a means of keeping in touch with the group, even if you cannot meet with them. In this chapter I've listed many of the organizations of interest to the fly fisherman. I've highlighted two of them, Trout Unlimited and the Federation of Fly Fishers, because of their wide appeal and because they are effective both on the local level and the national level. The other organizations that I'm at all familiar with are also described, and the remainder are simply listed so that you may write for more information.

CONSERVATION ORGANIZATIONS

Fly Fishing Organizations

We all have dues to pay in this sport, as we do in every part of our lives. To take pleasure from trout fishing without trying to return something to the sport shows a lack of responsibility that we can no longer afford. The streams and lakes in our country today are in trouble, and, therefore, the sport is in trouble. If we are to enjoy trout fishing in the years to come, we must act together to protect our fisheries now. The best way to start to do this is to join one or more of the conservation groups listed here.

The Federation of Fly Fishers (FFF) and Trout Unlimited (TU) are widely-known conservation groups.

Their interests are far-reaching, and members are active in everything from legislative influence to local stream improvement projects.

Other groups listed here are limited to an interest in a species or an interest in a particular geographical area. The Atlantic Salmon Foundation, for instance, is concerned with the rehabilitation of salmon runs, and Oregon Trout is concerned with trout fishing in Oregon.

It's often difficult to think that the $15 or $20 you spend on annual dues is worth the investment, but I think it is. Organizations like TU and FFF are doing a lot to help protect the quality of our trout fishing. I've seen the results locally with stream improvement projects and political pressure to clean up effluents. It may appear that most of the real gains are made by local members working together, and often they are. But those members are together because they've joined TU or FFF or California Trout. Membership in these organizations is the springboard from which the leap is made to effective stream conservation efforts.

Do something nice for a trout today. Join in the effort to protect its environment.

Trout Unlimited
Box 1944
Washington, D.C. 20013

TU is a non-profit conservation organization dedicated to the protection and enhancement of coldwater fisheries. Founded in Michigan in 1959, TU now has well over 30,000 members in 300 clubs around the country. It is in a period of rapid growth.

Although TU is a large organization operating out of Washington, it is most proud of its grassroots work. Local chapters are active in stream improvement projects and in assisting local wildlife officials in stream samples and other work. Chapters also provide clinics and public information services within their communities.

TU recognizes that the solution to habitat problems is often political and social, as well as biological and environmental, and it works to influence legislation and to educate the public. The group's success in these matters is undeniable.

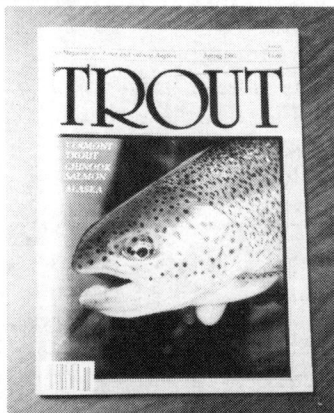

One of the strongest parts of TU organization is the state level council. Each council represents the working of national TU in miniature. The influence these councils have on state legislation is critical, since many decisions crucial to habitat are made on that level.

On the local level, TU clubs are active socially as well as environmentally. Participation at the local level can give the angler the opportunity to affect the quality of fishing in his own backyard, but it also provides lots of fun.

Membership is $15 and includes a subscription to *Trout*, TU's national magazine.

The Federation of Fly Fishers
Box 1088
West Yellowstone, Montana 59758

FFF is another major national organization for fly fishermen concerned with the sport and the environment. Founded in Colorado in 1964, the group now has over 10,000 regular members and many other supporters.

FFF has many notable on-going educational and stream improvement projects. The Whitlock-Vibert box program is one example. The boxes with trout eggs are "planted" in streams where natural spawning success may be limited. Fish hatched from the boxes are wild, which makes them much more desirable than the hatchery-reared clones usually dumped into streams with in-adequate reproduction. Over the past eight years, over 17,000 boxes have been distributed.

The Federation is also building the International Fly Fishing Center in West Yellowstone. The goal of the project is to provide a building for exhibits dedicated to the sport of fly fishing and the conservation ideals of FFF. Money for the Center is being raised through the efforts of local clubs.

Education of the public is one concentration of the Federation. The International Fly Fishing Center is an example of their dedication to the idea that an informed angler will respect the environment and help protect it.

Membership in FFF is currently $20. Members receive *The Flyfisher*, FFF's fine magazine.

Atlantic Salmon Foundation
100 Park Avenue
New York, New York 10017
Restoration of Atlantic Salmon in America, Inc.
Box 164
Hancock, New Hampshire 03449

These two organizations are concerned with the plight of the Atlantic salmon. The numbers of this tremendous gamefish have been seriously reduced over the years, and only the dedication of the salmon angler to his sport will improve the environment and help the salmon regain its place in the world. Write for details on membership fees and the activities of these organizations.

CalTrout project on Hat Creek

California Trout
Box 2046
San Francisco, California 94126

CalTrout was formed in 1970 to protect the trout and steelhead fisheries in California. The group works to promote natural trout fisheries and quality angling opportunities as opposed to stocked fisheries. It concentrates on the state level. Funds are raised through sale of a Wild Trout Stamp and through memberships. Regular membership is $20.

Oregon Trout
Box 19540
Portland, Oregon 97219

This is a relatively new state organization with the intent to protect the fisheries in Oregon, including the great steelhead streams there.

Other Conservation-Oriented Groups

American Rivers Conservation
317 Pennsylvania Avenue, S.E.
Washington, D.C. 20003

Association of Northwest Steelheaders
6168 N.E. Highway 99, Suite 102
Vancouver, Washington 98665

British Columbia Steelhead Society
Box 33947, Station D
Vancouver, British Columbia
Canada V6J 3J3

California Fisheries Restoration Foundation
1212 Broadway
Oakland, California 94612

Friends of the River
Fort Mason Center, Building C
San Francisco, California 94123

Izaak Walton League of America
1800 North Kent Street, #806
Arlington, Virginia 22209

Michigan United Conservation Club
Box 2235
Lansing, Michigan 48911

The Nature Conservancy
1800 North Kent Street
Arlington, Virginia 22209

If you've ever fished Idaho's Silver Creek or dreamed of it, you have The Nature Conservancy to thank. The organization saved the creek from development by purchasing the surrounding farm lands in 1976. It has stayed on to manage the stream and land in the most ecological manner possible.

Purchasing land to protect wildlife and plant life is the goal of The Nature Conservancy. Since its inception in 1951, it has purchased over 2 million acres. Most of the land is eventually turned over to state organizations, but Silver Creek has been maintained by the organization because of its unique management problems.

The Nature Conservancy depends on its membership and endowments for its monies. Money must still be raised to retire the debts associated with the purchase of the Silver Creek property. Donations for that fund can be sent to The Nature Conservancy, Box 624, Picabo, Idaho 83348.

I've visited the Silver Creek property and the Sonoita Creek Sanctuary near Patagonia, Arizona, a birder's paradise. Without the organization's efforts, both those properties would be private and unavailable for the public's use. If you support this kind of direct intervention in the face of loss of habitat, be it for birds or browns, then start by joining The Nature Conservancy. Memberships are $10 and include a quarterly magazine.

Stripers Unlimited
Box 45
South Attleboro, Massachusetts 01703

Theodore Gordon Flyfishers
24 East 39th Street
New York, New York 10016

OTHER ORGANIZATIONS
Special Interest Organizations

American Medical Fly Fishing Association
401 Bogle Street
Somerset, Kentucky 42501

The American Museum of Fly Fishing
Manchester, Vermont 05254

The American Museum of Fly Fishing is devoted to the collection of memorabilia concerning fly fishing. Most notable in the collection are the antique rods, reels, and other equipment and the out-of-print books. Visitors to the museum can also view actual equipment used by historical figures.

The heritage of the sport in America is protected by the collection and by the educational work of the Museum. Housed for many years in the Orvis retail store, the Museum now has a new location down the road a few miles. Visitors to Vermont can enjoy the excellent displays and historical presentations, and anglers around the country may soon be able to visit traveling displays. In the meantime, membership includes a subscription to *The American Fly Fisher*, the Museum's magazine. Each issue contains articles about the history of the sport, including excerpts from books long out of print. Photos of antique equipment and illustrations from elderly publications bring the Museum's collection to people who can't visit in person. Memberships begin at $20.

Bass Research Foundation
Box 99
Starkville, Mississippi 39759

Catskill Fly Fishing Center
Roscoe, New York 12776

The Catskill Fly Fishing Center features historical and educational displays. Special programs are scheduled throughout the year at their building on the banks of the Willowemoc.

International Association of Fish and Wildlife Agencies
1412 16th Street, N.W.
Washington, D.C. 20036

International Game Fish Association
3000 East Las Olas Boulevard
Fort Lauderdale, Florida 33316

RodCrafters
C.T. Building
Route 2, Box 860-D
Wescosville, Pennsylvania 18106

RodCrafters brings together rod builders for two-day seminars at several locations around the country. The organization is about 10 years old. Included in the membership of $12 is a subscription to RodCrafters Journal, a magazine devoted to all types of rod building. It's edited by one of the top people in rod building, Dale Clemens, whose books are standards in the field.

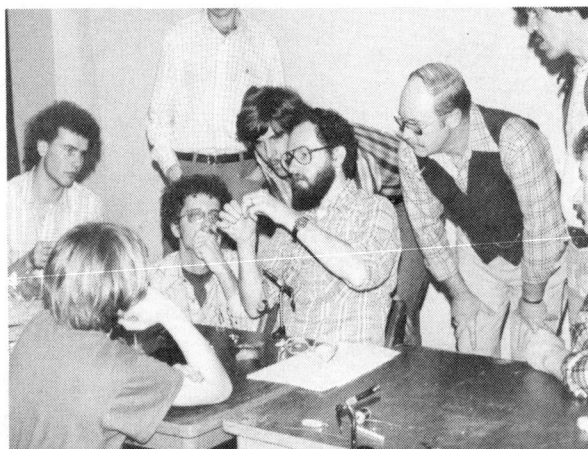

United Fly Tyers, Inc.
Box 220
Maynard, Massachusetts 01754

Founded in 1959, United Fly Tyers, Inc. is devoted to the art of fly tying. Included in membership dues is a subscription to Roundtable, a fly tier's magazine with innovative patterns and historical articles of interest to the tier. Membership dues are $15.

Other Groups of Interest

American Casting Association
7328 Maple Avenue
Cincinnati, Ohio 45321

An organization of local casting clubs, the American Casting Association promotes fly casting through educational programs and casting competitions.

American Fisheries Society
5410 Grosvenor Lane
Bethesda, Maryland 20014

American League of Anglers
810 Eighteenth Street, N.W.
Washington, D.C. 20006

Sport Fishery Research Institute
608 13th Street, N.W., Suite 801
Washington, D.C. 20005

Supported by the fishing industry, this organization is devoted to research concerning sport fishes in America. Lots of information is available to affiliate members.

U.S. Fish and Wildlife Service
Department of Interior
Public Affairs Office
Washington, D.C. 20240

Wildlife Legislative Fund of America
50 West Broad Street
Columbus, Ohio 43215

Game and Fish Departments

The state agencies listed here can provide valuable information for trip planning. Upon request, they will often send not only regulation booklets but also fishing maps and lists of public waters. You might also ask for a list of publications they have for sale.

Alabama
Game and Fish Division
64 North Union Street
Montgomery, Alabama 36104
Alaska
Department of Fish and Game
Juneau, Alaska 99801
Arizona
Game and Fish Department
2222 West Greenway Road
Phoenix, Arizona 85203
Arkansas
Game and Fish Commission
Little Rock, Arkansas 72201
California
Department of Fish and Game
1416 Ninth Street
Sacramento, California 95814
Colorado
Division of Wildlife
6060 Broadway
Denver, Colorado 80216
Connecticut
Environmental Protection
State Office Building
Hartford, Connecticut 06115
Delaware
Division of Fish and Wildlife
Tatnall Building
Dover, Delaware 19901
District of Columbia
Environmental Services
1875 Connecticut Avenue, N.W.
Washington, D.C. 20009

Florida
Fresh Water Fish Commission
620 South Meridian Street
Tallahassee, Florida 32304
Georgia
Game and Fish Division
270 Washington Street, S.W.
Atlanta, Georgia 30334
Hawaii
Fish and Game Division
1179 Punchbowl Street
Honolulu, Hawaii 96813
Idaho
Fish and Game Department
Box 25
Boise, Idaho 83707
Illinois
Division of Fisheries
605 State Office Building
Springfield, Illinois 62706
Indiana
Fish and Wildlife Division
607 State Office Building
Indianapolis, Indiana 46204
Iowa
Fish and Wildlife Division
300 Fourth Street
Des Moines, Iowa 50319
Kansas
Fish and Game Commission
Box 1028
Pratt, Kansas 67124

Kentucky
Fish and Wildlife Department
Capital Plaza Tower
Frankfort, Kentucky 40601
Louisiana
Fisheries Commission
400 Royal Street
New Orleans, Louisiana 70130
Maine
Department of Fisheries
284 State Street
Augusta, Maine 04330
Maryland
Natural Resources Department
580 Taylor Avenue
Annapolis, Maryland 21401
Massachusetts
Natural Resources Department
100 Cambridge Street
Boston, Massachusetts 02202
Michigan
Natural Resources Department
Stevens Mason Building
Lansing, Michigan 48926
Minnesota
Natural Resources Department
Centennial Office Building
St. Paul, Minnesota 55155
Mississippi
Game and Fish Commission
Box 451
Jackson, Mississippi 39205

Missouri
Department of Conservation
Box 180
Jefferson City, Missouri 65101

Montana
Department of Fish and Game
Helena, Montana 59601

Nebraska
Game and Parks Commission
Box 30370
Lincoln, Nebraska 68503

Nevada
Department of Fish and Game
Box 10678
Reno, Nevada 89510

New Hampshire
Department of Fish and Game
34 Bridge Street
Concord, New Hampshire 03301

New Jersey
Fish and Game Division
Box 1809
Trenton, New Jersey 08625

New Mexico
Department of Fish and Game
Santa Fe, New Mexico 87503

New York
Division of Fish and Wildlife
50 Wolf Road
Albany, New York 12201

North Carolina
Wildlife Resources Commission
Box 27687
Raleigh, North Carolina 27611

North Dakota
Department of Game and Fish
2121 Lovett Avenue
Bismarck, North Dakota 58505

Ohio
Natural Resources Department
Columbus, Ohio 43224

Oklahoma
Wildlife Conservation
Box 53465
Oklahoma City, Oklahoma 73105

Oregon
Wildlife Commission
Box 3503
Portland, Oregon 97208

Pennsylvania
Fish Commission
Box 1673
Harrisburg, Pennsylvania 17120

Rhode Island
Division of Fish and Wildlife
83 Park Street
Providence, Rhode Island 02903

South Carolina
Wildlife and Marine Resources
Box 167
Columbia, South Carolina 29202

South Dakota
Department of Game and Fish
State Office Building No. 1
Pierre, South Dakota 57501

Tennessee
Game and Fish Commission
Box 40747
Nashville, Tennessee 37204

Texas
Fish and Wildlife Division
John Reagan Building
Austin, Texas 78701

Utah
Division of Wildlife Resources
1596 West North Temple
Salt Lake City, Utah 84116

Vermont
Department of Fish and Game
Montpelier, Vermont 05602

Virginia
Marine Resources Commission
Box 756
Newport News, Virginia 23607

Washington
Department of Game
600 North Capitol Way
Olympia, Washington 98504

West Virginia
Division of Wildlife Resources
1800 Washington Street, East
Charleston, West Virginia 25305

Wisconsin
Bureau of Fish and Wildlife
Box 450
Madison, Wisconsin 53701

Wyoming
Game and Fish Department
Box 1589
Cheyenne, Wyoming 82001

Habitat Improvement Firms

Trout streams, like automobiles, sometimes need repairs. These can range from tune-ups to major overhauls, and since trout streams are just as complicated as today's cars, the backyard trout habitat repairman is likely to do as much damage as good.

The firms listed here often have aquatic biologists, hydrologists, entomologists, and other specialists who work together to improve all aspects of a stream. By improving the overall health of the stream, of course, the number and size of trout can be increased.

If you're fortunate enough to own trout water or if you belong to a club with private water, investment in the services of one of these firms may be returned to you many times over. In selecting a firm, check the credentials of the personnel, compare costs, and get a list of references from projects they have already undertaken. If possible, visit the projects and talk with people who fish the water. The firms are listed here in alphabetical order.

Aquatic Resource Consulting
R.D. 6 Box 6308
Stroudsburg, Pennsylvania 18360
(717) 629-1691

ARC is a team of aquatic biologists which evaluates trout stream habitat and management regulations and develops a plan to enhance the fishery based on that evaluation. They also provide water and wastewater analysis and legal testimony, as well as educational services.

In general, ARC limits their work to the northeastern and mid-Atlantic states, but they are open to inquiries from other areas.

Inter-Fluve, Inc.
408 North Bozeman
Bozeman, Montana 59715
(406) 586-6926

IFI focuses on the creation and restoration of streams and wetlands, with services including planning, design, and construction of wildlife habitats. They also provide landscape improvements, water analysis, population surveys, and land surveys.

IFI operates nationwide and has done work in 28 states and Canada.

Stream Team
10515 Ute Highway
Longmont, Colorado 80501
(303) 776-4050

Stream Team offers stream habitat improvement services, including analysis, construction supervision, and management planning.

Stream Team concentrates its work in the western states but welcomes inquiries from other regions.

Timberline Reclamations, Inc.
127 West Main
Bozeman, Montana 59715
(406) 587-9004

TRI includes a staff of biologists, hydrologists, entomologists, soil scientists, and engineers working on design of stream habitat for enhancement, rehabilitation, and relocation. They also provide services in riparian management, legal testimony, flood control, population surveys, and silt removal.

TRI has worked worldwide and has completed over 100 projects since its inception in 1978.

Trout Habitat Specialists
2720 West Main Street
Bozeman, Montana 59715
(406) 586-1113

THS offers a full range of habitat services including habitat analysis, management supervision, habitat construction, and population inventory. They work with lakes and ponds, as well as streams, and can aid in the enhancement of warmwater fisheries.

THS has done projects across the country, but the bulk of their work has been in the Midwest and West.

An Improved Egg Incubator

News of a new egg incubator will not seem especially important to the average fly fisherman, but many trout clubs across the country are involved with trout population enhancement projects that utilize incubators.

In this type of "stocking", live eggs are placed in a nest box-incubator. The box provides protection and a constant water flow to the eggs and the hatched fry until they are able to swim free. The advantage of this system is that the fish introduced into the stream in this fashion are wild trout. As such they are vastly superior to the stocked clones dumped on top of the wild trout population.

The best known system is the Whitlock-Vibert box. It's a plastic box with a screen bottom. The eggs are retained by the screen, but the hatched fry can work their way through the screen and into the gravel below and around the box, thus simulating natural hatching.

Now, VMG Industries is manufacturing an improved box developed 20 years ago by Neil Van Gaalen, then superintendent of the Crystal River Hatchery in Colorado. The VMG Instream Incubator features a catch lip top that faces into the current, directing the water flow through the box. The lip is adjustable to compensate for different currents. This improvement is designed to eliminate one of the main problems with egg boxes, siltation that suffocates the eggs.

Hatch percentages with the VMG Instream Incubator are impressive. Installation of the boxes can be done by novices with a minimum of instruction. Of course, all enhancement projects such as this should only be done with the permission of the appropriate state agencies and/or private land owners.

Cost of the Instream Incubators is $5 each in lots of 100. Smaller lots may be available. For information, contact VMG Industries, 858 Grand Avenue, Grand Junction, Colorado 81501 (303) 242-8623.

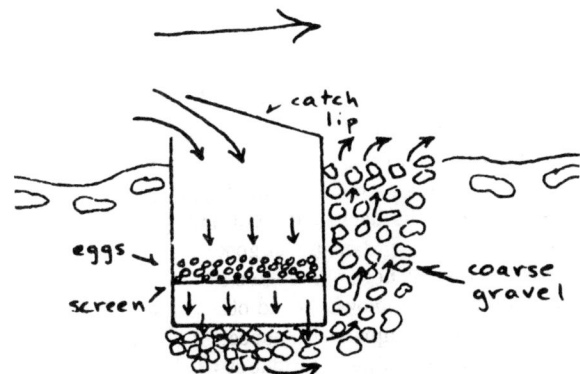

14. Catalogs and Fly Shops

CATALOGS ARE A SOURCE not only of our fly fishing equipment but of our fly fishing dreams. They are a cherished part of the sport, as much as is the local fly shop. They are better read than many magazines, occasionally better written, and at least as welcome in the mailbox. They open our fishing horizons, take us to better waters, and reassure us about our sport. They tell us about and sell us on the newest equipment and teach us the value of what we already own. Catalogs are a source . . . of conversation, of entertainment, of information, of dreams, and, rather incidentally, of equipment.

In writing this "catalog", I've worked with over 50 mail order companies. They range from relatively small concerns, like Egger's in Georgia, Murray's in Virginia, and Rangeley Region Shop in Maine, to the biggest companies in the industry, Orvis in Vermont, Kaufmann's in Oregon, and Thomas & Thomas in New York. For a few months now, I've had the biggest fly shop in the world right in my living room. It's been fun.

You, of course, won't have 50 catalogs. You don't need 50 catalogs, you just need one or two good ones. This part of the book is designed to help you find the best catalogs for you, but first, a word about catalogs and your local fly shop.

When to use a catalog. For many people, this is a simple issue. They don't have a local fly shop, and catalogs are their only source of equipment. For the rest of us, the issue is more complicated. It involves some thought, some philosophy.

My prejudice is clear. If you have a local fly shop and if that shop gives good service at reasonable prices, buy your equipment there. We receive a lot more than goods from a local shop. There's advice, comraderie, locations of local hot spots, a meeting place for the subculture. We're not charged for all this, but perhaps we should be. It would make us appreciate what we have.

The one concern that pulls people away from their local shop and attracts them to catalogs is price. Most shops carry products at full retail price; several catalogs have discount prices. But consider what I've said already—we get a lot more from a fly shop than equipment and we should be willing to pay for that. Second, I don't know anybody who's getting rich from owning a fly shop, and most shop owners are just scraping by. Full retail is standard business practice and shouldn't be looked upon as a gouge. If you enjoy having a local fly shop, the extra bucks you may spend to deal there are worth it.

One thing I want you to know is that fly shop owners know when someone is in the shop to get information so that he can go order an item from a catalog. It's a despicable thing, I think, to use the resources of the locals and not recompense them for it. Would you go into a garage and pump the mechanic for information so you could work on your own car?

Still there are plenty of times when catalogs are the only way or simply the best way to go. Maybe your local fly shop isn't that good in terms of service or politeness. Maybe they are unable to special order equipment for you. If you're planning a trip to the Northeast for Atlantic salmon or to West Yellowstone for Madison River trout, a catalog from that region can help in planning, especially in fly selection. At those times, you'll want a good catalog.

What makes a good catalog company. The same thing that makes a fly shop good makes a catalog company good . . . service and selection. You can't judge the service very well until you've ordered from a catalog, but there are a few things that will give you an indication ahead of time.

First, there should be a clearly stated return policy and guarantee, and you should read it. A catalog company should allow full return of goods with which you are not satisfied. That return should give the choice of exchange or refund. All catalogs require that the items be unused (which only makes sense) and that they be returned within a specific period of time, five to ten days in most cases.

Second, you can learn a lot about the company's attitude by reading the material in the catalog, especially the ordering information. If you had a choice on fly shops, you'd deal with the one where you felt most welcome and appreciated. It's no different with catalogs. Some of them will make you feel comfortable, and those are the ones you should deal with.

Selection is also important, of course, and you can only judge that from the catalog itself. You'll want a catalog that features equipment for the kind of fishing you do. Depending on your level of involvement, you may appreciate a catalog that offers only a few items selected by the staff and recommended by them or you may prefer a large selection from which you make the choice.

Finally, there's the catalog itself. It should be well illustrated, and the product descriptions should be factual and sincere. You can tell the difference between a sales pitch based on hype and one based on belief in the product. Ordering information should be clear, and there should be some way for you to indicate whether you want items not in stock to be back ordered or the money refunded to you. If there's no place to indicate this on the order form, write a note on your order stating your wishes and telling them they should have a place to indicate this on the form.

It's also helpful if the catalog takes a credit card. That allows phone orders and means that your order can be shipped without waiting for a check to clear.

The catalogs listed here. My criterion for including a catalog was simple. If the catalog was advertised in fly fishing magazines, I wrote for it. If it came, I put it in.

A couple of things resulted from this selection process. First, there are some catalogs here that are of only minor interest, mostly because the real emphasis of the catalog is something other than fly fishing. Second, there are some good catalogs missing. Some arrived too late or the company had run out of catalogs when I asked for one. Other companies declined to reply, perhaps because of fear of the press or because I didn't want to pay them. (I figured they would get more than $2 worth of publicity from my efforts.)

Many companies now charge for their catalogs. The high cost of printing has made this necessary. Charging reduces the number of people who ask for a catalog to those who are serious customers, a good business practice. Some companies refund the catalog charge when you order, and I approve of the system, since it reduces overhead. Prices on products don't have to be raised to cover printing, and people who actually order don't pay for the catalog for themselves or for anyone else. Most of the catalogs with a cover charge are worth it just for the entertainment value.

In the initial parts of the listings, you'll find telephone numbers, hours, credit cards, shipping charges, and the charge for the catalog. I've also included a brief run-down on the types of products offered (with the most predominant types listed first) and the number of pages in the

catalog (but bigger does not necessarily mean better). There are some omissions where information was not given.

Credit cards include American Express (AE), Mastercard (MC), Visa (V), Carte-Blanche (CB), and Diner's Club (DC). Shipping rates are given as room permitted. Most shipping charges are based on cost of the order. They're listed with the shipping charge followed by the cost of the order. For example, "$2.50/$30" means the shipping charge for orders up to $30 is $2.50. Some catalogs have a flat rate which is indicated in the following manner: "$3.75 flat". The complete schedule is seldom given, but enough information is available for comparison.

The three-letter code given in the upper right of the descriptions corresponds to the listings of sources in this book. With few exceptions, the code is simply the first three letters of the company's common name. If the code is missing, that catalog is not included in the source listings.

You'll also find a "review" of each catalog. I've tried to give you the flavor of the catalog and an idea of who might be interested in it. Whichever catalogs you order, enjoy them. Good shopping to you.

CATALOG COMPANIES

Angler's Junction   **AnJ**
5606 Alameda N.E.
Albuquerque, New Mexico 87113

Owner: John Wirth, Jr. Manager: Bill Fiorino
Phone #, orders: (800) 645-9292
Phone #, information: (505) 821-0500
Hours: 8:30-5, Mountain Time, Mon.-Fri. (for orders)
Credit cards: MC, V Shipping: $2.50/$14.99; $3.50/$29.99
Charge: none Pages: 35, color and b&w
Products: fly fishing, tying, flies, other fishing, clothing

Like The Tackle Shop in Texas, Angler's Junction might seem suspect because of its location. I've been to Albuquerque and I can't remember too many trout streams running through town. However, there are evidently a number of trout fishermen running through town. And just up the road a piece are mountains with rivers and lakes and trout. Bass may be lurking even closer.

This catalog features a very basic selection of equipment. There is, for instance, only one fly reel, the Scientific Anglers Systems One, and only one brand of fly rod, Reliance. The fly selection is fairly complete and displayed with full-color photos.

If you're a beginner in the sport, you may appreciate the fewer number of choices in the catalog. The people at Angler's Junction have chosen what they consider to be reliable equipment at reasonable prices, and that's all they offer right now. They've written me that they intend to add a section on salmon/steelhead (not many of those around Albuquerque either) due to customer requests. So the Angler's Junction catalog will continue to grow. (Ask for their woodworking catalog, too, if you're interested in that hobby.)

Angler's Ruff, Ltd.   AnR
19 Glen Head Rd.
Glen Head, New York 11545

Owners: Val and Lauren Antonucci
Phone #: (516) 676-0087
Hours: 10-6, Eastern Time, Tue.-Sat. (till 8, Wed., Fri.)
Credit cards: AE, MC, V Shipping: $2/$25; $2.75/$50; $3.25/$50 +
Charge: $1 Pages: 21, b&w
Products: fly fishing, tying, flies, books

The Angler's Ruff catalog is first class. It's printed on heavy, glossy paper which gives it a feel of quality and also reproduces photos exceptionally well.

The catalog features top-line equipment. There are Scott rods, Hardy reels, Orvis products, Xuron vises, and Wheatley boxes. You will find Thompson vises here, but nothing from India. Perrine didn't even make the cut.

I suspect the flies, which are among the most expensive, are also among the best. All are American-made. An unusual number of salmon patterns, over 40, makes Angler's Ruff one of the best sources for those flies.

The fly tying materials section deserves the attention of any serious tier, and the prices here are comparable to other catalogs. You can expect top quality. The descriptions are top quality, too, aiding those who aren't quite sure why they need a Macaw tail or Silver Monkey hair or Pearsall's Pure Silk Floss. An excellent place for salmon fly tiers to look for that hard-to-find material.

A ruff, incidentally, is a collar of feathers or hair on an animal.

Anglers Warehouse   AnW
Box 158
Wellsville, Pennsylvania 17365

Phone #, orders: (717) 432-8611
Phone #, customer service: (717) 432-8651
Hours: 8-midnight, Eastern Time, Mon.-Fri. (9-5 Sat.)
Credit cards: none Shipping: $3/$20; $4.50/$50; $5.50/$100
Charge: none Pages: 111, b&w
Products: other fishing, fly fishing

Most of this catalog is given over to fishing equipment other than fly fishing gear. It's a fat catalog with lots of items.

The fly fishing equipment in the catalog includes rods, reels, waders, vests, and some accessories. Prices are very competitive. Examples include Fenwick Boron-X rods for $186 and Hardy Lightweight reels for $73. Anglers Warehouse carries the Daiwa reel that is virtually identical to the Scientific Anglers System One reel. The Daiwa reel retails for $17.

Beartooth Fly Rods   Bea
Box 734
West Yellowstone, Montana 59758

Owner: Daniel Delekta
Phone #: (406) 646-9023
Credit cards: none Shipping: $3.50/$50; $4/$100; $5/$100 +
Charge: none Pages: 18, b&w
Products: fly fishing, rod building

Dan Delekta is a believer. He believes in his product, the Beartooth Rod, and anyone who's tried one will understand why. Dan's catalog, of course, is mainly concerned with the rods.

There are Marryat reels in the current catalog, and the Beartooth braided leaders are, I'm sure, included now. What other things are in store, I couldn't say, but Beartooth strikes me as a company on an upward swing. I think the rods will be successful, and with success, all things are possible.

If you're shopping for a rod, I think you should take a look at this catalog. The rods are among the most handsome, and their power curve is something else. Beartooth, incidentally, grants a lifetime guarantee. They'll replace any broken rod section, no matter what the cause, for as long as ye shall be able to cast and Dan able to repair.

You'll also find blanks and high-quality components, along with a brief introduction to rod building.

Big Sky Custom Flies   Big
Box 4981
Missoula, Montana 59801

Owner: Doug Brewer
Phone #: (406) 273-2535
Credit cards: none Shipping: $1.50 flat
Charge: none Pages: 18, b&w
Products: flies, materials, some equipment

Big Sky Custom Flies offers interesting bass flies and a full selection of trout flies, including some exclusive patterns. Most notable are the "wide wing" dry flies with extra-wide hen hackle tip wings, larger and more opaque than traditional wings. The flies show up better on the water which, in itself, means you'll probably catch more fish with them, but Doug Brewer also believes the wings represent the natural mayfly wings more accurately.

If your bass are getting tired of the standard flies (it happens in bass fishing; I knocked them out with Hair Moths one year and couldn't turn a fish with them the next), order some of Doug's patterns that you and your bass are unlikely to have seen. The Wooly Bass Bugger, for instance, is tied on a stinger hook, and it has yellow doll's eyes top and bottom, rather than on the sides. All flies are American-tied, actually Montana-tied, and Doug sounds like the picky type.

Custom orders are welcome at Big Sky without additional charge (except those flies requiring exotic materials). You'll also find materials at very good prices, a few books, some miscellaneous equipment, and exclusive Walton Powell graphite rods. They include three nine-foot models for line weights 2-3, 4-5, and 8-9.

Blue Ribbon Flies   Blu
Box 1037
West Yellowstone, Montana 59758

Owners: Craig and Jackie Mathews
Phone #: (406) 646-9365
Credit cards: MC, V Shipping: $2.50 flat
Charge: none Pages: 23, b&w
Products: flies, materials, some eccentric and esoteric equipment

You'll find the Mathews' catalog to be as entertaining as most magazines (and more entertaining than some), and if you don't feel as if you know all the folks at and around Blue Ribbon Flies after reading their catalog, then you weren't paying attention.

The issue I have begins with a run down on the last year's fishing in their area and includes a nifty map. There's enough information here to plan a trip to the West Yellowstone area. Interspersed with the listings of fly patterns (of which you'll find many, including some locally-proven patterns unavailable elsewhere) are recipes for flies. This issue also has an article by Jack Gartside entitled "What To Do With a Pheasant Skin". Included are several of his favorite pheasant recipes (for flies, that is).

For now, the catalog lists only flies and materials and a few equipment oddities. Major among those is a French silk fly line, an exclusive product. Look for this catalog to catch on and expand into other areas.

Bob Jacklin's Fly Shop   Bob
Box 310
West Yellowstone, Montana 59758

Owners: Bob and Chris Jacklin
Phone #: (406) 646-7336
Hours: 9-5, Mountain Time, 7 days a week
Credit cards: MC, V Shipping: $2.50 flat
Charge: none Pages: 24, tabloid, b&w
Products: fly fishing, tying, flies

Bob Jacklin is one of the most highly regarded guides in one of the most highly regarded fishing areas in the world. Nothing more need be said about his expertise, except that it shows up in his catalog.

In the catalog, you'll find a wealth of information about local hatches and the flies that take fish. The issue I have now also includes a full-spread map and complete article on the Yellowstone area. Interspersed in the listings are short articles on such worthy topics as nearby camping, fishing the Henry's Fork, streamer fishing, and Montana regs.

In short, you're getting a lot more than a catalog. You'll find, however, that the catalog is plenty interesting in itself. It has fine line drawings, some of which I've borrowed for this book with the Jacklins' kind permission. Most impressive is the fly section. The illustrations and descriptions are very helpful, and from them you can plan your Yellowstone fly needs.

You'll also find a good materials section, lots of interesting equipment, books, and a number of photos of people with huge fish. It's enough to make you sick with envy. To get well, go to West Yellowstone (and stop at Bob's shop while you're there).

Bud Lilly's Trout Shop   Bud
Box 698
West Yellowstone, Montana 59758

Owner: Fred Terwilliger
Phone #: (406) 646-7801
Hours: 9-6, Mountain Time, Thurs.-Mon. (7-7 every day in summer)
Credit cards: MC, V Shipping: $2.50 flat
Charge: none Pages: 70, b&w
Products: fly fishing, flies, tying, clothing, art

You'll find Fred Terwilliger behind the counter at Bud Lilly's Trout Shop now instead of Bud, but that's about the only change you'll find in one of the nicest shops in the West. Fred is in the enviable position of having been able to buy his favorite fly shop. We're all jealous, Fred (except in the dead of Montana's winter).

The catalog's about the same as usual, too—complete, well done, and always interesting. There's a lot of equipment in every category. The rod selection includes Sage, Orvis, and Winston. There are Ross and Sage reels and Wheatley fly boxes.

I always study the flies they offer. Yellowstone is one of my favorite areas, and these are the patterns one needs for the Park and surrounding areas. The flies are shown in b&w photos.

The browsing is great in the Trout Shop's catalog, as it is in the shop. You'll find a number of unusual items, including the Ampersand belt buckles (which I will go broke collecting) and fishing prints. The Trout Shop also has an outstanding fishing art gallery. Some of the prints are illustrated in the catalog, and I think Fred would be happy to try to locate any print you're looking for. If the shop were nearby, you'd visit it often. Since it's not, try the catalog. It's not a poor second.

Bullard International   Bul
Box 38131
Dallas, Texas 75238

Phone #: (214) 341-4981
Hours: 8:30-5:30, Central Time, Mon.-Fri.
Credit cards: MC, V Shipping: $3 flat
Charge: none Pages: 97, b&w
Products: rod building, fly fishing

Bullard has a super catalog for rod builders. Some 65 pages are given over to rod building products, and although much of that deals with rods for other types of fishing, you'll find some excellent components and tools here.

Among the components of note are Benchmark and Struble reel seats. You'll find blanks from Lamiglas, Fenwick, and G. Loomis. Fin-Nor reels are in the catalog, but that's the only reel of interest to fly fishermen. Ultra lines are here for $22.50, and Mustad hooks are part of the line-up. And that's about all folks.

Rod builders, however, should add this catalog to their collection.

Cabela's   Cab
812 13th Ave.
Sidney, Nebraska 69160

Phone #, orders: (800) 237-4444
Phone #, customer service: (800) 237-8888
Hours: 8-5, Mountain Time, 7 days a week
Credit cards: MC, V Shipping: $2.60/$25; $3.40/$50; $4/$100
Charge: none Pages: 145, color throughout
Products: fly fishing, flies, rod building, other fishing, tying, hunting, clothing, boating, camping

I had done no fishing but fly fishing for several years when my first Cabela's catalog arrived with its Mister Twister Sassy Shiners and Mad Dad Wounded Crawdads.

For several evenings I relived youthful bass fishing expeditions and restored some balance to my life.

When you find the fly fishing equipment among the wounded crawdads, you'll find quality gear at very competitive prices. Air Cel Ultra Fly Lines, for instance, are $25.95.

Cabela's also offers an exclusive line of graphite rods. They are nicely finished, and the one model that I've tried performed very well. For the money ($64.95-$92.95; blanks $31.95 and up), they are exceptional values. There are two pages of tying materials and one of flies. The fly section includes a full offering of Whitlock patterns, making this one of the best sources for bass bugs.

My Cabela's orders have been shipped quickly, and the return policy is generous. Cabela's will take anything back for whatever reason or no reason. The only problem I've had is that they operate seasonally in part, so some fly fishing equipment may be out of stock late in the year. Call first to avoid disappointment.

Cascade Lakes Tackle
23 Elm Street
Manchester, Massachusetts 01944

President: Jeffrey R. Henry
Phone #: (617) 526-7936
Credit cards: none Shipping: $10/$100; $20/$250
Charge: none Pages: 7, b&w
Products: fly fishing

Cascade Lakes Tackle produces wooden landing nets that are a standard in the field. The nets are available from many catalogs, and considering the shipping charges direct from the company, I'd suggest you deal with a regular retailer.

They carry some canoe accessories, such as yokes and motor mounts, that are more difficult to find, and you may want the catalog for them.

Classic & Custom Fly Shop   C&C
477 Pleasant Street
Holyoke, Massachusetts 01040

Phone: (413) 533-0433
Hours: 9-5, Eastern time, Mon.-Sat. (till 8 Thurs.)
Credit cards: V, MC Shipping: $2.50 flat
Charge: none Pages: 47, b&w
Products: fly fishing, tying

I learned of the C&C catalog too late to include it in very many of the source listings in the book. This is unfortunate since the catalog has a nice selection of rods, reels, and other equipment.

One exclusive offering is the rod line of L. A. Cavalieri. These bamboo rods retail for $575-$595. C&C's fly tying materials section is also noteworthy. C&C carries a full line of Cortland rods, Lee Wulff Triangle Taper lines, a fine selection of salmon flies, and Regal fly tying vises.

Coren's Rod and Reel Service   Cor

6424 N. Western
Chicago, Illinois 60645

Phone #: (312) 743-2980
Hours: 9-5, Central Time, Mon.-Sat. (noon-8 Thurs.)
Credit cards: MC, V Shipping: $2/$10; $2.60/$25; $2.85/$50
Charge: $1, refunded 1st order Pages: 57, b&w
Products: fly rod building, other rod building, fly fishing, tying, camping

There are two things that make this catalog interesting to the fly fishermen. The first is the rod building section. Among other things, there are a couple of fairly unusual brands of blanks available, including Loomis Composites and G. Loomis.

The components are standard brands, although there's a great variety since rod building is the company's specialty. You'll have to search through the spinning-salt-water-trolling-boat rod blanks and components to find the fly rod items. Experienced rod builders who know their brands and models won't mind this, and they'll also be intrigued by a number of special tools available, including power rod winders.

The second item of interest is rod and reel repairs. Since no other catalogs offer this service and so many fly fishermen are some distance from local sources of help, Coren's provides a valuable service. Anglers needing equipment repairs would be wise, I think, to call ahead to see if parts and expertise on particular models are available.

Custom Fishing Tackle   Cus

Box 16, Cemetery Road
Arbovale, West Virginia 24915

Owner: Stephen Fleckenstein
Phone #: (304) 456-3305
Credit cards: MC, V Shipping: $1.95/$10; $2.50/$25; $3.50/$50
Charge: none Pages: 24, b&w
Products: fly fishing, flies, tying

This isn't one of your slick catalogs, but it has some of the slickest prices. The Custom Fishing Tackle catalog has a down home list of equipment. The one I have is done on a typewriter, printed on inexpensive paper, and stapled together. There's not a lot of description, so it's a good thing you have this book. In short, no effort has been spared to save money on the production of the catalog, but the money saved is passed along to you in the form of lower-than-average prices.

You'll find Cascade Lakes nets for $18.90, and Ultra lines for $23.75. Fenwick Boron-X rods come in at under $200. For an unprepossessing catalog, these are some impressive prices. The issue I have is the first fly-fishing-only issue, so you can expect some improvements in years to come.

Going through the minute listings in the catalog is kind of like going through a sale bin. You have to pick through it all to find what you're looking for (and the other things you can't live without), but once you find it, the price is worth it. The most interesting of the items may be the West Virginia Spinner Fly, a lightweight spinner blade

with trailing fly. It's an unusual idea but an intriguing one. Cost of the spinner fly is about $1.

The Cutthroat Hook Co.   Cut

Box 127
Verdugo City, California 91046-9990

Owner: Taylor Walke
Phone #: none given
Credit cards: MC, V Shipping: $3/$20; $3.50/$40; $4/$75
Charge: none Pages: 4, b&w
Products: hooks and only hooks

If the key to success in the mail order business is specialization, Taylor Walke will surely be successful. His company carries only hooks, only Mustad hooks, and only those Mustad hooks "that people want the majority of the time".

The Cutthroat "catalog" is a list of 47 Mustad hooks, each with a concise description. These include such esoteric items as the #277, a gold-plated midge hook in size 32 for "when you want to impress your few remaining friends".

Obviously, there are a lot of hooks here. If you think you want a hook Cutthroat doesn't offer, you're probably wrong. In any case, the best thing about ordering from The Cutthroat Hook Company is the price you'll pay. Walke made friends with the Mustad people during WWII. Seems he was an expert on Norway's salmon rivers and surrounding territory. That friendship (and his ability to buy in lots of 1,000,000) lets Walke sell his hooks at (excuse the phrase) cutthroat prices.

The standard Mustad dry fly hook, #94840, is priced at $2.65 per hundred. Of course, you'll have to order a lot of hooks to really save. Postage on orders under $20 adds about $.50 to a box. Incidentally, my order was back in seven days. Good, fast service.

Dale Clemens Custom Tackle   Dal

Route 2, Box 860
Wescosville, Pennsylvania 18106

President: Dale Clemens
Phone #: (215) 395-5119
Hours: 9-5, Eastern Time, Mon.-Fri.
Credit cards: $1 Shipping: $2/$10; $2.60/$25; $3.40/$50
Products: fly rod building, other rod building, fly fishing, tying

If you build rods, you probably own something from Dale Clemens already, his books. They are standards in the field. His expertise and writing skills show up in the catalog, too. All descriptions are concise and clear, and the catalog is illustrated very well.

The Clemens catalog is the most comprehensive for rod builders. There are more choices, more tools, more innovative ideas than anywhere else. The company is, according to Dale, the largest supplier of rod building components and specialty tools in the world. No rod builder should be without this one.

There are so many exclusive items in this catalog that I can't begin to list them. Most have to do with rod building, and many are specialty tools that rod builders will go crazy about.

In addition, you'll find other fly fishing equipment and a good selection of tying tools and materials. One item of note here are the hard-to-find Renzetti vises.

Rod builders will also be interested in RodCrafters Journal, a magazine with them in mind. See the chapter on publications for more information.

Dan Bailey's Flies   Dan
Box 1019
Livingston, Montana 59047

Owner: John Bailey
Phone #: (406) 222-1673
Hours: 8-5, Mountain Time, Mon.-Sat.
Credit cards: AE, MC, V Shipping: $1.50/$19.99; $2.50/$39.99; free/$40
Charge: $2 (includes fishing map) Pages: 63, color and b&w
Products: fly fishing, tying, flies, clothing

Dan Bailey's holds a place close to the heart of every western angler, just as Dan Bailey himself held a place in the heart of all who knew him. The shop is a required stopping place for Montana trips. The Wall of Fame is worth a trip in itself. The shop and the catalog business are now maintained in the spirit of their original owner by his son, John.

Green Drake Wulff

This is a good sources for flies. They're all American-tied, most right there in the shop, and the catalog carries full-color photos of all of the over-300 patterns. This makes ordering a pleasant experience, devoid of the fear of what you'll get when the order comes. Pre-packaged fly selections help first-timers to the area.

Other products of note include French nylon leaders and Stream Cleats, those ingenious slip-on felt soles with cleats that are so helpful on the Madison and other slick streams. Although found in other catalogs, they're made right there in Livingston.

Bailey's offers an excellent equipment selection. The rods, for instance, include Sage, Scott, Fenwick, Orvis, and Winston. Like the rest of the products, these are items for the serious angler.

No trip planning for the Yellowstone area can be complete without the When-Where-How Map that you'll receive with the Bailey catalog.

Donegal Inc.   Don
Box 569
Monroe, New York 10950

Phone #: (914) 782-4600
Hours: 9-5, Eastern Time, Mon.-Sat.
Credit cards: AE, MC, V Shipping: $3.40/$29.99; $4/$49.99
Charge: none Pages: 57, b&w and color
Products: fly fishing, tying, flies, rod building

Here's another wonderful catalog with lots of photos and excellent descriptions. There are plenty of rods to choose from—Leonard, Sage, and Rodon—and plenty of reels—Fenwick, Scientific Anglers, Fin-Nor, and Hardy. A good, basic selection of accessories backs up these quality names.

The real strength of this catalog, however, are the flies and tying materials. The fly selection includes many salmon flies, including hard-to-find featherwing patterns. Saltwater, steelhead, and bass flies complement the standard offerings. Not every fly pattern is illustrated, but if you know what you're after, this is a good source.

The materials section is a must for every salmon fly tier, and even a plain old trout fly tier will feel like he's in heaven. Some of the more unusual items include polar bear, natural black squirrel, nutria, English grouse, Reeve's pheasant, black heron substitute, kingfisher skins, macaw tail, and bustard quills.

And if you're just beginning salmon fly tying, you'll enjoy the specific pattern kits that have enough materials for two flies. Instructions are included.

Dunn's, Inc.   Dun
Box 449
Grand Junction, Tennessee 38039-0449

Phone #: (901) 764-6901
Hours: 7:30-7:30, Central Time, Mon.-Fri. (till 5 on Sat.)
Credit cards: AE, CB, DC, MC, V Shipping: $2.50/$25; $3.50/$75
Charge: none Pages: 65, full-color throughout
Products: hunting, clothing, tack, fly fishing

Dunn's catalog concentrates on hunting equipment and clothing. It has about four pages devoted to fly fishing, but in those few pages, there's some good equipment.

Most notable is the line of Hardy graphite rods, including the Smuggler, the amazing 6- to 8-piece travel/pack rod. The selection of the hard-to-find Hardy rods and other quality gear earned the catalog a place in this book.

You won't find much else to recommend this catalog if you're interested only in fly fishing, but if you have an interest in duck hunting and bird dogs, Dunn's makes for good shopping. Horse lovers will enjoy a tack section that includes a special bird hunter's saddle and such practical accessories as a saddle holder for your Stanley vacuum bottle (which is, incidentally, the best vacuum bottle around, for horse lovers or trout lovers). The clothing and outdoor wear section is good, too.

With so many fascinating products here, you may end up expanding your interests just so you can order an item or two.

Eddie's Flies   Edd
303 Broadway
Bangor, Maine 04401

Owner: Ed Reif
Phone #: (207) 945-5587
Credit cards: MC, V Shipping: $1.25/$10; $1.75/$20; $2.25/$20 +
Charge: none Pages: 29, b&w
Products: fly fishing, tying, flies, rod building

This small catalog has an impressive selection of equipment and rod building supplies, but the best part, and the one that might convince you to order it, is the fly selection.

With its proximity to some of the best Atlantic salmon waters, Ed Reif's shop seems certain to be a reputable source of salmon flies, and the catalog lists a very complete selection at excellent prices. For example, mixed-wing salmon flies such as the Mars Lodge are $2.75. Eddie's Flies also offers tandem streamers, a regional favorite, as well as all the "regulars".

The catalog has Cortland and Fisher rods and other quality equipment.

Egger's   Egg
Box 1344
Cumming, Georgia 30130

Owners: Hart and Marj Egger
Phone #: none given
Credit cards: none Shipping: $1.75/$20; $2/$30; free/$30 +
Charge: none Pages: 13, b&w
Products: fly fishing, tying, rod building

Egger's catalog is primarily of regional interest. For those who live in or visit the southern Appalachians, this catalog is the nearest mail order source of equipment and tying materials. It's also directed to those who fish the area.

A couple of items are of interest to any fly fisherman. Egger's offers a wood backpacking net, either in kit form or finished. These are light, small, and handsome. Second, you'll find a number of fly tying tool sets, including a complete streamside kit, at reasonable prices.

E.J. Hille, The Angler's Supply House   EJH
Box 996
Williamsport, Pennsylvania 17703

Owner: C.W. O'Connor
Phone #: (717) 323-7564
Hours: 9-4:30, Eastern Time, Mon.-Fri. (Mon.-Sat. from ½ to 4/30)
Credit cards: MC, V Shipping: $2.65/$25; $3.50/$50; $4/$100
Charge: none Pages: 59, b&w
Products: fly fishing, tying, rod building, other fishing

E.J. Hille's catalog is about 90% fly fishing equipment and materials with some additional goodies for other fishermen. It's kind of nice to think about the hardware fishermen having to shuffle through the fly fishing gear to find their spoon blades.

There's also a concentration on rod building products. In fact, there are no finished rods in this catalog. The same goes for fly tying materials, lots of materials and tools but no finished flies.

The materials section is very complete and includes a number of unusual materials. The explanations are helpful, and the beginner will appreciate ordering from this catalog.

You won't find much pocket fluff here. All the products are very practical, and I like that. You won't have to worry about ending up with something silly.

My only objection is the occasional use of the Hille name in place of the manufacturer's name. I recommend against buying house names when brand names are available, even though most house brands are from well-known manufacturers. But Hille's can be forgiven for this minor offense because they've included an index, right on the back cover. And right on.

Fly-Rite   FIR
7421 S. Beyer Road
Frankenmuth, Michigan 48734

Owner: David M. McCann
Phone #: (517) 652-9869
Credit cards: none Shipping: not announced
Charge: $1, refunded 1st order Pages: 14, b&w
Products: tying, flies, fly fishing

Fly-Rite products, especially the synthetic dubbing materials, are well known in the business. Fly-Rite Dubbing is carried by more catalogs than any other single material.

The Fly-Rite catalog doubles, I'm sure, as a retail catalog and as a wholesale catalog, although wholesale prices are not included for the retail customer. It has 14 pages printed on one side only, so there's not a great number of items here. Most are found in other catalogs, but the brass thumb bobbin and the bronze hackle pliers are not very common. There's also a wooden landing net for $15.

Fly-Rite products are very popular, especially among tiers, and if you use a lot of them, you may prefer to deal directly with the company.

The Fly Shop

The Fly Shop   **Fly**
4140 Churn Creek Road
Redding, California 96002

Phone #, orders: (800) 533-3474 or from CA (800) 535-3474
Phone #, local conditions: (916) 222-3555
Hours: 9-6, Pacific Time, 7 days a week
Credit cards: MC, V Shipping: $3 flat
Charge: none Pages: 61, b&w
Products: fly fishing, tying, flies, rod building

The Fly Shop is one of the largest fly fishing concerns in the West. Its catalog reflects this. It's very complete, well designed and illustrated, and has very good product descriptions.

The range of products offered is excellent, with good quality standard items and higher-priced top line items in equal share. In landing nets, for instance, you'll find the standard Cascade Lakes nets, the special purpose Insta-Net, and the top line Chris Brodin nets. In vises, there's everything from the Crest 200 to the Regal to the HMG, representing a price range of $26.95-$184.

The book section is one of the best. It includes popular titles as well as some unusual books. The River Why, that wonderful novel, is here, as are regional titles such as Fly Patterns of Alaska and Pacific Northwest Fly Patterns.

The Fly Shop also offers worldwide booking for fly fishing trips as well as guided trips to waters like the famous Hat Creek. They also have a fly fishing school.

The Folks on Buck Hill   **Fol**
Box 306
North Industry, Ohio 44707

Phone #, orders: (800) 321-0200; OH (800) 362-6540
Credit cards: MC, V Shipping: $3.35/$50; $4/$100; $4.75/$150
Charge: $4.95 (Note: Mine came free.) Pages: 500, color
Products: hunting, other fishing, fly fishing, camping

Considering the stated charge for this catalog, you need to like all the things listed under "products" to make the investment worthwhile. However, I got my catalog free without soliciting it, and it could be that a simple request will get you one.

Of the fly fishing items in the catalog, some have excellent prices. Ultra lines, for instance, are $21.45. Others, like Fenwick Boron-X rods, have good prices ($204) but better prices are available.

However, if you enjoy hunting with firearms or bows and other outdoor activities, especially other types of fishing, you'll enjoy the catalog from The Folks on Buck Hill. It has color photos throughout, and with 500 pages, it can give you several evenings of enjoyment.

Fred Reese's Fly Fisherman Shop   **Fre**
1145 Allegheny Street
Jersey Shore, Pennsylvania 17740

Owner: Fred Reese
Phone #: (717) 398-1318
Credit cards: MC, V Shipping: $3/$20; free/over $20
Products: fly fishing, tying, flies, rod building

Although Fred Reese was unable to send me a full catalog in time to be included in this book, he did send a tabloid supplement that's larger than many of the catalogs listed here. There is a wide range of offerings that will please beginner and experienced angler alike. Fly tying vises, for instance, range from the "AA" import at about $15 to the HMH at about $150. If the supplement is any indication, the full catalog will be worth sending for.

HIGH COUNTRY Flies

High Country Flies   **Hig**
Box 1022
Jackson, Wyoming 83001

Owners: Jay and Kathy Buchner
Phone #: (307) 733-4944
Credit cards: AE, MC, V Shipping: $1.50/$20.99; $2.50/$49.99
Charge: none Pages: 35, b&w
Products: fly fishing, flies, tying, clothing

From the country north of me comes another fine catalog. The Buchners, of Wyoming's High Country Flies, have put together a nice selection of equipment, flies, tying materials, accessories, and clothing for the fly fisherman.

Many catalogs are pretty sterile. They have only hard line equipment. This isn't true of High Country Flies. They feature accessories and clothing, all the things people who have equipment needs under control go into a shop for.

High Country Flies offers top line equipment, American-tied flies, and Patagonia outdoor clothing. In addition to the Patagonia line, you'll find some great fishing T-shirts.

If I were giving awards for catalogs, this one would be in line for the layout award. The catalog is so well-designed and easy to get around in that it has the feeling of a nice magazine. Even with the classy design, the catalog is obviously from a family-run business, and that makes it comfortable to order from.

Incidentally, Jay has the best handlebar moustache in the industry. He gets that award.

The Hook & Hackle Company — H&H

Box 1003
Plattsburgh, New York 12901

Phone #: (518) 561-5893
Credit cards: AE, MC, V Shipping: $2.80 flat
Charge: none Pages: 37, b&w
Products: fly fishing, tying, rod building, flies

Hook and Hackle's intention is to bring you good fly fishing equipment at the most competitive prices possible. A means to this end is publishing a no-frills catalog. It's barely coach. Before it sounds like I'm complaining about the miniscule descriptions and the lack of illustrations, let me tell you that I appreciate the bargain prices, the lack of hype, and the committment to the Intention.

You can buy a Caddis Deluxe float tube for $67.50, a Thompson A vise for $22.30, and a Lamiglas G-1000 graphite rod for as low as $44.40. American-tied dry flies are less than a buck. Other products carry price tags among the best in the marketplace.

How does H&H do it? Partly by minimizing the cost of their catalog. That means brief descriptions and no illustrations. You'll have to salivate over the prices rather than the pictures.

Beginners may have some problems with the catalog because it assumes the buyer has confidence in his decisions about equipment. No effort is made to convince him to buy.

Hunter's Angling Supplies — Hun

Central Square
New Boston, New Hampshire 03070

Owners: Bill and Simone Hunter
Phone #: (603) 487-3388
Hours: 9-5, Eastern Time, Tues.-Sat. (till 8 on Thurs.)
Credit cards: MC, V Shipping: $3/$125; free/$125+
Charge: $2 Pages: 63, b&w and color
Products: fly fishing, tying, flies, rod building

This catalog turned out to be one of the few that I referred to when I had a question about equipment. So well illustrated and documented is it that it provided guidance on products I was not familiar with. And I respect the opinion of the Hunters.

As I've suggested, the descriptions are generous, and the photos are plentiful and excellent. The Hunters have included only quality equipment in their catalog. Their rod selection, for instance, includes Scott, Orvis, Leonard, and Cortland. Each of the rods, incidentally, is matched to a Hardy, S/A Systems One, or, in the case of saltwater and big game rods, to Catinos or Fin-Nors and packaged with line and backing at discount prices for the outfit.

You'll find a wonderful selection of flies here, also. Special attention is given to salmon flies, and their offering of these patterns is excellent. Prices are in line with other catalogs carrying American-tied flies.

You'll also find many "goodies" in Hunter's catalog. There are Hardy thermometers, REC rod components, and a number of other hard-to-find items. And how can you not give consideration to the Master Tyer's Chest? No matter that it has a price tag of $1,870.

This catalog is a pretty piece. You should try a copy.

Kaufmann's Streamborn — Kau

Box 23032
Portland, Oregon 97223

Owner: Randall Kaufmann
Phone #: (503) 639-6400 (or, on Sat. 639-7004)
Credit cards: AE, MC, V Shipping: $2.50/$20; $3/$40; $3.50/$75
Charge: none Pages: 87, color and b&w
Products: fly fishing, flies, tying, rod building, clothing

Kaufmann's catalog has lots of everything. It's one of the most complete catalogs available. In reels, for instance, you'll find Ross, Sage, Hardy, Orvis, Cortland, Scientific Anglers, Pflueger, Billy Pate, and Fin-Nor. Rods include Rodon, Sage, Orvis, Fenwick, and Leonard.

I could give a list like those in many of the equipment areas, but let's just say that Kaufmann's is a big operation with a high volume and they've used their resulting resources to provide as many choices for the angler as they can.

In addition to that strength, Kaufmann's is one of the best places to shop for mail order flies, because each fly is illustrated with a color photo and described with a paragraph suggesting its use. I couldn't find any specific declaration, but I assume the flies are American-tied. They look like it, and the prices are right.

In addition to the traditional patterns, you'll find Randall Kaufmann's interesting nymph patterns, Iwamasa-style flies, a fine selection of saltwater flies, all the popular Whitlock patterns, LaFontaine's caddis patterns, Janssen minnows, and an outstanding selection of steelhead flies. This last makes the catalog a must for steelheaders. The descriptions provide a mini-course in the sport and the inspiration to take it up.

Letort, Ltd.   Let
Box 417
Boiling Springs, Pennsylvania 17007

Owner: Thomas E. Baltz
Phone #, orders: (800) 321-2264; PA (717) 258-3010
Phone #, customer service: (717) 258-3010
Hours: 9-6, Eastern Time
Credit cards: MC, V Shipping: $1.25/$10; $2.75/$10 +
Charge: $2, refunded 1st order Pages: 47, b&w
Products: fly fishing, tying, flies

You can tell the people in Boiling Springs are excited about the sport of fly fishing. Their catalog conveys that feeling in its descriptions and articles.

Speaking of the articles, you'll find interesting writing from the likes of Vince Marinaro, Joe Humphreys, and Ed Shenk. Ed's piece on terrestrial fishing in the issue I have in hand is informative and amounts to a regular magazine article. It doesn't try to sell you on anything but fishing with terrestrials. The company, incidentally, is in an area where terrestrials are a mainstay of the trout's diet and the fisherman's repertoire.

Marinaro contributes a piece on hooks, which is appropriate since he has developed a new midge hook for Partridge. Letort, Ltd. is the distributor for Partridge hooks in this country, incidentally, so you'll find the entire line here, including the Swedish dry fly hook that LaFontaine's book on caddis is making popular.

You'll find some items of special interest in the catalog. One is Ed Shenk's Flea Rod, all five and a half feet of it. Richardson Chest Fly Boxes are also included. They're as popular on the Yellow Breeches as vests are. The best recommendation for the catalog remains the descriptions of the products. It's much like enthusiastic advice to a friend.

L.L. Bean   LLB
Freeport, Maine 04033

Phone #: (207) 865-3111
Hours: 24 hours a day, 7 days a week
Credit cards: AE, MC, V Shipping: free
Charge: none Pages: 71, color throughout
Products: clothing, outdoor gear, fly fishing, other fishing, tying, flies

If you're over 12 and you love the outdoors and every piece of gear designed for man's (and woman's) enjoyment of it, you already know about L.L. Bean. What you may not know is that the venerable Maine company is now in the fly fishing business.

The spring issue I have offers nine pages of equipment and an invitation to write for a list of fly patterns (over 500!) and a materials list, as well as a brochure on their fly fishing school. Unfortunately, the catalog supplements weren't sent to me in time to be included in this book, so Bean's involvement in the fly fishing market is greater than may appear from the listings here.

The Bean product line, which includes S/A lines and Marryat reels features their own line-up of graphite rods, made for them by REC, Inc. of Vermont. The product line is being developed with the help of Dave Whitlock. Expect more equipment and greater diversity in the future (or now, since I'm writing this in the past).

My orders to Bean have always been handled with speed and accuracy, and their guarantee is absolute. Bean's support of Trout Unlimited and other conservation groups is admirable and not surprising. This is a great company to add to the list of fly fishing merchants. Welcome, L.L. Bean.

Merrick's Tackle Center   Mer
2655 Merrick Road
Bellmore, New York 11710

Phone #: (516) 781-6777
Hours: 9-6, Eastern Time, Mon.-Sat.; 9-3 Sun.
Credit cards: AE, MC, V Shipping: $4/$25; $5/$75; $6.50/$75 +
Charge: $1, refundable 1st order Pages: 153, b&w
Products: fly fishing, flies, tying, rod building, other fishing

When you open Merrick's catalog, you may feel as if you've just walked into a fly fishing surplus store. The setting does not at all appeal to delicate sensibilities, but just like the surplus store, once you start looking at all the stuff, you'll be mesmerized, at least through the two hours or so it may take for the first go-through and probably for a long time thereafter as you try to remember on which page you saw the Brown Spotted Snipe skin for $15. There's an incredible amount of gear (none of it surplus).

If any catalog needed an index, this one does. And there is one, but you need an index to find it. It's buried on page 72 (which is announced on the cover, I must admit). On second thought, maybe an index is a bad idea. A supermarket-type directory would take some of the fun out of shopping in a surplus store. A prominent index might do the same here. Besides, every time you go through Merrick's catalog, you'll discover something you missed.

The illustrations are awful or non-existent, the organization is "creative", but the prices are good, the selection is among the best, and no other catalog is quite as much an adventure. Whether you're looking for Capercailizie wings or a good deal on a rod blank, Merrick's is a catalog you'll want.

Murray's Fly Shop   Mur
Box 156
Edinburg, Virginia 22824

Owner: Harry Murray
Phone #: (703) 984-4212
Credit cards: MC, V Shipping: $1.75/$15; $2/$30; $2.50/$50
Charge: none Pages: 19, b&w
Products: fly fishing, flies, tying, rod building

You may recognize Harry Murray's name from his articles in fly fishing magazines, or you may have been fortunate enough to hear him speak at one of the many Trout Unlimited meetings at which he's been the featured guest.

Harry's expertise, combined with his geographical location, makes this catalog especially informative. I mention the location of the shop because it's on the Shenandoah, a renowned smallmouth fishery, and near the mountain trout streams of the Appalachians. Harry has a thorough knowledge of both of these kinds of fishing.

Nowhere does this provocative combination show up better than in his fly selections. There are many unique patterns here, including the Mr. Rapidan Dry trout fly and Murray's Shenandoah River Hair Bass Bugs. The latter features renditions entitled Krazy Kicker Frog and Homely Hair Mouse, among others. You'll find standard Whitlock patterns and unusual patterns from well-known regional people like Ed Shenk, who offers things (and I mean things) like the Mr. Ugly Sculpin.

You'll also find a good selection of equipment including Walt Carpenter bamboo rods and the complete line of Scott rods. If you live near bass or near Harry, either one, you should have this catalog.

National Feather-Craft, Co.,   Nat
Box 186
Florissant, Missouri 63032

Owner: Ed Story
Phone #: (314) 427-1707
Credit cards: none Shipping: $2.25 flat
Products: tying, fly fishing

This is not so much a catalog as a newsletter. Let me have Ed introduce it to you in his own inimitable style:

"New readers should note that we do not have time to edit or look back. For the beginning fly tyer we again describe new and old fly tying methods and patterns. Our regular readers (over 60,000) can expect the same old dragged out laborious bulletin with our regular tips on how to pick up girls, lose weight, gain wealth and of course back bite the slick publications . . . and some industry gossip."

There are lots of materials here, good ones. Tanned black bear from the people who make the "changing of the guard hats". Things like that. Many kinds of duck feathers: canvasback, gadwall, widgeon, and the regulars.

Mostly it's adventuresome reading, this newsletter. Ed Story is irreverent, iconoclastic, and a lousy typist, but he's always got something to say that's entertaining and

has a point to it. He loves to zing the biggies, and that makes him something of a stand-alone and something of a folk hero to many people who don't want to "buy in" 100%. He'll hate me saying that, 'cause he's just a plain ole fisherman and duck hunter. But hell, Ed, it's true.

Netcraft Co.
2800 Tremainsville Road
Toledo, Ohio 43613

Owner: Herb Ludgate
Phone #: (419) 472-9826
Credit cards: MC, V Shipping: 10% order +$.85 (refunds)
Charge: none Pages: 162, b&w and color
Products: other fishing, fly fishing, flies, tying, rod building

Like some of the other catalogs here, Netcraft does not concentrate on fly fishing. Most of the products are for other kinds of fishing. If you're not a purist, these other items will be of interest. For many fly fishermen, however, things like electric fish scalers come from some other planet.

Netcraft carries some very interesting rod building tools. Their rod wrapping tools, for instance, are inexpensive and look very practical. A little searching through the other fishing equipment may turn up some goodies. (Note: The Netcraft catalog arrived too late to be included in the listings.)

The North Fork   Nor
417 Delaware
Kansas City, Missouri 64105

Phone #, orders: (816) 421-3344
Phone #, customer service: (816) 474-1236
Hours: 9-5, Central Time, Mon.-Fri.
Credit cards: AE, MC, V Shipping: $2.75/$20; $3.50/$50;
$3.95/$100
Charge: none Pages: 31, color throughout
Products: fly fishing, fly tying, flies, clothing

My review of the initial North Fork "magalog" read, in part: "What we have here is a company with good intentions and high-quality products, but without a strong sense of where they're at." They offered, among other things, a Sony Walkman with the suggestion that you take it to a mountain stream for "a little entertainment".

With their second catalog, North Fork has shown they've discovered what all us fly fishermen already knew—the music of the stream is entertaining enough. Gone are the Walkmans, the baby blue waders, and the other odd items. North Fork now has a handsome catalog with reasonable products for the angler.

Added are fly tying materials, selected rods from Leonard, Cairnton, Fisher, and Cortland, and fly lines and leaders. Of course, you'll still find some unusual items, such as the digital watch you can submerge to read water temperature (listed, of course, under stream thermometers in Chapter 6).

The North Fork reels and quality accessories are also of interest. If you didn't favor the first "magalog", give them another try. I think they know where they're at now.

The Orvis Co., Inc.   Orv
10 River Road
Manchester, Vermont 05254

President: Leigh Perkins
Phone #, orders: (802) 362-1300
Phone #, customer service: (802) 362-3434
Phone #, technical questions: (802) 362-3166
Hours: 8 a.m.-11 p.m., Eastern Time, Mon.-Fri.; 9-4, Sat.-Sun.
Credit cards: AE, MC, V Shipping: $3.50 flat
Charge: none Pages: 85, color throughout
Products: fly fishing, tying, flies, rod building, other fishing,
hunting, clothing, accessories

A Sporting Tradition Since 1856. The Orvis motto says
just about everything that needs to be said. They've been
around longer than any other company I know of and
have always been highly regarded. They are the American
tradition in fly fishing.

Let's just put it this way. If you don't recognize the
Orvis name, you are, prima facie, a rank beginner in fly
fishing. If you don't have a well worn Orvis catalog, you
are deprived as a fly fisherman. If you don't own Orvis
equipment, you will someday.

Orvis handles only first-rate products, from their rods
and reels, to their flies and materials. Orvis rods and
reels are among the best available. Orvis rods, including
bamboo as well as graphite and boron/graphite, are
well-designed and distinctive not only in appearance, but
also in performance. The CFO reel is excellent and
competitively priced in its part of the market.

You'll have nothing to fear from the standpoint of
quality or service when ordering from Orvis. Their
catalog is a treasure, one of the best in fly fishing in terms
of the overall quality of presentation (which is always
important in fly fishing), organization, and photos. If you
don't have one, shame on you. Call or write immediately.
Just put the book down and do it.

Pennsylvania Outdoor Warehouse   Pen
1508 Memorial Ave.
Williamsport, Pennsylvania 17701

President: Charles L. Matter, II
Phone #: (800) 441-7685; PA (800) 282-8731; others (717) 322-3589
Hours: 9-9, Eastern Time, Mon.-Sat.
Credit cards: MC, V Shipping: $3.40/$50; $4/$100; $4.75/$150
Charge: $2 Pages: 70, b&w, some color
Products: fly fishing, flies, tying

Pennsylvania Outdoor Warehouse offers a complete
line of fly fishing equipment, much of it at discount prices.

Air Cel Ultra lines, for instance, are $23.98. Fenwick
Boron-X rods are under $200.

Not all the equipment is discounted, but major items
like rods, reels, float tubes, and the like are, and their
prices are among the best for those products.

The catalog offers very good descriptions of its
products. The fly line section, for example, is well
organized and has complete descriptions of the lines,
including sink rates. It should serve as a model for other
catalog companies that often assume we customers know
more than we do.

Black-and-white photos are used generously throughout, and the fly section has six pages of color plates.

If you order this catalog, specify the spring fly fishing
issue. I don't know what else the company offers, but like
Cabela's and other catalogs, the spring catalog is the one
you're after.

Pfeiffer's Tackle Crafters   Pfe
14303 Robcaste Road
Phoenix, Maryland 21131

Owner: C. Boyd Pfeiffer
Phone #: (301) 667-6464 or 472-2555
Hours: 9-5, Eastern Time, Mon.-Fri.
Credit cards: MC, V Shipping: $1.95/$10; $2.50/$25; $3.30/$50
Charge: $1, refundable 1st order Pages: 59, b&w
Products: fly rod building, other rod building, lure making

Begun as a result of C. Boyd Pfeiffer's book, *Tackle
Craft*, this catalog concentrates entirely on supplies for
the rod builder and lure maker.

If you're just getting into rod building, you should order
this catalog. With its specialization in rod building, it
provides much more information about blanks, components, and tools than you'll find in general catalogs. Those
catalogs simply can't devote the space to rod building
products that a beginner needs in order to make sound
decisions.

In addition, Boyd will include informational pamphlets
that he's written for each type of rod building. These
aren't definitive guides to rod building; for that, you'll
want his book or one of the others on rod building. They
do serve, however, to give a concise rundown on the steps
involved and the items you'll need to build your own fly
rod.

In addition, because this is a specialty business, you
can get the expert advice you may need as you order and
later as you proceed with your rod building. Not all
companies have experience with rod building even though
they may carry some supplies.

Ramsey Outdoor   Ram
226 Route 17 North
Paramus, New Jersey 07652

Phone #: (201) 261-5000
Hours: 9-6, Eastern Time, Mon.-Sat.
Credit cards: MC, V Shipping: $2.25/$25; $3/$50; $4/$100
Charge: none Pages: 65, b&w
Products: outdoor equipment, camping, fly fishing, clothing

The Ramsey Outdoor catalog has only nine pages of fly fishing equipment. The brand names include James-Scott, Sage, Hardy, and Stream Designs, so although the selection is limited, it's good equipment.

The prices are also good. Caddis float tubes, for instance, are $69.95. Ultra lines are $22.95.

Even if I never order any fly fishing equipment from Ramsey Outdoor, there are lots of other items I see here that I'd enjoy. Backpacking equipment, camping gear, and clothing highlight the offerings, but I also like things like the "Think Trout" T-shirt and the juggling set for the complete klutz.

If you enjoy other outdoor sports along with your fly fishing, I think you'll enjoy the Ramsey Outdoor catalog. It's nicely done and completely illustrated. And while you're browsing through it, you might end up with a bargain or two in the fly fishing section.

Rangeley Region Sport Shop   Ran
28 Main Street, Box 400
Rangeley, Maine 04970

Owners: Dick and Joan Frost
Phone #: (207) 864-3309
Credit cards: MC, V Shipping: $1.25/$10; $1.75/$20; $2.25/$20 +
Charge: $1 Pages: 21, b&w
Products: fly fishing, tying, flies, rod building

The Rangeley Region is one of the most beautiful areas in our country. An area of large lakes and many rivers, it's an ideal, fairly out-of-the-way vacation spot for fly fishermen. It also has lakes with the most unusual names in the world. My favorite is (and I'm about to spell the name of a lake from an old memory of how I thought it was pronounced, so don't try to find this one on the map) Lake Mooselookemeguntik. Dick and Joan and all good Mainers may be groaning, but I know they all recognize this lake and wish they were there right now, fishing. So much for geography.

The Rangeley Region catalog has a little bit of everything in it, including materials, rod building, and flies. It does not presently include rods, reels, or other big ticket items. The regional flies are the most interesting. They include local favorites, such as the Doodle Bug and tandem trolling streamers, and salmon flies.

The catalog I have, incidentally, says the shop's for sale. The Frosts want to devote full time to the catalog business. So, if you've been looking for a fly shop in a wonderful fishing area . . .

Reed Tackle   Ree
Box 1348
Fairfield, New Jersey 07007

Phone #: (201) 227-0409
Credit cards: MC, V Shipping: $2.25/$20; $2.50/$30; free/$30 +
Charge: none Pages: 49, b&w
Products: other fishing, fly fishing, tying, rod building

Reed Tackle concentrates on tying materials and rod building supplies. You won't find finished rods or other equipment such as reels in their catalog.

What you will find is a good materials selection, including lots of Mustad hook models, rod building components, and house-brand blanks. The fact that Reed doesn't identify the manufacturer for its blanks is unfortunate, I think, because they're probably quality rods.

You'll find some items of special interest in the tying and rod building tool sections. For example, Reed offers a pedestal base for vises for $13.95 and an exclusive hackle trimmer.

R.L. Winston Rod Companuy   RLW
Box 248
Twin Bridges, Montana 59754

Owner: Tom Morgan
Phone #: (406) 684-5533
Credit cards: MC, V Shipping: $4 flat
Charge: none Pages: 36, b&w and color
Products: fly rods, fly fishing, rod building

The Winston catalog is a great place to shop for a high-quality bamboo, graphite, or fiberglass rod. Not only are the rods exceptional, but the descriptions are the best in the business.

You will find the rods categorized by their intended use, such as light trout, saltwater, steelhead or salmon, and within each category there are specific suggestions on which rod to order for the kind of fishing you'll be doing. It's almost like being in the shop with Tom Morgan discussing the perfect rod for your favorite river.

You'll find the shopping to be comfortable, and the guarantee reassuring. Winston would like you to call and discuss your rod purchase, unless you're familiar with their rods. They want you to be happy with the rod, and they are obviously aware that such a purchase through the mail is chancy. If you're not happy with your new rod, you may return it within five days (as long as it hasn't been fished) for an exhange or refund. You can count on that.

This catalog is one of the most informative and enjoyable to be found. There's a lot of information that will help you select the proper rod, whether it turns out to be a Winston or not. The supplement includes such goodies as leather rod cases, Ross reels, and Brodin nets, but the main things here are the wonderful Winston rods.

Shoff Tackle Supply   Sho
Box 1227
Kent, Washington 98032

Phone #: (206) 852-7304
Hours: 9-5, Pacific time, Mon.-Fri.
Credit cards: AE, V Shiping: $2.60/$10; $3.40/$25; $3.90/$50
Charge: none Pages: 32, b&w
Products: rod building

Shoff Tackle Supply deals entirely in rod building
supplies. Included in their selection of rod blanks are
Lamiglas S-Glass, graphite, and boron, Sage and Sage
Graphite II, and Fenwick fiberglass, graphite, and boron.
Struble components are also offered, as are a number of
rod building tools.

Simon Peter   Sim
28 Deerfield Drive
Franklin, New Jersey 07416

Owners: Ed and Linda Rembish
Phone #: (201) 827-6875 (collect for orders)
Hours: 9-5, Eastern Time, Mon.-Fri.
Credit cards: MC, V Shipping: $2.60/$25; $3.40/$50; $4/$100
Charge: $2, refundable 1st order Pages: 119, b&w
Products: fly fishing, other fishing, boating

Simon Peter, of course, was the Biblical Ernie
Schwiebert. A worthy name for a worthy catalog
company.

Simon Peter is a relatively new company, but there's
something about its catalog that gives the impression of
success in the making, perhaps because it's attractive and
well-illustrated.

The emphasis in the catalog is not on fly fishing, but
you'll find enough fly fishing equipment offered at
excellent prices to make your browsing worthwhile. They
offer many marine products, depth-finders and so on, not
typically found in fishing catalogs.

Prices are one good reason for getting this catalog.
Examples: Air Cel Ultra—$21.50; Cascade Lakes landing
net—$13.35-$14.65. (As I said in the text of this book,
the price on the landing net almost has to be a mistake.
It's about half the going price.)

With all these cut-rate prices, the catalog and the
ambience is first class, so I'm confused. We have other
discount houses in the business, but they all look like
discount houses. Nobody expects K-Mart prices in a
Bloomingdale's store. I hope this company prospers and
adds more fly fishing equipment to their line.

Sportsman's Supplies   Spo
2924 South Avenue
Toledo, Ohio 43609

Manager: Dave Jann
Phone #: (419) 381-9777
Hours: 9-5, Central Time, Mon.-Fri. (Sat. 9-12)
Credit cards: MC, V Shipping: $1.85/$20; $2.45/$50; $3.10/$50 +
Charge: none Pages: 35, b&w
Products: rod building, tying, lure making

Fly fishing is only a minor part of this catalog, but you
will find rod building supplies and a basic selection of

tying materials. Much of the catalog is given over to lure
making and rod building for other types of fishing. The
people at Sportsman's Supplies sound like good folks, and
if you live in the general region, this would be a good
place to deal.

Stewart Custom Tackle   Ste
17310 N.E. Halsey
Portland, Oregon 97230

Phone #: (503) 254-2359
Hours: 9-9, Pacific Time, Tues.-Fri. (12-9, Mon.; 9-6, Sat.)
Credit cards: MC, V Shipping: $3.50 flat (excess refunded)
Charge: none Pages: 21, b&w
Products: fly fishing, flies, tying

This well-illustrated catalog features Orvis products,
as well as other top brands. You'll find some unusual
items, like the Teeny vest and Teeny fly lines, and several
products of special interest to steelheaders.

The fly selection, for instance, includes many steelhead
patterns, including some unusual ones. The book section
has many titles about steelhead fishing.

Since the shop also offers guided trips and clinics,
anglers planning a steelhead trip would be wise to send
for this catalog.

Streamlife Innovations   Str
Box 266
Hailey, Idaho 83333

Owner: Fred Arbona, Jr. and Roger Lampman
Phone #: (208) 788-3649
Credit cards: MC, V Shipping: $1/$25; $2/$25 +
Charge: none Pages: 9, b&w
Products: flies, tying

Fred Arbona, Jr. is the author of *Mayflies, the Angler,
and the Trout*, so it's not surprising that the featured
items in this catalog are mayfly patterns.

These are not standard patterns, however. There are
cut-wing emergers, duns, and spinners as well as
extended body cut-wing patterns. Other patterns in the
catalog include Arbona's Ostrich Nymphs and more
standard patterns such as scuds and hairwing caddis
dries. All flies are American-tied.

In addition to the unusual patterns, you'll find wing
burners and a few materials specifically for tying those
patterns. Streamlife Innovations is also one of the few
sources for Climax leader material.

Tackle Chandlers
Box 3041
Wilmington, Delaware 19804

Phone #: (302) 998-7584
Hours: 9-5, Eastern Time, Mon.-Fri.
Credit cards: MC, V Shipping: $1.90/$10; $2.40/$20; $2.90/$50
Charge: $1 Pages: 48, b&w
Products: fly rod building, other rod building

For rod builders only, Tackle Chandlers offers blanks,
components, and tools. You will, however, have to look

through a lot of products designed for other types of rods. Fly rods are a minor part of the catalog's offerings.

There are good tools here, including a finishing motor and stand, so experienced rod builders may be interested in the catalog.

(Note: Because of the limited number of fly fishing items in this catalog, it was not included in the source listings.)

Tackle-Craft   TCr
Box 280
Chippewa Falls, Wisconsin 54729

Phone #: not given
Credit cards: none Shipping: by weight, see catalog
Charge: none Pages: 89, b&w
Products: tying materials, lure-making supplies

This catalog carries only fly tying materials and tools and jig-making supplies. There's a good selection of materials, hooks, and basic tools. Tying materials include Fly-Rite products and Hareline Dubbin. The tools include a set of brass tools in a velvet-lined case for $18.50.

My request for a catalog was answered promptly, and a friendly note accompanied the catalog. Makes me think that dealing with Tackle-Craft would be an entirely pleasant experience.

The Tackle Shop   Tac
Box 369
Richardson, Texas 75080

Owner: Bill Barlow
Phone #: (214) 231-5982
Hours: 9-6, Dallas time, Monday-Friday
Credit cards: MC, V Shipping: $2.45/$20; $2.70/$40; $2.95/$40+
Charge: none Pages: 129, b&w, some color
Products: fly fishing, tying, rod building, other fishing

Okay, I'll admit that it's difficult to believe that a firm in Texas can have something to offer to trout fishermen from Montana or Oregon or Vermont. I mean, I almost didn't write for their catalog. Geographic prejudice, I guess.

But this is a good catalog. They offer a lot of fly fishing equipment with quality brand names and good prices. More than that, The Tackle Shop offers such a complete line of fly tying materials and tools that it puts some of the traditionally favorite catalogs to shame. And the materials section has full-color photos of most of the feathers and hair. The photos aren't great, but they're good enough. If I were a beginning tier without a fly shop nearby, I'd get this catalog.

In the materials section of this book, you'll find Tac mentioned often, sometimes by itself. They are one of the few companies, for instance, to offer Eagle Claw (as well as VMC and Mustad) dry fly hooks.

Yes, you'll have to fight your way through jig molds and triple wing buzz blades to find the fly fishing products, but the prices and selection will make it worthwhile.

Thomas & Thomas   T&T
Box 32
Turners Falls, Massachusetts 01376

Phone #: (413) 863-9727
Hours: 9-5, Eastern Time, Mon.-Fri. (closed for 2 wks. in August)
Credit cards: AE, MC, V Shipping: $3/$100; free/$100+
Charge: $3 Pages: 83, color and b&w
Products: fly fishing, tying, flies, rod building, clothing

This catalog is really a wish book for me. For one thing, I wish that the Thomas & Thomas showroom was just down the road.

Few catalogs have T&T's diversity, nor is there any other catalog with better descriptions of its products. Each is original, rather than something from the manufacturer, but be warned—T&T's style of enthusiastic understatement can be quite compelling. Nearly every product is illustrated. All in all, things that might not have even caught your attention in another catalog can cause you to get out your Visa card.

I have only one complaint, and you've heard it before. T&T sometimes likes to put its name on products made by other manufacturers. The one product that must bear their name is the famous T&T rods. I have a friend whose greatest passion in fishing is T&T cane rods. He had six of them last I asked, but there was one more he had his eye on. They are rods to be cherished.

You'll also find informative bits and pieces throughout the catalog, including the fact that trout like insects because they have 10%-20% fat compared to about 3% fat for minnows. And there are articles on equipment and flies for bass, saltwater, and salmon fishing. You can even order a fishing trip to Norway. Get this catalog.

Tidewater Specialties   Tid
U.S. Rt. 50, Box 158
Wye Mills, Maryland 21679

Phone #, orders: (800) 638-3696; MD 820-2076
Phone #, customer service: (301) 820-2079
Hours: 9-5, Eastern Time, 7 days a week
Credit cards: AE, MC, V, DC Shipping: $3 flat
Charge: none Pages: 61, color throughout
Products: duck hunting, fly fishing, clothing

Tidewater Specialties' catalog is similar to those offered by Orvis, L.L. Bean, and Dunn's. Clothing, hunting items, and outdoor art are offered along with high quality fly fishing equipment.

The fall edition of their catalog that I used rightfully carries a lot of duck hunting gear. I suspect the spring catalog may be the one for the fly fisherman, but you'll enjoy any issue.

Among the fly fishing equipment featured in the catalog are Ross reels, Deerfield rods, and Fothergill vests, and that's an impressive sample.

Wulff's Fishing Things   Wul
Box CC
Livingston Manor, New York 12758

Owners: Joan and Lee Wulff
Phone #: (914) 439-4060
Hours: 9-5, Eastern Time, Mon.-Fri.
Credit cards: MC, V Shipping: $1/$10; $2/$30; $3/$30+
Charge: none Pages: 9, b&w
Products: fly fishing, flies

The contemporary patron saints of both men and women fly fishers have recently entered the catalog business, and whatever Joan and Lee Wulff decide to do is always interesting. Fishing Things offers a basic selection of equipment and an interesting fly selection. We'll have to assume that people like the Wulffs could lay hands on any piece of equipment they wanted for their catalog, so the products bear a high-level recommendation just from being included.

Rods and reels for specific uses are offered, and in a departure from standard catalog procedure, the Wulffs have selected individual models rather than entire product lines, so you'll find two Scott rods, one Leonard rod, and so on. All in all, it's kind of like having Joan and Lee advise you personally on equipment selection.

You'll also find some specific Wulff products, including his and her vests (from the man who invented the vest), several Wulff fly patterns tied to Lee's specifications, and Wulff's Triangle Taper fly lines. You can even order a Wulff original, tied without aid of vise, in a frame, signed and numbered in a limited edition. Price: $125.

FLY FISHING SCHOOLS

Fly fishing, like a lot of other things, is better when you know how. A fly fishing school can save you years of "learning" in a day or two.

Skilled fly fishing does take a long, long time to learn. I'm reminded of a slogan for some popular parlor game of years ago: A moment to learn, a lifetime to master. It's not true of fly fishing, so I don't know why I thought of it. Fly fishing takes a lifetime to learn and another to master, and some of us haven't gotten it down even on our second try.

I don't always think school is an appropriate place to learn things (and that comes from a former school teacher), but there are a couple of good reasons why you may want to consider one for fly fishing. First, a fly fishing school isn't like a regular school, or shouldn't be. It's a hands-on experience carried on in the outdoors. The teachers love their subject. Attendance isn't taken, and you don't have to recite lines from Schwiebert.

Second, fly fishing is complicated. That's not to say the individual parts of the sport, like casting, are difficult to

learn, but there are a lot of parts to it and they must all fit together pretty well if you're to be an accomplished fly fisherman. Not only are there a lot of parts, but some of them are very difficult to learn from a book or from observation.

An illustration of this is casting. Without help (and sometimes with help), nothing is likely to work correctly for the beginning fly caster. If you try to teach yourself, you can expect a lot of frustration. That frustration can cause you to quit the sport, and that would be too bad. Even if you survive self-taught casting (as many of us have), you'll likely have enough bad habits to keep an instructor busy for three days on that alone. In the casting clinics I've given, I prefer the student who has never cast. It's easier to teach good habits than to correct poor ones.

Incidentally, I'm the director of one of the schools listed here, so I'm prejudiced about their value.

What to look for in a school. It's a bit more difficult to shop for a school than it is to shop for a rod, for instance. You can't try one out, for one thing. So a little homework (excuse the expression) is in order.

Location of the school will be a prime consideration. It will either be close to home or in a place you want to vacation or in a hot dog fishing place, like West Yellowstone. There's not likely to be a fishing school in a place without decent water, but you may wish to pick a school that is in an area similar to the one you'll be fishing. If you're traveling with family, you'll want a school in a place where there's plenty to do for everyone.

Cost will be another factor most of us consider. Compare the rates between several schools before choosing. Try to conjure up comparable packages. Some schools include lodging and some let you arrange that. If you're on your own, the school should send you a list of nearby motels and their rates. The ideal arrangement would be a school with lodging included at good rates but with the option to separate the lodging cost so you can stay where you wish. I'm a budget motel person myself, but in arranging lodging for a school I would choose a nicer motel than I'm used to personally just to make sure nobody was unhappy.

Find out what you'll be learning in the school. The basic list should include casting, reading water, equipment selection, knot tying, leader selection, fly selection, and basic entomology. You may also find a school that offers fly tying, but that's more unusual. The important thing here is to make sure the school is designed for a student at your level of the sport.

You should also check for equipment needs. If you are an absolute beginner, you'll want to be sure the school has equipment for your use, either as a rental or as part of the school. If you have equipment you'll be using after the school, it's better to use it during the school. Your instructor will tell you if the equipment is hurting your chances of success. Some of the schools associated with rod companies will issue you a rod for use during the school. Their hope, of course, is that you'll love the rod and have to own one. That's fine as long as we all understand this.

You should check the student/teacher ratio. An instructor can demonstrate casting to a fairly large group, but you'll need lots of individual attention when it comes time for you to cast. A ratio of 4 to 1 or less is good. I've tried to teach six people at once, but I always feel like a marathon runner by the time the clinic is over and I always feel like I haven't had enough time with each person.

You might ask for references from people in your town or area, but I don't know how successful you'll be. I guess that if, after talking with the school personnel, you still feel uncertain, you should look around some more.

You'll find some opportunities to study under some well-known names in fly fishing. It's always fun to rub shoulders with the biggies and many of them are fine teachers. It will often be more expensive, of course. Just make sure the class is at the appropriate level for you and that there are a limited number of students in the class.

The schools listed here. This is probably a very limited list. I found advertisements for schools in magazines and catalogs, but there are a great number of schools that are regionally known that didn't make the list. They, of course, are welcome to let me know of their existence in case we have a later edition of this book.

The schools are listed by state. Can't make any recommendations here, except one, of course. I've listed the rates and other information that was available to me. The months during which the schools are offered are listed by numbers 1-12 (for instance, "Months: 8,9" means schools are offered in August and September). I didn't have time to write for all the brochures, so you'll find some voids indicated by "n/a" or "write". I've also listed other recreational prospects when they were given in the advertisement.

Remember, as usual, that these are old rates. But, they're in the ballpark and will serve as comparison.

Alaska

Fenwick Bristol Bay School   # Days: 7 Cost: $2,750
7003 Glen Court   Lodging: included
Frederick, Maryland 21701   Meals: included
(301) 663-3966   Months: 9
Director(s): Jim Gilford
Nearby waters: waters in the Wood-Tikchik area
Other recreation: gourmet dining, sauna-ing

Fenwick Alaska River School # Days: 7 Cost: $2,600
2633 Clay Road   Lodging: included
Arcata, California 95521   Meals: included
(707) 839-1117   Months: 9
Director(s): Bob Kelly
Nearby waters: rivers in Togiak National Wildlife Refuge
Other recreation: story telling

Fenwick King Salmon School # Days: 7 Cost: $2,500
790 27th Avenue   Lodging: included
San Francisco, California 94121   Meals: included
(415) 752-0192   Months: 8
Director(s): Mel Krieger
Nearby waters: Naknek River, many other trophy fish rivers
Other recreation: who needs anything else

Fenwick Iliamna School # Days: 7 Cost: $2,700
309 S. 11th Avenue   Lodging: included
Wausau, Wisconsin 54401   Meals: included
(715) 842-9872   Months: 8
Director(s): Gary Borger
Nearby waters: Iliamna Lake and other rivers and lakes
Other recreation: a day's fishing here is enough

Arizona

Fenwick Arizona School   # Days: 2 Cost: $290
790 27th Avenue   Lodging: unclear
San Francisco, California 94121   Meals: included
(415) 752-0192   Months: 5
Director(s): Mel and Fanny Krieger
Nearby waters: located in Scottsdale
Other recreation: located at resort, golf

Fenwick Striped Bass School # Days: 5 Cost: $395
7816 Center Street, RR2   Lodging: included
Mohave Valley, Arizona 86440   Meals: lunches only
(602) 768-4093   Months: 5
Director(s): Dave and Freddie Cox
Nearby waters: Colorado River
Other recreation: casinos in nearby Nevada

Fenwick Saltwater School # Days: 6 Cost: $1,050
7816 Center Street, RR2   Lodging: included
Mohave Valley, Arizona 86440 Meals: included
(602) 768-4093   Months: 9
Director(s): Dave and Freddie Cox
Nearby waters: saltwater areas near Bahia de los Angeles
Other recreation: swimming, other outdoor activities

California

The Fly Shop # Days: 3 Cost: $395
4140 Churn Creek Road
Redding, California 96002   Lodging: included
(916) 222-3555   Meals: included
                             Months: 5,6,7,10
Director(s): Brad Jackson
Nearby waters: Hat Creek, Fall River
Other recreation: located at private lodge

Fenwick California Schools # Days: 2 Cost: $230-$340
790 27th Avenue   Lodging: unclear
San Francisco, California 94121   Meals: included
(415) 752-0192   Months: 4-9
Director(s): Mel and Fanny Krieger
Nearby waters: variety of locations
Other recreation: all schools located at resorts

Orvis California Schools # Days: 3 Cost: $325-$460
166 Maiden Lane   Lodging: varies
San Francisco, California 94108   Meals: varies
(415) 392-1603   Months: 6,7,9,10
Director(s): Orvis staff
Nearby waters: located in Tahoe City, Bishop, Sonoma, and others
Other recreation: California dreaming

Colorado
Colorado School of Fly Fishing # Days: 1,2
                                   Cost: $65, $125
Box 1848   Lodging: not included
Estes Park Colorado 80517   Meals: lunches only
(303) 586-8812   Months: 5-9
Director(s): Scott Roederer, Chuck Christensen
Nearby waters: Big Thompson, Colorado, South Platte Rivers, mountain lakes
Other recreation: Rocky Mountain National Park, full resort town

Columbine School of Flyfishing # Days: 2 Cost: $135
4305 Hwy. 50   Lodging: not included
Salida, Colorado 81201   Meals: lunches only
(303) 539-3136   Months: 5,7,8
Director(s): Don Puterbaugh, Paul Fling
Nearby waters: Arkansas River, mountain lakes
Other recreation: mountain setting

Del Canty's Colorado Fly Fishing School # Days: 5
                                   Cost: $325
4039 Highway 91   Lodging: included
Leadville, Colorado 80461   Meals: not included
(303) 486-0769   Months: 6,7
Director(s): Del Canty, Rick Christmas
Nearby waters: Arkansas River, mountain lakes
Other recreation: located at Colorado Mountain College

Taylor Creek Fly Shop # Days: 2 Cost: $150
Box 1295   Lodging: included
Basalt, Colorado 81621   Meals: breakfast only
(303) 927-4374   Months: n/a
Director(s): Bill Fitzsimmons, Ted Isaacson
Nearby waters: Fryingpan, Roaring Fork, Colorado Rivers, mountain lakes
Other recreation: Aspen nearby

Maine
L.L. Bean Fly Fishing School   # Days: n/a
                                   Cost: write
L.L. Bean, Inc.   Lodging: write
Freeport, Maine 04033   Meals: write
(207) 865-4761   Months: spring
Director(s): Dave Whitlock
Nearby waters: streams and lakes of Maine
Other recreation: shopping at L.L. Bean

Maryland
Fenwick Maryland School   # Days: 2 Cost: $135
7003 Glen Court   Lodging: not included
Frederick, Maryland 21701   Meals: not included
(301) 663-3966   Months: 3,4
Director(s): Jim Gilford
Nearby waters: Big Hunting Creek and other mountain streams
Other recreation: historic spot hopping, hiking, sightseeing

Michigan
Orvis Michigan School   # Days: 2 Cost: write
Box 133   Lodging: write
Ada, Michigan 49301   Meals: write
(616) 676-0177   Months: 6
Director(s): Dick Pobst
Nearby waters: Pere Marquette, Rogue Rivers, other streams and lakes
Other recreation: n/a

Minnesota
Fenwick Minnesota School   # Days: 3 Cost: $400
Life of Riley Resort   Lodging: included
Cook, Minesota 55723   Meals: n/a
(218) 666-5453   Months: 6
Director(s): Ms. Lee Gibson
Nearby waters: Lake Vermillion, other lakes and streams
Other recreation: located at full resort, tennis, golf, riding

Montana
Fenwick Montana School   # Days: 3 Cost: $325
Box 729   Lodging: not included
Westminster, California 92683   Meals: lunches, dinners
(714) 897-1066   Months: 6-9
Director(s): Bob Kelly
Nearby waters: Madison, Henry's Fork, Firehole, many others
Other recreation: Yellowstone National Park

Yellowstone Angler # Days: 2 Cost: $200
124 N. Main Street   Lodging: not included
Livingston, Montana 59047   Meals: not included
(406) 222-7130   Months: 6-9
Director(s): George Anderson
Nearby waters: Armstrong Spring Creek, Yellowstone River, many others
Other recreation: Yellowstone National Park

Montana School of Fly Fishing # Days: 7 Cost: $595
Nye,   Lodging: included
Montana 59061   Meals: included
(406) 328-8294   Months: 5-10
Director(s): Charles S. Mouat
Nearby waters: Stillwater River, Yellowstone River, others
Other recreation: located at full service dude ranch, mountain setting

Nevada

Fenwick Nevada School   # Days: 2 Cost: $290
790 27th Avenue
San Francisco, California 94121
(415) 752-0192
Lodging: unclear
Meals: included
Months: 4
Director(s): Mel and Fanny Krieger
Nearby waters: located in Las Vegas
Other recreation: almost anything

New Hampshire

Hunter's Fly Fishing Schools   # Days: 2 Cost: $190
Central Square
New Boston, New Hampshire
(603) 487-3388
Lodging: not included
Meals: not included
Months: 6
Director(s): Bill Hunter
Nearby waters: with Lefty Kreh, other classes scheduled
Other recreation: n/a

New Mexico

Fenwick New Mexico School   # Days: 3 Cost: $595
Vermejo Park, Drawer E
Raton, New Mexico 87740
(505) 445-3097
Lodging: included
Meals: included
Months: 6,7
Director(s): Gary Borger
Nearby waters: mountain lakes, streams
Other recreation: located at full resort dude ranch

New York

Fenwick New York School   # Days: 2 Cost: $135
7003 Glen Court
Frederick, Maryland 21701
(301) 663-3966
Lodging: not included
Meals: not included
Months: 4-6
Director(s): Jim Gilford
Nearby waters: mountain streams and lakes
Other recreation: hiking, sightseeing

Fenwick Whiteface School   # Days: 2 Cost: $135-$160
7003 Glen Court
Frederick, Maryland 21701
(301) 663-3966
Lodging: not included
Meals: not included
Months: 7
Director(s): Jim Gilford
Nearby waters: Ausable, Saranac, Bouquet Rivers
Other recreation: hiking, sightseeing

Wulff's Fishing School   # Days: write Cost: write
Box CC
Livingston Manor, New York 12758
(914) 439-4060
Lodging: write
Meals: write
Months: write
Director(s): Joan and Lee Wulff
Nearby waters: Beaverkill River and other Catskill streams
Other recreation: n/a

Fenwick Entomology Schools   # Days: 2 Cost: $125
7003 Glen Court
Frederick, Maryland 21701
(301) 663-3966
Lodging: not included
Meals: not included
Months: 2,3,8
Director(s): Jim Gilford
Nearby waters: located in Washington, D.C., New York state, Philadelphia
Other recreation: variety of activities at each location

North Carolina

Orvis North Carolina School   # Days: 3 Cost: write
4369 S. Tryon
Charlotte, North Carolina 28210
(704) 523-9094
Lodging: write
Meals: write
Months: 6,7
Director(s): Joe Hedrick
Nearby waters: mountain streams
Other recreation: n/a

Fenwick North Carolina School   # Days: 2
7003 Glen Court
Frederick, Maryland 21701
(301) 663-3966
Cost: $255-$280
Lodging: included
Meals: included
Months: 6
Director(s): Jim Gilford
Nearby waters: streams and lakes of the Blue Ridge Mountains
Other recreation: located at full service resort, skeet, trap, tennis, golf

Oregon

Fenwick Oregon School   # Days: 2 Cost: $250
790 27th Avenue
San Francisco, California 94121
(415) 752-0192
Lodging: unclear
Meals: included
Months: 6
Director(s): Mel and Fanny Krieger
Nearby waters: Deschutes River, other waters
Other recreation: located at full service resort

Orvis Oregon School # Days: 3 Cost: $460
166 Maiden Lane
San Francisco, California 94108
(415) 392-1600
Lodging: included
Meals: included
Months: 7-9
Director(s): Orvis staff
Nearby waters: private spring creeks near Ft. Klamath
Other recreation: located at full service resort

Rogue River Anglers # Days: 3 Cost: $400
3156 Rogue River Highway
Gold Hill, Oregon 97525
(800) 528-0001
Lodging: included
Meals: included
Months: 6,7,9
Director(s): Al and Nancy Perryman
Nearby waters: private spring creeks, steelhead rivers
Other recreation: located at private resort;

Kaufmann's Fly Fishing Schools # Days: 3 Cost: $295
Box 23032
Portland, Oregon 97223
(503) 639-6400
Lodging: included
Meals: included
Months: 5-10
Director(s): Kaufmann's staff
Nearby waters: Deschutes River

Pennsylvania

Fenwick Poconos School   # Days: 2 Cost: $135
7003 Glen Court
Frederick, Maryland 21701
(301) 663-3966
Lodging: not included
Meals: not included
Months: 5,9
Director(s): Jim Gilford
Nearby waters: mountain streams and lakes
Other recreation: tennis, sailing, hiking, sightseeing

Fenwick Spruce Creek School # Days: 2 Cost: $160–$185
7003 Glen Court   Lodging: not included
Frederick, Maryland 21701   Meals: not included
(301) 663-3966   Months: 6,7
Director(s): Jim Gilford
Nearby waters: mountain streams and lakes near State
College, PA
Other recreation: hiking, sightseeing

Orvis Pennsylvania School # Days: 3 Cost: write
Slate Run Tackle Shop   Lodging: write
Slate Run, Pennsylvania 17769   Meals: write
(717) 753-8551   Months: 6-8
Director(s): Thomas Finkbiner
Nearby waters: mountain streams and lakes

Orvis Pennsylvania School # Days: 2 Cost: write
306 E. Baltimore Pike   Lodging: write
Media, Pennsylvania 19063   Meals: write
(215) 565-6140   Months: 7
Director(s): Barry Staats

Letort Ltd. Schools # Days: 3 Cost: $215
Box 417   Lodging: not included
Boiling Springs, Pennsylvania 17007 Meals: included
(717) 258-3010   Months: 4-9
Director(s): Ed Shenk, staff
Nearby waters: Yellow Breeches, Letort, Falling Spring,
Big Spring
Other recreation: located at Allenberry Inn, theatre,
tennis

Texas
Fenwick Texas Schools   # Days: 2 Cost: $290
790 27th Avenue   Lodging: unclear
San Francisco, California 94121   Meals: included
(415) 752-0192   Months: 5
Director(s): Mel and Fanny Krieger
Nearby waters: one school near Dallas, one on Lake
Conroe
Other recreation: both schools located at resorts

Orvis Houston School # Days: 3 Cost: $175
5848 Westheimer Rd.   Lodging: not included
Houston, Texas 77057   Meals: not included
(713) 783-2111   Months: 6-9
Director(s): Jim Davis, Dave Hayward
Nearby waters: area bass ponds, saltwater flats
Other recreation: shopping

Vermont
Orvis Fly Fishing School   # Days: 3 Cost: $365
10 River Road   Lodging: included
Manchester, Vermont 05254   Meals: included
(802) 362-3434   Months: 6-8
Director(s): Orvis staff
Nearby waters: Battenkill, White Rivers, mountain lakes
Other recreation: antique shopping, hiking

Virginia
Murray's Fly Fishing Schools   # Days: 2 Cost: $85
Box 156   Lodging: not included
Edinburg, Virginia 22824   Meals: not included
(703) 984-4212   Months: 4-9
Director(s): Harry Murray
Nearby waters: Shenandoah, Rapidan Rivers, Mossy
Creek for bass and trout

Fenwick Virginia School # Days: 2 Cost: $135
7003 Glen Court   Lodging: not included
Frederick, Maryland 21701   Meals: not included
(301) 663-3966   Months: 3
Director(s): Jim Gilford
Nearby waters: mountain streams and lakes
Other recreation: hiking, sightseeing

Washington
Fenwick Washington School   # Days: 2 Cost: $260
790 27th Avenue   Lodging: unclear
San Francisco, California 94121   Meals: included
(415) 752-0192   Months: 6
Director(s): Mel and Fanny Krieger
Nearby waters: Olympic Peninsula streams and lakes
Other recreation: located at resort, Olympic National
Park

Wisconsin
Fenwick Wisconsin School   # Days: 2 Cost: $175
309 S. 11th Avenue   Lodging: not included
Wausau, Wisconsin 54401   Meals: not included
(715) 842-9879   Months: 5
Director(s): Gary Borger
Nearby waters: various Wisconsin streams and lakes
Other recreation: located at historic lodge

Wyoming
Orvis Wyoming School   #Days: 3 Cost: write
315 Columbine Street   Lodging: write
Denver, Colorado 80206   Meals: write
(303) 322-5014   Months: 6-8
Director(s): Ken Walters, Mike Clough
Nearby waters: North Platte River, mountain lakes and

Other Countries
Orvis U. K. School   # Days: n/a Cost: write
10 River Road   Lodging: write
Manchester, Vermont 05254   Meals: write
(802) 362-3434   Months: write
Director(s): Orvis staff
Nearby waters: Rivers Test and Itchen, other
chalkstreams
Other recreation: sightseeing, travel

Fenwick British Columbia School # Days: 2 Cost: $275
790 27th Avenue   Lodging: unclear
San Francisco, California 94121   Meals: included
(415) 752-0192   Months: 7
Director(s): Mel and Fanny Krieger
Nearby waters: Harrison Lake, other waters
Other recreation: located at resort, golf, tennis

FLY SHOPS

The names and addresses here were gleaned from a number of sources, including fly fishing magazines. The list is not entirely accurate, since shops move and disappear regularly, nor are all the shops devoted to fly fishing. The list is also by no means complete, and I invite other shops to send me information for another edition. From all shops, including those listed here, I'd like addresses, phone numbers, geographical area served, nearby rivers and lakes, and a brief list of fly patterns recommended for those areas. Such a fly shop directory for the country is overdue. (Send information to me in care of Spring Creek Press, Box 1848, Estes Park, Colorado 80517.)

If you travel, contact the shops listed here. Phone for information on fishing licenses, areas to fish, and fly patterns. Visit the shops and support the good people in them.

Alaska

Anglers Habitat
808 East 36th
Anchorage, Alaska 99503
(907) 561-7312

Gary King, Inc.
202 East Northern Lights Boulevard
Anchorage, Alaska
(907) 272-5401

Mountainview Sports
134 South Fork
Anchorage, Alaska 99507
(907) 277-9733

Northwest Outfitters, Inc.
5801 Arctic Boulevard
Anchorage, Alaska 99502
(907) 561-8286

Arizona

Allen's Fly Fishing Shop
31 West Baseline
Tempe, Arizona 85281
(602) 838-9775

The Fisherman
8625 East McDowell Road
Scottsdale, Arizona 85252

The Hatch
Box 5624
Tucson, Arizona 85705

Arkansas

Claridads-Singer Sporting Outfitters
21 West Mountain, Box 3090
Fayetteville, Arkansas 72701
(501) 442-2193

California

Anglers Emporium
1332 West Hillsdale Boulevard
San Mateo, California 94403
(415) 572-0100

Buz's Fly and Tackle Shop
219 North Encina Street
Visalia, California 93291
(209) 734-1151

Creative Sports Enterprises
2333 Boulevard Circle
Walnut Creek, California 94523
(415) 938-2255

Dale's Hackle & Tackle
2634 West Orangethorpe
Fullerton, California 92633
(714) 525-1827

Doug Kittredge's Sport Shop
Box 598
Mammoth Lakes, California 93546

Eddie Bauer
220 Post Street
San Francisco, California 94108
(415) 986-7600

Fall River Fly Shop
Star Route Glenburn
Fall River Mills, California 96028

Fly Fishing Unlimited
2929 Fulton Avenue No. 3
Sacramento, California 95821

Hackle & Tackle
27324 Camino Capistrano
Laguna Niguel, California 92677
(714) 643-9252

Hackle 'n Tackle Shop
458 North Humboldt Avenue
Willows, California 95988

Hat Creek Angler
3369 Main Street
Burney, California 96013
(916) 335-3165

Hidden Rod Shop
2623 Gardenia Avenue
Signal Hill, California 90806

High Sierra Fly Fisher
2122 South Sunland Drive
Ridgecrest, California 93555
(619) 375-5810

Intermountain Fly & Tackle
Highway 299C, Box 430
Fall River Mills, California 96028
(916) 336-6600

Johnny's Sport Shop
1402 Lincoln
Pasadena, California 91103

King's Western Angler
532 College Avenue
Santa Rosa, California 95401
(707) 542-4432

Kittredge Sports
Highway 203, Box 598
Mammoth Lakes, California 93546

Light's Fly Shop
4947 Folsom Boulevard
Sacramento, California 95816

Ned Gray's Sierra Tackle
Box 338
Montrose, California 91020

North Country Fly & Tackle
150 Bellam No. 250
San Rafael, California 94902

Ojai Fisherman
218 North Encinal Avenue
Ojai, California 93023

Orvis - San Francisco
166 Maiden Lane
San Francisco, California 94108
(415) 392-1600

Pat's Tackle Shop
Box 595
Bridgeport, California 93517

Powell Fly Shop
2797 Esplanade, Box 3966
Chico, California 95927-3966
(916) 345-3393

Riverside Ski & Sport
6744 Brockton Avenue
Riverside, California 92506
(714) 784-0205

San Francisco Flyfisher's Supply
1545 Clement Street
San Francisco, California 94123

Sport Chalet
920 Foothill Boulevard
La Canada, California
(818) 790-9800

Sportsmen's Den
404 North Mt. Shasta Boulevard
Mt. Shasta, California 96067

The Fisherman's Spot
Van Nuys, California 91401
(213) 785-7306

The Fly Hutch
3423 El Camino Real
Santa Clara, California 95051

The Fly Shop
4140 Churn Creek Road
Redding, California 96002
(916) 222-3555

The Grand Garage
Corona Del Mar, California 92625
(714) 760-6850

The Midge Fly Shop
2132 O'Toole Avenue
San Jose, California 95131
(408) 263-8877

The Millpond
10893 North Wolfe Road
Cupertino, California 95014
(408) 996-8916

The Millpond North
1601 Douglas Boulevard
Roseville, California 95678

The San Francisco Fly Fisherman
530 Bush Street
San Francisco, California 94108

World Wide Outfitters
425 Tesconi Circle
Santa Rosa, California 95401
(707) 545-4657

Wray's Fly & Tackle
2039 Montecito Avenue
Santa Rosa, California 95404
(707) 526-4968

Colorado

All Pro Fishing
633 South Santa Fe
Littleton, Colorado 80120
(303) 795-3473

Angler's All Ltd.
5211 South Santa Fe
Littleton, Colorado 80120
(303) 794-1104

Angler's Covey, Inc.
917 West Colorado Avenue
Colorado Springs, Colorado 80905
(303) 471-2984

Beaver Creek Sports
2851 North Avenue
Grand Junction, Colorado 81501
(303) 245-4353

Colorado Angler
1457 Nelson Street
Lakewood, Colorado 80215
(303) 232-8298

Dan's Fly Shop
Box 118
Lake City, Colorado 81235
(303) 944-2281

Duranglers Flies and Supplies
801 B Main Avenue
Durango, Colorado 81301
(303) 385-4081

Elk Trout Lodge
Box 313
Kremmling, Colorado 80405
(303) 724-3343

F.I. Sherman
2404 Pearl
Boulder, Colorado 80302
(303) 444-9315

Fothergill's Outdoor Sportsman
Box 88
Aspen, Colorado 81611
(303) 925-3288

Front Range Anglers, Inc.
685-D South Broadway
Boulder, Colorado 80303
(303) 494-1375

Gardenswartz Sporting Goods
863 Main Avenue, Box 1620
Durango, Colorado 81301

Match The Hatch
254 Bridge Street
Vail, Colorado 81657
(303) 476-5337

Nelson Fly and Tackle
72149 Highway 40, Box 336
Tabernash, Colorado 80478
(303) 726-8558

Roaring Fork Anglers
2114 Grand Avenue
Glenwood Springs, Colorado 81601
(303) 945-0180

Straightline Fly & Tackle
703 Lincoln Avenue, Box 3510
Streamboat Springs, Colorado 80477
(303) 879-7568

Taylor Creek Angling Services
160 Highway 82, Box 1295
Basalt, Colorado 81621
(303) 927-4374

The Complete Angler
8255 South Holly Street
Littleton, Colorado 80122
(303) 694-2387

The Fisherman's Fly
161 Virginia Dr., Box 4512
Estes Park, Colorado 80517
(303) 586-8843

The Flyfisher Ltd.
315 Columbine Street
Denver, Colorado 80206
(303) 322-5014

The U.S. Angler
3609 Austin Bluffs Parkway
Colorado Springs, Colorado 80907
(303) 594-6262

Western Angler
122 West Laurel Street
Fort Collins, Colorado 80521
(303) 221-4777

Connecticut

Autumn & Greenleaf, Riverdale Farms
136 Simsbury Road
Avon, Connecticut 06001
(203) 677-8258

Clapp & Treat, Inc.
674 Farmington Avenue
West Hartford, Connecticut 06119
(203) 236-0878

Joe Garman
Manchester, Connecticut 06040
(203) 643-2401

Oakdale Gun & Fly Shop
RFD 2, Rt. 82
Oakdale, Connecticut 06370
(203) 859-1454

Ridgefield Sports
23 Governor Street
Ridgefield, Connecticut 06877
(203) 438-5090

The Compleat Angler
979 Post Road, East
Westport, Connecticut 06880
(203) 226-5503

The Trail
Litchfield, Connecticut 06759
(203) 567-9339

The Upstream Studio & Fly Shop
Knowalot Lane
Norwalk, Connecticut 06851

Westport Tackle, Inc.
14 Riverside Avenue
Westport, Connecticut 06880
(203) 227-5702

Florida

Catino Custom Rods and Reels
599 East Sherwood Avenue, Box 2088
Satellite Beach, Florida 32937
(305) 777-2793 or 777-5706

Downeast Sporting Classics
538 Park Avenue, South
Winter Park, Florida 32789
(305) 645-5100

Great Outdoors
13499 U.S. 41 SE, Bell Tower, Suite 211
Ft. Myers, Florida 33907
(813) 433-2040

Shorelines South
831 N.E. Second Avenue
Ft. Lauderdale, Florida 33304
(305) 467-1786

Georgia

Anglers Afield
3271 Roswell Road
Atlanta, Georgia
(404) 262-1772

The Fish Hawk, Inc.
283 Buckhead
Atlanta, Georgia 30305
(404) 237-3473

The Quail Call, Ltd.
605 Victoria Square, Box 1218
Thomasville, Georgia 31792
(912) 226-3333

Idaho

Caldwell Sporting Goods
812 Main Street
Caldwell, Idaho 83605
(208) 454-3666

Henry's Fork Anglers, Inc.
Box 487-A
St. Anthony, Idaho 83445
(208) 558-7525 (summer) 624-3595 (winter)

Lakefork Flies
Highway 55, Route 1, Box 43
McCall, Idaho 83638

Renegade Fly Shop
280 South Idaho Street
Wendell, Idaho 83355
(208) 536-2407

Rocky Mountain Angler's
1008 Vista
Boise, Idaho 83705
(208) 336-3336

Silver Creek Outfitters
507 North Main Street
Sun Valley, Idaho 83340
(208) 726-5282

Snug Fly Fishing
Box 598F
Sun Valley, Idaho 83353
(208) 622-9305

South Fork Expeditions
Box 2584
Idaho Falls, Idaho 83401
(208) 483-2722 (summer) 524-1589 (winter)

Streamside Adventures
6907 Overland Avenue
Boise, Idaho 83709
(208) 375-6008

Will Godfrey's Fly Fishing Center
Box 68
Island Park, Idaho 83429

Illinois

Coren's Rod & Reel Service
6424 North Western
Chicago, Illinois 60645
(312) 743-2980

Trout & Grouse
1147 Wilmette Avenue
Wilmette, Illinois 60091
(312) 215-8090

Indiana

Jorgensens, Inc.
6226 Covington Road
Ft. Wayne, Indiana 46804
(219) 432-5519

T.D. Brooke, Ltd.
8702 Keystone Crossing North
Indianapolis, Indiana 46240
(317) 846-6868

Kansas

Backwoods Equipment Co., Suite 221
221 North Main
Wichita, Kansas 67202
(316) 267-4297

The Gun Shop
708 South Rogers Road
Olathe, Kansas 66062
(913) 782-6900

Maine

Eddie's Flies & Tackle
303 Broadway
Bangor, Maine 04401
(207) 945-5587

Hook & Feathers
28 Main Street
Rangeley, Maine 04970-0400
(209) 864-3309

Joe's Tackle Shop
Route 1, Box 156
Danforth, Maine 04424
(207) 448-2909

Kittery Trading Post
Route 1, Box 488
Kittery, Maine 03904
(207) 439-2700

L.L. Bean
Freeport, Maine 04033
(207) 865-4761

Loring's Custom-Made Fishing Rod
R.R. 1 Box 3322
Sebago Lake, Maine 04075

Rangeley Region Sport Shop
28 Main Street, Box 400
Rangeley, Maine 04970
(207) 864-3309

Sebago Fly Shop
Steep Falls, Maine 04085

Woodman's Sporting Goods Store
223 Main Street
Norway, Maine 04268

Maryland

Anglers, Inc.
11812 Hunting Ridge Court
Potomac, Maryland 20854

Custom Tackle
Rte. 9 Box 181
Pasedena, Maryland 21122

Sporting Adventure
9191 Baltimore, Natl. Pike, Route 40
Ellicott City, Maryland 21043
(301) 465-1112

The Rockville Trading Post
250 North Washington Street
Rockville, Maryland 20850
(301) 762-8030

Tidewater Specialties
188 Main Street
Annapolis, Maryland

Tidewater Specialties
U.S. Route 50, Box 158
Wye Mills, Maryland 21679
(301) 820-2079

Massachusetts

Classic & Custom Fly Shop
477 Pleasant Street
Holyoke, Massachusetts 01040
(413) 533-0433

Cote's Fly Shop
115 Manville Street
Leicester, Massachusetts 01524
(617) 892-3765

Orvis Shop of Boston, Inc.
213 West Plain Street
Wayland, Massachusetts 01778
(617) 653-9144

Stoddard's
50 Temple Place
Boston, Massachusetts 02111
(617) 426-4187

The Outdoorsman, Inc.
201 West Boylston Street
West Boylston, Massachusetts 01583
(617) 835-3555

Thompsons Sport Shop
Route 6, 1479 Fall River Avenue
Seekonk, Massachusetts 02771
(617) 336-9588

Michigan

Ann Arbor Rod & Gun Co.
2261 West Liberty Road
Ann Arbor, Michigan 48103
(313) 769-7866

Bear's Fly Shop
311 South Clinton
Grand Ledge, Michigan 48837
(517) 627-7606

Gates AuSable Lodge
Rt. 2, Box 2336, Stephan Bridge
Grayling, Michigan 49738
(517) 348-8462

The Sportsman
184 Pierce
Birmingham, Michigan 48011
(313) 646-1225

Thornapple Orvis Shop
Box 133
Ada, Michigan 49301
(616) 676-0177

Minnesota

Bright Waters Fly Fishing
3803 Grand Avenue, South
Minneapolis, Minnesota 55409
(612) 825-5524

Missouri

Bass Pro Shop
1935 South Campbell, Box 4046
Cassville, Missouri 65625

Kelley Sporting Goods Co.
751 Old Frontenac Square
St. Louis, Missouri 63131
(314) 991-4724

Ozark Custom Rod & Fly Shop
1925K East Bennett
Springfield, Missouri
(417) 881-8340

Spring View Tackle Shop
Brice Route
Lebanon, Missouri 65536

St. Louis Trout Shop
9010 St. Charles Rock Road
St. Louis, Missouri 63114
(314) 427-1707

Montana

Angler's Roost
Route 1, Box 1209
Hamilton, Montana 59840

Big Sky Fly Shop
Box 4981
Missoula, Montana 59801
(406) 273-2535

Bighorn Angler
Fort Smith, Montana 59035
(406) 666-2233

Blue Ribbon Fly Shop
Box 1037
West Yellowstone, Montana 59758
(406) 646-9365

Bob Jacklin's Fly Shop
105 Yellowstone Avenue, Box 310
West Yellowstone, Montana 59758
(406) 646-7336

Dan Bailey's Flies
209 West Park Street
Livingston, Montana 59047
(406) 222-1673

Fly Fisher's Retreat
825 8th Avenue South
Great Falls, Montana 59405
(406) 453-9192

Four Rivers Sport Shop
205 South Main
Twin Bridges, Montana 59754

Frontier Anglers
27 South Atlantic
Dillon, Montana 59725
(406) 683-5276

Frustrated Fisherman
950 Highway 93
Victor, Montana 59875
(406) 961-3401

Headwaters Angling
Box 964
Ennis, Montana 59729
(406) 682-7451 or 682-7269

Madison River Outfitters
112 Canyon, Box 1106
West Yellowstone, Montana 59758
(406) 646-9644

Montana Fly Goods Co.
330 North Jackson
Helena, Montana 59601
(406) 442-2630

Montana River Outfitters
820 Central Avenue
Great Falls, Montana 59401
(406) 761-1677

Parks' Fly Shop
Box 196
Gardiner, Montana 59030
(406) 848-7314

Pat Barnes Tackle Shop
105 Yellowstone Avenue
West Yellowstone, Montana 59758

Streamside Anglers
1109 West Broadway
Missoula, Montana 59801

The Artful Angler
Box 969, Madison Avenue
West Yellowstone, Montana 59758
(406) 646-7662

The River's Edge
2012 North Seventh Street, Box 4019
Bozeman, Montana 59715
(406) 586-5373

The Tackle Shop
Box 625
Ennis, Montana 59729
(406) 682-4263 (summer) 388-6870 (winter)

The Trout Shop (formerly Bud Lilly's)
39 Madison Avenue, Box 698
West Yellowstone, Montana 59758
(406) 646-7801 (summer) 222-0022 (winter)

Western River Fly Shop, Inc.
120 East Sixth Avenue
Helena, Montana 59601
(406) 443-7431

Wild Wings Orvis Shop
2720 West Main Street
Bozeman, Montana 59715
(406) 587-4707

Nebraska

Back Woods
3724 Farnam Street
Omaha, Nebraska 68131
(402) 345-0303

Burden Sales
1000 West "O" Street
Lincoln, Nebraska 68501
(402) 474-4366

Cabela's, Inc.
812 13th Avenue
Sidney, Nebraska 69162
(800) 237-4444

Canfields Sporting Goods
2415 Cuming Street
Omaha, Nebraska 68131
(402) 342-1517

Nevada

Mark Fore & Strike Sporting Goods
490 Keitzke Lane
Reno, Nevada 89502
(702) 322-9559

New Hampshire

Hunter's Angling Supplies
Central Square
New Boston, New Hampshire 03070
(603) 487-3388

North Country Angler
Route 16
North Conway, New Hampshire 03860
(603) 356-6000

Opechee Trading Post
13 Opechee Street
Laconia, New Hampshire 03246
(603) 524-0908

The Fly Shop
3 Empire Boulevard
Hollis, New Hampshire
(603) 882-7007

Wood Stream Ltd.
One Eagle Square, Suite 100
Concord, New Hampshire
(603) 228-0766

New Jersey

Antler & Fin
Star Route A, Box 120, Route 12 West
Flemington, New Jersey 08822
(201) 996-6416

Efinger Sporting Goods Co.
513 West Union Street
Bound Brook, New Jersey 08805

Mastodon Sport Center, Inc.
Highland Lakes Road, Star Rt., Box 54
Vernon, New Jersey 07462
(201) 764-2206

Olivers Orvis Shop
44 Main Street
Clinton, New Jersey 08809
(201) 735-5959

Ramsey Outdoor
Route 17
Ramsey, New Jersey

Ramsey Outdoor
Route 46
Ledgewood, New Jersey
(201) 261-5000

Ramsey Outdoor
Route 17
Paramus, New Jersey 07652
(201) 261-5000

Ray's Sport Shop, Inc.
559 Hiway 22
North Plainfield, New Jersey 07060
(201) 561-4400

Reed Tackle
U.S. Highway 46
Fairfield, New Jersey 07007
(201) 227-0409

Sportsman's Sanctuary
770 River Road
Fair Haven, New Jersey 07701
(201) 747-6060

The Fly Fisherman's Source
12 Godwin Place
Midland Park, New Jersey 07432
(201) 447-6707

The Flyfisher's Den
Route 46, Kenvil Plaza
Kenvil, New Jersey 07847
(201) 584-2004

Wilderness Shop
23 Main Street
Madison, New Jersey 07940
(201) 377-3301

Wilderness Shop
348 Springfield Avenue
Summit, New Jersey 07901
(201) 273-7887

New Mexico

Back Woods
6307 Menaul, NE
Albuquerque, New Mexico 87110
(505) 881-5223

Charlie's Sporting Goods
7401 H. Menaul Boulevard
Albuquerque, New Mexico 87110
(505) 884-4545

New York

Angler's Ruff
19 Glen Head Road
Glen Head, New York 11545
(516) 676-0087

Chenago Sporting Gallery
Binghamton, New York
(607) 724-7332

Clarks Flylyte Tackle
Lake Placid, New York 12946
(518) 523-3468

Don's Tackle Service
4 Morton Street
Poughkeepsie, New York 12601
(914) 471-0020

Donegal Fly Tying Materials
677 Route 208, Box 569
Monroe, New York 10950
(914) 782-4600

F & H Sporting Goods
Flushing, New York 11358
(212) 598-9780

Folkerts Brothers, Inc.
Main Street
Phoenicia, New York 12464
(914) 688-9936

Fur, Fin & Feather
DeBruce Road
Livingston Manor, New York 12758
(914) 439-4476 (days) 439-4301 (nights)

Goldstock's Sporting Goods, Inc.
121 North Broadway
Schenectady, New York 12305

H.L. Leonard Rod, Inc.
Central Valley, New York 10917
(914) 928-2303

Hawkeye Traders
12 Adams Lane
Suffern, New York 10901

Henyan's Athletic Shop, Inc.
40 East Market Street
Corning, New York 14830

John's Gun & Tackle
10 Maple Avenue
New Rochelle, New York 10801

Jones Outfitters, Inc.
37 Main, Box 147
Lake Placid, New York 12946
(518) 523-3468

Merrick Tackle Center, Inc.
2655 Merrick Road
Bellmore, New York 11710
(516) 781-7766

Orvis - New York
355 Madison Avenue
New York, New York 10017
(212) 697-3133

Paragon Sporting Goods
871 Broadway 18th Street
New York, New York 10003
(212) 255-8036 and 255-8037

Sawyer's Sporting Goods
Clifton Park, New York 12065
(518) 371-6729

The Beaverkill Angler
Broad Street
Roscoe, New York 12776
(607) 498-5194

The Bedford Sportsman
25 Adams Street
Bedford Hills, New York 10507
(914) 666-8091 and 666-8092

The Hatch
Box T
Livingston Manor, New York 12758
(914) 439-4944

The Orvis Shop
5655 Main Street
Williamsville, New York 14221
(716) 631-5131

The Orvis Shop
900 Panorama Trail
Rochester, New York 14625
(716) 248-8390

The Orvis Shop
1478 Marsh Road
Pittsford, New York 14534
(716) 248-8390

The Salmon Shop
333 West First Street
Oswego, New York 13126

North Carolina

Brookstown Angler
200 Brookstown Avenue, Suite One-1,
Brookstown Mill
Winston-Salem, North Carolina 27101
(919) 724-2133

Great Outdoor Provision Co.
3114 Hillsborough Street
Raleigh, North Carolina 27607
(919) 833-1741

J. Powell Fly Shop
5704 Rail Fence Road
Raleigh, North Carolina 27606
(919) 851-6895

Jesse Browns, Inc.
4369 South Tryon
Charlotte, North Carolina 28210
(704) 523-9094

Roger's Fly Shop
Box 297
Etowah, North Carolina 28729

Sportsman's Pro Shop
Highway 19-23, Box 475
Chandler, North Carolina 28715
(704) 667-9965

Trail Shop
405 West Franklin
Chapel Hill, North Carolina 27514

Ohio

Boone & Crockett
3158 Kingsdale Ctr.
Columbus, Ohio 43221
(614) 451-1200

Pine Lake Pro Shop
17021 Chillicothe Road
Chagrin Falls, Ohio 44022
(216) 543-8322

Sportside Trading Co., Inc.
Suite 104, 408 North Summit
Toledo, Ohio 43604
(419) 242-7550

Sportsman's Supplies
2924 South Street, Box 6024
Toledo, Ohio 43614-0024
(419) 381-9777

The Backpackers Shop at Ohio Canoe
Adventures
5128 Colorado Avenue
Sheffield Lake, Ohio 44054
(216) 934-5345

TMF Sport Shop
107 East Main Street
Ravenna, Ohio 44266
(216) 296-2614

Oklahoma

Back Woods
5011 South 79 East Avenue
Tulsa, Oklahoma 74145
(918) 664-7850

Oregon

Caddis Fly Shop
131 A East 5th Street
Eugene, Oregon 97401
(503) 342-7005

Cascade Tackle Co.
2425 Diamond Lake Boulevard
Roseburg, Oregon 97470

Don Hill Riverboats and Whitewater
Guide Service
1075 Clearwater Lane, Box CC
Springfield, Oregon 97477
(503) 726-8951

Don's Tackle Shop
7622 S.E. Foster Road
Portland, Oregon 97206

Fishing Outfitters, Inc.
3340 Commercial S.E.
Salem, Oregon 97302
(503) 588-7688

Fly Bench-Carl Snelling
88029 Hwy 101 North
Florence, Oregon 97439
(503) 997-6328

Fur, Hook & Hackle
828 South Central
Medford, Oregon 97501
(503) 772-3456

Kaufmann's Streamborn Fly Shop
12963 SW Pacific Hwy., Box 23032
Portland, Oregon 97223
(503) 639-6400

Lamplight Trout Flies
Box 196
Alsea, Oregon 97324

McNeese's Fly Fishing Shop
330 Liberty Street, S.E.
Salem, Oregon 97301
(503) 588-1768

Price's Anglers Corner
15637 Sherrie Way
La Pine, Oregon 97739

Stewart Custom Tackle
17310 N.E. Halsey
Portland, Oregon 97230
(503) 254-2359

Streamborn Flies
7725 S.W. Cirrus
Beaverton, Oregon 97005
(503) 639-6400

The Barbless Hook
23 N.W. 23rd Place
Portland, Oregon 97210
(503) 248-9651

The Fly Box
923 S.E. 3rd
Bend, Oregon 97702
(503) 388-3330

Pennsylvania

Angler's Pro Shop
18 East Third
Lansdale, Pennsylvania 19446
(215) 362-0122

Anglers Warehouse
Zeigler Road, Box 158
Wellsville, Pennsylvania 17365
(717) 432-8651

Archer & Angler Pro Shop
RD #1, Route 534
Whitehaven, Pennsylvania 18661
(717) 443-8111

Beckies Sporting Goods
1336 Orange Street
Berwick, Pennsylvania 18603
(717) 752-2011

Blair's Sporting Goods (Penn. Outdoor
Warehouse)
1508 Memorial Avenue
Williamsport, Pennsylvania 17701

Clouser's Fly Shop
101 Ulrich Street
Middletown, Pennsylvania 17057
(717) 944-6541

Cross Fork Tackle Shop
Main Street, Box 261
Cross Fork, Pennsylvania 17729
(717) 923-1960

Dale Clemens Custom Tackle
Route 2, Box 860
Wescosville, Pennsylvania 18106
(215) 395-5119

Dave's Fishermen's Shop
Route 611
Doylestown, Pennsylvania
(215) 766-8000

Dave's Fly Shop
Box 8514
Erie, Pennsylvania 16505

E.J. Hille's Angler's Supply House, Inc.
Box 996
Williamsport, Pennsylvania 17703
(717) 323-7564

Evening Rise Fly Tyers
510 Chestnut Street
Perkasie, Pennsylvania 18944
(215) 257-7888

Eylers, Inc.
895 Penn Street
Bryn Mawr, Pennsylvania 19010
(215) 527-3388

Ferences Orvis Shop
1150 Old Freeport Road
Pittsburgh, Pennsylvania 15238
(412) 782-2222

Fly Fisher's Paradise
Pike Street, Box 448
Lemont, Pennsylvania 16851
(814) 234-4189

Flys 'N Flintlocks
512 West Walnut Street
Perkasie, Pennsylvania 18944
(215) 257-5662

Forest County Sports Center
Elm Street
Tionesta, Pennsylvania 16353
(814) 755-3644

Forsyth Sporting Equipment Co.
145 Mapledale Drive
Munhall, Pennsylvania 15120

Fred Reese's Trout Shop
1145 Allegheny Street
Jersey Shore, Pennsylvania 17740
(717) 398-1318

Hoffman's Fly & Sport Shop
41A Stoney Creek Road
Dauphin, Pennsylvania 17018
(717) 921-2020

Jack's Tackle
1262 Valley Forge Road
Phoenixville, Pennsylvania 19460

Jim's Sport Center
17 North Third Street
Clearfield, Pennsylvania 16830
(814) 765-3582

Len's Fly & Tackle
878 Alter Street
Hazelton, Pennsylvania 18201

Salty's Tackle and Game
2802 Sterrettania Road
Erie, Pennsylvania 16506
(814) 833-0828

Skip's Flies and Supplies
415 Roslyn Avenue
Erie, Pennsylvania 16505
(814) 833-8425

Slate Run Tackle Shop
Box 3
Slate Run, Pennsylvania 17769
(717) 753-8551

Steckler Tibor
Stoneboro, Pennsylvania 16153
(412) 376-3358

The Fishing Post
121 North Main Street
Greensburg, Pennsylvania 15601
(412) 832-8383

The Sporting Gentleman
1306 East Baltimore Pike
Media, Pennsylvania 19063
(215) 565-6140

The Yellow Breeches Fly Shop
Rt. 174, Box 200
Boiling Springs, Pennsylvania 17007
(717) 258-6752

Windsor Fly Shop
348 North 9th Street
Stroudsburg, Pennsylvania 18360

Rhode Island

Mac's Sport Room
West Warwick, Rhode Island 02893
(401) 821-5549

South Dakota

Black Hills Fly Shop
Box 616
Hill City, South Dakota 57745
(605) 574-2030

Tennessee

Choo Choo Fly & Tackle
739 Ashland Terrace
Chattanooga, Tennessee
(615) 875-0944

Dunn's
Highway 57, Box 449
Grand Junction, Tennessee 38039-0449
(901) 764-6901

Gordon Marine, Inc.
930 West Watauga Avenue, Box 1676
Johnson City, Tennessee 37601
(615) 929-3151

Oak Ridge Sporting Goods
115 Broadway
Oak Ridge, Tennessee
(615) 483-8545

The Sporting Life
3092 Poplar
Memphis, Tennessee 38111
(901) 324-2383

Texas

Austin Angler
312½ Congress
Austin, Texas 78701
(512) 472-4553

Back Woods
3212 Camp Bowie
Ft. Worth, Texas 76107
(817) 332-2423

First In Sports
101 West Wall Street
Midland, Texas 79701
(915) 684-8853

Hunter Bradlee Co.
East 4025 N.W. Parkway
Dallas, Texas 75225
(214) 363-9213

Orvis - Houston
5848 Westheimer Road
Houston, Texas 77057
(713) 783-2111

The Tackle Box
111 East Martin
San Antonio, Texas 78205
(512) 222-8311

The Tackle Shop
451 North Central Expressway (Hwy. 75
North)
Richardson, Texas 75080
(214) 231-5982

Toepperweins
111 East Travis
San Antonio, Texas 78205
(512) 226-1421

Utah

Angler's Inn
2265 Highland Drive
Salt Lake City, Utah 84106

The Fly Line, Inc.
2935 Washington Boulevard
Ogden, Utah 84401

Vermont

Briggs, Ltd.
Main Street
White River, Vermont 05001
(802) 295-7100

Orvis - Manchester
Route 7
Manchester, Vermont 05254
(802) 362-3434

Schirmer's Fly Shop
South Burlington, Vermont

The Fly Fishing Shop, Inc.
1291 Williston Road
South Burlington, Vermont 05401
(802) 658-6128

Timberline Sports
67 Lincoln Street, Box 147
Essex Junction, Vermont 05452

Virginia

Bob's Gun & Tackle Shop
746 Granby Street
Norfolk, Virginia 23510
(804) 627-8311

Murray's Fly Shop
Box 156
Edinburg, Virginia 22824
(703) 984-4212

VanDoren's Orvis Shoppe, Ltd.
5703 Grove Avenue
Richmond, Virginia 23226
(804) 282-5527

Washington

7-S Guide Service and Fly and Tackle Shop
1501 Walnut Street
Everett, Washington 98201
(206) 259-5916

Angler's Workshop
1350 Atlantic Avenue, Box 1044-STS
Woodland, Washington 98674
(206) 225-8601

Compleat Archer & Angler
11714 15th N.E.
Seattle, Washington 98125

Creative Angler
Cedar Road, Box 40
Loon Lake, Washington 99148

Kaufmann's Streamborn Fly Shop
15015 Main Street
Bellevue, Washington 98007
(206) 643-2246

Monson's Custom Tackle
Box 518
Ephrata, Washington 98823

Neal's Fly & Tackle
5427 Pacific Avenue
Tacoma, Washington 98408

Patrick's Fly Shop
2237 Eastlake Avenue E
Seattle, Washington 98102

The Sport Cove, Inc.
E. 6630 Sprague
Spokane, Washington 99206

Ullis Company
3721 South Lawrence, Box 11303
Tacoma, Washington 98411

West Virginia

Upstream
954 Maple Drive, Suite 3
Morgantown, West Virginia 26505
(304) 599-4998

Wisconsin

Laacke & Joys
1433 North Water Street
Milwaukee, Wisconsin 53202
(414) 271-7878

Vern Lunde's Fly Fishing Chalet
2491 Highway 92
Mount Horeb, Wisconsin 53572
(608) 437-5465

Wyoming

H & K Sales
164 North 3rd
Laramie, Wyoming 82070

High Country Flies
565 North Cache Street, Box 1022
Jackson, Wyoming 83001
(307) 733-4944

Jack Dennis Outdoor Shop
Jackson, Wyoming 83001
(307) 733-3210

Wyoming Waters Fly Shop
1588 Sheridan Avenue
Cody, Wyoming 82414

Foreign Countries
Australia

Compleat Angler
19 McKillop Street
Melbourne, Australia 3000
(03) 67 2518

Canada

Angler's Craft
7 North Street
Corner Brook, Newfoundland Canada
A2H 2K9
(709) 634-4716

Bob's Sporting Goods
4150 East Hastings Street
Vancouver, British Columbia Canada
V5C 2J4
(604) 298-8551

Cleve's Sporting Goods
1558 Argyle Street
Halifax, Nova Scotia Canada B3J 2T3
(902) 422-9324

Country Pleasures
No. 130 1935-37th Street, S.W.
Calgary, Alberta Canada T3E 3A4
(403) 249-8996

Hook and Hackle Ind., Ltd.
Box 6
Lethbridge, Alberta, Canada T1J 3Y3
(403) 328-7400

Island Rods & Flies
Box 2163
Charlotte Town, PEI Canada CIA 8B9

Phinney's
1678 Barrington Street
Halifax, Nova Scotia Canada B3J 2A2
(902) 423-1316

Ruddick's Fly Shop
3730 Canada Way
Burnaby, British Columbia Canada
V5G 1G5
(604) 434-2420

Searles Shooting Supplies
141 Highway 8
Stoney Creek, Ontario Canada L8E 2Y4
(416) 561-0422

Denmark

Flyfishing Equipment
Adalsparkrej 11
2970 Horsholm, Danmark
02-86 2829

Japan

Amon Co.
Tokyo, Japan
03-234-2665

Holland

Heron Hengelsport
Kadoelen 25
8326 BA Sint-Jansklooster, Holland
05274-6987

West Germany

RST-Angelgerate GmbH
Schwaninger Strasse 31
8871 Ellzee/Stoffenried, West Germany
(0 82 83) 461

Traun River Products
Haupstrasse 4-6
Siegsdorf, West Germany
8662-9338

Feinste Fliegen Fischer
Munchberg, West Germany
09251-80444

Switzerland

Harvis AG
Schaffhausertr 514
CH-8052 Zurich, Switzerland
01/301 22 21

Jenzer & Co.
4012 Basel 12
Basel, Switzerland
061-25-5122

Sweden

Skarps Fly Fishing AB
Floda, Sweden
0302-35187

Sportag Handels AB
Akerogatan 5
212 24 Malmö, Sweden
040-18 30 60

Index